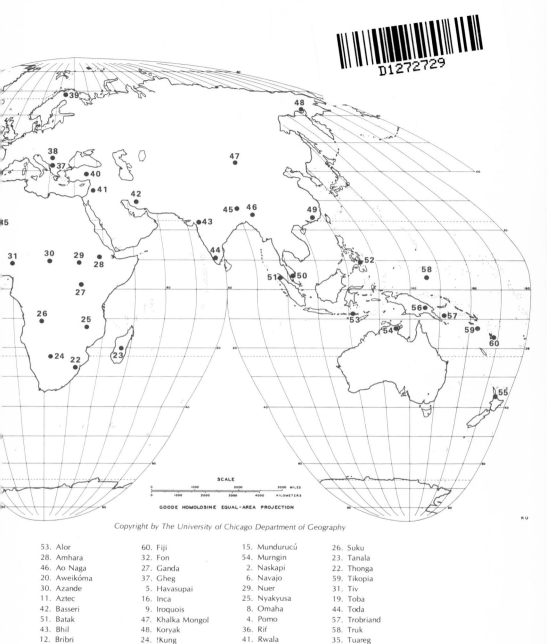

GOODE HOMOLOSINE EQUAL-AREA PROJECTION

53. Alor	60. Fiji	15. Mundurucú	26. Suku
28. Amhara	32. Fon	54. Murngin	23. Tanala
46. Ao Naga	27. Ganda	2. Naskapi	22. Thonga
20. Aweikóma	37. Gheg	6. Navajo	59. Tikopia
30. Azande	5. Havasupai	29. Nuer	31. Tiv
11. Aztec	16. Inca	25. Nyakyusa	19. Toba
42. Basseri	9. Iroquois	8. Omaha	44. Toda
51. Batak	47. Khalka Mongol	4. Pomo	57. Trobriand
43. Bhil	48. Koryak	36. Rif	58. Truk
12. Bribri	24. !Kung	41. Rwala	35. Tuareg
14. Callinago	3. Kwakiutl	50. Semang	40. Turk
49. South China	39. Lapp	38. Serb	13. Warao
7. Comanche	45. Lepcha	18. Shavante	34. Wolof
1. Copper Eskimo	52. Manóbo	56. Siane	21. Yahgan
33. Dogon	55. Maori	17. Sirionó	10. Yaqui

THE ORIGINS OF THE ECONOMY

A Comparative Study of Distribution in Primitive and Peasant Economies

By the Same Author

The Communist Foreign Trade System (1963)
Public Expenditures in Communist and Capitalist Nations (1968)
Property and Industrial Organization in Communist and Capitalist Nations (1973)

This is a volume in

↓ STUDIES IN SOCIAL DISCONTINUITY

A complete list of titles in this series appears at the end of this volume.

THE ORIGINS
OF THE
ECONOMY

A Comparative Study of Distribution
in Primitive and Peasant Economies

FREDERIC L. PRYOR

Swarthmore College

ACADEMIC PRESS New York San Francisco London
A Subsidiary of Harcourt Brace Jovanovich, Publishers

ACADEMIC PRESS, INC.
111 Fifth Avenue, New York, New York 10003

United Kingdom Edition published by
ACADEMIC PRESS, INC. (LONDON) LTD.
24/28 Oval Road, London NW1

Library of Congress Cataloging in Publication Data

Pryor, Frederic L
    The origins of the economy.

    (Studies in social discontinuity series)
    Bibliography: p.
    Includes index.
    1.   Economics, Primitive.   I.   Title.   II.   Series:
Studies in social discontinuity.
GN448.P78   301.5'1   77-6609
ISBN 0–12–566650–0

To
ROBERT Y. DAVIS, FRANK C. PIERSON,
HAROLD A. RAMSEY, AND LLOYD G. REYNOLDS

Some my teachers, some my colleagues, some both;
all educators in the finest sense

CONTENTS

LIST OF TABLES

LIST OF FIGURES

ACKNOWLEDGMENTS

A joint grant given by the Social Science Research Council and the Center for International Studies at the University of California in Berkeley financed the initial stages of research for this book. The middle stages were, in part, paid for by the Swarthmore College Faculty Research Fund. And the final stages were funded by the United States National Science Foundation. I would like to express my deep appreciation to these groups for the trust they placed in me.

Early drafts of several chapters were published in *American Ethnologist* III, 4 (1976); *Journal of Comparative Economics* I, 1 (1977); *Journal of Money, Credit, and Banking* IX, 3 (1977); *Journal of Political Economy* LXIV (August 1976); and *Social Exchange: Advances in Theory and Research,* ed. Kenneth J. Gergen et al. (New York: Wiley, 1977). I greatly appreciate receiving permission to republish some of the materials from these essays.

Steven Piker and Zora Pryor read the entire first draft and made many valuable suggestions. Duane Ball, Kenneth E. Boulding, George Dalton, Raoul Naroll, William N. Parker, Frank C. Pierson, Mary S. Pryor, Millard H. Pryor, Sr., and Alexandra Rummel read the entire second draft and also gave me extremely helpful comments. Frederick Kettering selected the drawings and carried out the art work. To all these people I express my deepest gratitude.

A number of colleagues and friends read individual chapters and for their many useful suggestions I would like to thank: Barbara Bergmann, James Brow, Karl Fox, Peter Kemper, J. M. Montias, James Morgan, Mancur Olson, Van Dorne Ooms, Sidney Pollard, Millard H. Pryor, Jr., Jenny-Keith Ross, Marc Ross, Bernard Saffran, T. W. Schultz, and James Tober. Nelson H. H. Graburn coauthored Chapter 4 and Appendixes B.4, B.5, and C.2, and we received valuable comments and assistance for this work from Judith Kleinberg, Larissa Lomnitz, Nabil Mourad, and Gary Wolfram.

In carrying out the research on the various societies comprising the sample, I consulted with many anthropologists and other experts. I asked many to serve

xviii   **Acknowledgments**

as informants and to fill out long questionnaires or to supply detailed answers to large numbers of questions. I wrote others to clear up particular points, to supply bibliographic references, or to provide other help. Some were repeatedly contacted by letter and telephone to clarify additional problems which had arisen. For all this help, I would like to express my great appreciation to: Burt Aginsky, David Ames, James N. Anderson, Fredrik Barth, Ralph Beals, Paul Bohannan, Lloyd Cabot Briggs, Helen Codere, Cora DuBois, Richard E. Elkins, Murray B. Emeneau, William N. Fenton, Raymond Firth, David Gamble, Ward H. Goodenough, Geoffrey Gorer, Nelson H. H. Graburn, Joel M. Halpern, David M. Hart, Allan Hoben, E. Adamson Hoebel, W. C. Holden, Paul P. Howell, Hatip Jemali, Igor Kopytoff, Owen Lattimore, Donald N. Levine, Michael J. Lowy, David Mandelbaum, John Franklyn Martin, David Maybury-Lewis, Margaret Mead, Simon D. Messing, Elmer S. Miller, Robert Miller, George Murphy, Robert F. Murphy, T. B. Naik, Johannes Nicolaissen, Robert Oswald, Denise Paulme, Conrad Reining, Hassan Risilia, Ronald Rohner, Hjørdis Ruud, Richard F. Salisbury, Stuart A. Schlegel, Haifdan Siiger, Edmund H. Spicer, Paul Stirling, Doris Stone, Douglas Taylor, Elizabeth Tooker, Aziz Veliu, Anthony F. C. Wallace, Ernest Wallace, Robert Wharton, Johannes Wilbert, Monica Wilson, and C. K. Yang. All the people in this large group answered my questions with patience and good will, and they should not be held responsible for my use (or misuse) of their information. Owen Lattimore asked that specific mention be made of his disagreements both with my research methods and with my eventual conclusions (whatever they might be) and undoubtedly others felt this way too.

1

INTRODUCTION

Guarda com' entri e di cui tu ti fide:
Non t'inganni l'ampiezza dell' entrare!
DANTE[1]

MAJOR THEMES AND PURPOSES

Many scholars have speculated about the major differences between the economies (comprising consumption, production, and distribution) of human beings and their primate cousins. Certainly the economies of men, as well of apes and monkeys, feature consumption. And insofar as we label as "production" primitive man's gathering of plant food, both groups of economies feature production. The economies of the two groups do differ greatly in the matter of the distribution of goods and services, an activity resulting in consumption of something by someone other than the producer. Leaving aside the distribution by parents to their offspring, the economies of human beings encompass a wide variety of other types of distribution, while the economies of other primates feature almost no distribution. Along these lines of argumentation many have made a good—but not completely airtight—case that distribution represents the distinctive feature of homo sapiens in comparison to other known primate groups.[2] Such a notion undoubtedly explains much of the great interest, as well

---

Design from a Baiga door; Bilaspur District, Madhya Pradesh, India.

[1]Dante Alighieri, *La divina commedia: Inferno,* Canto V: 'Watch how you enter and in whom you trust; do not let the wideness of the gate deceive you!'

[2]Most recently this has been forcefully argued by Morton H. Fried, *The Evolution of Political Society* (1968), p. 44. While containing a very strong element of truth, this argument seems somewhat overstated; isolated instances of systematic extrafamilial distribution among primates have been recorded. Some of these are discussed in two articles by Melvin C. Fredlund, "Economics of Animal Systems," in *Frontiers of Economics* (1975), ed. Gordon Tullock; and "Wolves, Chimps and Demsetz," *Economic Inquiry* XIV (June 1976): 279–290.

as the controversy, concerning questions about the origins of various types of distribution.

Violently conflicting opinions can be found on a wide variety of topics in this subject area. How did money begin? Why do some societies have slavery while others do not? Can we fruitfully define primitive and peasant economies in terms of distribution, rather than by reference to the primary mode of food production? Is exchange between friendly social equals always reciprocal? If not, how can we explain such imbalances? How can we predict which societies feature net marriage payments from the family of a prospective groom to the family of his prospective bride and which societies feature the reverse net flow of resources? Do cooperative labor exchanges disappear at higher levels of economic development? If so, why? Many more such controversial questions about distribution in primitive and peasant societies can be found in the literature. Unfortunately, up to now these questions have not, for the most part, been answered in a very convincing manner. They number among the questions that I attempt to explore in the following chapters in a more satisfactory fashion.

This book is a study in comparative primitive economic systems, economic anthropology, and economic prehistory. It focuses on the conditions within societies which have led to the employment of different types of distributional mechanisms and institutions. I investigate all major types of exchange and transfers of goods and services both within and between precapitalist economies and test a variety of hypotheses about the origins of such distributional patterns, using a worldwide sample of 60 primitive and peasant societies.[3]

[3]This book is, as far as I have been able to determine, the only systematic cross-cultural study of all aspects of distribution. There are, of course, numerous studies which provide comparative case materials on selected aspects of distribution and which attempt to synthesize the major trends; but usually only several aspects of distribution are considered. Of these, the most relevant for this study are: Marcel Mauss, The Gift: Forms and Functions of Exchange in Archaic Societies (1967) [originally published 1925]; Elizabeth E. Hoyt, Primitive Trade: Its Psychology and Economics (1926); Margaret Mead, ed., Cooperation and Competition Among Primitive Peoples (1966) [originally published 1937]; Karl Polanyi et al., eds., Trade and Market in the Early Empires (1957); Yehudi A. Cohen, "Food and Its Vicissitudes: A Cross-Cultural Study of Sharing and Nonsharing," in his edited book Social Structure and Personality (1961), pp. 312–350; and Marshall Sahlins, Stone Age Economics (1972). In addition, a number of specialized comparative studies on transfer transactions (particularly slavery), comparative work exchanges, money, and so forth are duly noted when I discuss these topics in the following chapters. Furthermore, a number of useful treatises in economic anthropology focus considerable attention on distribution as a whole. In the English language these include: Richard Thurnwald, Economics in Primitive Communities (1932); Stephen Viljoen, The Economics of Primitive Peoples (1936); D. W. Goodfellow, Principles of Economic Sociology (1939); Melville J. Herskovits, Economic Anthropology: The Economic Life of Primitive Peoples (1952) [originally published 1940]; Manning Nash, Primitive and Peasant Economic Systems (1966); and Harold K. Schneider, Economic Man: The Anthropology of Economics (1974). A number of treatises on economic anthropology in languages other than English have appeared; the most useful of these are referred to in later chapters of this study. Finally, there are a great many theoretical studies or highly specialized empirical studies concerning distribution in particular primitive and peasant societies, a great number of which have been listed by H. T. Van der Pas, Economic Anthropology, 1940–1972: An Annotated Bibliography (1973).

The major emphasis is on the empirical testing of a set of interrelated propositions which are mostly "middle level hypotheses." I hope that the propositions generated in the process of framing such statements to allow empirical testing will displace many of the vague generalizations now found in the literature. It must be emphasized that I do not attempt any grandiose tasks such as "reformulating" economic anthropology, "determining the relative primacy" of distribution or production, or building a theoretical structure to embrace all man's economic activities. Rather, I attempt the more modest but important task of analyzing on a theoretical and empirical level a set of hypotheses of interest to economists, anthropologists, and historians and letting the reader draw his own philosophical and ideological conclusions. I do have an analytic framework for orienting my course, but it is consistent with a wide number of broader philosophical approaches.

Several subsidiary purposes also deserve brief mention. First, I wish to bring into sharper analytic focus a series of neglected aspects of distribution so that others may see the value of collecting new types of data. Second, I wish to develop a series of new concepts and analytic techniques so that problems of distribution in different economic systems can be more rigorously handled. Finally, I hope to offer a new perspective by which problems concerning the origins of economic institutions can be studied.

The remainder of this introductory chapter is to orient the reader to the general conclusions of the study, to the methods used to reach these conclusions, to the data used in the empirical analysis, and to the manner in which I attack the subject.

AN OVERVIEW OF THE RESULTS

In the next chapter, I develop an exhaustive typology of modes of distribution. The first major distinction is between the concepts of exchange and transfer. An exchange is a transaction in which the goods and services going from one group to another are "balanced" by a counterflow of goods and services. Exchanges are sometimes called "two-way transactions." A transfer is a transaction in which the goods and services going from a person or group to another are not "balanced" by a counterflow. Transfers are sometimes called "one-way transactions" or "grants." I then distinguish two types of exchange transactions: market exchange and reciprocal exchange, the differentiating characteristic being the visibility of the underlying supply and demand forces. I also distinguish two types of transfer transactions: centric and noncentric transfers, the differentiating characteristic being the degree to which the system of transfers is structured with a focal point such as a political or religious leader or institution.

Some Conclusions

In the paragraphs below I briefly review some of the important theoretical and empirical conclusions reached in the following chapters. At this point some of the propositions discussed below may appear counterintuitive or even wrong; detailed argumentation of these propositions is found in the following chapters.

Many different modes of distribution appear related to the levels of economic development of primitive and peasant societies. For societies at low levels of economic development, the most important distributional modes include the reciprocal exchange of goods and of labor and noncentric transfers of goods. For societies at high levels of economic development, the most important distributional modes include the market exchange of goods and of labor and centric transfers of goods and of labor. Thus, we can say that in an important sense reciprocal exchange of goods and of labor and the noncentric transfers of goods are the types of distributional systems which emerged first in human history.

Although such an evolutionary approach takes us a certain distance in understanding the origins of various modes of distribution, we must also pay attention to a series of other causal variables as well if we are to achieve an acceptable degree of explanatory power. Some of these variables can be classified as economic. For instance, the principal source of food production—hunting, gathering, herding, fishing, or farming—appears to play an important role in determining the presence of the market exchange of labor, the reciprocal exchange of goods, and the noncentric transfers of goods. Other variables usually classified as "economic" also play a role: For instance, the relative scarcity of land plays a causal role in the presence of land rentals, and the capital intensiveness of production plays a causal role in the presence of an interest rate.

Some of the variables playing a causal role in the presence or absence of particular modes of exchange can be classified as "social." For instance, the size of the major production and consumption unit seems to play an important role in the presence of noncentric transfers of goods and centric transfers of labor. The economic role of women and particular marriage institutions play important causal roles in the presence of markets for goods, the presence of a market for land, noncentric transfers of goods, and the presence of slavery (a noncentric transfer of labor). Indeed, my entire theory of slavery is based on the homologous role of women and slaves in the functioning of society. Some political variables also seem to play a causal role: For instance, certain types of slavery can be linked to the presence of a fairly high degree of concentration of political power.

At the same time that theoretical and empirical evidence is presented to argue these propositions, additional evidence is provided showing that other hypotheses do not explain the results. A good portion of many chapters is devoted to discussion of propositions offered by others to explain the presence or absence of some particular mode of distribution; I also try to outline briefly how I tested these propositions and the negative results I obtained. In the course of research, literally thousands of propositions found in the literature were tested; most had to be decisively rejected.

In addition to the kinds of propositions just discussed, I also examine a variety of other types of hypotheses. I look at a number of conjectures about the relative levels of economic development at which certain types of distributional modes appeared. For instance, I find that the empirical evidence supporting the oft-stated proposition that external trade emerged at a lower level of economic development than internal trade (or similarly, that "external money" emerged before "internal money") quite unconvincing. I also explore a series of hypotheses about the relative frequencies of different types of distributional modes and reach conclusions running counter to common beliefs. For instance, I find the frequency of occurrence of various types of transfers to be almost as great as the frequency of different types of exchange, a proposition running contrary to the enormous emphasis in the last few decades on the essentially reciprocal nature of distribution in precapitalist societies.

In the final chapter I reexamine the concept of primitive economic systems and provide a new classification based on distributional criteria and the way in which certain clusters of societies deviate from the pattern predicted by reference to the level of economic development. The usefulness of the classification schema is demonstrated by showing how economic systems variables can be successfully included as causal variables for explaining certain features of primitive and peasant economies which are not directly related to the economy.

Some Observations

Although the relationships which I find between various modes of distribution and the level of economic development have also been argued by a number of evolutionists, I believe my linkage between the theoretical and empirical evidence on these matters to be quite novel. Furthermore, the isolation of a wide number of other causal variables represents, I believe, a distinct improvement over the approach of the evolutionists who focused their sole attention on the development variable.

In arguing the various propositions and in carrying out the different statistical tests, I am approaching the subject of the origins of distribution in a manner quite different from others now working in the field. It should be clear that I am an adherent of none of the various warring factions in economic anthropology or economic prehistory. Rather, I try to reframe the questions asked by all the factions in a manner which will permit systematic empirical testing. It should also be clear that my approach is quite different from that traditionally followed by economists, who have been content to limit themselves to a narrower set of questions and to explore only a small set of causal variables.

The Analytic Approach

A BRIEF METHODOLOGICAL PERSPECTIVE[4]

I am trying to derive general laws that are valid in different economic systems rather than to investigate and explain the particular features of the economy of any given society. However, in all of the analyses I try to keep in mind that a major purpose in making generalizations is to aid in the investigation of individual cases. The reader will quickly see that in none of the various statistical analyses do I explain more than a part of the variation of the phenomenon under investigation. But if I am able to explain a significant part of this variation, I am reducing (but not eliminating) the difficulties of explaining the phenomenon in a specific historical context of a particular society.

A serious problem in such an analysis arises because of difficulties in isolating specific traits as general causal factors in a complex context without destroying the cultural web which allegedly gives meaning to the phenomenon under investigation. I try to circumvent some of these problems by employing multivariate techniques of statistical analysis so that I can take into account a number of different variables at the same time and determine the relative importance of each. Furthermore, I try to pay some attention to deviant cases so as to explore some of the possible causal variables not included in the analysis. Finally, I not only examine the various individual types of exchange and transfer in isolation from each other but also, at the end of the book, examine overall patterns. Such techniques by no means solve the problem of the destruction of integument, but I hope that they minimize some of the major difficulties.

Closely related to this difficulty is the problem of how much one must analyze an economic system in terms of the cognitive and moral perceptions of the members of the society, in contrast with analyzing the economy with one's own concepts. In order to make cross-cultural comparisons, one must employ a carefully defined and consistent set of concepts, but I try to meet some of the objections to my techniques in several ways. First, for many phenomena I use multiple definitions in the statistical analysis; although none of these may correspond to native usages in a particular society, they give the reader some feeling of how the results of the analysis are affected by changes in definition and meaning. Second, for certain parts of the study I try to explore the different native cognitions and perceptions. Finally, in Chapter 4 and in Appendix B, I specifically carry out some studies designed to explore these problems of meaning and how they affect our conclusions in a systematic fashion.

----

[4]In the next few paragraphs I state briefly the underlying position of this study regarding the issues in the ideographic–nomothetic debate, the holism–particularism debate, and the emic–etic debate. (These issues are discussed in an illuminating fashion on a more abstract basis by Neil Smelser, *Comparisons in the Social Sciences* (forthcoming) and Marvin Harris, "Emics, Etics, and the New Ethnography," *The Rise of Anthropological Theory* (1968), pp. 568–605.)

This book is the third volume of a trilogy on comparative economics, and my methodological position on certain issues is spelled out in greater detail in these books. The other two volumes are: *Public Expenditures in Communist and Capitalist Nations* (1968) and *Property and Industrial Organization in Communist and Capitalist Nations* (1973).

A final problem concerns the way in which I delineate the "economy" from the rest of "society." Although I sometimes speak of "economic," "social," or "political" variables, these should not be interpreted as anything more than convenient labels. Any act of exchange or transfer has economic, social, and political implications, and it is no more possible to separate one group of activities as purely economic and another group of activities as purely political than it is to separate physically the blue part of a flame from the yellow or the red part of a flame. But as these parts of the flame have different temperatures and for certain purposes can be analytically distinguished, so we can focus our major attention on the economic aspects of the various activities and omit from current consideration other aspects of the subject.

SELECTION OF HYPOTHESES

The hypotheses studied in this book are not generated deductively from some overarching general model of primitive and peasant economies. Rather, I have combed the anthropological and economic literatures for hypotheses of others and, in addition, have generated a large number by myself on the basis of simple economic considerations that scarcely warrant the rodomontade appellation of "model." Some of the hypotheses, based on different economic considerations, conflict; but this is not necessarily bad since in many cases it is quite unclear as to which economic considerations we must properly take into account. In short, I have tried to use the method of "intelligent plausibility," so that this study can be classified neither as strictly deductive nor inductive. Economists may well request more elaborate models, but the subject matter of anthropology is sufficiently more complicated than economics that this may be a counsel of perfection. Anthropologists may well desire fewer deductions, but they must be advised that I am trying to introduce some rigor into the analysis of propositions that are usually treated as *obiter dicta*.

Because I focus attention on only the most important causal forces, the explanations for the occurrence of particular phenomena under investigation are seldom complete. For this reason I use probabilistic techniques in testing the various hypotheses, assuming that these unspecified minor causal factors act in a random fashion.

Almost every chapter begins with a survey of the most interesting propositions regarding the phenomena under investigation. Such efforts would be unnecessary if some economic anthropologist had published a propositional inventory similar to those appearing in other subareas of anthropology.[5] In order to clarify my methods of hypothesis selection, it is useful to consider briefly several types of hypotheses which are neglected both in the discussion and in the empirical analysis.

First, I generally avoid propositions resting exclusively on psychological considerations not only because comparable data are extremely difficult to obtain

---

[5]E.g., William J. Goode, *Social Systems and Family Patterns: A Propositional Inventory* (1971).

but also because it is almost impossible to determine whether psychological correlates to economic phenomena are causes or effects. In addition, the chains of reasoning from psychological to economic phenomena are sufficiently tenuous that the value of collecting relevant data to test them can be questioned. For instance, Yehudi Cohen has advanced some propositions relating food sharing practices between adults to child-raising methods,[6] and although neither his evidence nor his argumentation seemed particularly convincing to me, I dutifully collected comparable information on infant feeding practices and disciplinary techniques to see if I could replicate his results, which I could not. Other hypotheses relating toilet training and similar considerations to societal processes of exchange and transfer of goods and services were originally considered, but the costs of the expenditure of time to collect comparable information on such matters appeared sufficiently greater than the possible benefits from such information that I chose not to pursue such approaches. Of course, I am aware that a number of psychological explanations of social phenomena in primitive societies have been successfully demonstrated[7]; for this study, however, none seemed very promising.

Second, I generally pay little attention to "functional" propositions of any sort unless they can be translated into a form permitting cross-cultural testing.[8] One example might illustrate some of the logical and empirical problems involved in such propositions. The late E. E. Evans-Pritchard once noted: "It is therefore a common-sense inference that payment of bridewealth [goods and money given by the family of a groom to the family of the bride—FLP] has a stabilizing action on marriage."[9] He argued this proposition by reference to the difficulties a bride's family has in returning the bridewealth in case of a divorce and the pressures they would exert on the bride to remain with her husband if marital difficulties occur. What does this proposition really mean? Aside from the difficulties concerning some crucial terms (e.g., "bridewealth," "stabilizing," and even "marriage"), it is unclear whether this proposition refers only to the single society he was examining (if so, it becomes one of those arguments which is "true" only because it is a rationalization to "explain" and observe relationships in a single case) or to all societies. If it is the latter, then it is unclear whether this is a general proposition or whether additional modifications and conditions are necessary to specify. If we interpret this "functional" proposition without modifiers and look at actual data rather than

[6]Cohen, *Social Structure and Personality*. In fairness to Yehudi Cohen it should be noted that in a later article, "Macroethnology: Large Scale Comparative Studies," in *Introduction to Cultural Anthropology* (1968), ed. James A. Clifton, pp. 402–450, he repudiates this psychological approach to societal exchange relations and advocates an approach toward the analysis of sharing which bears some strong similarities to that which I follow in this study.

[7]A number of such studies are summarized by Charles Harrington and John W. M. Whiting, "Socialization Process and Personality," in *Psychological Anthropology* (1972), ed. Francis L. K. Hsu, pp. 469–509.

[8]As Carl G. Hempel ("The Logic of Functional Analysis," in *Symposium of Sociological Theory* [1959], ed. Llewellyn Gross, pp. 271–307) has pointed out, many "functional" propositions do not reach this state of precision.

[9]E. E. Evans-Pritchard, *Kinship and Marriage among the Nuer* (1951), p. 90.

sit in our armchair and idly speculate, it turns out that this "obvious" proposition is quite untrue.[10]

Other "functional" propositions refer to such vague phenomena as "social solidarity," and these could not be tested except if they permitted an interpretation based on relative frequency of the phenomenon under investigation. That is, if Institution A is supposed to promote social solidarity to a greater extent than Institution B, and if societies adopting either of these institutions face difficult survival problems, then we would expect to find more societies with Institution A than B, other things being equal. Unfortunately, many "functional" arguments that I came across in the literature were tautologies or were stated in a manner that did not permit statistical testing with any kind of data. In the following chapters I generally omit from discussion such examples of anthropological alchemy, that is, the attempt to transmute verbiage into laws of human behavior.

In order to explain the various types of exchange and transfer, I have tried to employ as wide a set of causal variables as possible: "social variables" such as measures of social inequality or size of family; "social structural variables" such as type of lineages, postmarital residence rules, and so forth; "political" variables such as relative frequency of internal or external disputes, the relative degree of political centralization, and similar variables; "economic" variables such as the level of economic development, the relative importance of women's work, the presence of various types of economic institutions and practices, and many others; "environmental" variables such as average temperature and temperature variations, average length of growing season, soil conditions, vegetation, and so forth (but very few of these proved very useful in the analysis).[11] I also occasionally employ what may be described as "atmosphere" variables, which are variables reflecting particular values or beliefs, as manifested by some measurable phenomenon. Although, as noted above, I believe that most activities in society contain social, social structural, political, and economic elements, I categorize the variables into boxes labeled "social" or "political" for matters of convenience, where the label reflects that aspect of the activity that seems relatively most important in some general sense.

THE USE OF STATISTICAL TECHNIQUES

In testing the various propositions, I have used multivariate statistical techniques that are quite standard in economics but are seldom applied in anthropology. These techniques are employed because I usually want to test several allegedly conflicting hypotheses at the same time; in many cases it turns

[10]The data underlying this contention are presented in Appendix C.1.   The proposition also appears untrue for important subsamples of the 60 societies, for example, for those societies which are stateless or which have had no extensive contact with the West.

[11]It turned out to be extremely difficult to obtain comparable information about these environmental variables since there are few standardized statistics in this field which are available for the entire planet. The two most useful sources I found were: I. A. Gol'tsberg, ed., *Agroklimaticheskii atlas mira,* Glavnaia gidrometeorologicheskoi sluzbi (1972); and Heinrich Walter and Helmut Lieth, *Klimadiagramm Weltatlas* (various years).

out that rival explanations for a given phenomenon both turn out to be true and that the best explanation combines both. Furthermore, by the inclusion of a number of different independent variables, we are much more able to take into consideration the "context" of a particular phenomenon than approaches that use unicausal statistical models permitting only one causal variable to be examined at a time.

In most cases hypothesis testing is carried out by calculating a multiple regression of the form:

$$D = a + bl_1 + cl_2 + dl_3,$$

where D is the dependent variable (or variable to be explained), the ls are the independent variables (or explanatory variables) and the small letters are the calculated regression coefficients. The coefficient of determination (R^2) shows the percentage of the variance of the dependent variable that is explained by the calculated regression. For all of the statistical tests (usually performed by comparing the standard error of the calculated coefficient to the coefficient; the standard error is always placed below the coefficient in parentheses) I consider a relationship statistically significant only if there is less than 1 chance in 20 that the observed relationship occurred as a result of random events.

In many cases I use as independent variables certain variables which take on only two values (i.e., 1 = a specified phenomenon is present; 0 = a specified phenomenon is absent). The calculated coefficients of these "dummy variables" are interpreted in the same manner as the coefficients for continuous variables.

Three major statistical problems arise in the analysis that deserve brief mention. First, in certain cases the independent variables did not meet the requirement for regression analysis that they be statistically unrelated. When the explanatory variables are correlated (which can be easily determined), then two techniques can be employed. If the intercorrelations are not great, the inaccuracies in the calculated regression coefficients are small and can be neglected. If the correlations are considerable, particular steps must be taken, of which the easiest is to drop one of the explanatory variables. (Thus, in the analysis of Eskimo exchange accounts in Chapter 4, I find that hunting productivity and income of Eskimo men are highly correlated; I drop the former variable from the statistical analysis since the latter is, for my purposes, a more appropriate variable.)

A much more serious problem arises because in many cases the dependent variable (variable to be explained) takes on only several values. In this case, according to standard statistical theory, ordinary least squares techniques for calculating the regression are often inappropriate because they allegedly cause the error term in the regression to be heteroskedastic.[12] Certain fancy statistical techniques such as the use of logit or probit analysis can be used for circumventing such problems, and I dutifully calculated logit regressions for every

---

[12]A detailed discussion of this problem is by Jan Kmenta, *Elements of Econometrics* (1971), pp. 425–428.

relationship presented in the text for which this was feasible.[13] In almost every case, the logit analyses gave practically the same results as the ordinary least squares regressions. Since the results of a logit regression are not easily interpretable without carrying out certain transformations requiring a calculator and a table of logarithms, it seems worthwhile to present the easily interpretable least squares regression results in the text and to present for the statistical purists the results of the logit analysis in Appendix B.1.

A third problem involves the robustness of my regression results. Since I am not presenting the reader with most of the regressions showing negative results (but merely mentioning that such results were obtained, a technique reducing the size of this book by about 50%), a number of legitimate questions can be raised. In carrying out such regression experiments, I paid considerable attention to the robustness of the results which I present. In most cases my regression results are quite robust, that is, my regression coefficients remain roughly the same when new variables are added. Those few regression results which are not robust are explicitly noted in the text.

A final problem concerns interaction of causal forces. Although the use of the linear regression form implies that the various causal forces act in an additive fashion, it is certainly possible to define the variables in such a manner as to take into account particular types of interactive processes between the independent variables. A number of experiments along these lines were carried out and proved unsuccessful. The simple additive causal model which I use was not blindly chosen but was selected because it served well the statistical investigation.

In some analyses in this study, I examine the regression "residuals." These are the differences between the predicted value of the dependent variable for the various societies (which are calculated for each society by plugging into the regression equation the relevant independent variables) and the actual value of this variable. One example of such an analysis of residuals occurs in the search for diffusion effects; another case occurs in trying to test the impact of kinship relations on imbalances of Eskimo exchange accounts. What I am doing in such analyses is roughly the same as an analysis of "deviant cases," which is sometimes used by social scientists.

Most economists will find the statistical analysis employed in this study to be quite elementary and my various explanations of the methods employed to be tedious. Many anthropologists and historians will find the statistical analyses to

---

[13]A general discussion of problems underlying logit analysis can be found in Daniel McFadden, "Conditional Logit Analysis of Qualitative Choice Behavior," in *Frontiers in Econometrics* (1974), ed. Paul Zarembka, pp. 105–146; or Marc Nerlove and S. James Press, *Univariate and Multivariate Log-Linear and Logistic Models* (1973).

The logit program which I used was written by Charles Mansky of Carnegie-Mellon University, who cooperated with me above and beyond the normal call of scholarly duty. I also received help from Larry Mannheim, Barry Fishman, and E. M. Mullins.

Logit regressions were calculated for all ordinary least squares regressions presented in the text except for those where the dependent variable had more than two values. In several cases the algorithm used in calculating the logit regressions did not converge; such cases are noted in the text. Further notes on the logit analysis, as well as all the logit results, are presented in Appendix B.1.

be overcomplicated and my various explanations too terse. A reverse discontent may arise when I discuss kinship relations or certain social structural concepts. A short glossary of technical terms employed is presented in Appendix D. I ask the forbearance of all groups.

THE DATA

Selection of the Sample

The basic thrust of this study is to test a series of propositions using cross-section data and then use these results to generalize about events over time. Such an approach raises many problems, and my procedures to avoid the obvious pitfalls are discussed in detail in Chapter 3. In addition, the selection of the cross-section sample raises a number of practical difficulties that deserve brief consideration now.

In selecting a sample, two general methods may be chosen to determine empirically whether variable A "causes" the presence of variable B, given the presence of variables C, D, and E. Following a research design designated as the "most similar systems" design,[14] we select a sample in which all of the various societies are the same with regard to variable C, D, and E, and then we see if A and B vary in the expected manner. In short, we control for the possible influence of other variables by holding them constant. Following the "most different systems" design, we select a random sample where we hope that there is no systematic clustering of the explanatory variables B, C, D, and E, and then we see if A and B vary in the expected manner. In short, we control for the possible influences of other variables by randomizing them. I use a "most different systems" design but take the analysis one further step: With the use of multivariate statistical techniques I not only test for the expected variation of A and B but also, at the same time, often test whether variations in other variables for which data are available are or are not related to variations of A.

Given such a research design, the selection of the sample of 60 units followed certain procedures. I use communities, rather than societies, as my basic unit of observation because of the obvious difficulties of comparing complex societies such as the Chinese with hundreds of millions of people with isolated primitive societies of only several hundred people such as the Havasupai Indians of Arizona.[15] For nonnomadic societies these communities consist of vil-

---

[14] I use the terminology of Adam Przeworski and Henry Teune, *The Logic of Comparative Social Inquiry* (1970), pp. 31–39.

[15] I have handled this problem (sometimes named "Flowers' problem" and named after the person who apparently first raised it in conjunction with cross-cultural research) in a standard way, which is discussed and justified by John W. M. Whiting, "Methods and Problems in Cross-Cultural Research," in *The Handbook of Social Psychology*, ed. Gardner Lindzey and Elliot Aronson, Vol. II (1968), pp. 693–728.

lages; for nomadic societies the community is the group that travels together in some type of closely coordinated fashion. In some cases the basic ethnographic data consist of a description of a "culture" rather than a single community, so that a "representative community" had to be hypothesized; since ethnographers generally have described the "culture" in terms of the few communities they have visited, this backward inference procedure does not seem unreasonable. For expositional convenience all of the communities are labeled "societies" or are sometimes called after the larger society in which they are located; for example, Nanching village in Kwangtung Province, China, is simply called "China," and the Sirionó group with which the ethnographer Allen Holmberg traveled in Bolivia is labeled "Sirionó." For my results to be valid, it is not necessary to believe that the various communities necessarily "represent" their larger societies. In addition, each community is pinpointed in time so that my sample represents a set of very specific groups existing at a specific time in a specific place.

In selecting the communities, some rules were followed: First, the communities had to come from all over the earth and, to lessen problems arising from diffusion of cultural traits, had to be as far in distance from each other as possible. Second, to lessen diffusion problems still further, the communities had to have mutually unintelligible languages.[16] Third, in order to avoid the clustering of potential causal variables and to obtain as heterogeneous samples as possible (as well as to less diffusion problems), the various communities had to vary from each other in as many significant features as possible. Fourth, the ethnographic materials about the communities had to be reliable and sufficient to obtain answers for a large number of questions about their economies and societies. Finally, there had to be sufficient overlap between my sample and those used in other cross-cultural studies so that certain checks could be made about the accuracy of my codings and also so that certain materials might be drawn from these other samples. Each of these selection principles deserves brief comment.

Regarding the selection of a worldwide sample, a rather simple procedure was employed. I started with a 1957 study by George Peter Murdock that presented the "World Ethnographic Sample" and that divided the earth into 60 separate cultural areas.[17] I tried with considerable success to draw one society for my sample from each of these areas.[18] The map of the sample societies at the beginning of the book shows sample points from all over the world. A more

---

[16]With this principle I am following the suggestion provided by Raoul Naroll, "The Double Language Boundary in Cross-Cultural Surveys," *Behavior Science Notes* VI, 2 (1971): 95–101.

[17]George Peter Murdock, "World Ethnographic Sample," *American Anthropologist* LIX (August 1957): 664–687.

[18]I could find no society in Caucasia with sufficient data for this study and so substituted a nearby culture (the Turks), so that two Near Eastern societies are presented (the Rwala Bedouin is the other). I also did not include any society among the "overseas European" and instead picked an additional Arctic American culture (the two are Copper Eskimo and the Naskapi). Thus, 58 of Murdock's 60 areas are represented.

TABLE 1.1

Distances between Pairs of Societies in the Sample[a]

Distance		Pairs of societies	
Miles	Kilometers	Absolute number	Percentages
0–400	0–644	6	0.3
401–800	645–1288	26	1.5
801–1200	1289–1932	41	2.3
1201–1600	1933–2576	48	2.7
1601–2000	2577–3221	58	3.3
2001–2400	3222–3865	63	3.6
2401–3000	3866–4831	83	4.7
3001–3600	4832–5797	92	5.2
over 3600	over 5797	1353	76.4
	Totals:	1770	100.0

[a] The distances are straight-line distances, measured between the two communities, calculated by use of a tape measure on a large globe. These data underlie the analysis of diffusion described in Chapter 3.

adequate method of gauging the geographical distribution of my sample societies is to investigate the distances between each pair of societies, an exercise carried out in Table 1.1.

A glance at the table shows that roughly 90% of the pairs of societies are over 2000 miles (3221 km) from each other. If the 60 societies were evenly distributed over the entire land area of the earth, the nearest distance that any two would be from each other would be about 900 miles (this would be 1800 miles if we were considering both the land and the sea area); only roughly 2.5% of the pairs of societies are less than this distance from each other, a relatively small percentage. The six pairs of societies that are within 400 miles (644 km) from each other are different in language and are also quite different in their economies and culture, so that cultural diffusion does not seem to be a great problem in these cases.[19]

Regarding the mutual unintelligibility of languages, certain difficulties arose in making decisions about this matter. As the basis of my investigation I used the Voegelins' language index of the world[20] and employed as my criterion of mutual unintelligibility whether or not the various languages were no more closely related than being in the same language "branch." Although I believe

[19] The six pairs are: the Batak of Sumatra and the Semang of Malaysia; the Lepcha of Sikkim and the Ao Naga of Assam; the Serbs of Yugoslavia and the Ghegs of Albania; the Omaha Indians of the Central United States and the Comanche Indians of the south central United States; the Havasupai of Arizona and the Navajo of New Mexico in the United States; and the Warao of Venezuela and the Callinago of the Lesser Antilles Islands.

[20] C. F. and F. M. Voegelin, "Index of Languages of the World," *Anthropological Linguistics* VIII (June 1966): 1–222; and (October 1966): 1–202.

that all of the languages represented by communities in the sample are mutually unintelligible, certain ambiguities arose in the application of the criterion so that in several cases I cannot be entirely sure that the sampling principle was met.[21]

Regarding the selection of "different" societies, only a rather subjective method could be employed. More specifically, after I had gained a rough idea of the outlines of the culture, I would stop and ask myself whether or not it strongly resembled any other society in the sample which had already been coded, especially in the same geographical area. In certain cases similar societies in different global areas (e.g., the Rwala Bedouin of Syria and Arabia and the Somali Bedouin of Somali) could be easily spotted, and one was omitted; in other cases I could take into account only gross cultural or economic differences and similarities.

Examining the sample to see if the desired heterogeneity is achieved can be carried out in several different ways. Since I tried to select societies as different as possible from each other, particularly in the same geographical area, one indication of such heterogeneity is whether we find a relatively even distribution over the scale of economic development of the societies in each major geographical area. Data on these matters are presented in Table 1.2.

Although each major geographical area usually contains societies in the four categories of development (the scale is described in detail in Chapter 2), the distribution is not as even as we might have hoped. Nevertheless, from a statistical point of view the situation is not particularly alarming.

Another indication of heterogeneity of the sample is whether or not we have societies whose major ways of obtaining food represent the different possibilities that are available. The characteristics of the communities in the sample in this regard, cross-classified by relative level of economic development, are presented in Table 1.3.

Although 60% of the societies in the sample have a subsistence economy such that the most important food source is agriculture, other modes of subsistence production are also represented. As I note in what follows, a comparison of the distribution of major modes of subsistence production in my sample and in a sample of 1170 societies in the *Ethnographic Atlas* shows no significant

[21]In most cases the languages of the societies in the sample are at least in different language "branches" in the Voegelins' index. There are four important groups of exceptions. A group of five of the African societies (Ganda, Nyakyusa, Suku, Tiv, and Thonga) have languages in the Bantu branch of the Benue-Congo family of languages; however, each of these is in a different "Guthrie Zone" where the assumption of mutual unintelligibility seems plausible. The other exceptions occur for pairs of societies. Both Tikopian and Maori languages are in the Polynesian subfamily of the Austronesian family of languages; however, they are classified as belonging to different "clusters." The languages of the Ao Naga and the Lepcha have given rise to some confusion, according to the Voegelins, ibid., but probably they are in different language branches of the same language family. The languages of the Rif and the Tuareg are both in the Berber family of languages but are classified in different "groups." A native Rif speaker assured me that he could not understand a Tuareg speaker. It appears, therefore, that probably all of the languages spoken by members of the 60 societies of my sample are mutually unintelligible.

TABLE 1.2

Relative Levels of Economic Development and Major Geographical Areas of the Societies in the Sample[a]

	Number of societies in the sample					
	Sub-Sahara Africa	Circum-Mediterranean	East Eurasia	Insular Pacific	North America	Central and South America
Lowest 15 societies in economic development scale	1	0	2	2	3	7
Second lowest 15 societies in economic development scale	1	1	2	3	6	2
Second highest 15 societies in economic development scale	5	2	3	5	0	0
Highest 15 societies in economic development scale	4	6	2	0	2	1
Total	11	9	9	10	11	10

[a]The data come from Appendix A, Series 1 and 22. The concept of economic development employed in this study is explained in Chapter 2.

TABLE 1.3

Relative Levels of Economic Development and Major Modes of Obtaining Food of Societies in the Sample[a]

	Number of societies in the sample					
	Gathering	Hunting	Fishing	Animal husbandry	Incipient agriculture	Agriculture
Lowest 15 societies in economic development scale	7	4	0	1	2	1
Second lowest 15 societies in economic development scale	1	1	2	5	1	5
Second highest 15 societies in economic development scale	0	0	0	3	1	11
Highest 15 societies in economic development scale	0	0	0	0	0	15
Total	8	5	2	9	4	32

[a]The data come from Appendix A, Series 5 and 22.

difference.[22] Although it may have been desirable to overrepresent societies relying on fishing and hunting in my sample, I do not feel that lack of heterogeneity with regard to major source of food production is a very serious problem.

One other means of obtaining heterogeneity was employed, namely, selecting societies that do not have strong Western influence. In a few cases this did not prove possible. In other cases this required pinpointing the variables of the society at a date before the anthropologist visited the community, usually at the time just before initial contact with the West or at a time when Western influence was not strong. In these cases I usually followed the reconstruction of the society in this period by the anthropologist who, like me, was interested in factoring out Western influences in order to determine what features of the community were truly "aboriginal." Such an exercise is, of course, fraught with difficulties; the obtained results warrant, I believe, such efforts. A listing of each society, along with the pinpointed date, is given in Appendix E.

Regarding the availability and sufficiency of ethnographic materials, several procedures were adopted. In initially selecting societies for analysis, I tried to choose only those societies in which an educated observer had spent one or more years, could speak the native language, and had written sufficiently on the economic aspects of the society for most of my questions to be answered. Whenever possible, I also tried to select societies which had been visited by more than one such observer so that different viewpoints could be gained. Unfortunately, it did not prove possible to meet these demanding criteria in all cases.

Regarding the overlap of my sample with others, the situation is quite simple. When this study was started, the most intensive attempt to make comparisons of the relative levels of economic development of a large group of primitive and peasant societies was by Robert Carneiro.[23] In order to take advantage of his

[22]In making such comparisons, two questions arise. First, to what degree is my perception of the principal source of food production similar to the ratings of other observers? Second, to what degree does the distribution of societies of my sample according to the principal source of food production differ from a similar distribution from a larger sample? To answer both questions, my data must be recoded to correspond with the definitions used by others.

After such recoding is carried out, it is clear that my coding of the principal source of food production corresponds closely with the ratings of others. Of the 45 societies in my sample that are also reported by George P. Murdock and Douglas R. White, "Standard Cross-Cultural Sample," *Ethnology* VIII (October 1969): 329–369, my ratings are the same as theirs for 44.5 cases (in 1 case I rate a society as a gathering/hunting society, while Murdock and White rate it as a hunting society). Of the 59 societies of my sample which are also reported in the *Ethnographic Atlas,* 53 are rated similarly with regard to the major mode of food production. Of the six differences in ratings two are due to the selection of different parts of the same larger society or the society at greatly different points in time; three differences are due to whether or not agriculture is considered "incipient" or "full"; and one difference is due to a disagreement about the relative importance of agriculture and animal husbandry in a society in which both are quite important.

The comparison of the distribution of societies according to the major mode of food production was carried out with the *Ethnographic Atlas* sample. This is discussed below.

[23]Robert L. Carneiro has made a number of these studies, which are summarized in his essay, "Scale Analysis, Evolutionary Sequences, and the Rating of Cultures," in *A Handbook of Method in Cultural Anthropology* (1973), eds. Raoul Naroll and Ronald Cohen, pp. 834–872. Carneiro very generously gave me access to the data on which he made his estimates, and I would like to express my appreciation to him for this help.

calculations, I tried to select societies for which he made such development ratings. During the course of research, however, other articles were published presenting much simpler methods of calculating levels of economic development. Since these methods led to results highly correlated with Carneiro's findings,[24] this permitted me to stray from Carneiro's sample. Most of the societies in my sample are either in the sample of Carneiro or in the "Standard Cross-Cultural Sample" of Murdock and White.[25] In a number of places in this study I compare my codings for particular variables with theirs so that the reader may gain some idea about the replicability of my results. The actual comparisons are, of course, rather boring to the general reader and for this reason are usually placed in footnotes.

How adequate is my sample for carrying out cross-cultural testing of hypotheses? The major statistical criterion is "independence," which, in the context of cross-cultural studies, has two meanings. One meaning refers to the historical independence of the societies and whether or not my results are influenced by cultural diffusion; for my sample I do not believe that this is a problem, and I discuss such matters in great detail in Chapter 3. A more common meaning refers to the degree to which the sample was randomly selected. I must emphasize that this is not a random sample; therefore, the statistical results must be cautiously interpreted. In a standard regression analysis with a sample of 60 a calculated coefficient is generally considered to be statistically significant (at the .05 level) if the t test (the calculated coefficient, divided by its standard error) is slightly above 2.00. My level of acceptance is only for those cases where the t statistic is 2.25 or above. In the various regressions presented in the following chapters, I designate with an asterisk whether or not the calculated coefficient meets this acceptance test.

One final important question to be asked about the sample concerns its "representativeness." Since we have no complete catalogue of world societies, it is difficult to make very firm judgments on this matter; nevertheless, certain useful comparisons can be made with larger samples.

Comparison of the geographical spread of the societies in my sample with a listing of over 2000 cultures suggests that my sample somewhat underrepresents the number of cultures from Africa and the Circum-Mediterranean area and overrepresents the number of societies from Oceania and from North and South America.[26] This judgment can only be very tentative since we have no

[24]The most useful of these studies for my purposes was: George P. Murdock and Caterina Provost, "Measurement of Cultural Complexity," *Ethnology* XIII (October 1973): 379–392.

[25]George P. Murdock and Douglas R. White, "Standard Cross-Cultural Sample," pp. 329–369.

[26]George Peter Murdock, *Outline of World Cultures*, 3rd ed., rev. (1963), has listed somewhat over 2100 which are classified with a double capital letter and a number (some additional societies are sometimes included within a single double-capital-letter-and-number category). The number of these societies are divided into the following regions: Sub-Sahara Africa, 21%; Circum-Mediterranean (Europe plus Middle East plus European Russia and Caucasia), 21%; East Eurasia (Asia excluding Middle East but including the Asian parts of the U.S.S.R.), 13%; Insular Pacific or Oceania, 15%; South and Central America (plus Caribbean Islands) 14%; and North America (excluding Central America), 15%. My own sample has the following breakdown for these six areas respectively: 18%, 15%, 15%, 17%, 18%, and 17%. My sample has a considerably better approximation to this list of over 2100 societies than the *Ethnographic Atlas*, 1972 version.

way of knowing how complete the larger listing is and to what extent the societies in this larger listing represent distinct cultural units.

If we judge representativeness in terms of the distribution of the population of my sample and of the distribution of the population of the world, then clearly my sample underrepresents East Eurasia (especially India, China, and Japan) and highly overrepresents North and South America.

Another way of investigating the representativeness of my sample is in terms of the distribution of various characteristics vis-à-vis such a distribution drawn from a much larger sample of the world's societies. Comparisons were made between my sample and the 1170 societies in the *Ethnographic Atlas* for 30 different variables covering marriage and the family (premarital sex norms, types of major marriage payments, types of preferences for cousin marriage, forms of marriage, and composition of families living together), social structure (lineage structure [four different variables], kin terminology, postmarital residence, class structure, presence of castes, presence of slavery [two variables], inheritance patterns [four variables]), community structure (settlement patterns [nomadic, stationary, etc.], local community size, community organization, and levels of jurisdictional hierarchy in the community and larger society [two variables]), and the economy (major mode of subsistence, type of agriculture, major crop, employment of animals in plow cultivation, predominant type of animal husbandry, and milking of domestic animals).[27] For none of these variables was the distribution of traits in my sample and in the larger sample very different. Despite the nonrandom manner in which my sample was selected, I ended up with a sample that appears representative regarding the distribution of important characteristics of a much larger sample. Although we do not know whether the 1170 societies in the *Ethnographic Atlas* adequately represent the entire number of societies in world history, this was the largest collection of consistently coded ethnographic information that I could obtain.

Collection and Coding of the Data

Unlike many cross-cultural studies that employ overworked and underpaid students to collect and code the data, I carried out this work myself. At one time several students were employed to collect data; but this was primarily to check the degree of coding similarity that could be obtained, and their data are not

[27]Several problems occurred in making these comparisons. I have coded communities, while the *Ethnographic Atlas*, 1972 version, contains codings for larger societies. Furthermore, many of my codings rest on quite different definitions than those of the *Ethnographic Atlas*. To circumvent these difficulties, I used the codings of the *Ethnographic Atlas* for the larger societies in which my societies were located and compared these with the codings for the entire *Ethnographic Atlas*. Because I disagree with some of the codings in the *Ethnographic Atlas*, because I believe that some of their concepts are ambiguous, and because some of their codings for the societies in my sample refer to different groups or different time periods than those I have chosen, such a procedure has some obvious problems. But for the very rough purposes for which I use the results, I believe that such a procedure is adequate.

used in the major part of the analysis. By plowing through the various ethno-graphic studies myself, several purposes were served. First, I learned a good deal about anthropology and anthropologists, information that is inaccessible if one limits one's reading to more theoretical studies. Second, I could gain some idea about the accuracy of various sources by comparing them. In many cases, ethnographic sources give exactly opposite opinions about certain allegedly factual matters, so that I became more sensitized to different definitions that are employed, different field methods that are used, and the impact of carrying out fieldwork in different places or at different times.[28] And third, I gained sufficient familiarity with the societies in the sample that when it became necessary to recode certain variables, I could carry out such a task with a minimum of trauma. In many cases my original conceptualizations of particular phenomena were inadequate, and I had to employ new definitions. In other cases I saw the necessity of using multiple definitions of particular concepts (e.g., in the analysis of money, I use nine different definitions of money; in the analysis of slavery, four). Finally, I gained insight into the ways in which anthropologists and ethnographers attempt to explain certain phenomena; in addition, I could collect hypotheses for further cross-cultural testing.

Whenever possible, I tried to read the complete primary ethnographies on each society and, for the 60 sample societies, consulted over 1200 different sources. The most useful sources are listed in Appendix E. I had no hesitation in writing, telephoning, or visiting with anthropologists who had carried out fieldwork in the sample societies in order to explore particular problems. With few exceptions, these informants were most patient and accommodating, even when I followed lines of inquiry that they felt were unproductive or when I argued with them about their interpretations. Let me emphasize the usual disclaimer that these informants are not responsible either for my interpreta-tions of their materials or for any of my conclusions.

Some of the variables that I coded concern just the communities used in the sample, while other variables concern the larger society in which the com-munities are located (e.g., the level of economic development). Some of the variables concern one simple and relatively unambiguous phenomenon (e.g., is there extensive use of irrigation?), while other variables deal with a complex of different phenomena and represent a judgment on my part (e.g., are more than 5% of the goods produced in the society distributed through a market?). For many of the judgmental variables, the proper data are really not available, so that I had to try to quantify the ethnographer's adjectival descriptions (e.g., the market was "extremely unimportant" or only a "few unimportant" goods were transferred through the market). Sometimes this could be done by deter-mining how the author described cases in which more evidence was provided;

---

[28]In some cases in which disagreement about fact appeared in different ethnographic reports after all these considerations had been taken into account, a decision about relative reliability still had to be made. In these cases, I tried to make such decisions on the bases of whose supporting materials were the more adequate.

TABLE 1.4

Hypothetical Cases of the Impact of Coding Errors[a]

	Case 1				Case 2			
	Real world		My coding		Real world		My coding	
	A present	A absent	A present	A absent	A present	A absent	A present	A absent
B present	100	0	80	20	50	50	50	50
B absent	0	100	20	80	50	50	50	50

[a]*General assumption:* I make a random error in coding the presence or absence of each variable in 20% of all cases.

sometimes this could be done only by reference to intuitive notions such as the exactitude of the author's style. Of course, in many cases my codings contain a considerable element of guesswork since the evidence for making judgments was unsatisfactory. Such a method of coding introduces a general bias, namely, to muddy any causal relationship which may be present. This is because random errors in coding are introduced on both sides of the causal relationship being studied. To see this quantitatively, two numerical examples are presented in Table 1.4.

It is noteworthy that the relationship in Case 1 is muddied, but it is still observable. In Case 2, no relationship can be found between the two variables to start with, and if my coding errors are random, no relationship is found after the coding is completed. In short, I might miss finding a particular relationship because of random coding errors, but I would never find a relationship that does not exist.

The problem of systematic errors or bias, either on my part or on the part of the ethnographers on whose work I am basing the coding, raises difficult problems as well. In order to control for systematic bias on my part, as noted above, I compare my coding results with those of others whenever possible. In addition, for many of the variables I have coded, I feel some uncertainty, and to alert the reader, these are designated in Appendix A with a special sign. In some cases I have explored the hypothesized relationship not only with the data for the entire sample but also with the data from a subsample of cases for which I am more confident of the coding evaluations.

Systematic bias on the part of individual ethnographic reports could be detected only by reading the reports of as many different ethnographers studying the society which I could obtain. A glance at the bibliography in Appendix E shows that for most societies the ethnographic reports of at least two observers were used.

PLAN OF ATTACK

In the next chapter, I define some crucial terms used throughout this study. This includes not only a detailed delineation of the different types of exchange and transfer but also a discussion of the meaning of such terms as the "level of economic development" and the "consumption and production units."

Then in Chapter 3 I explore the various problems involved in using the results of cross-section analysis to generalize about events over time. In this discussion I show how I overcome "Galton's problem" and explain the statistical tests carried through the book which I use to show that the cross-section data are sufficiently uncontaminated by cultural diffusion that they can be used for historical generalizations. In the following chapter I present a case study of Eskimo distribution to show how the conceptual apparatus of the study, as well as the analytic techniques, permit us deep understanding into the distributional system of a single community.

Chapters 5–10 constitute the core of analysis and are composed of the cross-cultural analyses of the origins of the major modes of distribution: market exchange, reciprocal exchange, noncentric transfers, and centric transfers. Each chapter contains a survey of propositions, a derivation of the propositions I intend to test, and cross-cultural testing of these propositions, using the evidence from the worldwide sample of 60 societies. I also include a special chapter on the origins of money and of slavery (which, as noted earlier, is a special type of noncentric transfer of labor).

In the final chapter, I examine the determinants of the various modes of distribution together and, using this information, present a method of classifying primitive and peasant economic systems according to distributional criteria. In addition, I also show how such concepts of primitive economic systems can be successfully used in further analyses of some new hypotheses. Finally, I try to show the significance of the results obtained in previous chapters in the broader contexts of anthropology, economics, and history.

2

SOME IMPORTANT
DEFINITIONS

La trop grande subtilité est une fausse délicatesse, et la véritable délicatesse est une solide subtilité.

LA ROCHEFOUCAULD[1]

In "nature" or in the "real world" there are no such phenomena as "reciprocity," "transfers," or "markets"; rather, these are constructs of the mind used to organize particular types of observations and experiences. Disputes over what these concepts "really" mean are sterile except insofar as such arguments lead toward more serious analysis of underlying theoretical differences about causal relations.

Since there is no standard terminology used by scholars in analyzing problems of distribution, I shall explicitly define the various concepts used in this study. These definitions, which differ from those of others, have proved useful for analyzing the various propositions discussed in the following chapters. Of course, definitions and their explications are always dull to read; but this imposition on the reader is necessary to avoid disputes arising from confusions about the way in which I have organized and labeled ethnographic materials. It must be emphasized that neither defining particular concepts nor constructing typologies based on these definitions "explains" any phenomenon; rather, such activity is merely preliminary to investigating causal relations. The "adequacy" of my definitions can only be judged by their clarity and by determining whether the propositions using such concepts illuminate the operations of

---

Design from a Beti stone for playing the game *Abbia;* southern Cameroon.

[1]François VI de La Rochefoucauld, *Réflexions ou sentences et maximes morales*, Maxim No. 128: 'Excessive subtlety is a false refinement; true refinement is a genuine subtlety.'

the various economies in a manner which could not be achieved by using other conceptual schemas.

I start the discussion by outlining some key concepts of distribution which are used to define a typology embracing all types of distributional activities. This typology is used to organize much of the factual materials in the following chapters. Then I examine the concept of "unit of observation," which serves to distinguish between the extrafamilial distributional transactions which I study and the intrafamilial transactions which I do not. Finally, I set forth the definition of "economic development" which serves as one of the key explanatory variables in this book.

MODES OF DISTRIBUTION

Before the individual types of distributional mechanisms can be defined, some very basic terms deserve brief examination.

"Distribution" refers to those transactions that result in goods and services being used or consumed by those who did not directly produce them; "householding" refers to production of goods and services for the sake of immediate consumption by the producer and does not involve distribution. Although the concept of "goods" does not warrant definition, the concept of "services" raises difficulties. Some of the definitional problems concerning "services," which are both an input and an output, have received attention in the social science literature,[2] and they warrant brief consideration here.

As used in this book, "services" refer to productive activities of a nonmaterial sort which are organized in such a manner as to create a "close" connection between the performance of the activity and the performer's obtaining material means to satisfy his wants. This "close" connection may be direct, for example, wage labor or the selling of the use of skills by such diverse professionals as lawyers or prostitutes. This "close" connection may also be somewhat more indirect, for example, reciprocal work exchanges (Person A helps Person B plow his field in return for the same favor by B sometime in the future, a type of delayed reciprocity) or the case of a shaman appealing to the supernatural for aid in curing a sick man in return for a sacrifice to the supernatural by the patient, which the shaman then consumes. Contrariwise, the connection is not "close" in such cases as a person's participating in a sporting or a ceremonial event without pay, a person giving another person friendly advice, or a person helping his child learn to talk. These are not services since, although they may ultimately result in the obtaining of materials means for satisfying the provider's wants, the linkage is quite distant. It should be clear

---

[2]An extremely useful analysis is provided by Walter C. Neale, "On Defining 'Labor' and 'Services' for Comparative Studies," *American Anthropologist* LXVI (December 1964): 1300–1307. Neale also summarizes the definitions of "services" used by a number of others.

that drawing the line between services and other activities requires not only a knowledge of how the society works (since a given activity may be a service in one society and not in another) but also a judgment about the closeness of connection between the activity and the reward. Although this dividing line between services and other activities is somewhat fuzzy, it should be sufficiently clear for most activities to be easily classified.[3]

In the following discussion, I define four modes of distribution covering all types of such mechanisms: market exchange, reciprocal exchange, centric transfers, and noncentric transfers. A society may have none or several of these modes; and the "system of distribution" characterizing a particular society depends on the relative importance of the different modes. For instance, the existence of a "market" does not necessarily imply a "market system," for other modes of distribution may be more important or the markets may be quite peripheral to the important economic processes of the society.[4]

The Distinction between Exchange and Transfer

A key distinction in this study is the differentiation of exchanges and transfers. An exchange is a transaction where the goods and services going from one person or group to another are "balanced" by a counterflow of goods and services. Exchanges are sometimes called "two-way transactions." A transfer is a transaction where the goods and services going from a person or group to another are not "balanced" by a directly observable counterflow. Transfers are sometimes called "one-way transactions" or "grants." This distinction has a number of ambiguities that need to be cleared up.

"Balance" depends, of course, on the standard of value used in evaluating the transaction. With one important modification, I use the definition or the standard of value that is accepted in the society under investigation. That is, if the society has a range of acceptable exchange ratios for particular goods and services, and if the exchange ratios of the transactions under investigation fall within this range, the transaction is considered "balanced" even though by other criteria the transaction may be considered "unbalanced." The determination of balance does not involve consideration either of equity or of any abstract theory of value (e.g., a labor theory requiring that goods should embody the same labor content) or of any evaluation as to the effectiveness of the trans-

---

[3]This definition differs somewhat from that of Neale, ibid., p. 1305, who makes several distinctions:

> [S]ocially integrative activities which provide the material means to action or of satisfying wants are 'labor' and those other activities which 'recreate social relations' and are organized in the same way by the same institutions which organize the provision of material means are economic 'services'.

Reciprocal exchanges of work which Neale might consider labor, I include as services.

[4]This point is elaborated in an interesting manner by Paul Bohannan and George Dalton, "Introduction," *Markets in Africa* (1965), pp. 1–35 [originally published 1962].

action (e.g., the returns from some type of sacrifice or cursing ritual may be worthless at least from our viewpoint). In certain cases the exchange ratios are not explicit and must be induced; a case study of such a process with its attendant difficulties of interpretation is presented in Appendix B.2. In other cases cross-exchange ratios are not consistent, a matter analyzed in Appendix B.3.

The important modification that I introduce is the exclusion of most "social invisibles" that are often invoked by the participants or by observers to be the counterflows which "balance" a flow of goods and services. When A gives B some goods or service and receives none in return, this is often rationalized by saying that B returns "deference" or "respect" or "recognition of prestige" or by asserting that B gives A "protection" or "social recognition" or "permission" (when B permits A to share in some of his "social privileges"). The first set of invisibles is often invoked when B has a lower status than A; the second set of invisibles is often invoked in the reverse social case. Analytic focus on the flow of invisibles can often provide many insights, particularly in laboratory experiments where the implications of these invisibles can be carefully controlled[5]; but such invisibles can also be invoked as "explanations" of particular transactions in a tautological manner (the transaction appears unbalanced, so the analyst dreams up some counterflow of invisibles to "restore" balance) which may obscure the real situation. In this study I exclude considerations of all invisibles except those that have an observable market value. Examples of such invisibles with market values include rental payments for the use of land, interest payments for the use of money or some object, or payments for patents, chants, hunting rights, or some other type of nonmaterial property right.

Some may feel that such an exclusion of invisibles from the classification system gives a "materialistic bias" to the analysis and that it is too "economic oriented" even though such an approach permits cross-cultural comparisons, while the inclusion of such invisibles may not. In reply, let me say that although such invisibles are excluded from the definitions used in classifying transactions, it is not necessary to exclude them from the interpretation of the results. For example, I *classify* the services supplied by a hard-working field slave to his master as a transfer of labor services even though the master may be nice to his slave, protect him from other slaves and slaveholders and feed and clothe him; in *interpreting* the slavery phenomenon, such social invisibles and occasional counterflows can be taken into account. Further, in an intensive case study presented in Chapter 4 I am able to quantify such social invisibles and to test statistically whether they actually do balance the transaction, one of the first such analyses in the economic and economic anthropology literatures. Contrary to the conventional wisdom in anthropology, I find that transfers in this society cannot be explained by status differentials or other invisibles which are usually invoked to interpret such imbalances.

[5]One interesting example of such a study is: Kenneth J. Gergen, Phoebe Diebold, M. Seipel, and Christine Maslach, "Obligation, Donor Resources, and Reaction to Receiving Aid in Three Cultures," *Journal of Personality and Social Psychology* XXXI, 3 (1975) 390–400.

It must be emphasized that attention is focused primarily on the transaction itself and not on the benevolent or malevolent motives underlying the transaction. Reciprocal exchange, which some anthropologists consider to be a distributional mode that furthers social solidity, can be quite hostile, while market exchange can be based on friendly motives.[6] Self-interest and altruism take many forms, and neither can be tied exclusively to "economic motives."[7] In any transaction motives may be quite mixed, and they are, of course, extremely difficult to separate. Linguistic evidence about motives in particular types of exchange also point to very mixed purposes for participation.[8]

In the classification of distributional transactions, attention is paid to the content and not to the form. "Gift giving" is considered to be exchange or transfer only when we determine whether a countergift of equal value is or is not invoked. Many types of transactions are structured to resemble an exchange or transfer but turn out in actuality to be the reverse when the return flow is examined. A particularly interesting example of an ostensibly reciprocal exchange actually turning out to involve important transfer elements is shown in the analysis of Eskimo distribution in Chapter 4; a case of the reverse is the ostensible gift which, in actuality, requires a countergift in return.[9]

A particularly serious problem for the study of distribution concerns the time period of analysis. A particular transaction may appear to be a transfer, but if the long run is taken into account, it is a reciprocal exchange. Indeed, at any given point in time most reciprocity arrangements or relationships are never balanced[10]; they only are balanced in the long run. On the other hand, in a community featuring a great deal of in-and-out mobility, ostensibly delayed reciprocal transactions actually turn out to be transfers since the long-term debts are never collected. In classifying transactions, I have tried to take such long-run considerations into account.

[6]Malevolent reciprocity occurs in some of the societies in the sample. For instance, among the Sirionó of Bolivia we read that although a person is "required" to share food with his closest kinsmen, "reciprocity . . . is almost forced, and is sometimes even hostile (Allan R. Holmberg, *Nomads of the Long Bow: The Sirionó of Eastern Bolivia* [1969], p. 87 [originally published 1950])." On the other hand, as many have pointed out, market exchange can be a peacemaking initiative.

[7]The concepts of "self-interest" and "economic motives" have often been used extremely unrigorously. For a first-rate conceptual analysis, see Talcott Parsons, "The Motivation of Economic Activities," *Canadian Journal of Economics and Political Science* VI (May 1940): 187–203. Another extremely interesting exploration of economic motives is made by Barry Schwartz, "The Social Psychology of the Gift," *American Journal of Sociology* LXXIII (July 1967): 1–11.

[8]For instance, among the Chukchee of Northeast Russia the root of the old word for 'to exchange' (*Elpu'rlrkln*) was also used to designate a vendetta; while the more recent Chukchee word 'to trade' (*vili'urkln*) corresponds to a word of a neighboring society meaning 'to make peace with'. (This example is cited by Claude Lévi-Strauss, *The Elementary Structures of Kinship*, rev. ed. [1969], trans. J. H. Bell et al., p. 60 [originally published 1949]. It must be added that Lévi-Strauss used this example to demonstrate a point almost completely opposite to that which I am making.)

[9]This type of transaction was analyzed in detail by Marcel Mauss, *The Gift, Forms and Functions of Exchange in Archaic Societies* (1967), trans. Ian Cunnison [originally published 1925].

[10]This point receives particular emphasis by: Alvin W. Gouldner, "The Norm of Reciprocity: A Preliminary Statement," *American Sociological Review* XXV (1960): 161–179; and Marshall Sahlins, "On the Sociology of Primitive Exchange," in his *Stone Age Economics* (1972), pp. 185–277.

   This type of classification focuses attention on the degree of balance between the participants of single transactions and is thus somewhat different from other types of classifications. What is sometimes called "generalized exchange" or "generalized reciprocity" (where A gives x to B, who gives x to C, who in turn gives x to A) I classify as a series of transfers. Designating such a series of transactions as "exchange" or "reciprocity" obscures an important fact: These chains of transactions are seldom completed, so there are almost always net gainers and losers.

   In the discussion that follows, I distinguish between several different kinds of exchanges and transfers; in the subsequent chapters, I also distinguish several important dimensions of these transactions. The "intensity" of such exchanges or transfers refers to the relative shares of goods and services of the society that are distributed in such ways. In this book I focus primary attention on those types of distributional modes which account for 5% or more of the goods or services produced; although this quantification must sometimes be carried out somewhat arbitrarily, it means we are examining only the most intense modes of distribution and are omitting from consideration the occasional occurrence of other modes. The "area" of exchanges or transfers refers to how extensively such transactions are carried out. Other important concepts distinguishing transactions within the four distributional modes are advanced whenever I feel they can aid the analysis.

   Economists' notions about exchange, which have often been criticized in the past as limited in conception and application, have recently experienced a sudden wave of popularity among social scientists in other disciplines. In various fields—anthropology, macro- and microsociology, social psychology, and political science—economists' ideas about exchange have been adopted and adapted to analyze particular problems that have not proved amenable to traditional approaches.[11] Particular attention has been focused on one particular type of exchange, namely, reciprocity.[12] This intellectual movement has

[11]In anthropology: Mauss, *The Gift*; Lévi-Strauss, *Elementary Structures*; and Karl Polanyi, "The Economy as Instituted Process," in *Trade and Markets in the Early Empires: Economies in History and Theory* (1957), ed. Karl Polanyi, Conrad M. Arensberg, and Harry W. Pearson, pp. 243–270.

   In macrosociology: Talcott Parsons and Neil J. Smelser, *Economy and Society: A Study in the Integration of Economic and Social Theory* (1956). In microsociology, George Caspar Homans, *Social Behavior: Its Elementary Forms* (1961); and Peter M. Blau, *Exchange and Power in Social Life* (1964).

   In political science and international relations: R. L. Curry, Jr. and L. L. Wade, *A Theory of Political Exchange* (1968); Warren F. Ilchman and Norman Thomas Uphoff, *The Political Economics of Change* (1969); or Wilton S. Dillon, *Gifts and Nations* (1968).

   In social psychology: John W. Thibaut and Harold H. Kelley, *The Social Psychology of Groups* (1959); or Kenneth J. Gergen, *The Psychology of Behavior Exchange* (1969). In recent years there has been a flourishing of experimental studies of exchange relations, many of which are summarized by Kenneth J. Gergen, Stanley J. Morse, and Mary M. Gergen, "Behavior Exchange in Cross-Cultural Perspective," in *Handbook of Cross-Cultural Psychology*, ed. H. Triandis et al., forthcoming.

[12]An enormous theoretical literature on the concept of reciprocity exists, and the most interesting recent studies to me are: Fredrik Barth, *Models of Social Organization*, Occasional Paper No. 23, Royal Anthropological Institute of Great Britain and Ireland (1966); Peter P. Ekeh, *Social Exchange Theories: The Two Traditions* (1974); Richard M. Emmerson, "Exchange Theory, Part II; Exchange

occurred at the same time that some economists have begun to feel uneasy about the adequacy of their approach toward exchange and have begun to explore transfers. I hope that this study will induce those of other disciplines also to place greater attention on transfers.

The Distinction between Market Exchange and Reciprocal Exchange

Exchange transactions can be arranged along a continuum defined according to the visibility of supply and demand forces. At one end of the continuum is market exchange, where such economic forces are highly visible. Market exchange requires neither money (barter is carried out without money) nor predesignated market places nor even fluctuating prices (since market forces can manifest themselves in ways other than price changes, as I discuss later). At the other end of the continuum is reciprocal exchange where supply and demand forces are suppressed and other forces manifest themselves. The most obvious examples are those in which exactly the same items are exchanged (e.g., in modern societies, Christmas cards, dinner invitations, and so forth); less obvious examples include the exchange of dissimilar items according to a traditional exchange rate in which the transaction may ostensibly be economically disadvantageous to one of the partners (e.g., in the Trobriand Islands off the southeast coast of New Guinea we find an exchange of yams from an inland village with fish from a lagoon village at a particular exchange rate, even though the men from the lagoon could have earned much more diving for pearls than obtaining fish for this exchange).[13]

Both market exchange and reciprocal exchange are characterized by exchange ratios (often called a "price" in market exchange). Both can be carried out with a wide or narrow set of goods and services and with a wide or narrow group of partners. Both can involve credit (credit in a reciprocal exchange is sometimes called "delayed reciprocity"). These two types of exchange deserve brief comment.

MARKET EXCHANGE

Economists seem to have little difficulty in discussing or locating markets, but they have enormous difficulties in trying to define markets.[14] The traditional

---

Relations, Exchange Networks and Groups as Exchange Systems," in *Sociological Theories in Progress*, Vol. II (1972), ed. Joseph Berger, Morris Zelditch, and Bo Anderson; Gouldner, The Norm of Reciprocity; Polanyi, *Trade and Markets*; and Sahlins, *Stone Age Economics*.

[13]Bronisław Malinowski, *Argonauts of the Western Pacific* (1961), Chap. VI, p. 189 [originally published 1922].

[14]See, for example, the discussion of Peter O. Steiner, "Markets and Industries," in *International Encyclopedia of the Social Sciences* (1968), ed. David L. Sills, Vol. IX, pp. 575–581. The most extensive attempt in the recent economic literature to deal with problems arising in defining markets is by John Michael Montias, *The Structure of Economics Systems* (1976), Chaps. VIII and IX. Unfortunately, both authors deal primarily with modern industrial economies and do not closely consider this difference between reciprocal and market exchange.

Marshallian approach,[15] which defines markets in terms of that area in which a given commodity or service is selling for a single price (plus or minus transportation costs), does not take into consideration certain types of imperfect competition, information costs, or market adjustment processes which affect price.

> To define a market according to the price behavior exhibited destroys any possibility of using the market so defined to say anything about price behavior, and it prejudges the question of which market structure is the relevant one for making predictions. An empirically useful market definition must be independent of the alternative theoretical models of market structure, if we wish to test or to apply those theories.[16]

Defining a market in terms of visibility of supply and demand forces, which is one way around this problem, presupposes certain conditions deserving explication.

In a market, transactions are solicited and can be accepted or rejected without wide-scale social repercussions, regardless of whether the operation of the market is peripheral or central to the economy. There is a voluntariness and a mutuality in which decisions by the participants dealing with prices, quantities, qualities, and delivery and payment conditions reflect supply and demand conditions in a manner never occurring in reciprocal exchange. On the supply side we are able to make a number of simple predictions. For instance, if a service is of higher quality than another service, we can expect that its price will probably be higher (e.g., if there are several grades of shaman, the more "powerful" shaman usually receives a higher gift/fee or else requires larger sacrifices on the part of the patient). If the costs of producing something rise, the seller will probably either try to raise his price and/or cut back on his production and look for something else to produce and/or seek out less costly production processes. On the demand side we are also able to make a number of simple predictions. For instance, if the services of a single specialist (e.g., a boatbuilder or housebuilder) are required immediately, the buyers will probably offer the specialist a higher price than less skilled workers. Or if the price of a particular commodity is increased, the buyers will probably either reduce their purchases or look for alternative suppliers.

A fixed price can rule, yet a market can still exist. This concept of the market differs from that of others such as Karl Polanyi. In several different places Polanyi describes situations in which prices are allegedly fixed yet there is enormous "haggling" over qualities or quantities, and in which the results of such negotiations seem to depend on supply and demand conditions[17]; although according to my definition such situations indicate market exchange, he treats them as some type of reciprocity. It must be added that the existence

---

[15]Alfred Marshall, *Principles of Economics*, 8th ed. (1948), Book V, Chap. I [originally published 1890].

[16]Steiner, "Markets and Industry."

[17]The haggling over qualities is described by Karl Polanyi and Abraham Rotstein, *Dahomey and the Slave Trade* (1960), p. 83; the fixed prices and quantity variations are described in the case of "state trading" by Karl Polanyi, "Marketless Trading in Hammurabi's Time," *Trade and Markets*, ed. Polanyi, Arensberg, and Pearson, pp. 12–27.

of a fluctuating price does not necessarily indicate a market rather than recip-rocal exchange; for instance, a fluctuating exchange ratio in reciprocal ex-change occurs in certain transactions such as marriage payments (which are analyzed in detail in Appendix B.1).

RECIPROCAL EXCHANGE

In reciprocal exchange, transactions are carried on without money[18] and usually at fixed exchange ratios, at least in the short run. Reciprocal exchange can be carried out in a highly formal or ceremonial way (e.g., the oft-discussed Kula ring which featured the ceremonial exchange of necklaces for bracelets in a highly organized fashion) or in a highly informal manner between friends. The exchange can be initiated either by a tied gift (Person A gives Person B a gift, and Person B is obligated to make a return of equal value if he accepts it) or a tied request (Person A requests something from Person B and then gives B in return something of equal value). Reciprocal exchange can either be forced (in the sense that any initiated exchange must be accepted) or voluntary (in the sense that the initiated exchange can be rejected).

It must be noted that reciprocity involves a mechanism for enforcement, but these mechanisms can be embodied in social rather than legal institutions. If no enforcement mechanism exists, then an intended reciprocal exchange may turn into a transfer.

My concept of reciprocity is somewhat different from that of others[19]: As noted earlier, it excludes transactions which Claude Lévi-Strauss labels "generalized exchange" (or which Peter Ekeh labels "chain reciprocity"); it also excludes transactions which Marshall Sahlins calls "generalized reciproc-ity" and "negative reciprocity" as well as Karl Polanyi's "redistributive ex-change." However, it does not necessarily exclude what Ekeh calls "net generalized exchange," if such exchanges are consciously balanced.[20]

---

[18]An exception to this generalization occurs when the reciprocity directly concerns money, for example, a friend making an interest-free loan to another. Sometimes reciprocity is accompanied by the transfer of a pseudomoney, an example of which is the case of the alleged chocolate box "currency" in Geneva, Switzerland. According to the story which I heard, in a certain social stratum in Geneva, a dinner guest always brings a box of chocolates to his host; furthermore, the host never opens the box but passes it on to the person who invites him to dinner at a later time, who later also gives it away. If a person's inventory of chocolate boxes is low, this is a sign that it is time to host a dinner in order to replenish his supply. The chocolate boxes are a pseudomoney (this is defined and discussed in Chapter 6). Although I have been unable to verify whether this story accurately reflects the ethnographic facts of Geneva, it illustrates the conceptual point.

[19]Claude Lévi-Strauss, *Elementary Structures*; Peter Ekeh, *Social Exchange Theories*, pp. 52–53; Marshall Sahlins, *Stone Age Economics*, pp. 191–196; Karl Polanyi, "The Economy as Instituted Process."

[20]Ekeh, ibid., p. 53, distinguishes several different types of "net generalized exchange." "Indi-vidual focused net generalized exchange" occurs when a "group as a whole benefits each member consecutively until all members have received the same amount of benefits and attention. In a five-party generalized exchange it operates as follows: ABCD→E; ABCE→D; ABDE→C; ACDE→B and BCDE→A." "Group focused net generalized exchange" occurs when "individuals involved . . . successively give to the group as a unit and then gain back as part of the group from each of the unit members . . . Hence, it operates as follows: A→BCDE; B→ACDE; C→ABCE; D→ABCE; and E→ABCD."

The Distinction between Centric and
Noncentric Transfers

The feature distinguishing transfer from exchange transactions—the lack of a balanced counterflow—can arise either because no counterflow usually takes place or because the counterflow has only a very inexact relationship to the value of the original goods or services in the transaction. Transfers can arise from benevolence (a parent giving a gift to his child without expecting or desiring a counterflow) or malevolence (e.g., theft or the forcing of tribute payments).[21] They can also arise from the structure of society and have no relationship to malevolent or benevolent motives, a type of transaction receiving considerable attention in Chapter 4. Transfers can be classified as progressive (if they represent a flow of goods and services from the rich to the poor), regressive (if the reverse flow occurs), or neutral (if they represent either a flow between individuals of equal income or if there is no systematic relationship between the relative income status of the givers and receivers). Transfer relationships can arise between only a small set of people (e.g., a family) or can embrace larger groups up to the entire society.

Transfer transactions can be arranged along a continuum defined according to the "centricity" of focus of the pattern of transactions,[22] that is, the degree to which the transfers are patterned so as to focus on either an institution or an individual carrying out a societal-wide role (these are centric transfers) or to focus on the relationship between distinct pairs of individuals who are not tied in their transactions to a societal-wide pattern (these are noncentric transfers). An example of a centric transfer is a political redistribution scheme, where goods or services are collected by a political figure and then redistributed in a manner not corresponding to the amounts given. An example of a noncentric transfer is the personal exploitation of a slave (whose work corresponds in no way to what is given him by his master in return). Another example of a noncentric transfer occurs in a situation I designate as "floating centricity," that is, when particular individuals from time to time institute a series of transfers with other individuals such as holding a large feast to enhance their prestige but when this transfer does not reflect any permanent societal-wide political, social, or religious role. It must finally be emphasized that centric and noncentric transfers are not distinguished by what is transferred; a noncentric transfer occurs when individuals donate blood to their friends in time of need, while a centric transfer occurs when individuals donate blood to the Red Cross, which then redistributes it).[23]

---

[21]A number of analytic propositions concerning benevolent and malevolent transfers are analyzed by Kenneth E. Boulding, *The Economy of Love and Fear: A Preface to the Grants Economy* (1973).

[22]The term is borrowed from Polanyi, "The Economy as Instituted Process."

[23]Such transfers are analyzed in an extremely interesting manner by Richard M. Titmuss, *The Gift Relationship: From Human Blood to Social Policy* (1971).

NONCENTRIC TRANSFERS

Noncentric transfers, as a genus, have received relatively little systematic attention in the anthropology literature; indeed, some have denied their existence. However, certain species of such transfers, e.g., slavery, have received considerable treatment. Further examples of noncentric transfers include personal philanthropy (particularly of an anonymous sort), theft, Lévi-Strauss's "generalized exchange," and the payment of food by a Trobriand Island male to his sister's husband in return for very irregular amounts of work and occasional gifts in which the equivalencies involved are extremely inexact so that balance is not obtained.[24] A poignant example closer to home appears to be the high school dating pattern in America in the late 1940s where the boys paid all the expenses of the date and received very little or nothing in return.[25]

Certain kinds of noncentric transfers such as a system of widespread hospitality to any and all travelers represent transactions embracing a large number of people; while other kinds of noncentric transfers (the Trobriand case just cited) represent a transfer that is limited in scope only to brothers-in-law. Although some of these noncentric transfers possibly result from, or are strongly influenced by, benevolent or malevolent motives (e.g., philanthropy and theft), such motives do not play an important role per se in other cases such as the Trobriand and the dating examples. Although the ingenious "theorist" can undoubtedly find various social invisibles that will "balance" such transactions so that they become "reciprocal," hence, "stable," such "explanations" tell us little. The important questions are the determinants of such transfers and the impact of such transactions on the rest of society.

CENTRIC TRANSFERS

Most of the centric transfers discussed in the anthropology literature concern either political or religious focal points. Typical examples are the political or religious authority collecting tribute, taxes, or tithes and then either using such collected goods and services for personal use or redistributing them to the population in ways unrelated to the contributions paid. In such redistribution the subject either gets nothing in return or else has a very small probability of

---

[24]Malinowski, *Argonauts*.

[25]It should be added that the male generally received and expected to receive very little in return in the realm of sexual pleasure. The usual justification of such an ostensibly unbalanced transaction was that the male received "the pleasure of the female's company"; this represented a rationalization that a flow of social invisibles "balanced" the transaction. Such invisibles are excluded from my definition of balance. Such a justification is also peculiar in that the female not only received the material benefits of the interaction, but she also received "the pleasure of the male's company." The difficulties in deciding whose company benefited the other more illustrates the absurdity of introducing social invisibles to "balance" such transactions and of refusing to recognize the transactions as a transfer. (Another rationalization of this transfer transaction was that the female had to spend considerable money on clothes for the date, but it must be noted that the males had to make considerable expenditures for nice clothes as well.) Since this footnote raised enormous controversy among those who read the manuscript in draft, it should be added that the ethnographic facts of this situation seem still uncertain and have since changed considerably in America.

getting in return something of equal value (either a good, service, or "public good") to what was given to the authority. Such a redistribution can be either regressive (e.g., if the political authority keeps for his personal use what is collected), progressive (e.g., if the goods are collected from the rich and given to the poor), or neutral. A different kind of political centric transfer occurs in quite primitive hunting and gathering societies where the political leader, who is often the best hunter, gives much of the game he kills to his followers in order "to retain their loyalty." Another type of centric transfer is a mobilization drive, where goods and services are collected by the political authorities in order to build or produce something (e.g., a fortification) that presumably benefits the entire community.

Some Concluding Notes on Classification

The typology of distributional modes that I outline is exhaustive. However, different criteria are used to draw the distinctions within each of the two major categories (exchange and transfer) so that the typology is not symmetrical. The purpose of the typology is to permit me to assemble together for discussion those transactions that I believe have similar determinants. The usefulness of the typology depends on the kinds of propositions that can be produced and the degree to which such hypotheses explain the ethnographic facts. In classifying transactions using the typology, several problems occur.

First, difficulties arise in classifying "border cases." For instance, is gambling an exchange or a transfer? Is the returning of a borrowed pot with a little bit of food in it an exchange or a transfer? Fortunately, such cases are relatively rare. Particular problems of classification are discussed in detail in Chapters 5–10, where the four major distributional modes are systematically reviewed.

Second, some types of distributional transactions embody both exchange and transfer elements. For instance, in a number of hunting societies there is considerable sharing of game because of problems of storage. Reciprocal elements occur when successful Hunter A gives successful Hunter B some meat, and the latter returns the favor the next week when he obtains game; transfer elements occur when successful Hunter A gives chronically unsuccessful Hunter C some meat, and the latter is never able to return the favor. In such cases the transaction must be included as both an exchange and as a transfer.

Third, some types of transactions occur between groups, not individuals per se, for example, one group feasts another, which later returns the favor.[26] In such cases I consider the group as a fictitious person and ask whether the transactions between such fictitious persons is balanced in order to determine if the activity represents an exchange or a transfer.

[26]Such a system of exchange is discussed by Mauss *The Gift*, p. 3 ff. In a system of "total prestations" Mauss argues that "it is groups, and not individuals, which carry on exchange, make contracts, and are bound by obligations."

Finally, for many people it is an article of faith that all transactions of importance are balanced. From the previous discussion it should be clear that I consider this issue a matter to be investigated in an empirical and systematic fashion rather than an assumption.

COMPARABLE UNITS OF OBSERVATION

The Problem

The "unit of observation" of exchange and transfer transactions is that grouping of individuals within which distributional transactions are excluded from analysis. The choice of such a unit for this study raises some difficult problems.

Suppose we are examining exchange and transfer transactions in each of three almost identical societies. If we choose as the unit of observation individuals alone in the first society, nuclear families in the second society, extended families in the third, then we might arrive at three quite different evaluations of the relative importance of various types of transactions in these similar societies. In the first society we might find noncentric transfers of an individual with his nuclear family to be the most important mode of distribution, with all other modes of distribution playing relatively secondary roles. In the second society we might find reciprocal exchange between individuals in the same extended families to be the most important mode of distribution, with all other modes of distribution playing relatively secondary roles. And in the third society we might find market exchange between individuals of different extended families as the most important mode of distribution, with all other modes playing relatively secondary roles.

If all societies had the same family and social structure, this problem would raise no difficulties. We would merely select as the unit of observation either the individual alone, the nuclear family, or the extended family and use this as the basis of our analysis of every society in our sample. But if this similarity in family and social structures does not occur, for example, if extended families do not exist in some societies, then we run into difficulties in making comparisons. These comparability problems may be seen quite concretely in a study on competition and cooperation in primitive and peasant economies by Margaret Mead, who classifies the Thonga of Mozambique (who are also in my sample) as a highly "cooperative" society. However, if we look at the degree of reciprocal labor exchanges or noncentric labor transfers between members of different extended families, we find little to justify this characterization.[27] Because Mead is interested in certain psychological vectors, she focuses on the individuals of this society alone, and since the Thonga live in extended families,

[27]Margaret Mead, "Interpretative Statement," in *Cooperation and Competition among Primitive Peoples,* rev. ed. (1966), ed. Margaret Mead, pp. 458–516 [originally published 1947].

within which there is considerable cooperativeness, she characterizes the society as a whole as cooperative. If we are interested in general propositions about distribution and use the individual alone as our unit of observation, then we might find great cooperativeness in any society with extended families, which is not a very interesting proposition. (Although intrafamilial cooperation and sharing are variable among societies, in any given society they are usually much greater than interfamilial cooperation and sharing.)

One alleged escape from this problem is to use the "household" as the basic unit, but this raises a number of other difficulties. As some have pointed out,[28] the concept of household contains some ambiguities: Are we talking about a family unit (defined by kinship), a coresidence unit (defined in terms of who lives together, even if those living together participate in no common activities other than those directly connected with sleeping under the same roof), or a unit serving certain domestic functions (cooperating for economic or social purposes)? It is quite possible for these three units to be quite different in a given society: For a set of given nuclear families, the husbands may live in the village men's house, while the wives may live in separate huts around the village; and certain activities such as hunting may be carried out by men living in several different men's huts, while agriculture may be carried out by groups of cooperating women from several different families.

I select the basic unit of observation through a two-step procedure. First, I isolate the major "units of production" and "units of consumption" of each society in the sample. Second, if these are the same, I use them as the basic unit of observation; if they differ, I apply criteria specified in the next section to select one of them as the basic unit of observation. This procedure requires us to explore what these units of production and consumption are and how they are distributed in the sample societies.

Units of Production and Consumption

The concepts of "unit of production" and "unit of consumption" have been used in the anthropology literature for some years. They are employed by a diverse group of anthropologists ranging from the French Marxist Emmanuel Terray to the American formalist Edward E. LeClair, Jr.[29] Rarely, however, are the concepts very precisely defined.

I define "units of production" as groups of people who, by means of some type of decision-making process among themselves, are able to produce together in an organized fashion particular goods or services. In modern industrial

[28]This has been argued most forcefully by Donald R. Bender, "A Refinement of the Concept of the Household: Family, Co-Residence, and Domestic Functions," *American Anthropologist* LXIX (October 1967): 493–504.

[29]Emmanuel Terray, *Marxism and 'Primitive Societies'*, trans. Mary Kloppen (1972); Edward E. LeClair, Jr., "Economic Theory and Economic Anthropology," *American Anthropologist* LXIV (1962): 1179–1203. My definitions of these concepts differ somewhat from those employed by these or by others.

societies a variety of different types of production units exist: the factory, the store, and the service establishment (e.g., the office of the doctor or the school). In primitive and peasant societies we find as production units nuclear families as well as larger family groupings (e.g., extended family or lineages) and special work teams (e.g., agricultural work teams, herding "camps" or "tents," hunting bands, and so forth). For primitive and peasant societies in this study I focus primary attention on production units which produce the most important foods.

Some of the production units in a given society may be quite temporary (e.g., a group of men participating in a single hunt), while others consist of the same individuals over a long period of time. Some are aimed at a single purpose (e.g., the annual buffalo hunt), while others may embrace many different types of production. In some societies there is a single major production unit, while in other societies there are a large number of production units. The anthropology literature on production units is rich and voluminous.

Units of consumption are groups of people who receive a set of goods and services and who, by means of some type of internal decision-making process, divide these goods and services and consume them together. I pay particular attention in this study to the group consuming food together, which some anthropologists call the commensal unit. In modern industrial societies, the major consumption unit is the nuclear family, although other units such as the boarding school, the army unit, the "commune," or the "crowd watching a basketball game together" also exist. In primitive and peasant societies we can find nuclear families and larger family groups as consumption units, as well as other groupings such as men's houses, herding "camps," and so forth.

Some of the consumption units in a given society may be quite temporary (e.g., a group enjoying a feast together), while others may consist of the same individuals over a long period of time. Some are aimed for a single purpose (e.g., consumption of a sacred food), while others may serve many different consumption needs (e.g., consumption of food, housing, rituals, services, and so forth). In some societies there is a single major consumption unit, while in other societies there are several different and important consumption units (e.g., a men's house and the grouping of individual wives with their children).

Although it may be relatively easy to draw up a list of different production and consumption units in the society, some anthropologists have pointed out that in some cases it is quite difficult to designate a single most important unit of either.[30] In both cases we try to select that unit in which the most food is produced or consumed. For consumption, however, this appears more difficult, and several special difficulties arise.

A serious problem occurs because of the existence of multiple obligations regarding the sharing of food. A person may eat with his nuclear family, but he may be obligated to share certain parts of the meat he obtains with several

[30]See especially the remarks of Daryll Ford and Mary Douglas, "Primitive Economics," in *Man, Culture, and Society* (1956), ed. Harry L. Shapiro, pp. 330–344.

relatives outside his ostensible commensal unit. If such meat is an unimportant food in the society, then the nuclear family can be considered as the primary consumption unit. However, if the shared meat is an important part of the diets of the recipients, then the situation can be treated in alternative ways: We might include the group with whom the meat is shared in the consumption unit; or else we might still conveniently consider the nuclear family as the consumption unit and define such meat sharing as a manifestation of a narrow "area" (defined above) of distribution. In any case, we must take into account the intensiveness and extensiveness of the meat sharing before arriving at a final judgment. In most cases I end up following the second of the two alternatives.

Another problem in interpreting empirical evidence on these matters arises because ethnographers have often not bothered to investigate or describe the consumption unit very carefully. For instance, it is very difficult to determine whether the basic consumption unit among the Iroquois Indians of New York is the nuclear family or the long house because very little information on the subject is available in the literature.

Despite the difficulties in defining the most important consumption and production unit, we must tackle this task if we wish to carry out cross-cultural studies of exchange and distribution. Let me add that I have been unable to devise any rule which allows one to predict very successfully in advance whether such a task will be difficult for a given society.[31]

Analyses of exchange and transfer transactions are relatively straightforward when production and consumption units are the same in a given society. When they differ, some new considerations must be taken into account.

Let us first examine those societies in which the production unit is larger than the consumption unit, a situation that can arise because of the importance of economies of scale in production. In modern industrial societies this occurs because the factory (production unit) is larger than the individual family (consumption unit). In herding societies this occurs when families travel together and combine their herds (so that the herding camp is the production unit), while maintaining the individual families as the consumption units. In hunting societies the men may hunt together in groups (so the hunting band is the production unit), while family groupings are the consumption units.

The major problem of distribution is the following: If production is carried out together, how is the income or the other results of production split among the participants? Several solutions are available to a society.

One solution is to determine in some manner the relative contribution of each person and divide the production or income accordingly. Another solution is for production or income to be divided in some manner which does not

---

[31]One might expect that for societies at the lower end of the development scale, it might be more difficult to designate the most important production or consumption unit; but this did not turn out to be the case.

correspond to relative productivity, in which case important transfers occur. Or some compromise between these two solutions can occur. More insights can be gained by examining several specific enthnographic situations.

Both among the Lapps of northern Scandinavia and the Koryak of the far east of the U.S.S.R., reindeer herding was carried out by all men of the herding group working together, with the herds combined and each man contributing roughly the same amount of work.[32] If Man A with a small herd and Man B with a large herd traveled together and if, as was common among the Lapps, the major economic rewards which each received were the products of his flock and also the increase of his flock, then Man A was giving Man B a gift of labor since he contributed more work to B's flock than B did to his flock (i.e., a noncentric transfer which, by the way, is regressive). Among the Koryak the situation was apparently handled differently: Both men would work together and do roughly the same amount of work, but Man A would be considered to be "working for" Man B, and Man B's payment (in kind) to Man A would apparently depend on the relative size of the herds; the situation was probably that the more equal the sizes of the herds belonging to the two men, the lower A's pay would be (since he would be devoting relatively more time to his own herd and less time to B's herd).[33] Both would receive economic rewards in the form of products and increases in their respective flocks. Among the Lapps greater social equality existed, but at the same time there were regressive noncentric labor transfers; among the Koryak there was apparently less social equality but at the same time more reciprocal exchange in work (i.e., payment for labor).

[32]My interpretation is controversial and directly contradicts that of V. V. Antropova, Kul'tura i byt koryakov (1971). Since both Antropova and I base our interpretations on the ethnographic materials of Waldemar Jochelson, Material Culture and Social Organization of the Koryak, American Museum of Natural History, X, Part II (1908), a brief explanation is necessary. In Jochelson's account the following descriptions are found: Sometimes hired herders lived with their employers and shared their food, while sometimes they lived in separate tents; the herders sometimes had a fixed wage (usually those living in their own tents) and sometimes they did not; there were, however, no general wage standards for the whole society; herders also received special gifts from their employers; herd sizes of individuals and families often fluctuated greatly so that employers of herders often became employees of others if their herds were decimated; and there was not massive discontent with the labor system. Antropova argues that the fluidity of wages reflected an exploitative situation where the bosses extracted varying amounts of unpaid work from their herders, depending on individual circumstances; however, it is doubtful that Jochelson would have missed the discontent arising from such an unfair situation. If my interpretation is correct, there was no wage standard because herders brought in different-sized herds and would thus devote different amounts of time to their own herds and those of their employers; furthermore, the variable wage would reflect whether the herder was living with the employer or living in a separate tent. The gifts might represent a payment if the employer was especially pleased with the job the herder was doing, a type of quality bonus which can not be easily negotiated in advance. The situation which I describe would not necessarily give rise to massive discontent and is consistent with the previously stated facts. Unfortunately, it does not appear as though ethnographic evidence is available to determine whether Antropova's or my interpretation is correct, even though mine appears more consistent with Jochelson's description.

[33]The ethnographic sources for these two societies, both of which are in my sample, are given in Appendix E.

In a hunting group the problem is in some ways more complex. If the hunting technique requires a large number of men (e.g., to surround the game and force them toward the center), then it is clear that all men participate in production, quite independently of which man actually kills the animals. Often hunting groups assign "responsibility" for killing the game in a relatively arbitrary manner (e.g., whose arrow first touched the animal, whose hand first touched the animal, and so forth) and then require the "responsible" person to divide up the meat among the other members of the group.[34] In this manner the "successful" hunter shares the produce with those who helped him, so we have a case of reciprocal exchange. If the "successful" hunter were allowed to keep the game for himself, we would have noncentric labor transfers since the "unsuccessful" hunters contributed to production and received no compensation.

The consumption unit can also be larger than the production unit. One kind of case, which appears rare, occurs in extended families in which food is shared in common but groups of individual members of the family (e.g., a husband and his wife) cultivate individual garden plots. Another case arises in which the men in a community live in the village "men's house" and share their food (while the women and children of a particular man live in separate huts near the men's house and eat as a semifamily unit separately) but in which the individual family units of husband and wife are the basic production unit. In the former case the consumption unit embraces the individual production units; in the second case the consumption unit embraces only part of the production unit.

Different kinds of redistribution can occur. If consumption products are allocated according to the amount contributed to the common pot, then we would have a correspondence between work and income but, at the same time, an inequality in consumption levels and, in addition, no net transfers. If consumption products are allocated in roughly equal amounts, then those contributing the most would be transferring goods to those contributing the least. (Given the circumstances, such a transfer might be either progressive or regressive.) If consumption products are allocated in unequal amounts which do not correspond to work input, then transfers occur which may also be either progressive or regressive. Of these three cases, the second and the third seem most likely to occur. The second case might arise in the case of men living in the men's house. The third case would occur in an extended family in which each nuclear family farms its own land and contributes the food to the common pot, from which it would be redistributed by a leader who might contribute the least amount of work since he is the oldest. In both cases the transfers would probably be regressive.

[34]This matter is discussed in much greater detail by John H. Dowling, "Individual Ownership and the Sharing of Game in Hunting Societies," *American Anthropologist* LXX (June 1968): 502–507. I would, however, take exception to Dowling's functional explanation.

TABLE 2.1

A Classification of Production and Consumption Units in the Sample Societies[a]

	Number of societies in sample						
	Major mode of food production						
	Gathering	Hunting	Fishing	Herding	Incipient agriculture	Full agriculture	Total
Part A: Societies where major consumption and production units are the same							
Nuclear or small extended family (e.g., stem family)	5	2	2	5	3	22	39
Large extended family	1	0	0	0	0	3	4
(Subtotal)	(6)	(2)	(2)	(5)	(3)	(25)	(43)
Part B: Societies where major consumption and production units are different							
Societies with major consumption unit larger than major production unit	0	0	0	0	0	1	1
Societies with major production unit larger than major consumption unit	0	2	0	3	0	1	6
Societies with several major consumption units	0	0	0	1	0	3	4
Societies with several major production units	0	0	0	0	0	1	1
Societies with several major consumption and production units	2	1	0	0	1	1	5
(Subtotal)	(2)	(3)	(0)	(4)	(1)	(7)	(17)
Grand total	8	5	2	9	4	32	60

[a]The data underlying this table are presented in Appendix A, Series 4, 18, 19, and 20.

In order to gain a more concrete idea about the relative importance of these various cases, it is useful to examine briefly the kinds of production and consumption units found in the sample of 60 societies used in this study. Several difficulties in coding arose. In at least one society (the Amhara of Ethiopia) the major production unit seemed to vary according to the population density of the area. In a number of other societies in which related families lived either together or closely together, it was difficult to decide whether the small families or the large family grouping was the consumption unit. Such coding problems fortunately did not occur with great frequency.

Since the production unit often depends on technological considerations in carrying out the most important subsistence activity, I have cross-tabulated the production and consumption units with the major mode of food production. Relevant data are presented in Table 2.1.

Several features of the results of Table 2.1 are noteworthy. For slightly over 70% of the societies in the sample, the problems arising from differences in major consumption and production units did not arise. Furthermore, multiple consumption or production units or differences in the units appear proportionately more numerous in hunting and herding societies. Finally, Part B has proportionately more uncertainties in the codings than Part A of the table.

Selection of the Comparative Unit and Some Empirical Implications

With information about the production and consumption units the comparative unit of observation can now be specified. The following criteria were observed in making the choice.

First, the minimum size of this unit is defined to be either the monogamous, polygynous, or polyandrous family. Although in certain societies with polygyny, each individual wife produces her own food and eats alone with her children, the husband usually has sufficient power to participate in basic production decisions (since often he must carry out a key portion of the work for each wife) and to redistribute food among the wives if his children by one wife are going hungry.

Second, in those cases where the major production and consumption units are the same, this unit is chosen as the unit of observation. Thus, for 43 societies out of 60, difficulties do not arise on this account.

Third, whenever major production and consumption units differ, additional criteria must be invoked, and two strategies of solution are available. One solution is to use a rule and to select that unit which is largest (or smallest). But such a mechanical approach does not permit us to distinguish which of the two units plays a more important role in economic processes. A second solution is to make a determination of which of the units is the most "basic" decision-making unit, in which "basic" is defined in terms of usual precedence of interest when conflicts arise. In the case of the society with the men's house a man may have strong loyalty to this group, but in conflict situations he may tend to side more often with his family, so the latter is chosen as the unit of observation. In the case of an extended family as the consumption unit and individual families as the production units, the former usually engenders the most basic loyalties and greatest stability, although not always. I have chosen this second solution—trying to determine the most "basic" unit—and have examined each society where production and consumption units differ in order to apply this somewhat vague criterion. Although in a few cases a decision was extremely difficult to make, fortunately such cases were rare; nevertheless, a regrettable subjective element entered my choice in these instances.

In all 60 societies the unit of observation was a kin-based grouping. Some notion of the distribution of sizes of these units of observation can be gained from the data presented in Table 2.2, in which the size of the unit is cross-classified by major mode of production and also relative level of economic development. (The latter concept is explored in the next section.)

The data in Table 2.2 reveal several useful facts. In 51 out of 60 societies, the unit of observation chosen for this study is the nuclear or the small extended family; the existence of "basic" production or consumption units of a large extended family occurs only in a small minority of societies in the sample. Furthermore, such large units of observation occur proportionately more in agricultural societies and in societies at the higher end of the economic development scale. It must be added that after a certain point in economic development, the large units seem to break up into smaller units, a process observable in the history of the various societies of the sample, particularly markedly among the Serbs of Yugoslavia and the Dogon of Mali.

What kind of impact do these choices of the unit of observation have on the verification of propositions about exchange and transfer? We can distinguish direct effects (which concern the coding of the variable) from the indirect effects (which concern the impact of the unit of observation on the functioning of distribution in the society).

The direct effects of the choice of the unit of observation on the codings of market exchange are nil because very few societies feature very much market exchange between members of the same family, defining family either very narrowly or very broadly. It turns out empirically that the choice of the unit of observation does not have a great effect on the codings of reciprocal exchange and centric transfers. However, the codings of certain types of noncentric transfers are strongly affected by the choice of the unit of observation. The designation of the nine societies with units of observation of large extended families reduces markedly the types of noncentric transfers in these societies since most such transfers occur within the extended family and are thus excluded from consideration.

The indirect effects of the choice of the unit of observation on the propositions about different modes of distribution are quite interesting. For instance, in comparing two societies which are similar in important ways except that the

TABLE 2.2

Units of Observations in the Sample Societies at Different Levels of Economic Development and with Different Major Modes of Subsistence Production[a]

| Groups of societies classified according to their relative levels of economic development | | Number of societies in sample | | | | | | |
| | | Major mode of food production | | | | | | |
		Gathering	Hunting	Fishing	Herding	Incipient agriculture	Full agriculture	Total
Lowest 15 on economic development scale	N[b]	6	4	0	1	2	1	14
	L[b]	1	0	0	0	0	0	1
Second lowest 15 on economic development scale	N	1	1	2	4	1	4	13
	L	0	0	0	1	0	1	2
Second highest 15 on economic development scale	N	0	0	0	3	1	8	12
	L	0	0	0	0	0	3	3
Highest 15 on economic development scale	N	0	0	0	0	0	12	12
	L	0	0	0	0	0	3	3
Total	N	7	5	2	8	4	25	51
	L	1	0	0	1	0	7	9

[a] The data underlying this table are presented in Appendix A, Series 4, 21, and 22.
[b] N = nuclear or small extended family (e.g., stem family);
L = large extended family

"basic" unit is the nuclear family in the first and is the large extended family in the second, we can hypothesize that reciprocal exchange is more likely to occur in the former than the latter if there are any kind of important economies of scale in production. That is, in a society with nuclear families a family might specialize in production and then exchange its goods with members of other nuclear families, while in the other society the various families within the extended families might specialize and then, through a series of intrafamilial transfers, obtain the other goods. This conjecture, by the way, receives empirical support in the analysis presented in Chapter 7. In other chapters conjectures of a similar nature are explored.

Problems arising from the indirect impact of the choice of the unit of observation can be quite simply handled in the empirical analysis, for we can use dummy variables indicating the size of the unit of observation when calculating the regressions. Use of such a technique is based on the reasonable assumption that the impact of the size of the unit of observation on the modes of distribution in the community is much more important than the reverse relationship. In other words, the boundaries of the unit of observation come first in the causal chain, an assumption which must rest on theoretical evidence since it is extremely difficult to test empirically.

Problems arising from the direct choice of the unit of observation on the coding cannot be easily handled in the type of analysis carried out in this study. However, many of these difficulties can be taken into account in the interpretation of the results.

RELATIVE LEVELS OF ECONOMIC DEVELOPMENT

Some Important Aspects of the Problem

In analyzing modern industrial economies, comparable measures of per capita production or income are readily available, and other comparable measures of the level of economic development can be calculated with a small expenditure of effort. In analyzing primitive and peasant economies, we have no such advantage. Furthermore, we face an additional problem, namely, that in primitive and peasant societies, the rankings of societies diverge greatly when the level of economic development is measured by per capita productivity and per capita production (or per capita consumption).

The nature of this problem is shown in a stimulating essay by Marshall Sahlins, who argues that members of societies which rank the lowest in terms of total per capita production or consumption—the nomadic hunting and gathering societies—often spend very little time engaged in obtaining food and thus show a very high per capita productivity (measured in terms of outputs per labor hour) in contrast to settled societies which produce (and consume) more per person but which also use a great deal more effort to obtain this small increment in per capita production and consumption.[35] A stark illustration of the facts underlying this assertion can be seen for the !Kung Bushmen, a nomadic gathering and hunting society in Botswana and one of the most "primitive" societies in the world, in which the average adult spends only about 15 hours a week in activities to obtain food.[36] Sahlins adduces similar evidence of high productivity from a number of other hunting and gathering societies as well.

The same problem in agricultural societies is illustrated in a controversial and brilliant book by Ester Boserup, who presents data showing that productivity per man among slash-and-burn agriculturalists is a good deal higher than in societies using technologically more sophisticated farming techniques such as plowing, irrigation, systematic crop rotation schemes, and so forth.[37] She argues that as population density in a farming area increases, agricultural techniques become more intensive, per capita production may increase, but production per man hour decreases, even though the adoption of more intensive techniques is accompanied by new farming innovations.[38]

Underlying these paradoxical theses by Sahlins and Boserup is a simple idea well known to all economists, namely, that labor productivity may be very high, even with the use of technologically backward techniques, if the amount of cooperating factors of production is great. As long as an area is sparsely populated so that the available land per capita is very great, labor productivity in food production may be very high; however, as the population density increases, diminishing returns set in which are not completely offset by more advanced technological techniques; as a result, productivity per worker declines. However, per capita production may still increase if the hours worked per worker increase at a faster rate than the labor productivity declines.[39] Although the degree to which this description fits all primitive and peasant societies is open to considerable debate, the dilemmas in measuring the level of economic development of such societies should be evident.

What is the meaning of the concept of "economic development" when the correlation between such indicators as per capita production (and consumption) and labor productivity is found among industrialized economies but not among hunting, gathering, or farming economies? It seems to me that the underlying idea of the concept of economic development is tied neither di-

[35]Marshall Sahlins, "The Original Affluent Society," pp. 1–41.

[36]Richard B. Lee, "What Hunters Do for a Living, or, How to Make Out on Scarce Resources," in Man the Hunter (1968), ed. Richard B. Lee and Irven DeVore, pp. 30–48.

[37]Ester Boserup, The Conditions of Agricultural Growth: The Economics of Agrarian Change under Population Pressure (1965).

[38]This thesis is extremely controversial, and some contrary evidence is presented by Bennet Bronson, "Farm Labor and the Evolution of Food Production," in Population Growth: Anthropological Implications (1972), ed. Brian Spooner, pp. 190–218.

[39]Such a notion leads us to an interesting interpretation of the story of the Garden of Eden, namely, that the garden represents nature and the ease of obtaining food in nature before diminishing returns set in.

rectly to per capita production nor to labor productivity but to the more fundamental notion of economic complexity. By "economic complexity" I refer not only to the levels of technology utilized in the economy but also to the organization of the economy, as manifested by the extensiveness of the division of labor and by the variety of qualitatively different types of economic interactions. Thus, the !Kung Bushmen or some slash-and-burn agricultural economy are considered less developed than the Incan or Aztec economies, not because labor productivity in the former group of economies is less (it probably is not) but because the latter economies have much more extensive divisions of labor and a much greater variety of different types of economic interactions. It appears, incidentally, that per capita production and consumption are usually greater in societies with considerable economic complexity than in societies with little economic complexity, but such per capita production is not logically a necessary condition for complexity. It appears that in industrialized societies both labor productivity and per capita production (and consumption) are tied to complexity, while in primitive societies they are not necessarily so correlated.

The Carneiro Technique for Determining Relative Complexity

As far as I have been able to determine, there are no studies of relative per capita production or relative labor productivity in a large number or primitive and peasant societies, so that comparisons can be made. Nevertheless, a number of studies measuring societal complexity of such economies have appeared on which we can draw.[40]

The most detailed and extensive comparative studies of complexity in primitive and peasant societies are those carried out by Robert L. Carneiro.[41] Experiments with Carneiro's data show that his measures for societal complexity are extremely strongly correlated with a subset of his measures for economic com-

[40]Such studies include: Edgar Bowden, "An Index to Sociocultural Development Applicable to Precivilized Societies," *American Anthropologist* LXXI (June 1969): 454–461; Charles W. McNett, Jr., "A Settlement Pattern Scale of Cultural Complexity," in *A Handbook of Method in Cultural Anthropology* (1973), ed. Raoul Naroll and Ronald Cohen, pp. 502–507; George P. Murdock and Caterina Provost, "Measurement of Cultural Complexity," *Ethnology* XIII (October 1973): 379–392; and Terrence A. Tatje and Raoul Naroll, "Two Measures of Societal Complexity: An Empirical Cross-Cultural Comparison," in Naroll and Cohen, ibid., pp. 766–834.

[41]A summary article is by Robert L. Carneiro, "Scale Analysis, Evolutionary Sequences, and the Rating of Cultures," in Naroll and Cohen, ibid., pp. 834–872. Carneiro and his associates have written a series of essays on the subject, which include: "Scale Analysis as an Instrument for the Study of Cultural Evolution," *Southwestern Journal of Anthropology* XXVIII (Summer 1962): 149–169; (with Stephen F. Tobias) "The Application of Scale Analysis to the Study of Cultural Evolution," *Transactions of the New York Academy of Sciences,* 2nd series, XXVI (1963): 196–207; "On the Relation between Size of Population and Complexity of Social Organization," *Southwestern Journal of Anthropology* XXIV (Winter 1968): 354–374; and "The Measurement of Cultural Development in the Ancient Near East and in Anglo-Saxon England," *Transactions of the New York Academy of Sciences,* 2nd series, XXXI (1969): 1013–1023.

plexity, so that we can use the former as a proxy for the latter.[42] Carneiro used a special statistical technique—scalogram analysis—devised by Louis Guttman,[43] and since this technique may be unfamiliar, a brief explanation is warranted before I turn to the way in which I used and extended Carneiro's data to measure the level of development of the 60 societies in the sample.

The key idea behind the scalogram analysis is the "dichotomous cumulative trait." A trait is dichotomous if it can take only two possible ratings. For instance, for a person the trait "being 6 feet tall or over" is dichotomous (a person either is or is not), while height per se in feet is not dichotomous, as a person's height can take an infinite number of values.

For a group of societies, a set of traits is "cumulative" if a society with a higher ranking has all the traits of a society with a lower rank plus a number of additional traits. This also means that, if Trait A ranks above Trait B, Trait A is possessed by all the societies that possess Trait B and is also possessed by a number of additional societies. A different way of looking at this "cumulative" phenomenon is to examine rankings of societies or traits using different subsets of societies and traits; a society that ranks higher than another on one scale (i.e., using one subset of traits) maintains this relative position when another scale is used; and a trait that is possessed by more societies than another also maintains this relative position with other scales (i.e., using another subset of societies).

A simple example of a set of dichotomous, cumulative traits is a set of traits based on the height continuum. Let us suppose that we have four traits: (a) being 4 feet tall or over; (b) being 5 feet tall or over; (c) being 6 feet tall or over; (d) being 7 feet tall or over. Each of these is a dichotomous trait. Furthermore, if a person scores positive on only one trait, it must be the first; on two traits, the first two on the list, and so forth. If one person has a higher number of positive ratings than another, then he must score the same or numerically higher for all the traits in the scale than the other.

The scalogram technique can be extended to the measurement of the level of economic complexity quite easily. Let us measure the degree of economic complexity by reference to the division of labor and select the following four traits: the existence of a political leader who is a full-time specialist (i.e., does not regularly engage in subsistence food production); the existence of a full-time teacher (i.e., professional or secular instructor); the existence of a special full-time religious practitioner (e.g., shaman); and the existence of a full-time craft specialist (e.g., brewer, lapidary, cooper, tailor, tanner, and so forth).

---

[42]Such experiments were made by calculating correlation coefficients between a special scale containing 156 economic characteristics (reported in Frederic L. Pryor, "Property Institutions and Economic Development: Some Empirical Tests," *Economic Development and Cultural Change* XX (April 1972): 406–437) and Carneiro's scale containing a large number of political, social, and other types of variables.

[43]There are numerous analyses of Guttman scaling techniques; one useful short book on the subject is: Warren S. Torgerson, *Methods of Scaling* (1958).

TABLE 2.3

Existence of Full-Time Occupations in Four Societies: Unarranged Data[a]

| Societies | Traits[b] | | | | Total traits per society |
	Political leader	Secular teacher	Religious practitioner	Craft specialist	
Rwala	1	0	1	0	2
Incas	1	1	1	1	4
Thonga	1	0	1	1	3
Semang	0	0	1	0	1
Total societies per trait	3	1	4	2	—

[a]These data come from unpublished worksheets of Robert Carneiro, whom I would like to thank not only for this assistance but also for his general guidance on the whole subject of empirical measurements of economic development in primitive and peasant societies. The four societies used in this example are also in my sample. The Incas lived in Peru; the Rwala are Bedouins of Syria, Jordan, and Arabia; the Semang live in Malaysia; and the Thonga come from Mozambique.

[b]1 = presence; 0 = absence.

Taking four communities (represented by the name of their larger society), we can obtain the data which are presented in Table 2.3.

If the rows and columns can be rearranged in such a manner that the 1s form a "triangle," then we have a set of cumulative traits forming a "Guttman scale." As a start, it is useful to rearrange the rows and columns in ascending order of total traits. The results are given in Table 2.4.

A Guttman scale can indeed be formed from the societies and traits since the 1 values form a triangle. Thus, the extent of the division of labor appears to be a unidimensional scale. The results tell us that the Semang have the lowest and the Incas the highest level of economic development, a conclusion which accords with general opinion about such matters.

TABLE 2.4

Existence of Full-Time Occupations in Four Societies: Rearranged Data

| Societies | Traits[a] | | | | Total traits per society |
	Secular teacher	Craft specialist	Political leader	Religious practitioner	
Semang	0	0	0	1	1
Rwala	0	0	1	1	2
Thonga	0	1	1	1	3
Incas	1	1	1	1	4
Total societies per trait	1	2	3	4	—

[a]1 = presence; 0 = absence.

Before turning to more specific problems of calculating a Guttman scale for the problems at hand, several general observations about Carneiro's scale are offered in order to avoid misunderstanding.

First of all, the use of this method does not rest on any theory as to how specific societies function or change. There is nothing in this technique that is based on any particular theory of economic development, except insofar as any theory is predicated on the notion that "economic development" or "complexity of the society" is a unidimensional continuum.

Second, this approach does not imply that all aspects of societies, especially those in which economic elements may play minor roles (e.g., family structure, religious beliefs, or political forms) are necessarily related to the derived rankings of economic development or societal complexity; indeed, experiments along these lines show that most of the common social structural variables are not related.[44]

Third, the proof that the traits selected actually form a cumulative scale can only be seen in the process of rearranging the rows and columns to form such a scale. That is, although the traits are originally chosen on the basis of various a priori hypotheses about the relation of the traits to economic development or societal complexity, the only indication of whether we chose the traits correctly is whether or not they form a unidimensional (cumulative) scale.

Fourth, if a unidimensional ranking exists but if errors are made in the coding, or if the presence or absence of a trait is sometimes affected by random circumstances, then a series of technical problems arises with the use of this technique. Tests of statistical significance can, however, be performed.[45]

Robert L. Carneiro calculated such Guttman scales of societal complexity using 354 traits for 100 cultures (his "fourth edition") and another scale using 618 traits for 56 cultures (his "sixth edition"). He used a series of economic traits that can be conveniently divided into traits relating to: the division of labor, production of goods embodying "advanced" technological processes in production (such as pottery), production of specialized goods and services over and above those goods and services needed for bare subsistence, and existence of complex economic institutions (such as various property regulations, large urban settlements, and so forth). In addition, he included a number of traits reflecting complexity of social organization and stratification, complexity of political organization, complexity of law and judicial process, special knowledge and practices (such as use of writing), and so forth. He shows that strong rank order correlations exist between societies when different subsets of traits are used even though the societies have sufficient differences to be characterized as "relatively more advanced politically and less advanced economically for a society of its overall complexity." An inspection of his trait list reveals relatively few traits that can be considered to depend on environment

---

[44]Results of this experiment are reported by Pryor, "Property Institutions," pp. 406–437.
[45]These are discussed in the context of Carneiro's scales by Pryor, ibid.

(e.g., the Eskimos have no chance to show whether they can develop advanced agricultural techniques) or to be inappropriate in other ways.[46] Although objections can be raised about the details of Carneiro's work (especially some of his codings), the results show an impressive consistency and an enormous amount of careful work.

The Measure of Economic Development Used in This Study

Of all the attempts to measure societal complexity that have been proposed, Carneiro's work seems most appropriate, both methodologically and substantively, for use in this study. Certain small problems did arise, however.

For the first step I had to splice together the results of Carneiro's fourth and sixth editions in order to enlarge the sample of societies that he had rated. This task did not prove difficult because the rank order of societies in the two samples were highly correlated. (Kendall rank order correlation coefficient equals .88.) This combined list overlapped with my sample for 39 societies,[47] so other means had to be worked out to determine the rank on the development scale of the remaining 21, short of using Carneiro's technique, which would have taken an enormous amount of time.

Murdock and Provost recently developed a quite different method of ranking cultural complexity of societies using 10 traits, each of which could assume four values. Calculating the Murdock–Provost scale for the 39 societies for which I had Carneiro ratings and comparing the two rank orders of societies revealed a highly significant correlation. (Kendall rank order correlation coefficient equals .77). Therefore, Murdock-Provost scores for the remaining 21 societies in my sample were calculated, and the societies were spliced into the series of the 39, which had been ranked using the Carneiro scale. The final rankings are given in Appendix A, Series 21.

[46]One allegedly worrisome feature of Carneiro's data arises because he sometimes used data for an entire society, rather than for a specific community. Since the underlying ethnographic materials on which he based his ratings are usually reports on one or several communities visited by anthropologists, this problem does not seem very severe in most cases. However, in selecting societies rather than communities, one problem arising from different scales of society must be noted. A very small society, no matter how high its level of technology or complexity, will have certain limitations placed on its division of labor, while a society composed of a large number of people is likely to have a certain division of labor, even though its level of technology is quite low. For instance, a large society which is politically centralized might be able to support a number of full-time political and religious officials which could not be supported in a very small society. Acting to offset this factor, however, is the possibility that a society with a complex division of labor might find it advantageous to grow (e.g., through conquest) in order to utilize more fully their advanced technologies through a more extensive division of labor. The degree to which this size factor gives Carneiro's ratings of economic development an upward bias to societies which are large in size and the reverse bias to societies which are small in size is not clear. However, it does not seem likely that this is a very severe problem either.

[47]Since Carneiro and I generally used similar rules for selecting the period for which the community or society is coded, as well as the same ethnographic sources, this does not present a problem in using his ratings.

In examining the relationship between particular traits and the scale of economic development, I experimented with a number of techniques to investigate possible mistakes in the development rankings and also the coding of the trait. One simple technique proved especially useful. Suppose that the presence of Trait A, which occurs in 36 of the sample societies, is allegedly correlated with the level of economic development of societies. If we line up the societies in the sample by their relative level of economic development, we should find that most of the societies which, according to my ranking, number among the most highly developed 36 societies (for this example, 36 is called the "cutoff line") should have the trait and that most of the societies which are below the cutoff line should not have it. The greatest concentration of "errors" (societies which have the trait but which, according to their developmental rank, "should not"; and societies which do not have the trait but which, according to their developmental rank, "should") should occur among those societies in a narrow band around the cutoff line.[48] By comparing the percentage of errors in the total sample to the percentage of errors in a band of six (this proved a convenient number) societies on either side of the cutoff line, we can gain a clear notion of whether this expected result occurred. Although we cannot determine the degree to which errors in scaling and errors in coding contributed, we can see if the predicted error pattern appears. If the percentage of "errors" in the entire sample is low and if most of the "errors" appear in the band around the cutoff line, then we have good grounds for believing that the trait is really correlated with the relative level of economic development.

A problem deserving serious consideration is the degree to which my ratings of economic development predetermine the results of the statistical investigation of determinants of various modes of distribution. Such circularity could occur in several different ways.

Direct circularity occurs when the traits under examination actually form the units of the scale used in measuring the level of economic development. Indeed, several of the phenomena which I examine in the following chapters are included in Carneiro's trait list (e.g., existence of money, existence of markets for goods, and existence of markets for services), although most are not. This means that complete independence between the explanatory variable (the level of economic development) and the explained variable in these cases does not exist. However, since Carneiro used from 354 to 618 different traits in his ratings, the impact of this overlap is very small and can certainly be neglected.

The problem of indirect circularity is more severe. To what extent do the traits used in making this economic development scale cause or bring about the various distributional modes in a manner unrelated per se to the level of eco-

---

[48]Several reasons can be advanced to support this argument. First, it is among the societies in this band around the cutoff line that mistakes in the economic development ratings would most likely affect the results. Second, it is among these societies that the forces determining the presence or absence of the trait are most equally balanced, so that random factors play a relatively more important role than elsewhere. Third, it is among these societies that the greatest difficulties in coding would occur.

nomic development? For instance, various features associated with a centralized government are used in the development scale, and these are, in a serious sense, predicated on centric transfers (e.g., taxes). Sufficient information is not available to be able to make a judgment about such matters, but one extremely important aspect of the problem must be noted. The use of multivariate statistical techniques permits a number of determinants of a particular mode of distribution to be investigated at the same time. Although indirect circularity may exist between the particular distributional mode and the scale of economic development, this does not affect the analysis of the causal role of the other variables. Some may consider the results I obtain linking particular modes of distribution with the level of economic development to be tautological, but the determination of other causal variables (or the determination that no other variables play a causal role) still has validity. In other words, even though the evolutionary hypotheses advanced in the following chapters may be questioned by those worried about circularity, the other propositions can be accepted. I should also add my own subjective assessment that such indirect circularity is probably as unimportant as the direct circularity in most cases.

The end result of the calculations is a development ranking of the 60 societies; this tells us nothing, however, about absolute levels of economic development that must be used in the regression analysis. In order to calculate this variable, we must somehow convert the rankings to an absolute scale, and to this end I investigated three different assumptions about how this conversion could be made. In the first experiment I assumed that: $ALED = a + b(RLED)$, where $ALED$ = the absolute level of economic development, $RLED$ = the rank of the level of economic development computed by the method discussed above, and a and b are constants. This meant that in the regressions I merely used the rank of the level of economic development as my development variable (so that the development variable ranged from 1, the lowest level, to 60, the higher level). In the second experiment I assumed that: $ALED = a + b(RLED)^2$, a nonlinear relation between the ranks and the absolute scale. This meant that in the regressions, I used the square of the rank of the level of economic development as my development variable (so that it ranged from 1 to 3600). In the last experiment, I assumed that: $ALED = a + b \ln(RLED)$, where $\ln$ is the natural logarithm. This meant that in the regressions I used the natural logarithm of the rank of the level of economic development as my development variable (so that it ranged from 0 to 4.094). These experiments, carried out with most of the dependent variables studied in the following chapters, showed that if the second assumption gave the best results, the third assumption gave the worst results, or vice versa. Since the first assumption usually gave results quite close to the best results in almost all cases, this conversion method is used throughout this book, especially since there was no clear superiority of the latter two assumptions.

The other exaplanatory variables that I use are much less complicated than the development variable and are defined and explained when I come to them.

A BRIEF SUMMARY

I start by defining the difference between exchange and transfer transactions and then distinguish two components of each, ending up with an exhaustive classification of all types of distributional transactions into four modes: market exchange, reciprocal exchange, noncentric transfers, and centric transfers. A variety of different types of distributional transactions compose each mode, but this typology provides the framework for the initial classification.

A difficult problem arises concerning the distributional transactions that I include or exclude from analysis. In particular, I examine whether transactions within the nuclear family, the extended family, or larger family groupings such as the lineage should be excluded. This choice of the societal level at which the distributional transactions are analyzed is important, as the relative importance of certain modes of distribution (particularly noncentric transfers) is quite sensitive to the choice of the unit of observation. The unit of observation used in this study (i.e., the unit within which consideration of distributional transactions is excluded from analysis) is based on the production and consumption units of the society.

The definition of economic development, which is one of the explanatory variables used most frequently in the analysis, is based on the notion that economic complexity is the most basic concept underlying our understanding of economic development. The use of complexity allows us to sidestep many problems arising when certain indicators of economic development such as labor productivity and production per capita show divergent trends among a group of societies. I use as my measurement a ranking of societal complexity devised by Robert Carneiro.

I would like to reemphasize that in this chapter I have not explained anything about the reality of primitive and peasant economies but have merely described some of the conceptual tools which I will use in constructing the propositions to explain this reality. Whether or not these definitions are useful depends on the propositions which I or others can derive employing them.

3

USING CROSS-SECTION
EVIDENCE TO MAKE
INFERENCES ABOUT
EVENTS IN THE PAST[1]

... nullumque habere [deum] in praeterita ius praeterquam oblivionis ...
PLINY THE ELDER[2]

... the Present is the living sum-total of the whole Past ...
THOMAS CARLYLE[3]

The relationships between cross-section and time-series evidence (or, as some-times called by anthropologists, synchronic and diachronic evidence) are intri-cate; and perplexities abound on these matters with distressing frequency. For the most part we cannot easily study distribution in primitive societies from historical or archaeological records, for many matters of vital concern to the topic were never written down (assuming the society had a written language at the time) or are undetectable from archaeological evidence. If we wish to know something about the past, we are forced to generalize from our knowledge of present-day primitive societies; and this requires us to face squarely two ques-tions about our methods of analysis linking cross-section with time-series generalizations: To what extent do the correlations that are discovered by statistical analysis of present-day societies represent causal relationships in some fundamental sense and to what extent are the discovered relationships brought about by historical circumstances unrelated to the hypothesis under investigation? And assuming that the correlations uncovered in the cross-

Design from a body painting of an Australian aborigine; Arnhem Land, Northern Territory, Aus-tralia.

[1]Portions of this chapter are reproduced from the *American Ethnologist* 3 (1976): 731–750.

[2]Gaius Plinius Secundus, *Naturalis historia,* Book II, Verse 27: '[God] has no power over the past except to obscure it.'

[3]"Characteristics," (1831), *Critical and Miscellaneous Essays,* Vol. III (London: Chapman and Hall, n.d.).

section analysis represent causal relationships, to what extent may we use these to make inferences about the past?

The first question—the interpretability of cross-section results—has been discussed much more intensively by anthropologists than by economists. The focal point of most such anthropological analyses is the extent to which the results of cross-sectional statistical results are influenced by cultural diffusion (the process by which one society borrows traits from another society; or the process of the geographical spreading of particular cultural traits through societal migration). This problem was first raised in anthropology by the famous statistician Francis Galton when commenting on a pioneering cross-cultural study by Edward Tylor and, in his honor, is designated as "Galton's problem" (actually, of course, it was Tylor's problem).[4] In recent years Raoul Naroll has published a number of papers on this topic, and others, stimulated by his work, have also devoted considerable efforts in trying to devise statistical tests with which to determine whether cross-section results are contaminated by diffusion.[5] Most methods for dealing with the problem follow one of two basic approaches: (a) Either comparisons are made of the results from geographical subareas with the entire sample, a method which requires a large sample size and involves some difficult problems of interpretation; (b) or else clustering tests are performed, which, up to now, leave much to be desired.

In the following discussion I propose a new method (called the "diffusion possibility method") that is subsequently applied throughout this book. The method is based on an analysis of different kinds of prediction errors to determine if a particular pattern of errors suggesting diffusion occurs for societies which are geographically close to other societies which possess the trait under investigation. This method is both more flexible and more powerful than previously proposed tests. And its application shows quite clearly that the correlations presented in the following chapters are not, by and large, contaminated by cultural diffusion in previous eras.

The second question—the differences between the nature of causal processes over time and at a single point in time—has been discussed much more intensively by economists than by anthropologists. The contexts of most such economical analyses are the investigations of relationships of cross-section and time-series results for modern industrial societies that have considerable contact with each other. In the context of this study the basic issues of this question are more simple and are briefly outlined after the topic of diffusion has been analyzed.

---

[4]Tylor's paper (1889) and Galton's comments are reprinted in *Readings in Cross-Cultural Methodology* (1961), ed. Frank W. Moore, pp. 1–26.

[5]The various issues as well as the past literature on the subject are ably discussed by: Raoul Naroll, "Galton's Problem," in *A Handbook of Method in Cultural Anthropology* (1973), ed. Raoul Naroll and Ronald Cohen, pp. 927–946; Harold E. Driver, "Cross-Cultural Studies," in *Handbook of Social and Cultural Anthropology* (1973), ed. John J. Honigmann, pp. 327–447; C. J. J. Vermeulen and A. de Ruijter, "Dominant Epistemological Presuppositions in the Use of Cross-Cultural Survey Methods," *Current Anthropology* XVI (March 1975): 29–52; and by various authors in *Studies in Cultural Diffusion: Galton's Problem* (1974), ed. James M. Schaefer.

This chapter may be skipped by those readers who: (a) are sufficiently impressed by the evidence presented in Chapter 1 that the societies in my sample are too far from each other to permit any kind of important cultural borrowing; (b) are, therefore, willing to admit that the cross-section results represent uncontaminated functional relations; (c) and are also willing to accept the reasonable notion that causal laws valid for present-day societies are also valid for societies in the past.

GALTON'S PROBLEMS

The problems raised by Galton pertain to inductive studies, and legitimate questions can be raised about their applicability to deductive studies such as those carried out in this book. That is, if we have a formal deductive model, derive certain hypotheses from it, and then test the hypotheses using a randomly selected sample of societies, then we need not worry about Galton's problems. Unfortunately, two conditions of this statement are not always met in the following chapters. First, some of the hypotheses investigated in this study are not derived rigorously from deductive models but instead are based on "common sense" considerations that ultimately may be inductively arrived at. Second, as noted in Chapter 1, the sample is not randomly drawn from the universe of primitive and peasant societies in the world. It behooves us, therefore, to pay some attention to Galton's problem or, more accurately, to the two problems which are usually discussed in this context. Although these problems are quite interrelated, their separation permits the problem to be viewed from two useful perspectives.

The Problem of Causal Identification

Let us assume for the moment that in isolated societies Trait Y is caused solely by Trait X. We would never expect to find Trait Y without X and vice versa. Suppose that Trait Y is such that once it is invented or brought about, it can be easily carried to or borrowed by some other society. If societies are no longer isolated from each other, then we might argue that Trait Y has two different causes: an ultimate (functional) cause and a historical cause (related to the process of cultural diffusion). This raises some knotty problems for empirical investigators.

Although X may be the ultimate cause of Y, we may find no positive relationship between the two variables in a cross-section investigation if Y has spread primarily by diffusion. In this case (which Naroll has designated as "hyperdiffusion" and which Driver designates as "nonfunctional diffusion"), the borrowing has obscured the basic functional causal relationship. If Trait X is also such that it can be easily borrowed, then Y and X may diffuse together. In this case (which Naroll has designated as "semidiffusion") we find the expected correlation between the two variables in the sample of societies, but the results are not necessarily brought about by the posited causal mechanism but by a different mechanism which really does not support (or refute) the functional hypothesis. Only if Trait X is borrowed and then brings about Trait Y in the borrowing society can a correlation between Y and X be found which reflects the posited functional mechanism.

Other analytic difficulties arise if we have diffusion in the situation where our hypothesized causal relationship between Y and X is incorrect. If X or Y diffuse separately, then no relationship between the two may be found, and the hypothesis will not be statistically validated. Suppose, however, that the traits diffuse together (e.g., in a situation where an original society by chance had the two traits, and the various societies which emerged from the original society kept the two traits). In this case statistical analysis might reveal a correlation between the two variables which validates an incorrect hypothesis.

How can we guard against allowing diffusion effects to mislead us so that we reject functional hypotheses (e.g., Trait X causes Trait Y) that are actually true or accept functional hypotheses that are actually false? First, of course, we might decide on the basis of a priori information the likelihood that the phenomena under investigation diffused in a manner to cause false inferences. Certainly, the diffusion of some inconsequential technological device (e.g., a particular type of bowl) is more likely than the diffusion of a complex social variable because the assimilation of this latter variable in other societies might require extensive societal changes. Fortunately, most of the variables investigated in further chapters seem to be closer to the latter than to the former example. Unfortunately, this is a very intuitive procedure, and more formal methods for investigating the problem are desirable.

If diffusion occurred, then we would expect to find a geographical clustering of the variables under investigation. One obvious step would be to examine the average distances between all pairs of societies, both of which have the trait, and compare this either with the average distance between all pairs of societies which do not have the trait or else with the average distance between all pairs of societies, only one of which has the trait.[6] For various reasons the latter type of comparison seems preferable.[7] A similar type of analysis can also be carried

---

[6]In carrying out this and the other analyses of distance described in this chapter, one shortcut was followed in measuring the distances the 1770 pairs of societies. For all societies within 3600 miles of each other the distances were classified into one of the categories shown in Table 1.1, with the midpoint of the interval used as the distance. For all societies more than 3600 miles from each other, I assumed that the distance is 6600 miles, a distance which is the average distance between the middle of the six geographical areas (North America, South America, Sub-Sahara Africa, Circum-Mediterranean area, Eurasia, and Insular Pacific) from which the sample societies were drawn.

[7]The most important reason is that there may have been diffusion, but of the "negative-trait," that is, the elimination of a trait may have spread by diffusion such as the elimination of indigenous moneys which resulted after Western contact. Therefore, it seems better to compare the average distances between pairs of societies that both have the traits under investigation with the average distance between pairs of societies, only one of which has the trait.

out with regard to the hypothesized causal variable. (If more than one such variable exists, we might also investigate the average distances between all pairs of societies for which we *predict* both to have the trait, and so forth, using as our basis of prediction various combinations of the alleged causal variables.)[8]

The lack of a significant degree of geographical clustering suggests that diffusion did not occur between the societies in the sample. The presence of a significant degree of geographical clustering does not definitely prove that diffusion occurred; but detection of such clustering sends up warning signals that we should be careful and that we should employ more rigorous statistical tests to detect diffusion.

The Problem of Independence of Sample Societies

In discussions of Galton's problems the term *independence* is used in two senses. The first meaning relates to the manner in which the sample is selected; if the societies in the sample are drawn at random, there is statistical independence. For the sample used in this study, such matters are discussed in Chapter 1. The second meaning relates to the historical contact of the sample societies. If, for instance, we draw a random sample of 500 societies, and 60 of them are in China, the latter subset of societies may in actuality represent only one case since such strong historical contact between ethnic groups in China has taken place that they may be considered for all intents the same society.

Ultimately, both of these meanings of *independence* boil down to a technical question, namely, how many degrees of freedom we should use in making tests of statistical significance when we are examining the various hypotheses. As noted in Chapter 1, a probabilistic model is employed since there are many reasons why the posited causal relationships do not occur in every society in the sample. It is therefore necessary to make tests of statistical significance, and here is where our problems arise. As I argued in Chapter 1, the lack of statistical independence in the selection of the sample requires us to reduce the number of degrees of freedom (or, equivalently, to raise the numerical level of the level of acceptance of the various computed statistics). The lack of historical independence of the sample societies might require the same procedure. In the example cited in the previous paragraph, if the Chinese societies are considered as a single case, we have only 441 degrees of freedom rather than 500.

We need a systematic way of determining whether or not we need to reduce the number of degrees of freedom because of the absence of a significant degree of historical independence. Before turning to this matter, however, one last problem concerning the degrees of freedom used in the statistical analysis deserves brief consideration.

[8]The basis of making predictions in this study is the regression formula which is calculated. Some problems of using this method of prediction are discussed later.

In both the simple clustering tests described earlier or the more complicated test of historical independence described below, we are examining distances between pairs of societies. In a sample consisting of N societies, we have $(N)(N-1)/2$ pairs to examine. However, because the societies are located on a spherical surface, we do not have $(N)(N-)/2$ independent distances; that is, if a subset of distances between pairs of societies is designated, the distances between the remaining pairs can be calculated. (For instance, if we have four societies and are given the distances between five out of the six pairs of societies, we can calculate the distance between the remaining pair of societies.)

What this means in terms of our investigations is quite simple. All of our tests are set up to determine if a certain kind of geographical clustering exists, that is, whether the average distances between a set of societies is significantly less than between another set. If we assume that there are $(N)(N-1)/2$ degrees of freedom when calculating our standard deviations and standard errors, we may accept as a "significantly" smaller distance, a difference in distance that, if fewer degrees of freedom had been employed in the calculation of the statistics, would not be considered statistically significant. More simply, if we assume that the degrees of freedom are equal to $(N)(N-1)/2$, we are applying an overly strong significance test and may pick up cases of alleged diffusion where none exists in reality.

Unfortunately, I have been unable to find or to devise any formula which would tell us how many degrees of freedom we should use for our sample of 60 societies spread over a sphere. Since I am willing to err more in the direction of detecting diffusion where none exists than overlooking diffusion where it actually occurred, I assume that there are $(N)(N-1)/2$ degrees of freedom when calculating the statistics used in the clustering tests.

THE PROPOSED SOLUTION [9]

The Method

Underlying the method I propose for dealing with certain problems of diffusion are some simple considerations about the pattern of errors which occur when making predictions based on functional relations if diffusion occurred. Let us assume that we are testing the hypothesis that Trait X brings about the occurrence of Trait Y and that we find a statistically significant relationship between these two variables in our sample of societies. Let us also suppose that

[9]A more general solution to this problem is presented in my essay, "The Diffusion Possibility Method: A More General and Simpler Solution to Galton's Problem," *American Ethnologist* 3 (November 1976): 731–749. The following discussion is tailored to the actual tests which are carried out in this study.

the single most important factor conducive to diffusion is geographical proximity, measured in terms of straight-line distances between the societies under examination.

If diffusion occurred in such a manner that Trait Y was borrowed from Society 1 by Society 2, then we might be able to predict successfully the presence of Trait Y in Society 1 (because Trait X is present) but not in Society 2 (because Trait X is absent). If such a type of diffusion is an important phenomenon, then this type of prediction error should occur relatively more often between societies that are geographically close to each other than far away. A rarer instance of the same type of diffusion would occur if, by chance, Society 1 possessed Trait Y (even though it did not possess Trait X) and if it were borrowed by Society 2; in this case, we might predict the absence of Trait Y from both societies (because Trait X is absent) and make prediction errors in both cases.

If diffusion occurred in such a manner that Trait X was borrowed from Society 1 by Society 2 and if not enough time elapsed in Society 2 for Trait X to bring about the occurrence of Trait Y, then we might be able to predict successfully the presence of Trait Y in Society 1 (because Trait X is present) but not in Society 2 (because of the time lag). If such a type of diffusion is an important phenomenon, then this type of prediction error should also occur relatively more often between societies that are geographically close to each other than far away.

The only societies for which we can be quite sure that diffusion did not occur are pairs for which we predict the presence of Trait Y in one but not the other (because of the presence of causal Trait X in one but not the other) and for which in both cases our predictions are incorrect.

If we do not know if diffusion occurred but are able to find a significant relationship between Variables X and Y among the societies of the sample, then we begin our search for diffusion by looking at prediction errors. More specifically, we examine each pair of societies in the sample and classify them according to the schema presented in the discussion above and summarized in Table 3.1. After this is done, we simply calculate the average distance (and the standard deviation and the standard error of the distance) between the societies in each of the four groups and compare them.

If Trait Y diffused, but not Trait X, then we would expect that the average distances between the societies in Group P or Group P' would be significantly less than between the societies in Group R. If Trait X diffused but not Trait Y, then we would expect that the average distances between the societies in Group Q would be significantly less than between the societies in Group R. For these types of diffusion, therefore, we have quantitative methods with which to deal with certain aspects of the problem.

This method of detecting diffusion by examining prediction errors allows us to avoid an error which might arise in simple clustering tests. In the latter tests

TABLE 3.1

A Representation of the Grouping of Pairs of Societies for the Analysis of Diffusion

Prediction of presence of Trait Y (dependent variable)		Actual presence of Trait Y (dependent variable)		Group designation	Comments
First society	Second society	First society	Second society		
Yes	No	Yes	Yes	Group P	Possible diffusion of Trait Y without diffusion of "causal" Trait X
No	Yes	Yes	Yes	Group P	
No	No	Yes	Yes	Group P'	Possible diffusion of Trait Y without diffusion of "causal" Trait X
No	No	Yes	Yes	Group P'	(a rare case)
Yes	Yes	Yes	No	Group Q	Possible diffusion of "causal" Trait X without diffusion of Trait Y
Yes	Yes	No	Yes	Group Q	
Yes	No	Yes	Yes	Group R	Diffusion definitely could not have occurred
No	Yes	Yes	No	Group R	
All other combinations				Group S	Dropped from further consideration

we may find a geographical clustering of a particular variable that is not due to diffusion but to the simple fact that the societies in this cluster also possess the same causal traits (e.g., a relatively high level of economic development or the same type of harsh climate).

This type of analysis permits us to detect diffusion occurring not only from a single point but also from several points. However, the more polycentric the diffusion process, the more difficult the detection of the phenomenon becomes with the methods I have proposed. Several other problems in using this method of detecting diffusion also occur.

Underlying the procedure is the assumption that straight-line geographical distance is an adequate measure for the probability of diffusion between one society and another (the greater the distance, the less the probability). In early stages of research I made a number of experiments to see if other measures might be more adequate, for example, measuring distances at sea as one-half similar distances on land or measuring distances in mountainous terrains as somewhat more than similar distances in miles on flat land. None of these had much effect on the results, so this type of investigation was dropped and straight-line geographical distances are exclusively employed.

Since the level of economic development plays an important role in most of the causal relationships that I investigate, and since I may have made mistakes in the relative rankings of the various societies on the development scale, the results of the diffusion analysis might be affected. Such an impact could especially occur at the "cutoff line," the critical level of development where the trait under investigation appears or disappears. Therefore, other experiments were performed where the societies in a band of three or six societies around this critical developmental level were omitted from the analysis. Such a procedure made little difference to the results; therefore, this line of investigation was also dropped.

A hidden assumption underlying the application of this method is that we are examining for the presence of diffusion in societies at roughly the same point in time; since this condition is not met in the sample of 60 primitive and peasant societies, certain difficulties arise. Since the codings for most of the societies in the sample refer to the second part of the nineteenth century, this is the period for which the diffusion analysis is made. Societies for which the data refer to either earlier or later periods are excluded from the analysis unless I have positive evidence that for the variables involved, the situation in the second half of the nineteenth century was the same as for the period to which my data refer. Usually 50 to 54 societies are included in the diffusion analysis.

An Important Assumption

If we can establish a low probability that the cross-section results of functional causal relationships are contaminated by diffusion, then only one major step remains to be taken—generalizing the cross-section results to events over time. This requires an assumption that the nature of causation for the phenomenon investigated was the same in the far past as it has been in the near past.

A purist might contend that this is not difficult, for a social law is a social law, wherever and whenever it occurs. But the problem is more complicated than this, for the context in which social causal forces operated in the far past might be sufficiently different from the context of the near past, so that relationships between the most important observed causal variables and the variables to be explained might be different in the two time periods. That is to say, a different causal force might have been operating in the far past that is not detected by analysis of the data from the near past.

The main contextual difference is usually said to be the occurrence of cultural diffusions, and this matter has already been discussed. For the phenomena under investigation I spent a good deal of time trying to conjure up situations in which *other* contextual differences in the past might nullify the social laws discovered from the cross-section evidence. I considered a variety of factors such as the impact of differences in climate, in "consciousness," and many other phenomena. Given the nature of the causal forces unearthed through the cross-cultural analysis, I was unable to come up with any kind of credible examples which would force me to abandon the procedure of generalizing about past events from the cross-section evidence, once the absence of diffusion has been established. If the reader still has reservations about generalizing from cross-section results to time-series, then he can read this book as strictly a cross-section study.

Some Caveats

The technique described above for dealing with the detection of diffusion must be used cautiously, and several caveats deserve explicit attention.

First, this technique is designed primarily to handle cases of diffusion where a relationship between variables X and Y is found, but we are not sure whether this association is due to diffusion or not. The technique does not handle cases where diffusion acts to obscure causal relations, unless we are lucky enough that the relationship is not totally masked (a situation that might occur if diffusion of the variable under investigation did occur, but not very often). That is, the analysis of prediction errors summarized in Table 3.1 rests on the assumption that a relationship between the dependent and independent variables can be detected. Given the phenomenon with which I am dealing in this book, I feel this is a reasonable assumption. But the reader must bear in mind that the technique is biased toward rejecting relationships that may actually exist but that may be masked by diffusion processes.

Second, this technique does not handle cases of "fast" diffusion, that is, diffusion occurring over long distances in a rapid manner because of special circumstances. Such diffusion occurs, for instance, when long-distance traders introduce practices that they learned abroad or when armies on long-distance crusades bring back foreign customs from afar. In such cases the assumption about the greater likelihood of diffusion between close than distant neighbors does not hold. However, recorded instances of "fast" diffusion can be taken into account in the interpretation of the results.

Third, this technique does not handle cases where the particular traits and their hypothesized causal traits diffuse together at roughly the same time. Such cases would show clustering of the dependent variable as well as clustering of the independent variable, but no diffusion would be shown in the analysis of prediction errors. If one or the other set of traits diffused at a different time, then the third test would show the presence of diffusion. Given the nature of the sample and the type of phenomena under investigation, such cases of simultaneous diffusion (semidiffusion) do not seem very likely.

Interpretation of the statistical results can not be carried out in a mechanical fashion. Nevertheless, the tests I have outlined can detect a number of different types of diffusion, and their application gives us greater confidence in the results.

SUMMARY

For each case where I investigate whether the cross-section results are influenced by diffusion, three sets of numbers are presented. First, I give data on average distances and the standard deviations of distances between pairs of societies, both of which have the trait under investigation, both of which do not have the trait, and one of which has the trait, so that a simple clustering analysis can be performed. Second, I present data on average distances and standard deviations of distances between pairs of societies, both of which I *predict* to have the trait, both of which I *predict* not to have the trait, and one of which I *predict* to have the trait, so that another simple clustering analysis can be performed. Finally I present data on the average distances and standard deviations of distances between pairs of societies grouped in the manner presented in Table 3.1 (except, for simplicity, Group S is omitted). This latter analysis, which focuses on particular patterns of predictive errors indicating different types of diffusion, is the most powerful test.

The first two simple clustering tests alert us to the possibility of diffusion occurring; if the results of these tests are negative, there is little need to perform the analysis of errors discussed above. However, if they suggest that diffusion might have occurred, then the more powerful test must be used. If this third test suggests diffusion, then the statistical analysis must be reformulated to take into account the diffusion process. As it turns out, in only one important case in the following chapters did this prove necessary, namely, the analysis of gambling. Here I then tried to take diffusion into account by including in the regression analysis a special location variable.

If the cross-section results are shown to be uninfluenced by the presence of diffusion, then the results are used to generalize about the past in this study. This procedure rests on certain assumptions about the nature of social causation and the similarity of causal laws in different time periods. In science, as well as religion, a certain amount of faith is required if we wish to enjoy ourselves while participating in its rites.

4

EXCHANGE AND TRANSFER: A CASE STUDY

Mensch, bezahle deine Schulden,
Lang ist ja die Lebensbahn,
Und du musst noch oftmals borgen,
Wie du es so oft gethan.

HEINE[1]

This chapter has two major purposes: to provide a case study of distribution in a single community so that the analytic categories of this book and the interrelations of different distributional modes may become clearer; and to examine the usefulness of current approaches in the anthropology literature toward the subject of reciprocal exchange.

The case study, jointly written with Nelson H. H. Graburn,[2] explores data on every major type of distributional transaction in a small Eskimo village, one of the few precapitalist societies for which such information is available. The data permit us to calculate in a bookkeeping fashion distributional accounts of every individual in the community so that particular exchange and transfer elements can be viewed quite concretely. The data for individuals, as well as for collections of similar individuals (e.g., all men, all people from wealthy families, or all people with political power) show considerable imbalances (transfers), which are further explored with the aid of a regression analysis. The regressions permit us not only to isolate a number of important causal variables of such

---

Design from a Goajira cotton belt; northern Columbia.

[1]Heinrich Heine, "Die Heimkehr," Section 36, Stanza 2: 'Brother, pay off all your debts, as life's a long and weary way; for in the future you might borrow, as you borrowed yesterday.' This banal thought is embodied in equally bad verse in other languages as well. For instance, Ralph Waldo Emerson once wrote (in his poem "Solution"): "Wilt thou seal up the avenues of ill? Pay every debt, as if God wrote the bill."

[2]The data contained in this chapter are from Graburn's fieldnotes. The first-person plural adopted in this chapter is not a stylistic affectation but denotes a close cooperation between us.

transfers but also to show that social invisibles such as "prestige" or "status" play a relatively small or negligible role in explaining the results.

The subject of reciprocal exchange has received inordinate attention in the anthropology literature, so much so that the subject of transfers has been quite neglected. In part, this attention toward reciprocity can be traced to the high ethical value placed on such exchange, a valuation which has impelled many investigators to study the phenomenon. In part, this is also because reciprocity has been tied to certain notions about social stability. For instance, Marcel Mauss argued that various types of domestic and foreign reciprocal exchange serve not only as a cohesive force internally but also as a substitute or a replacement for external conflict.[3] Curiously, most anthropological analyses of reciprocal exchange have focused on rather vague ethnographic impressions rather than on any type of quantitative evidence.[4] And few of the theoretical discussions about reciprocal exchange have been accompanied by empirical evidence which permits any type of rigorous testing of hypotheses.[5]

We explore and test a number of common hypotheses about reciprocal exchange and are able to show their inadequacy for explaining the data of the case study. From such evidence we argue that reciprocity among Eskimos is a myth—not only to natives but also to previous outside observers. We include a brief analysis of myths of exchange and transfer in general and the role such myths have in bringing about situations exactly opposite to that characterized by the myth.

RECIPROCITY THEORIES AND SOME EMPIRICAL IMPLICATIONS

By "reciprocity theory" we mean the attempt to use the concept of reciprocal exchange as an analytic tool rather than as an ex post rationalization of some exotic native custom. The concept of reciprocal exchange has too rich an intellectual history and too many ramifications to be discussed in full in a few pages. We wish only to consider a few of the most important theories as to the nature of reciprocal exchange that may shed light on our more general concerns about exchange and transfer transactions.

Over the centuries it has been a commonplace among writers on ethics to emphasize the "goodness" of reciprocal exchange. Heine's philistine verse, serving as the chapter's epigraph, incorporates an oft-repeated injunction to

---

[3]Marcel Mauss, The Gift (1967) [originally published 1925].

[4]A notable exception is Jules Henry, "The Economics of Pilagá Food Distribution," American Anthropologist LIII (1951): 187–219. He had a different kind of sample, handled the data differently, and examined a different set of questions than we do. It should be added that the Pilagá are very strongly related to the Toba of Argentina, one of the sample societies in this study.

[5]A notable exception is Marshall Sahlins, "On the Sociology of Primitive Exchange," in his Stone Age Economics (1972), pp. 185–277. An earlier version of this essay was published under the same title in The Relevance of Models for Social Anthropology (1965), ed. Michael Banton, pp. 139–236.

make a reciprocal exchange which might otherwise become a transfer. Furthermore, reciprocal exchange (as defined in this study) is supposed to characterize a relationship between social equals (which is also "good") and not a hierarchical relationship (which is "bad"). From such a train of sentiments it is but a small step to argue that "good" people engage in reciprocal exchange.

Ideas about the inherently reciprocal nature of distribution in primitive and peasant societies appear to derive essentially from the romantic movement in Western intellectual life that idealized the people and the life in these societies. The degree of emphasis on reciprocal exchange in such societies may well have also depended on the author's alienation from the norms of his own society and on his concern with reform. For instance, one might contrast the romantic views of Rousseau on the supposed state of natural man before the imposition of the state with the views on ancient society outlined by Henry Maine, who saw not one whit of egalitarianism or reciprocity.[6]

In his well-known essay on the gift, in 1925, Marcel Mauss first raised the concept of reciprocity to a central place in anthropology. Although he discussed several different types of transfers, he focused his analytic energies on an examination of the importance of reciprocity in primitive and peasant societies, delimited by the simple rules of the obligation to give, the obligation to receive ("One does not have the right to refuse a gift or a potlatch. To do so would show fear of having to repay and of being abased in default."), and the obligation to repay ("[This] is imperative. Face is lost forever if [a worthy return] is not made or if equivalent value is not destroyed.").[7] Mauss's attempted systematization of the nature of reciprocity was based on a number of ethnographic accounts, two of which—those of Thurnwald on the Buin and of Malinowski on the Trobriand *kula*—focus on reciprocity as a key to the economic life of the peoples under study. In a later monograph Malinowski elevated the concept of reciprocity to a central position in his analysis of the social organization on the Trobriand Islands. He declared that the principle of "give and take" pervades all of tribal life, that it is the basis of the social structure, and that "the whole division into totemic clans, into sub-clans of a local nature and into village communities, is characterized by a system of reciprocal services and duties, in which the groups play a game of give and take. . . . Reciprocity, the give-and-take principle, reigns supreme also within the clan, nay, within the nearest group of kinsmen."[8] From these writings it seems fair to draw the hypothesis that in primitive and peasant societies, most distributional transactions are reciprocal exchanges, a matter investigated in later chapters.

In the past few decades the analysis of reciprocity has taken several divergent paths in anthropological theory. One path lies in the field of social structure

[6]Jean-Jacques Rousseau, *The Social Contract* (1955) [originally published 1791]; Henry Maine, *Ancient Law* (1861).
[7]Mauss, *The Gift*, pp. 37–41.
[8]Bronisław Malinowski, *Crime and Custom in Savage Society* (1926), p. 47.

known as "alliance theory," in which analysts have developed Mausssian notions of reciprocity as the foundation of human social structure and as the fundamental quality of the human/social mind. In a famous early book Claude Lévi-Strauss combines Mauss's ideas about reciprocity with Tylor's ideas about the importance of exogamy to analyze marital exchange and stabilizing elements of social structures.[9] Furthermore, he introduces the notion that there is a hierarchy of "things" to be exchanged among groups, with women the most valuable, followed by goods and services. Lévi-Strauss further argues that the natives may not be consciously aware of the kinds of reciprocities involved and may not actually calculate or deliberately balance the accounts of women, goods, or services; but such balance is nevertheless achieved.

A second path has been blazed by Edmund Leach[10] in a reply to Lévi-Strauss. Leach agrees with the latter's ideas on the essential reciprocal nature of exchange in precapitalist economies but disagrees that women are necessarily "the highest good" or that transactions of women, goods, or services necessarily need to be balanced in terms of "tangibles." Rather, he argues, part of the balance may be in terms of intangibles such as rights of a territorial and political nature, or relative "status" or "prestige." (These terms, he notes, cannot be defined except in terms of the cultural situation: Prestige may be derived from murder in one society, philanthropy in a second, economic success in a third.) Turning away from marital exchange, a number of anthropologists have since analyzed imbalances in the exchange of goods and services in terms of counterflows of prestige, the most extensive study being a book-length monograph about festive and ritual giving in a Mayan community.[11]

A final path is that followed by anthropologists of the "substantivist" persuasion, based on many of the ideas of Karl Polanyi. Of these, Marshall Sahlins has presented the most sophisticated attempt to analyze reciprocity and other modes of distribution and has propounded a number of interesting propositions.[12] He argues that transfer transactions of an altruistic nature[13] characterize the transactions between kinsmen. Among kin there is an obligation to give, but the obligation to receive and, more importantly, to return are considerably more vague. Reckoning is not overt (in contradistinction to the approach of Mauss and Malinowski). Sustained transfer transactions with goods moving toward one person (often a "have-not") occur sometimes for a very long period. According to Leach this would be balanced by the flows of intangibles in the opposite direction, but Sahlins makes no such assertion. Sahlins also argues that transactions between strangers or enemies are characterized often

      [9]Claude Lévi-Strauss, The Elementary Structures of Kinship, 2nd ed. (1969) [originally published 1949].
      [10]E. R. Leach, "The Structural Implications of Matrilateral Cross-Cousin Marriage," Journal of the Royal Anthropological Institute LXXXI (1951): 24–53.
      [11]Frank Cancian, Economics and Prestige in a Maya Community: The Religious Cargo System in Zinacantan (1965).
      [12]Sahlins, Stone Age Economics, pp. 185–277.
      [13]He labels this "generalized reciprocity," but we feel this label is confusing and have used our own terminology.

by transfers of a malevolent nature.[14] That is, the participants attempt to get something for less than its customary value by haggling, chicanery, theft, or other means; as a result, the transactions are often unbalanced. Finally, Sahlins argues that transactions between those whose social distance is somewhere between kin and enemies is usually characterized by a reciprocal exchange.[15] He emphasizes that the exchange accounts may not be balanced at any single point in time but that in the long run the accounts are balanced.

If we can somehow calculate transactions accounts between individuals, we can test some of these ideas. If Mauss is basically correct, we should find relatively balanced transactions accounts; if Leach is correct, we might find unbalanced transactions, but the imbalances would be counterbalanced by a flow of social invisibles (Leach only considers "good" invisibles such as prestige; however, "bad" invisibles such as "force" can also be included); if Sahlins is correct, we might find unbalanced transactions, but the imbalances can be explained by the social distance between the transactors. These are the key hypotheses for which evidence is needed.

The case study presented in this chapter examines these hypotheses for a particular village. It can be argued that theories of such general nature cannot be disproved in an absolute manner by a single contrary case. However, these reciprocity theories and their many variants are usually argued in the literature on the basis of "plausibility" rather than quantitative evidence. Therefore, a single contrary case employing a serious quantitative analysis shifts the burden of proof to the shoulders of those affirming rather than those denying such theories.

THE ETHNOGRAPHIC SETTING

The Society

The quantitative analysis is carried out on the Eskimo village of Sugluk, which is a settlement on the southwest side of the Hudson Strait, connecting Hudson Bay to the Atlantic Ocean. The 254 inhabitants of the village belong to the Taqagmiut Eskimo and have been the subject of extensive ethnographic analysis.[16]

The shores of Sugluk Inlet have been inhabited by the winter and summer camps of the Taqagmiut for many centuries. Sporadic contact with the whites began in the second half of the nineteenth century with the establishment of

---

[14]He labels this "negative reciprocity," but we feel that this label is even more confusing and have also used our own terminology.

[15]He labels this "balanced reciprocity."

[16]The principal ethnographer is Nelson H. H. Graburn and his major publications on this society are: *Taqagmiut Eskimo Kinship Terminology* (1964): *Eskimos Without Igloos: Social and Economic Development in Sugluk* (1969); "Eskimo Law in Light of Self and Group Interest," *Law and Society Review* IV (1969): 45–60; and "Traditional Economic Institutions and the Acculturation of Canadian Eskimos," in *Studies in Economic Anthropology* (1971), ed. George Dalton, pp. 107–122.

trade relations with distant Western posts: The Eskimos traded fox, seal, and caribou skins for metal implements, especially knives, guns, and powder, and more recently for textiles and flour. The first permanent trading post at Sugluk was established in 1916, and resident missionaries arrived after World War II. Until recently, however, the Eskimos lived by hunting and trapping and followed a nomadic life in kin-based camp groups. Major changes came about in the late 1950s with increasing involvement of the Canadian government in the form of a local administrator. A generator was installed, a day school was started, and by the end of the decade an extensive building program was begun which aimed to move all the Eskimos into prefabricated houses in settlements.

By 1959, the time of investigation, the Sugluk residents (called *Sallumiut*) lived in their settlement throughout the fall and winter, apart from all-male trapping expeditions. They formed smaller camp groups in the spring and summer for hunting and fishing, but increasing numbers stayed in the settlement the whole year, especially as more wage labor positions became available as a consequence of various governmental building and educational programs. Many adults also carved soapstone sculpture for sale for cash income since permanent wage jobs were confined to less than 10% of the adults and since seasonal wage employment was irregular and only for the most physically fit. Economically, therefore, Sugluk was a somewhat mixed community; nearly all Eskimos hunted, fished, and trapped when they could and when they did not have other employment. Furthermore, all desired and attempted to live from "native foods," although they also ate bannock (pan-fried bread) and drank tea in quantity.

The sociopolitical organization of 1959 reflected in part the traditional Eskimo economy and in part economic and technological changes (particularly in the use of motorized boats) introduced in recent years. Larger than any traditional Eskimo community, the Sallumiut divided themselves residentially and economically into five kin-based groups, or bands. The cores of these groups were sibling groups which ran and co-owned (or hoped to do so) large motorized hunting vessels, the Peterhead boats. These kin-based groups had originally been independent, mobile camp groups from different areas of the Hudson Strait coast which were attracted to Sugluk by the physical amenities and by the presence of white agencies. Each group had a traditional leadership pattern vested in the senior effective male, and all but one group was exogamous. Like all Eskimo groups the bands had a bilateral kin structure (i.e., a kin structure something like our own) and an ambilocal residence pattern (i.e., the initial postmarital residence was with the kin of the wife, but after the birth of the first child or two, the couple lived with the kin of the husband). Thus, band members were close kin or affines (related by marriage), but not all close kin were members of one's own band. (Further details on the designation of these bands are contained in Appendix B.4, Item 2.)

The major production units were the bands and also the smaller hunting groups, which were usually composed of band members. The major consumption units were the households, which were usually composed of a nuclear family or a small extended family but which, sometimes, might be composed of several families who chose to live together.

The community-wide sociopolitical structure in 1959 appeared to be a weak and artificially superimposed layer depending for the most part on white agencies: The Anglican Church had a senior and other catechists; the Canadian government had an Eskimo clerk with some power, and it encouraged the election and maintenance of an almost powerless community council; and the Hudson's Bay Company had an Eskimo assistant manager who enjoyed considerable community power because of his economic influence and his interpreting abilities. In actuality, the key elements in the community-wide layer were the various white personnel, but this layer was not of great importance to the Sallumiut qua community in 1959.

In some ways Sugluk was certainly not an aboriginal Eskimo village since some Western techniques of production and certain Western innovations in trade were readily apparent. However, by 1959 we believe that these Western influences were still not sufficiently strong to obliterate the century-old distributional patterns existing between these Eskimos. All ethnographic evidence obtained in Sugluk suggests that the kinds of transfers that we uncover existed for many hundreds of years before Western influence was noticeable.

Data Gathering

The data on exchange transactions were gathered between July and September, 1959. A few of the men of the village were away for the first part of the period, engaged in wage labor in other settlements. A few other men were doing some unskilled labor in the settlement. Most of the men were engaged in typical activities for the season: hunting by boat for seals and walrus, hunting by foot and boat for migrating wildfowl, and fishing. One or two government ships came into the settlement bringing back families and taking others to work as janitors at meteorological stations. Many families were building wooden winter houses for the first time, so that probably somewhat fewer families were out at hunting camps than in any previous year in the community's history. The 6-week period represents a fairly typical time slice in Eskimo life, as further research showed that the exchange patterns in the spring and fall months were quite similar. In the wintertime the exchange system began to break down; in years previous, many groups would leave the camp for better hunting areas.

In Sugluk it was permissible to visit any residence at any time. The ethnographer (Nelson H. H. Graburn) undertook a systematic series of visits to every household in the community to determine who was visiting whom and what was being distributed. He made slightly over 300 visits and recorded 1250 instances of different types of distribution (or nondistribution, if no other visitors appeared in the residence).

Ideally, the ethnographer would have visited each household the same number of times and at the same times throughout the day. The fieldwork conditions and original intentions of the research precluded absolute perfection in sampling; therefore, the data used in the analysis had to be adjusted so as to reflect ideal sampling conditions. Three types of adjustment problems arose. First, not all families were visited the same number of times. If the average number of visits by the ethnographer to each family in the village were 6 and if one family with 10 exchange transactions had been visited only 3 times (or 12 times), their transactions were multiplied by 2 (or 0.5). Second, during the period of observations several families had moved into the same residence to form extended families. If this occurred early in the sampling period, the two families were treated as one family for the entire period; if this occurred late in the sampling period, the two families were treated as separate families for the entire period. Third, the visit times by the anthropologist did not occur in the desired random pattern. However, analysis of the data revealed no important biases arising from this deviation from the ideal; therefore, no adjustments were made. Results based on these data published in previous analyses[17] were not adjusted in this way because they were originally presented for different purposes.

Data on three different kinds of distributional transactions were collected: length of visit, material goods changing hands, and services extended. The ethnographer made a record of each visitor who came into the residence where he was, taking notes, which person or persons the visitor was visiting (the "visit unit" was allocated two-thirds to the prime visitee and one-third to the secondary visitee; if there were no secondary visitee, then the entire visit unit was attributed to the prime visitee), how long the visit lasted, what distribution of material goods or services occurred, what the apparent purpose of the visit was, and in what kinship relation the visitor stood with the prime visitee. The authors ended up with a giant matrix recording these various transactions of every person with every other person in the village. The analytic problem of this chapter is to relate imbalances in the transaction flows to certain key socioeconomic variables.

To this end a census was also made, so that age, marital status, occupation, family income, individual income, social status of the family, individual prestige, relative space of house, family wealth, political status, and other variables could be calculated. (Appendix B.4 has a description of the variables and the methods employed.) The classification of individuals and families in this census according to such socioeconomic factors was performed independently of, and before, the examination of the distribution accounts; thus, the possibility of biasing the analysis with ex post rationalizations does not arise. In addition, it must be stressed that most of the classifications use native categories and were derived from native informants long before this quantitative analysis was conceived.

[17]Nelson H. H. Graburn, ibid.; and Eskimos Without Igloos, ibid.

SETTING UP THE EMPIRICAL ANALYSIS

Carrying out an empirical analysis of all major distributional transactions requires solution to a number of knotty problems. In the discussion below we catalogue the different types of transactions and examine briefly a number of statistical difficulties which must be surmounted before the regression calculations can be made.

Types of Transactions

Distributional transactions took place among the villages in the following contexts:

1. Distribution between members of a single household. Due to data-gathering difficulties, such transactions were not systematically recorded. We thus omit both regular and irregular (e.g., inheritance) intrahousehold transactions and focus on distribution only between household members and members of other households. In short, the household is considered the unit of observation (a concept discussed in Chapter 2).

2. Distribution between villagers taking place within the dwellings. The Eskimos spent most of their leisure time either visiting or being visited; thus, exchange of hospitality was an important type of distribution. A great deal of distribution of food accompanied this hospitality, so much so that a considerable proportion of most people's diet was obtained in households other than their own. Such data were collected and are analyzed below.

3. Distribution between people within the village but outside the dwellings. Such transactions included the borrowing of dogs, sleds, boats, gasoline, and ammunition; gambling and prostitution; and exchanges with white men (trading furs, sale of carvings, wage labor, welfare, and so forth). Borrowing, gambling, and prostitution were not recorded; however, transactions occurring during gambling or prostitution (other than the acts themselves) were minor. Transactions with white men were recorded separately and are not included in the analysis of intra-Eskimo distributions. However, the results of such transactions are taken into consideration when classifying the various individuals according to money income, family wealth, size of dwelling, and so forth.

4. Distribution between people outside the limits of the village. These transactions included most importantly the mutual help in hunting and subsequent sharing of the kill. Data on such activities were not collected; we may assume, however, that since the work in such hunting expeditions was shared, the catch was also shared, that is, that a reciprocity arrangement of a particular type was followed. Another such transaction is intervillage exchange; instances of such exchange were so few during the period of observation that they were neglected in the quantitative analysis.

5. One other type of distributional transaction included exchanges of women and children (through marriage, wife exchange, or adoption). These

were recorded but not included directly in the analysis of distributional transactions. However, many aspects of such transactions are included when they were components of such census categories as marital status, number of children, and prestige.

We have also treated visits per se as a type of distribution. Although in our culture it is not necessarily clear what type of distributional transaction occurs when a visit takes place, among the Sallumiut the hosting of a visit was considered an act of giving and so is included in our analysis, albeit in an account separate from the transactions in material goods. Particular interrelations between transactions in material goods and in visits occurred and are discussed in Appendix B.5; however, these interrelations do not affect the conclusions presented in this chapter.

In short, we focus our quantitative attention on the distribution that occurred within the residences. However, we try to take other types of transactions into account in a qualitative manner in the analysis of the results at a later stage.

Classification of Transactors

A problem arose in the analysis on how the individuals in the community should be grouped, especially since distributional activities of Eskimos of different ages were quite different. Following Eskimo age categories, we classify all individuals in Sugluk into groups as they were in fact labeled by the Sallumiut themselves: babies (ca. 0 through 4 years); children (ca. 5 through 13 years); youth (boys, ca. 14 through 19 years; girls, ca. 14 through 18 years); adults (men, ca. 20 through 50 to 60 years, according to how the Sallumiut spoke of each individual; women, ca. 19 through apparent menopause); and old persons.

Various experiments with the data suggested that the quantitative results are most meaningful when babies are omitted from the calculations and when the society is divided up into two groups: children and unmarried youth; and married youths, adults, and old persons. For analysis of visiting and gift transactions, we have found it illuminating to consider three separate exchange universes: transactions between all members of the society except babies; transactions only between married youth, adults, and old persons; and transactions only between children and unmarried youth. These three groups are designated below, respectively, as Universes A, B, and C.

Problems in the Analysis of Distribution Accounts

In the initial stages of analysis we use a narrow definition of reciprocity, namely, the relative degree of balance of the exchange of visits and goods. Later, we examine broader definitions of reciprocity. Using the data on distribution, we can compute different types of visiting and gift accounts for each individual as well as for groups of individuals sharing specified similar social characteristics. In carrying out such exercises, two kinds of problems arise: First, how can we aggregate the different types of visits or the different types of material distributions so that we can deal with 1 or 2 different types of consolidated accounts rather than 10 or 20 different accounts, 1 for each type of gift or visit? Second, what kind of statistic can we calculate which will reveal the closeness to perfect balance of an individual's account? Each is discussed briefly below.

THE PROBLEM OF WEIGHTS

How should visits of a certain length be converted so that they are comparable with visits of another length? Initially, the visits were classified into four groups: very short (0–5 min), medium short (6–30 min), medium long (31 min to 3 hr), and long (more than 3 hr). How do we weigh the visits in each category so that we need deal only with an aggregate visit unit?

Two obvious solutions suggest themselves, both of which we rejected. We could have given all visits the same weight, so that a 1-min visit would be counted the same as a 5-hr visit, a procedure which does not seem reasonable. Or we could have weighted each visit according to the number of minutes, so that a 3-hr visit would be considered equal to 36 5-min visits, a procedure which does not seem to accord with common sense, either. Upon close inspection of the data, it turned out that there was a strong correlation between the degree and direction of imbalances in the accounts of all visit categories, which means that any weighting schemes would give roughly the same results. We chose to give the four classes of visits weights, respectively, of 1, 2, 3, and 4; in order, however, to have some check on the results, we also tried another weighting scheme, giving the four classes of visits weights, respectively, of 0, 2, 3, 4, and got very similar results in the regression analysis. For reasons of limited space, the control results are not presented.

A similar problem arises in the analysis of gift transactions. We classified the gift transactions by the host of the visit into the following categories: no gifts; tea; bannock or porridge; bannock plus butter and jam; meat broth; meat (including fish, bird, mussels); and "other." Gifts by the visitor to the host household were also recorded. It turned out that "other" gifts by the host and gifts by the visitor were so infrequent that they could be neglected. As noted in Appendix B.5, the donation of labor services did not seem to influence gift giving and was also quite minor, so that these visits did not need to be specially weighted. We are therefore left with six categories of gifts which were given weights, respectively, of 0, 1, 2, 3, 4, and 5. The order of weighting of these categories parallels native evaluations in that it follows the almost universal Eskimo predilections for these foods, from the commonest of the imported to the most valued of the local fare. Detailed inspection of the data revealed (as it did in our analysis of visit lengths) a strong correlation between the direction and degree of imbalance for the accounts of each gift category, so that the exact weighting system used would not greatly affect the results. (If this had not been the case, we could have adopted a type of statistical approach presented in Appendix B.2 to impute exchange rates.)

How should visit and gift indices be computed so that they are interchangeable? Sahlins has suggested that gifts of food are not equivalent to other categories of socioeconomic transactions,[18] but we did not want to prejudge our analysis by assuming Sahlins to be correct. From inspection of our data and from ethnographic evidence it was quite unclear whether visits and gifts served as an alternative "currency" or whether the people of Sugluk considered these as two different types of social transactions which could not be compared (i.e., exchange spheres, a phenomenon explored in Appendix B.3). Rather than risk combining such categories, we analyze each type of transaction separately and then compare the results. In general, both types of transaction have roughly the same determinants and can be considered as a single type of exchange, but this is a result derived at the end of the analysis and not assumed at the beginning.

THE PROBLEM OF THE OVERALL INDEX FOR THE DISTRIBUTION ACCOUNTS

Since we have a narrow definition of reciprocity (the closeness to absolute balance) we can use for quantitative analysis a single index to describe the degree to which a person is a net giver (or host) or receiver (or visitor). The following simple formulas are used[19]:

$$\text{Net account index of visits} = \frac{\text{Weighted visits to others} - \text{weighted visits by others}}{\text{Weighted visits to others} + \text{weighted visits by others}}$$

$$\text{Net account index of gifts} = \frac{\text{Weighted gifts received} - \text{weighted gifts given}}{\text{Weighted gifts received} + \text{weighted gifts given}}$$

If a person only visited others and received gifts from others (i.e., received their hospitality or gifts), his net account indices are 1.00; if a person was only visited and only gave gifts, his net account indices are −1.00; and if a person received as many visits and gifts as he gave, his net account indices are 0.00. Or, more simply, hosts and gift givers have negative net accounts, while visitors and gift receivers have positive net accounts. The definitions of the net account

---

[18]Sahlins, *Stone Age Economics*, p. 170. Herbert Spencer, *The Principles of Sociology*, Vol. II (1882), Chap. V, has some interesting hints on the relationship between visits and gifts.

[19]It would have been desirable to analyze the degree to which every person's accounts were balanced with every other member of the society; unfortunately, there were not enough data to do this; therefore, we focus the analysis on the aggregate balance of each individual's accounts. Such a procedure obliterates the existence of those transfers described as "generalized exchange" in the previous chapter (where A gives x to B, who gives x to C, who gives x to A), but the ethnographer did not feel that such types of chain transactions occurred to any significant degree in the society.

indices introduce a certain statistical bias into the regression results, but this should not make much difference.[20]

When the net account indices are calculated for each individual, their imbalances are striking, and few of them show perfect balance. The most simple aggregative measure of the variations of these net exchange indices around the mean (which, for the society as a whole, is zero since the amount of giving is equal to the amount of receiving) is the standard deviation of these indices for all individuals in the sample. Such standard deviations show that roughly one-third of the Sallumiut have net exchange indices which are greater than +.70 or −.70, which represents considerable imbalance.[21] These results do not immediately disprove Mauss's theory about strict reciprocity since they may merely reflect temporary imbalances.

Another way to examine the imbalances is to aggregate the various individuals in the society according to certain criteria for similarity, for example, all men, all poor people, all people living in large houses, all people with political power, and so forth. These also show great imbalances, which suggests that the variations in the individual net account indices were structured and were not random. Unfortunately, such types of aggregation permit only one variable at a time to be examined. To test properly any of the hypotheses about reciprocity discussed above, we need more sophisticated statistical techniques which permit examination of several different causal forces at once.

EXCHANGE AND TRANSFER AMONG THE ESKIMO: A REGRESSION APPROACH

Steps in the Analysis

We carried out the quantitative analysis of the 1250 transactions according to the following steps:

1. We calculated aggregated net account indices for a wide number of social groups and for a large number of universes in order to gain insight into the surface appearance of the distribution networks. In particular, we carefully

---

[20]The bias occurs because the dependent variable is bounded between +1.00 and −1.00, while the regression model assumes no such upper and lower limits. In looking at the data, however, most cases did not appear to have the dependent variable exactly at these limits. Given the nature of the data, we do not believe that the impact of using a least squares regression technique, rather than a more suitable technique such as probit analysis, is sufficiently great to warrant much worry. In a different context this problem is discussed in Chapter 1.

[21]We refer the reader curious to know the distribution of the net account indices to Table 4.2, which presents more summary measures. The large deviations from exact balance in the accounts (where the net account score is 0.00) are indicated by the large standard deviations.

examined the data to see whether or not there were interactions between particular potential causal variables which would render inappropriate the type of linear regression model we proposed to use. Fortunately, such interactions could be properly taken into account, and no problems arose from this potential source of difficulty.

2. Since we had a large number of conjectures about possible factors influencing the numerical values of the net account indices, it seemed useful to approach the problem inductively. Therefore, we took every variable from the census for which we had some reason for believing that it might prove important, a procedure leaving us with 30 hypothesized causal variables. We recoded each of these variables on a 12-point scale so that the calculated regression coefficients would represent in a quantitative fashion the relative influence of these variables. Then we calculated a series of preliminary regressions using various combinations of these variables and examined the results.

3. We reduced the number of explanatory variables by using two criteria. First, several explanatory variables that were highly correlated with other independent variables were removed in order to eliminate problems of interpretation arising from multicollinearity. Thus, since hunting productivity was highly related to income and sex (reflecting the fact that traditional food gathering by males constituted a major portion of income), the various hunting variables were excluded from further consideration since the income variable is somewhat broader. (It embraces hunting and other sources of income as well.) Second, variables with little explanatory power (low t tests) were eliminated. We then calculated a new set of regressions, and an additional group of variables with little explanatory power were removed. This process was repeated several times, with close attention paid to the impact of removing or adding variables on all of the calculated regression coefficients.

Results of the Regression Analysis

The final regression results using a simple least squares method of calculation are presented in Table 4.1. Each calculated regression coefficient in the main part of the table indicates the impact of that particular variable on the net account index, with all other variables held constant. In the parentheses below each calculated regression coefficient is the standard error, so that a t test of statistical significance can be performed. In order to ease the burden on the reader, all calculated coefficients that are statistically significant at the .05 level are marked with an asterisk.

In five out of the six cases, the explanatory variables contained in the linear regressions explain between one-quarter and one-half of the variance of the net exchange indices. The exact explanatory power is measured by the coefficient of determination, which is the square of the coefficient of multiple correlation. Comparing such explanatory power to economic studies analyzing consumption or savings behavior in capitalist economies, our coefficients of determination are relatively high. The only disappointing result is the regression analyzing gifts exchanged among children and unmarried youth (Universe C). Since gift giving in this universe is relatively unimportant, random factors appear to have a much more marked effect than in the other regressions. The conclusion to be drawn from such results is simple and powerful: The exchange imbalances (dependent variable) are patterned, and strict reciprocity, which we infer from the writings of Mauss, did not seem to occur.

The regressions in Universe A (all members except babies) and B (married youth, adults, and older persons) are "well behaved" in the sense that large calculated coefficients are also those coefficients which are statistically significant; similarly, the small coefficients are not statistically significant. The regressions in Universe C do not show such behavior in all cases, so that interpretation there is more difficult.

For the remainder of this subsection we focus on the individual coefficients and note the explanatory variables that were tried and rejected. In the following subsection we will try to interpret these results from the standpoint of the entire social context of distribution.

The constants in the various regressions express the net exchange indices when all the explanatory variables are zero. They have no real meaning for the problem under consideration and are simply an artifact arising from the way in which we defined our explanatory variables.

Four "personal quality" variables (sex, marital status, physical disability, and a variable indicating whether or not the individual was continually present in the community throughout the sampling period) are included in the final regressions. The following personal quality variables were included originally but were later removed because of lack of explanatory power: age, individual prestige, type of major occupation, adoption status (whether the person was adopted or not), and legitimacy status (whether the person's birth was legitimate or not). The lack of statistical relation between the prestige variable and the variable indicating transactions imbalances, once other factors had been taken into account, is an important result for evaluating Leach's theory of reciprocity, a matter taken up later in the chapter.

Within Universes A and B, the calculated regression coefficients show that females acted more as hosts and gift givers (i.e., had more negative indices) than did males. In the total universe, females had a net exchange index .036 lower than males; all other factors held constant. Furthermore, married people more often acted as hosts and gift givers than did unmarried people. The calculated coefficients show that married women had the most negative accounts; that single adult women or married men had roughly balanced accounts; and that single adult men had the most positive exchange accounts, other things being equal. This suggests that married men turned over their income (including hunting products) to their wives, who acted as redis-

TABLE 4.1

Regression Analyses of the Net Exchange Indices (Explained Variable) of the Sallumiut Eskimo[a]

| | Explained variable: Exchange invoices of members of different universes | | | | | |
| Explanatory variables | Universe A[b] | | Universe B[c] | | Universe C[d] | |
	Visit index	Gift index	Visit index	Gift index	Visit index	Gift index
Constant	0.766	1.442	1.053	1.924	2.002	0.643
Sex (0 = male; 12 = female)	−.036*	−.021*	−.059*	−.029*	−.014	−.009
	(.007)	(.008)	(.010)	(.013)	(.013)	(.016)
Marital status (0 = single, divorced, widowed; 12 = married)	−.035*	−.023*	−.039*	−.023	—	—
	(.009)	(.010)	(.010)	(.012)		
Physical disability (0 = totally disabled; 12 = able-bodied)	.040*	.020	.057*	.013	—	—
	(.018)	(.020)	(.018)	(.023)		
Individual presence in community (0 = absent; 6 = absent part of time; 12 = always present)	−.006	−.022	.014	−.012	−.107	.002
	(.023)	(.026)	(.026)	(.032)	(.062)	(.076)
Individual income (0 = lowest; 12 = highest)	−.032	−.051*	−.063*	−.062*	−.064	−.101
	(.016)	(.019)	(.020)	(.025)	(.084)	(.104)
Average family wealth (0 = lowest; 12 = highest)	−.051*	−.033	−.051*	−.032	−.190*	−.107*
	(.019)	(.022)	(.024)	(.030)	(.039)	(.048)

Size of house (0 = smallest house; 12 = largest house)	-.038 (.020)	-.090* (.023)	-.064* (.024)	-.127* (.030)	.046 (.043)	-.000 (.053)
Relation to band leader (0 = no or distant relative; 4 = children or sibling; 8 = wife; 12 = identity)	-.012 (.017)	-.001 (.020)	-.021 (.017)	-.044 (.022)	-.236* (.104)	-.073 (.129)
Belong to band 1 (0 = no; 12 = yes)	-.030* (.009)	-.029* (.011)	-.043* (.011)	-.055* (.014)	-.008 (.019)	-.005 (.023)
Belong to band 2 (0 = no; 12 = yes)	-.001 (.009)	-.001 (.011)	-.013 (.011)	-.011 (.014)	.073* (.020)	.028 (.024)
Belong to band 5 (0 = no; 12 = yes)	.002 (.011)	-.026* (.013)	-.002 (.013)	-.040* (.017)	.014 (.021)	-.014 (.026)
Size of sample	182	182	112	112	67	67
Coefficient of determination	.3824	.2767	.4558	.3212	.3777	.1213

[a] All people who did not receive or give at least one visit in the universe under examination are eliminated from the analysis. A person could be a member of Universe A without being in Universe B or C if his or her transactions were only with people in the other age category. If a person made or received visits but neither gave nor received any gifts, his net gift index is calculated as 0.000. The numbers in the top part of the table are the calculated regression coefficients for each variable, and the numbers in parentheses are their standard errors. An asterisk denotes statistical significance at the .05 level.

[b] All members of the society excluding babies.

[c] Married youth, adults, and old people among each other.

[d] Children and unmarried youth among each other.

*Statistically significant at the 0.5 level.

tributors,[22] while unmarried men, being unable easily to entertain in their own homes, acted as freeloaders. The lack of a marital status category among children is the reason why this variable was not important in Universe C.

A small complication enters at this point with regard to the disabled. Concerning visiting, the regressions show that disabled people had more negative accounts than the able-bodied because, of course, they could not easily go out of their homes to visit others. However, the calculated regression coefficients of gift giving by the disabled are not statistically significant, which suggests (because individual income is held constant) that the disabled did not often reward their visitors with gifts because of the economic uncertainties they faced.

Individual presence in the community (expressed as 0 = absent all the time; 6 = present part-time; 12 = present during the entire data collection time except for short hunting trips) is not a statistically significant explanatory variable in any of the regressions. However, the calculated coefficient is negative and quite large for visiting behavior among children, which suggests that many children and unmarried youth took greater pains to renew their contacts upon returning to the village than did married youth and adults.

Three "income and wealth" variables (individual income, average family wealth, and size of house) are included in the final regressions. The following income and wealth variables were included in the first stages of analysis but were later removed because of lack of explanatory power: average total family income, individual money income, average family money income, and type of house. Individual hunting productivity and average family hunting productivity were removed because of multicollinearity.

In Universes A and B, the regression results show that individuals with high total incomes appear to have served as hosts and gift givers vis-à-vis low-income individuals. In three out of the four regressions, the calculated coefficient is negative and statistically significant, and in the fourth regression statistical significance at the .05 level is missed just by a hair. Among children individual income does not appear to play a significant role.

In all three universes individuals in families with high material wealth appear to have served an important role as hosts to people from families with less wealth. With regard to gift giving, average family wealth also appears an important explanatory factor among the children and unmarried youth, the only variable we found to be statistically significant.

The regression results show that the size-of-house variable appears to have played an exactly opposite role in Universe B than in Universe C. Among married youth, adults, and older people, individuals in relatively large

---

[22]In the ritual distribution of hunting products, which took place in every household after a reasonably successful hunt, this pattern was repeated. The family and visitors squatted around the game that lay in the center of the floor; the hunter made the first effort to apportion the meat by slicing into a prime cut with his knife; and he would give the first morsel to the most important visitor. He then handed over the knife and/or the rest of the game to his wife who completed the distribution to those present.

dwellings served as hosts to those from smaller houses; that is, the people in this universe appear to have placed some value on spaciousness for their social interaction. However, among children and unmarried youth, individuals from small houses appear to have acted as hosts to those from larger houses; that is, the children in Universe C appear either to have placed some positive value on crowdedness or else to have felt that they had no place to go other than the small houses because the adults might be entertaining in the large houses. The calculated regression coefficient for this house-size variable in Universe C is not, however, statistically significant, so we can not be completely sure of these conclusions. Among adults, house spaciousness appears related to gift giving as well.

Four "band-related" variables (relation to leader, belonging to Band 1, belonging to Band 2, and belonging to Band 5) are included in the final regressions. Band 1 is the band with the highest prestige; "Band" 5 is not really a band but the aggregate of all bandless people. Two band-related variables were originally included but were later removed because of lack of explanatory power: belonging to Band 3 and belonging to Band 4.

The band-related variables acted very differently in the different universes. Relation to band leader (children of leader) seemed to have played a very important role in the visiting pattern among children and unmarried youth; but it did not seem important for visiting patterns in the other two universes or for gift giving in all universes. Among married youth, adults, and older persons, as well as in the entire community, excluding babies, Band 1 members acted as hosts and gift givers to Bands 2, 3, and 4. Members of Band 5 appeared also as net gift givers. Among children and youth the members of Band 2 did a great deal more visiting of others than receiving of visitors. Although a certain social ranking of bands existed in this village, such a ranking would not be discoverable from the regression results.

Several "family-related" variables were included in the first regression runs but were later removed for lack of explanatory power. These included social status of the family, whether or not the family was nuclear (in contrast to joint or extended or to a situation in which the husband or wife was lacking) and whether or not the head of the house was always present in the village during the period of data collection. The lack of relationship between social status and exchange imbalances, once other variables were held constant, has important implications for Leach's theory of reciprocity, which is discussed in a later part of the chapter.

Several "community-related" variables were also originally included in the regression analysis and were later removed either because of multicollinearity or because of low explanatory power. These included political status (no status, leader of weak subband, leader of strong band); community leadership (no leader, past or present member of community council, part or present head of community council); and other status in the community (none, subcatechist, catechist).

The regression results in Table 4.1 represent a considerable culling process of possible explanatory variables. The meaning of the various coefficients should be sufficiently clear so that we can consider what these results mean in terms of the entire economy of the village of Sugluk.

Interpretation of the Results

CHILD AND ADULT UNIVERSES

The regression results for the entire community (Universe A) and for the married youth, adults, and older persons among each other (Universe B) are relatively similar, but both differ from the results recording the transactions only between children and unmarried youth. Three explanations may be offered for such a discrepancy:

First, children did not have certain social attributes (e.g., marital status or physical disability) that occurred among adults, so that exchange mechanisms arising from these sources did not come into operation. Similarly, children had very much less control over resources than did adults (because few had very large independent sources of income), so that causal factors arising from these sources did not come into play. Another difference may be seen in regard to band membership: For children band membership was a social and residential phenomenon, but for adults it also was important as an economic phenomenon. In short, the social position of children was such that their behavior was, of necessity, less structured. In the previous discussion we suggested that the exchange mechanisms arising from sex and marital status are not operative among children and unmarried youth, which is another example of this structural phenomenon.

Second, children might not have been well socialized into the society, so that their behavior among themselves was not guided by the same norms as those guiding their behavior with adults or those guiding behavior between adults themselves. The possible desire of children for crowded conditions for social interaction and the failure of the children and unmarried youth of Band 1 to act as hosts and gift givers are examples of this second explanation.

Finally, the behavior of the two groups could have been equally well structured, but the structural principles might have been different. Such a phenomenon could arise if assimilation of Western norms were more advanced among the children than among the adults, a situation which we do not think characterized Sugluk at the time the data were collected. It could also arise if the children were socialized to norms different from those operative among adults, and their behavior was expected to change at entry to adulthood.

VISITS VERSUS GIFT GIVING

In all three universes we are able to explain a higher percentage of variation of the net account indices of visits than of gift giving. At first sight this variation

TABLE 4.2

Standard Deviations of the Various Net Account Indices of the Sallumiut Eskimo[a]

	Universe A		Universe B		Universe C	
	Visits	Gifts	Visits	Gifts	Visits	Gifts
Size of sample	182	182	112	112	67	67
Standard deviation	.648	.693	.652	.731	.699	.725

[a]The samples used in the calculation are the same as in Table 4.1. Universes A, B, and C are also defined in the same table.

is puzzling, for one would think that the pattern of visiting would be more random than that of gift giving. One possible explanation is suggested by Sahlins' discussion of the special role of food exchanges vis-à-vis other types of exchanges. "Staple foodstuffs cannot always be handled just like anything else."[23] Food has a special element of sociability, so that more of it might be given away without expectation of return than other types of goods. According to this approach net account indices in food would be more unbalanced than such indices for other goods or services; furthermore, food distribution would be, in a sense, less structured since the rational, calculating element in individual decision making would play a less important role.

One way to test these ideas is to look at the variations in the net account indices of food gifts (which constitute all of our gift-exchange index) and other gifts (visits) to see if the former is more unbalanced. In statistical terms this would mean that the standard deviation (a measure of dispersion) of the individual net account indices for gifts would be greater than for visits. Relevant data are presented in Table 4.2.

The data show that in all cases the standard deviation of the net account indices of gift giving is larger than that of visiting, although the differences are not quite statistically significant at the .05 level when an F test is performed. In some following tables calculated by subdividing each universe into subsamples and holding constant the variables listed in Table 4.1, a roughly similar pattern of differences between the standard deviations of the net account indices of visits and gifts also appears, but few of these differences are statistically significant, either. The results in Table 4.2 provide only a suggestion of positive evidence for the first part of Sahlins' hypothesis—that distribution accounts are more unbalanced for food than for other goods or services. The possible correctness of the first part of the hypothesis provides plausibility for the second part—that food exchange is less structured—thus, our results appear less paradoxical.

[23]Sahlins, *Stone Age Economics*, p. 170.

Although food and visit accounts have certain differences, their similarities should not be overlooked. In Universes A and B, the same explanatory variables play either a statistically significant role or else a statistically nonsignificant role in both food and visit regressions (Table 4.1) in 13 cases, while the explanatory variables differ in statistical significance (i.e., one is significant, the other is not) in 9 cases. Concerning certain variables (e.g., the different role of physical disability in visiting and gift giving), a reasonable explanation can be given for the differences. Although food gifts and visits may be in different exchange spheres, as Sahlins suggests, the causal factors underlying the net account indices appear sufficiently similar that for many analytic purposes the two kinds of transactions could be combined into a single index without a great loss of information.

REGRESSION RESULTS IN THE LIGHT OF
NONINCLUDED TRANSACTIONS

The most important types of intra-Eskimo transactions not included in our data are those within family groups sharing the same residence and those taking place between the time of the kill and the return home from the hunt. When large game (sea mammals or large land animals) or large amounts of small game were killed, the products of the hunt were divided among the party of hunters present, according to who was responsible for the kill, and who assisted.[24]

The exact impact of these transactions on the regressions in Table 4.1 is difficult to determine, but a qualitative examination of their effects did not suggest that this omission was very important. Two types of evidence were used to arrive at this assessment. First, the ethnographer received no indication during his many months spent in Sugluk that methods of distribution of game at the time of the kill had any appreciable impact on distributional patterns within the village, except insofar as the income of the hunters was directly affected (the income variable is contained in the regressions). Second, experiments with a hunting productivity variable revealed nothing suggesting that the conclusions drawn from Table 4.1 would be modified if such extravillage hunting activities had been included. It must be added, however, that certain statistical problems made these experiments more ambiguous than desired.

Other transactions between Eskimos outside the residences, gambling occurring within the homes, or exchange of women or children are not taken into account in the analysis except insofar as they might affect the explanatory variables (e.g., marital status or adoption status). We believe, however, that such transactions of goods formed a quantitatively small part of the total of Eskimo exchange transactions, and we do not see how their inclusion in the net exchange indices would significantly change the results in any direction.

As noted above, transactions between Eskimos and whites do not enter our analysis except insofar as they affect explanatory factors such as individual

[24]Graburn, *Eskimos Without Igloos*, pp. 66–70.

income, material wealth, employment, and welfare status. Since the regression results in Table 4.1 concern only intra-Eskimo exchange, this omission should not be of great importance.

Finally, we believe that the results are not specifically an artifact of the 6-week period during which the data were collected. The community was also under intensive observation during the months before and after this period and during various times of the year in 1964 and again in 1968. It was not until 1968 that major changes in community structure, hospitality and generosity patterns, and, above all, the distribution of family income were observed. If we had numerical data for the entire year of 1959–1960 it would probably show that sex, marital status, physical disability, individual income, average family wealth, space in house, and relation to band leader would still be the determinants of imbalanced exchange (and perhaps, also, belonging to the various bands). We must also stress that the period of observation was neither a feast nor a famine period. Furthermore, although some fortunate families were able to cache foods so as to build up a reserve for themselves, they did so in a way that was not significantly different from other periods of observation. Food in such caches was not expected to be distributed to others at a later time but to serve personal food needs.

The concept of building up "social credit" by being more generous and hospitable than one feels like in order to draw upon it in time of famine or starvation was foreign to Eskimo ideology and practice, and two circumstances of Eskimo life contributed to this situation. First, there was a great deal of mobility in and out of the village, so that there was a high probability that long-term "social creditors" might never be able to locate their debtors to collect. Second, in times of famine or starvation, everyone would be badly off; as a matter of fact, the rules of generosity and reciprocity would break down.[25] (Other aspects of this problem are discussed in Appendix B.5.)

MAJOR AND MINOR EXPLANATORY FACTORS

We have used a multivariate analysis because we believe that a number of factors must be taken into account to analyze the pattern of negative and positive net account indices. Since every variable used in the regressions was defined on a scale of 12, we can use the calculated regression coefficients to determine the relative importance of broad groups of causal factors. More specifically, we can determine the relative importance of personal, social, and economic factors by summing up the absolute values of the statistically significant calculated regression coefficients.

When we began the preliminary work on the regression analysis, we distinguished five different groups of possible explanatory variables: personal quality variables, economic variables, band-related variables, family-related variables, and community-related variables. None of the specific variables in the latter two categories proved to have significant explanatory power, and they were

[25]Ibid., pp. 72–76.

dropped before the final regressions were run. Therefore, the major explanatory factors seem to be personal quality, economic, and band-related variables.

For gift giving, the economic variables play the most important role, followed by the band-related variables (except for Universe C). For visiting, on the other hand, the results were mixed: Personal quality variables played the most important role in the society as a whole (Universe A); economic variables, for interactions between married youth, adults, and old people (Universe B); and band-related variables for interaction among children and unmarried youth (Universe C).

The different relative importance of these major sets of variables must be taken into account by anyone inclined to construct a formal model of Eskimo decision making with regard to gift giving or visit transactions. Among the economic variables account must also be taken of certain ecological considerations (high uncertainty of any particular individual's obtaining food) besides more mundane factors such as the space within each family's house or income and wealth. The reason why wealth plays a causal role equal to that of income in the exchange transactions may be due to uncertainty of income. The most puzzling results concern the importance of membership in particular bands as a causal factor underlying the net account indices. To explain why certain bands act as hosts while others act as guests, we need a much deeper knowledge of the dynamics of band structure and interband relations, a task on our future research agenda. A rigorous justification of the relative importance (or nonimportance) of particular variables cannot be supplied until an Eskimo decision-making model can be constructed which will permit deductions about factors underlying exchange. Without such a model we must be content with these inductive results. However, the regression equations suggest that a theory of neither strict economic nor strict social determinism can explain our results and that any Eskimo decision-making model must take into account a variety of considerations.

NATIVE INTERPRETATIONS VERSUS OUR INTERPRETATIONS OF EXCHANGE TRANSACTIONS

Before we end these broad interpretations, two last questions must be posed: To what extent are the categories used for this analysis significant to the Eskimos of Sugluk? And to what extent are our results consistent with native understanding of the exchange process?

The Sallumiut concept of reciprocity is the same as that used in this analysis, namely, balance of goods and services exchanged between gross status equals.[26] Thus, our interpretation of the net account indices would be similar to that of the Sallumiut. Moreover, it is important to note that most of the categories chosen for quantification are those used in the community (Appendix B.4). The villagers recognized the importance of factors such as sex, age,

[26]Graburn, "Traditional Economic Institutions," pp. 108–109.

and marital status in social transactions. Furthermore, native criteria were used in rating each individual according to prestige and each family according to its social status. But, in addition, we have introduced a number of categories which we felt were important for analysis but which the natives would not recognize or, if they did, would believe to be irrelevant. The purpose of the regression analysis is to determine the actual determinants of Eskimo exchange behavior, not the ideology rationalizing such behavior. Indeed, by comparing our regression results with how the natives might explain or justify the pattern of transactions, we can determine the gap between the two and obtain a clearer view of the relation between native theory and native practice.

In explaining the pattern of transactions and the net exchange indices, the natives of Sugluk would use the following model, which is an ideal used as a mental guide for action and also which is the way the Sugluk villagers believe reality is structured. In the economic sphere prestige was derived by being a successful hunter and conspicuously distributing the game according to the ideal. After the rules of the division during the hunt were followed (before the animal is brought to the village), one had the duty to share with members of the following social groups: one's own family and household, one's parents, one's restricted *ilagiit* (bilaterally reckoned relatives), one's band, and lastly, the whole community either as individuals or as an invited group. In addition, one was expected to visit and render services to these groups in the same order. Naturally, without significant hunting productivity or other useful skills, one could fulfill little of the overall model of generosity.

The prescribed sharing patterns ensured that amounts of game totaling approximately 300 lb and up and brought into the community would be shared among others besides one's household and close relatives and that truly large kills would be celebrated by feasts to which the host and hostess might invite all the men and women in the community to eat and carry away bags of meat. To host such an occasion was the epitome of Eskimo success. On a more mundane level, household members and all visitors were supposed to be able to partake of any food or drink that was available in a household without asking; a good host did, however, offer and might even make available comestibles that were not in sight. Visitors from settlements outside Sugluk would be accorded more generous hospitality, especially if they were previously known to the host. In fact, a number of such transactions were recorded in our data, but they were not recorded in our final analysis because their number was too small and because the other half of the possible reciprocal socioeconomic relationships could not be observed.

Like many Western social scientists, the Sallumiut argued that generosity and prestige were correlated and that between those equal in prestige exchange accounts were roughly balanced. Both aspects of this proposition deserve further analysis, especially because distributional accounts are highly unbalanced in this egalitarian society and because prestige and status are not related to net generosity when other important factors are taken into account. In short, the

Sallumiut did not fully perceive the discrepancies between their model and their behavior, nor did the ethnographer until we performed the regression analysis.

The Sallumiut perceptions of the relationships between generosity and prestige were maintained because they had many tautological elements. These relationships were so powerfully held that aspects might be violated without shaking their beliefs. For instance, we found that many people of low social status were very generous in their gift transactions, yet they continued to be labeled as low-status individuals, in part because their members broke some of the other moral rules but mainly because most of the Sallumiut hardly ever visited them and were therefore able to accuse them of lack of hospitality. On the other hand, some of the most productive families were only irregularly generous but were able to maintain their high prestige by occasional conspicuous giveaways on a scale that those who were physically unable or who were poor in hunting equipment were unable to maintain. Furthermore, conspicuous giveaways or successful families were long remembered, and what people said about the rules of sharing sometimes counted for more than what people did: For instance, the high-prestige persons always vehemently upheld the ethics of the system and the necessity of total generosity, whereas some of the poorest questioned the need to continue a distribution system that had been functional among much smaller traditional social groups. Yet, as our analysis indicates, some of the former were net takers (even after the giveaways had been taken into account) and some of the latter, net donors! In short, high prestige people could maintain their position by manipulating the symbols of generosity rather than by their actual behavior.

The notion that social equals had roughly balanced distributional accounts had a similar ideological reinforcement and, in addition, did not make it necessary for the natives of Sugluk to keep an exact mental accounting. Thus, again no confrontation occurred between the facts of social behavior and the ideology of exchange.

One other factor influencing differences between the reality and ideology of exchange deserves brief mention. Most individual Sallumiut were more attracted to modern conveniences as opposed to traditional virtues than they liked to admit; thus, wealth in terms of modern material possessions significantly affected the net exchange indices (Table 4.1), although conveniences had no place in their traditional ideology.

MYTHS OF EXCHANGE AND TRANSFER

An extremely important general hypothesis can be drawn from this discussion: The myth that distributional accounts are roughly balanced between social equals allows unbalanced accounts to be maintained without rancor, while a society with the myth that everyone is trying to cheat everyone else might show much more balanced net account indices because both partners to a transaction would make sure that the accounts were balanced at all times.

That is, the myths of exchange and transfer may be the most important causal factor in bringing about the reverse situation in actual behavior.

A crucial element in such situations is the mechanism preventing the myth from changing. Among the Sugluk villagers we have argued that the myth was maintained because of certain tautological elements between perceptions and behavior and that activities in other spheres of society acted to reinforce such relationships between perception and behavior in the distributional sphere.

TESTING VARIOUS RECIPROCITY THEORIES

General Observations

Extracting testable propositions about reciprocity from the writings of Marcel Mauss or Bronisław Malinowski is quite difficult. We believe, however, that our empirical results showing structured imbalances would be extremely difficult for these anthropologists to explain with their formally stated notions about the nature of reciprocity between gross social equals. Furthermore, the regression results showing that a certain portion of these imbalances can be traced to variables reflecting general economic, social, and political circumstances provide concrete counterhypotheses to vague notions about "credit" or "delayed reciprocity" which may be invoked by followers of Mauss or Malinowski to interpret such results in an ex post facto fashion.

The theories suggesting that the flow of goods and services can be counterbalanced by a flow of social invisibles are also inadequate for explaining our results. We have tried to include all of the social invisibles which the Eskimos and/or the ethnographer felt to be important as variables in the regression and have found that they do not serve to explain the imbalances. It must be added that in this village there are no unilineal descent groups, preferred cross-cousin marriages, brideprices or dowries, social classes or castes, or other sociological features which might place into question our interpretation of the regression results.[27]

It must be stressed that we do not deny the existence of reciprocal exchange in this village. But on top of such exchanges there are also unilateral transfers which, in part, can be traced to the variables which we have included in the regression results. None of these explanatory variables alone cause marked transfers; but in combination, the net transfers resulting therefrom can be considerable, indeed far more than enough to belie the Eskimo belief that strict reciprocity prevails.

---

[27]Those readers who, for mystical reasons, believe that all interpersonal transactions must be balanced will undoubtedly be able to find social invisibles which we have not discussed which will "balance" the transactions; similarly, those who, for mystical reasons, believe that all interpersonal transactions must be unbalanced will undoubtedly be able to find still more social invisibles which will make the transactions accounts unbalanced again. Such foolish games can be played indefinitely.

Reciprocity and Kinship Distance

As we discussed above, Marshall Sahlins has argued that distributional transactions between close kin should be characterized by transfers; that distributional transactions between strangers or enemies should also be characterized by transfers; and that distributional transactions between covillagers
who are not kin or enemies should be characterized by reciprocity. Since
Sugluk is a relatively small and closed community, we cannot test Sahlins'
ideas about exchange between strangers or enemies. But we can examine the
other parts of his hypothesis. And since there was no community leader in
Sugluk in the sense of a person who pooled food and redistributed it (the band
leaders sometimes assigned parts of large sea mammals caught by other community members, but this activity was less a redistribution function than an
assignment function), we do not have a formal organization of reciprocities in a
redistribution arrangement to complicate the analysis. We can, in other words,
make a relatively clean test of Sahlins' approach.

Sahlins framed his hypothesis strictly in terms of individuals, and in presenting his propositions about reciprocity and kinship distance, he noted that such
distance may be reckoned in two ways: either by segmentary distance (group
membership in clans or bands) or by genealogical distance and interpersonal
kinship status. These two groups may or may not coincide, so that it is necessary to test his proposition using both approaches.

We can examine the balance of exchange within and between bands in two
ways. The simplest method is to calculate net exchange indices of each individual for these two groups and then see whether the former have greater
imbalances. Since the imbalances can be either positive or negative, the easiest
way to make the comparison is to calculate standard deviations of the net
exchange indices. The more unbalanced the exchange accounts, the higher the
standard deviations.

One problem with such an attempt to test Sahlins' proposition is to hold
other factors constant since merely examining the standard deviations without
doing so would produce a spurious analysis. Our approach assumes that the
various factors (e.g., sex, marital status, size of house, and other explanatory
variables discussed in conjunction with Table 4.1) operate in the same manner
in transactions within bands; furthermore, we assume that the same type of
individuals participate in visiting and gift giving in transactions within and
between bands, so that imbalances arising from special individual characteristics do not influence the results.

The easiest way to "hold all factors constant" is to take the regressions
presented in Table 4.1 and examine the residuals, that is, the differences between the actual values of the net exchange indices and the predicted values.
According to Sahlins we would expect greater imbalances (regression residuals) for those individuals who carry out most of their transactions within their
band than for those individuals who carry out most of their transactions with
other bands.

For such an analysis the first step is to calculate an index ($= Q$) indicating the relative amount of transactions (both positive and negative) within the band ($= X$) and with other bands ($= Y$). The formula used is: $Q = (X-Y)/(X+Y)$, which is equal to $+1.0$ if the person only visited and received visits from his fellow band members, and is equal to -1.0 if a person only visited and received visits from nonband members. A similar index was used for gifts given and received. The people in each universe were then arranged according to the increasing value of Q for visits and for gifts. Standard deviations of the residuals (indicating imbalances other than those expected from the regression equation) were calculated for three groups of people according to their Q value. According to Sahlins we would expect the standard deviations to increase as the Q index increases. Relevant data are given in Table 4.3.

Universe B gives exactly the results predicted; and Universe A gives the predicted results with one exception. (A decline occurs in the standard deviation between the second and third group in the gift index.) For neither universe are the differences between these standard deviations generally significant at the .05 level when an F test is performed. The results for Universe C (children and unmarried youth among each other) are much different from Sahlins' prediction, and it is difficult to explain such results except by the hypothesis that this age group has not yet been "properly" socialized into the general communal pattern of visiting and gift giving. It should also be pointed out that the standard deviations for gift giving in Universe C are based on very small

TABLE 4.3

Standard Deviations from the Regression Line of Estimated Net Exchange Indices according to Degree to which Transactions are Made with Band Members among the Sallumiut Eskimo[a]

	Universe A		Universe B		Universe C	
	Visits	Gifts	Visits	Gifts	Visits	Gifts
Group, $Q = -1.00$ to $-.40$ (visit or gifts primarily with members of other bands)	.490	.554	.449	.565	.571	.737
Group, $Q = -.41$ to $+.40$ (visits or gifts primarily balanced between band members and members of other bands)	.508	.633	.497	.628	.552	.401
Group, $Q = .41$ to 1.00 (visits or gifts primarily with band members)	.569	.577	.535	.662	.528	.616

[a] The samples used in the calculation are the same as in Table 4.1. All transactions of "Band 5" are classified as extraband. If a person has no transactions with a particular group (with extraband members), his net exchange ratio is defined as zero. In this calculation secondary hosts and gift givers are not included, and the entire visit or gift is attributed to the prime host. Universes A, B, and C are defined in Table 4.1. Data on sample sizes are presented in Appendix C.2.

figures, as children are not often gift givers. In spite of the negative results for the universe of children and unmarried youth, Sahlins' proposition receives some confirmation for the adults of the society.

If we measure kinship distance by genealogical distance, then we can examine the data in a similar manner, comparing the standard deviations of the individual accounts with nonkin, distant kin, and close kin. For the purpose of this particular calculation close kin are defined as those within two links (consanguineal or affinal) of Ego; this includes all those who are or were members of one's own, one's parents', one's siblings', one's spouse's, or one's children's nuclear family households. Distant kindsmen are defined as all others recognized as relatives by the Sallumiut but *not* including those between whom only the ethnographer was able to trace relationships or those to whom the Eskimos could trace a relationship, but one which was not dignified by a kinship term. Nonkin are all those whom a speaker would not address by a kinship term on a genealogical basis.

The first step is to devise an index to measure the relative importance of transactions with the three groups. We weighted the percentage of visits (both to and from) with nonkin by -1.00; the percentage of visits (both to and from) with far kin by 0.00; and the percentage of visits (both to and from) with near kin by $+1.00$; divided the total by 100; and ended up with an index ranging from -1.00 (if all visits were with nonkin) to $+1.00$ (if all visits were with near kin). If all visits were with far kin, or if all visits were evenly balanced between nonkin or near kin, the index is 0.00. Such an index (designated below as the kin distance index, *KDI*) corresponds to the index devised for the visits within and outside the band.[28]

The second step is to examine the standard deviations of the regression residuals of the individuals with different *KDI*s. If Sahlins is correct, we should expect that the standard deviations of the residuals increase with a rising *KDI*. Relevant data are presented in Table 4.4.

The data do not support the hypothesis; out of 14 pairs for which comparisons can be made, 7 show the predicted direction of differences in the standard deviations, and 7 show just the opposite. Two explanations for this failure can be given.

First, the bonds of band membership seem stronger than the bonds of kinship, probably because band membership was centered around much closer economic cooperation. Thus, kin who were not in the band received treatment more like that of other nonband members than that of equivalent kin who were within the band.

Second, reciprocal kinship duties were highly structured and reflected imbalances that would not be completely explained by the factors listed in Table 4.1. These imbalances can be seen clearly by aggregating all distributional

---

[28]We are assuming a linearity in the changes of the standard deviations such that the standard deviations of regression residuals of people dealing with a balanced mix of near kin and nonkin are roughly the same as those of a person dealing just with distant kin.

TABLE 4.4

Standard Deviations from the Regression Line of Estimated Net Exchange Indices According to the Degree to Which Transactions Are Made with Kin among the Sallumiut Eskimo[a]

	Universe A		Universe B		Universe C	
	Visits	Gifts	Visits	Gifts	Visits	Gifts
Group, KDI = −1.00 to −.40 (visits or gifts primarily with nonkin)	.542	.562	.552	.521	.512	.813
Group, KDI = −.41 to +.40 (visits or gifts primarily with far kin)	.515	.611	.430	.609	.581	.606
Group, KDI = .41 to 1.00 (visits or gifts primarily with near kin)	.429	.597	.480	.719	*	*

[a] See footnote to Table 4.3. An asterisk indicates that too few transactions were recorded for meaningful comparisons; most of the close kin of children and unmarried youth were living in the same household; thus, most of their transactions with near kin are not recorded. Universes A, B, and C are defined in Table 4.1. Data on sample sizes are presented in Appendix C.2.

transactions occurring between people standing in a reciprocal kinship relation and then grouping these data according to kin distance. (Such an exercise is carried out in Appendix B.5.) A possible result of these factors might be to increase the role of random or other elements in the calculations presented in Table 4.4.

The results of this analysis of reciprocal exchange and kin distance can be quickly summarized. Some positive evidence can be found to support Sahlins' proposition that kin distance affects net account imbalances, especially when kin distance is defined in terms of band membership. Nevertheless, we cannot be completely sure about these matters because the results are not statistically significant. Furthermore, a considerable part of the imbalances in the net account indices can be explained by the factors listed in Table 4.1 that have nothing to do with kin distance.

In addition to these hypotheses about the nature of reciprocity, a large number of other propositions and conjectures about the nature of reciprocal exchange can be found in the literature. Analysis of these propositions in the light of our data would lead us too far from the major themes of this chapter. However, additional discussion on some of these matters is presented in Appendix B.5.

SUMMARY AND CONCLUSIONS

This is a study designed to show how the major concepts defined in the previous chapters can be used for empirical analysis and, at the same time, to test a series of hypotheses about the nature of distribution which particularly focus on reciprocal exchange. The data are drawn from a sample of distributional transactions which took place in an Eskimo village, combined with evidence from a census of population characteristics which was taken at the same time. Distribution accounts were calculated for all village inhabitants. Although the sample of transactions is, unfortunately, not complete, sufficient qualitative evidence on the missing transactions is available to believe that our results would not be substantially different if a complete sample could have been drawn.

Extracting testable propositions from the writings of social scientists discussing the "inherently" balanced nature of exchange among social equals in primitive and peasant societies is quite difficult. In this chapter we focused on three such theories:

1. According to Marcel Mauss, transactions in such societies are generally balanced in the sense that the flows of material goods or services are roughly equal between individuals in the long run. This in turn suggests that the pattern of imbalances in any period should be essentially random and not influenced by social, economic, or political factors.

2. According to E. R. Leach, transactions in such societies are generally balanced in the long run, but he includes among the balancing items certain social invisibles such as prestige or status, for example, high prestige persons may be either net givers or receivers, depending on the ways in which prestige or status are defined and manifested in the society. This in turn suggests that the pattern of imbalances in any period should be influenced by certain pre-specified social invisibles which a sensitive ethnographer can detect.

3. According to Marshall Sahlins, transactions in such societies are generally balanced if they are between nonkin who are friendly social equals; however, transactions between kin (defined in some way) where there are certain feelings of affection or transactions between enemies may be unbalanced in the long run.

Our data from an Eskimo village show that there are great distributional imbalances; furthermore, a certain patterning of these imbalances can be detected. We are not denying that reciprocal exchange took place. But in addition to such exchange, there are also some extremely important transfers which can be traced in part to the action of certain economic, social, and political variables which we have isolated. Thus, the views of Mauss and others who believe that exchange in precapitalist societies is essentially reciprocal seems belied by our results. Furthermore, the Eskimos in our village who believed in the reality of strict reciprocity between social equals were also incorrect.

By including in our calculations a number of social invisibles such as "prestige" and "status," we tried to test the notion that distributions "balanced" by a counterflow of such invisibles. Our regression experiments showed that these did not seem to play a sufficiently important role to yield significant results. It seems to us that it is always a dangerous procedure for analysts to invoke the use of counterbalancing social invisibles to "explain" transfers, and in the ethnographic case under consideration such a procedure seems clearly wrong. Thus, the views of E. R. Leach and his followers appear incorrect in this regard.

We have found the views of Marshall Sahlins more promising, although in this instance as well we provide evidence that he is only partially correct. In addition to the net exchange indices being influenced by the economic, social, and political factors which we isolated, we found that kin distance—defined in terms of membership in certain bands—also appeared to influence the results. However, this influence does not appear completely certain since the statistical tests did not yield results significant at the .05 level.

It must be finally emphasized that the native belief that reciprocal exchange does or does not occur does not necessarily reflect the reality of the situation since the existence of such a belief may bring about a reality which is exactly opposite. That is, a belief in the occurrence of reciprocity makes it unnecessary for close attention to be paid to the exact balance of transactions, and as a result balanced transactions may never be achieved; while a belief that recip-rocal exchange seldom occurs may make participants in any type of distri-butional transaction extremely sensitive about any types of imbalances which may occur so that, as a result, transactions are generally balanced. In short, the concept of "reciprocity" has certain mythic qualities to both Western social scientists and natives. Although myths are important social entities and, as such, deserve to be studied, this does not mean that we, as scholars, need to believe them.

Several less dramatic methodological conclusions also warrant summary. First, the distinction drawn in Chapter 2 between exchange and transfer can be quite successfully employed in quantitative analysis of distribution using ac-counting data. Second, the analysis of transfers does not need to be tied to any analysis of individual motives since transfers can arise not only from benevo-lent or malevolent reasons but also from certain structural features of the soci-ety that can be empirically isolated and explored as we have done in the regression analysis. Third, using quite simple quantitative methods, data on distributional transactions can be explored in a manner to permit much deeper insight to be gained in a particular case study than by using traditional field interviews and generalizing solely from qualitative evidence.

This study of Eskimo distribution patterns has been primarily inductive. If we wish to study the determinants of distribution, ideally we need a set of general propositions derived deductively from theoretical considerations which permit us to examine all kinds of transactions in a systematic fashion. After this long four-chapter introduction to this book, it is to such matters that we now turn.

5

THE DETERMINANTS OF MARKET EXCHANGE

I saw you, Walt Whitman, childless, lonely old grubber, poking among the meats in the refrigerator and eyeing the grocery boys.
I heard you asking questions of each: Who killed the pork chops? What price bananas?

GINSBERG[1]

Exploration of the determinants of the different modes of distribution begins with this analysis of market exchange, a type of distribution that includes the buying and selling of goods, services, and intangibles such as rights of ownership in incorporeal and corporeal property. In the social science literature a great deal of attention has been focused on the origins of various types of market exchange, and we begin our study of determinants of distribution in relatively familiar territory. A major task of this chapter is to enlarge the existing boundaries of analysis of the subject by examining a new set of determinants, an undertaking that becomes necessary because so many of the current theoretical notions about the causal forces underlying market exchange turn out either to be wrong or to be quite incomplete.

The analysis presented in this chapter reveals four major sets of determinants of market exchange. First, almost all types of market exchange are positively related to the level of economic development; the higher the level of development, the more likely we are to find such exchange. Second, several major types of market exchange are linked to the form of marriage and the degree of participation of women in food production: The exact causal connections are developed in the analysis of my theory of "alternative paths to wealth." Third,

Design from a Santal *banam* fiddle; Santal Parganas, Bihar, India.

[1]Allen Ginsberg, "A Supermarket in California," in *The New American Poetry, 1945–1960* (New York: Grove Press, 1960), comp. Donald M. Allen, p. 181. "A Supermarket in California" was originally published in *Howl and Other Poems* by Allen Ginsberg, copyright © 1956, 1959 by Allen Ginsberg, and is reprinted here by permission of City Lights Books.

certain types of market exchange can be traced to the principal mode of food production in the society. Finally, other types of market exchange are related to scarcities of such factors of production as land and capital. The specific propositions containing these determinants are first argued on theoretical grounds and then tested empirically using the sample of 60 primitive and peasant economies.

For expositional simplicity I have separated the empirical and theoretical analyses of the following four markets: goods, labor, credit, and land. Although there are common analytic threads running through the discussion of all four types of markets, the results of the empirical analyses of each yield somewhat different results, a complexity which places a certain burden on the memory of the reader until the final section, in which the major conclusions are drawn together.

A SURVEY OF MARKET EXCHANGE

Some General Considerations of Definition

In order to delineate the subject of this chapter, it is necessary to make some distinctions about market exchange. It is quite possible to have market exchange without money (e.g., in barter transactions) and to have money without market exchange (where money serves a number of noncommercial purposes, a topic discussed in the next chapter). It is also possible to have market exchange without having formal "marketplaces" or specialized market personnel. And, of course, it is possible for an economy to have a certain amount of market exchange without such exchange greatly influencing or dominating important production and distribution decisions. Therefore, when I speak of market exchange, I refer to a phenomenon that is independent of money, marketplaces, market personnel, or all-embracing market systems, even though these may accompany some types of market exchange.

In Chapter 2, I defined market exchange as a type of balanced distributional transaction involving goods or services where the forces of supply and demand are visible, in contrast to reciprocal exchange which is also balanced but where such economic forces are not so visible. By visible, I mean that important changes in the relative prices, the quantities of goods offered or sought, or the quality of the goods can be easily traced to changes in supply or demand forces. The balanced nature of market transaction and this visibility of economic forces in market exchange are acknowledged among the Fon of Dahomey and the Dogon of Mali, who post signs depicting twins wherever market exchange transactions are supposed to take place.[2]

---

[2]Both the Fon and the Dogon number among the sample societies of this study, and the reader is referred to the ethnographic references in Appendix E.

Although market and reciprocal exchange differ with regard to the ostensible role of economic forces, the ultimate role of such forces may be similar. That is, both types of exchange can involve fixed or fluctuating exchange rates over the long run, both can involve credit, and both can be carried out with a wide or narrow set of goods and services. The visibility of the economic forces, the distinguishing criterion of the two types of transactions, has a number of social implications that have often been stressed, for example, there is a voluntariness and an openness in the decision making concerning exchange rates (or prices), quantities, qualities, and delivery and payment conditions; and transactions can be accepted or rejected without wide-scale social repercussions. By defining market exchange in terms of the visibility of economic forces rather than these secondary phenomena, I have outlined a concept which is both more general and, at the same time, easier to apply in trying to code particular kinds of balanced distributional transactions.

Since many, if not most, distributional transactions in primitive and peasant economies are embedded in a social matrix, market exchange in these societies has certain social elements not usually present in such exchange in modern industrial societies. Indeed, some analysts have found it useful to classify market exchanges by the type of social mixture, a practice which unfortunately yields few useful propositions. This mixture of elements sometimes gives rise to difficulties in distinguishing market and reciprocal exchange, especially since a certain amount of market exchange in primitive economies is carried out in an ostensible framework of reciprocity. That is, market exchange of goods may take place in a given society almost exclusively between "trade partners" who may have considerable social and ritual obligations to each other. Yet, these trade partners may negotiate in some manner about prices, quantities, qualities, and delivery and payment conditions, and the ultimate outcome may depend greatly on supply and demand forces. The social structuring of the relationship between trade partners may be quite irrelevant to the visibility of the economic factors that dominate the exchange side of their transactions.

In market exchange the visibility of the economic forces can be structured so that the actual negotiations are either heated or ostensibly perfunctory. Although negotiations are usually carried on directly, they can also be carried out quite indirectly. For instance, in the phenomenon of "silent trade" where goods are left by one partner and where the other trade partner takes what he wants and leaves what he thinks is of equal value, dissatisfaction with the proffered exchange can be manifested in several different ways, such as the first partner leaving untouched what the second partner has left.[3]

---

[3]Some types of "silent trade" are really "silent reciprocity." The most extensive study on the subject is by P. J. Hamilton Grierson, *The Silent Trade* (1903); this book is useful even though many of his examples have subsequently been shown to be in error. The subject invites perpetual interest, witness its treatment by Melville Herskovits, *Economic Anthropology: The Economic Life of Primitive Peoples* (1952), pp. 185–187.

Numerous cases of silent trade can be found in modern industrial societies. An amusing example

Specific Types of Market Exchange

The most commonly discussed type of market exchange in the anthropology literature is the exchange of one good for another or of one good and money. This can involve casual bartering between isolated individuals or groups at a single point in time; or a formal marketplace with particular rules, an elaborate mechanism for maintaining the "peace of the market" and all sorts of subsidiary market institutions. The anthropology literature documents a variety of different types of markets, including rotating or periodic markets, trade fairs, trade feasts, trade enclaves and ports of trade, and so forth.[4]

Market exchange can also involve different sorts of intangibles. In a number of primitive or peasant societies we find the buying and selling of ownership to particular songs or permission to perform particular rituals.[5] In some societies there are even primitive futures markets, that is, markets involving the buying and selling of claims on goods in the future that may not be yet produced.[6] Another type of buying and selling of intangibles involves rights in land and will be discussed further.

A labor market has several manifestations. There is the buying and selling of services, where the provider of the service maintains a certain degree of independence in his work; and the buying and selling of wage labor, where the provider of labor primarily follows the orders of the buyer. Although one can imagine a situation where the payment for one service is a return service (with bargaining, fluctuating prices, and so forth), I have found no ethnographic examples of such a phenomenon; rather, I have found only payment for services or wage labor in terms of money or goods (the latter is the so-called "truck system" and may involve some of the goods which the service provider produces or cares for such as the shepherd receiving cattle for his labor).

For the most part labor markets in primitive and peasant economies do not involve fluctuating prices, so that problems arise in distinguishing market and

---

is recorded by Myres S. McDougal, Harold D. Lasswell, and M. Michael Reisman ("The World Constitutive Process of Authoritative Decision," *Journal of Legal Education* XIX 3 (1967): 254), who tell of a package of pictures of the moon taken from the Soviet satellite Luna 9 that was found by custodians when opening up the U.S. State Department in Washington on May 26, 1966. No letter of explanation was included; such a picture exchange was not part of the U.S.S.R.–U.S. cooperative agreements; and the pictures were unsolicited. Five days later, the Soviets found a package of lunar photos taken by the American satellite, Surveyor 1, on the doorstep of their Washington embassy with no message, either. (Perhaps this is an example of silent reciprocity rather than silent trade.)

[4]Various forms of markets for goods are surveyed by Richard F. Salisbury, "Trade and Markets," in *International Encyclopedia of the Social Sciences* (1968), ed. David L. Sills, Vol. XVI, pp. 118–122; or Herskovits, *Economic Anthropology*, pp. 180–204.

[5]A number of different cases of markets for incorporeal or intangible things are surveyed by Herskovits, ibid., pp. 371–395.

[6]An interesting case of a futures markets for cigarettes is discussed by R. A. Radford, "The Economic Organization of a P.O.W. Camp," in *Economic Anthropology: Readings in Theory and Analysis* (1968), ed. Edward E. LeClair, Jr. and Harold K. Schneider, pp. 403–415. Cases of rudimentary futures markets in more primitive economies can occasionally be found.

reciprocal exchanges of labor. Some cases of labor exchange are clearly recip-rocal: various types of work exchange; cooperative labor; and labor rings. Some cases of labor exchange are clearly market exchange: the herd owner hiring the shepherd; the specialist selling his services for a fee; the various grades of shaman accepting different fees (according to their alleged curing powers) or consuming various amounts of sacrificial goods (according to the same criterion); or the work team selling its group services. If the transaction of labor exchange is accompanied by certain ritual or other social elements, yet at the same time features negotiations concerning quantity of work, quality, or conditions of payment and delivery, classification becomes more difficult; for-tunately, such mixed cases were sufficiently rare that I do not believe my results are greatly affected by arbitrary classification decisions.

Two types of markets concerning land can be distinguished. The first occurs with the renting of a plot of land, which is, in essence, the buying of rights to use a piece of land for some purpose for a specified time.[7] This is designated below as a "land rental market." The second occurs with the buying and selling of the particular ownership rights in land, which I label a "land market." In this latter situation, only particular rights in some cases may be sold (e.g., hunting rights), while in other cases a whole bundle of rights and obligations concerning a piece of land may be sold.

In the land rental market two closely related phenomena must also be distin-guished. "Gift rents" are gifts made to the owner of a piece of land by someone using the land. The amount of the gift rent bears no relation to the size of the crop or the value of the land; it is usually quite small in size and is determined by the land user, not the landowner. For instance, among the Tikopia (in the British Solomon Islands of the Western Pacific), a person could farm any piece of land he chose without the owner's permission; after the crop was harvested, the land user would deliver a basket of produce to the landowner. "Tax rents" are payments made to a political leader for permission to farm a piece of land in his territory, a phenomenon which occurred, for example, among the Ganda of Uganda.[8] The gift rents are too small in amount to deserve much attention

---

[7]It might be argued that such rental transactions (and the interest transactions discussed below) are really noncentric transfers since the land renter (or interest payer) is really receiving in return an "invisible" that should not be taken into calculation in determining if the counterflow balances the original payment. This argument might be restated somewhat differently: My distinction in Chapter 2 between exchange and transfer transactions is not internally consistent since I do include several types of invisibles (i.e., those in rent and interest transactions) as suitable counterflows in determin-ing whether the transactions are balanced, but not other types of invisibles. However, the causal forces underlying the existence of rent and interest phenomena seem sufficiently similar to those underlying other types of market transactions that clarity is gained by making these exceptions to my general rule concerning the treatment of invisibles. I have, nevertheless, separated my analyses of land rental markets and credit markets so that their differences with other types of market transactions can be clearly seen, and the reader, if he wishes, may mentally transfer the conclusions of these analyses to the chapters dealing with transfer payments.

[8]These societies are included in my sample, and the ethnographic sources are given in Appendix E.

(technically, they would be classified as a noncentric transfer); the tax rents are classified as a centric transfer since they are primarily a political phenomenon.

In land markets the society may place limitations on the set of individuals or families to whom a landowner may sell his land. Although the set often includes just close kin, in certain nomadic societies both land renting and land buying and selling are carried out primarily with those who do not belong to the society, for example, a person buys land at an oasis, rents or resells it to a villager, and (in the case of renting it) collects his rental once or twice a year. Thus, in some cases we must distinguish between internal and external land and land rental markets.

A final type of market exchange is reflected in interest payments, that is, the payments for the privilege of borrowing something now and returning it later. I label this the "credit market." It is important to distinguish between "real" and "pseudo" interest payments. Real interest occurs when the interest phenomenon is explicitly recognized by the participants (i.e., it is either negotiated, or else a prevailing societal norm of the interest is charged) and can be manifested in a variety of different ways.[9] Among the Fon of Dahomey, borrowing is accompanied by the sending of a person as a pawn to the lender, such that the latter reaps the benefit of the pawn's work until the loan is repaid. Among the Nuer of the Sudan, cattle debts must be repaid with better quality cattle than were lent. If prohibitions against interest exist, the interest may be disguised in various ways in the same manner that "mortgage points" are used in the selling of houses in the United States to avoid state usury laws on mortgage interest rates. In many societies interest is charged on certain types of loans (particularly loans for productive purposes) and not for others (particularly loans for consumption purposes). In some societies (e.g., apparently among the Lepcha of Sikkim) interest is charged only on loans when repayment exceeds a particular length of time. Some societies have rotating credit associations, where all contribute and the funds are sequentially lent to members.

Pseudointerest occurs in several forms. One case is where payment for borrowing is in the form of a gift which is not agreed upon in advance and which may bear no relation to the thing borrowed, for example, the Semang of Malaysia may leave a bit of food in a pot which they borrow and return. Another case occurs when cattle are borrowed and returned with any natural increase which may have occurred, a type of transaction found particularly in herding societies. And still another case occurs when borrowers on their own account return more than they borrowed only if they used the borrowed goods for productive purposes.[10]

---

[9]The ethnographic examples in this paragraph are all drawn from societies in my sample, whose references are given in Appendix E.

[10]The Semang are in my sample, and the ethnographic sources are given in Appendix E. An interesting discussion of certain types of pseudointerest payments among the Maori is by Marshall Sahlins, "The Spirit of the Gift," in his Stone Age Economics (1972), pp. 149–185.

THEORIES OF MARKET EXCHANGE

Specific Determinants of Market Exchange

The discussion concerning determinants of market exchange is quite muddled in the literature. In this section I try to sort out some major arguments and, in addition, to propose a number of new hypotheses.

DETERMINANTS OF THE GOODS MARKET

In 1776, in his great economic opus, Adam Smith wrote:[11]

> The division of labour . . . is not originally the effect of any human wisdom. . . . It is the necessary, though very slow and gradual, consequence of a certain propensity in human nature, which has in view no such extensive utility: the propensity to truck, barter, and exchange one thing for another. Whether this propensity be one of those original principles in human nature . . . ; or whether, as seems more probable, it be the necessary consequence of the faculties of reason and speech, it belongs not to our present subject to enquire. It is common to all men, and to be found in no other race of animals.

Anthropologists, seizing upon the word "barter" (and neglecting truck and exchange), have reacted for the last century with scorn for this generalization. The counterpropositions that they have offered vary considerably, and in this brief survey I can focus only on those that appear the most plausible.

The most frequently stated counterproposition is some variant of the commonplace evolutionist argument: The presence of market exchange is a function of the level of economic development, and such exchange does not occur or is of little importance in the most primitive communities.[12] A number of quite reasonable justifications for this relationship have been offered. For instance, market exchange is unimportant in highly primitive communities because: Technology is sufficiently simple that anyone can produce any good that he wants for himself; production in such communities is not sufficiently varied in quality or sufficiently great in quantity to warrant such exchange; or the social and kinship bonds in communities at low levels of economic development are too strong to permit this type of distributional mode, just as in the modern family no market exchange occurs between family members. Certain more dubious arguments have also been advanced: The motive for economic gain is not "basic" to man and therefore will not be found in highly primitive communities; in these communities other types of distribution crowd out market

---

[11]Adam Smith, *An Inquiry into the Nature and Cause of the Wealth of Nations* (1961), Book I, Chap. II, paragraphs 1 and 2 [originally published 1776].

[12]Several elaborate twentieth-century justifications of this proposition are: Elizabeth Ellis Hoyt, *Primitive Trade: Its Psychology and Economics* (1968) [originally published 1926]; and Karl Polanyi, "The Economy as Instituted Process," in *Trade and Market in the Early Empires: Economies in History and Theory* (1957), ed. Karl Polanyi, Conrad M. Arensberg, and Harry W. Pearson, pp. 243–270.

exchange; and at low cultural-economic levels the separation of a person's personality from the goods that he has produced does not occur.

The proposition that the presence of market exchange and the level of economic development are positively correlated is too unqualified to be completely correct, for few societies have ever been found that have no type of market exchange at all. If we modify the proposition to read that the presence of an important amount of market exchange and the level of economic development are positively correlated, then I believe that this is a reasonable first approximation to the relationship found for most types of market exchange. In the regressions presented below, the calculated coefficient for the economic development is positively correlated, usually to a statistically significant extent, with every type of market exchange that is explored.

Analytic difficulties arise in the isolation of variables other than the level of economic development that contribute to the presence or absence of different types of market exchange. Evolutionists have posed this problem in terms of understanding the sequence of events by which market exchange emerged or evolved, and opinions differed about the correct scenario. For some such as Karl Marx, Heinrich Schurtz, Richard Thurnwald, and Karl Polanyi[13] market exchange began with external or foreign trade (i.e., transactions "at the boundaries of the community"); later, internal trade arose as an extension of such external trade.[14] Such a sequence has been justified because external trade is not inhibited by close social or kinship bonds[15] and because the goods obtainable in external trade often cannot be produced locally, so that the benefits of complementary exchange of goods outweigh the possible social costs of engaging in such transactions. Linguistic evidence is also apposite: the English word "trade" originates from a German word referring to the path of a ship (*trade* or *trâ*), so that "trade" originally had a foreign commerce connotation.

For others, however, internal market exchange arose through an evolution of domestic distribution by itself. For instance, Karl Buecher argued that there has been an evolution from noncentric transfers (which he labels "presents") to reciprocal exchange (which he calls "gift exchange") to barter, while Marcel Mauss appears to believe that there has been an evolution from reciprocity between groups ("total prestations") to reciprocity between individuals ("gift

---

[13]Karl Marx, *Capital*, Vol. I, Part I, Chap. II [originally published 1867]; Heinrich Schurtz, *Grundriss einer Entstehungsgeschichte des Geldes* (1898); Richard Thurnwald, *Economics in Primitive Communities* (1932); and Karl Polanyi, *The Great Transformation: The Political and Economic Origins of Our Times* (1957), Chaps. IV and V [originally published 1944]. Other references on this topic are given in Chapter 6 of this book.
[14]The proposition that foreign trade began at a lower stage of economic development than domestic trade is logically independent of the proposition that very primitive societies feature no trade at all. Max Weber, *General Economic History* (1966), trans. Frank H. Knight, Chap. XIV [originally published 1923] and Thurnwald, Ibid., to argue the former proposition without accepting the latter.
[15]Marshall Sahlins, "On the Sociology of Primitive Exchange," in his *Stone Age Economics*, pp. 185–277, argues this proposition at length and supplies some extremely interesting evidence bearing on it.

exchange") to barter and trade.[16] These schemes are justified primarily by reference to the loosening of social bonds, a phenomenon in primitive communities that allegedly accompanies economic development. Such arguments have a certain intuitive appeal.

Evolutionary arguments of this type are, unfortunately, framed in a manner to blur causal forces other than the influence of the level of economic development. If we recast the problem in terms of exploring causal forces inhibiting or encouraging market exchange at particular levels of economic development, then we can attack it more systematically. But before engaging upon this enterprise, a few evolutionary ideas must be put to rest.

First, the notion that market exchange does not occur in highly primitive communities because of the absence of motive for gain or because the personality of the producer and his object can not be separated rings hollow when we consider that almost all societies engage in some sort of trade with other societies. For instance, the Australian aboriginees, who number among the least economically developed societies in the world, have elaborate foreign trade networks which extend thousands of miles.[17] In addition, such psychological explanations often have a certain odor of ex post facto rationalization which is out of step with the approach adopted in this study.

Second, the notion that trade is *necessarily* due to specialization and a division of labor is also false. Of course, trade between communities often does arise because of a division of labor, which can be traced to differences in environment, availability of resources, or technological knowledge between the two communities. But Paul Einzig has advanced the argument that trade can also occur where no occupational specialization exists or where there is even no private property of the means of production.[18] As examples of the former type of exchange he notes the great scope for bartering one kind of cattle against another (e.g., an ox for a cow, two young animals for one which is mature, one good quality ox for two poorer quality oxen, and so forth) or one type of crop against another (which might occur if a person's harvest of one crop failed while his harvest of other crops were successful). He also argues that primitive religions provide a strong motive for barter when various types of consumption taboos are imposed, and, in addition, totemism might also lead to barter between different totemic groups. Although I believe that Einzig's logic is correct, I also believe that the type of trade he mentions is, in actuality, relatively unimportant. Nevertheless, such an approach forces us to be more cautious in making easy generalizations about the "earlier emergence" of external

[16]Karl Buecher, *Industrial Evolution* (1907), trans. S. Morley Wickett, pp. 60 ff. [originally published 1893]; Marcel Mauss, *The Gift: Forms and Functions of Exchange in Archaic Societies*, trans. Ian Cunnison (1967), Chap. I [originally published 1925].

[17]Frederick D. McCarthy, " 'Trade' in Aboriginal Australia and 'Trade' Relationships with Torres Strait, New Guinea and Malaya," *Oceania* IX (June 1939): 405–438; X (September 1939): 81–104; and (December 1939): 171–195.

[18]Paul Einzig, *Primitive Money: In Its Ethnological, Historical and Economic Aspects* (1966), 2nd ed., pp. 338–340.

than internal trade based on theoretical considerations concerning the division of labor.

Third, most of the evolutionists seem to posit that the primitive communities are composed of tightly knit kin groups or friends, so that such social bonds in the community overshadow economic forces. But if the community is composed of groups that spend a good part of the year separated from each other (e.g., seminomadic hunters, gatherers, or herders), then one might not find the type of close social ties between community members that would inhibit trade whenever the community periodically reassembles.

Moving away from the evolutionary arguments to explain the presence or absence of the market exchange of goods, a number of other considerations appear fruitful to take into account:

1. The prevailing form of marriage (i.e., polygyny or monogamy) and the degree of female participation in subsistence production interact in an interesting fashion to encourage or inhibit the market exchange of goods; given the configuration of these two elements, alternative paths to wealth accumulation are open to the society. *Ceteris paribus,* market exchange is more likely to appear in societies characterized by monogamy and high participation of women in subsistence production than in societies characterized by polygyny and low participation of women in subsistence production. Several factors enter into the underlying causal mechanism: A monogamous family is less likely to achieve economies of scale in production than a polygynous family. Furthermore, the carrying out of trade gives a person a certain degree of marital power over one's spouse, so that there is an important tie between production and trade. Finally, participation in trade requires time to carry out, and this factor must be also taken into consideration in the analysis.

The way these three factors interact can be seen more concretely by examining four configurations and by assuming *ceteris paribus* conditions. With a monogamous marriage pattern and high female participation in food production the husband is released to produce certain specialized articles which can be traded for other specialized articles; trade is encouraged because a family cannot obtain economies of scale in the production of everything it needs, and men will carry out most of the trading. With a polygynous marriage pattern and low female participation in production, trade is inhibited because the husband will spend most of his time engaged in subsistence production for his large family, and the wives will have little to trade. The converse cases are more interesting. With a polygynous marriage pattern and high female participation in production, a family might experience a food surplus since the amount of food production would grow faster than food consumption with the acquisition of each additional wife (since the overhead cost of feeding the husband would be spread over more wives). Market exchange of food surpluses would be encouraged; since the husband would be occupied in providing certain complementary labor tasks for each wife, and since the wives would have considerable incentive to trade, such activity would be carried out by the women. (This pattern for West Africa has received considerable analysis in the anthropology literature.) Finally, in a society characterized by monogamy and low female participation in production, market exchange would be encouraged because of the economies of scale problem, but it is likely that the husband would carry out such activities if it occurred.

The presence of these alternative paths to wealth encouraging or inhibiting the presence of a market for goods can be easily examined by looking for a positive relationship between market exchange and the degree of participation of women in subsistence production and a negative relationship between such exchange and the degree of polygyny. Both relationships are confirmed by the empirical analysis below. It should be added that my theory of alternative paths to wealth is based on the reasonable assumption that the causal forces run from the two social structural considerations to the mode of distribution rather than in the reverse direction. The reader should also be warned in advance that the mechanism of interaction between the form of marriage and the degree of female participation in subsistence production is somewhat different in the study of the determinants of the presence of a goods market than for a land market, which is discussed later.

2. The importance of external trade should be inversely related to the population of the entire society, other things being equal. That is, the larger the population, the less likely the society is to have a relatively important foreign trade sector.[19] This is due to the obvious consideration that the larger the population of a society as a whole, the more likely members of that society will have extensive contacts only with people from the same society rather than foreigners. Such an argument gives insight why some highly developed but very populous societies such as the Chinese or the Incas seem to have had relatively small external trade relations in comparison with their total production, even when we take their relative geographical isolation into account.

3. External trade also depends in part upon contact with other societies, particularly the West. In this latter case trade is either forced on the primitive society, or else the benefits of obtaining certain Western wares (e.g., metal goods) are sufficiently great that the natives find it more advantageous to enter into trade relations than to forego the dangers of contact with a militarily more powerful society by trying to remain isolated.

In addition to these hypotheses a number of other promising propositions were tested and rejected; for completeness these deserve brief mention. One

[19]This is a well-known proposition in foreign trade theory and is discussed in many places, for example, Karl W. Deutsch et al., "Population, Sovereignty, and the Share of Foreign Trade," *Economic Development and Cultural Change* X (July 1962): 353–366. If the level of economic development is not held constant, population and foreign trade growth may be positively, not negatively, related to each other (e.g., the case of Western Europe after the Dark Ages); this is the reason for the *ceteris paribus* clauses.

such hypothesis rests on the notion that since trade does not often occur within family units,[20] it is possible that societies characterized by small family units might have more market exchange than societies with large family units. In the regression experiments, I defined "size of the family unit" in terms of the unit of observation (discussed in Chapter 2) and also in terms of the presence of lineages (defined in several different ways). Although the calculated regression coefficients of these variables with the market exchange of goods (as well as other types of market exchange) generally showed the expected sign, their statistical significance was never sufficiently great to warrant reporting.

In the literature I found conjectures that the primary mode of food production could influence the presence of the market for goods, other things remaining equal. Although some plausible arguments can be offered to support these ideas, I found that for the market for goods the influence of such factors did not seem greatly to influence the presence of markets, *ceteris paribus*. Other factors such as population density, frequency of internal or external strife, and other similar variables have also been advanced as determinants of the market for goods. In the regression experiments such factors also did not seem to play a statistically important role.

Aside from such propositions about factors inhibiting or encouraging the market exchange of goods one can find in the literature other propositions about particular types of goods markets. For instance, Karl Polanyi has argued that "in primitive and archaic society" there is a "universal banning of transactions of a gainful nature in regard to food and foodstuffs."[21] This proposition can be interpreted either in a literal sense or else more loosely as meaning that the market exchange of food arises at higher stages of economic development than market exchange of other products. Melville Herskovits once suggested that in primitive and peasant societies, external trade consists primarily of utilitarian products, while internal trade consists primarily of prestige goods.[22] Others have advanced propositions about market characteristics: that although domestic trade may occur in societies at relatively low levels of development, formal markets or marketplaces occur only in societies at higher levels of development and that specialized market personnel appear only at a still higher stage of economic evolution.

DETERMINANTS OF THE LABOR MARKET

The appearance of labor markets seems also a function of the level of economic development. Following the doctrines of Adam Smith, economists have argued that labor markets are a function of the division of labor. Since the division of labor is often an indicator of the level of economic development,

---

[20]The Kapauku of New Guinea is probably the most commercialized primitive society that has been extensively analyzed by anthropologists, and even they have limited commercial relations between family members, according to Leopold J. Pospisil, *Kapauku Papuan Economy* (1963).

[21]Karl Polanyi, "The Economy as Instituted Process," p. 255.

[22]Herskovits, *Economic Anthropology*, p. 181.

certain problems of circularity arise when the relationships between economic development and labor markets are empirically examined.

Many economists and anthropologists have also recognized exceptions to this relationship between development and labor markets. For instance, it is possible to have a division of labor without a labor market in situations where a caste system or where slavery occurs. It is also possible to find labor markets in societies with very low levels of development if one group in the society controls a scarce resource and where neither slavery nor a caste system occurs. However, it is usually felt that these exceptions represent relatively secondary phenomena. I wish to approach the subject in a somewhat different manner, and it seems useful to start the analysis by separately considering the markets for unskilled and skilled labor, an extremely important distinction which is seldom made.

Both the demand for and the supply of unskilled wage labor can arise when the stock of productive factors complementary to labor (e.g., capital) is subject to erratic changes among producers, so that some producers suddenly find themselves without the needed complementary factor, while others suddenly find that they have too much of the complementary factor to use by themselves in production. Such a situation occurs frequently in herding societies, especially of the nomadic variety, where an individual's herd can be wiped out very quickly in adverse environmental circumstances, while the herd of another can increase naturally to the point where the owner and his family can not supply sufficient manpower to shepherd the flock. That is, under certain circumstances a complementary need for employment and a need for additional shepherds can arise simultaneously, so that there is a serious labor allocation problem. One solution is for the large herd owner to hire the unlucky herd owner, paying the latter in kine or money (as noted in the next chapter, the Latin word for cattle *pecus* is related to the word for money *pecunia*), so that the latter can accumulate enough capital (a word ultimately stemming from a Latin word used for head of cattle) to become an independent herd owner again.

Another causal force underlying unskilled labor markets might be contact with the West, which could influence unskilled employment in two different ways. First, employment of unskilled workers among Western societies might serve as an example of a new type of market process, so that we have a case of diffusion. Second, the contact with the West might result in employment of unskilled workers to produce the trade goods which are exported.

For skilled labor it is more difficult to find or to conjure up propositions which might inhibit or encourage markets.[23] One promising hypothesis is based on the notion that in nomadic societies the exigencies of travel force

---

[23]A proposition found in the popular press, but not in the scholarly literature, is that prostitution is the oldest profession (i.e., the labor service appearing at the lowest level of economic development). Although in some (but not all) societies food is used as a payment for sexual services, the recipients are usually not full-time professionals. In societies at very low levels of development the most likely professionals to be found are priests and curers.

individuals to become adept at a wider range of activities than in a settled society where the availability of people with specialized skills is more assured. Another likely hypothesis is that skilled labor markets are less likely to be found in societies with large family units since intrafamilial labor specialization has more opportunity to arise. Again, family unit size can be measured either in terms of the size of the unit of observation or in terms of the presence of lineages. A final promising hypothesis concerns the positive impact that a market for goods might have on the presence of a skilled labor market. Empirical investigation of these and similar propositions, unfortunately, proved unrewarding.

DETERMINANTS OF THE CREDIT MARKET

Arguments linking the presence of credit markets with the level of economic development can be made in ways quite similar to those by which I argued this relation for the goods market. Propositions about other determinants of the credit market can also be advanced.

One important causal factor is the relative scarcity of capital. The third of the three major reasons for the existence of interest which is listed in Böhm-Bawerk's classical treatment of the subject discusses this matter in terms of the productivity of capital.[24] In societies where production is carried out with capital intensive technologies, that is, where massive accumulations of capital are profitably used in production, we would expect to find an interest rate; while in societies where production does not employ much capital, the phenomenon of interest is less likely to be found. A corollary to this proposition is that interest is more likely to be levied on loans for production than loans for consumption.

Another proposition links the existence of interest and the existence of a domestic commercial money in the following manner[25]: So long as goods can not be easily exchanged for other goods, the opportunity costs of temporarily lending particular goods to someone else can not often be easily measured. If goods have prices in terms of an accepted medium of exchange, loans can be more easily viewed in terms not only of foregone consumption but also of missed investment opportunities; that is, the cost of a loan becomes more apparent to the lender. Therefore, the phenomenon of interest might be more likely to occur with the presence of money. Unfortunately, once the level of economic development was held constant, this proposition did not receive verification in the empirical investigation.

---

[24]Eugen von Böhm-Bawerk, Capital and Interest: A Positive Theory of Capital (1959), Book IV, Chap. I [originally published 1889]. I would like to thank Bernard Saffran for his discussion of this proposition with me.

[25]This proposition is argued at greater length by Frederic L. Pryor, "Property Institutions and Economic Development: Some Empirical Tests," Economic Development and Cultural Change XX (April 1972): 406–437.

A final consideration that must be taken into account is the religious or moral attitude of the society toward interest, which can be illustrated by the following passage from Aristotle[26]:

> The most hated sort [of wealth-getting], and with the greatest reason, is usury, which makes a gain out of money itself, and not from the natural object of it. For money was intended to be used in exchange but not to increase at interest. And this term interest, which means the birth of money from money, is applied to the breeding of money because the offspring resembles the parent. Wherefore of all modes of getting wealth this is the most unnatural.

A number of societies for such moral reasons have banned interest, and although such bans may not be completely successful, they often make it difficult for the outside observer to detect the presence of interest. Such observation problems aside, quantifying these moral attitudes to calculate a variable for use in the regression analysis proved impossible, so the relationship between moral attitudes and the presence of interest could not be tested.

DETERMINANTS OF LAND AND LAND RENTAL MARKETS

The relationship between the occurrence of land and land rental markets and the level of economic development occurs not only for reasons already adduced for other markets but also because such markets rest on private property rights in land which allegedly do not occur in highly primitive economies. And, indeed, there is strong empirical evidence that an important relationship exists between the level of economic development and the presence of different private ownership rights in land.[27] But land and land rental markets are influenced by other causal forces as well.

One important causal factor is the relative scarcity of land. Some observers have falsely tied land scarcity solely to the level of economic development. For instance, Melville Herskovits offered the following dubious generalization: "Among nonliterate cultivators, scarcity of land is almost unknown, except occasionally in such thickly settled portions of the nonliterate world as West Africa or Mexico or the highlands of Peru or Indonesia."[28] As I argue in Chapter 8, scarcity of land is more likely to be reflected in the population density and in the type of fallowing system which is employed. That is, a society with a low population density but with employment only of very land-using agricultural techniques (i.e., employing long fallowing periods or using slash and burn methods) may have greater land scarcity than a society with a much higher population density but with employment of double cropping, land-saving techniques of agricultural production. These two factors must be considered

---

[26]Aristotle, *Politics*, Book I, Chap. X [trans. Jowett] in *The Basic Works of Aristotle* (1941), ed. Richard McKeon, p. 1141.

[27]For instance, the investigations of L. T. Hobhouse, G. C. Wheeler, and M. Ginsberg, *The Material Culture and Social Institutions of the Simpler Peoples: An Essay in Correlation* (1930), pp. 243 ff.; or Pryor, "Property Institutions."

[28]Herskovits, *Economic Anthropology*, p. 354.

together in analyzing land scarcity; for this purpose, a special variable (whose construction is described in Appendix C.3) is used.

Another set of causal factors underlying the presence or absence of land and land rental markets arises from consideration of alternative paths to wealth arising from different configuration of marital forms and female participation in subsistence production. In particular, let us consider two agricultural societies at the same level of economic development, one of which is characterized by considerable polygyny and a high participation of women in subsistence production. If a man has extra land, in the former society his path to wealth lies clearly in the accumulation of wives who will work this extra land; in the latter society accumulation of wealth can not occur in this way but through the renting of this land to tenant farmers or the selling of the land to others so that resources can be obtained for investment. Thus, we predict that the presence of land and land rental markets should be inversely related to the participation of women in agricultural production and also inversely related to the importance of polygyny.

The interaction of female subsistence production and the marriage form is thus somewhat different (and also less complex) from that discussed previously concerning the market exchange of goods. Nevertheless, both interaction mechanisms are manifestations of the fact that different social structural configurations yield quite different paths toward wealth accumulation, which influences the presence or absence of market exchange. This line of argumentation receives impressive verification.

A number of other hypotheses concerning the determinants of land and land rental markets were also examined. The results of these regression experiments were sufficiently negative that they do not deserve further mention.

Developmental Relationships of Different Types of Market Exchange

Since market exchange can occur for goods, labor, credit, and land, many anthropologists and economists have speculated about the relative levels of economic development at which these different types of exchange first appear. These matters deserve brief consideration.

There seems to be general agreement that labor markets arise at higher stages of development than goods markets, but the arguments justifying such propositions leave something to be desired. Some analysts seem to think that this is because the wage earner must have something on which to spend his earnings,[29] an argument which overlooks the possibility of payments in kind or in kine. Some argue that payment for services implies a subordination and that this type of social relation is strongly resisted by all free men as a type of slavery which must be avoided until they no longer have the means (land, cattle, or

[29]E. H. Phelps-Brown, *The Economies of Labor* (1962), p. 11.

tools) for self-employment.[30] This type of reasoning seems to confuse wage labor, which implies a certain subordination, with the buying and selling of services in which social subordination need not necessarily occur at all. Some have made another type of argument: Labor markets occur only when free labor is separated from land, that is, when land becomes salable and when the economic and social spheres of the society have separated, a situation arising only at high levels of economic development.[31] Although such an argument may be true regarding the existence of extensive markets for wage labor, it does not necessarily apply to services per se or to the existence of wage labor in herding or agriculture.

For the credit market I have not been able to find any rigorously stated propositions about the relative level of development at which interest payments arise. It is well known that the phenomenon of interest has existed for a very long period of time[32] and, furthermore, that usury laws prohibiting interest are also very ancient.[33] The difficulties in stating a proposition about the emergence of interest which takes such historical evidence rigorously into account should be quite apparent.

The conventional wisdom of the evolutionists was that land and land rental markets arise at much higher levels of economic development than goods markets, and they offered two major rationalizations for this state of affairs. First, since private property in land occurs only in societies at relatively high levels of economic development, and since land can not be sold or rented without such rights, land and land rental markets therefore arise at relatively high levels of development. As I noted above, the first clause of this proposition seems empirically correct; however, the second clause is sufficiently dubious (unless it is interpreted tautologically) that the conclusion does not follow. That is, even though land is, in some mystical-social sense, not "owned" privately but held by a family or lineage group, the notion of transferring rights for using the land for a particular purpose can still arise, and payments can be made by the person or group wishing to use the land to the head of the family or lineage. In other words, rental payments or even peculiar types of land sales can arise, even before all rights to the land are alienable or before the society recognizes a distinction between sovereignty over land and ownership of land. Second, it is argued that land only becomes "scarce" when societies reach high levels of development. I have already commented on one aspect of this notion; another

[30]Ibid., pp. 10–11.

[31]This type of argument was argued forcibly by Marx in various places (e.g., *Grundrisse der Kritik der Politischen Oekonomie* [n.d.], Chap. III, 2nd Section, pp. 375 ff.) and is reformulated by others such as Karl Polanyi (*The Great Transformation,* Chap. V). The Marxist view on these matters is not stated fully in any single place and is complex, for example, Frederick Engels (*The Origins of the Family, Private Property and the State* [1972], Chap. IX, p. 226 [originally published 1884]) explicitly recognized certain types of wage labor in the time of slavery, although he does not discuss these matters in any detail.

[32]A nice summary is by Sidney Homer, *A History of Interest Rates* (1963), which discusses interest rates back to 3000 B.C.

[33]See esp. Weber, *General Economic History,* Chap. XXI.

aspect deserves brief comment. Even though land may not in general be "scarce," land of a particular quality or in a particular location may be "scarce" so that land sales or rental may occur. Although it turns out empirically that land and land rental markets do emerge only at relatively high levels of economic development, the theoretical explanations of this phenomenon are uncomfortably weak.

Another developmental relationship was advanced by Frederick Engels, who asserted that money and private property in land arose at about the same stage of development (the reasons he gives are, however, obscure) and that both lead inexorably to a land market with all of its social ill effects.[34]

Some Impact Propositions about Markets: A Digression

In addition to propositions about the determinants of markets, the social science literature contains many propositions about the influences of markets on the economy and the society. Many of these are quite commonplace, for example, trade brings greater interdependency between groups, introduces certain types of new risks, encourages greater specialization of labor, and widens spheres of personal acquaintanceships, and hardly bear repeating. Others provide some useful leads for research and, although I do not test them except in the most casual manner, deserve brief mention.

One oft-stated proposition is that increased trade acts as an important stimulus for domestic production. European historians have long told us that production declined with the fall in trade in the Dark Ages and increased with the revival of trade in the succeeding centuries. In more primitive societies the same correlation is observed: For example, we find herd sizes increasing among the Lapps of Scandinavia when trade contacts with the Norwegians and the Swedes increased and domestic agricultural production (and brideprices) increasing among the Nyakyusa of Tanzania with the rise of trade with the West.[35]

It is often argued that trade requires law and order to be carried through, and thus we find institutions such as "the peace of the market" arising in diverse societies (e.g., the Batak of Sumatra; the Dogon of Mali; and the Rif of Morocco) as well as peaceful free ports of trade and trade enclaves also occurring around the world (e.g., the Hittites of the Eastern Mediterranean and the

---

[34]Engels, *Origins of the Family,* Chap. IX, p. 226. Engels' argument is extremely condensed, and his reasoning is quite unclear. He ends with a stirring oration: "Scarcely had private property in land been introduced than the mortgage was already invented (see Athens). As hetaerism and prostitution dog the heels of monogamy, so from now onward mortgage dogs the heels of private land ownership. You asked for full, free alienable ownership of the land and now you have got it—*'tu l'as voulu,* Georges Dandin'." (The phrase in the inner quotations refers to a ninth-rate play by Molière concerning the misadventures of a cuckolded landowner and seems to have little to do with Engels' argument except as a rhetorical flourish.)

[35]The Lapps and the Nyakyusa societies used in the examples below are in the ethnographic sample of this study and references are given in Appendix E.

Aztecs and Mayans of Mexico).[36] It is but a short argumentative step from this to the proposition that trade and peace are correlated or that trade is a substitute for war.[37] Supporting evidence is quite varied, ranging from anecdotes about peaceful neighbors engaging in trade or belligerent societies ceasing trade to broad historical demonstrations that trade increases with the spread of peace (e.g., a situation which occurred with the Ao Naga of Assam following British colonialization and pacification of Assam) to native analyses of the situation (e.g., the Iroquois statement to the New York State governor in 1835: "Trade and peace we take to be one thing.")[38] But we also know that in some cases trade has been the cause of war between primitive societies (e.g., in the trade wars of the Iroquois of New York)[39] and that trade can take place between belligerent parties actively engaged in war. The interrelations between trade and war are complex and require sensitive treatment[40]: Some of the complexity is due to the ambivalent motives of market exchange—the benevolent motive of exchange of goods or services for mutual benefit and the malevolent motive of exchange in order to obtain a better trade deal or to cheat the other person.[41] Cross-cultural investigation of particular propositions regarding the interrelations between trade and peace are very difficult and are not attempted below. It must be noted, however, that I tried to code the relative frequency of both internal and external strife in the various sample societies but found no significant positive or negative correlation in any of the many multiple regressions

[36]The Batak, Dogon, and Rif are all in the sample of societies used in this study, and ethnographic references are given in Appendix E. Ports of trade and trade enclaves among the Hittites, Aztecs, and Mayans are discussed in Polanyi, Arensberg, and Pearson, Trade and Market, in essays by Richard B. Rovere (pp. 38–64) and Anne C. Chapman (pp. 114–154).

[37]Variants of this proposition are argued by many. Edward B. Tylor, Anthropology: An Introduction to the Study of Man and Civilization (1896), p. 286 [originally published 1881] has a paean to the peace induced by foreign commerce and Mauss, The Gift, seems also to see a strong link between these two phenomena. In actuality, this proposition as argued by the anthropologist is merely a more sophisticated version of the vulgar mercantile proposition that was current at that period about the relationship of trade and peace. A more cautious version of this idea is formulated by Robert H. Lowie, An Introduction to Cultural Anthropology (1934), Chap. IX, who argues that trade fosters peaceful relations, at least for the time in which the transaction transpires, but this notion is trivial.

[38]The information on the Ao Naga comes from sources cited in Appendix E. The Iroquois citation comes from William N. Fenton, "The Iroquois in History," in North American Indians in Historical Perspective (1971), ed. Eleanor Burke Leacock and Nancy Oestreich Lurie, pp. 139–140.

[39]This is the subject of a notable study by George T. Hunt, The Wars of the Iroquois: A Study in Intertribal Trade Relations (1960).

[40]Two particularly interesting explorations of this subject are by Hoyt, Primitive Trade, pp. 125–133; and P. J. D. Wiles, "Trade and Peace," in his Communist International Economics (1968), pp. 524–557.

[41]Although trade has a benevolent aspect (both sides presumably gain in market exchange or else they would not agree to the transaction), malevolent aspects of this distributional mode can be seen, especially in certain connotations of words connected with trade. For instance, the English word "barter" originates from the archaic French word barater, which means 'to cheat.' A similar type of argument is offered by William Graham Sumner and Albert Galloway Keller, The Science of Society, Vol. I (1927), p. 155, who point out the similarities in the German language between the words Handel ('trade') and Händel ('quarrel') and tauschen ('to trade') and täuschen ('to deceive'). We might also add enttäuschen ('to disappoint').

which I calculated between any of the market variables and either of the strife variables.

A number of social scientists have pointed toward other relationships between market exchange and primitive economies. For instance, the opportunities of profitable trade often lead to much closer delineations and defense of property rights. For example, among the Montagnais Indians of the Canadian Labrador peninsula, the expansion of external trade in beaver pelts led to the carving up of the common hunting lands into individually held beaver hunting areas, even though for other purposes the use rights of the land were still held by the community as a whole.[42] Trade sometimes acts to increase the inequality of income in a society, especially when it can be monopolized—a situation occurring often in the case of external trade (e.g., among the Azande of Zaïre, Sudan, and the Central African Republic).[43] External trade can also have a considerable impact on exchange spheres (a phenomenon discussed in Appendix B.3) leading to their creation (e.g., among the Lele of Zaïre) or their destruction (e.g., among the Tiv of Nigeria).[44]

Many observers have pointed to important social influences of market exchange. It is argued that trade acts to strengthen those particular social groups which produce goods for trade. For example, in some societies where trade goods are produced primarily by women, trade has resulted in structural changes (e.g., introduction of matrilocal marriage patterns among the Mundurucú of Brazil or strengthening of the matrilineage among the Suku of Zaïre) enhancing the role of women.[45] Propositions about the impact of market exchange on social or political inequality can also be found in profusion, for example, monopolized external trade enhances the power of the political leaders or internal goods market act to increase social inequality. My investigation of some of these propositions using multiple regression techniques were quite unrewarding: With the exception of a positive correlation between the existence of important land rental markets and social inequality, none of the market variables proved to have much explanatory power for social and political inequality variables.

Finally, many propositions have been offered about the impact of market exchange on the culture or values of societies, particularly with regard to external trade. Blanket generalizations about such trade leading to cultural

[42]This is the subject of a classic essay by Eleanor B. Leacock, "The Montagnais 'Hunting Territory' and the Fur Trade," Memoir No. 78, American Anthropologist LVI (October 1954), Part 2: 1–76. A more technical economic analysis of this situation is by Harold Demsetz, "Toward a Theory of Property Rights," American Economic Review LVII (May 1967): 347–359. It should be emphasized that increasing delineation of private property rights is not the only response that a primitive society might make to such a situation.
[43]Ethnographic references for the Azande are given in Appendix E.
[44]The Lele are discussed by Mary Douglas, "Raffia Cloth Distribution in the Lele Economy," in Tribal and Peasant Economies: Readings in Economic Anthropology (1967), ed. George Dalton, pp. 123–136. References for the Tiv, which is one of the sample societies of this study, are given in Appendix E.
[45]Ethnographic references for the Mundurucú and Suku are given in Appendix E.

impoverishment as enculturation ensues are certainly incorrect, for in certain cases external trade has acted to enrich or to increase cultural activities, a situation occurring in quite different ways among the Kwakiutl of Vancouver Island during the nineteenth century or among the Siane of the New Guinea highlands when trade contacts with the West were first made.[46] Certainly external trade may act to change values not only through the personal contact which such transactions may bring but also because of the social changes wrought in the society as a result of trade or the introduction of new products. For instance, the destructive impact of imported liquor on the American Plains Indians and the subsequent rise of peyote and other types of cults is well known; and numerous cases of the long-term impact of trade dependencies on previously relatively autarkic societies have been long discussed in the acculturation literature.[47] However, many propositions in this literature, for example, market exchange leads to greater covetousness,[48] seem a bit farfetched.

These are but a sample of the types of impact propositions about market exchange which can be found. This area of economic anthropology begs for systematic investigation.

EMPIRICAL TESTS OF IMPORTANT HYPOTHESES

Coding Problems

The most important coding problem to overcome is the development of a criterion for determining the importance of a market exchange activity. If one looks very closely, one can generally find the presence of a number of different types of market activity in almost every society, although this may consist only of the most casual type of barter or payment for services. In the empirical studies that follow, I generally use as a criterion of importance that such market activity must embrace 5% or more of total production of all goods or total work activities of the labor force. Since the proper data to make such an evaluation in an accurate manner are, of course, not available for any of the sample societies, coding was carried out in several different ways. I tried to determine what goods were traded in market exchange and how important these were in the

[46]For the Kwakiutl a combination of the cessation of wars, the introduction of trade goods such as Hudson's Bay Company blankets, and a population decline brought about a fantastic increase in the role of potlatches (giveaway ceremonies that are discussed in greater detail in Chapter 9) and associated economic institutions. For the Siane the introduction of steel axes from the West led to an increase in leisure of men (who previously used stone axes) and an increase in the tribal ceremonial life. Ethnographic references for both societies are given in Appendix E. Data for most societies in the sample refer to conditions before Western influence was strong.
[47]An interesting attempt to deal systematically with the impact of external trade on indigenous cultures is by Mary W. Helms, "The Purchase Society: Adaption to Economic Frontiers," *Anthropological Quarterly* XLII (October 1969): 325–342.
[48]A proposition advanced by several social scientists, for example, H. H. Nieboer, *Slavery as an Industrial System* (1971), p. 395 [originally published 1910].

total production pattern of the economy; or, with labor, I tried to decide how important those services were that were sold. In other cases I tried to determine what type of quantitative judgments the ethnographers were making when they described market exchange as "considerable" or "occasional." It should be clear that guesswork was involved, but by attempting to use such a quantitative criterion in the coding process, I tried to eliminate from consideration those types of market exchange which were "unimportant" or "casual."

In general, great difficulties did not arise in the coding for the presence of markets for goods, although some problems in the separation of external and internal markets appeared. (These are discussed in Chapter 6.) I have been able to locate only one other extensive coding of the presence of markets—a study carried out by Robert Carneiro—and in comparing his results with mine, I find that our ratings are significantly correlated but that we disagree in certain cases, especially where I code the presence of market exchange, and he does not.[49] I suspect such differences occur because his implicit criteria of importance are somewhat higher than mine. For other variables associated with goods markets, for example, the presence of permanent marketplaces, Carneiro and I are in closer agreement.[50]

In coding the presence of labor markets, some problems arose in dealing with part-time market participants. If an important part of their income stemmed from labor market activities, they were considered to be full-time sellers of labor skills. Comparison of the results of my codings with those of others can only be carried out with Robert Carneiro's ratings for unskilled labor; in this case considerable agreement is obtained.[51]

Of all the market variables, the credit market proved the most difficult to code even when the coding was for the single occurrence of any type of interest levy in the individual societies. Such difficulties arose in part because of problems in separating true interest from pseudointerest payments; in part because interest may be charged only on one particular type of transaction which is only vaguely discussed by the ethnographers; and in part because religious injunctions against the charging of interest often made it difficult for the ethnog-

[49]Robert L. Carneiro carried out such codings in a series of articles, including his "Scale Analysis, Evolutionary Sequences, and the Rating of Cultures," in A Handbook of Method in Cultural Anthropology (1973), ed. Raoul Naroll and Ronald Cohen, pp. 834–872. The data used in this and the following comparisons came from his unpublished worksheets, and I would like to thank him for permission for obtaining them. For the 33 where our samples overlap (he uses a "presence of market exchange" variable, but I assume that he means domestic market exchange and compare this with my domestic market exchange variable), we are in agreement in 75% of all cases (a chi square with Yates correction of 4.73 can be calculated). Of the eight cases in which we disagree, in seven I code the presence of a market and he does not. It is quite possible that he paid closer attention to the presence of marketplaces than I, which means that my definition is broader and would include more cases. This interesting alternative explanation of our differences was suggested by George Dalton.
[50]In this case we agree in 88% of all cases.
[51]Of the 33 cases in which our samples overlap for the coding of markets for unskilled labor, our judgments agree in 85% of all cases (a chi square with Yates correction 4.64 can be calculated). Of the five cases in which we disagree, in four I code the presence of a labor market and he does not.

raphers to obtain much accurate information about the subject. Comparison of my codings for the presence of interest with those of Robert Carneiro and also of George P. Murdock and Diana O. Morrow reveal significant correlations, but I am somewhat dubious about the quality of the basic ethnographic information on which both they and I based our ratings.[52]

Determination of the existence of land and land rental markets did not generally prove difficult. Distinguishing between real and pseudorents also raised few problems. On the other hand, evaluation of the relative importance of land and land rental markets introduced certain judgmental difficulties, and the codings are more problematic. Comparison of my results with the codings of Robert Carneiro reveal relatively high agreement.[53]

With all of the market variables the same pattern appears when comparisons are made with the codings of others, namely, that disagreements arise primarily in situations where I have coded the presence of the variable and they have not. This may arise in part from differences in professional perspectives between the other coders and me since all of them are primarily social anthropologists rather than economists.

Cross-Section Tests

AN OVERALL VIEW

In the preceding theoretical discussion I hypothesized that the level of economic development acted as a determinant for every market exchange variable. By looking at the presence of these variables in groups of societies arranged according to their relative levels of economic development, we can not only test this idea but also gain a quick overall view of the various phenomena which I then examine more thoroughly in a regression analysis. Relevant data are presented in Table 5.1.

For the most part the relationship between economic development and the presence of market exchange can be easily seen. The two noticeable exceptions to this generalization are the external trade of goods and the unskilled internal labor market; when other causal factors are held constant in the regression experiments, the expected relationship between development and market

[52]Codings are made by George P. Murdock and Diana O. Morrow, "Subsistence Economy and Supportive Practices: Cross-Cultural Codes 1," *Ethnology* IX, No. 3 (July 1970): 302–330 for their variable No. 9. In the 38 societies that are in both of our samples, we find agreement in 74% of all cases (a chi square with Yates correction of 5.34 can be calculated). Of the 10 societies in which we disagree, in 7 I code the presence of interest and they do not. In the 30 societies in which my sample overlaps with that of Robert Carneiro, we agree in our ratings of 77% of them (a chi square with Yates correction of 7.83 can be calculated). Of the 7 cases in which we disagree, all are cases where I code the presence of interest, and he does not.

[53]Of the 32 societies in which our samples overlapped, we agree in our judgments about the presence of a land rent in 91% of all cases (a chi square with Yates correction of 5.70 can be calculated). In the three cases in which we disagree, all were societies in which I code the presence of land rents, and he did not.

TABLE 5.1

Market Exchange and Market Phenomena Occurring at Different Levels of Economic Development[a]

	Number of societies				
	Groups of societies classified according to relative levels of economic development				
	Lowest 15 societies[b]	Second lowest 15 societies[b]	Second highest 15 societies[b]	Highest 15 societies	Total
A. Market characteristics					
1. Market exchange of food	0	4	7	15	26
2. No marketplaces (formal markets)	14	12	10	1	37
3. Occasional marketplaces (formal markets occur less than 4 days a week)	0	0	2	4	6
4. Frequent use of marketplaces of other societies	0	2	2	2	6
5. Permanent marketplaces (formal markets occur 4 or more days a week)	1	1	1	8	11
B. Goods markets[b]					
1. Internal market exchange	3	3	5	13	24
2. External market exchange	5	12	6	3.5	26.5
3. Total (internal + external) market exchange	7	12	10	14	43

C. Labor markets[c]

1. Skilled internal labor market	1	4	6	11	22
2. Unskilled internal labor market	1	4	1	7	13
3. Total (skilled + unskilled) internal labor market	2	7	6	13	28
4. External labor market (societal members working in other societies)	0	0	0	1	1
5. Total (skilled + unskilled) labor market (internal + external)	2	7	7	14	30

D. Credit markets

1. Occurrence of a real interest rate (pseudointerest rates excluded)	2	6.5	10	9.5	28

E. Land markets (internal only)

1. Occurrence of land sales	0	1	3	8	12
2. More than occasional land sales	0	0	1	4	5

F. Land rental markets (internal only)

1. Occurrence of pseudorents	0	1	1	1	3
2. Occurrence of tax rents	0	0	2	4	6
3. Occurrence of real rents	0	0	4	7	11
4. Real land rents amount to 5% or more of agricultural production	0	0	0	6	6

[a] The data come from Appendix A, Series 23 through 36. In cases where no information about the variable is available for a given society, I have arbitrarily coded the variable as .5; and for this reason 3.5 of the societies in the 15 societies with the highest level of economic development have external market exchange. For the following tables, the cases where no data are available are omitted from analysis unless otherwise noted.

[b] Coded only if 5% or more of produced goods are exchanged in the designated type of market.

[c] Coded only if 5% or more of total workers' services are purchased in the designated type of market.

exchange is far from perfect, so that we still have much to explain and can fruitfully introduce additional variables into the analysis of determinants.

With regard to Polanyi's proposition that market exchange of food is suppressed in "primitive and archaic society," the data suggest that he is quite wrong, for such trade can be found in even quite primitive economies.

DETERMINANTS OF THE GOODS MARKET

Empirical testing of the various propositions about the determinants of the internal goods market turned out to be very straightforward, for few difficulties were encountered in obtaining suitable indices or codes for the proposed explanatory variables. For testing the "alternative paths to wealth" hypothesis linking the presence of market exchange to marriage form and female participation in subsistence production, problems arise in calculating the latter variable. The actual estimate was made in three steps: First, I estimated the relative proportion of food originating from various types of subsistence activities (i.e., hunting, gathering, fishing, herding, and farming); then I estimated in a rough manner the relative share of work hours in each of these activities that was carried out by women; finally, I calculated a weighted average of these relative shares of work hours, using as weights the relative proportion of food originating from the various types of subsistence activities.[54] In order to check my rough estimates against those of others, I correlated them with a similar type of index that was derived from data from the *Ethnographic Atlas* and found a statistically significant relationship between the two series.[55]

For analysis of external trade, few difficulties arose in devising suitable explanatory variables. The population variable was in most cases supplied in the various ethnographies. The variable representing contact with the West created certain problems since contact with Western traders usually indicated external trade and thus gave rise to certain tautological features in the variable. However, since the presence of Western traders does not necessarily imply external trade amounting to more than 5% of production, and since contact with the West also included extensive missionary contact or Western governmental

[54]For calculation of the relative proportion of food originating from various types of subsistence activities, I used calorie estimates or, when these were not available, rough estimates of the relative weights of the different types of foods. For calculation of the relative hours of work by men and women in these activities I assumed that the family consisted only of one husband and one wife.

[55]The 1972 version of the *Ethnographic Atlas* (computer cards obtained from the Department of Anthropology, University of Pittsburgh) contains estimates of the relative proportion of food originating from various types of subsistence activities (Card EA-1, columns 6–10) and rough estimates of female labor force participation (Card EA-2, columns 18–26). For the rating "females alone or almost alone" I assigned a score of 100%; for "females appreciably more," 75%; for "equal participation," 50%; for "males appreciably more," 25%; for "males alone or almost alone," 0%. For several societies the *Ethnographic Atlas* had no estimations for female participation for a particular activity, in which case I substituted my own rating; if several estimates were missing, I dropped the society from the comparison. The R^2 between our ratings for 57 societies is .45, which is statistically significant at the .05 level. On the whole, my ratings indicate greater female participation (by roughly 10 percentage points) than the ratings of the *Ethnographic Atlas*.

contact, I feel that it is legitimate to include such a contact variable into the analysis.

For the analysis of total trade (internal + external) I used as independent variables those variables which played a role for the two components alone. These were then culled so that only the statistically significant variables re-

ABLE 5.2

Determinants of the Markets for Goods[a]

Internal market exchange

. $IME = -.3250 + .0138*ED - .2643*PG + .0095*WSP$ $R^2 = .3402$
      (.0031)   (.1098)   (.0035) $n = 60; PCP = 76.67\%$

External market exchange

. $EME = .5586 - .0042ED$ $R^2 = .0212$
      (.0039) $n = 55; PCP = 45.45\%$

. $EME = 1.4385 + .0104*ED - .2845*PO + .4632*CW$ $R^2 = .4305$
      (.0049)   (.0644)   (.1220) $n = 55; PCP = 80.00\%$

Total market exchange

. $TME = .4717 + .0080*ED$ $R^2 = .0953$
      (.0032) $n = 60; PCP = 76.67\%$

. $TME = 1.1023 + .0169*ED - .1680*PO + .3032*CW - .2685*PG$ $R^2 = .3812$
      (.0046)   (.0602)   (.1103)   (.0965) $n = 60; PCP = 81.67\%$

Key:

IME = Internal market exchange accounts for distribution of 5% or more of all produced goods (1 = yes; 0 = no) [mean = .4000].

EME = External market exchange accounts for exchange of 5% or more of all produced goods (1 = yes; 0 = no) [mean = .4364].

TME = Total (internal + external) market exchange accounts for 5% or more of all produced goods (1 = yes; 0 = no) [mean = .7167].

ED = Rank on economic development scale (1 = lowest; 60 = highest) [mean = 30.50 when $n = 60$; mean = 29.00 when $n = 55$].

PG = Society has more than occasional polygyny (i.e., polygyny is a quantitatively important marriage form) (1 = yes; 0 = no) [mean = .4500].

WSP = Percentage of subsistence production carried out by women [mean = 40.70].

PO = Population of total society [mean = 5.117 when $n = 60$; mean = 5.000 when $n = 55$].
     2 = under 100   5 = 10,000–99,999   8 = 10,000,000 and over
     3 = 100–999   6 = 100,000–999,999
     4 = 1000–9999   7 = 1,000,000–9,999,999

CW = Contact with the West (1 = significant contact, e.g., traders, missionaries, many visitors, colonists, etc.; 0 = no significant contact) [mean = .2667 when $n = 60$; mean = .2545 when $n = 55$].

R^2 = Coefficient of determination.

n = Size of sample.

PCP = Percentage of correct predictions.

( ) = Standard error.

* = t statistic for calculated regression coefficient is over the acceptable limit (2.25) defined in Chapter 1.

[a]Cases for which data are missing are omitted from the regressions, a treatment different from that employed in Table 5.1. The data come from Appendix A, Series 3, 8, 11, 22, 24, 25, 26, and 69. Logit regressions are presented in Appendix B.1 and yield very similar results.

mained. The results of the regression analysis are presented in Table 5.2. The logit regression calculations, which yield very similar results and which are used as the basis of further calculations in this chapter, are presented in Appendix B.1.

As the evolutionary hypothesis presented in the preceding discussion predicts, the presence of internal market exchange is directly related to the level of economic development; as the "alternative paths to wealth" hypothesis suggests, the presence of internal market exchange is directly related to the importance of subsistence production carried out by women and inversely proportional to the presence of a socially significant degree of polygyny. Other hypotheses relating such market exchange to variables such as the unit of observation, the presence of lineages, and so forth are not validated.

Additional insight into these results can be gained by glancing at those cases where differences between predictions and observed results (i.e., the regression residuals) are the greatest. For this discussion I use the results of the logit regressions, but practically the same results occur for the least squares regressions. Of the eight greatest prediction errors, four concern societies for which the data were rated as "uncertain" before the regressions were calculated. (These cases are specified in Appendix A.) Two societies with very low relative levels of economic development for which internal trade is coded but which (according to the regression calculations) I predict should not have such trade are the Copper Eskimo of northern Canada and the Yahgan of Tierra del Fuego at the tip of South America. Both societies were relatively nomadic and traveled about in small groups; neither had unilineal kin structures or very much contact either with the West or other societies. Moreover, neither society had the close-knittedness of large groups, which is often (but falsely) associated with all primitive societies and which, allegedly, directs distribution toward reciprocal exchange or various types of transfers. And both conducted considerable amounts of barter, particularly for handicraft items, whenever small groups met other groups of the same society. Explanations for the other type of prediction error—where market exchange is predicted from the formulas but not observed—are more difficult to find. However, in several cases the societies lived in very close contact with other societies, so that external trade appears to crowd out internal trade.

Turning to external trade, we see that the simple evolutionist hypothesis is incorrect: External trade is not related strongly to the level of economic development until we hold other factors constant (formula 3, Table 5.2). As predicted, external trade is positively related to contact with the West and inversely related to the population of the total society. (A slight statistical difficulty arises in these calculations because the economic development variable and the population variable are somewhat correlated with each other; this should not, however, greatly affect the interpretation below.) What the regression formula does not show are the important differences in the manner in which the contact and trade with the West has influenced the economy of the primitive society. Certain highly primitive societies such as the Naskapi of Labrador carried on trade with the West through infrequent visits to Western trading posts, so that long periods of time elapsed before Western culture had much influence on these people. On the other hand, cultural disintegration occurred quickly in some societies when such trading contact occurred, even when Western political and economic power was exercised in relatively benign ways. In short, the regression analysis explains certain quantitative, but not qualitative, differences in external trade.

If we glance at the most important prediction errors (again the logit regressions are used for this discussion), we see that of the eight societies with the largest regression residuals (differences between observed and predicted results), three out of these eight occur for societies for which the data were rated as uncertain before the regressions were run (these are noted in Appendix A). Two of the four societies in this group of eight for which external trade is falsely predicted to be relatively unimportant (namely, the Alorese of Indonesia and the Toba of northern Argentina) were in quite close geographical proximity with other primitive societies; and three out of the four societies in this group of eight for which external trade is falsely predicted to be important (namely, the Aweikóma of Brazil, the Copper Eskimo of northern Canada, and the Tikopians of the western Pacific) were relatively isolated from other primitive societies.

A final step in the analysis of goods markets is to look at the presence of market exchange without distinguishing whether such exchange is internal or external. It seems most reasonable to use the individual determinants of the two different types of exchange in the regression experiments, and the results are presented in formulas 4 and 5 in Table 5.2. The results confirm such an approach, for only the calculated regression coefficient for the percentage of subsistence production carried out by women appears to lose statistical significance even though its predicted sign is still maintained. Of the eight societies for which the greatest prediction errors are made, the data for a majority (in both the logit and least squares regression) were classified as uncertain before the regressions were calculated.

Several other matters concerning the determinants of market exchange can now be cleared up quickly. It can be shown by a similar type of regression analysis that a variable indicating the presence of market exchange of food is related to the degree of economic development and, to a much lesser extent, to some of the other determinants of the goods markets. Furthermore, a variable indicating the type of market (where "no marketplace" is coded 0; "occasional marketplaces" is coded 1; "frequent use of marketplaces of other societies" is coded 2; and "permanent marketplaces" is coded 3) also reveals similar relationships.

Although the hypotheses relating the presence of market exchange of goods to the level of economic development, to the role of women in the accumulation of wealth, to the contact of the society with the West, and to the population of the society appear to receive a certain validation, two additional matters deserve brief mention. It could be argued that the results arise because the direction of causation between the independent and dependent variables is in the opposite direction to that which I have posited. Given the particular variables under consideration, this does not appear very plausible. It should also be pointed out that although the calculated regression formulas show quite satisfactory coefficients of determination, we are still far from explaining the presence or absence of a market for goods in every society. The PCP data show that the regression formulas in Table 5.2 lead to correct predictions on these matters in roughly three-fourths to four-fifths of all cases.

DETERMINANTS OF THE LABOR MARKET

The analysis of the market for labor turns out to be very much less complicated than the analysis of the goods markets. This is because most of the hypotheses which were tested did not prove very satisfactory. The positive results are presented in Table 5.3.

For the presence of an internal market for skilled labor, the only statistically significant results were obtained by using the simple evolutionist's hypothesis (formula 1). Tests of other hypotheses discussed in the theoretical section were negative, and attempts to find other variables providing significant explanatory power (e.g., community size) proved fruitless. Part of the difficulty arose because of uncertainties in coding this labor force variable: In many cases the primary skilled workers whose services are purchased in some type of market transaction are part-time priests, shaman, and others of the religion and healing professions, so that the "5% criterion" is difficult to apply.

Some additional insights can be gained by looking at the prediction errors (again the logit regressions are used in this discussion). Of the eight societies with the largest differences between predicted and actual results, the data for four were rated as uncertain before the regressions were run (Appendix A). Among these eight societies are some such as the Toba of northern Argentina, for which we predict the absence of a labor market for skilled workers but in which we seem to find such a market present. The Toba had a number of shaman who charged extremely high fees (in food) but then later redistributed these fees to the entire community, so that, at one level of analysis, the skilled labor market can be considered part of a broader redistributive mechanism. Such a mechanism appeared in a considerably less dramatic form in several other of the eight societies for which a similar prediction error is made. Among the societies in this group of eight for which we predict but do not find a skilled labor market are the Serbs of Yugoslavia. The Serbs had only recently evolved from a herding society when the sample was taken and used a simple type of agriculture; in addition, priests, shaman, curers and the like were numerically unimportant. Thus, among the most strikingly divergent societies from the generalization contained in the regression analysis, a heightened or diminished role of religious leaders seems to have an important influence on the results.

TABLE 5.3

Determinants of the Markets for Labor[a]

Internal market for skilled labor
1. $IMSL = -.0784 + .0146 *ED$ $R^2 = .2749$
                    (.0031) $n = 60; PCP = 71.67\%$

Internal market for unskilled labor
2. $IMUL = .0098 + .0068 *ED$ $R^2 = .0812$
                   (.0030) $n = 60; PCP = 78.33\%$[b]
3. $IMUL = -.1171 + .0081 *ED + .5740 *H$ $R^2 = .3256$
                 (.0026)   (.1263) $n = 60; PCP = 83.33\%$

Internal market for skilled and unskilled labor
4. $IML = -.1085 + .0160 *ED + .5854 *H$ $R^2 = .4302$
              (.0029)   (.1406) $n = 60; PCP = 80.00\%$

Total (internal + external) market for skilled and unskilled labor
5. $TML = -.1034 + .0171 *ED + .5512 *H$ $R^2 = .4519$
             (.0028)   (.1382) $n = 60; PCP = 78.33\%$

Key:
IMSL = Skilled labor purchased through some type of internal market accounts for 5% or more of the total labor outside the home (1 = yes; 0 = no) [mean = .3667].
IMUL = Unskilled labor purchased through some type of internal market accounts for 5% or more of the total labor outside the home (1 = yes; 0 = no) [mean = .2167].
IML = Skilled and unskilled labor purchased through some type of internal market accounts for 5% or more of the total labor outside the home (1 = yes; 0 = no) [mean = .4667].
TML = Skilled and unskilled labor purchased through some type of internal or external market accounts for 5% or more of the total labor outside the home (1 = yes; 0 = no) [mean = .5000].
ED = Rank on economic development scale (1 = lowest; 60 = highest) [mean = 30.50].
H = The most important sources of food come from herding (i.e., meat and dairy products) (1 = yes; 0 = no) [mean = .1500].
R^2 = Coefficient of determination.
n = Size of sample.
PCP = Percentage of correct predictions.
( ) = Standard error.
* = t statistic for calculated regression coefficient is over the acceptable limit (2.25) defined in Chapter 1.
[a]The data come from Appendix A, Series 4, 22, 28, 29, 30, and 32. Logit regressions are presented in Appendix B.1 and show similar results.
[b]No cases of markets are predicted.

For the presence of an internal market for unskilled labor, the simple evolutionary hypothesis performs poorly (formula 2). However, if we take into account the hypothesis about the influence of herding in such a market, we obtain very much more impressive regression results (formula 3).

Glancing at the eight societies for which prediction errors are greatest (in the logit regressions), we find four societies for which the data were rated as "uncertain" before the regressions were carried out. Among the eight societies with the largest prediction errors are the nomadic herding societies of the Khalka Mongols of Mongolia and the Tuareg of the Sahara; it is quite unclear to me why these two societies did not develop the predicted labor markets for herders.

In regression equations 4 and 5 in Table 5.3, I have combined the various types of labor markets; the hypotheses that appear validated are those that have been discussed individually for the unskilled and skilled labor markets. I have not made any separate analysis of societies with external labor markets (in which workers in the society sell their labor to other societies), for only one society in my sample—the Yaqui of Sonora, Mexico—appears to have such a market to an important extent. Again, many of the prediction errors are for societies for which the original data were classified as uncertain before the regressions were calculated. A number of other regression experiments were carried out to see if other causal variables for the dependent variables in Table 5.3 could be isolated, but these proved fruitless.[56]

The negative results of testing these other hypotheses are disturbing because of all the types of distribution examined in this book, a tautological relationship between one important explanatory variable (the level of development) and one variable to be explained (skilled labor) seems most apparent. This arises because an important component of my measure of the level of economic development is the extent of the division of labor, which is particularly manifested by the presence of various types of skilled labor. Although the extent of the tautology can not be measured, this means the most important discovery presented in Table 5.3 is the relationship between unskilled labor and the presence of a herding society, a relationship for which no tautological elements enter.

An important and fortunate negative result in the various regression experiments is that the inclusion of a variable representing the presence of a goods market accounting for distribution of 5% or more of total production did not prove to be a significant explanatory variable or to greatly affect the other results. This means that, *ceteris paribus,* the existence of labor markets is independent of the existence of goods markets in a society; since market activity in one sphere does not seem to encourage market activity in the other sphere, the determinants of both types of exchange must be analyzed separately.

DETERMINANTS OF THE CREDIT MARKET

Although the presence of interest rates in primitive societies has caught the imagination of a number of economists, the topic is extremely difficult to

[56]The polygyny variable was one on which I focused particular attention. One could argue that this variable should be positively related to the presence of labor markets since the older men who were unable to obtain wives (e.g., because they had little land) might simply hire themselves out; on the other hand, the "alternative paths to wealth" approach would suggest a negative relationship. Actually, the latter seems to prevail, but the calculated coefficient of the polygyny variable appeared interesting only in one regression (the total internal labor market). Since it added very little to the coefficient of determination, it is omitted from presentation in Table 5.3.

analyze empirically. As noted in the discussion concerning coding problems, considerable problems arose in trying to determine whether this phenomenon was present, and in none of the societies in the sample did such payments appear to amount to a very large percentage of total income.

Other difficulties arose in trying to test Böhm-Bawerk's approach to the presence of interest by determining whether interest is correlated with capital intensiveness of production. To derive such a variable, I adopted the following procedure: All hunting and gathering societies are coded as noncapital intensive; fishing societies are coded as capital intensive only if fishing in the society was carried out primarily in boats; all herding societies are coded as capital intensive (since flocks represent a considerable accumulation of capital); and agricultural societies are coded as capital intensive only if the societies used two out of three common capital intensive agricultural techniques (namely, plow agriculture, irrigation, or terracing).

Given the nature of these coding problems, we should not expect very high coefficients of determination in the calculated regressions, and such expectations are not disappointed. The various hypotheses discussed in the preceding theoretical section were tested, and the only ones which appeared validated by the data are presented in Table 5.4.

The predictions that the presence of an interest rate is directly related to the level of economic development and to the capital intensiveness of production appear confirmed. It is important to note that the presence of an interest rate appears independent of the presence either of an internal commercial money or a goods market (holding the level of economic development and the capital

TABLE 5.4

Determinants of Markets for Credit[a]

1. $PI = .1259 + .0113*ED$	$R^2 = .1577$
$\quad\quad\quad\quad (.0036)$	$n = 56; PCP = 67.86\%$
2. $PI = .1249 + .0082\ ED + .3124*CI$	$R^2 = .2285$
$\quad\quad\quad\quad (.0037)\quad\quad (.1416)$	$n = 56; PCP = 71.43\%$

Key:
PI = Presence of an interest rate (1 = yes; 0 = no) [mean = .4643].
ED = Rank on economic development scale (1 = lowest; 60 = highest) [mean = 30.01].
CI = Capital intensiveness of production (1 = relatively capital intensive production methods; 0 = relatively non capital intensive production methods) [mean = .3036].
R^2 = Coefficient of determination.
n = Size of sample.
PCP = Percentage of correct predictions.
( ) = Standard error.
* = t statistic for calculated regression coefficient is over the acceptable limit (2.25) defined in Chapter 1.
   [a]Cases for which data are missing are omitted from the regressions. The data come from Appendix A, Series 17, 22, and 33. Logit regressions are presented in Appendix B.1 and show similar results.

intensiveness of production constant). No other reasonable causal factors un-derlying the presence of an interest rate could be found.[57]

Although the coefficient of determination is low in formula 2 of Table 5.4, correct predictions concerning the presence of interest are made in roughly two-thirds of the societies in the sample. When we examine the eight societies for which the greatest prediction errors are made, some of the difficulties in the analysis of the presence of interest become clearer. The prediction errors (in the logit regressions) do not appear for many of the societies for which the data are particularly uncertain (only two out of the eight fall in this category) but reflect very special circumstances.

Among these eight societies the absence of interest is predicted for the Siane of the New Guinea highlands and the Naskapi of Labrador, but such a phe-nomenon is actually found. However, among the Siane the only interest pay-ment occurs when a pig is borrowed for mating purposes, so this interest rate lies on the border between a pseudo and a real interest rate. Among the Naskapi there is no interest rate on any credit transaction, even of money, except for goods lent in order for the borrower to obtain a canoe. Thus, in both societies the interest phenomenon appears only for a narrow range of transac-tions connected with investment. Among these eight societies with largest prediction errors, interest does not appear in the Rif of Morocco society when, according to the formula, we would expect the presence of this phenomenon. However, in this society there was a strong religious (Moslem) injunction against the charging of an interest rate, so the ethnographer might not have been able to observe transactions involving interest easily. For the Wolof of Senegal and Gambia (which does not number among the eight with the largest prediction errors) a similar circumstance probably arose.

DETERMINANTS OF LAND AND LAND RENTAL MARKETS

Among the societies in the sample land and land rental markets did not appear among hunting, gathering, or fishing societies and, among herding societies, appear only in several that are nomadic and that have land dealings with nonnomadic peoples. Since it should be clear that land and land rental markets do not appear likely in societies where land is not a factor of produc-tion (and, hence, is not scarce in an obvious sense), I limit myself in this analysis only to analyzing such markets among agricultural societies.

Testing of the various hypotheses that are discussed in the theoretical section above proved relatively simple. As noted previously, few difficulties arose in the coding of the presence of land and land rental markets. The "alternative paths to wealth" hypothesis, which leads us to predict that the presence of land

---

[57]In carrying out the regression experiments I made a programming error and found that inclusion of a variable indicating the pattern of postmarital residence raised the coefficient of determination considerably. Since there is no theoretical reason why, *ceteris paribus*, an interest rate should be associated with patrilocal residence, and the absence of such an interest rate with matrilocal residence, this correlation was judged to be spurious.

and land rental markets is inversely related to the presence of polygynous marriage forms and also to the relative importance of female subsistence work, could be easily tested since the data were already available. Certain problems did arise in devising a suitable measure indicating the scarcity of land. In Appendix C.3 I describe the construction of such an index, taking two factors into account: the population density and also the length of time that a piece of land was permitted to lie fallow before it was planted again. The regressions using these variables are presented in Table 5.5.

The regression results for the land rental market are almost too good to be true. As predicted, land rentals occur in a direct relation to the level of economic development and to the scarcity of land and in an inverse relation to the presence of polygyny and the percentage of subsistence production carried out by women. Since the calculated regression coefficients have standard errors above the acceptable limit (except for the female subsistence production variable, where the calculated coefficient is a shade below the limit), we can consider that these hypotheses receive impressive confirmation. Prediction errors for the presence of rent appear in only about one-fifth of the cases, which is also impressive.

Turning to the eight societies with the largest prediction errors (no logit results are available, so the formula in Table 5.5 is used), we see that two out of the three societies for which the value of the predicted dependent variable is below the observed dependent variable actually have land rents, but not to the degree predicted. Of the five societies for which the dependent variable is predicted to have a value which turns out to be considerably higher than observed, two (the Dogon of Mali and the Maori of New Zealand) have pseudorents.

We can dispose of other types of land rents quite quickly. The data in Table 5.1 indicate that only three societies in the entire sample appear to have pseudorents. Since formula 1 in Table 5.5 predicts that two of these "should" have real land rents instead, it appears likely that such pseudorents are a transitional form between a no-rent and a rent situation. Tax rents pose a more difficult explanatory problem. The only variable I could find that seems related to the presence of such rents is an index of political inequality. Such an index does not, of course, shed much light on the situation because of the tautological element between the two variables.

For the analysis of the presence of the buying and selling of land, the results are less spectacular. In testing the "alternative paths to wealth" hypothesis and also the land scarcity proposition, I found that the posited causal variables had the correct signs, but only two—the level of economic development and the percentage of subsistence production carried out by women—had calculated regressions coefficients with t statistics above the acceptable limit. It is noteworthy that other hypothesized causal variables such as the presence of strong lineages, the presence of goods markets, or the use of commercial money had no statistical influence on the dependent variable.

TABLE 5.5

Determinants of Markets for Land and Land Rentals in Agricultural Societies[a]

Land rental market

1. $LR = .1793 + .0238*ED + .0970*SLDC - .5213*PG - .0156 \ WSP$

   $\quad\quad\quad\quad (.0066) \quad\quad (.0382) \quad\quad\quad (.1968) \quad\quad (.0070)$

   $R^2 = .6212$

   $n = 36; PCP = 80.56\%$

Land market

2. $LS = -.4645 + .0235*ED$

   $\quad\quad\quad\quad\quad (.0079)$

   $R^2 = .2070$

   $n = 36; PCP = 63.89\%$

3. $LS = .6411 + .0177*ED - .0185*WSP$

   $\quad\quad\quad\quad (.0077) \quad\quad (.0074)$

   $R^2 = .3328$

   $n = 36; PCP = 75.00\%$

Key:

LR = Occurrence of land rents (0 = no land rents; 1 = land rents occur but are not economically important; 2 = land rents account for 5% or more of total agricultural production) [mean = .4772].

LS = Occurrence of land sales (0 = do not occur; 1 = occur but infrequently; 2 = occur and relatively frequently) [mean = .4722].

ED = Rank on economic development scale (1 = lowest; 60 = highest) [mean = 39.85].

$SLDC$ = Scarcity of land as measured by a scale taking into account population density and crop rotation system (Appendix C.3) (0 = land not scarce; 6 = land very scarce) [mean = 3.222]

PG = Society has more than occasional polygyny (i.e., polygyny is a quantitatively important marriage form) (0 = no; 1 = yes) [mean = .4444].

R^2 = Coefficient of determination.

n = Size of sample.

PCP = Percentage of correct predictions.

( ) = Standard error.

* = t statistic for calculated regression coefficient is over the acceptable limit (2.25) defined in Chapter 1.

[a]The data come from Appendix A, Series 8, 13, 22, 34, 36, and 69. Agricultural societies are defined as those in which the value of the variable in Series 4 is 1 or 2. No logit regressions are calculated since the dependent variables have three values.

These results are difficult to interpret. Rather than consider the women's subsistence production variable as an indicator of the "alternative paths to wealth" hypothesis, it could be argued that it really reflects a family structural situation. That is, only in societies which have relatively high levels of economic development and where men carry out most of the subsistence production do rights in land become sufficiently "individualized" that commercialization of such rights is possible. Although conjectures about the dynamics underlying such a situation can be easily made, I see no easy way in which these propositions can be sorted out and tested in a rigorous fashion.

Unfortunately, examining the eight societies with the largest prediction errors (again the formula in Table 5.5 is used) provides little assistance in solving these problems. For six out of the eight the data are reasonably certain; and the societies in the groups with high positive or negative prediction errors appear quite heterogeneous.

DEVELOPMENTAL RELATIONSHIPS OF DIFFERENT TYPES OF
MARKET EXCHANGE

Do goods markets appear at lower levels of economic development than labor markets? Do internal goods markets emerge from external goods markets or vice versa? How do credit and land rental markets fit into an evolutionary schema? Since the various types of market exchanges appear to have different sets of determinants, we can not directly compare the various regression formulas to answer such questions. Fortunately, two quite different analytic methods can be applied to these problems.

One technique (designated hereafter as "Technique A" or the "*ceteris paribus* technique") involves using the regression formulas already calculated to derive the determinants of the various types of market exchange. By placing in these formulas the average value of all of the independent variables except that for the level of economic development, we can easily determine the lowest level of development which would lead to the prediction that the particular market exchange would be present (i.e., which level of economic development would yield more than a fifty–fifty chance that the dependent variable is over .5 when all other explanatory values are held at their average value).

A second technique (designated hereafter as "Technique B" or the "*mutatis mutandis* technique") involves lining up the various societies along the developmental scale and seeing at what levels particular types of market exchange appear. Data for this technique can be found in Table 5.1. For this technique no attention is paid to the other causal factors.

It must be emphasized that these two methods for determining relative developmental levels of emergence may not necessarily yield the same answer because they are focused on somewhat different questions. In Technique A all factors are held constant except the level of development; in Technique B all factors other than the level of development are not taken into consideration. If it turns out that factors other than the level of economic development also play

TABLE 5.6

Emergence Levels of Development of Different Types of Market Exchange[a]

Type of market exchange	Technique A: Holding other causal factors constant		Technique B: Relative frequency in different developmental groups (number)	
	Corresponding formula numbers	Emergence level of economic development (rank of society)	15 societies at lowest level	15 societies at second lowest level
Internal goods market	B5-2-1	40	3	3
External goods market	B5-2-3	37 (49)	5 (2)	12 (7)
*Total goods market	5-2-5	18 (23)	7 (5)	12 (10)
Internal market for skilled labor	B5-3-1	41	1	4
Internal market for unskilled labor	B5-3-3	53	1	4
Internal market for labor	B5-3-4	34	2	7
*Total market for labor	B5-3-5	32	2	7
*Credit market	B5-4-2	34	2	6.5
*Land rental market (value = 1)	5-5-1	42	0 [0]	1 [0]
*Land market (value = 1)	5-5-3	42	0 [0]	2 [1]

[a]The emergence levels are numbered from 1 (the society with the lowest rank on the development scale) to 60 (the society with the highest rank on this scale). The asterisks are explained in the text.

For Technique A, the first two numbers in the formula number refer to the table; the last number refers to the formula number in the specific table; and the B refers to whether the logit regression formula in Appendix B.1 is used. No logit regressions are available for the land and land rental markets because the dependent variable has more than two values; and for the total goods market, the logit algorithm which I used did not appear to converge within a reasonable number of iterations. The emergence levels using the logit and ordinary least squares regressions are very similar for almost all cases. The numbers in parentheses for the external goods market and the total goods market designate the developmental level of emergence when the variable designating contact with the West is valued at zero (a technique discussed in the text). For technique B the data come from Table 5.1 and include those few societies for which a determination of the dependent variable could not be made by adopting the expedient of valuing this variable at .5 in such cases. The data in parentheses for the goods markets represent the relative frequencies when those societies for which trade with the West is the prime source of external trade are removed. The data in brackets for the land markets represent the relative frequencies when external land markets (i.e., land dealings between members of the society and

an important role, and if some of these other causal factors are more likely to be found in societies at a low level of economic development, then the derived "emergence level" might be much lower using Technique B than Technique A. The results of the analysis of developmental relationships using both techniques are presented in Table 5.6.

The easiest way to proceed in the analysis of this important table is to look first at the major types of markets (which are preceded by an asterisk) and later to turn to the various components. However, one preliminary note of explanation must be given. As noted above, a determinant of the external goods market and also the total goods market is contact with the West. If we wish to use the cross-section results for generalizing about events over time, this influence must be eliminated. For Technique A this involves merely placing the value of the variable indicating Western contact at zero (rather than at its average value) when calculating the emergence level. For Technique B, this involves removing from the sample those societies for which Western contact appears to be the most important determinant of external trade. The results of these calculations are placed in parentheses. (The data in brackets for the land markets are explained below.)

Both Techniques A and B show that the goods market appears at earlier levels of economic development than other types of markets. At somewhat higher levels of economic development both the labor market and the credit market appear to emerge. Finally, at still higher levels of development we begin to find land and land rental markets. Such a derived developmental sequence appears to validate the conventional wisdom about such matters that has been discussed in the theoretical section of this chapter. However, as I noted in this theoretical discussion, the predictions by some about the developmental sequence appeared to be correct empirically but incorrect theoretically (e.g., the proposition of Phelps-Brown that the goods market arose before labor markets because the workers had to be able to buy something with their wages, a conjecture which does not take into account the possibility of wages in kine).

In turning to examine the components of various types of market exchange, one seeming difficulty appears to arise. For Technique A the total market for goods and also for labor emerge at lower levels of economic development than their individual components. This occurs because most societies at the lowest levels of economic development that have these markets have only one type of goods market or one type of labor market. Since the total number of societies at these low developmental levels that have at least one type of market is much greater than the number of societies having any particular type of market, the slope of the calculated regression line is influenced as to yield the results presented in the table.

As noted in the theoretical discussion, a good deal of controversy has arisen concerning the question of whether external or internal goods markets arise at lower levels of development; the results presented in Table 5.6 support neither position. Part of the difficulty arises because neither side of the dispute considered very carefully the role of other causal factors underlying these different types of goods markets. The influence of these other factors provides the complicating factor when we try to interpret the results from the table.

According to Technique A, internal goods markets appear to emerge at roughly the same level of economic development as external goods markets if we do not worry about the influence of contact with the West on external trade. If we exclude the influence of this Western trade, it appears as though internal goods markets emerge at a somewhat lower level than external goods markets. Technique B leads to an even more mixed picture: Internal goods markets appear somewhat less frequent at lower levels of development than external goods markets; however, if we exclude from consideration those societies whose external trade is primarily due to Western contact, then internal goods markets appear more or less frequent, depending on whether the lowest 15 or 30 societies on the development scale are examined.

From such contradictory results we see that the concepts of "origins" or "emergence" are considerably more complicated than they appear at first sight. "Emergence," defined in terms of holding all causal factors constant except the level of development (and excluding the influence of contact with the West), suggests that internal goods markets precede external goods markets on the development scale. "Emergence," defined in terms of simple relative frequencies at different levels of development (and excluding the influence of contact with the West), gives mixed results, depending on the cutoff limit chosen for the sample.

From this confusing picture one extremely important negative conclusion can be drawn: No clear evidence supports hypotheses that external goods markets arise at lower developmental levels than internal goods markets or vice versa. A tentative hypothesis combining the results of Technique A and Technique B would be that external trade occurs earlier on the development scale than internal trade but that the number of societies with such trade does not reach a sufficient level to permit a fifty–fifty chance of correctly predicting such external exchange until a developmental level is reached at which internal goods markets appear in a predominant number of societies.

Difficulties similar to those encountered in the goods market appear when we examine the different components of the labor market. Technique A suggests that the market for unskilled labor appears at considerably higher levels of economic development than for skilled labor. Technique B suggests that the two different labor markets emerge at roughly the same levels of economic development. The explanation for this state of affairs appears simple: Unskilled labor markets appear not only at high levels of development but also in herding societies at relatively low levels of development; emergence defined in terms of *ceteris paribus* focuses less attention on these particular herding societies than emergence defined in terms of *mutatis mutandis*.

Although the credit market appears to emerge at roughly the same level of economic development as labor markets, it should be emphasized that the credit market is defined merely by the presence of an interest rate phenomenon, while the labor market is defined in terms of a 5% cutoff limit. If the credit market is defined in terms of relatively important transactions bearing interest charges, its level of emergence would be considerably higher.

Land markets and land rental markets seem to emerge at roughly the same levels of economic development, at least with regard to their initial appearance. Since Technique A is used only with data concerning internal land markets (i.e., markets for the sale or rental of land between members of the society), the results are not directly comparable with the results of Technique B, which include all land and land rental markets. However, if we exclude such markets between nomadic peoples and peoples of other societies (the results are placed in brackets), our conclusions are not changed. If, however, we define land rental and land sale markets in terms of importance (i.e., for the former, land rents equal to 5% or more of total agricultural production; for the latter, land sales made relatively frequently), then both techniques lead to the conclusion that land rental markets appear at earlier stages of economic development than markets for the buying and selling of land.

Time-Series Tests

Contact with the West does influence at least one type of market transaction in primitive and peasant societies, as I show in Table 5.2. This is a type of "fast" diffusion (defined in Chapter 3) and leads us to wonder if the results presented up to now are influenced by other types of diffusion processes. In order to explore this possibility in a systematic manner, we must employ the statistical technique discussed at length in Chapter 3 that permits us to examine diffusion arising from the slow transfer of cultural traits from one society to its neighbors. The analysis is carried out in three steps; the data for all steps are presented in Table 5.7.

First, it is necessary to calculate the average distances between three groups of pairs of societies: a group where both societies have the particular market exchange under examination; a group where only one society of the pair has the designated market exchange; and a final group where neither of the societies has the market exchange being studied. I omit from these calculations all those societies for which the data do not apply to the latter half of the nineteenth century or for which I do not have additional data on market exchange for the society for this nineteenth-century period (a procedure also followed in the other chapters as well).

In all cases there appears to be a greater clustering of societies with the market exchange (Group K) than societies where one member of the pair has the exchange and the other does not (Group L). In most cases this clustering

TABLE 5.7

Average Distances between Groups of Pairs of Societies for Making Diffusion Tests[a]

Type of market exchange	Formula number	Total	Between societies with and without designated market exchange			Between societies with and without predicted designated market exchange			Between societies with and without designated market exchange after taking causal variables into account			
			K	L	M	X	Y	Z	P	P'	Q	R
Internal goods market	B5-2-1	5519 [1964] (1326)	5152 [2104] (231)	5560 [1953] (660)	5652 [1878] (435)	4316 [2330] (120)	5605 [1883] (576)	5670 [1881] (630)	5670 [1769] (112)	5954 [1625] (28)	4393 [2437] (28)	5544 [1851] (16)
External goods market	B5-2-3	5531 [1965] (1176)	5488 [1973] (210)	5709 [1829] (588)	5279 [2128] (378)	5519 [1909] (171)	5737 [1801] (570)	5266 [2150] (435)	5472 [2046] (90)	5880 [1837] (15)	5540 [1951] (60)	5492 [1980] (24)
Total goods market	5-2-5	5519 [1964] (1326)	5450 [1986] (703)	5629 [1899] (532)	5415 [2129] (91)	5405 [2009] (630)	5708 [1819] (576)	5217 [2288] (120)	5811 [1719] (165)	5680 [1842] (10)	5749 [1745] (99)	5907 [1774] (15)
Internal market for skilled labor	B5-3-1	5519 [1964] (1326)	5183 [2120] (153)	5522 [1953] (612)	5609 [1921] (561)	3355 [2047] (105)	5793 [1749] (555)	5632 [1913] (666)	5428 [2015] (80)	5760 [1849] (45)	3255 [2076] (56)	5720 [1865] (70)
Internal market for unskilled labor	B5-3-3	5519 [1964] (1326)	4871 [2180] (55)	5520 [1896] (451)	5562 [1978] (820)	4921 [1979] (28)	5438 [2015] (352)	5567 [1940] (946)	5170 [2089] (30)	3860 [2303] (15)	4527 [1995] (15)	3644 [2176] (18)
Internal market for labor	B5-3-4	5519 [1964] (1326)	5135 [2121] (253)	5678 [1836] (667)	5499 [2031] (406)	4228 [2278] (276)	6096 [1425] (672)	5438 [2079] (378)	6417 [882] (90)	5040 [2390] (10)	4231 [2280] (108)	6600 [0] (30)

Average distances, standard deviations, and size of sample[b]

Total market for labor	B5-3-5	5519 [1964] (1326)	5172 [2096] (300)	5681 [1841] (675)	5505 [2036] (351)	4392 [2275] (300)	6047 [1490] (675)	5467 [2063] (351)	6321 [1044] (114)	5560 [2085] (15)	4569 [2248] (114)	5611 [1874] (36)
Credit market	B5-4-2	5549 [1942] (1176)	4928 [2170] (276)	5823 [1745] (600)	5573 [1965] (300)	4371 [2264] (190)	5971 [1549] (580)	5498 [2048] (406)	5451 [1908] (140)	5447 [2060] (45)	4826 [2217] (84)	5613 [1932] (60)
Land rental market	5-5-1	5165 [2131] (435)	4522 [2248] (36)	5258 [2029] (189)	5191 [2182] (210)	4716 [2209] (55)	5180 [2084] (209)	5290 [2143] (171)	4850 [2262] (8)	0 [0] (0)	5067 [2034] (24)	6600 [0] (3)
Land market	5-5-3	5165 [2131] (435)	4684 [2264] (55)	5255 [2030] (209)	5209 [2188] (171)	4300 [2252] (66)	5281 [2021] (216)	5374 [2140] (153)	5139 [2160] (18)	6600 [0] (1)	4544 [2013] (27)	6600 [0] (6)

Key:

Group K: All pairs of societies that have the designated type of market exchange.

Group L: All pairs of societies, one of which has and the other of which does not have the designated type of market exchange.

Group M: All pairs of societies that do not have the designated type of market exchange.

Group X: All pairs of societies that the explanatory variables lead us to predict the presence of the designated type of market exchange.

Group Y: All pairs of societies, one of which we predict to have and the other of which we predict not to have the designated type of market exchange.

Group Z: All pairs of societies that the explanatory variables lead us to predict the absence of the designated type of market exchange.

Group P: All pairs of societies, one of which is predicted to have and the other of which is predicted not to have the designated type of market exchange, but both of which actually have the designated type of market exchange.

Group P': All pairs of societies, both of which are predicted not to have the designated type of market exchange, but both of which actually have the designated type of market exchange.

Group Q: All pairs of societies, both of which are predicted to have the designated type of market exchange, but one prediction is incorrect.

Group R: All pairs of societies, one of which is predicted to have and the other of which is predicted not to have the designated type of market exchange, and both predictions are incorrect.

[a] The data used in these calculations come from the sources discussed in previous tables. The formulas preceded by a B indicate that the logit regressions presented in Appendix B.1 are used. No such regressions are made for the land rental and land markets because the dependent variable has more than two values. The ordinary least squares regression is used for the total goods market because of problems of conversion of the logit algorithm. However, using the logit regression B5-2-5 gives practically the same results as that presented in the table.

[b] The standard deviation is enclosed in brackets and the size of sample in parentheses.

appears statistically significant (using a one-tailed test and a .05 level of significance). This is due primarily to the fact that the level of economic development is an important causal variable, and there is a clustering of societies with roughly similar development levels in the sample.

Second, it is necessary to calculate the average distances between the societies that we predict to have the various types of market transactions and also between the pairs of societies, one of which we predict to have such market transactions, the other of which we predict the absence of such exchanges. We find that there is a clustering of societies for which we predict such market exchanges (Subgroup X) for every type of market exchange vis-à-vis the comparison group (Subgroup Y). Again, most of these differences are statistically significant. If we examine the data for the internal market for skilled labor, which has only the level of economic development as its explanatory variable, we see a marked clustering reflecting the fact that throughout the world the primitive and peasant societies within large geographical areas appeared to have somewhat similar levels of economic development.

Such results suggest that the results of the regression analyses in this chapter may have been due to some sort of diffusion phenomenon rather than to the different causal variables which I have isolated. It is, therefore, quite necessary to apply the more sophisticated analysis based on the diffusion-possibility method that is outlined in Chapter 3 to make a conclusive judgment about these matters. This more powerful statistical method requires investigation of the prediction errors of the various regressions to see if they fall in a particular pattern, namely, when we find examples of geographically close societies where we predict one society to have the particular type of market exchange and the other not to have it, but where, in actuality, both societies feature this type of exchange. We compare the average distances of the societies in this subgroup (P) with the average distance between societies where we have reasonably good evidence that diffusion did *not* take place (Subgroup R). Some additional subsidiary tests are also described in Chapter 3.

In applying such a test, one problem arises that deserves brief attention. In certain cases the group of societies that reflect possible diffusion is very small. If the number is less than 5% of the total pairs of societies in the sample, then it seems very likely that diffusion did not occur, and we need pay no further attention to the distances between subsamples. A similar but more difficult problem arises when the comparison subgroup (Subgroup R) is extremely small (for this and the following chapters this is considered to be 30 or less). In such cases it seems most simple to make comparisons between the clustering of the possible diffusion group and the average distance between all the societies in the sample. (Since the number of pairs of societies in Subgroup P is usually less than 10% and almost never more than 15% of the total number of pairs of societies, the amount of bias introduced because the samples overlap is quite small.)

Turning to the data we find no case for which diffusion appears to have played an important role. For a number of different types of market exchange, the number of pairs of societies in the possible diffusion group fall under the 5% limit; and for the other cases, no statistically significant clustering is found vis-à-vis the comparison group. Nor does the application of the subsidiary tests suggest the presence of diffusion to any important degree. Although the exact results of the various tests are not presented, sufficient data are presented in Table 5.7 for the reader to carry out a variety of statistical tests to allay any lingering suspicions.

Thus, although the societies that have the various types of market exchange appear to exhibit some geographical clustering, the analysis of prediction errors leads us to believe that diffusion did not influence the results of the regression analysis. We need, therefore, have no second thoughts about the conclusions of such a regression analysis, at least with regard to problems arising from the "slow" diffusion which can be detected by the statistical tests performed. As noted above, however, "fast" diffusion (as represented by the variable reflecting contact with the West) does influence external market trade and also the total market exchange. It must also be emphasized that I am not arguing "independent invention" of particular types of market exchange, for the different types of market exchange and their causal factors may have diffused together—a process which can not be easily detected either from the data or the currently available ethnographic and historical source materials.

SUMMARY AND CONCLUSIONS

From the mass of theoretical and statistical evidence several quite simple conclusions can be drawn.

First, the general argument of the evolutionists that various types of market exchange are functions of the level of economic development seems generally correct. For every type of market exchange investigated, the level of economic development has a significantly positive relation with the presence of such exchange, although in certain cases this appears only after other variables have been held constant. For the labor markets, however, certain problems of interpretation arise because the level of economic development has been defined partly in terms of the division of labor, which might be reflected in a market for skilled labor.

Second, for almost every type of market exchange, other factors play important causal roles encouraging or inhibiting the presence of such market exchange. The hypothesis about "alternative paths to wealth" successfully links the form of marriage and the relative amount of subsistence production performed by women to the presence of markets for goods and also land rental markets. For these two markets the mechanisms underlying the causal link between such social structural variables and the presence of particular markets are somewhat different; nevertheless, both the theoretical and empirical evidence supported this "alternative paths to wealth" approach. In addition, the principal mode of food production seems to influence several types of market exchange: Other things remaining equal, herding societies seem more likely to feature markets for unskilled labor than other societies, and agricultural societies seem more likely to feature markets for land. Furthermore, the relative scarcities of certain factors of production also seem to play an important causal role: Credit markets appear when there are shortages of capital, and land rental markets appear when there are shortages of land. Several other miscellaneous causal factors are also isolated for other markets.

Third, cultural diffusion, as represented by a variable designating contact with the West, appears to influence the market exchange of goods by affecting external trade. However, the statistical analysis for the detection of "slow diffusion" which is carried out in the previous section suggests that certain other types of diffusion appear not to have played an important causal role.

Fourth, the analysis of the relative levels of economic development at which different types of markets emerge leads to several important conclusions: In general, the market for goods appears to occur at the lowest levels of economic development; the markets for labor and for credit (i.e., the presence of interest) emerge at roughly the same higher levels; and the land and land rental markets generally occur only at still higher levels of development. Because of certain ambiguities in the concept of "emergence," we can not make unqualified statements about the relative levels of emergence of particular components of these different types of market exchange. However, previous dogmatism about such matters as the relative level of emergence of internal and external markets for goods does not appear warranted. This negative conclusion receives some interesting additional support when the origins of money are examined in the next chapter.

Fifth, in trying to isolate the causal factors underlying market exchange, I have had to discard a number of propositions previously considered quite plausible. Of particular importance to note, the existence of labor, credit, land, and land rental markets appear independent of the existence of a goods market, other factors (such as the level of economic development) held constant. Furthermore, none of the markets appears significantly related to various family variables such as the existence of unilineal descent groups (defined in several different ways). The labor, credit, land, and land rental markets are also not related to the existence of money, other factors held constant.

Although this chapter has focused on only a subset of questions that can be asked about the origins and impact of market exchange in primitive and peasant societies, a great deal of ground has been covered. I have tried to show that the causal forces underlying the presence or absence of markets for goods, labor, credit, and land rents can be delineated on a theoretical level and shown to act in the hypothesized manner on an empirical level. Such a two-level approach has led to considering and testing of a number of new hypotheses about the determinants of market exchange, a process which has extended the boundaries hitherto confining analysis of this mode of distribution.

6

A DIGRESSION ON THE ORIGINS OF MONEY

Gold! Yellow, glittering, precious gold! . . . Thus much of this will make black white, foul fair, wrong right, base noble, old young, coward valiant. . . . This yellow salve will knit and break religions; bless the accurs'd; make the hoar leprosy ador'd. . . .

SHAKESPEARE[1]
Wine gladdens life, but money answers all things.
ECCLESIASTES[2]

This chapter is not a survey of woodpecker scalps and other esoterica which have served a money function[3]; nor is it a review of the archaeological and historical evidence about early coinage[4]; nor is it a set of armchair philosophical speculations about the origins of money[5]; nor is it a general theory of primitive moneys embracing all important aspects of the subject.[6]

Design from a Santa Cruz islander's carving of a fish; Melanesia.

[1]*Timon of Athens,* Act IV, Scene III.

[2]*Ecclesiastes,* Chapter X, Verse 19.

[3]For this purpose see Paul Einzig, *Primitive Money: In Its Ethnological, Historical and Economic Aspects,* 2nd ed. (1966), pp. 29–186; or A. Hingston Quiggin, *A Survey of Primitive Money* (1949). Although the anthropological profession has been extremely critical of Einzig's study, it is (in spite of its flaws) the single best descriptive and theoretical study on primitive money that I have found. Most of the critical literature on this book represents a retrogression from Einzig's standards.

[4]For this purpose, see Einzig, ibid., pp. 187–245; or Morris A. Copeland, "Concerning the Origin of a Money Economy," *The American Journal of Economics and Sociology* XXXIII (January 1974): 1–17.

[5]It is difficult to designate the apex of this dreary genre, but the nadir can be easily specified: It is Norman O. Brown's excremental theory of money, contained in his essay "Filthy Lucre," Chap. XV of "Studies in Anality," in his book *Life Against Death: The Psychoanalytical Meaning of History* (1959), pp. 234–306.

[6]Aside from the major studies of Einzig, *Primitive Money,* and Quiggin, *Survey of Primitive Money,* four other widely distributed books on the origins of money have appeared in the last quarter century: William H. Desmonde, *Magic, Myth, and Money* (1962); Wilhelm Gerloff, *Die Entstehung des Geldes und die Anfaenge des Geldwesens,* 3d ed. (1947); Jacques Melitz, *Primitive and Modern Money* (1974); A. Hingston Quiggin, *The Story of Money* (1956). The most important recent essays on the topic are: Helen Codere, "Money-Exchange Systems and the Theory of Money," *Man* III (December 1968): 557–577; George Dalton, "Primitive Money," in *Tribal and*

Rather, the purpose of this analysis is to test empirically some propositions about the origins of money. The results provide an interesting perspective on the origins of market exchange and, in addition, yield insights into the determinants of other types of distribution.

The first major problem is to arrive at a workable definition of money. Unlike many of my predecessors who have written on this topic, it is not my intention to plunge the reader into the metaphysical depths of the concept but to derive a definition that is related to the propositions I intend to test and that can be used for empirical analysis. One aspect of such an approach is an investigation of how the empirical results obtained apply to different definitions of money.

The second major problem is to derive and test some propositions about the origins of money. It is not my intention to march the reader through the thicket of theories that have been advanced on this matter but to prune from this literature the most important propositions, which are then carefully examined. In particular, I explore and test propositions relating the origin of money to two basic purposes: the "requirements" of trade and the "needs" for certain noncommercial payments. The empirical results show that the presence of money used for both purposes is strongly related to the level of development. Although the money for noncommercial payments seems to appear at lower levels of development than money used for commercial payments, exceptions to this latter generalization are sufficiently frequent that no firm generalizations can be drawn. From evidence relating the presence or absence of money and various kinds of market, I also show that the linkage between market exchange and money is, at low levels of development, much stronger for external than for internal trade. From such data I further demonstrate that previous dogmatism about the earlier emergence of external than internal commercial moneys (i.e., moneys for foreign and domestic trade) is quite unwarranted. Finally, by examining the relationship between the money stuff and the purposes to which the money is put, I explore other aspects of the determinants of money. Although the statistical tests are carried out primarily using cross-section data, I investigate the validity of using some of these results to generalize about events over time, using the same analytic techniques as presented in the previous chapter.

Almost three-quarters of a century ago, Karl Buecher marveled: "How much has been written and imagined about the many species of money among primitive peoples."[7] I would like to add: How unsystematic this literature has

Peasant Economies (1967), ed. George Dalton, pp. 254–284; Mary Douglas, "Primitive Rationing," in Themes in Economic Anthropology, (1967), ed. Raymond Firth, pp. 119–148; Melville J. Herskovits, "Money and Wealth," Chap. XI in his Economic Anthropology: The Economic Life of Primitive Peoples (1952), pp. 238–268; Jacques Melitz, "The Polanyi School of Anthropology on Money: An Economist's View," American Anthropologist LXX (October 1970): 1020–1040; Karl Polanyi, "The Semantics of Money-Uses," in Primitive, Archaic and Modern Economies: Essays of Karl Polanyi (1968), ed. George Dalton, pp. 175–206; and Harold K. Schneider, "Money," Chap. V in his Economic Man (1974), pp. 157–177. Earlier theories of money are summarized by Einzig, ibid.
[7]Karl Buecher, Industrial Evolution (1907), p. 67.

been and how few have been the attempts to test empirically the many fanciful notions that have been advanced. It is time to repair this deplorable state of affairs.

PROBLEMS IN DEFINING MONEY

An endless literature is concerned with the question of what money "really" is. No useful purpose would be served in entering this debate because, for the most part, such types of analyses seldom move beyond the problem of classification—what phenomena should be included in the definition—to the theoretical differences underlying the definitional quarrels.

For the purpose of this book I define money as any standardized object serving actively as a medium of exchange for commercial purposes (either for domestic or foreign transactions) or as a medium of payment for domestic noncommercial purposes. The terms employed in this definition are explained below. To put this definition in context, it is useful to explore briefly some of the monetary distinctions that have been made so that it becomes clearer what I have included and excluded in my approach. It must be emphasized that my definition is not a universal definition of money but is selected for a very specific theoretical purpose.

All-Purpose and Limited-Purpose Moneys

Karl Polanyi and his followers have emphasized repeatedly that modern societies have impersonal all-purpose moneys while primitive economies have limited or special-purpose moneys.[8] The extent to which money in modern economies is actually "all-purpose" can be questioned[9]; nevertheless, such a distinction contains many useful insights. Primitive moneys are limited in the "functions" they fill, the extent to which they facilitate exchange, and the degree to which they possess the "necessary" physical characteristics of money.

The question of the "functions" of money has evoked the most extensive discussion, for many puzzles arise. From Aristotle onward money has been defined as something fulfilling a number of functions such as: a medium of exchange, a store of value, a unit of account or a standard of value, and a standard and means of deferred payments.[10] Difficulties arise in using such lists of functions in determining the existence of money in a particular society because the functions are overlapping. In addition, although in advanced

[8]See especially Dalton, "Primitive Money," and Polanyi, "The Semantics of Money-Uses."
[9]This has been done in considerable detail by Melitz, "The Polanyi School."
[10]The history of ideas about these functions of money is briefly reviewed by Joseph A. Schumpeter, *History of Economic Analysis* (1954), pp. 62–63, 296–297, and 1087–1090; and Melitz, *Primitive and Modern Money*, pp. 4–9.

capitalist economies one particular thing might serve all of these four functions, in most primitive economies these functions are divided among a series of different things and not embodied exclusively in any single one. If we wish to analyze empirically the existence of money in primitive and peasant societies, it seems advisable to select one or several of these functions on which to focus. But which ones?

Clearly any kind of inventory (food, ornaments, household goods) or capital good (spears, canoes, looms) can serve as a store of value, so this function of money does not seem to be a useful differentiating criterion for money. Similarly, a standard or a means of deferred payment also does not appear to be a useful criterion since a great deal of credit in various kinds of goods and services is extended in primitive economies, a mode of exchange that is often designated as "delayed reciprocity."

The money function of a standard of value or a unit of account is more difficult to handle. (These terms appear to have slightly different meanings: A standard of value is an abstract unit that serves as a *numéraire* for calculating wealth, while a unit of account is an abstract unit that serves as a *numéraire* for calculating exchange values. Such a distinction is not necessary to maintain for the discussion that follows.) It is certainly possible to have exchange without either a standard of value or a unit of account: If the society produces or exchanges only a few goods, a person can remember the equivalencies of any one good in terms of each other good, so that the abstract *numéraire* is not necessary. And it is also possible to have a standard of value without having a great deal of exchange, a situation arising also in modern societies with inconvertible currencies.

The relations of a standard of value or a unit of account to a medium of exchange are complex. It is certainly possible to have a standard of value or a unit of account without a medium of exchange and several notable examples are frequently discussed in the literature, for instance, the copper weight standard used in domestic trade of Middle Kingdom Egypt or the various fictitious units used in foreign trade of a number of West African societies several centuries ago.[11] However, it does not seem likely that a society would have a medium of exchange without having a standard of value or unit of account since the medium of exchange can be easily used for such purposes.

Certain serious ethnographic problems also arise in determining whether a society has a standard of value or a unit of account, especially since the

[11]Egyptian copper units of account are discussed by Pierre Montet, *Everyday Life in Egypt in the Days of Rameses the Great* (1958). Einzig, *Primitive Money*, pp. 193–201 also has some interesting comments on this situation. The fictitious foreign exchange units of account of West Africa are discussed by: Karl Polanyi and Abraham Rotstein, *Dahomey and the Slave Trade* (1960), Chap. X; and Einzig, ibid., pp. 146–150 and 436–440. Several examples are provided by Einzig, ibid., pp. 436–440; and Schneider, *Economic Man*. In modern times the British guinea and the Chinese tael might be used as examples of a unit of account unembodied in any specific unit of currency, but these do have a direct and obvious relationship to the currency. A better example occurred during the 1950s in the U.S.S.R., when a constant value ruble was used as a unit of account for certain purposes even though a current ruble was used as the medium of exchange.

existence of abstract units of calculation can not be easily identified by observation of behavior. Of course, in some societies such an abstract unit is clearly and openly articulated (e.g., in certain cattle-raising societies, many transactions are carried out in terms of cattle units even though cattle are not part of the exchange); but in other societies the situation is not so dramatic. Indeed, it may be quite difficult to formulate questions to find out whether the respondents use a standard of value at all or whether they think about their medium of exchange as a unit of account. In the various ethnographies for the societies used in the following empirical examination, few of the anthropologists looked deeply into this matter of a standard of value or a unit of account except when the society had a very visible and obvious medium of exchange; thus, it is impossible to determine whether such value *numéraires* existed for a large number of societies in the sample.

Thus, a first limitation of primitive moneys is that they may not fulfil all of the commercial functions of a modern money. I have taken this notion further in this chapter by defining the commercial aspect of money only in terms of one of these functions, namely, as a medium of exchange, and by omitting reference to the other three traditional functions.[12]

A second limitation of primitive moneys occurs in their uses as media of exchange. As I analyze further in Appendix B.3, the medium of exchange in many primitive economies is used to obtain only a small subset of the goods that are produced; some goods may not enter into exchange at all, while other goods may belong to an exchange sphere that is different from that of the medium of exchange under consideration. In addition, the medium of exchange may not be used by all people in the society. Thus, most primitive moneys are not universal media of exchange. The criteria I use for determining a medium of exchange are: if there is a "thing" that can be directly exchanged for a large number of other goods or services or valuables, if it possesses this characteristic more than most other "things," and if it serves this transfer function between other goods frequently.

A third limitation of primitive moneys concerns particular characteristics of the money stuff. According to Stanley Jevons' oft-cited list of characteristics of a universal money, such money must have: (a) utility and value; (b) portability; (c) indestructibility; (d) homogeneity; (e) divisibility; (f) stability of value; (g) cognizability.[13] Many primitive money stuffs are not very portable, not indestructible, not divisible, and unstable in value even though they seem to serve as a medium of exchange. If we were to use these seven characteristics to designate moneys, then we would find few primitive societies with money. It does not seem useful to tie the existence of money to the technical characteristics of the substance used for money, although, it must be added, we can advance some interesting propositions about the easy availability of particular

---

[12]It should be noted that a designation of this particular function runs counter to the approach of some recent work such as that by Melitz, *Primitive and Modern Money*.

[13]W. Stanley Jevons, *Money and the Mechanism of Exchange* (1875), p. 31.

things that have some of the previously mentioned properties with the existence of money. One such proposition, linking money in societies at very low
levels of development with the availability of livestock, is discussed and tested
below.

Other Useful Monetary Distinctions

EXTERNAL AND INTERNAL MONEYS

A number of economic anthropologists have advanced the notion that
money arose out of foreign trade activities. In order to examine such matters
empirically, it is useful to separate moneys used in foreign trade and domestic
trade.[14] Although it is possible that the same money stuffs are involved in both
kinds of trade, it is also possible that societies may use two quite different
moneys for these activities. Although some commentators on primitive moneys
have decried the possibility of making this distinction,[15] the ethnographic materials of most of the societies in the sample permitted easily the separation of
domestic and foreign trade activities and the types of moneys used for both. By
"internal trade" I mean trade with people under the same overall political
leadership or, if overall political leadership is different, with people with greatly
similar language, culture, and economy. "Foreign trade" is all other trade.

COMMERCIAL AND NONCOMMERCIAL MONEYS

A widely used distinction by anthropologists differentiates between commercial money (a medium of exchange) and noncommercial money (sometimes designated as a "means of payment"). Noncommercial money is a standardized stuff which is employed in a variety of social transactions. Drawing on
an extensive literature on these matters, I have distinguished 12 such uses: in
marriage payments, for taxes or tribute, in sacrifices, in other religious ceremonies, in festive gifts, in blood money, in fines, in peace offerings, in funerals,
in other ceremonial purposes, in payment for skilled or sacred labor, and in
ornaments and prestige tokens. As I discuss in greater detail later, noncommercial moneys are coded as present if a standardized stuff is used for a subset of
these 12 possible purposes.

[14]The distinction between internal and external moneys was strongly emphasized by Heinrich
Schurtz, *Grundriss einer Entstehungsgeschichte des Geldes* (1898) and has been employed by
many later writers on the topic.
[15]For instance, Max Schmidt (*The Primitive Races of Mankind* (1926), pp. 158–159) argues:

> Schurtz divides money into two kinds—the money used in home transactions and that
> used in dealing with other peoples. This classification is irrelevant because, in the first
> place, the narrower and wider economic communities are so intermingled among primi-
> tive peoples that it is impossible to draw a sharp distinction between "home" and "for-
> eign" money; and, secondly, many peoples use the very same commodities in the very
> same way for both purposes.

I believe Schmidt greatly overdraws the difficulties in distinguishing these two types of money and
that by and large his objections are baseless.

This distinction between commercial and noncommercial moneys is important because a great number of anthropologists have argued that money was used for noncommercial functions of money before its use as a commercial medium of exchange. It is perfectly possible to have a noncommercial money without having the presence of a commercial money and vice versa. The two types of money are logically quite distinct; by maintaining the distinction between the two, a variety of propositions about the origins of money can be tested.

ACTIVE AND PASSIVE MONEY

In modern commercial society money is a necessary and sufficient condition for obtaining some good on the market; in such a case, we say that money is active. Passive "money" is something that appears at first glance as a medium of exchange but which does not have this property. Although such "moneys" are excluded from my definition of commercial money (the distinction does not apply to noncommercial moneys), several different types of passive "money" (labeled for convenience as "pseudomoney" and "true passive money") deserve brief consideration.

"Pseudomoney" is something that accompanies a great many different types of economic transactions, yet is unrelated to the values that are involved and, in itself, is insufficient to bring the transaction about. An example of such "pseudomoney" is the use of wampum (shell beads) among the Iroquois Indians of New York before they had much contact with the white settlers. Wampum was transferred at any important transaction to serve as a symbol and mnemonic device of the transaction. The giving of wampum was also a sign that trust should be placed in the transaction (thus when a scout reported to his tribe about the movement of enemy soldiers, he gave a strip of wampum to the leader of the group as a surety, rather than receiving a wampum strip as a payment). The amount of wampum exchanged did not matter so much as the fact that it was exchanged. Thus, wampum can not be considered as a commercial money, although it does fit into my definition of a noncommercial money.[16]

A "true passive money" occurs in some special circumstances in modern industrial societies and is a sufficiently interesting curiosum to have received some comment in the economic literature. Since such cases of a "true passive money" did not occur in my sample of 60 societies, it does not seem worthwhile to pursue these matters further.

[16]This brief account is based on: Frank G. Speck, The Functions of Wampum among the Eastern Algonkian; Memoirs of the American Anthropological Association, VI (1919), pp. 3–71; J. S. Slotkin, "Studies of Wampum," American Anthropologist LI (April–June 1949): 223–236; and a conversation with Professor Elizabeth Tooker of Temple University. It is noteworthy that only when the white settlers, mistaking such wampum for a commercial money, began to use it as a medium of exchange did it change its function among the Indians to parallel this usage. This interpretation of wampum is at wide variance with the older view that is reflected in Einzig, Primitive Money, pp. 170–175.

SOME LESS USEFUL DISTINCTIONS

A great many other distinctions concerning particular aspects of primitive moneys have been made. For instance, recently, Helen Codere has suggested that we distinguish four different types of money, each having different symbolic roles.[17] Other authors have set up different criteria and have distinguished between different types of money.[18] Since these distinctions do not play any role in the propositions that I intend to test, I do not pursue these matters further.

The Definition of Money Employed in This Study

In a widely acclaimed article George Dalton has written:

> One source of ambiguity in the literature is the quest for a single all-purpose definition of money. . . . To concentrate attention on what all moneys have in common is to discard those clues—how moneys differ—which are surface expressions of different social and economic organizations. . . . Money traits differ where socioeconomic organization differs. To concentrate attention on money traits independently of underlying organization leads writers to use the traits of Western money as a model of the real thing . . .[19]

Unfortunately, if we wish to compare money in two different societies, we must use a single definition if the comparison is to have any meaning. Although it is true that with such a definition we cannot consider small differences in money traits in the various societies, we may extract some helpful generalizations that can be used to place such differences in greater perspective.

One other shoal in studying money must be mentioned, namely, defining the concept so narrowly that all hypotheses about the origins of the phenomenon are excluded but one.[20] The definition I employ is relatively broad; in the empirical analysis, however, I also examine the origins of money using a number of narrower alternative definitions as well so that particular facets of the results derived from my definition may be visible.

Inclusion of noncommercial moneys in the definition of money raises certain problems. For quite practical reasons I have limited designation of such noncommercial functions to domestic transactions.[21] Undoubtedly, certain questions can be raised about inclusion of particular noncommercial functions in

[17]Codere, "Money Exchange System." This approach receives some criticism by Schneider.
[18]Einzig, Primitive Money, has virtually a catalogue raisonné of such distinctions.
[19]Dalton, "Primitive Money," p. 280.
[20]The definition of money employed by Jacques Melitz in his book Primitive and Modern Money, (which is different from the one used in his article "The Polanyi School ") seems sufficiently narrow to exclude any but a trade origin of money hypothesis, so his conclusions about the origin of money seem to spring more from this definition than from any other source.
[21]The instances where a means of payment might be used externally, that is, for noncommercial purposes with other societies, are not recorded in the ethnographic literature in a sufficient number of societies to warrant inclusion in the definition.

my list.[22] Resolving these questions in a different manner would not greatly affect the conclusions presented in the discussion below, an assertion based on the comparison of the results employing two different ways of empirically defining the presence of noncommercial moneys. It must finally be reiterated that my definition of a commercial money excludes passive moneys; that no commercial functions of money other than the medium of exchange are considered; and most of the particular characteristics of the money stuff, as defined by Jevons, are dismissed as irrelevant.

Although my use of the term "money" may not be in accord with the metaphysical truths that have been discovered by others, it does permit the carrying out of a relatively unambiguous empirical examination of the phenomenon embraced in the definition. Some aspects of money (as the term is commonly employed), especially its use as a standard of value and a unit of account, cannot be incorporated because of the paucity of good ethnographic materials on this point[23]; other aspects of money are not included because they are too restrictive or too broad. The propositions using this definition do not by any means cover all aspects of money, but rather the most important ones that permit statistical testing.

THEORIES ABOUT THE ORIGINS OF MONEY

Most arguments about the origins of money are rather loose. The general strategy is to make a plausible argument for some thesis, usually based on some implicit notions about relative costs and benefits of particular economic institutions or about relative strengths of particular social forces, and then to use

---

[22]The list of noncommercial payments deserves several brief comments. I consider the use of standardized objects in sacrifices and other religious ceremonies as a transaction between the individual and his gods. The use of a standardized object in payments for skilled labor is considered "noncommercial" because in many such cases (especially payments for the services of shaman and priests), the sacral and commercial character of the transaction are inextricably mixed; on the other hand, the use of payments for nonskilled labor is considered sufficiently "commercial" to be excluded. The exclusive or extensive use of a standardized object as an ornament or as a prestige token does not necessarily mean that they were actually used as payments in many transactions but that they had a strong potentiality for such use at any time. As it turns out in the empirical analysis (especially Table 6.4) this particular noncommercial purpose is very unimportant since rarely did ornaments consist primarily of one type of object.

[23]Melitz, *Primitive and Modern Money,* has an interesting argument that money in its medium of exchange function should be separated from its standard of value (and unit of account) function because these two functions of money have quite different causal origins. He also argues that a standard of value appeared at a much earlier stage of societal development than a medium of exchange, but unfortunately he offers no empirical evidence to back up this interesting proposition. Copeland similarly believes that the standard of value function (especially in foreign trade) arose before the medium of exchange function. Unfortunately, his evidence rests primarily on speculations. Paul Einzig, *Primitive Money,* p. 358, holds a modified version of this position, namely that more often than not, the standard of value arose first.

several examples drawn from the copious ethnographic literature on the subject of money to demonstrate that the plausibility is actually a strong possibility. Contrary evidence is then dismissed as representing special circumstances that do not normally hold. Since anthropologists and economists differ on their acceptance of different kinds of implicit arguments, it should not be surprising that, by and large, the conventional wisdom about the origins of money is quite different in the two disciplines.

Most economists seem generally to favor the notion that the origins of money lay in the costs of conducting trade by barter. This approach, which began with Plato and Aristotle[24] and continued through Adam Smith and Stanley Jevons[25] to the present day,[26] is based on a simple cost/benefit consideration. As societies develop economically, trade increases, and a greater quantity and a wider variety of goods and services are exchanged. As trade expands, it becomes increasingly difficult for a person wishing to barter A for Z to find another person wishing to barter Z for A, a problem enshrined in the phrase "the double coincidence of wants." Thus, as trade expands both quantitatively and qualitatively, the benefits of a medium of exchange become increasingly greater. Sometimes the argument is fancier, so that search costs (including information costs and inventory storage costs) are brought in, but the same trading problems are focused on. The proposition implies, among other things, that markets developed at a lower level of economic development than money, a matter that will be explored.

This simple proposition has received a number of elaborations in the literature. First, resting on the notion that market exchange with other societies preceded internal market exchange, a diverse group of social scientists, including Karl Marx, Heinrich Schurtz, Karl Buecher, Max Weber, and Karl Polanyi, have argued that money as a medium of exchange arose first in the foreign trade sector.[27] Such theorists part company on the question of what the money stuff is (whether it is an important good that acquired a money use, an imported money, or an exported staple)[28] and also on the question of whether such external money arose independently between pairs of nations or whether its use diffused from several centers, a matter explored in considerable detail at the end of this chapter.

Second, the use of money depends in part on the technology of making money stuffs: If suitable materials are not available, or if it is very laborious to

[24]A short history of doctrine on this matter is presented by Gerloff, Die Entstehung.

[25]Adam Smith, The Wealth of Nations (1776), Book I, Chap. IV; Jevons, Money, Chap. I. The analyses of both are incredibly superficial.

[26]Since the origins of money are seldom discussed in any reputable modern book on economics, most economists draw from the collective unconsciousness of the profession on such matters, that is, the lore that has been passed on in elementary economics courses over the century that is rooted in the Plato–Aristotle–Smith–Jevons tradition.

[27]Karl Marx, Capital, Vol. 1, Chap. II; Schurtz, Grundriss; Buecher, Industrial Evolution, pp. 67 ff.; Max Weber, General Economic History (1961), Chap. XIX, [originally published 1923]; Karl Polanyi, "The Semantics of Money-Uses."

[28]Einzig, Primitive Money, Book III, Part II, Section 8 has a doctrinal review of these variants.

obtain or make the money stuff, then the probability of a society having money at a given level of development is lower. On the other hand, if some useful movable such as cattle is available, then the probability of a society at a given level of development having money is higher.[29] (Some interesting linguistic evidence is sometimes offered to support this contention. Reference is made not only to the ox units mentioned in the Homeric epics but the fact—as noted in the previous chapter—that the Latin word for money *pecunia* derives from the word *pecus*, which means 'cattle'; that the English word "fee" derives from the Germanic word *fehu* meaning 'cattle', whence the modern German word *Vieh* stems; and that the monetary unit of the *kesitah* mentioned in the Old Testament means 'lamb' or 'sheep'.)

Third, if the society places great stress on reciprocal exchange or on various types of redistribution, then the probability of the society having money is low, for trade is allegedly unimportant. (A variant of this is Thurnwald's questionable assertion that if a society is characterized by a single social class or by "clan rule," then money is superfluous since there is little trade.)[30] Finally, if the religion of the society places great emphasis on strong personal relations between the individuals of the society, and if a negative value is placed on impersonal transactions between individuals, then the probability of a society having money is low unless it has a very high level of economic development.

Such arguments that the origins of money stem from the needs of trade have several weaknesses. First, the problem of the double coincidence of wants is considerably less acute if multilateral trade can easily be carried out or if credit is freely requested and given, that is, if a person can obtain a particular good or service by promising to give in return in the future some other type of good or service. Second, the cost/benefit analyses are usually rather casually argued.[31]

The introduction of credit into the analysis allows us to make one last proposition. Since it is more likely that individuals will grant credit to members of the same society rather than foreigners (because the risks involved are greater for loans to the latter group), the coincidence between the rise of foreign trading and the introduction of an external money should be closer than that between the rise of domestic trading and the introduction of an internal money.

Many anthropologists seem to favor the notion that money did not originate from trade but from noncommercial payments. Those of this persuasion differ

---

[29]Among others who argued this proposition was Karl Marx, *Capital*, Chap. II.

[30]Richard Thurnwald, *Economics in Primitive Communities* (1932), p. 105.

[31]Melitz, *Primitive and Modern Money*, pp. 57–67, has a rigorous cost/benefit analysis of the use of a medium of exchange; his discussion omits, I believe, several important considerations. In recent discussions about monetary theory a number of other economists have begun to examine carefully benefits and costs of holding money rather than other assets (e.g., Jürg Niehans, "Money and Barter in General Equilibrium with Transactions Costs," *American Economic Review* LXI (December 1971): 773–784; Karl Brunner and Allan H. Meltzer, "The Uses of Money: Money in the Theory of Exchange," *American Economic Review* LXI (December 1971): 784–805; or Robert A. Jones, "The Origin and Development of Media of Exchange," *Journal of Political Economy* LXXXIV (August 1976): 757–775. Although such articles raise pertinent issues, I have been unable to see any way in which their insights can be employed in the analysis of the origins of money.

concerning which noncommercial function was the most important. In a brilliant book Bernhard Laum argued that money originated from religious ceremonies, more particularly the sacrifice in which livestock was used.[32] Others have supported this with ethnographic evidence that many primitive peoples consider money to have magic qualities or with linguistic evidence that in many societies the word for "money" has strong religious connotations (e.g., in Fiji *tambus* are used for many payments; the word stems from the word *tambu* which means 'sacred'). Others have tried to tie the origins of money to ornaments and status tokens, drawing heavily on evidence of shell moneys and on the manipulation of particular payment media by high status individuals.[33] Still others have linked the origins of money to the development of the state and the need for payment of taxes or fines or peace offerings to the state.[34] Other theorists have advanced still other noncommercial payments as the original source of money.[35]

Such arguments also raise uncomfortable queries which some social scientists such as Polanyi have explored. Exactly why does the use of a standardized payment media for such noncommercial purposes necessarily precede rather than follow the use of a commercial medium of exchange? Why does the use of such a noncommercial money necessarily occur for one particular type of transaction and not another? Why is there a necessary link between the introduction of a noncommercial money and the later introduction of a commercial medium of exchange?

A number of social scientists have also held complicated amalgams of the trade and the noncommercial payments theories of the origin of money. Max Weber argued that money as a medium of exchange originated in foreign trade, but that domestic noncommercial uses of money preceded internal commercial money.[36] Karl Polanyi supported this view that external and internal moneys have different origins but felt that the noncommercial purpose from which internal commercial money originated depended on particular social structural features such as stratification.[37] Paul Einzig appears to argue that money developed out of domestic barter but that the media chosen were originally used for noncommercial payments.[38]

[32]Bernhard Laum, *Heiliges Geld: Eine historische Untersuchung ueber den sakralen Ursprung des Geldes* (1924).

[33]This theory has several variants which, among others, have been argued by Gerloff, *Die Entstehung*, and, more recently, by R. F. Salisbury, *From Stone to Steel: Economic Consequences of a Technological Change in New Guinea* (1962).

[34]Such a theory has been argued with great vigor by Karl Knies, *Das Geld*, 2nd ed., Vol. I, *Geld und Kredit* (1885); and G. F. Knapp, *The State Theory of Money* (1924).

[35]Again Einzig, *Primitive Money*, has the most complete summary. On his own Einzig advances a "matrimonial theory" that suggests that payment for marriage purposes might have been an important early noncommercial payment, a theory that receives considerable empirical support from my data.

[36]Max Weber, *Economic History*, Chap. 19. Weber merely sketches this theory and does not develop it.

[37]Karl Polanyi, "The Semantics of Money-Uses," especially pp. 201–202.

[38]Einzig, *Primitive Money*, pp. 345–346.

A final set of theories about the origin of money will be mentioned only briefly: These are the propositions that the functions of money such as a store of value or a means of deferred payments or a standard of value appeared at lower levels of economic development than the medium of exchange function of money.[39] As noted before, the proper information to test such propositions is not available, nor, I should add, is it likely to ever be available in sufficient quantity to provide any kind of convincing demonstration.

Whatever their belief about the particular origins of money, almost all who have written on the subject assume, either implicitly or explicitly, that societies at higher stages of economic development are more likely to have money than those at lower levels. The argument why noncommercial functions of money are more likely to be found at higher stages of economic development rests, in turn, on a number of assumptions about the relationships between different types of noncommercial functions (especially those related to taxes) and economic development. Such matters can be easily investigated.

EMPIRICAL TESTS OF IMPORTANT HYPOTHESES

Data Problems

Three topics will be briefly discussed: problems arising in the original collection of ethnographic data on money, problems arising in coding these data, and problems of comparability of my results with others.

If the society had a medium of commercial exchange at the time of the original fieldwork, it does not seem likely that the first ethnographers would overlook its existence. Indeed, the expenses of fieldwork give most ethnographers a particular sensitivity to money and its manifestations. If the commodity serving a money function is not obviously "money," its use may still be keenly noted and reported in terms of its usefulness in trade or in various noncommercial transactions. Several problems do, however, arise. The ethnographer may report the existence or nonexistence of money with no very clear discussion of his definition or his evidence. Furthermore, the ethnographer may not systematically examine all noncommercial transactions but may report only on several "major" types of such payments.

In coding the information from the ethnographic sources, it was sometimes difficult to decide whether a particular thing serves as a medium of exchange or a medium of barter. In several cases, it was also difficult to decide whether trade is domestic or foreign, that is, whether the group with which a society trades is sufficiently different to be designated as foreign.[40] In coding noncommercial moneys, additional problems arose. In particular, how many noncom-

---

[39]Such theories are summarized by Einzig, ibid., pp. 428–463. See also footnote 23.
[40]This problem arose with the Ao Naga, Copper Eskimo, Fiji, Khalka Mongol, and Koryak, since the boundaries of these societies are especially indistinct.

mercial functions must a standardized object serve to be included as noncommercial money? Since an arbitrary decision must be made, I have used two different definitions. As a broad definition of noncommercial moneys I have included any standardized thing serving 2 of the 12 specified noncommercial purposes; for a narrower definition I have included any standardized thing serving 3 of the 12 noncommercial purposes. By "serving" I mean either used almost exclusively (which is counted as a "full use") or used extensively (which is counted as "half of a full use"). If a particular thing is used only in an unimportant manner in a noncommercial transaction, it is not considered to serve this noncommercial function at all. Thus, a noncommercial money coded according to the "criterion of three" might be a money stuff that is used almost exclusively in at least three noncommercial transactions or extensively in at least six such transactions.

In assessing the reliability of the codings, several subjective impressions are worth noting. I encountered relatively few difficulties in coding the presence or absence of commercial moneys, and I have reasonable confidence in the codings for most societies. However, in coding the noncommercial moneys, two major uncertainties deserve mention. First, it was often difficult to determine whether a particular standardized object was used exclusively, extensively, or just in a trivial manner since the ethnographers often did not make such an assessment. Second, it was often difficult to obtain information on all 12 noncommercial functions; in many cases, several functions were simply not discussed by any observer, and in such circumstances I had to assume that no standardized object fulfilled this purpose. Thus, for the noncommercial money the data are much less firm. Nevertheless, I believe that they are sufficient for the relatively rough purposes for which I employ the data.

To gain a more concrete notion about such coding reliability, it is useful to compare my coding results with those of others. However, other codings of money that I have seen are not very explicit about their definitions. I think, but I can not be sure, that they cover only internal commercial moneys, that is, domestic media of exchange. If we compare my coding of such a money with that of Robert Carneiro,[41] the greatest differences arise because I was more willing than he to consider that a particular commodity served as money. If we

---

[41] I am referring to the fourth edition of Carneiro's scale analysis trait list which is summarized in: Robert L. Carneiro, "Scale Analysis, Evolutionary Sequences, and the Rating of Cultures," Chap. XLI in A Handbook of Method in Cultural Anthropology (1973), ed. Raoul Naroll and Ronald Cohen, pp. 834–871. The actual codings on money were taken by permission from Carneiro's worksheets, and I would like to express my appreciation to Carneiro for this assistance. Although Carneiro does not give the dates to which his codings of various societies refer, he informed me that he tried to code the society in its form shortly before extensive Western contact—a rule similar to my own. His sample and mine contain 33 of the same societies, and our codings (using my coding for domestic, commercial money) of the presence or absence of money are the same in 27 cases (82%). For 1 society (the Inca) he coded money, whereas I coded its absence; in 5 societies, I coded money, whereas he coded its absence. Our results are, however, significantly correlated at the .05 level (chi square with Yates correction = 9.19).

compare my coding with that of George Peter Murdock and Diana Morrow,[42] the causes of our differences are impossible to isolate. It is noteworthy that in none of the cases in which I coded a society as lacking an internal commercial money and either Carneiro or Murdock–Morrow coded the existence of money did the society fail to have a noncommercial money or a money used for external trade. This suggests that these analysts may, on occasion, have included as (internal commercial) money something serving these functions as well.

As far as I know, no one else has ever tried to code for a sample of societies the existence of noncommercial moneys separately from commercial moneys. A replication experiment of my results using materials drawn from the Human Relations Area File was attempted but was not very successful because not all of the 12 noncommercial payments are covered in these materials in a manner to permit easy extraction.[43] The major conclusion from this failed experiment is that to determine the existence of noncommercial moneys, it is necessary to read whole ethnographies.

Tests Using Cross-Section Data

The analysis proceeds in three steps. First, I show the strong positive relationship between the use of money and the level of economic development. Second, I examine the appearance of both commercial and noncommercial moneys in the set of societies at the lowest levels of economic development in order to see which type of money appears first and whether such money is correlated with the presence of a significant amount of trade. Finally, I look at the various types of money stuffs in order to explore which money stuffs are used for similar purposes, an exercise that gives important clues about borrowing from one money function for use in another function.

THE RELATIONSHIP BETWEEN MONEY AND THE LEVEL OF ECONOMIC DEVELOPMENT

To determine the strength of the relationship between the presence of money (defined in various ways) and the level of economic development seems a

---

[42]George Peter Murdock and Diana O. Morrow, "Subsistence Economy and Supportive Practices: Cross-Cultural Codes 1," *Ethnology* IX, No. 3 (July 1970), pp. 302–330. Their sample and mine contain 46 of the same societies, of which 3 must be eliminated because we use quite different time periods. Of the 43 remaining cases, we agree on our codings (using my coding for domestic, commercial money) of the presence or absence of money in 32 cases (74%). For 5 societies, they coded money, whereas I coded its absence; in 6 societies, I coded money, whereas they coded its absence. Our results are, however, significantly correlated at the .05 level (chi square with Yates correction = 8.24).

[43]This replication experiment was carried out by Mr. John Hartung, working under my direction. In addition, he conducted a number of other replication experiments using the Murdock–Morrow sample which, for lack of space, are not presented below.

TABLE 6.1

Relationships between the Existence of Money and the Level of Economic Development[a]

		Other statistics	Emergence level
1. Commercial internal money [mean = .4667]	$= -.0318 + .0163*ED$ (.0031)	$R^2 = .3217$ $n = 60; PCP = 73.33\%$	33 [33]
2a. Commercial external money [mean = .4912]	$= .1134 + .0129*ED$ (.0036)	$R^2 = .1904$ $n = 57; PCP = 66.67\%$	30 [30]
2b. Commercial external money [mean = .4912]	$= .0590 + .0108*ED$ (.0033) $+ .4340*CW$ (.1284)	$R^2 = .3323$ $n = 57; PCP = 71.92\%$	41 [39]
3a. Commercial money (internal + external) [mean = .5667]	$= .1844 + .0125*ED$ (.0034)	$R^2 = .1918$ $n = 60; PCP = 63.33\%$	26 [25]
3b. Commercial money (internal + external) [mean = .5667]	$= .1391 + .0110*ED$ (.0033) $+ .3455*CW$ (.1275)	$R^2 = .2840$ $n = 60; PCP = 71.67\%$	33 [33]
4. Noncommercial money (criterion of two) [mean = .6667]	$= .2835 + .0126*ED$ (.0032)	$R^2 = .2129$ $n = 60; PCP = 78.33\%$	18 [18]
5. Noncommercial money (criterion of three) [mean = .5500]	$= .2202 + .0108*ED$ (.0035)	$R^2 = .1416$ $n = 60; PCP = 65.00\%$	26 [26]
6. Internal money (commercial + non-commercial, criterion of two) [mean = .7667]	$= .2682 + .0163*ED$ (.0024)	$R^2 = .4476$ $n = 60; PCP = 91.67\%$	15 [15]

7. internal money (commercial + non-commercial, criterion of three) [mean = .7000] $= .1660 + .0175*ED$ (.0026) $R^2 = .4377$ 20 [19] $n = 60; PCP = 85.00\%$

8. All money (internal + external commercial + noncommercial, criterion of two) [mean = .8000] $= .3558 + .0146*ED$ (.0024) $R^2 = .3975$ 10 [13] $n = 60; PCP = 91.67\%$

9. All money (internal + external commercial + noncommercial, criterion of three) [mean = .7500] $= .2931 + .0150*ED$ (.0026) $R^2 = .3589$ 14 [15] $n = 60; PCP = 85.00\%$

Key:

ED = Rank on economic development scale (1 = lowest; 60 = highest) [mean = 30.5 when n = 60; mean = 29.33 when n = 57].

CW = Appreciable contact with West (0 = no; 1 = yes) [mean = .2667 when n = 60; mean = .2632 when n = 57].

R^2 = Coefficient of determination.

n = Size of sample.

PCP = Percentage of correct predictions.

( ) = Standard error.

* = t statistic for calculated regression coefficient is over the acceptable limit (2.25) defined in Chapter 1.

[ ] = Emergence level using the logit regressions (from Appendix B.1).

[a]The data come from Appendix A, Series 3, 22, 37, 38, 39, and 40. The level of emergence is calculated by determining that level of development which would lead to the prediction of the presence of money (i.e., where the dependent variable would be .5 or above). In cases where a variable representing contact with the West is included in the regression, the CW variable is set at zero in making such calculations of the level of emergence so that the influence of diffusion on the regression results would be minimized.

simple task. Since contact with the West (and Western money) appears to be a determinant for some types of money, the regressions were calculated both including and excluding an appropriate variable for this phenomenon. Relevant data are presented in Table 6.1.

Several conclusions can be immediately drawn from these data. First, a strong positive relationship exists between the level of economic development and the presence of money no matter how money is defined.[44] Second, contact with the West (broadly defined) is important in determining whether an external commercial money is used, and this, in turn, influences the use of all (internal + external) commercial moneys. Third, the relationship between money and the level of economic development is considerably stronger when both noncommercial and commercial moneys are embraced in the same definition.

Although a number of false predictions occur, the errors fall into certain quite recognizable patterns, which can be examined by defining the "emergence level" as the level of economic development that would lead us to the prediction of the presence of the particular type of money under examination. For the equations with the level of economic development as the only explanatory variable, this can be easily calculated. For equations 2b and 3b, which contain a second explanatory variable, the calculation is somewhat more complicated. Since we wish to determine such an emergence level independently from any influences from the West, we need merely to set the value of the Western contact variable equal to zero and carry out the same type of calculation as for the other types of money. Once such a calculation is performed (the results are reported in Table 6.1), a clustering of prediction errors around this emergence level can be seen, which reflects the expected pattern of such errors.[45]

Several of the propositions discussed above give us clues as to what types of prediction errors we might find. On the low end of the development scale we might expect to find that many of the societies, which have money, although we predict the opposite, are societies in which the availability of domesticated animals presents a convenient (and ostensibly costless) money stuff.[46] Using as

---

[44]One peculiarity of the data is that the correlation between the level of economic development and the presence of a commercial money is lowered when external and internal moneys are combined. Nevertheless, all the regression coefficients more than pass the test of significance established in Chapter 1.

[45]This pattern of errors can be seen in a simple way by examining the errors of prediction in the band of six societies around the emergence limit. If the prediction errors were randomly distributed, the percentage of errors found in this band should be 20%. In actuality, these percentages for the regressions (the least square results are cited; the logit calculations give almost the same results) in the order they appear in the table are, respectively: 31%, 21%, 31%, 38%, 24%, 38%, 37%, 50%, 55%, 80%, and 25%. In contrast to the results obtained in the regression analyses in Chapter 5 the prediction errors do not appear more frequently in the codings about which I have some misgivings and have so designated with a rating of "A" or "B" in Appendix A.

[46]Of course, a livestock money is not costless, for labor costs are involved in caring for and guarding the animals as well as the costs induced by overgrazing that stems from hoarding such livestock money. In such societies, however, the opportunity costs of the money use are very low for these costs would be borne anyway.

our criterion of such availability whether 10% or more of the society's foodstuffs come from domesticated animals, we find, indeed, that such a proposition receives considerable support.[47] Other types of investigations of these prediction errors proved fruitless.

On the high end of the development scale two rather vague hypotheses which are sometimes encountered in the anthropology literature might help us: Money would not appear in societies in which its presence is predicted if various sorts of transfers play a particularly important role in the circulation of goods; or, as others such as Thurnwald have argued, such prediction errors might appear when strong unilineal kin groups are present. However, such relationships are not validated by the evidence.[48] Unfortunately, the societies on the high end of the development scale for which incorrect predictions are made compose a very heterogeneous group, and I was unable to find any unifying characteristic.

Although the positive relation between the presence of money for commercial purposes and the level of economic development should be clear, a number of questions might be asked about the forces underlying such a relationship for noncommercial moneys. This matter can be easily investigated by examining what noncommercial money purposes are met at different levels of economic development. Such a study would also tell us which noncommercial purposes of money are most important. Relevant data are presented in Table 6.2.

The data in Table 6.2 show us that the various noncommercial uses of money respond in quite different ways to changes in the relative level of economic development. Religious and ceremonial uses of noncommercial moneys,

---

[47]This proposition is examined by looking at those societies that are more than six societies below the emergence limit (so that errors arising from an incorrect determination of the relative level of economic development and errors arising from the influence of random factors around the emergence level are minimized) and then making various kinds of comparisons. I present three kinds of data (for the least square regressions) for each type of money: the number of errors of prediction; the percentage of such errors occurring in societies in which animal husbandry products account for 10% or more of the diet and the percentage of societies in this entire lower development group in which animal husbandry products account for 10% or more of the diet. If a relationship exists between the existence of animal husbandry and money, the second percentage should be larger than the third; if no relationship exists, they should be the same. Using the data from Table 6.1 and Appendix A, Series 5, we obtain the following data (presented in the same order as the type of money specified in Table 6.1): 6, 67%, 35%; 8, 50%, 33%; 10, 40%, 32%; 6, 50%, 17%; 8, 62%, 35%; 1, 100%, 9%; 4, 75%, 17%; 0, 0%, 0%; 2, 100%, 14%; 0, 0%, 0%; and 0, 0%, 0%.

[48]The measure that was used of relative importance of such transfers was whether the number of important modes of transfers of goods (i.e., centric transfers and noncentric transfers) was greater than the important modes of exchange of goods (i.e., market exchange and reciprocal exchange). (These data come from Appendix A, Series 26, 44, 54, and 57.) The results of this test were inconclusive. For the relationship between the presence of unilineal kin groups and prediction errors among the societies with higher developmental levels, a test similar to that described in footnote 48 was performed, using data from Appendix A, Series 64 and 65. Such calculations showed that the presence of strong unilineal kin groups (defined either with economic or social criteria) had no positive relation with prediction errors; they suggested a slight negative relation (i.e., fewer prediction errors when unilineal kin groups were present) instead.

TABLE 6.2

Societies at Different Levels of Economic Development Using Noncommercial Moneys for Particular Purposes[a]

Noncommercial purposes	Noncommercial money defined according to the criterion of two					Noncommercial money defined according to the criterion of three				
	Groups of societies classified according to their levels of economic development									
	Lowest	Second lowest	Second highest	Highest	Total	Lowest	Second lowest	Second highest	Highest	Total
Political										
Taxes	0	3	5	5.5	13.5	0	3	4	5.5	12.5
Fines	0	4.5	7	6	17.5	0	4.5	6	6	16.5
Blood money	3	4.5	6.5	5	16	2	4.5	6	4.5	17
Peace offering	0	1	0	0	1	0	1	0	0	1
Religious										
Sacrifice	1.5	4.5	5.5	1	12.5	1.5	4.5	5	1	12
Other religious	.5	1	4	2.5	8	.5	1	4	1.5	7
Festive										
Marriage payment	2	10	9	9	30	1	8.5	8.5	8	26
Festive gifts	0	2	2	.5	4.5	0	1.5	2	.5	4
Funeral ceremonies	1.5	6	4	1.5	13	1	5	3.5	1.5	11
Other ceremonies	0	2.5	2.5	2	7	0	2	2.5	1.5	6
Other										
Ornamental	0	1	1.5	2	4.5	0	1	1.5	2	4.5
Pay for skilled and sacral labor	0	2.5	4.5	5	12	0	1.5	3.5	4	9
Total societies with noncommercial moneys	3	12	13	12	40	2	10	11	10	33
Total societies in group	15	15	15	15	60	15	15	15	15	60

[a]The sources underlying the calculation of this table are the same as those used in Table 6.1. Since no calculations are made from these data, I have not listed the specific data in Appendix A. If a noncommercial money is used almost exclusively for a given function, it is scored equal to one; if it is used extensively but not almost exclusively in this function, it is scored equal to one-half.

which appear relatively important at the lower part of the developmental scale, lose their importance at the high end of the scale, a trend that perhaps reflects the growing differentiation between the religious and economic spheres that accompanies economic development. Over the course of development the use of noncommercial money for political purposes seems to increase, as does payment for skilled and sacral labor. Both trends are, of course, quite expected. The rise in political uses of noncommercial moneys reflects the correlation between the level of economic development and the increasing importance of state institutions with the power to tax and to administer justice. Moreover, at higher stages of economic development in which the central political authorities are geographically and socially more isolated from their subjects, it should be apparent that the need (i.e., greater benefits) to carry out tax and judicial transactions with a standardized medium of payment is greater.

The data in Table 6.2 also show that the single most important use of noncommercial moneys is in marriage transactions and that all other single purposes are considerably less important.[49] With the exception of Paul Einzig and A. Hingston Quiggens,[50] no theorist whom I have read has suggested such a proposition. Theories linking the origins of money to political payments also receive a certain amount of support, provided that we consider a number of different types of political payments together. Theories linking the origin of money with ornamental or prestige tokens receive very little support.[51]

The strong correlation that I have found between the appearance of money (by almost any definition) and the relative level of economic development would be expected and certainly is not disputed in the literature. Moreover, such a relationship can be easily shown using other sets of available data.[52]

[49]Doubtless some psychiatrically oriented "theorist" will use these data for demonstrating yet another relationship between sex and money, and I would like, at this point, to disclaim any responsibility for such misuse of my data. Nevertheless, the matrimonial link between sex and money seems more plausible than the orthodox Freudian view linking money with the anal functions of the body, as argued, for instance, by Brown, Life against Death.

[50]Einzig, Primitive Money, pp. 382–385 and Quiggen, A Survey, pp. 7–9. Although I do not believe that either was seriously defending this proposition, they both offer evidence that it is a plausible conjecture.

[51]Certain prestige-token theories are not so easily dismissed, especially those linking money to exchange spheres (discussed in Appendix B.3). Of the five societies known with certainty to have exchange spheres, only two (Tiv and Siane) have either internal or external commercial moneys, while four have noncommercial moneys. In both cases in which commercial moneys occur, the money stuff falls in the prestige sphere. The lack of commercial moneys in the other three societies with exchange spheres suggests that this linkage between particular types of prestige token and money is not a promising way of looking for the origin of money.

[52]Using the Carneiro fourth edition sample of 100 societies, the chi square (with Yates correction) of his coding of money and his definition of development level is 12.76 (data obtained from his unpublished work sheets). Using the Murdock sample of 186 societies, the Murdock–Morrow ("Subsistence Economy") codings for money and the Murdock–Provost (George P. Murdock and Caterina Provost, "Measurement of Cultural Complexity," Ethnology XIII [October 1973]: 379–392) measurements of economic development, a chi square (with Yates correction) of 46.76 is obtained. The latter result is not, however, totally "clean" because the presence of money is used as one of the 10 indicators for the level of economic development. (For the Carneiro sample, the presence of money is only one of the 354 indicators used in determining the level of economic development.)

TABLE 6.3

The Existence of Different Types of Money and the Presence of Market Exchange in Societies at Different Levels of Economic Development[a]

Characteristic of society	Groups of societies classified according to levels of economic development			
	Lowest 15 societies	Second lowest 15 societies	Second highest 15 societies	Highest 15 societies
Societies with a noncommercial money (criterion of two)	3 (3)	12 (12)	13 (13)	12 (9)
Societies with a noncommercial money (criterion of three)	2 (2)	10 (10)	11 (11)	10 (7)
Societies with an internal commercial money	1 (1)	6 (3)	7 (6)	14 (10)
Societies with significant internal trade	3 (3)	3 (3)	5 (5)	13 (9)
Societies with both internal commercial money and significant internal trade	0 (0)	1 (1)	4 (4)	13 (9)
Societies with neither internal commercial money nor significant internal trade	11 (11)	7 (7)	7 (7)	1 (1)
Societies with an external commercial money	2 (1)	8 (3)	8 (2)	11.5 (7.5)
Societies with significant external trade	5 (4)	12 (7)	6 (3)	3.5 (1.5)
Societies with both external commerial money and significant external trade	2 (1)	8 (3)	4 (1)	2 (1)
Societies with neither external commercial money nor significant external trade	10 (10)	3 (3)	5 (5)	2 (2)
Societies in which data unavailable for determining dual presence of external money and markets	0 (0)	0 (0)	2 (2)	6 (4)
Societies with a commercial money (external or internal)	2 (1)	9 (4)	8 (6)	14 (10)
Societies with significant trade (external + internal)	7 (6)	12 (7)	10 (9)	14 (10)
Societies with both a commercial money (internal or external) and significant trade (internal + external)	2 (1)	9 (4)	7 (6)	14 (10)

Continued

TABLE 6.3—*Continued*

Characteristic of society	Groups of societies classified according to levels of economic development			
	Lowest 15 societies	Second lowest 15 societies	Second highest 15 societies	Highest 15 societies
Societies with neither a commercial money (internal or external) nor significant trade (internal + external)	7 (7)	3 (3)	4 (4)	1 (1)

[a] The data for this table come from Appendix A, Series 22 and 37 through 40, and from Table 5.1. For those societies for which a determination of the presence of money or markets could not be made, I assume a value of .5. The data in parentheses are calculated by removing those societies from the sample in which the specified money is primarily of Western origin. (For the noncommercial moneys these include the Bhil, Gheg, and Rif; for the internal commerical moneys these include the Basseri, Bhil, Gheg, Kwakiutl, Lapp, Rif, Tanala, and Yaqui; for the external commercial moneys these include the Ao, Basseri, Batak, Bhil, Gheg, Khalka Mongol, Kwakiutl, Lapp, Manóbo, Naskapi, Rif, Rwala, Tanala, Toda, Tuareg, and Yaqui; for the combined commercial moneys these include the Basseri, Bhil, Gheg, Kwakiutl, Lapp, Manóbo, Naskapi, Rif, Tanala, Toda, Tuareg, and Yaqui.) This list of societies differs from those classified as "foreign currency" in Table 6.4 for two reasons. First, they include only Western foreign currencies; second, Table 6.4 permits a fractional counting system in which multiple moneys exist so that a more exact determination is permitted than a simple decision as to whether the Western currency is "primarily" used or not.

Nevertheless, establishing this relationship on a firm basis is an important first step in the analysis that prepares us for the crucial empirical comparisons.

MONEY IN SOCIETIES AT VERY LOW LEVELS OF
ECONOMIC DEVELOPMENT

A serious difficulty in statistically analyzing the determinants of money, particularly variables such as the presence of markets, arises because of a correlation between such determinants and the level of development. Furthermore, since some factors seem to play an important role at one stage of development and not at other stages, additional statistical problems arise. Given the nature of these problems, we are forced in the following paragraphs to adopt relatively simple analytic methods.

One approach is to examine the relative levels of economic development at which various types of money appear. We can compare the emergence levels which are calculated from the regression equations presented in Table 6.1, a technique described in Chapter 5 and designated as the "*ceteris paribus* approach"; or we can examine the relative frequencies of money appearing in societies at different levels of development, a technique described in Chapter 5 and designated as the "mutatis mutandis approach." Data for the latter approach are presented in Table 6.3. One complication immediately arises because Western moneys were used in certain primitive and peasant societies (especially in foreign trade) at the time for which I have sampled. For the regression equations we can handle this by including a variable indicating close contact with the West and then calculating the emergence level by assuming that this variable is zero, that is, that no contact with the West occurred. For the analysis of relative frequencies, we can merely remove these societies from the sample, a procedure carried out in Table 6.3 by placing the "purified" sample in parentheses. By examining the relative level of emergence or the relative importance of different kinds of money at very low levels of economic development, several important conclusions can be drawn.

First, some evidence exists to support the proposition that noncommercial moneys preceded commercial moneys on the economic development scale, but such evidence is certainly not overwhelming. Table 6.3 shows that noncommercial moneys appear in more societies at the early levels of economic development than commercial moneys and that such noncommercial moneys appeared in some societies without commercial moneys, even those which had markets. Such a generalization also holds for the societies when societies with Western moneys have been removed. Table 6.1 also shows that the emergence levels of noncommercial moneys are somewhat lower than commercial moneys. However, it must be emphasized that there are a number of societies which form an exception to this generalization—a sufficient number to require that we state the generalization about relative precedence of noncommercial to commercial moneys in probabilistic terms, permitting us to acknowledge the exceptions which are found.

Second, the proposition that external commercial moneys appeared at lower economic levels than internal commercial moneys receives very mixed support from the evidence. If we define emergence in terms of relative frequency and use the data from Table 6.3, we find that external moneys appear with a slightly greater frequency at the lowest levels of economic development. However, if we exclude Western external moneys, both types of money appear to emerge at the same level. On the other hand, the emergence levels calculated in Table 6.1 predict the earlier emergence of internal commercial moneys. The same type of discrepancy is found when we examine the emergence of internal and external markets in Chapter 5, and the explanation is, I believe, quite similar. Although external moneys may have appeared before internal moneys in some societies at very low levels of economic development, the relative number of these societies in the universe of societies at this developmental level is quite small; when finally a level of economic development is reached at which the relative number of societies with commercial moneys predominates, it turns out that the number of societies with internal moneys are more numerous.

Third, the relationship between the presence of money and of markets in Table 6.3 appears complex but interesting. Among the societies at the lowest levels of economic development, we find no correlation between the appearance of significant internal trade and the appearance of an internal commercial money, although these two variables are highly correlated in societies at higher levels of economic development. On the other hand, if we examine external trade and the presence of external money, we find a number of societies among those at the lowest developmental levels which have significant trade without external moneys but no societies with external moneys which do not have significant external trade. Taking both external and internal commercial moneys and trade together, we find the same relationships that we find for external trade and moneys. From such empirical evidence we conclude that the relationship between the appearance of money and the relative importance of trade among societies at very low levels of economic development appears primarily in the external, not the internal sector, and that at such low levels of development neither the presence of money nor the presence of an important amount of trade necessarily imply each other.

This conclusion suggests that the "double coincidence of wants" problem in primitive economies is considerably more important in foreign trade (where credit involves more risks) than in domestic trade. The appearance of commercial money without a significant degree of trade also implies certain links between noncommercial and commercial moneys which deserve further exploration, a problem which is most easily attacked by focusing briefly on the standardized object which is used for the money.

COMMERCIAL AND NONCOMMERCIAL MONEY STUFFS

To investigate further the links between noncommercial and commercial moneys, it is useful to know whether the same or different money stuffs are used for the two different purposes. From such an investigation we can determine whether the *actual* money stuff was carried from one purpose to another rather than merely the transfer of the *idea* of money.

Before turning to the data, one problem must be mentioned in passing. Some of the sample societies have several different moneys for a given purpose. The Aztec, for instance, had four media of commercial payments: ornamental copper ax blades, quills of gold dust, cloth mantles, and cocoa beans, each of which was convertible into the other and each of which was often used in trade. In other societies it sometimes occurred that substances different from the primary money were used as small change; however, the existence of multiple moneys used for the same purposes was relatively infrequent among the 60 sample societies: For example, among the 28 societies with an internal commercial money, only 5 cases of such multiple moneys for this single purpose can be found. In these cases of multiple moneys I have employed fractional evaluations in the tables recording such data.

Turning now to the analysis of multiple moneys for different purposes, the first step in the analysis is to categorize the money stuffs into the most important groups and then to investigate the particular money stuffs used for noncommer-

TABLE 6.4

Money Stuffs in Societies at Different Levels of Economic Development[a]

Money stuffs	Groups of societies classified according to levels of economic development				
	Lowest	Second lowest	Second highest	Highest	Total
Noncommercial internal money (criterion for two)					
None	12	3	2	3	20
Livestock	3	7	7.5	1	18.5
Shells	0	1.5	1	2	4.5
Food staples	0	1	2	1	4
Other	0	2.5	2.5	2	7
Domestic currency	0	0	0	3	3
Foreign currency	0	0	0	3	3
Commercial internal money					
None	14	9	8	1	32
Livestock	1	1	.75	0	2.75
Shells	0	1.5	1	3	5.5
Food staples	0	0	2.25	.25	2.5
Other	0	1.5	1.25	1.75	4.5
Domestic currency	0	0	0	4	4
Foreign currency	0	2.5	1.75	5	8.75
Commercial external money					
None	13	7	7	2	29
Livestock	1	1	1	0	3
Shells	0	1.5	1	1.5	4
Food staples	0	0	0	0	0
Other	0	.5	1.5	1.5	3.5
Domestic currency	0	0	0	3	3
Foreign currency	1	5	4.5	4	14.5
Don't know	0	0	0	3	3
Total societies	15	15	15	15	60

[a] For those societies with a multiple money for a single purpose I use fractional evaluations, so that each society has money for a particular purpose that add up to one. The method by which the existence of noncommercial moneys is determined minimizes such problems, the reason being that if a society used Substance A exclusively for one noncommerical purpose and Substance B exclusively for another type, it is not considered to have a noncommerical money according to the criterion of two.

There are some problems of replication of these data. For those societies for which Murdock–Morrow "Subsistence Economy" and I agree that there is money, we seldom differ on the question of whether or not it is a currency. We often differ, however, on whether such currency is of foreign or domestic origin. My definition of "domestic origin" is narrow, that is, anything that is produced in the society by natives of that society, an approach that means that currency of occupying powers or of societies intermingled with the society under investigation is considered to be of foreign origin. Thus, Murdock–Morrow classify the Gheg money (which was of Turkish origin since the Turks occupied Albania) as domestic, while I classify it as a foreign money. In contrast to Table 6.3, foreign currency includes both Western and non-Western foreign currencies. Furthermore, the use of fractional units in this table means that the number of societies classified as using foreign currency can be made more finely.

cial, internal commercial, and external commercial moneys.[53] The requisite data for such an analysis are presented in Table 6.4.

A number of important generalizations can be drawn from the data of this table.

First, the types of money stuffs that are used for the different types of money vary greatly. This means that many societies have multiple moneys, each money stuff used for a different purpose. In turn, this raises the question of what we mean when we speak of the "origin" of money—does B "originate" from A if they are embodied in two quite different substances?

Second, although livestock appears to be a favorite noncommercial money, its use as a commercial money, either internal or external, appears quite limited. The various hypotheses about the origins of money that focus attention on livestock may be somewhat misdirected; it may not be livestock per se that influences the development of money so much as the mentality developed through the care of livestock (especially the hoarding and counting of livestock, i.e., its store of value function) that may encourage the development of a commercial money.

Third, as we might suspect, the use of domestic currency as a money occurs only in societies at the highest level of economic development. The use of a foreign currency, especially from a Western nation or neighboring society that is more highly developed or that is much larger in terms of population, can occur at a very much lower level of development.[54] Even societies at relatively high levels of economic development may use a foreign rather than a domestic currency; this can occur either because of military occupation or because it has not been felt economically worthwhile to create a domestic currency.

Fourth, foreign currencies have been adopted for use not only as commercial external moneys but also as commercial internal moneys and even, in a few cases, as a noncommercial money. We have a clear case of diffusion in this situation.

Fifth, propositions tying the money stuff of an internal money exclusively to either an exported domestic staple, an imported good, or a foreign money is quite ill advised. Instances of each, as well as instances in which the domestic money is in no manner connected with foreign trade activities, can be easily found.

---

[53]It should be noted that some primitive moneys are incorporeal, so that the money stuff is unembodied. For instance, if the large Yap stones are considered to be a representation of a true money that are too large to move (or are lying at the bottom of the ocean and can not be moved), then it is the nonwritten titles to these stones that are the actual money in this society. Among the societies in my sample, however, no such cases are recorded.

[54]The Naskapi, a Labrador society at quite a low level of economic development, were able to adapt to a money-script system of the Hudson's Bay Company with apparent ease; and particular groups of the Semang (one of the most primitive societies in the entire sample, which I have classified as moneyless) were able to employ Malay money in their dealings with this group. If various types of animal primates can be taught to use different types of coins to operate in exchange situations with their keepers, then surely the cultural and intellectual level required to understand the use of money is not very high.

TABLE 6.5

Number of Societies at Different Levels of Development with Similar and Different Moneys[a]

	Groups of societies classified according to levels of economic development				
	Lowest 15 societies	Second lowest 15 societies	Second highest 15 societies	Highest 15 societies	Total
Pairwise comparisons					
Same NCM and ICM	1	2.5	3.5	9	16
Different NCM and ICM	0	2.5	1.5	2	6
Same NCM and ECM	1	1	2	7.5	11.5
Different NCM and ECM	0	5	4	.5	10.5
Same ICM and ECM	0	4.5	4.5	9	18
Different ICM and ECM	0	.5	2.5	1	4
Three-way comparisons[b]					
Same NCM, ICM, and ECM	0	1	1	8	10
Different NCM, ICM, and ECM	0	3	4	0	7

Key:
NCM = Noncommercial money
ICM = Internal commercial money
ECM = External commercial money

[a]The data used in this table come from Table 6.4. If the money stuff used as a commercial money is the same as one of the two money stuffs used as a commercial currency, a rating of one-half is assigned to the box designating similarity, and a similar rating is assigned to the box designating differences. Other problems arising with the use of multiple moneys for the same purposes are handled in a similar manner.

[b]Only societies with all three are included.

The similarity of money stuff for different purposes can be examined in a more sensitive manner by making comparisons for each society. The results of such an investigation are presented in Table 6.5. These data provide tantalizing clues to a number of important equations.

To what extent are the origins of noncommercial moneys and external commercial moneys related? Although in roughly half of the societies, these two moneys are made of the same money stuffs, in the critical second lowest stage of development when both money functions appeared to emerge, quite different money stuffs were employed in five cases out of six. This means that although noncommercial moneys appear to have originated at a somewhat earlier stage of economic development than external moneys, there does not appear to be a direct transfer of money usage from one to the other. In short, noncommercial moneys and external moneys seem to have different origins in an important sense.[55]

To what extent are the origins of internal and external commercial moneys related to each other? The important clue to this question can be found in the data for the second lowest stage of economic development when both types of money appear to emerge. It is apparent at this stage that the same money stuff is quite likely to be used for both kinds of commercial money. Furthermore, the likelihood that the same money stuff is used for one commercial purpose and for the noncommercial purpose is considerably lower than the likelihood that the two commercial purposes use the same money stuff.

What is the relationship between the existence of multiple moneys and the level of economic development? The data from both the pairwise and the three-way comparisons show clearly that, at higher stages of development, a single money stuff is increasingly used, at least with regard to the three different purposes specified in the table.[56]

Time-Series Tests

In analyzing the origins of money using cross-section data, some particular problems arise because of the influence of cultural diffusion. Some qualitative facets of the problem deserve brief discussion before the quantitative analysis.

First, in some ultimate sense the use of internal commercial moneys has diffused almost entirely over the world by the last third of the twentieth century;

[55]Although Melitz (*Primitive and Modern Money*, pp. 39–42) implies that noncommercial moneys preceded commercial moneys, he refuses to consider the possibility that the former was the origin of the latter because he is so intent to demonstrate that the existence of trade and markets erodes the foundation of noncommercial moneys. My data suggest that his refusal to consider the former as the origin of the latter has some empirical justification even though his conclusions about erosion may be incorrect.

[56]This generalization may not hold for multiple moneys for a given purpose. In the sample, five societies have multiple internal commercial moneys (Aztec, Khalka Mongol, Kwakiutl, Pomo, and Rwala), and six societies have multiple external commercial moneys (Bribri, Khalka Mongol, Pomo, Rwala, Tuareg, and Wolof). Several of these societies number among the 15 most highly developed in the sample.

TABLE 6.6

Average Distances (Miles) between Groups of Pairs of Societies for Making Diffusion Tests[a]

			Average distances, standard deviations, and size of sample[b]									
			Between societies with and without designated money			Between societies with and without predicted designated money			Between societies with and without designated money after taking causal variables into account			
Type of money	Formula number	Total	K	L	M	X	Y	Z	P	P'	Q	R
Commercial internal money	B6-1-1	5519 [1964] (1326)	5083 [2127] (300)	5621 [1893] (675)	5697 [1898] (351)	4207 [2289] (253)	6023 [1514] (667)	5510 [2019] (406)	6317 [1030] (126)	5205 [2245] (21)	4348 [2377] (90)	6231 [1225] (35)
Commercial external money	B6-1-2b	5590 [1918] (1176)	5288 [2026] (300)	5746 [1786] (600)	5581 [2033] (276)	5025 [2133] (210)	5796 [1756] (588)	5585 [1970] (378)	5583 [1873] (144)	5475 [1986] (36)	5118 [2130] (80)	5487 [2115] (45)
Commercial money (internal + external)	B6-1-3b	5519 [1964] (1326)	5199 [2086] (465)	5726 [1817] (651)	5588 [2029] (210)	4959 [2184] (406)	5864 [1706] (667)	5510 [2108] (253)	5989 [1510] (184)	5093 [2237] (28)	5429 [2025] (138)	5562 [2051] (48)
Noncommercial money (criterion of two)	B6-1-4	5519 [1964] (1326)	5185 [2145] (595)	5900 [1648] (595)	5320 [2108] (136)	5040 [2174] (595)	6050 [1501] (595)	5293 [2187] (136)	6049 [1580] (150)	4850 [2679] (10)	5413 [2013] (150)	5504 [1972] (25)
Noncommercial money (criterion of three)	B6-1-5	5519 [1964] (1326)	5065 [2171] (378)	5766 [1801] (672)	5541 [1937] (276)	4670 [2269] (351)	5990 [1558] (675)	5454 [2054] (300)	5633 [1849] (171)	5681 [1953] (36)	4901 [2195] (152)	5751 [1846] (72)
Internal money (commercial + noncommercial, criterion of two)	B6-1-6	5519 [1964] (1326)	5239 [2119] (741)	6003 [1521] (507)	5038 [2323] (78)	5135 [2152] (666)	6018 [1528] (555)	5322 [2170] (105)	5904 [1721] (108)	6600 [—] (3)	5419 [1949] (36)	5000 [2263] (3)

	B6-1-7										
Internal money (commercial + non-commercial, criterion of three)	5519 [1964] (1326)	5112 [2151] (595)	5956 [1613] (595)	5390 [2099] (136)	4972 [2192] (561)	6087 [1459] (612)	5256 [2202] (153)	6076 [1513] (124)	5183 [2077] (6)	5588 [1927] (93)	5800 [1789] (12)
	B6-1-8										
Total money (internal + external commercial + noncommercial, criterion of two)	5519 [1964] (1326)	5269 [2095] (820)	6074 [1455] (451)	4707 [2464] (55)	5277 [2095] (780)	5913 [1642] (480)	5517 [2047] (66)	5871 [1616] (114)	6600 [—] (3)	6350 [961] (76)	6050 [1230] (6)
	B6-1-9										
Total money (internal + external commercial + noncommercial, criterion of three)	5519 [1964] (1326)	5200 [2117] (703)	5977 [1587] (532)	5312 [2193] (91)	5135 [2152] (666)	6018 [1528] (555)	5322 [2170] (105)	5891 [1596] (105)	6600 [—] (3)	5657 [1866] (70)	5800 [1789] (6)

Key:

Group K: All pairs of societies that have the designated type of money.

Group L: All pairs of societies, one of which has and the other of which does not have the designated type of money.

Group M: All pairs of societies that do not have the designated type of money.

Group X: All pairs of societies in which the explanatory variables lead us to predict the presence of the designated type of money.

Group Y: All pairs of societies, one of which we predict to have and the other of which we predict not to have the designated type of money.

Group Z: All pairs of societies in which the explanatory variables lead us to predict the absence of the designated type of money.

Group P: All pairs of societies, one of which is predicted to have and the other of which is predicted not to have the designated type of money, but both of which actually have the designated type of money.

Group P': All pairs of societies, both of which are predicted not to have the designated type of money, but both of which actually have the designated type of money.

Group Q: All pairs of societies, both of which are predicted to have the designated type of money, but one prediction is incorrect.

Group R: All pairs of societies, one of which is predicted to have and the other of which is predicted not to have the designated type of money, and both predictions are incorrect.

[a] The data come from the logit regressions which are presented in Appendix B.1. In the column labeled "formula number," the B refers to the logit regressions, the 6.1 refers to the original table in this chapter, and the number on the left refers to the specific number of the fomula. A dash indicates that no calculation is made because the set was empty.

[b] The standard deviation is enclosed in brackets and the size of sample in parentheses.

few primitive societies that have come into contact with the West have long resisted adopting the use of Western moneys, a diffusion process that was undoubtedly influenced by the great imbalance of economic and political power between these simpler societies and modern industrial states. This ultimate diffusion of money appeared at a period that was somewhat later than the period for which I sampled most of the societies; furthermore, this ultimate diffusion of money does not necessarily mean that the use of money diffused greatly before this time when the imbalances in relative political and economic power were less.

Second, in the discussion about the various societies using money, it was shown (Table 6.3) that a number of societies have adopted Western moneys, particularly for the purpose of external trade. Such evidence does not necessarily imply that these societies would not have used money if this foreign currency had not been available. Furthermore, by including in the regressions a variable indicating contact with the West, such factors could be taken into account for those societies for which the codings refer to a period when they were not in completely aboriginal conditions.

Third, a number of anthropologists have pointed out that the use of money appears in geographical clusters of societies, and, indeed, my data (Table 6.6) bear this out quite clearly. But since societies with roughly the same levels of economic development (the explanatory variable) seem also to cluster, the clustering of societies with money does not prove that diffusion occurred.

Fourth, some theorists have argued cultural diffusion by claiming that few examples of independent invention of money can be located. Most recently (1974), Jacques Melitz has argued that "valid examples of money among primitives are principally, therefore, the result of diffusion from a Eurasian civilized center"[57] which existed between 2000 and 800 B.C. He notes only three exceptions to this general rule: the cocoa-bean money of the Aztecs, the shell money of the Kapauku Papuans of New Guinea, and the red feather money of the Santa Cruz Islands of the Western Pacific. Those, including Melitz, who have argued such a proposition usually give little or no evidence on how hard they have searched the ethnographic literature for such "exceptions." Certainly in my sample of 60 societies I found few instances where the societies appear to have adopted the money of other societies except from the West. What we need, of course, are reconstructions of the monetary histories of these societies, but unfortunately such evidence does not usually exist, and we must resort to other analytic techniques.

The major argument against the importance of any type of diffusion is very simple. The relationship between the relative level of economic development and the use of money (Table 6.1) is so strong that most cases can be explained by reference to this single factor alone. If any kind of diffusion of the use of money occurred, it must be considered as a very secondary explanatory factor.

[57]Melitz, *Primitive and Modern Money*, p. 83. Among authorities cited by Melitz to add plausibility to his diffusion argument is Bronisław Malinowski.

As noted in Chapter 3, we have a technique that permits us to use cross-section evidence to detect the presence of one type of diffusion, namely, the diffusion occurring when a society borrows a particular cultural trait from one neighbor and passes it to another neighbor, where the process is repeated. The relevant data are presented in Table 6.6.

By comparing columns K with L and M, we see that for most definitions of money a geographical clustering of societies with such money occurs and that in a number of cases the degree of clustering is statistically significant. As noted previously, this arises because the major independent (explanatory) variable is the level of economic development and that societies with similar levels of development are clustered. This phenomenon is seen even more clearly in comparing columns X with Y and Z, which show that the societies in which money is predicted are even more clustered than the societies in which money actually appears.

As I have argued in Chapter 3, the really crucial tests are made when we examine the prediction errors and compare columns P and P' with column R. In certain cases we rule out diffusion when the cases in column P' are fewer than 30. And for several other types of money, there are too few cases (30 or less) in column R to use as a base of comparison, and we must use the averages for the entire sample. After making these adjustments, we find no evidence of a significant geographical clustering of a nature to suggest the occurrence of slow diffusion of a normal variety.[58]

Although the statistical analysis suggests that the results of the regression analysis and other statistical investigations in the previous pages are not affected by "slow" diffusion, "fast" diffusion of money did occur, especially after contact with the West; this type of diffusion could be taken in part into account in the regression analysis. However, as I have noted previously, my statistical analysis does not detect the occurrence of diffusion when both money and the explanatory factors diffused together. I do not believe that the occurrence of this latter type of diffusion was sufficiently important to affect greatly the conclusions that I have drawn.

SUMMARY AND CONCLUSIONS

The definition of money employed in this chapter focuses on the use of a standardized object as a medium of exchange for foreign or domestic trade transactions or as a means of payment in noncommercial transactions. Since most theories about the origins of money rest on some type of intuitive cost/benefit analysis in which the costs and the benefits of using money can only be

---

[58]For commercial money (formula 6-1-3b) we find a clustering suggesting that money diffused from one society in which we do not predict the presence of money to a nearby society in which we make the same prediction. Since this type of diffusion does appear in the two components of commercial money, this result may well represent merely a statistical artifact and be of no empirical importance.

specified in a qualitative fashion, they lack a certain credibility, so that it has been useful to approach the origins of money in a quasi-inductive fashion.

The empirical analysis shows a strong relationship between the presence of money, however specifically defined, and the level of economic development of the society. At the very lowest levels of development primitive societies have relatively little market exchange and, in addition, usually lack all types of money. In more cases than not, at higher stages of development, money used for noncommercial payments appears before money used for commercial purposes. However, sufficient exceptions to the rule that noncommercial moneys appear before commercial moneys exist, so that a firm conclusion on these matters can not be made.

Regarding the earlier emergence of external and internal commercial moneys, the evidence is even more mixed, and no conclusions can be drawn. Depending on the analytic technique employed, different generalizations can be obtained. Such a situation also occurred in Chapter 5 in the analysis of the relative emergence levels of external and internal market exchange and is thus quite consistent with the money analysis. In any case, previous dogmatism about such matters is quite unwarranted.

Although the presence of extensive market exchange and the presence of money are highly correlated at higher levels of economic development, this linkage is much weaker at lower levels of development. More specifically, a linkage between trade and money is more likely to be found in external commercial transactions than internal commercial transactions, a difference which can be interpreted in part by the relative risks of extending credit in the two situations.

Investigation of the money stuff used reveals that the money stuffs for commercial purposes (either external or internal) are very often different from the money stuff used for noncommercial purposes. This result raises some questions about what we mean by the "origin" of money: Are we referring to the idea of money or to the actual substances used as money?

Although the analysis is carried out using a cross-section sample of 60 societies, the data are subjected to a particular type of statistical analysis that shows that the conclusions drawn are probably not affected by the presence of "slow" diffusion. Although "fast" diffusion did occur, insofar as a number of primitive societies have adopted Western moneys, measures were taken so that the impact of such diffusion on the conclusions is minimized.

Many facets of primitive moneys are not explored in this study: Most importantly, I have not examined the occurrence of "standards of value" or "units of account." This means that I have been unable to test some interesting hypotheses, although it must also be added that we will probably never have the data to test these ideas.[59]

[59]Although Melitz, *Primitive and Modern Money*, pp. 42–52, has perhaps given the most stress to the importance of the unit-of-account function of money and its emergence before the medium-of-exchange function, he provides little data to back up his contentions and presents some theoreti-

Primitive moneys have exercised a fascination on social scientists of many disciplines. Now it can be argued that this fascination is illogical; that money is a mere superstructural element of the economy masking much more important underlying social forces; and that money receives attention primarily because the subject evokes passionate and irrational feelings, samples of which are provided in the chapter's epigraphs. But the evidence presented on noncommercial moneys and on the presence of money in societies without extensive market exchange suggests that such dismissal is unwarranted. Much about the origins of money needs further exploration; and investigation of the impact of money on society, once it has been introduced, presents a valuable type of inquiry. The subject of primitive moneys exercises its fascination, I believe, because it provides important clues to the operation and changes of these economies.

---

cal considerations which raise a number of serious questions. A good deal of his argument rests on the notion that a unit of account has very low costs and quite high benefits in even very primitive societies. But many of his arguments about the necessity of a cardinal scale of value can be applied to ordinal rankings of value as well which do not imply a unit of account. Furthermore, many societies do not have systems of numbers or sufficient knowledge of arithmetic operations to use a cardinal scale. Finally, I believe that Melitz underestimates the ability of people to function without cardinal value scales; certainly most of our personal social dealings with different individuals are carried out without our needing to score such individuals on a cardinal "friendliness" or "trust" scale.

7

THE DETERMINANTS OF RECIPROCAL EXCHANGE

La donna gli mostrò la gallina.
"Non posso accettare" rispose don Paolo. "I preti non possono accettare regali."
La donna protestò.
"Allora non vale" ella disse. "Se non prendete la gallina, la grazia non vale. . . ."
"La grazia è gratuita" disse don Paolo.
"Grazie gratuite non esistono" disse la donna.

SILONE[1]

Reciprocal exchange raises much different problems of analysis than market exchange. In empirical research certain problems of identification and investigation are encountered (some of which are discussed in Chapter 4 and Appendix B.2) that do not occur in the exploration of market exchange. In theoretical research a vast literature seems to be available, but most of this is unusable for hypothesis testing. More specifically, a large part of this literature is on a very high level of generality without clear specification of the limiting conditions; and another part focuses primarily on the phenomenon of reciprocity in one or several specific situations without clear specification of the general circumstances that might apply to other situations. The residue of propositions that can be used in this cross-cultural study when the empirical theoretical literature on reciprocity is distilled is disappointingly small.

Fortunately, a number of propositions can be generated from quite simple economic and social considerations, so that we do not need to worry about a deficiency of analytic tasks to provide scholarly employment. Furthermore, these propositions can be tested using the sample of 60 primitive and peasant

---

Design from a Kiowa baby-carrier; southern plains of the U.S.A.
[1]Ignazio Silone, *Vino e pane,* Chap. VII: 'The woman showed him the chicken. "I dare not accept," replied Don Paolo. "Priests can't take gifts." The woman protested. "Then the whole thing isn't any good," she said. "Unless you take the chicken, the grace isn't any good. . . ." "Grace is free," said Don Paolo. "There is no such thing as free grace," said the woman.'

societies. However, it should become readily apparent that the propositions explored in this macrosocietal analysis of reciprocal exchange are quite different in nature from the microsocietal hypotheses used in particular case studies such as the exploration of Eskimo reciprocity presented in Chapter 4.

The theoretical and statistical analyses in this chapter show that the presence of an important degree of reciprocal exchange of goods is more likely to occur in societies with low rather than high levels of economic development. Furthermore, the size of the unit of observation and the principal modes of food production also play important causal roles for the presence of such reciprocal exchange. For particular types of this exchange the division of society into lineages also seems another important causal element. In the analysis of the reciprocal exchange of labor the theoretical literature is richer, but the statistical results are more disappointing. However, such labor reciprocity appears inversely related to the level of economic development, directly related to the presence of lineages, and for particular types of such exchange also related to the principal mode of food production. I also show that the reciprocal exchange of labor appears to persist to an important degree at much higher levels of economic development than the reciprocal exchange of goods.

A SURVEY OF RECIPROCAL EXCHANGE

General Considerations of Definition

As I define terms in Chapter 2, reciprocal exchange is a balanced distributional transaction in which the forces of supply and demand are masked, in contrast to market exchange where such forces are highly visible. Of course, determination of "masking" requires a judgment by the analyst about the ways in which such exchange is structured. I exclude from reciprocal exchange those transactions that are "balanced" by flows of social invisibles and consider only those transactions in which the counterflow is a good or labor service of roughly equal value. In reciprocal exchange transactions are carried on without a true money (although a pseudomoney may be present), usually at fixed exchange ratios. An archtypical example of reciprocal exchange occurs in the Trobriand Islands off the southeast coast of New Guinea in which the coast and inland dwellers exchange fish and yams at fixed exchange rates even though the coast dwellers would be economically better off by devoting their time to other pursuits.[2]

Reciprocal exchange can be carried out in many different ways—ceremonially, formally, informally, secretively. The exchange can be initiated either by a tied gift (Person A gives Person B a gift and Person B feels obligated to make a return of equal value) or a tied request (Person A requests something

[2]Bronisław Malinowski, *Argonauts of the Western Pacific* (1961), p. 188 [originally published 1922].

from Person B and then gives B in return something of equal value). Such exchange can also be forced (in the sense that any initiated exchange must be accepted) or voluntary (in the sense that the initiated exchange can be rejected). It should be clear that if reciprocal exchange is initiated, there are usually mechanisms for enforcing the transaction so that it is balanced; but such mechanisms seem most often embodied in social or religious rather than political or legal forces and institutions. If no enforcement mechanisms exist, then an intended reciprocal exchange may turn into an unintended transfer.

Considerable analytic attention has been paid to the fact that at any given point in time the accounts of people engaged in reciprocal exchange are rarely balanced; that such imbalances are said to bind the parties of the transactions more closely together and thus have a positive social function; and that the exchange accounts are balanced only in the long run. It is, I believe, most useful in the coding of transactions to define "balance" over the long run, a decision that raises some obvious difficulties in the empirical research.

It must be emphasized that I define reciprocal exchange in terms neither of the motives of the participants nor of the social consequences of the transaction. Many anthropologists in the Maussian tradition[3] have emphasized that people enter into such transactions to cement social bonds and that such transactions produce a greater societal solidarity. But I also include as reciprocity various types of balanced transactions that occur as a form of unfriendly competition[4] as well as various types of balanced transactions accompanied by considerable suspicion.[5] (Indeed, reciprocal transactions might be avoided because of worries about the inability of the receivers to reciprocate.[6]) Many of the transactions I classify as reciprocity may contribute nothing to social solidarity, however this vague concept may be defined.

Let me add that I do not classify transactions as reciprocal if they are intended to be reciprocal but turn out not to be (e.g., the giving of baby or wedding presents in the United States is sometimes intended to be reciprocal, but often one of the transactors has more babies or marriages; I have been informed, however, that in certain social strata arrangements are made so that

[3]Marcel Mauss, The Gift (1967) [originally published 1925].

[4]Inasmuch as potlatches and similar institutions can be considered as structuring reciprocal exchange (a problem discussed briefly later), several studies have emphasized the way in which such exchanges are initiated for malevolent purposes, for example, Helen Codere, Fighting with Property: A Study of Kwakiutl Potlatching and Warfare, 1792–1930 (1950); and Michael W. Young, Fighting with Food (1971).

[5]This is exemplified by the Sirionó, as reportedly by Allen R. Holmberg, Nomads of the Long Bow: The Sirionó of Eastern Bolivia (1969) [originally published 1950] who notes (p. 151): "Indeed, sharing [in this case he means reciprocal exchange—F.P.] rarely occurs without a certain amount of mutual distrust and misunderstanding."

[6]This is exemplified by the Copper Eskimo of Northwest Canada, as reported by Diamond Jenness, Report of the Canadian Arctic Expedition, 1913–18, Vol. XII, The Life of the Copper Eskimo (1922) who notes (p. 90): "In the winter, when each housewife cooks in her own hut, she can hide away some of the choicer portions of the meat for her husband and herself to eat after all the visitors have left; but in summer when most of the cooking is done out of doors, everyone gathers round the pot to eat and no concealment is possible."

such transactions are actually balanced by a reverse flow of services such as babysitting). I further base judgments about the quantitative importance of such reciprocal transactions on the actual frequency of the exchanges and value of goods involved rather than the ethical stress placed on such transactions by the society.

Reciprocal exchange, as I have defined it, is different from the concept of "sharing" since the latter does not involve an obligation to return something of equal value and, thus, may turn out to be a transfer. It is also different from the concept of "mutuality," a situation in which two people or groups have rights over and obligations to each other but in which these do not necessarily result in balanced exchange.[7] Of course, if sharing or mutuality involve balanced exchange, than I would classify such transactions as reciprocal.

Any definition of reciprocity raises problems of classification at the borders, and mine is no exception. Difficulties in drawing the line between market and reciprocal exchange are discussed in Chapter 5. In addition, some difficulties arise in drawing the border between reciprocal exchange and certain types of noncentric transfers, and these will be examined in several specific contexts.

Given my definition of reciprocal exchange, we can distinguish several different dimensions for analytic purposes. Clearly, it is useful to determine the relative economic importance of reciprocal exchange, that is, the proportion of total goods or services in the society that are exchanged in this manner. It also seems useful to separate reciprocal exchange of food from other goods and services since the former may (as I discuss in Chapter 4) have some special determinants. For some purposes we might also separate reciprocal exchange taking place only between closely related persons with such exchange occurring between individuals belonging to different kin groups or communities. Other analytic purposes can be served by distinguishing between reciprocal exchanges involving the same good or service, a small set of different goods or services, or a large set of different goods and services.

For certain purposes it is also useful to distinguish between simple reciprocal exchange and reciprocal exchange that is embedded in some type of system of such exchanges. For instance, there might be reciprocal relations between two groups such that each member in one group has an exchange partner in the other group. Or, within a single group, reciprocal relations can be structured in several different ways. In a labor exchange ring an entire group may together work the fields of each of its members so that each person gives to and receives the same amount of labor from every other person. Or in a mutual feasting group each member invites the entire group to a feast so that each person gives to and receives the same number of feasts from every other person.[8] It must be

---

[7]For instance, Melville Herskovits, *Economic Anthropology: The Economic Life of Primitive Peoples* (1965), p. 157 [originally published 1940], speaks of "reciprocal obligations" between tribes in the Nilgiri Hills of India, but he described a situation where exchange is highly unbalanced and, according to my definition, is therefore not reciprocal.

[8]Peter P. Ekeh, *Social Exchange Theory* (1974), p. 53 labels these two types of reciprocal exchange structures "individual-focused net generalized exchange" and "group-focused net generalized exchange."

explicitly noted that I exclude from such group reciprocal exchange arrangements what is sometimes called generalized or chain reciprocity (where Person A gives X to B, who gives something of equal value to C, who in turn gives an equal value to A) since exchange between any two people is not balanced.

From this brief exposition it should be clear that my definition of reciprocity is quite different from those of Mauss, Lévi-Strauss, Sahlins, and others who have written extensively on the subject.[9] Determination of whose conceptualization is better or worse can only be made by comparing the various analyses in which the different concepts are employed and the type of propositions that are generated.

Types of Reciprocal Exchange

INTRODUCTION

Three types of transactions, which might be considered reciprocal exchange by my definition, are excluded from the analysis in the rest of this chapter: the exchanges of goods and services between families that center around a marriage between members of the two families; the goods and labor parents give to their children that are then repaid when the children reach adulthood and help support their elderly parents; and borrowing of specific goods that are then returned. Each of these deserves brief consideration.

In a number of the sample societies the various types of reciprocal exchanges occurring once in a lifetime at marriage are the most important economic transactions of a person's life. Since these transactions have been the subject of statistical analysis in Appendix B.2, I exclude them from consideration in this chapter to avoid duplication and focus instead on more repetitive types of transactions.

The exchanges between a person and his parents over the life cycle are often described as representing reciprocal exchange. Unfortunately, quantitative information about such transactions is quite scanty for most societies, so that it is impossible to determine whether we have a transfer or an exchange transaction. Since such exchanges occur within the basic unit of observation (defined in Chapter 2) in most societies, this type of transaction is also excluded from consideration.

Reciprocal exchange embraces cases where a good is borrowed at one time and then an equivalent value is returned at another time. If it is exactly the same good that is returned, certain analytic problems arise. Also, most ethnographers have paid little attention to these types of ordinary borrowing except if an interest rate is charged, so that our data base is quite incomplete. So for practical reasons this type of transaction is also left undiscussed and uncoded in the analysis below.

---

[9]Mauss, The Gift; Claude Lévi-Strauss, The Elementary Structures of Kinship, 2nd ed. (1969); Marshall Sahlins, Stone Age Economics (1972); Ekeh, Social Exchange Theory.

In most discussions of reciprocity three types are distinguished: goods for goods; labor hours for labor hours; and goods for labor hours. For reasons given in Chapter 5, I have classified instances of exchange of goods for labor hours as labor exchange, so that primary attention in this chapter is focused on "goods reciprocity" and "labor reciprocity" (which embraces exchange of labor hours for labor hours as well as goods for labor hours).

GOODS RECIPROCITY

The most simple type of goods reciprocity is the exchange of similar goods—a dinner party for a dinner party, an arrow for an arrow—where the predominance of "social" over "economic" forces is clearly seen since there is no apparent economic gain. Such a type of exchange can be found in a large number of societies.

If we turn to the reciprocal exchange of different kinds of goods, then we introduce several additional problems, of which difficulties centering around the exchange rate are the most important. Often the exchange rates are recognized and ostensibly fixed. For instance, in the oft-discussed Kula ring, which involves a ceremonial exchange of necklaces for bracelets between and within various island groups off the east coast of New Guinea, the exchange rate is one for one.[10] When more complicated equivalencies occur, there are not only problems of general recognition of the exchange rate but also difficulties arising in the change of such exchange rates.[11] Furthermore, the existence of reciprocal exchange of two different types of goods at a specified exchange rate gives rise to the possibility that at least one of the participants in such exchange may economically gain in the transaction. For instance, if two Xs are worth one Y to a particular individual (for personal reasons), and if the exchange rate in the society is 1X = 1Y, then by exchanging reciprocally his Xs for Ys through a series of reciprocity transactions, the individual will benefit economically from such "social" transactions by collecting, in the jargon of economists, a "consumer rent."

The mechanics of the reciprocal exchange of goods appear quite simple—at least until we investigate processes of enforcement—but the forms and variety of circumstances at which such exchanges take place are quite varied. Ceremonial aspects of such exchange especially vary from society to society. Since various investigators have detailed the variety of forms through which such exchange takes place, at this time there is no special need to illustrate such forms through a long list of anecdotes.

[10]This example of simple one-to-one reciprocity refers only to the domestic Kula exchange. In the external Kula exchange the situation is more complicated since the items exchanged are not homogeneous and each carries a different "history" which may give it a differential value. Although the exchange is still one-for-one, a particularly valuable necklace requires in return not just any bracelet but a bracelet of roughly equal value.

[11]In a different context a number of these problems are discussed by Marshall Sahlins, "Exchange Value and the Diplomacy of Primitive Trade," in Sahlins, *Stone Age Economics*, pp. 277–315.

Some difficulties in distinguishing market and reciprocal exchange arise, especially when trade is carried on in a framework of ostensible reciprocity, for example, with "trade" partners who exchange ceremonial gifts. In several such cases we must code the transactions as representing both market and reciprocal exchange since elements of both are so inextricably mixed. More difficulties arise in situations involving both reciprocal exchange and transfer elements, and several cases are worth considering.

In some simple hunting societies game is often shared by the hunter with others, either in his hunting party or in the community.[12] In part, this occurs because storage of meat is difficult, so that the hunter and his family have three choices: either to gorge themselves on whatever game is killed (an alternative almost exclusively taken in some societies such as the Sirionó of Bolivia); to use the meat for some type of delayed exchange (either market or reciprocal); or to give it to others. The latter two choices result in a more even distribution of meat consumption over time than if one had to rely solely on one's own hunting efforts. Often the meat is distributed by "sharing," which involves both reciprocal exchange and transfer elements, even though such "sharing" is carried out within a framework of ostensible reciprocal exchange. That is, if meat is generally "shared," it should be clear that reciprocity extends only between hunters of similar skill and that under such an arrangement over time good hunters will always be net givers to bad hunters. Sometimes the rules about who is the "owner" of the fallen game are structured so as to break this link between hunting ability and net givers or receivers, for example, in situations where the first person in a hunting party to see the game is the "owner" or where there is extensive lending of arrows and the owner of the arrow felling the game is the owner of the game (a situation occurring among the !Kung Bushmen of the Kalihari desert in southern Africa). Clearly, such sharing of game has both reciprocal and transfer elements and must therefore be considered in the analysis of both modes of distribution.

Another intricate case is the potlatch, which are giveaway feasts occurring in a number of societies on the western coast of Canada and the northwestern coast of the United States, as well as in other parts of the world. Different observers have emphasized the reciprocal and the transfer elements of this institution.[13] Certainly, there are strong reciprocal elements at several levels: A potlatch host invites people whose potlatches he has attended; and within the

[12]These issues and a number of cases, including those mentioned later, are analyzed by John H. Dowling, "Individual Ownership and the Sharing of Game in Hunting Societies," *American Anthropologist* LXX (June 1968): 502–507.

[13]The reciprocal elements of a potlatch are emphasized by Mauss, *The Gift*, and, to a certain extent, John W. Adams, *The Gitksan Potlatch: Population Flux, Resource Ownership and Reciprocity* (1973). The transfer elements of a potlatch are emphasized in varying degrees by Codere, *Fighting with Property*, and Homer G. Barnett, *The Nature and Function of the Potlatch* (1968) [originally written as Ph.D. dissertation, 1938]. In the considerable literature on the potlatch, a consensus on the relative importance of the exchange and transfer elements does not yet appear to be reached.

host's kin group those who stand most likely to benefit when invited to other potlatches contribute the most to the potlatches their group is sponsoring (or, conversely, those who contribute most to the host's potlatch receive the most in the distribution that the host makes when the host and his kin are invited to a potlatch). But there are also strong transfer elements, since a frequent motive of the host is to give his guests more than they have given him in the past or, perhaps, ever will give him in the future. As in the previous case, the institution contains both reciprocal and transfer elements and must therefore be considered in the analysis of both modes of distribution.

LABOR RECIPROCITY

The reciprocal exchange of labor has many parallels with the reciprocal exchange of goods. The most simple type of labor reciprocity is the exchange of man-hour for man-hour of unskilled labor. If different skills or strengths are exchanged, different equivalencies may obtain: For example, the Serb peasants considered the work of an adult man in a given time to be equal to the work of two children in the same time and the work of a man with a plowing team equal in value to the work of five men doing normal agricultural tasks in the same time.

As noted earlier, labor reciprocity can involve just two people or an entire group. Labor rings and other types of group labor reciprocity can be conducted quite informally or, on the other hand, can be highly ceremonialized. One type of ceremonialized reciprocal labor exchange that is often mentioned in the ethnological literature is festive labor, where the reciprocal element is the exchange of labor for a feast.[14] The convener of a festive labor group may or may not be required to participate in the festive labor groups convened by members of the group participating in his feast (i.e., A and B may both exchange food and labor, or else a single transaction of A's food for B's labor may occur).

A serious problem of definition of labor reciprocity arises when the unit of production includes members of different consumption units. For instance, are the participants of a hunting band or the workers on an agricultural plantation engaged in labor reciprocity when they "cooperate" in production, or should we omit such mutual assistance in our definition of reciprocity? Clearly, if the members of the production group are engaged by themselves in production (e.g., each person in a gathering group is gathering for himself), we do not have labor reciprocity. If members of the production group are hired or enslaved by the leader, and if they then cooperate among themselves in the production process, it does not seem useful to classify this as labor reciprocity since the

[14]The various types of reciprocal labor are systematically described and investigated in an unpublished Ph.D. dissertation by Charles John Erasmus, *Reciprocal Labor: A Study of Its Occurrence and Disappearance Among Farming Peoples in Latin America* (1955). The most accessible article based on this dissertation is his "Culture Structure and Process: The Occurrence and Disappearance of Reciprocal Farm Labor," *Southwestern Journal of Anthropology* XII (Winter 1956): 444–469.

organization of work is ultimately determined by the overseer. If, on the other hand, production cooperation is important and voluntary (e.g., hunting drives, joint ocean fishing in a large canoe, group clearing, and planting of land) and is not the result of their selling their labor services, then I believe we deal with phenomena which, given the requirement for balanced exchange, should be considered as labor reciprocity.

The requirement of balance in such situations raises certain problems, for it is often very difficult to determine whether the division of production among participants corresponds to the relative productivity (either average or marginal productivity) of the various participants. For some cases we have direct evidence that this is not the case, for example, the joint herding example cited in Chapter 2 where a man with a large flock shares herding duties on a fifty–fifty basis with a man with a small flock; or a situation where some of the participants get no share in the jointly produced product; or a situation where a participant who had done relatively little work obtained the lion's share of the final product. But for most cases such evidence does not exist; therefore, we must assume that the division of the jointly produced good corresponds roughly to relative productivity and that we have a case of labor reciprocity.

THEORIES OF RECIPROCAL EXCHANGE

Most of the theoretical literature on reciprocal exchange focuses on microsocietal rather than macrosocietal aspects of the question, on questions such as why does reciprocal exchange exist and what are the social forces inducing a receiver to return a good or service of equal value to the giver, rather than on questions about why reciprocal exchange is a more common mode of distribution in certain societies than others. That is, there is a much greater literature on why the woman cited in the chapter epigraph feels it necessary to pay the priest to receive grace than why such women are found in one society rather than another. Often, the notion of reciprocity is used as an organizing principle for certain factual materials rather than as an analytic tool with which to construct propositions. Sometimes the concept is used primarily for dramatic effect.[15]

Most of the propositions that I have been able to find in the literature or to generate myself deal with particular types of reciprocity. Two general propositions, however, are worthy of a brief glance. Helen Codere has conjectured that reciprocity is the dominant mode of distribution in primitive but not peasant societies and that reciprocity is the prevailing or dominant mode of distribution in a majority of societies up to the industrial revolution.[16] Although testing

---

[15]An egregious example of this is by Howard Becker, Man in Reciprocity: Introductory Lectures on Culture, Society and Personality (1956); in which the author explicitly refuses to define reciprocity (p. 1) and, as far as I could determine, expounds not one interesting and testable proposition about the nature, determinants, or occurrence of reciprocity in the entire 450 pages of the book.

[16]Helen Codere, "Exchange and Display," in International Encyclopedia of the Social Sciences, ed. David L. Sills, Vol. V (1968), pp. 239–245. Similar but less precisely stated propositions can be found in the writings of others.

these conjectures in a rigorous fashion is difficult with the data at hand, the evidence that follows casts a certain amount of doubt on them.

Determinants of Goods Reciprocity

In the anthropology literature one often finds hypotheses about the relationship between the importance of reciprocal exchange and the level of economic development; however, the nature of this relationship varies considerably according to the theorist. As I note in Chapter 5, a number of social scientists, especially the evolutionists, have focused their attention on the lower part of the economic development scale and have argued that reciprocal exchange occurs at lower levels than market exchange. Some, such as Karl Buecher, have hypothesized an evolution from noncentric transfers (which Buecher labels "presents") to reciprocal exchange (which he calls "gift exchange") to barter.[17] A variant on this theme can be found in the work of Marcel Mauss, who states that market exchange occurs at a later stage of development than "total prestations," which is a type of reciprocal exchange in which bundles of goods, services, social rights, and social duties are exchanged between groups.[18] More recently, Karl Polanyi has suggested that for the domestic economy (in this discussion he excludes external trade) reciprocal exchange probably appears at lower levels of development than market exchange because of the more social nature of the former type of transaction.[19]

The relationship between reciprocal exchange of goods and higher levels of economic development is seldom sketched as clearly. Karl Polanyi has argued that in primitive communities reciprocity is a vital feature of the economy but that at a higher level of development in "archaic" economies, redistribution of goods from a center (centric transfers) plays a key role in distribution instead.[20] Such a proposition must be taken in conjunction with his repeated reminder that almost all forms of distribution occur to a certain degree at all stages of economic development.

A reverse proposition seems to be argued by Margaret Mead, who seems to agree that reciprocal exchange can be found in highly primitive societies but who sees little relationship between the level of economic development (or, for that matter, the primary mode of production) and the psychological value

[17]Karl Buecher, *Industrial Evolution* (1907), pp. 60 ff. [originally published 1893].

[18]Mauss, *The Gift*, Chap. I.

[19]Karl Polanyi, *The Great Transformation* (1957), Chap. IV and V; and Karl Polanyi, "The Economy as Instituted Process," in *Trade and Market in the Early Empire: Economies in History and Theory* (1957), ed. Karl Polanyi, Conard M. Arensberg, and Harry W. Pearson, pp. 243–307. I use the term "suggest" in the text advisedly since this is an inference from his writings rather than a proposition which he baldly states.

[20]This proposition is explicitly stated in Karl Polanyi and Abraham Rotstein, *Dahomey and the Slave Trade* (1960), p. xx. George Dalton has pointed out to me that such redistribution occurs primarily between the villages and the top political leaders and that within the villages market and reciprocal exchange continue to play their important roles.

orientations (cooperativeness or competitiveness) that may underlie or be correlated with emphasis on different modes of distribution.[21]

In the statistical analysis we must look to see if reciprocal exchange is found in societies with very low levels of economic development and, in addition, whether the appearance of such exchange is more likely to be found at such levels of development than at higher levels. As I show below, this inverse relationship between reciprocity and development level is found, especially when other factors are held constant.

The mode of production might also have an influence on the presence of reciprocal exchange of goods through its impact on the certainty of the food supply or on the time pattern of when food is obtained. Two types of cases come to mind. First, if a society is highly dependent on a source of food for which production at any given time by any particular individual is quite uncertain, then the type of mixed distributional mode discussed above of half non-centric transfer, half reciprocal exchange might be very important. Such a situation would probably be most important in societies relying primarily on hunting or fishing as the main subsistence activity (a case study of such reciprocal exchange/transfers in these circumstances for the Eskimo is examined in detail in Chapter 5). Second, if a society is highly dependent on a source of food for which the time pattern of obtaining might vary from individual to individual but where the potential giver of food has visible evidence that the exchange will be reciprocal, then we might also expect to find considerable reciprocal exchange. Such a situation would probably be most important in agricultural societies. These propositions suggest, therefore, that reciprocal exchange of goods is more likely to be found (*ceteris paribus*) in hunting, fishing, and farming societies than in gathering and herding societies; such propositions also receive considerable support in the regression analysis below.

Another possible "economic" influence concerns the size of the unit of observation (defined in Chapter 2) and/or differences in the size of the production and consumption units. The larger the unit of observation, the more self-sufficient it might be, and the less need its members would have for engaging in exchange with other members of the community. Therefore, the size of the unit of observation and the presence of reciprocal exchange of goods should be inversely related, a proposition that also receives some confirmation in the empirical analysis below. We might also argue that if consumption and production units differ in size (a situation that occurs more frequently when multiple units of consumption and/or production exist), we might also find considerable reciprocal exchange of goods since a person would usually have close ties outside that unit which we use as the unit of observation. Although this proposition appeared promising at the early stages of empirical investigation, its effect was not sufficiently strong to warrant inclusion in the final calculations.

[21]Margaret Mead, "Interpretive Statement," in her edited volume *Cooperation and Competition among Primitive Peoples* (1966), p. 463 [originally published 1937].

It is useful to consider a number of propositions that were tested and did not appear to help explain the pattern of reciprocal exchange. The important presence of extensive lineages might encourage such reciprocity by tying members of individual nuclear families more closely to a broader set of people; furthermore, if kin ties encourage the distribution of goods between its members and at the same time discourage market exchange between them, then such distribution might well be carried on through reciprocal exchange. Lineages can be defined in several different ways, but none of these variables proved very useful predictors of reciprocal exchange of goods except with regard to the presence of ceremonial reciprocity (discussed later). I also tested a number of other hypotheses concerning social structural considerations and reciprocal exchange of goods, for example, a set of propositions dealing with the importance of such exchange in "harmonic" and "disharmonic" regimes or in societies with particular patterns of cousin marriages[22]; the empirical results of such tests were quite unpromising. I also tried testing a series of "atmosphere" variables, believing that the presence of great income differences, greatly unequal amounts of work performed by the spouses, widespread polygyny, and so forth might reflect value configurations that would be correlated with the absence of reciprocal exchange of goods. No such variables, however, proved to be significantly correlated with the reciprocity variable. Furthermore, I experimented with a series of hypotheses concerning the possible substitution of market for reciprocal exchange (i.e., that the social configurations accompanying market exchange act to discourage reciprocal exchange and vice versa). (A plausible reverse proposition can also be argued.) As it turned out, certain statistical problems of multicollinearity arose, and a conclusive test could not be performed; nevertheless, such propositions also did not seem promising. Finally, I tried to draw on some of the insights from the case study of Eskimo reciprocity in Chapter 4 to frame some additional hypotheses, but sufficient coding difficulties were encountered that such experiments had to be abandoned.

The components of the reciprocal exchange of goods also deserve brief attention. In the literature special attention has been devoted to examination of the reciprocal exchange of food. Partly this is because, in terms of total production, food is the most important good produced in almost every precapitalist economy. And partly this is because food has certain properties different from other goods. That is, since food is vital for life and therefore more "social" than other goods, some have argued that food is supposed to be more often transferred rather than exchanged and that it is supposed to be more often exchanged reciprocally at fixed rates rather than sold on markets. It is difficult to set up tests to examine these conjectures on a systematic basis, but as a first step I examined separately the various propositions discussed previously for food and nonfood items. I especially tried to see if any of the "atmosphere" variables

[22]Such propositions were drawn from certain provocative hints of Lévi-Strauss, *Elementary Structures of Kinship*, who also, as far as I know, coined these terms.

discussed, which have a strong "social" nature, would have a different impact on food and nonfood exchange but to no avail.

I also examined cases in which reciprocal exchange was accompanied by a great deal of ceremony, believing that certain "social" variables must underlie such festivities that are somewhat different from the other causes of reciprocal exchange. As I will show, the important presence of lineages seems to be particularly important.

Determinants of Labor Reciprocity

For the analysis of reciprocal labor exchange, we can build on the superb analysis of Charles J. Erasmus, who collected and tested a large number of propositions about the nature of this type of reciprocity.[23] Most of his propositions focus on microaspects of such exchange: Festive reciprocal labor groups are larger than other types of reciprocal labor groups; friendship, kinship, and proximity of residence all seem of equal importance in the composition of both exchange and festive work groups; the organization and direction of work parties tends to be more democratic when labor is highly reciprocal than when reciprocity takes some other form; tasks generally performed by reciprocal labor do not involve very extensive specialization; reciprocal exchange labor tends to occur among social equals, while festive exchange labor cuts across differences in wealth and status; and so forth. He also has a number of propositions about the determinants of reciprocal labor (which will be later discussed), the relative efficiency of various types of reciprocal labor, and the spread of reciprocal labor practices.

According to Charles J. Erasmus the basic factor underlying the reciprocal exchange of labor is the need for extrafamilial help, and this, in turn, arises with the occurrence of tasks that must be completed with particular urgency within a specified time period or tasks that require considerable strength applied at a single place (e.g., construction tasks in which weight is an important factor). But the "need" for reciprocal labor raises some analytic problems in situations where tasks can be performed in several different ways or by several different types of organizations of labor (e.g., plantation labor or wage labor). Furthermore, reciprocal labor exchanges might appear in production situations where no "absolute need" exists for such an organization of labor but where certain economic savings occur, for example, when there are economies of scale. In addition, reciprocal labor exchanges can arise for reasons of sociabil-

---

[23]Erasmus, *Reciprocal Labor*. It is unfortunate that his more accessible article on the topic, "Culture Structure," does not reflect the theoretical richness of the dissertation. I draw heavily from these writings in the discussion that follows.

Another interesting study of many of these problems is: Stanley H. Udy, Jr., *Organization of Work: A Comparative Analysis of Production among Nonindustrial Peoples* (1959). Unfortunately, this is written in a sociological code and is irritating to read. Since Udy examined problems of reciprocity at a different level of analysis than I have, I was unable to draw on his many suggestive propositions or, indeed, to compare my results with his.

ity rather than production necessity. The difficulties in specifying the determinants of reciprocal labor exchange should be quite apparent.

The relationship between reciprocal labor exchange and the level of economic development is generally not argued with as much confidence as in the case of the reciprocal exchange of goods. There are no compelling reasons why reciprocal labor exchanges should or should not be found at very low levels of economic development. At high levels of economic development it is likely that reciprocal labor exchange will not be found for several reasons. Advanced agricultural techniques and the introduction of simple mechanical devices or machines increase the speed at which a single agricultural worker can complete a task (thereby reducing the "urgency" problem) and the amount of power applied to a single task (thereby reducing the "considerable strength at a single place" problem). In addition, advanced agricultural techniques may require a greater specialization of labor, which, in turn, would make reciprocal group labor relatively less productive than other forms of labor organization.[24] I might also add that increased capital intensity of production in general might also be associated with a decline of reciprocal labor exchange because of problems arising with the responsibility for breakage of equipment or of equipment maintenance. The regression analysis does show that, other things being equal, the presence of labor reciprocity is inversely related to the level of economic development; however, the relationship is weaker than for goods reciprocity.

The causal links between the mode of production and the presence of reciprocal labor exchange are complex and raise some tantalizing problems. Hunting can be carried out for some animals by a single man; hunting for other animals may technologically require drive techniques that demand considerable cooperation (which may reflect labor reciprocity); while hunting for still other animals can be carried out with equal productivity by a single man or by a cooperating group. The situation for gathering is simpler, for cases in which gathering technologically requires reciprocal labor exchange seem rare; nevertheless, certain reciprocal exchange elements may be present in gathering for reasons of sociability (after all, gathering can be extremely monotonous work). Fishing can be carried out in large canoes by a group of men or singly by a man standing at the shore of a river or lake. Depending on the animal herded, animal husbandry can be carried out singly or may technologically require the joint efforts of several shepherds. In agriculture, land extensive methods of farming (e.g., slash and burn agriculture) may require cooperating groups for the heavy work of clearing[25]; and highly land intensive methods of farming using extensive irrigation techniques may also require cooperating work groups

---

[24]These propositions are argued in greater detail by Erasmus, *Reciprocal Labor.*

[25]Erasmus, *Reciprocal Labor,* argues that labor reciprocity is associated with the *milpa* system of agriculture in Latin America; my proposition is merely a generalization of his.

for the activities revolving around the common water source; but farming methods in the middle range of land intensivity may not require cooperating groups. I devoted considerable efforts to devise dummy variables reflecting these various conditions and to introduce them systematically into the regression analysis (especially variables designating land extensive and irrigation intensive agricultural techniques), but the results were extremely disappointing. As I will show in the empirical analysis, the only variable that seems to play a significant causal role is simply a dummy variable designating whether or not agriculture is the most important subsistence activity.

A plausible social structural variable influencing the reciprocal exchange of labor is the important presence of extensive lineages. These lineages would link through kin ties individuals who could be drawn on for such reciprocal labor exchanges; indeed, the presence of such ties might make it difficult for an individual to refuse to engage in exchanges. Lineages can be defined with reference either to economic or social activities; the latter definition proves more strongly related to reciprocal labor exchange than the former, although the additional degree of explanatory power is not great.

The combined explanatory power of the variables discussed up to now is not particularly high, and so it is particularly necessary to list the many tested hypotheses that turned out not to work at all. One economic factor that should play an important role is the size of the unit of observation; the larger this unit, the more labor power can be amassed without needing to go outside the family; the smaller this unit, the greater the necessity to obtain labor from other units. Although the sign of this variable was correct, the calculated regression coefficient was not statistically significant, and it was dropped from the final calculations. Nor did other economic hypotheses relating the absence of reciprocal exchange of labor to the presence of money or the market for goods work out. Testing whether the presence of reciprocal exchange of labor is inversely related to the presence of labor markets raised problems of multicollinearity, and a conclusive test could not be carried out, but this relationship also did not seem very promising.

Erasmus argues that a simple reciprocal exchange of labor occurs between social equals, while festive labor reciprocity often occurs when social inequalities exist. Tests were carried out to see if the social inequalities variable was related to reciprocal labor in toto or to particular components (festive and simple labor), but no significant relationships were observed. I also explored a variety of "atmosphere" variables, but none of the experiments proved very successful.

Erasmus has also advanced other propositions dealing with differences in the determinants of simple and festive reciprocity. Except for his contention that as the level of economic development rises, festive reciprocal labor disappears before simple reciprocal labor, none of his propositions on these matters could be easily tested.

The Impact of Reciprocal Exchange: A Digression

Although I do not formally test various propositions about the impact of reciprocal exchange, it is worthwhile to list briefly several propositions found in the literature that indicate some of the most important types of approaches toward the problem.

Many anthropologists in the Durkheimian tradition, especially those following Marcel Mauss, have argued that reciprocal exchange increases social solidarity by tying people together with bonds of mutual obligation and advantage. This is a difficult impact proposition to discuss for several reasons. First, it is quite unclear what "social solidarity" means. Second, a careful examination of the justifications that are offered suggests that many of the reasons that are used to argue the proposition are rather mystical and certainly not easily subject to any kind of rigorous test.

If "solidarity" refers to phenomena on the level of motives in human transactions, then the linkage between reciprocity and solidarity may have many exceptions. For, as I point out above, reciprocal exchange can be carried out for quite malevolent reasons or for reasons of private gain. If "solidarity" refers to social strife, then the linkage is also not clear. More specifically, a regression analysis I carried out with the sample societies revealed no significant or even important relationship between reciprocal exchange and internal disputes or fighting. If "solidarity" refers to durability of the society, then little convincing empirical evidence is really available. However, it is worth noting that societies that have other modes of distribution (e.g., transfers) show considerable durability, for example, the case of the Eskimo which I analyzed in Chapter 4. In short, the propositions linking reciprocal exchange with various manifestations of social solidarity need considerably more theoretical justification and empirical demonstration before we can accept them with a clean scholarly conscience.

Reciprocal exchange is said to have various influences on the distribution of income and wealth. For instance, Raoul Naroll once argued: "It seems clear that reciprocal type exchange systems (gift exchanges, official exchanges, most types of ceremonial exchanges) tend to spread wealth more evenly throughout a society whereas redistributive (taxation, socialism) or market types tend to concentrate wealth in a few hands."[26] And related to this proposition are hypotheses by a number of social scientists that the absence of reciprocal exchange and the presence of other types of distribution permits a concentration of wealth which, in turn, leads to greater investment and higher levels of economic development. Although it seems true empirically that the presence of reciprocal exchange of goods appears inversely related to the relative social-

[26]Raoul Naroll, "What Have We Learned from Cross-Cultural Surveys," *American Anthropologist* LXXII (December 1970): 1227–1289. This proposition is developed and explored empirically in his essay (with Walter Precourt, Terrence A. Tatje, Frada Naroll, and Enid Margolis) "Modes of Exchange, Wealth Concentration and Cultural Evolution," forthcoming.

economic inequality in the society,[27] the logical linkages between these ideas do not seem entirely convincing. Furthermore, there is empirical evidence that certain types of "redistributive" (i.e., centric transfer) systems do not concentrate wealth but rather accomplish the reverse.[28]

Other propositions relate the impact of reciprocal exchange both of foods and of services to production and productivity. For instance, Raymond Firth has argued that ritual activity stimulates production by making men more confident in the face of uncertainty and that whenever ritual has decayed in Oceanic communities, large-scale cooperation has declined, and production has decreased.[29] Others have offered propositions about the relative productivity of reciprocal labor exchange of various sorts vis-à-vis other types of labor organization or, more carefully, have offered propositions about the type of conditions necessary for reciprocal labor exchange to be more productive than alternative arrangements.[30]

EMPIRICAL TESTS OF IMPORTANT HYPOTHESES

Coding Problems

Following the procedure used in Chapter 5, I have used a 5% cutoff line for coding the presence of exchange (in this case, reciprocal exchange). That is, I have coded the presence of reciprocal exchange of goods only if such exchange accounts for 5% or more of the total goods produced in the society; and I have coded the presence of reciprocal labor exchange only if the exchange of labor for labor (or labor for goods in festive reciprocal exchange) accounts for 5% or more of the working hours outside the home (i.e., work excluding food preparation, house cleaning and repair, and the tending of children). For the components of reciprocal exchange of goods I also used the same 5% criterion with the total goods produced as the denominator.

Since I did not find in the ethnographies quantitative estimates either on the extent of such exchange or the extent of the total production of goods or the total working hours outside the home, my own estimates were made using a two-step procedure. First, I tried to determine the type of goods or the type of

---

[27]For instance, the presence of reciprocal exchange of goods (Appendix A, series 44) and social-economic inequality (Appendix A, series 66) are inversely and significantly correlated. Naroll et al., have further empirical evidence on this matter.

[28]In Chapters 9 and 10 I discuss "progressive transfers" which act to even out the distribution of income rather than concentrate it. In industrial societies socialist redistributive systems appear also to even out the distribution of income; empirical evidence can be found in "Property and Labor Incomes: Some Empirical Reflections," in my *Property and Industrial Organization in Communist and Capitalist Nations* (1973), pp. 67–90.

[29]Raymond Firth, *Primitive Polynesian Economy*, 2nd ed. (1965), pp. 172–183.

[30]Such matters are discussed in considerable detail by Erasmus, *Reciprocal Labor*, and Herskovits, *Economic Anthropology*.

labor that was exchanged reciprocally or the kind of occasions on which such reciprocal exchange took place. Then I tried to make an evaluation of the relative importance of such goods or labor or the frequency of occasions where reciprocal exchange took place in the total economy. This often involved trying to decide what the ethnographer's adjectival or adverbial descriptions meant (e.g., deciding that a statement such as "these festive labor parties did not often occur" means that such reciprocal labor fell below the 5% cutoff limit or deciding that a statement such as "this exchange of food was quite important in consumption" means that such reciprocal goods exchange was probably above the 5% cutoff limit).

How biased is such a procedure? Most ethnographers usually pay considerably more attention to the reciprocal exchange of goods (particularly food) than of labor; therefore, my data for the latter suffer from greater uncertainties. The relative lack of attention to labor reciprocity in the ethnographic literature suggests that estimates of labor reciprocity might be downwardly biased; to offset this, I have tried to be somewhat more "generous" in my estimates. I also have some doubts about my estimates for the reciprocal exchange of nonfood items since the relative importance of this phenomenon proved difficult to estimate for many societies. Since no one, to my knowledge, has coded the presence of reciprocity for the societies in my sample in any manner approaching my own,[31] and since this is the kind of phenomenon which requires reading whole ethnographies in order to code (rather than examination of slips in the Human Relations Area File), I have had no way of checking the accuracy of my estimates other than paying an independent coder for reading the same studies as I did and then making his estimates. Unfortunately, no funds for such a purpose were available.

Coding of the explanatory variables raised few problems, other than determining the important presence of extensive lineages. Two methods were employed. For coding the presence of lineages defined by economic criteria, I used the following rules: First, the lineages had to have some generational depth, and "shallow lineages" were not counted as "extensive." Second, the kin groups had to have certain joint production or other economic functions; if they had exclusively a ceremonial function, they were not counted. Third, the kin groups had to have some type of corporate or formal group structure, which meant, for instance, that kin structures of the type found in most modern societies (bilateral kin structure) were not counted. As long as the kin group met these criteria, it was counted; so my sample includes societies with unilineal, duolineal, and ambilineal kin structures. Determination of the presence of

[31]Naroll et al. have coded a number of societies and whether the reciprocal exchange of goods is the predominant form of distribution; their definition of reciprocity, however, differs considerably from mine; furthermore, I have made no judgment about which form of distribution is the most important. (In retrospect, I believe I was remiss in this respect when coding the ethnographic materials.)

lineages defined by social criteria was considerably simpler, for I merely used the codings of Murdock and associates in the Standard Cross-Cultural Sample, supplemented by the codings of Murdock and associates in the *Ethnographic Atlas* and, in several cases, my own codings or corrections of Murdock's estimates.[32] Generally speaking, our estimates were relatively similar.[33]

Cross-Section Tests

GENERAL HYPOTHESES

Propositions about the ubiquity or dominance of reciprocity in precapitalist economies are, as mentioned previously, usually hard to test. To be sure, instances of the reciprocal exchange of goods or of labor can be found in most societies, but so can instances of other modes of distribution. If we use the criteria that the particular mode of distribution has to account for at least 5% of the total production of goods or work hours outside the home, we find that both market exchange of goods and noncentric transfers of goods occur in more societies in the sample than the reciprocal exchange of goods but that the reciprocal exchange of labor occurs in more societies than any other mode of labor distribution.[34] If we exclude all societies where agriculture represents 50% or more of subsistence activities (assuming that there are few "peasant" societies below this limit), we obtain the same results for "primitive" societies. Unfortunately, I did not code the data in a manner that permits determination of the "dominant" mode of distribution. Nor, I may add, am I able to decide exactly what others mean by that term. Are they referring to the relative value of goods or services distributed through that mode? Or are they referring to the social ramifications of the distributional system, that is, which mode of distribution has the greatest social impact on the society or which mode of distribution "sets the tone" for other economic processes?

Several conclusions can be drawn. First, such general hypotheses must be more clearly framed if they are to be rigorously tested. Second, if relative importance of a distributional mode is determined by a 5% cutoff line, then the proposition that reciprocal exchange is relatively important in more societies

---

[32]George P. Murdock and Suzanne F. Wilson, "Settlement Patterns and Community Organization: Cross-Cultural Codes 3," *Ethnology* XI, No. 3 (July 1972): 254–295; and the 1972 version of the *World Ethnographic Atlas*, the computer cards for which were obtained from the *Ethnographic Atlas* project of the Department of Anthropology, University of Pittsburgh.

[33]Although the Murdock groups and I used different criteria for defining lineages, we agreed in 51 out of 60 cases whether or not lineages were present; the major source of disagreement occurred in cases where the lineages were relatively shallow or unimportant. Considerably greater disagreements in the codings arose in the determination of the type of lineage structure, but for this chapter this was not important. My codings of "economic" and "social" lineages are reported in Appendix A, Series 64 and 65.

[34]The data come from Appendix A, Series 22 and 44. This issue is explored in more depth in Chapter 11.

than other modes of distribution may be true for the reciprocal exchange of labor but not of goods (if we assume my sample is representative). Third, limiting the sample to "primitive" societies does not change this conclusion.

DETERMINANTS OF THE RECIPROCAL EXCHANGE OF GOODS

The propositions about the determinants of the reciprocal exchange of goods that are discussed above suggest examination of a number of relationships. Some of the statistical tests of these hypotheses are presented in Table 7.1. I have included in the regressions several variables that fall somewhat short of statistical significance but that nevertheless appear to play some role. Results of the regression analyses yielding less positive results are not reported.

In all of the four regressions reciprocal exchange of goods is inversely related to the level of economic development, and in three out of the four regressions the calculated coefficient is statistically significant. This means that, *ceteris paribus*, the reciprocal exchange of goods is more likely to be found in societies with low levels of economic development rather than high levels of development, a result that offers support to the common notion previously discussed that reciprocal exchange occurs in the most primitive economies and then becomes replaced by other modes of distribution at higher levels of development.

Since the reciprocal exchange of all goods is dominated by the reciprocal exchange of food, the first two regressions are quite similar. Both show, as predicted, that reciprocal exchange of goods is more likely to occur in hunting, fishing, and agricultural societies than in gathering and herding societies. It is noteworthy that the reciprocal exchange in hunting and fishing societies is tied directly to these activities and the exchange of food and therefore does not seem to play a significant role in the reciprocal exchange of nonfood items. The presence of agriculture appears to play a very important causal role (indeed, perhaps too important, given its relatively weak logical justification in the preceding discussion). Its inclusion along with the economic development variable in the regressions suggests that it is in the relatively lower level agricultural societies that reciprocal exchange of goods is most likely to occur.

As predicted, the size of the basic family unit is also related to the presence of the reciprocal exchange of goods: The larger the unit, the less necessary it becomes to obtain particular goods from outside the family unit, therefore, the less likely extrafamilial reciprocal exchange occurs. For both the overall reciprocal exchange of goods and for nonfood items the calculated regression coefficients unfortunately fall somewhat short of my standard of statistical significance. I have still included the variable in the regressions because I feel the theoretical argument linking it to the presence of reciprocal exchange is strong. However, for food items the coefficient falls sufficiently below the predesignated significance limit not to warrant inclusion.

In the previous discussion I noted that many have alleged the exchange of food to have properties different from the exchange of other goods. In particu-

TABLE 7.1

Determinants of the Reciprocal Exchange of Goods[a]

All goods		
. $REAG = 1.0461 - .0189*ED + .5072*HF + .5596*AG - .2962\ UO$	$R^2 = .4311$	
$\quad\quad\quad\quad (.0039)\quad\quad (.1719)\quad\quad (.1464)\quad\quad (.1446)$	$n = 60;\ PCP = 83.33\%$	
Food		
. $REF = .7291 - .0198*ED + .5403*HF + .5312*AG$	$R^2 = .4127$	
$\quad\quad\quad\quad (.0040)\quad\quad (.1725)\quad\quad (.1474)$	$n = 60;\ PCP = 81.67\%$	
Nonfood items		
. $RENF = .8013 - .0108*ED + .3467*AG - .3443\ UO$	$R^2 = .1774$	
$\quad\quad\quad\quad (.0042)\quad\quad (.1493)\quad\quad (.1548)$	$n = 60;\ PCP = 73.33\%$	
Ceremonial reciprocity		
$CREG = .4688 - .0076\ ED + .3793*PLSC + .3017*AG - .3862*UO$	$R^2 = .3097$	
$\quad\quad\quad\quad (.0038)\quad\quad (.1196)\quad\quad (.1331)\quad\quad (.1354)$	$n = 60;\ PCP = 78.33\%$	

Key:

REAG = Reciprocal exchange of all goods accounts for distribution of 5% or more of all produced goods (0 = no; 1 = yes) [mean = .5333].

REF = Reciprocal exchange of food accounts for distribution of 5% or more of all produced goods (0 = no; 1 = yes) [mean = .5167].

RENF = Reciprocal exchange of nonfood items accounts for distribution of 5% or more of all produced goods (0 = no; 1 = yes) [mean = .2833].

CREG = Important ceremonial reciprocal exchange of goods in societies in which reciprocal exchange of all goods accounts for distribution of 5% or more of all produced goods (0 = no; 1 = yes) [mean = .2333].

ED = Rank on economic development scale (1 = lowest; 60 = highest) [mean = 30.5].

HF = Dummy variable designating whether the primary subsistence activity is hunting or fishing (0 = no; 1 = yes) [mean = .1333].

AG = Dummy variable designating whether the primary subsistence activity is agriculture (0 = no; 1 = yes) [mean = .6000].

UO = Size of unit of observation (defined in Chapter 2) (0 = nuclear or stem family; 1 = extended family) [mean = 1.1500].

PLSC = Presence of lineages defined by social criteria (0 = no; 1 = yes) [mean = .6833].

R^2 = Coefficient of determination.

n = Size of sample.

PCP = Percentage of correct predictions.

( ) = Standard error.

* = t statistic for calculated regression coefficient is over the acceptable limit (2.25) defined in Chapter 1.
[a] The data come from Appendix A, Series 4, 7, 21, 22, 42, 43, 44, 45, and 65. Logit regressions are presented Appendix B.1; the algorithm used in these latter regressions does not appear to lead to convergent results, however.

lar, more "social" elements are supposed to influence such exchange. Unfortunately, the results in Table 7.1 shed little light on these matters, for the determinants are roughly the same as for all goods combined. Certainly the reciprocal exchange of food is more predictable (i.e., it has a higher coefficient of determination) than of nonfood items, but this reflects in part the higher quality of the data for the reciprocal exchange of food. I found little indication from the many regression experiments that I conducted that more "social" factors enter into the reciprocal exchange of food.

To investigate social determinants of reciprocal exchange of goods more thoroughly, I conducted a number of regression experiments to isolate the causal factors underlying such exchange that is conducted with important ceremonial observances. The only additional causal variable that I could isolate is the important presence of lineages, one of the "social" factors entering in the preceding discussion of hypotheses. Although this variable did not prove a significant explanatory variable for all reciprocal exchange of goods, its importance for ceremonial reciprocity should be clear from the table.

To gain further insight into the determinants of reciprocal exchange, I also examined the regression residuals (the differences between predicted and actual values of the dependent variable) to isolate the eight societies with the largest prediction errors.[35] In the regression for the reciprocal exchange of all goods the data for four of these societies have been designated as containing some degree of uncertainty (see Appendix A) before the statistical calculations reported in Table 7.1 had been made, which suggests that coding errors might be responsible for some of the false predictions. Furthermore, the largest errors seem mostly to be cases in which I predict the absence of reciprocity when such exchange actually occurred; and of these societies many seem to be cases in which the reciprocal exchange was accompanied by strong ceremonial observances. It seems likely that a more complete explanation of the determinants of the reciprocal exchange of goods would include some type of variable to represent the social structural, political, or economic features of the society underlying such ceremonial practices. I have been unable to devise a suitable variable myself and must leave the solution of this puzzle to future investigators. Examination of the regression residuals for the other equations in Table 7.1 revealed for each equation only two societies for which uncertainties in the data might account for the prediction failures; other than the considerations discussed previously, no other insights could be gleaned from such an exercise.

I also carried out a number of experiments in which the dependent (explained) variable was recoded to reflect whether or not the reciprocal exchange was carried on by individuals with a small or a large set of other people. More specifically, a value to the reciprocal exchange variable of 2 was given if such exchange accounts for distribution of 5% or more of all produced goods and if this exchange is carried out by the various members of the society with a large set of other members of the society, and a value of 1 was given if only the first criterion is met. The conclusions drawn from this and similar exercises are roughly the same as those drawn from Table 7.1; therefore, the results are not reported. Investigation of the determinants of "forced reciprocity" proved much less successful and eventually had to be abandoned.

[35]This discussion refers to the residuals of the least squares regressions.

To summarize, the presence of the reciprocal exchange of goods appears inversely related to the level of economic development and to the size of the "unit of observation" and directly related to the importance of hunting, fishing, and agriculture. Ceremonial reciprocity has an additional causal element, namely, the important presence of extensive lineages. Further explanatory power could be achieved in all probability if further causal elements underlying ceremonial reciprocal exchange could be isolated.

DETERMINANTS OF THE RECIPROCAL EXCHANGE OF LABOR

Although the literature on the reciprocal exchange of labor contains many more propositions to test than the literature on the reciprocal exchange of goods, the explanatory power of the calculations is very much lower. In order to explore particular subsets of causal forces, I separated "festive" and "simple" reciprocal exchange of labor, in which the importance of these two types of reciprocal labor exchange is judged by social significance rather than by the quantitative extent of such exchange. The results of the experiments for isolating the determinants of the simple reciprocal exchange of labor are too disap-

TABLE 7.2

Determinants of the Reciprocal Exchange of Labor[a]

All labor

1. $REL = .6517 - .0077\ ED + .4204*PLSC$ $R^2 = .1018$
    $\qquad\qquad (.0039)\qquad (.1418)$ $n = 60; PCP = 71.67\%$

Festive reciprocal exchange of labor

2. $FREL = .5579 - .0134*ED + .3437*PLSC + .3552\ AG$ $R^2 = .2023$
    $\qquad\qquad\ (.0040)\qquad\ (.1452)\qquad\ (.1627)$ $n = 60; PCP = 71.67\%$

Key:

REL = Reciprocal exchange of labor accounts for distribution of 5% or more of labor outside the home (0 = no; 1 = yes) [mean = .6833].

$FREL$ = Important festive reciprocal exchange of labor in societies in which total reciprocal exchange of labor accounts for distribution of 5% or more of labor outside the home (0 = no; 1 = yes) [mean = .6167].

ED = Rank on economic development scale (1 = lowest; 60 = highest) [mean = 30.5].

$PLSC$ = Presence of lineages defined by social criteria (0 = no; 1 = yes) [mean = .6833].

AG = Dummy variable designating whether the primary subsistence activity is agriculture (0 = no; 1 = yes) [mean = .60].

R^2 = Coefficient of determination.

n = Size of sample.

PCP = Percentage of correct predictions.

( ) = Standard error.

* = t statistic for calculated regression coefficient is over the acceptable limit (2.25) defined in Chapter 1.

[a]The data come from Appendix A, Series 4, 22, 46, 48, and 65. Logit regressions are presented in Appendix B.1.

pointing to report; the most successful results of the regression experiments for other types of reciprocal labor exchange are presented in Table 7.2.

As predicted, the presence of reciprocal labor exchange is inversely related to the level of economic development. That is, the probability of finding such exchange in societies at the lower end of the development scale is greater than at the higher end, other things remaining equal. Furthermore, the presence of lineages also appears to raise the probability of such exchange by tying individuals to a broad net of kin who draw on such ties to obtain labor services at needed times. For festive reciprocity, as predicted, the presence of important agricultural activities also appears to be a causal variable.

I expended considerable efforts in trying to validate Erasmus's conjecture that reciprocal exchange of labor is particularly important when land extensive agricultural techniques are used. Since I have data on crop rotation patterns, population density, and other variables related to such land extensive farming technologies, devising suitable variables for testing did not prove difficult. Unfortunately, none of these experiments yielded very satisfactory results. Since reciprocal labor exchange is more likely to occur in agricultural societies at low levels of economic development than at high levels, the most I can assert from my statistical results is that such exchange appears to arise more from the stage of development than from extensive or intensive production technologies per se. Since the level of agricultural development was held constant when examining the impact of such extensive or intensive farming technologies, the aspects of these technologies which were included in the calculation of the developmental level are not taken into account. This problem of tautology is not, I believe, serious but nevertheless deserves mention.

Given the subjective manner in which festive labor exchanges are defined, it is ironic that the regression achieves greater explanatory power. Two of the three possible causal variables also appear in the regression for all types of reciprocal labor exchanges. The causal influence of social inequality, which is strongly argued by Erasmus, does not receive very convincing confirmation and is not reported: although the sign of its calculated coefficient is correct, the coefficient is low in magnitude and has a large standard error as well.

Part of the difficulty in both regressions appears to arise from uncertainties in the basic data on reciprocal labor exchanges. If we examine the regression residuals to determine the eight societies with the largest prediction errors,[36] we find uncertainties in the codings of five of the societies in equation 1 and four of the societies in equation 2. The societies comprising these sets of eight appear a quite heterogeneous group, and no useful clues about possible omitted causal factors can be gained.

I carried out a number of experiments examining reciprocal exchange of labor defined in different ways. For instance, festive and simple reciprocity were recoded with the elimination of the stipulation that total labor reciprocity

---

[36]This discussion refers to the residuals of the logit regressions. However, the results of such an analysis for the least squares regressions presented in Table 7.2 yield the same general conclusions.

had to equal or exceed the 5% level. The results are sufficiently similar to those reported in Table 7.2 that no useful purpose would be served by presenting them here. It is important to note, however, that these regressions had considerably higher coefficients of determination (R^2), which suggests that coding difficulties encountered in deciding whether a society's reciprocal exchange of labor fell above or below the 5% limit underlay in part the unimpressive statistical fits that were obtained. I also tried to recode the reciprocal labor exchange variable in a manner to distinguish between such exchange which was "technologically necessary" from such exchange which seemed to arise more from social considerations. Obviously, there were also enormous coding difficulties here as well and, as the reader might suspect, the explanatory powers of the various regressions were very low.

In summary, the important presence of reciprocal exchange of labor appears inversely related to the level of economic development and directly related to the presence of lineages. Festive reciprocal exchange of labor also appears to be positively influenced by the presence of agriculture. Although the calculated coefficients in the regressions are significant, the overall degree of explanatory power is disappointingly low. Part of this might be traced to particular coding difficulties.

DEVELOPMENTAL RELATIONSHIPS BETWEEN DIFFERENT KINDS OF RECIPROCAL EXCHANGE

The equations in Tables 7.1 and 7.2 show that the presence of reciprocal exchange is inversely related to the level of economic development and, other things being equal, such exchange tends to disappear as the developmental level increases. Some useful insights are gained by exploring this matter more deeply. I use the same two techniques of analysis that have been employed for these purposes in previous chapters.

For "Technique A," (the *ceteris paribus* technique) we hold all explanatory variables constant (at their average values for the entire sample) except the level of economic development and then determine at what level of development we can no longer predict the presence of reciprocal exchange. That is, we determine the level of development at which there is more than a fifty–fifty chance of successfully predicting the presence of reciprocal exchange. For "Technique B" (the *mutatis mutandis* technique) we do not worry about other causal variables and merely present relative frequencies of occurrence of the different types of reciprocal exchange at different levels of development. The results of these two types of calculations are presented in Table 7.3.

If we compare total goods and total labor reciprocal exchange, the results are quite unambiguous: Labor reciprocity appears to persist at much higher levels of economic development than goods reciprocity. This is shown both by the higher level of development at which labor reciprocity "disappears" (Technique A) and the higher frequency of labor reciprocity at high levels of development (Technique B).

TABLE 7.3

Levels of Economic Development of the "Disappearance" of Different Types of Reciprocal Exchange[a]

Type of reciprocal exchange	Formula number	Technique A: Holding other causal factors constant — Level of economic development (rank) in which predicted reciprocal exchange "disappears"	Technique B: Relative frequency at different developmental levels (number)			
			The 15 societies at the lowest level	The 15 societies at the second lowest level	The 15 societies at the second highest level	The 15 societies at the highest level
Total goods exchange	7-1-1	33	13	8	8	3
Food exchange	7-1-2	32	13	8	8	2
Nonfood exchange	7-1-3	11	5	6	5	1
Ceremonial exchange	7-1-4	n.m.	2	5	4	3
Total labor exchange	B7-2-1	54	10	11	11	9
Festive labor exchange	B7-2-2	38	9	10	10	8
Simple labor exchange	none	—	8	10	9	9

[a] The formula numbers refer to the number of the table (the first two numbers) and the equation number in the table (the last number); B stands for the logit regression presented in Appendix B.1; "n.m." stands for "not meaningful"; the defined development level for the disappearance of ceremonial exchange is negative. The least squares regressions are used for the various types of goods reciprocity because of lack of convergence of the logit calculations.

Several factors must be taken into account in interpreting these results. First, if we consider that market exchanges of goods and of labor are substitutes for reciprocal exchanges of goods and of labor, then it is worth noting that the market for goods appears at a lower stage of economic development than labor markets, other things remaining equal (Table 5.6). This means that alternative arrangements to reciprocal exchange occur earlier in the case of goods than of labor. Second, if we believe that the same "social necessity" for reciprocal exchange of both goods and labor exists, it is worth noting that the technological necessity for the reciprocal exchange of labor may well be greater than of goods. This is reflected by the fact that the reciprocal exchange of goods seems to "disappear" at roughly the same level of economic development at which the domestic markets for goods "appear" (comparing data from Tables 5.6 and 7.3), while the reciprocal exchange of labor "disappears" at a somewhat higher level of economic development than that at which markets for labor "appear." Both sets of considerations help explain why the important presence of the reciprocal exchange of labor persists at higher levels of development than the reciprocal exchange of goods.

The reciprocal exchange of food not only appears more frequently at all levels of economic development than the reciprocal exchange of nonfood items, but it also seems to persist to much higher levels of economic development. An important amount of ceremonial reciprocal exchange appears in only half as many societies as the total reciprocal exchange of goods; unfortunately, we can not make a meaningful generalization about its level of "disappearance." Thus, we must leave untested certain notions found in the literature that important ceremonial exchange persists even when the social meaning of this form of exchange has changed or disappeared.

Unfortunately, the data do not permit us to make comparisons between different types of labor reciprocity in an unambiguous fashion. So in this case we must leave untested Erasmus's conjecture about the disappearance of festive labor at lower stages of development than simple labor reciprocity.

Time-Series Tests

The anthropology literature contains considerable controversy over whether or not reciprocal exchange has spread by diffusion. Melville Herskovits, for instance, has argued that many of the reciprocal labor exchanges found among Negroes in the New World are survivals of African institutions, while Charles J. Erasmus has argued that such exchanges can easily arise indigenously in response to particular technological and social needs.[37] On the face of it, Erasmus seems to have the better of the argument since reciprocal exchange appears a distributional mode found in societies at the very lowest levels of economic development.

---

[37]A summary of this dispute is contained in Erasmus, *Reciprocal Labor.*

TABLE 7.4

Average Distances between Groups of Pairs of Societies for Making Diffusion Tests[a]

Type of reciprocal exchange	Formula number	Average distances, standard deviations, and size of sample[b]										
		Total	Between societies with and without designated reciprocal exchange			Between societies with and without predicted designated reciprocal exchange			Between societies with and without designated reciprocal exchange after taking causal variables into account			
			K	L	M	X	Y	Z	P	P'	Q	R
Total goods exchange	7-1-1	5519 [1964] (1326)	5679 [1906] (378)	5736 [1783] (672)	4775 [2260] (276)	5564 [1995] (351)	5887 [1673] (675)	4639 [2240] (300)	6003 [1568] (115)	5550 [1611] (10)	5617 [1908] (92)	5540 [1863] (20)
Food exchange	7-1-2	5519 [1964] (1326)	5639 [1946] (351)	5816 [1709] (675)	4711 [2276] (300)	5472 [2067] (325)	6010 [1531] (676)	4547 [2268] (325)	6167 [1315] (110)	5380 [1956] (10)	5631 [1890] (88)	5745 [2043] (20)
Nonfood items exchange	7-1-3	5519 [1964] (1326)	5223 [2173] (105)	5900 [1671] (555)	5249 [2098] (666)	5213 [2323] (15)	5813 [1802] (276)	5445 [1992] (1035)	4936 [2364] (44)	5578 [1866] (55)	5900 [1852] (8)	5909 [1748] (22)
Ceremonial exchange	7-1-4	5519 [1964] (1326)	5304 [2174] (55)	5704 [1826] (451)	5432 [2014] (820)	5739 [1883] (28)	5723 [1873] (352)	5437 [1993] (946)	5400 [2124] (28)	5567 [1918] (21)	6394 [799] (16)	5196 [2112] (28)

Total labor exchange	B7-2-1	5519 [1964] (1326)	5629 [1879] (595)	5496 [1981] (595)	5141 [2192] (136)	5553 [1946] (1225)	5102 [2133] (100)	6600 [—] (1)	5165 [2115] (34)	— [—] (0)	5501 [1986] (544)	6094 [1365] (16)
Festive labor exchange	B7-2-2	5519 [1964] (1326)	5622 [1902] (465)	5527 [1955] (651)	5270 [2102] (210)	5471 [2025] (666)	5630 [1864] (555)	5243 [2045] (105)	5824 [1668] (130)	4680 [2358] (10)	5512 [1981] (286)	5249 [2079] (55)

Key:

Group K: All pairs of societies that have the designated type of reciprocal exchange.

Group L: All pairs of societies, one of which has and the other of which does not have the designated type of reciprocal exchange.

Group M: All pairs of societies that do not have the designated type of reciprocal exchange.

Group X: All pairs of societies that the explanatory variables lead us to predict the presence of the designated type of reciprocal exchange.

Group Y: All pairs of societies, one of which we predict to have and the other of which we predict not to have the designated type of reciprocal exchange.

Group Z: All pairs of societies that the explanatory variables lead us to predict the absence of the designated type of reciprocal exchange.

Group P: All pairs of societies, one of which is predicted to have and the other of which is predicted not to have the designated type of reciprocal exchange, but both of which actually have the designated type of reciprocal exchange.

Group P': All pairs of societies, both of which are predicted not to have the designated type of reciprocal exchange, but both of which actually have the designated type of reciprocal exchange.

Group Q: All pairs of societies, both of which are predicted to have the designated type of reciprocal exchange, but one prediction is incorrect.

Group R: All pairs of societies, one of which is predicted to have and the other of which is predicted not to have the designated type of reciprocal exchange, and both predictions are incorrect.

[a] The formula numbers refer to the number of the table (the first two numbers) and the equation number in the table (the last number); B stands for the logit regression presented in Appendix B.1. The least squares regressions are used for the various types of goods reciprocity because of lack of convergence of the logit calculations.

[b] The standard deviation is enclosed in brackets and the size of sample in parentheses.

We can investigate such matters of diffusion as well as determine the validity of the cross-section regressions presented in Tables 7.1 and 7.2 by applying the analytic techniques discussed in Chapter 3 to the data on reciprocity. The relevant results of such an empirical investigation are presented in Table 7.4.

The first test is whether the average distances between societies with the different types of reciprocity (Group K) are significantly less than the average distances between societies, one of which has and one of which does not have the designated reciprocal exchange (Group L). Except for the reciprocal exchange of nonfood items this does not seem to be the case. It is noteworthy that in four out of the six cases, the average distance between pairs of societies, neither of which have the designated reciprocal exchange (Group M), is less than the control group (Group L). This suggests that if diffusion took place, it was of a negative sort, that is, that the absence of reciprocal exchange spread by diffusion (which could arise, for instance, if a more primitive society with reciprocal exchange copied a more advanced society without such exchange with which it came into contact). Such a negative diffusion, if it occurred, would cast doubt on the alleged strength of social solidarity which is supposed to be generated by reciprocal exchange.

The second test is whether the causal variables underlying the presence of the various types of reciprocity seem to appear in societies that cluster together, which involves a comparison between Groups X and Y (and Z and Y). For the total goods exchange and also for the reciprocal exchange of food, such a clustering appears to occur. For the other four types of reciprocal exchange such clustering is not observed. If we wish to worry about negative diffusion, we find that for all different types of goods reciprocity such clustering appears to occur. For the reciprocal exchange of all labor, no cases are recorded in the table where we would predict the absence of such reciprocity. In actuality, there were several such cases, but they occurred in societies that were dropped from the comparisons presented in Table 7.4 because the data refer to periods other than the latter part of the nineteenth century.

The crucial statistical tests to resolve some of these uncertainties are carried out by means of an analysis of prediction errors. Certain problems arise because in a number of cases the number of societies in the sample falls below the limit specified in previous chapters (i.e., 30 societies or less) for which meaningful comparisons can be made. In the cases where the comparison group R has less than this number, we can make comparisons with the entire sample (the first column in the table).

Applying this sophisticated test, we find no compelling evidence for the presence of positive diffusion except for the reciprocal exchange of nonfood items. It is difficult to know how to interpret this one result, but since little weight was placed on this particular type of reciprocal exchange in the preceding analysis, the major conclusions of this chapter still stand. If we examine the probability of negative diffusion in the same manner (part of the data for such a test are not presented in Table 7.4), we find no significant evidence to support such a hypothesis; as in previous chapters the simple clustering tests suggest more diffusion than actually seems to have occurred, at least with respect to the type of slow diffusion that the more sophisticated test is designed to detect.

In short, with the possible exception of the reciprocal exchange of nonfood items, the regression equations explaining the determinants of reciprocal exchange do not appear distorted by diffusion effects.

SUMMARY AND CONCLUSIONS

A great many anthropologists have argued that reciprocal exchange is the earliest type of exchange, and in this chapter and Chapter 5 I have provided considerable empirical and theoretical evidence to confirm this proposition. In addition, I have provided both theoretical and empirical evidence for other determinants of reciprocal exchange as well.

For the reciprocal exchange of all goods, as well as food in particular, the evidence shows that the presence of such exchange is more probable if the primary mode of subsistence production is hunting, fishing, or agriculture (and is less probable if the primary mode of subsistence production is gathering or herding). In hunting and fishing societies the daily uncertainties of obtaining food give rise to such exchange; in agricultural societies a different type of temporal uncertainty seems to play a causal role. For the reciprocal exchange of all goods it also appears that such exchange is more probable in societies in which the unit of observation is relatively small, thus forcing the members to obtain goods from others outside the family unit. The occurrence of ceremonial reciprocity of goods has one additional determinant, namely, the important presence of extensive lineages in the society.

The reciprocal exchange of nonfood items appears to have many of the same determinants as other types of reciprocal exchange of goods, but I was much less successful in obtaining a good statistical relation. Part of this may have been due to the poorer quality of data; and part may have been due to the possibility of diffusion effects.

Exploration of the determinants of the reciprocal exchange of labor proved much less successful than for the reciprocal exchange of goods, which is quite ironic given the much richer theoretical literature on such labor exchanges. The regression analysis provided evidence that such exchange is more likely to occur in societies at low levels of economic development, where we also find the important presence of extensive lineages. I have also provided some theoretical evidence that such lineage structures facilitate this type of labor exchange. The festive reciprocal exchange of labor is also more likely to be found in agricultural societies. In the discussion I provide some evidence that part of the reason why such unimpressive results are found in the regression analysis can be traced to difficulties in determining whether such reciprocal exchange of labor constitutes 5% or more of the total labor in the society outside the home.

Finally, I show that the reciprocal exchange of labor can be found in societies at much higher levels of economic development than the reciprocal exchange of goods. Part of this is because markets, which provide an alternative exchange mechanism, occur at lower levels of development for goods than for labor. And part may be due to greater technological necessities for reciprocal labor exchange.

Many of the hypotheses and conclusions reached in this macrosocietal analysis of reciprocal exchange are of a quite different order from the microsocietal analysis of reciprocal exchange such as the Eskimo distribution presented in Chapter 4. In many cases the insights gained from the two different types of analyses are complementary and result in a deepened understanding of the phenomenon under investigation. I hope that this is the case with this chapter and the study of Eskimo exchange, for they are dealing with quite different aspects of a complex subject and in no manner lead to conflicting hypotheses about reciprocity.

Moreover, both this chapter and Chapter 4 have supplied different kinds of theoretical and empirical evidence showing that many microsocietal analyses of the "universal norm" of reciprocity omit consideration of some extremely important determinants of reciprocal exchange, that the relative importance of reciprocal exchange is quite different from society to society, and that the alleged contribution of reciprocity to social solidarity (that has received so much analytic attention from others) is open to considerable doubt. I have tried to demonstrate that reciprocal exchange can be analyzed in the same manner as other modes of distribution and that its determinants can be isolated in relatively straightforward ways. In brief, I have tried to show that the lens of romanticism through which many social scientists have peered at reciprocity has led to a distorted view of this phenomenon and that the tenderhearted apologetics of reciprocity that are often found in the literature are really quite unnecessary to understand the phenomenon.

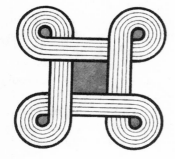

8

THE DETERMINANTS OF NONCENTRIC TRANSFERS: SLAVERY

It is thus clear that, just as some are by nature free, so others are by nature slaves, and for these latter the condition of slavery is both beneficial and just.

ARISTOTLE[1]

Zeus, who sees all, takes half a man's worth away on the day he becomes a slave.

HOMER[2]

In the social science literature sufficient materials are available on various types of exchange so that the surveys of market and reciprocal exchange in the last few chapters have dealt with phenomena whose boundaries are known. But for transfers, either centric or noncentric, we do not have such maps. To be sure, certain types of transfers have received considerable analytic attention, for example, slavery and taxes; but neither the borders of the territory nor the area within have been explored in any systematic fashion.

Slavery is a noncentric transfer of labor, that is, the appropriation of a person's labor without compensation related to any kind of established price or exchange rate; and it represents one of the most important species of noncentric transfers. It seems expeditious to begin the investigation of transfers by focusing on this relatively familiar phenomenon. Although the reality of slavery is repellent, the subject offers a host of fascinating intellectual puzzles. Although we have moved a considerable distance from Aristotle's judgment about the moral aspects of the institution and his bland acceptance of the asymmetry that the relationship entails, we have not moved so far in our analysis either of the causes of slavery or the impact of slavery on individuals and society. In short, much work on the subject remains to be done.

Design from a Fang brass armlet; northern Gabon.
[1] Aristotle, *Politics* (trans. Ernest Barker), Book I, Chap. V.
[2] *The Odyssey*, (trans. Ennis Rees), Chap. XVII.

In this chapter I explore the determinants of slavery in the same manner that I have investigated the causes of other types of distributional transactions in previous chapters. The first step in my argument is to show that slavery exists in several distinct forms and that the specific determinants of the institution depend very much on how the concept is defined. A particularly crucial distinction is between slavery representing "economic" capital and slavery representing "social" capital. I then propose a new approach toward the determinants of slavery, based on the notion that women and slaves serve as social homologs in the operation of the economy. I set forth certain measurable factors reflecting particular types of subordinate roles which women may play and then argue that such factors facilitate the introduction of slavery. This approach toward the subject is validated in the empirical analysis, while competing approaches, which are explored at length, do not yield successful predictions.

The results of such an investigation have important implications not only for the understanding of distribution but also for a host of other issues. They may aid us in evaluating the historical role of slavery as well as some important aspects of the internal dynamics of slave societies. In addition, the empirical results help to move us far from the position of the unilineal evolutionists, who mechanically see all societies passing through a period of slavery during their course of development.

DEFINITIONS OF SLAVERY

What is a "slave"? The bundle of rights that one person holds in another person varies enormously from society to society; and the particular subset of rights that constitutes "slavery" is far from clear. Which of the following situations can we define as slavery: When slaves can marry "free" persons and gain their "freedom"? When slaves can accumulate money and buy their freedom? When slaves can hold other slaves? When slaves cannot be transferred from one "master" to another without the slaves own permission? When a slave who does not like his master can transfer himself freely to another master? Or when slaves do no more work than anyone else, have the same standard of living as their masters, and are treated as family members by their masters? All these situations arise among the societies used in the empirical investigation below.

In certain types of analysis it is useful to consider the entire range of particular rights that may be held in different groups rather than designating any particular subset of rights as "slavery."[3] But if we wish to transcend the experience of one or two societies, then we must develop one or (more preferably)

---

[3]Among those stressing the importance of recognizing the continuum of rights that a master may have in his "slave" are: Moses I. Finley, "Between Slavery and Freedom," *Comparative Studies in Society and History* VI (April 1964): 233–249; and Bernard J. Siegel, "Some Methodological Considerations for a Comparative Study of Slavery," *American Anthropologist* XLVII (July–September 1945): 357–392.

several definitions of slavery that can be used for cross-cultural comparisons.

In its most general sense "slavery is a species of dependent labor and not the genus."[4] Before reaching a positive definition of slavery, it is useful to specify certain things which slavery is not. Most importantly, slavery is not characterized by totally unlimited powers over the slave by the master, an unpromising definition that is offered by Nieboer.[5] For in no society that I have come across does the slave appear totally without legal rights.[6] More specifically, although slaves have often been covertly abused, I have found no society in which the master could easily get away with open and unjustified physical abuse of slaves (e.g., open torture) for months on end.

Other common connotations of the term *slavery* should also be expurgated. First of all, slavery is not necessarily involuntary, and given the prospects of an economically precarious life as a free person and an economically secure life as a slave, it may be quite rational to choose the latter. Second, relationships between master and slave may not be openly coercive, and it is quite possible that in certain cases strong elements of mutual affection and love may exist between master and slave. In Roman literature, for instance, one often finds this theme (e.g., in Plautus's serious play *The Captives*). Third, slavery is not necessarily the lowest social status in the society; in classical Greece, for instance, the landless agricultural wage worker appeared to be even lower.[7]

Finally, slavery may not include economic exploitation as the term is commonly understood. As some have argued, slaves receive certain benefits (e.g., food and housing) from their masters, in which case a certain reciprocal element in the master–slave relationship may develop. A more important situation arises in some societies such as the Suku of Zaïre, where a person sold into slavery by his family did no more or less work than before; nor did the slave consume either more or less than the average person in his new surroundings. The major difference in the life of the slave was that he had to participate in the family rituals and wars of his master and to forego such participation in these events of his former relatives; he also had fewer social and legal rights than previously. For a slave to serve as "economic capital" to his master, the latter must obtain a marked economic advantage, which, in the case of the Suku, does not appear to have occurred; rather, among the Suku the slave served more as "social capital," supplying the manpower for particular social and

[4]Moses I. Finley, "Slavery," in *International Encyclopedia of the Social Sciences* (1968), ed. David L. Sills, Vol. XIV, p. 308.
[5]H. J. Nieboer, *Slavery as an Industrial System*, (1971) 2nd rev. ed., p. 5 [originally published 1910].
[6]This judgment echoes those of others, for example; William Linn Westermann, "Slavery and the Elements of Freedom in Ancient Greece," in *Slavery in Classical Antiquity* (1960), ed. Moses I. Finley, p. 18; or Finley, "Slavery."
[7]Finley, *The Ancient Economy* (1973), p. 66, discusses the Homeric passage in which Odysseus visits Hades and talks with the shade of Achilles. The latter is despondent and compares his lot to that of the lowest social class he can conceive, the landless agricultural worker. Perhaps the latter had a lower social status than a slave because he faced much greater economic uncertainties.

political events that gave a family and lineage prestige and power, the economic benefits of which were quite secondary or, indeed, nil.[8]

How can we define slavery in a positive manner that will permit us meaningfully to test various cross-cultural propositions? To this end I shall consider a broad definition so that we might include most of the relationships that various scholars have included as slavery and a narrow definition focusing on a type of labor relationship that seems central to some key propositions found in the literature.

In its broadest meaning (designated in the following discussion as "Slavery A" or "maximal slavery") I define slavery as a type of dependent labor of a nonfamily member in which *one* or more of the following three conditions is met: The superior has the right to kill the subordinate even when the latter has not committed a crime[9]; the superior has the right to transfer the subordinate any time over his lifespan to another superior without the subordinate's permission; or the superior has considerably more long-term legal rights than the subordinate not only with regard to participation in political decision making but also with regard to participation in all other kinds of activities.[10] These conditions are, of course, arranged according to decreasing severity, so that if the first condition is met, the other two are probably met as well. It must be explicitly noted that such a definition includes certain types of relationships that are often designated as serfdom[11] and that the definition excludes what is sometimes called "wage slavery" (allegedly found in some modern industrial societies) and also prison labor (since the prisoner fills such a role only for those few years in which he is serving his term).

It should be noted that such a definition includes situations in which slavery occurs in a society only quite casually. For instance, in England in 1772 there were 15,000 slaves, who mostly served as house servants.[12] Furthermore, it should be mentioned that this definition includes many types of slavery in which the slaves serve primarily as "social capital." To exclude these types of slavery, we can define the institution in such a way that the economic aspects

---

[8]The distinction between slaves as "economic" and "social" capital (which plays a crucial role in my analysis), as well as the description of Suku slavery, comes from a conversation with Igor Kopytoff, to whom I would like to express my appreciation.

[9]It can be argued that this particular right is tantamount to an absolute right over the slave, but this is not so. Although killing may be permitted, other types of abuse may not.

[10]It is convenient to define the legal rights of the subordinate on a relative rather than absolute scale. This excludes the type of relationship found in Incan Peru and other societies where almost all people had relatively few legal rights vis-à-vis the political leaders and, if slavery were based on absolute criteria, would be designated as slaves. Most definitions of slavery in the literature are based on the slave's absolute lack of legal rights and are considerably more vague than the definition of slavery which I offer; cf. the definitions of Finley, "Slavery"; Nieboer, *Slavery*, p. 5; or David Brion Davis, *The Problem of Slavery in Western Culture* (1966), p. 31.

[11]Slavery and serfdom can be distinguished, if it is necessary, by adding the condition that the subordinate is attached to a person, not to a piece of land. Since none of the societies in the sample had a feudal economic system or serfdom, this was not a problem in the empirical part of the study.

[12]This obscure but interesting fact comes from Robert William Fogel and Stanley L. Engerman, *Time on the Cross: The Economics of American Negro Slavery* (1974), p. 33, who cite no source.

of slavery that are generally considered most morally reprehensible will be central to the definition.

In its narrowest meaning (designated below as "Slavery C" or "narrow slavery") I define slavery as occurring when the conditions for Slavery A are met; furthermore: (a) such slavery constitutes more than 5% of the total labor force; and (b) such slaves serve as economic capital and are directly exploited in the production of food. By "exploitation" I mean that the slave has a markedly lower standard of living than his master, either because his consumption of goods and services is lower or because he has less leisure. In Slavery C I focus solely on "field slaves" and exclude situations where slaves work in factories or handicrafts (extremely rare among the societies in the sample), where slaves are used for the construction of public works and buildings (also very rare among the societies in the sample), or where slaves serve primarily as social capital. In short, Slavery C constitutes cases where the slaves serve as economic capital in agriculture.

In the early parts of the empirical investigation (Table 8.1) I investigate Slavery A and C. In a later part I find it useful to remove from Slavery A those cases where Slavery C occurs, so that Slavery A in those changed samples represents all cases of slavery where slaves are used only as social capital, together with only a few cases (outside of agriculture) where slaves are economically exploited. Such a procedure permits us to compare more directly the different properties of slavery as economic and social capital. In addition, I experimented with a number of other definitions of slavery (Slavery B, which represented a less inclusive definition than Slavery A, and Slavery D, which rested on a somewhat broader definition of economic exploitation). The results of the empirical analysis of these cases added little to the analysis and therefore are not included for further consideration. Data for all types of slavery are presented in Appendix A.

A number of ambiguities arise from these definitions of slavery, the most important of which deserve brief attention. First, should wives in a society where their husbands may kill them, transfer them to other men, or make them work long hours at extremely menial tasks be classified as slaves? The rights that husbands have in their wives (and vice versa) are sometimes hard for the ethnographer to disentangle. For this very practical reason, therefore, I exclude wives and concubines (other than war captives) from my definition of slavery. Children are similarly omitted from the definition of slaves, especially since the time period of their "slavery" is limited in duration. However, captive women from other societies who are forced to become wives or concubines and captive children who meet the conditions of slavery specified previously are included as slaves.

Second, can the definitions drawn above distinguish between slaves and lower classes, peons, subject peoples, war captives, debt pawns, and indentured servants, all of whom may be dependent laborers but who are generally considered not to be slaves? I believe that my definitions do allow such differences to be drawn but do not pursue these matters further in order to move more quickly to propositions about slavery. Greater problems arise with my definitions where *de jure* and *de facto* rights in subordinates diverge. In general, I tried to focus upon *de facto* rights, but in many cases only information on *de jure* rights was available.

THEORIES ABOUT THE DETERMINANTS OF SLAVERY

Stage Theories

A number of nineteenth-century social scientists proposed all-embracing unilineal stage theories of human evolution and posited that at some particular stage of societal development slavery emerged, while at a higher stage slavery disappeared and was replaced by some other way of organizing the labor force. These theories differ about what is meant by slavery, at what stages slavery arises and declines, whether the developmental stage is a sufficient or merely a necessary cause of the presence or absence of slavery, whether the mere presence of slavery or the existence of a "slave society" is the analytical focus, and what are the major causal factors and mechanisms bringing about this relationship between economic development and slavery. Most of these stage theories, for example, that of Herbert Spencer, have been discredited, and there is little need to explore them.[13]

At the present time the only general stage theory with any degree of acceptance among scholars is that proposed by Frederick Engels,[14] which was based in large measure on the path-breaking researches of the corporate lawyer who was the father of American anthropology, Lewis Henry Morgan. According to Engels, animal husbandry arose in the "lower stages of barbarism"; in the "middle stage of barbarism" horticulture began to be practiced, and in the field of handicraft the loom and metal smelting were developed. Although the cultivated land still remained tribal property, individuals began to have certain rights of possession. At this point

the increase of production in all branches—cattle raising, agriculture, domestic handicraft— gave human labor power the capacity to produce a larger product than was necessary for its

---

[13]However, remnants of stage theories can be found in the current writings of those who argue some type of benefit/cost theory of slavery and who tie such causal factors to the level of economic development. Such theories are considered in detail below. The most recent general stage theory of slavery that I have been able to locate was proposed by L. T. Hobhouse, G. C. Wheeler, and M. Ginsberg, *The Material Culture and Social Institution of the Simpler Peoples* (1930), Chap. IV. They seem to consider the level of economic development a necessary but not sufficient condition for the existence of slavery (which they do not carefully define).

[14]Frederick Engels, *The Origin of the Family, Private Property and the State,* ed. and intro. Eleanor Burke Leacock (1972) [originally published 1884].

maintenance. At the same time it increased the daily amount of work to be done by each member of the gens, household community, or single family. It was now desirable to bring in new labor forces. War provided them; prisoners of war were turned into slaves. With its increase of the productivity of labor, and therefore of wealth, and its extension of the field of production the first great social division of labor was bound, in the general historical conditions prevailing, to bring slavery in its train. From the first great social division of labor arose the first great cleavage of society into two classes: masters and slaves, exploiters and exploited.[15]

In this period, Engels argued, slavery was still in its beginning and was sporadic, but at a higher stage, when the second great division of labor took place (when handicraft separated from agriculture), slavery became

> an essential constituent part of the social system; slaves no longer merely help with production—they are driven by dozens to work in the fields and the workshops. With the splitting up of production into two great main branches, agriculture and handicrafts, arises production directly for exchange, commodity production; with it comes commerce, not only in the interior and on the tribal boundaries, but also already overseas.[16]

The threshold of "civilization" is approached and with it an increasing inequality of income and wealth.

Engels' doctrine about the decline of slavery is rather murky. He asserts that at a still higher stage of economic development, slavery is supplanted by serfdom, but he is extremely vague on the underlying causes. Presumably, Engels felt similarly about the decline of serfdom as Marx, whose scattered ideas on the subject point toward the notion that increases of agricultural technology, combined with the greater use of tools in agriculture, made for a greater productivity of serfs vis-à-vis slaves.

Engels did not stop to define slavery very carefully, nor did he really develop a very adequate theory about the causal mechanisms involved. The force of his theory—and the source of its greatest weakness—is the idea that at some point the level of economic development is a sufficient condition in itself to bring about the existence of a society whose economy is fundamentally based on the labor inputs of slaves.

In some of his manuscripts Marx appears to sketch a different evolutionary theory.[17] In addition to the line of historical development in which a society moves from primitive communism to a slave society to feudalism to capitalism and finally to advanced communism, alternative routes passing through different modes of production provide other developmental routes to capitalism

---

[15]Ibid., Chap. IX, p. 220.

[16]Ibid., Chap. IX, p. 222.

[17]Marx's major writings on slavery and serfdom can be found in Karl Marx, *Pre-Capitalist Economic Formations*, (1964), ed. and intro. Eric Hobsbawn. In addition, Marx's notes on the writings of Morgan and other anthropologists have been republished in *The Ethnological Notebooks of Karl Marx*, 2nd ed. (1914) ed. Lawrence Krader. Hobsbawn in his introduction shows quite clearly that although Marx and Engels had many interesting insights, neither had a well worked out theory about the transition from slavery to serfdom or from serfdom to capitalism.

that might bypass a genuine slave society.[18] Such other modes of production—sometimes lumped together under the rubric of "Asiatic modes"—are not clearly delineated, nor are the causal mechanisms leading societies along these evolutionary routes spelled out in any detail. The status of this alternative theory in the corpus of Marxist doctrine is extremely controversial, and it is not necessary to enter into this debate. But the issue which Marx raised—whether the level of economic development is a necessary or sufficient condition of slavery—is extremely important in analyzing any stage theory of slavery.

Such stage theories are intellectually dissatisfying because so much is left unexplained, particularly the crucial mechanisms through which the level of economic development brings about the rise or decline of slavery. They also leave us wondering what type of slavery they are describing, slavery as social or economic capital. Such objections do not necessarily mean, however, that such stage theories are inaccurate in describing empirically the relationship between economic development and the existence of some particular type of slavery. If we discard Engels' notion about "barbarism" and other matters relating to the level of development at which slavery becomes important, we find (as I show below) that as a descriptive device the approach has considerable merit with regard to Slavery A but not to Slavery C alone.

Benefit/Cost Theories

Appeals to benefit/cost arguments in order to explain the presence of slavery (Slavery C is almost always implied) are often found in the literature, and in recent years such arguments have been sharpened by quite explicit analyses of the specific benefits and costs associated with the presence of slaves as economic capital in various situations.[19]

[18]Karl Wittfogel, Oriental Despotism: A Comparative Study (1957), Chap. IX, reviews the early Marxist debate on the Asiatic mode of production and alternative routes to capitalism. He also shows how various Soviet authorites changed their minds about the importance of the Asiatic mode because of alleged implications of this debate on the current politics of that time. A number of Soviet writings about these matters are collected in Ancient Mesopotamia: Socio-Economic History (1969) ed. I. M. Diakonoff. And the most recent stages of the debate are summarized by Gianni Sofri, Ueber asiatische Productionsweise (1972) [originally published 1969 in Italian]. Some idea of the intensity of the discussion is recorded in a debate between French and Soviet Marxists that is summarized in a number of articles and abstracts in Soviet Anthropology and Archaeology IV (Fall 1965). Russian Marxists such as V. V. Struve strongly criticized the French notion of alternative routes to capitalism and placed the Asian mode of production as preceding slaveholding in all cases so that historical evolution is similar and unilineal for all nations. Abstracts of papers by French Marxists such as Maurice Godelier showed that they strongly supported the possibility of alternative routes to capitalism and the independence of the Asian mode of production from the orthodox (Engels) unilineal schema. A more extended argument along these lines is presented by Emmanuel Terray, Marxism and "Primitive" Societies (1972) [originally published 1969].

[19]A number of quite explicit benefit/cost arguments are found in Engels, Origins of the Family, and Nieboer, Slavery. More recently, these theories are developed by Mancur Olson, "Some Historic Variations in Property Institutions," a paper presented at the Southern Economic Association convention, Autumn 1967 and the Eastern Economic Association convention, Autumn 1974. I also used such an approach toward slavery in my article "Property Institutions and Economic

The benefit/cost argument in its most general guise appears quite unexceptionable: Slavery will only occur in a society when and where it is economically profitable for a person to hold slaves, and such economic profitability occurs only when the productivity of a slave is greater than the cost of maintaining and guarding him. Depending on additional assumptions, such a general argument can be used either to specify necessary or sufficient conditions for slavery. By specifying particular benefits and costs of slavery, a number of general propositions can be easily derived. It must be understood that for all these propositions, *ceteris paribus* conditions are assumed.

Some of the benefit/cost propositions focus on the benefits: At low stages of economic development the productivity of labor in general (and slaves in particular) is very low; therefore, slavery is not profitable in such societies. Furthermore, because of the lower productivity of slaves and the costs of guarding them, slavery does not appear in societies until they are well past the "subsistence level." Slaves are more likely to be found in societies with active commerce or with a large amount of handicraft production because the useful productivity of a slave (in terms of goods that the master can use himself or sell to others) is greater. However, others have argued that the greater the complexity of the goods produced in a society, the greater the capital intensiveness of production, or the greater the skills required in production, the lower the incidence of slavery because the net productivity (i.e., productivity after costs of supervision are removed) is less than that of free labor.[20]

Some of the benefit/cost propositions focus on the costs. Slavery is more likely to occur in agricultural and sedentary pastoral societies than in hunting and gathering or in migratory herding societies because the costs of guarding slaves are lower in the former group. For similar reasons slaves are more likely to be found in geographically isolated societies or in societies where large groups of people are clustered together. Extratribal slavery (where adult slaves are obtained by raiding other societies) is more likely to occur than intratribal slavery (where slaves are born and bred by the slave holder) in societies at low levels of economic development because the costs of raising and training slaves can be avoided in the former case, which lowers the average cost of maintaining slaves. Slavery is also less likely to occur in urban areas than in rural areas because of the higher costs of maintaining them and isolating them.

It should be clear that many of these benefit/cost arguments are complementary rather than antithetical to the stage theory approach if certain assumptions about the evolution of human societies are made (e.g., man evolves from

---

Development: Some Empirical Tests," *Economic Development and Cultural Change* XX (April 1972): 406–437; but my treatment of the benefit/cost approach in that study was, upon reflection, too uncritical. The most sophisticated benefit/cost approach to appear is by Ronald Findlay, "Slavery, Incentives, and Manumission: A Theoretical Model," *Journal of Political Economy* LXXXIII (October 1975): 923–933. Unfortunately, data necessary to test the propositions of Findlay may be impossible to obtain.

[20]Many such arguments have been invoked in analyzing "the natural limits of slavery" in the American South and are discussed by Fogel and Engerman, *Time on the Cross*, pp. 83, 94–97.

hunting and gathering to herding and thence to agricultural modes of production, and from rural, simple technology societies to urban, complex technology societies). Furthermore, although such propositions as previously presented express only the necessary conditions for the presence of slavery, some theorists have argued sufficiency conditions by making some additional assumptions. One such assumption is: Whenever the benefits of slavery are sufficiently greater than the costs, some people will take the opportunity to enslave others to obtain this gain. Another sufficiency assumption, sometimes found in the work of evolutionists, asserts that the specified benefits and costs of slavery are roughly the same for every society at a particular level of development, so that all societies follow the same developmental path through a slave-holding stage.

A number of objections have been raised to this approach, most of which focus on the implicit assumptions that underlie such arguments. First of all, such theories usually focus on slaves directly engaged in agricultural, herding, or manufacturing activities rather than those engaged in services or acting in the capacity of social rather than economic capital. Furthermore, the notion that slaves are less productive than free men, while seemingly "obvious," can be legitimately questioned in certain contexts. In the American South it has been argued that "the typical slave field hand was not lazy, inept, and unproductive. On the average he was harder working and more efficient than his white counterpart."[21] The lower productivity of slaves in classical Rome and Greece has also been recently questioned.[22]

Moreover, the costs of guarding slaves are very difficult to specify on a general level. In some cases the costs may be nil, especially in those societies where slaves are kinless people (either because their kin may be too far away to protect them, a situation arising among the Tiv of Nigeria, or because their kin may renounce the social tie when the person is captured, a situation arising among Indians in the northeastern woodlands of the U.S.). In such cases the slaves might as well stay where they are since they will be enslaved wherever they go. Costs of guarding slaves can also be low when terror is freely employed as a disciplinary tool.[23]

In addition, the alleged direct relationship between "low level of economic development" and "low productivity" may be quite incorrect. As I pointed out in Chapter 2, no necessary relationship exists between them; indeed, the two are often inversely related. Marshall Sahlins has amassed some interesting

---

[21]Ibid., p. 5. This quotation is the authors' summary of the cliometric literature on the subject; their own arguments for supporting this proposition are presented on pp. 192–232 and have been subject to considerable criticism.

[22]Moses I. Finley, *The Ancient Economy* (1973), pp. 83 ff. Finley's evidence is also open to challenge.

[23]In developed economies the monetary costs of terror (in terms of personnel expenditures) have been quite small in totalitarian societies. (Data on Nazi Germany and Stalinist U.S.S.R. are presented in my *Public Expenditures in Communist and Capitalist Nations* [1968], p. 242.) I think that this situation might also hold for precapitalist economies.

evidence that in highly primitive hunting and gathering societies productivity in the obtaining of food (as manifested by the few work hours per week that are invested in such activities) is very high.[24] Similarly, Ester Boserup has presented considerable evidence that labor productivity in highly primitive slash and burn agricultural systems is much higher than in more developed agricultural societies using more advanced agricultural techniques.[25]

The arguments about the lower likelihood of slavery in urban areas or when production is complex, highly capital intensive, or requiring high skills are also open to challenge. Furthermore, such arguments run counter to the arguments of the greater likelihood of slavery when manufacturing and commerce are important.

With the exception of the open resources argument (a variant benefit/cost argument that is discussed below), most benefit/cost arguments for the decline of slavery appear even more dubious than such arguments for the origins of slavery. For instance, according to many benefit/cost arguments, slavery in the southern states of the United States should have been declining during the middle part of the nineteenth century, yet a number of economic historians have recently provided convincing evidence that it was a profitable system for the slave holders up to the Civil War.[26]

Finally, one sufficiency argument—the assumption that whenever a source of profit arises, it will be exercised—is based on the assumption that there are no effective moral, religious, social, or political restraints on groups in society doing whatever they want to other groups in the society in order to obtain a profit. This assumption may be true empirically; however, it requires more evidence for theoretical justification than scholars have yet offered. Another sufficiency argument—the assumption about unilineal evolution and the cross-cultural similarity of benefits and costs of slavery—is even more controversial.

After taking into account this welter of arguments and counterarguments, what do we have left? Three important methodological conclusions can be drawn.

First, in societies with different modes of subsistence production, the benefits and costs of slavery are qualitatively very dissimilar. This suggests that for sensitive hypothesis testing it would be useful to examine groups of societies that all have the same subsistence production, a procedure that lends itself for the sample used in this study only to agricultural societies.

Second, buried in the various propositions advanced above are a series of *ceteris paribus* assumptions that make hypothesis testing very difficult unless the sample is quite large and a large number of variables can be held constant.

[24]Marshall Sahlins, "The Original Affluent Society," Chap. I in his *Stone Age Economics* (1972), pp. 1–40.
[25]Ester Boserup, *The Conditions of Agricultural Growth* (1973) [originally published 1965].
[26]Starting with the study of Alfred H. Conrad and John R. Meyer, "The Economics of Slavery in the Antibellum South," *Journal of Political Economy* LXIV (April 1958): 95–130 and their book *The Economics of Slavery* (1964), a flood of literature has recently appeared on the topic.

Third, further difficulties are encountered because some of the arguments raised above invoke variables which appear to be both causes and effects of slavery. For instance, it turns out, other things being equal, that the presence of slavery is directly related to the presence of a market for goods. But is this market variable a cause or an effect of slavery, or both? Certainly, if a market variable is placed in the regression calculations, a gratifyingly high coefficient of determination is obtained, but the results are impossible to interpret. The only way to handle this situation statistically is to set forth a simultaneous equation model that can capture such complex interactions, a procedure which I do not propose at the present time.

I devoted considerable efforts to test empirically the various benefit/cost hypotheses, and the results can be easily summarized: For the most part none of them appeared very promising. Perhaps if I could have held more factors constant or could have introduced complex simultaneous equations models, the situation would have been different. The only empirical validation of the approach appeared in the evidence that hunting and gathering societies do not generally have slaves, a proposition that can be argued from other grounds as well. In short, the benefit/cost approach toward slavery offers intriguing insights but does not appear to offer a very satisfactory way of distinguishing these societies in the sample that have and do not have slaves.

The Open Resource Theory

A number of historians and social scientists have wrestled with the problem of why slavery (again Slavery C seems to be implied) occurred in the sparsely populated lands of Africa but not in the densely populated societies of China and India; they have come up with a special type of benefit/cost argument that I designate the "open resource theory." This hypothesis was most extensively developed around the turn of the twentieth century by the Dutch anthropologist H. J. Nieboer[27] and has recently been resuscitated by Evsey Domar and others.[28]

According to Nieboer, open resources occur when agricultural land is easy to obtain and when little capital or complex technological knowledge is necessary for agricultural production. It would also be in the spirit of Nieboer's

[27]H. J. Nieboer, Slavery. Nieboer noted that various aspects of the open resource argument had been advanced by Walter Bagehot, J. E. Cairnes, A. Loria, Karl Marx, Werner Sombart, and Max Weber. He neglected to mention such Russian social scientists as A. V. Chayanov or V. Kliuchevsky. After taking proper account of such a distinguished and diverse group of predecessors, Nieboer developed the argument further and supplied more positive evidence from a wider range of societies than, as far as I have been able to determine, any other person.

[28]Evsey Domar, "The Causes of Slavery or Serfdom: A Hypothesis," Journal of Economic History XXX (March 1970): 18–31; and C. Baks, J. C. Breman, A. T. J. Nooij, "Slavery as a System of Production in Tribal Society," Bijdragen tot de Taal- Land- en Volkenkunde CXXII (1966) (Anthropologia VIII, 1966): 90–110. Although Domar used the argument to interpret the rise of Russian serfdom, its original and most general formulation refers to slavery in primitive and peasant societies.

approach to add that open resources occur when such agricultural land does not require enormous investments in time (i.e., human capital) to bring it into productive use. When open resources exist "every able-bodied man can, by taking a piece of land into cultivation, provide for himself. Hence it follows that nobody voluntarily serves another; he who wants a labourer must subject him and this subjection will often assume the character of slavery."[29] When open resources do not exist, "where all land fit for cultivation has been appropriated, slavery is not likely to occur."[30] This is because, as he noted in his favorable commentary on the ideas of A. Loria,

> the labourer has now no other resource but to sell his labour to the capitalist for such wages as the latter likes to give; he is compelled to yield to the capitalist the greater part of the produce of his labour. Now the latter need no longer use violence to get his profit; for it falls to him by the automatic operation of the social system.[31]

In the jargon of economic theory this theory focuses on divergencies between average and marginal productivities. In a situation in which land is roughly the same quality and rentless land is available, there is little incentive for wage labor unless a wage equal to that which could be earned by independent farming of the available land is obtained,[32] and such a situation would provide no profit for the landlord. As the ratio of the population to the land rises, land becomes "scarce" (i.e., its marginal productivity rises), and it earns a rent while at the same time the marginal productivity of labor (consequently, wages) declines. When there are open resources, the use of slave labor is the only way in which a landlord can obtain income from the land without actually working it himself; when there are no open resources, the landlord can obtain income without actually working the land. In the transition stage between these two situations, the choice of free or slave labor depends on whether the net productivity of a slave (the total production of a slave minus the cost of maintaining and guarding him) is more or less than the net rent the owner could obtain from a free man or else the net productivity of a free man (the total production of a free man minus his wages). The proponents of the open resource theory argue that it provides insight not only into the reasons underlying the absence of slavery in the densely populated oriental societies (where land rents indicate a land shortage) but also for the reasons why societies with slavery often abandon the institution at a higher stage of development when their land density becomes greater and land becomes relatively scarcer.

As outlined previously, the open resource theory provides necessary and sufficient conditions for the absence of slavery but only necessary (and not sufficient) conditions for the presence of slavery. To provide sufficient condi-

---

[29]Nieboer, *Slavery*, p. 298.

[30]Ibid., p. 303.

[31]Ibid., p. 305. He notes on the next page that although Loria confused capitalists with landlords, the gist of the argument is correct.

[32]Nieboer, ibid., does note some exceptions to this proposition, for example, on pp. 312–313 he argues that if the available unappropriated land lies a considerable distance away from the villages, some may prefer to work as wage laborers, rather than settling far away from others.

tions for the presence of slavery, it is necessary to introduce an additional causal variable. In some cases this is a political factor.[33] For instance, in a stimulating article Evsey Domar argues that we must also consider the willingness of the government to enforce slavery. He argues that of the

> three elements of agricultural structure that have been discussed—free land, free peasants, and nonworking landowners—any two elements but *never all three can exist simultaneously.* The combination to be found in reality will depend on the behavior of political factors— governmental measures—treated here as an exogenous variable.[34]

In some cases this is a social factor.[35] For instance, in a recent article Baks, Breman, and Nooij argue that social stratification in the society is the exogenous variable that must be introduced and that slavery cannot exist if there is not this hierarchical element in the free part of the society which acts to reinforce slavery.[36] In my own data there appears to be a certain correlation in the various societies between the degree of socioeconomic inequality and the degree of political inequality (or, equivalently, concentration of political power)[37]; testing the social inequality argument alone raises certain problems since such inequality seems more likely to be an effect of slavery rather than a cause.

The Nieboer form of the open resource argument can be, in principle, easily tested: We need merely look for the presence of Slavery C in societies in which open resources are no longer available. If slavery is found, the hypothesis is refuted. In practice, however, it is difficult to determine if open resources are available. Moreover, theoretical difficulties also arise, once we bring into consideration the type of land-fallowing technique which is employed. As Ester Boserup has argued, fallowing systems may vary with the density of the population, so that no "free land" exists in any society except those with rare frontier conditions.[38] In low density societies a slash and burn agricultural technique is employed that may result in a very high labor productivity but that may require land to lie fallow for several decades to regain its fertility. In high density societies much more labor is applied to each piece of land; in addition, fertilizers and irrigation water are applied, so fallowing is less necessary, and fertility can be maintained for longer periods.

To show the complications raised by this consideration more concretely, let us turn to the principal case analyzed by Evsey Domar to demonstrate the open

---

[33]Certain theorists, discussed below, claim political variables to be the cause of slavery and such theories can be combined with the Nieboer hypothesis.

[34]Domar, "Causes of Slavery," p. 6. Emphasis in the original.

[35]Certain theorists, discussed below, claim social variables to be the cause of slavery and such theories can also be combined with the Nieboer hypothesis.

[36]Baks, Breman, and Nooij, "Slavery."

[37]For the 60-society sample, the coefficient of determination (R^2) between the concentration of political power and socioeconomic inequality is .56. The coding of these variables is discussed below.

[38]Boserup, *Agricultural Growth*.

resources argument, namely, the enserfment of the Russian peasants between 1550 and 1650. One of the most important factors cited by Domar was an alleged depopulation from the center of Russia to the frontiers in the south and west as new lands were conquered. However, as Michael Confino points out in a thorough study of Russian farming techniques,[39] it was in the 1500s that the Russian farmers in the central area began to change from various forms of extensive farming (two-field rotation schemes, slash and burn systems, and "temporary" plantings) to a much more intensive type of farming that employed a three-field rotation system and that required more men per acre to farm. It is difficult to believe that both depopulation and the adoption of more intensive agriculture took place simultaneously; and the argument for the introduction of slavery or serfdom based exclusively on the sudden availability of free land on the frontier can legitimately be questioned. It must be added, however, that the introduction of the three-field rotation system acts in the same manner as the opening of a frontier on land rents and relative land "scarcity."

The open resources argument can also be applied to manufacturing production. In this case open resources occur when such production can be carried out with very few tools or other types of capital equipment, while the lack of open resources is manifested by production techniques requiring a great number of tools and other types of capital equipment. Some of the difficulties arising with the propositions about the lack of affinity of slavery in urban areas also arise here. We have, in addition, the problem of determining the critical capital/labor ratios when slavery is introduced.

For an economist the open resource argument has considerable appeal. Unfortunately, it suffers from some of the difficulties of all benefit/cost arguments about slavery and, more particularly, assumes a strong degree of economic rationality and individualism that may not be applicable to the situation under consideration.[40] In addition, the open resource hypothesis also focuses on the "field" (or "factory") slave rather than "house slaves." Furthermore, it implies an element of coercion that may not be present in slavery, that is, the options facing a particular individual may be such that he may voluntarily enter slavery, a situation not considered by the Nieboer approach. But the primary difficulty of the approach occurs when we try to test it empirically. If we informally consider several well-known cases of slavery, namely, classical Greece and Rome, we find two societies, neither of which apparently had open resources in land or manufacturing and both of which had considerable slav-

---

[39]Michael Confino, *Systèmes agraires et progrès agricole: L'assolement triennal en Russie aux XVIIIᵉ–XIXᵉ siècles* (1969). I would like to thank John Michael Montias for drawing my attention to this interesting study.

[40]This criticism is raised by a number of anthropologists; in concise form it is found in Bernard J. Siegel, "Slavery."

ery.[41] A more formal test can be applied by examining the 36 agricultural societies in my worldwide sample. I devoted countless days in trying to demonstrate conclusively this hypothesis but with no success. Although the calculated regression coefficient had the predicted sign, its level of significance was usually quite low.

Miscellaneous Theories

To complete this survey of theories about the determinants of slavery which have been proposed by others, I deal in a summary fashion with a few of the most interesting or plausible propositions that I have been able to locate.

GEOGRAPHICAL FACTORS INFLUENCING SLAVERY

Many geographical considerations, allegedly influencing the presence of slavery, are discussed in the literature. According to Nieboer,[42] societies forming a somewhat homogeneous group and maintaining constant relations with each other are more likely to keep slaves (and buy and sell them from each other) than other societies. Others have argued that, on the contrary, slavery is more likely to occur when an "inferior race" lives in the neighborhood. Still others have argued that slavery is less likely to occur if societies nearby are not carrying on a slave trade.[43] None of these theories rests, as far as I can determine, on any specification of the type of slavery. The first and third hypotheses are variants of a diffusion argument and are later tested; the empirical results suggest they do not appear promising. Since it is difficult to define "inferior races" except by the presence of slavery, the second hypothesis is not subjected to empirical testing; however, such an hypothesis should sensitize us to the question of whether or not the slaves belong to the same ethnic groups or races as the masters.

MARKET INFLUENCES ON SLAVERY

As noted previously, some have argued that the presence of slavery (presumably, slaves as economic capital) should be related to the presence of markets

[41]This situation is discussed in various previously cited articles and books by Moses I. Finley. Several problems arise in discussing these cases. First, can we really speak of closed resources when both societies were imperialistic and had "open" land on their frontiers that they were expanding? Second, there is some debate about the importance of slavery in agriculture, particularly in Greece; so that at least in Greece, we may not find the type of field slavery that I show the Nieboer hypothesis purports to explain. In the Roman empire it could be argued that most of the slave labor in agriculture was used in the large latifundia in which economies of scale, unobtainable in small farms, could be achieved. The importance of such economies of scale can, in turn, be questioned since such latifundia were apparently not characterized by monocultural production.

[42]Nieboer, *Slavery*, p. 256.

[43]This kind of argument is generally found in the context of analyses of particular societies, for example, explaining that the Nyakyusa of Tanzania did not have slavery, while their neighbors, the Ngonde, did because the latter were much closer to the routes of the Arab slave traders. This type of argument has been used also to explain why certain West African coastal societies had slavery only after, and not before, contact with European slave traders.

for goods, which is supposed to encourage the production of goods by slaves so that their owners can accumulate riches without limit. On the labor market side Moses Finley has suggested that slavery occurs when the labor markets in the society do not function "properly."[44] It is difficult to derive a measurement reflecting the manner in which labor markets function, although I do have measures for the occurrence of labor markets. For both the goods and labor market variables the same problems occur, namely, that these variables may be both cause and effect of slavery. It turns out empirically that both are correlated in the expected manner with slavery, but we can not include either in the regressions until the components of the reciprocal causation can be separated through some type of simultaneous equations approach to the problem, an approach that I do not attempt.

THE IMPACT OF SOCIETAL ETHOS

In those societies where egalitarianism is valued strongly or military achievement (in contrast to the amassing of wealth through production) is valued highly, slavery is supposed to be less likely to occur.

It is extremely difficult to obtain a measure of egalitarian ethos. I do have a variable representing social-economic inequality, and as expected, the greater the inequality, the more likely the presence of slavery. But since socioeconomic inequality is both an effect and possibly a cause of slavery, we run into some familiar problems and must drop this variable from the regressions because of difficulties of interpretation.

Devising a measure for military ethos also proved to be difficult. Using a behavioral variable such as frequency of wars is not satisfactory because wars may be fought for defensive as well as offensive purposes. Also, wars may provide a fertile source for captives who may be turned into slaves, so that this may counteract the ethos argument. Experiments with a war-frequency variable did not prove promising so this line of argument was abandoned.

Sometimes the ethos argument is also used to counter the benefit/cost arguments for slavery. More specifically, it is asserted that slavery is likely to persist in a society, even if it is unprofitable, if the slave holders have an aristocratic ethos which makes them indifferent to benefit/cost considerations except of the most gross nature.[45] Unfortunately, this proposition proved impossible to test with the data I was able to collect and therefore had to be dropped from empirical consideration.

A New Approach

The approach proposed in the following sections rests on two sets of considerations: certain family and social structural factors and certain political fac-

---

[44]Finley, *The Ancient Economy*, p. 70.

[45]In the literature on slavery in the American South, this position has been taken in part by Eugene D. Genovese, *The Political Economy of Slavery in the Economy and Society of the Slave South* (1965), as well as by many others.

tors. The theories that I present do not explain how slavery originally arose but focus instead on those factors which facilitate the introduction of the institution into a society.

A FAMILY AND SOCIAL STRUCTURAL THEORY

In these hypotheses I focus on several family and social structural variables that proved useful in explaining certain aspects of the appearance of markets (Chapter 5) embodied in the "several paths to wealth" theory. Such variables also play a successful role in the analysis of the determinants of the brideprice (Appendix B.2).

The key insight of my proposed theory of the determinants of slavery focuses on the societal parallels that one finds between a dominant husband and an exploited wife on the one hand and a master and his slave on the other hand. The exploited wife and the slave (either male or female) fulfill the same role, namely, to relieve the husband of work and to provide him with an opportunity to exercise power. This homologism between wife and slave can be seen not only in the myths of certain societies but also in much more concrete ethnographic facts as well, for example, in the Bismarck Archipelago male slaves are required to dress as women.[46]

Such an approach leads to some interesting hypotheses regarding the presence of slaves as economic and as social capital. For slaves as economic capital (Slavery C) we derive the proposition that slavery would most likely be found in societies in which women normally perform most of the work, so that the slave and the wife act as substitutes for each other. When slavery exists as social capital, the relative amount of work that women do is quite irrelevant to the presence of slavery since little economic advantage is gained from slaves. The role of the slave as social capital is more like the role of a wife in a polygynous situation—dominated in one sense by the husband but economically a relatively free agent. Thus, the presence of slavery as social capital should be related to the presence of polygyny and unrelated to the amount of work performed by women, while the presence of slavery as economic capital should be related to the amount of women's work and unrelated to the presence of polygyny.

It must be emphasized that I am not arguing that slavery is related to the "status" of women, for this kind of subjective consideration is quite irrelevant. (In order to test this assertion, an index of women's status was devised and tested in the regressions; I found no indications of any relationship between the two variables.) Rather, I am focusing on the social structural position of women

---

[46]Richard Thurnwald, *Economics in Primitive Communities* (1932), p. 215. Several pages later he speaks of slaves as people requiring patriarchal authority, a theme congruent to the theory that I propose. Ester Boserup, *Women's Role in Economic Development* (1970), p. 43, also has some extremely interesting insights on the complementarities between free women and other laborers, although my hypotheses are quite different from hers.

in terms of relative power vis-à-vis men and, wherever relevant, on the relative amount of work performed by women.

The hypotheses arising from such considerations are based on a particular type of causation that deserves brief comment. I am positing that slavery is most likely to occur in situations where a particular type of dominance pattern already exists; furthermore, that this dominance pattern permits the transplanting of slavery with a minimum of change occurring in the rest of society. In short, the ease of introduction of slavery appears crucial. If an empirical correlation is found between these family and social structural variables and slavery, it is likely that it represents a causal connection rather than a simple correlation because the possibility of the presence of slavery influencing these fundamental family and social structural variables appears remote. That is, the family and social structural variables that I have posited as determinants of slavery seem much more "basic" than the institution of slavery. I show in the statistical analysis that this social structural approach receives empirical confirmation.

A THEORY ABOUT MACRO- AND MICROPOLITICAL ASPECTS OF SLAVERY

In societies with slavery as economic capital, serious problems of ruling slaves exist because the slaves can see quite plainly their relatively low living standards vis-à-vis their masters. This problem has macropolitical and micropolitical aspects.

In order to prevent large-scale political disruptions by slaves or in order to quell slave revolts if they occur, a certain amount of political centralization is necessary. That is, political power must be sufficiently concentrated that decisive repressive actions can be taken whenever trouble might arise; indeed, the very existence of such political concentration is an important assurance that trouble will not arise. Therefore, we would hypothesize that the occurrence of political concentration is a necessary condition for the maintenance of slavery as economic capital, an hypothesis receiving empirical confirmation.

The micropolitical problem concerns the problem of directing the slaves at their tasks in a manner to obtain the greatest amount of goods and services from them (for the given costs of maintaining the human capital in good standing). A serious problem arises when the original slave holder dies and passes them to his heirs. Since in most societies with slaves as economic capital the slave owners are men, it can be argued that slave systems can be most easily maintained in patrilocal, patrilineal societies where future heirs live near their future inherited assets. The explanatory value of variables reflecting such societal conditions showed some initial promise but did not prove sufficiently high to be included in the final regressions.

For slavery as social capital, neither the presence of a high concentration of political power nor the existence of patrilocal, patrilineal social structures should make much difference since the political problem is not so important. In this case slavery refers primarily to a social, not economic, relationship for which redress through political means seems less likely to occur and less effective if it occurs. That is, the ills of slavery are less visible and less remediable. Therefore, we predict that the presence of slaves as social capital should be unrelated to either political concentration or to patrilocal postmarital residence structures, a proposition also receiving confirmation in the empirical analysis.

TESTS OF HYPOTHESES

Some Problems of Coding

WHAT IS SLAVERY?

The greatest difficulties arose when the ethnographer described a relationship as "slavery" but was not very explicit about what he meant by the term. In all cases I tried to go behind the actual use of the term and examine the rights which a master had in a slave. It is difficult to determine whether I erred more in including as slavery particular relationships falling outside my definition of slavery or in failing to recognize the existence of slavery when it occurred. Undoubtedly, the greatest possibility of error arose in the determination of Slavery C (narrow slavery), for this required an estimation not only of the relative importance of slaves in the population but also of the relative living standards of the superior and subordinate.

In comparing my codings of the existence of slavery with those of other observers, an amazing similarity is found between my maximal slavery definition (Slavery A) and those of others; in all cases a statistically significant degree of similarity was found. If my results of Slavery A are compared with the ratings of Nieboer, who allegedly used a much different definition, agreement on the presence or absence of slavery is found in 87% of the 30 societies in which our samples overlap[47]; and in the more recent ratings of Robert Carneiro, agreement is found in 94% of the 32 societies in which it is appropriate to make comparisons of our samples for slavery.[48] A comparison with the data from the

---

[47]Although Nieboer does not supply the dates to which his codings refer, I suspect that they are roughly the same as mine. Of the 30 societies that are contained in both of our samples, we agree in our ratings in 26 cases; for three societies he rated the presence of slavery, while I recorded the reverse; and for one society, the opposite occurred.

[48]I am referring to the fourth edition of Robert Carneiro's scale analysis trait list, which is summarized in his article "Scale Analysis, Evolutionary Sequences, and the Rating of Cultures," Chap. XLI in *A Handbook of Method in Cultural Anthropology* (1973), ed. Raoul Naroll and Ronald Cohen, pp. 834–871. The actual codings on slavery were taken by permission from Carneiro's worksheets, and I would like to thank him for this help. Although he does not give the dates to which his codings of various societies refer, I understand that he usually tried to code the society in its form shortly before intensive Western contact—a rule similar to my own. For the 32 societies for which comparisons are appropriate, our codings are the same in 30 cases; in one case of disagreement, I coded slavery, and he coded its absence; while in the other case, the reverse was true.

Ethnographic Atlas yields an equally impressive similarity.[49] Unfortunately, no other coder made as many distinctions of different kinds of slavery, so we have no such cross checks for other types of slavery.

WHAT ARE OPEN RESOURCES?

Testing the open resource hypothesis requires an operational definition of open resources, and this raises some difficulties. Nieboer used a legal definition of the term with regard to land: there is no open land "when every piece of land is claimed by someone as his property . . . when someone claims the use of it to the exclusion of all others."[50] As Nieboer notes, it is not always clearly stated in ethnographic reports whether all land has been appropriated. Another difficulty arises in situations where the king or various noble groups claim "ownership" of vast tracts of unused land that can be farmed by anyone who pledges a certain allegiance. Still other difficulties arise when one discovers that in many very sparsely populated areas, kin groups claim enormous tracts of land for their exclusive use, even though they do not use it for farming (e.g., the Maori in New Zealand before the coming of the English). Nieboer operationalizes the concept of "appropriation of land" by recourse to a demographic variable: the existence of a class of free men who are destitute of land.[51] But even this more specific definition raises problems: Are we to interpret "destitution" in an absolute sense or in the sense that there may be a group of people who do not have sufficient land and must rent some? Are we defining land destitution at a particular point in time or over the entire life cycle? How should we take into account priests or tradesmen who may not have land or need it but who could acquire land at any time?

I have tried to operationalize the concept in several different ways, taking into account a measure of the physical scarcity of land (Appendix C.3), the presence of rents, the relative amount of unfarmed land in the society and its value for farming (Appendix C.4), and farming techniques. No matter how I tried to construct an index of open resources, the index was not significantly correlated with the presence of slavery in agricultural societies.

OTHER PROBLEMS IN CODING

The construction of most of the other explanatory variables tested in the following empirical analysis was relatively straightforward and is explained in Appendix A. The only variable which gave rise to major difficulties was the variable indicating the concentration of political power (or political inequality). I tried to make a rough quantitative judgment on a five-point scale, taking into

---

[49]No ratings on slavery were made in the Murdock–White SES sample, so comparisons could not be made. If we compare my results to those in the 1972 version of the *Ethnographic Atlas* (obtained from the Department of Anthropology, University of Pittsburgh), which was supervised by George Peter Murdock, our samples overlap in 58 cases, and we have similar ratings in 54 cases (93%).

[50]Nieboer, *Slavery*, p. 310.

[51]Ibid., p. 311.

account the relative importance of the political leaders and the rest of the society in various decisions of political importance such as war making, dispute resolution, and so forth.

Cross-Section Tests

STAGE THEORIES

Testing whether or not slavery is an inevitable stage of economic development is quite simple: We need merely calculate a regression showing the relationship between the level of economic development and slavery. By placing in the regression not only the level of economic development but a squared term of this level, we can see whether slavery appears at one particular range on the economic development scale. This would be shown by a positive coefficient for the simple development variable and a negative coefficient for the squared term. The results are presented in Table 8.1.

It should be clear that the stage theories leave a great deal to be desired. For Slavery C none of the calculated coefficients is significant; and for Slavery A the coefficients are statistically significant but the coefficients of determination are

TABLE 8.1

Relationships between the Presence of Slavery and the Level of Economic Development[a]

1. $SC = .0305 + .0039\ ED$ $\quad(.0027)$	$R^2 = .0361$ $n = 60;\ PCP = 85.00\%$
2. $SC = -.0755 + .0142\ ED - .00017\ ED^2$ $\quad\quad(.0108)\quad\quad(.00017)$	$R^2 = .0520$ $n = 60;\ PCP = 85.00\%$
3. $SA = .0361 + .0108\,{}^*ED$ $\quad\quad(.0034)$	$R^2 = .1517$ $n = 60;\ PCP = 63.33\%$
4. $SA = -.2872 + .0421\,{}^*ED - .00051\,{}^*ED^2$ $\quad\quad(.0131)\quad\quad(.00021)$	$R^2 = .2328$ $n = 60;\ PCP = 75.00\%$

Key:
SC = Presence of Slavery C (narrow slavery) (0 = no; 1 = yes) [mean = .1500].
SA = Presence of Slavery A (maximal slavery) (0 = no; 1 = yes). These samples are not adjusted by removing Slavery C [mean = .3667].
ED = Rank on economic development scale (1 = lowest; 60 = highest) [mean = 30.5000].
R^2 = Coefficient of determination.
n = Size of sample.
PCP = Percentage of correct predictions.
( ) = Standard error.
* = t statistic for calculated regression coefficient is over the acceptable limit (2.25) defined in Chapter 1.

[a]The data come from Appendix A, Series 22, 50, 52. For equations 1 and 2, the PCPs are high because no societies are predicted to have slavery. Logit regressions are presented in Appendix B.1 for all four regressions.

TABLE 8.2

Determinants of Slavery as Economic Capital in Agricultural Societies[a]

1. $SCA = -.4526 + .2453*RWS + .1647*PC$ $\qquad\qquad\quad (.1031) \qquad\quad (.0697)$	$R^2 = .2593$ $n = 36; PCP = 86.1\%$

Key:

SCA = Presence of Slavery C (narrow slavery) in agricultural societies (0 = no; 1 = yes) [mean = .1667].

RWS = Relative work of spouses (+1 = wife spends considerably more time in economic activities than husband; 0 = spouses spend roughly the same amount of time in economic activities; −1 = husband spends considerably more time in economic activities than wife) [mean = .3889].

PC = Political concentration scale (political inequality scale) (1 = a low concentration of political power; 5 = a high concentration of political power) [mean = 3.1806].

R^2 = Coefficient of determination.

n = Size of sample.

PCP = Percentage of correct predictions.

( ) = Standard error.

* = t statistic for calculated regression coefficient is over the acceptable limit (2.25) defined in Chapter 1.

[a]The data come from Appendix A, Series 4, 9, 52, 63, 67. Both full and incipient agricultural societies are included. A logit regression is presented in Appendix B.1.

sufficiently low to suggest that there are numerous exceptions. Addition of a series of other variables suggested in the stage-theory literature added little explanatory power. The level of economic development may be a necessary condition of slavery, but it certainly is not a sufficient condition.

OTHER HYPOTHESES

In testing the various hypotheses previously discussed, I have adopted several procedures which deserve mention before the results are presented. First, I have isolated Slavery C ("narrow" slavery, i.e., slaves as economic capital in societies where they constitute a significant part of the labor force) and then removed these cases from the sample used in testing Slavery A. Thus, Slavery A embraces slaves as social capital plus a few cases where slaves as economic capital exist but are not important in the operation of the economy as a whole. Second, to simplify exposition, I do not present the many regressions of hypotheses which did not work but merely discuss these failures in passing in the text. The results of the most revealing regression experiments are presented in Tables 8.2 and 8.3.

As predicted, the presence of slavery is related to the relative work performed by wives (if the wife performs much more than the husband, slavery is more likely to be present) and the presence of a high concentration of political power. The level of economic development, the degree of nomadism, the

TABLE 8.3

Determinants of Slavery as Social Capital[a]

1. $SARSC = -.3176 + .0299*ED - .00035 \ ED^2 + .2476*PG$				$R^2 = .2732$
$(.0127)$	$(.00031)$	$(.1105)$		$n = 51; PCP = 80.39\%$

Key:
SARSC   = Presence of Slavery A (maximal slavery) in the reduced sample (excluding cases of Slavery
          C) (0 = no; 1 = yes) [mean = .2549].
ED   = Rank of economic development scale (1 = lowest; 60 = highest) [mean = 29.1176].
PG   = Important presence of polygyny (1 = more than occasional polygyny; 0 = monogamy,
          polyandry, or only occasional polygyny) [mean = .4314].
R^2 = Coefficient of determination.
n   = Size of sample.
PCP   = Percentage of correct predictions.
( )   = Standard error.
*   = t statistic for calculated regression coefficient is over the acceptable limit (2.25) defined in
          Chapter 1.
   [a]The data come from Appendix A, Series 22, 50, 52, and 69. A logit regression is presented in
Appendix B.1.

presence of open resources,[52] and other factors discussed previously do not
appear to play a role. If the entire sample of 60 societies is used, the relationships shown in Table 8.2 are weaker, but the factors shown in the table still
appear to be operating.

Since I implicitly argued in the theoretical discussion that the factors shown
in the regression calculation are necessary but not sufficient conditions for the
presence of slavery, some might feel that the method in which these hypotheses
are tested (in which the hypothesized causal factors are considered as sufficient
conditions for slavery) might lead to prediction problems. More specifically,
such a procedure might lead to a number of cases where slavery is predicted
when it does not actually occur. Examination of the regression residuals to
isolate such a prediction error does not reveal this confounding of necessary
and sufficient conditions to be a major source of difficulty; only the false
prediction of slavery in Turkey (which, of course, had slavery at one time) and
among the Ganda (of Uganda) might be traced to this problem. Little additional
information can be gained from such an exercise with the regression residuals.

The presence of slavery as social capital is related to the stage of economic
development and, as predicted, to the occurrence of polygyny. As I have

_____

[52]This is, as far as I know, the most extensive test of the open resources hypothesis using a
statistical approach. As noted in the previous discussion, the sign of the calculated regression
coefficient was usually correct but usually the calculated t coefficient was considerably lower than
the acceptable limit. Nieboer, *Slavery*, designated quite carefully the presence of slavery and a
series of other variables such as the open resources variable; but he never really performed a
critical statistical test. Domar, *Causes of Slavery*, uses the open resource hypothesis to interpret
events in various societies but also does not test it in a rigorous fashion. Baks, Breman, and Nooij,
"Slavery," do attempt some statistical tests but not for a worldwide sample.

predicted, it is not related to the degree of political concentration of power or the relative amount of work done by spouses. It is also not related to variables representing the other hypotheses that have been previously discussed. If only agricultural societies are examined (with cases of Slavery C removed), the presence of Slavery A appears related only to the presence of polygyny, and the relative importance of the level of economic development does not appear great. With regard to other variables the same results are obtained as reported for the larger sample.

As in the case of my previous calculations, I have assumed that the presence of the explanatory variables is not only necessary but sufficient to bring about Slavery A. Examination of the prediction errors does not reveal that this assumption is a major source of error. Again, little additional information is gained in the analysis of regression residuals.

SEVERAL OTHER FACETS OF SLAVERY

One hypothesis discussed in the survey of propositions deserves brief attention, namely, that extrasocietal slavery should occur at lower stages of economic development than intratribal slavery. Data pertaining to this matter are presented in Table 8.4.

The data show quite clearly that extrasocietal slavery does occur at lower levels of economic development than intrasocietal slavery. Furthermore, this relationship holds not only for Definitions A and C of slavery but also for others as well. It is not clear to me, however, that the economic explanation on which this hypothesis is based is correct. A plausible case can be made for the argument that extrasocietal slavery is socially "easier" to carry out than enslaving a

TABLE 8.4

Extrasocietal and Intrasocietal Slavery in Slave Holding Societies at Low Levels of Economic Development[a]

	Number of societies with slaves		
	Total	With extrasocietal slavery	With intrasocietal slavery
Slavery A (maximal slavery)[b]			
Lowest 40% on development scale	3	3	0
Lowest 60% on development scale	8	8	4
Slavery C (narrow slavery)[b]			
Lowest 40% on development scale	2	2	0
Lowest 60% on development scale	5	5	2

[a]Intrasocietal slavery includes enslavement of the children of slaves, enslavement for debts, and similar types of slavery. A less conclusive examination of this hypothesis is carried out by Pryor, "Property Institutions."

[b]Full sample of 60 societies.

person who has grown up in the society, so that intrasocietal slavery would not occur until the notion of slavery had become firmly embedded in the society.

Several additional insights can be gained by examining briefly the incidence of slavery in societies with different modes of food production. In Table 8.5 I present data on such matters, as well as information on the explanatory variables contained in the regression equations in Tables 8.2 and 8.3.

The data in Table 8.5 reveal that in hunting and gathering societies slavery is practically nonexistent. Of these societies only the Comanche Indians of the south central part of the United States had slavery, and for this society grave problems of coding arise since the alleged slaves were usually war captives who were often adopted into the tribe. Although the Comanche were a nomadic society, they were sufficiently isolated from other societies to make escape difficult, a characteristic giving rise to a particular literary genre of how-I-escaped-from-the-wild-Comanche-with-my-virtue-intact, which had some popularity in the late nineteenth century. To explain the absence of slavery in such hunting and gathering societies, we do not need to place great stress on the benefit/cost argument based on the high costs of guarding slaves since their relatively equal division of work among spouses, low concentration of political power, and low level of economic development go a long way in

TABLE 8.5

The Primary Mode of Food Production and the Presence of Slavery[a]

Primary mode of food production	Total number of societies	Societies with presence of slavery		Average levels			
		Slavery A	Slavery C	RWS	PC	ED	PG
Gathering	8	0	0	0.38	1.88	7.7	0.44
Hunting	5	1	0	0.00	1.90	9.1	0.30
Fishing	2	2	1	0.50	3.00	28.0	0.50
Herding	9	3	2	0.44	2.67	25.8	0.22
Farming	36	16	6	0.39	3.12	39.8	0.47
Total	60	22	9	0.37	2.78	30.5	0.42

Key:

PC = Political concentration scale (political inequality scale) (1 = a low concentration of political power; 5 = a high concentration of political power).

RWS = Relative work of spouses (+1 = wife spends considerably more time in economic activities than husband; 0 = spouses spend roughly the same amount of time in economic activities); −1 = husband spends considerably more time in economic activities than wife).

ED = Rank on economic development scale (1 = lowest; 60 = highest).

PG = Important presence of polygyny (1 = more than occasional polygyny; 0 = monogamy, polyandry, or only occasional polygyny).

[a]The data come from Appendix A, Series 4, 22, 50, 52, 63, 67, and 69. Because two of the societies are considered half-hunting, half-gathering, both are given weights of one-half for each of the respective groupings of societies.

explaining the situation. It should be added that addition of a variable representing the degree of nomadism had practically no effect on the regression results in Tables 8.2 and 8.3.

Slavery among fishing societies presents some interesting ethnographic features.[53] An extension of the open resource hypothesis would suggest that slavery would not be present if fishing boats were a particularly important piece of capital equipment in the societies. In both of the fishing societies in the sample, fishing was carried on at the shores of rivers or on ocean beaches where relatively little capital equipment was needed. The data in Table 8.5 reveal that the two fishing societies had other features which would suggest the presence of slavery: Wives carried on more of the work, the concentration of political power was high, and there was a relatively high incidence of polygyny. Slavery was indeed found in both these societies.

In the literature one often finds arguments as to why slavery should be unlikely in herding societies. For instance, the open resources argument would suggest the absence of slavery because the herds constitute an important closed resource; furthermore, as argued in Chapter 5, labor markets are quite frequent in herding societies, so slavery is not necessary to obtain labor power. The data in Table 8.5 do not greatly help us in deciding whether slavery should be present or absent in herding societies since for all explanatory variables except the presence of polygyny, the values for herding societies are roughly equal to the average values for the entire sample. Although it is sometimes argued that slavery should be infrequent in herding societies if they are nomadic (because escape would be easy), objections to this approach can be raised. For one example of the functioning of slavery in nomadic herding societies (and in the sample only the nomadic herding societies had slavery), we might recall from the Bible in the book of *Genesis* the story of the female slave Hagar or the unnamed male slave whom Abraham sent to get a wife for Isaac. In two of the three herding societies with slavery in the sample, the slaves were of a visibly different racial stock than their masters, which certainly increased the difficulties of escape.

Time-Series Tests

Several of the hypotheses surveyed above rest on the notion that slavery in one society occurs as a result of contact with another society with slavery. Such propositions rest on two different concepts of the diffusion process. As noted in Chapter 3, "slow diffusion" is that process which occurs when a given society adopts a particular trait from its neighbor and, in turn, passes it on to another neighbor, and so forth. This is the type of diffusion for which we can carry out statistical tests. "Fast diffusion" occurs when a given society adopts a trait from

---

[53]Some interesting remarks on slavery among fishing groups are made by IU. P. Averkieva, "Slavery among the Indians of North America," in *Slavery: A Comparative Perspective* (1972), ed. Robin Winks, pp. 165–171. Nieboer, *Slavery*, Part II, Chap. II also discusses such cases.

a society that is quite separated in geographical distance; this might occur, for instance, when a society adopts slavery after contact with a slave trader from a faraway land in order to supply both themselves and him with this new valuable commodity. There is historical evidence of such a process in some societies in West Africa,[54] and it is possible that such a process might also have occurred among some of the societies in the sample.

In using the technique described in Chapter 3 and employed in previous chapters to investigate the presence of slow diffusion, a problem arises. Since the regression analysis of Slavery C is confined to agricultural societies, since the sample is made even smaller by removal of societies for which we do not have information pertaining to the second half of the nineteenth century, and since the number of societies with Slavery C is relatively small, we should expect that the number of pairs of societies in some of the cells of the table are really too small for meaningful statistical tests to be performed. And the relevant data, which are presented in Table 8.6, bear out this expectation. A similar problem, although to a much lesser extent, also occurs for Slavery A. Therefore, our conclusions can only be quite tentative.

The data suggest that a certain geographical clustering of societies with both Slavery C and Slavery A (excluding cases of Slavery C) exists. There appears to be an even greater clustering of societies when such slavery is predicted, that is, the societies with the relevant explanatory variables. The data in the last four columns (especially comparing column P with the average distances between all pairs of societies since column R has too few cases to make adequate comparisons) suggest, however, that slow diffusion does not appear sufficiently great to affect our cross-section results. Let me repeat that we can not be completely sure about these matters because of the smallness of the sample.

Unfortunately, we do not have the historical evidence which is needed to be able to make a judgment about the presence of "fast diffusion." Although the hypothesis that "fast diffusion" was important does not seem very plausible, we can not reject it completely. It should be further added that in an ultimate sense the fast diffusion of antislavery attitudes in the nineteenth century played, as we know, an extremely important role in the elimination of slavery in many societies. However, this fast diffusion process of the elimination of slavery occurred for most societies in the sample at a much later point than the year for which the societies were sampled.

One other geographical factor deserves to be noted. One of the hypotheses previously mentioned attributes the presence of slavery to the presence of neighbors who are "inferior" peoples. In discussing this, I have pointed out that slavery occurs in several societies where the slaves belong to visibly different racial stocks than the slaveholders. The availability of neighboring societies of

---

[54]For a number of West African societies, Walter Rodney, "African Slavery and Other Forms of Social Oppression on the Upper Guinea Coast in the Context of the Atlantic Slave Trade," *Journal of African History* VII, 3(1966): 431–443, argues that slavery was introduced only after contact with European slave traders.

TABLE 8.6

Average Distances between Groups of Pairs of Societies for Making Diffusion Tests[a]

Type of slavery	Formula number	Total	Between societies with and without designated slavery			Between societies with and without predicted designated slavery			Between societies with and without designated slavery after taking causal variables into account			
			K	L	M	X	Y	Z	P	P'	Q	R
Slavery C (narrow slavery)	B8-2-1	5287 [2077] (435)	4500 [2304] (15)	4975 [2183] (144)	5492 [1974] (276)	2680 [1528] (10)	5030 [2162] (125)	5481 [1984] (300)	5178 [2088] (9)	5000 [2263] (3)	3033 [1834] (6)	4867 [2462] (6)
Slavery A excluding Slavery C	B8-3-1	5618 [1897] (946)	5089 [2151] (55)	5585 [1922] (363)	5695 [1840] (528)	4423 [2271] (78)	5846 [1713] (403)	5620 [1904] (465)	6062 [1507] (24)	5000 [2264] (3)	4295 [2295] (40)	6253 [1297] (15)

Key:

Group K: All pairs of societies that have the designated type of slavery.

Group L: All pairs of societies, one of which has and the other of which does not have the designated type of slavery.

Group M: All pairs of societies that do not have the designated type of slavery.

Group X: All pairs of societies that the explanatory variables lead us to predict the presence of the designated type of slavery.

Group Y: All pairs of societies, one of which we predict to have and the other of which we predict not to have the designated type of slavery.

Group Z: All pairs of societies that the explanatory variables lead us to predict the absence of the designated type of slavery.

Group P: All pairs of societies, one of which is predicted to have and the other of which is predicted not to have the designated type of slavery, but both of which actually have the designated type of slavery.

Group P': All pairs of societies, both of which are predicted not to have the designated type of slavery, but both of which actually have the designated type of slavery.

Group Q: All pairs of societies, both of which are predicted to have the designated type of slavery, but one prediction is incorrect.

Group R: All pairs of societies, one of which is predicted to have and the other of which is predicted not to have the designated type of slavery, and both predictions are incorrect.

[a] The formulas come from the logit regressions presented on Appendix B.1.

[b] The standard deviation is enclosed in brackets and the size of the sample in parentheses.

different races might encourage slavery because the cost of guarding slaves is lower (since an escaped slave can always be recognized); this, in turn, might encourage the diffusion of slavery in such boundary areas. Although such a phenomenon can be invoked to explain special cases, I do not believe that it would greatly influence the results obtained from our entire sample, that is, the general case.

SUMMARY AND CONCLUSION

A major message of this chapter is that the specific determinants of slavery depend very much on the type of slavery under consideration. I have particularly stressed the differences between slaves as economic and as social capital. Slavery as economic capital occurs when slaves constitute a significant part of the labor force and when they are economically exploited in the sense that their standard of living is markedly below that of their masters. Slavery as social capital occurs when slaves are not economically exploited but constitute a group lacking particular social and political rights and are forced to participate in the social life and rituals of their masters.

Whether we define slavery in terms of social or economic capital, the regression analysis suggests that slavery is not inevitable and that many societies have developed economically without passing through a slavery phase. Thus, a stage theory approach to slavery appears unpromising.

A major determinant of Slavery C (slavery as economic capital) is a family-social structure in which wives do considerably more economic work than their husbands. In this case slaves serve a homologous economic role as wives, and the social structure permits a relatively easy introduction of slavery into the work situation. Such a situation gives rise to an obvious political problem; therefore, another condition appears necessary: a concentration of political power that permits force to be applied quickly to any situation where the slaves might band together in order to gain their freedom. Although all of these factors are necessary but not sufficient reasons for slavery to occur, the statistical analysis suggests that their joint concurrence begins to approximate a sufficient condition for Slavery C.

For Slavery A excluding Slavery C (that is, in societies where slaves are primarily used as social capital) neither the economic nor the political considerations discussed above are relevant. A social structural argument parallel to the argument about the economic role of women focuses on the social relation between spouses: Slavery of this type is more likely in societies that also feature polygyny. Again, the causal mechanism focuses on the ease with which the institution can be introduced without introducing other profound changes in the social structure. For the entire sample the relative level of economic development appears also to be related to the presence of such slavery; for agricultural societies, on the other hand, this relationship appears unimportant.

Some negative results are also important to note. I have considerable data for the various societies in the sample and tested a large number of theories discussed only in passing in this chapter; none of these theories proved very helpful. As just noted explicitly in the analysis, the presence of slavery does not appear to be significantly correlated to the occurrence of "open resources." Furthermore, various types of benefit/cost theories about slavery do not appear useful in helping us predict the presence or absence of slavery except in some quite special cases. For instance, from such an approach we successfully predict that extrasocietal slavery occurs at lower levels of economic development than intrasocietal slavery. It is noteworthy, however, that other theories can lead to the same prediction.

Finally, I provide some evidence, but it is not conclusive, that the cross-section results are not influenced by diffusion, so that we can use the various conclusions to generalize about events over time.

This analysis of the determinants of slavery has left some important aspects of the topic undiscussed. I do not, for instance, explore empirically the interrelations between the presence or absence of markets for goods and for labor with the presence of slavery; nor do I examine similar types of interrelations between different types of inequality and the presence of slavery. Both of these types of analyses would require considerably more complicated models. I also do not consider rural nonagricultural slavery (e.g., for use in building and other public works projects) or urban slaves used in manufacturing and handicrafts primarily because neither type of slavery occurred in a sufficient number of societies in my sample to make such an attempt worthwhile. Although both of these types of slaveries may be present only when slavery as economic capital is present in agriculture (an hypothesis which I believe can be easily proved), not all of the societies having the latter type of slavery also have the former type; this forces us, in turn, to introduce more variables into the analysis.

I hope to have demonstrated that the phenomenon of slavery lends itself well to the approach toward distributional transactions followed throughout the study; that different types of slavery have different determinants; that slavery is not an inevitable stage of development; and that the major determinants of the appearance of slavery are social and political. By isolating these general causal factors that appear to operate across many societies, we gain perspective on those ostensibly "singular" systems of slavery occurring in particular societies.

9

THE DETERMINANTS OF NONCENTRIC TRANSFERS: TYPES OTHER THAN SLAVERY

My ne stol'ko liubim liudei za to dobro, kotoroie oni nam sdelali, skol'ko za to dobro, kotoroie my im sdelali.

TOLSTOI[1]

As we turn our analytic attention from slavery to other types of noncentric transfers, we advance into *terra incognita*. Few of these noncentric transfers have been studied by others, and we have no maps to guide us. In the analysis of this chapter we meet intellectual thickets at every turn. Conceptual problems abound, it is difficult to generate testable propositions, and the data leave something to be desired. But in spite of these difficulties of exploration, we are able to survey the terrain and to sketch a rough chart that may prove useful to those who wish to explore further these fascinating problems.

After examining different types of noncentric transfers, I propose a number of hypotheses about their determinants. For the noncentric transfers of goods I argue that such a mode of distribution should be found in societies with low levels of economic development, with the absence of certain risks associated with particular types of food production, with small "units of observation," and with particular "tolerances for nonreciprocities." The empirical evidence appears to confirm the first two hypotheses and provides support but not convincing evidence for the last two propositions. For a particular type of noncentric transfer of goods, namely, gambling, the determinants bear some similarity to the more general case. However, some additional specific determinants related to special properties of the transaction are derived from theoretical consider-

---

Design from a Solomon Islands dance shield; Melanesia.

[1]Lev Tolstoi, *Voina i mir*, Book I, Part 1, Chap. 25. 'We do not only love others for the good that they have done us, but also for the good that we have done them.'

ations and demonstrated in the regression analysis. Experiments in testing various hypotheses purporting to explain noncentric transfers of labor other than slavery proved much less successful and eventually had to be abandoned. The time-series tests add further positive evidence to the results obtained from the cross-section analysis.

A SURVEY OF NONCENTRIC TRANSFERS

Some General Considerations of Definition

Although slavery appears at first sight unambiguously to be a noncentric transfer, the distinction between slavery as economic and social capital which is discussed in the previous chapter illustrates some of the difficulties in analyzing transfers. For the discussion in this chapter, it is useful to examine the concept of noncentric transfer in some detail.

In Chapter 2 I define a transfer as a transaction in which goods or services going from a person or a group to another person or group are not "balanced" by a counterflow. "Balance" is defined to exclude the flow of social invisibles. The lack of a balanced material counterflow can arise either because no material counterflow takes place or because the material counterflow is very uncertain or has only a very inexact relationship to the value of the original goods and services. In the terminology now emerging in economics[2] I am talking about "grants," and this chapter concerns the noncentric aspects of the "grants economy."

Centric transfers are characterized by the high degree they radiate to or from a single individual (e.g., a political or religious leader) or a single community-wide institution (e.g., the government or religious establishment). The pattern of these transfers throughout the society has a focus. Noncentric transfers are characterized by a relationship between individual pairs of people throughout the society (e.g., the slavery relationship, which occurs between individual masters and their slaves), and the pattern of these transfers throughout the society does not have a single focus. In some cases such transactions between pairs of individuals presupposes a central institution (e.g., as I pointed out in the previous chapter, some types of slavery depend, in part, on the existence of a strong political center), but they are still considered noncentric. In the following discussion I examine only noncentric transfers and leave analysis of centric transfers to the next chapter.

This type of definition of transfer embraces both positive transfers (in which the initiator gives something, such as a gift), negative transfers (in which the

---

[2]See particularly: Kenneth E. Boulding, *The Economy of Love and Fear: A Preface to the Grants Economy* (1973); and Martin Pfaff, *The Grants Economy*, Research Report, Computer Institute for Social Research, Michigan State University (n.d.).

initiator takes something, which occurs in a theft), and transfers which contain elements of both (for instance, the giving of a handout to a large and menacing beggar). This approach defines transfers in terms other than the motives of the participants, for as I have argued, transfers can arise from benevolence (e.g., the giving of food to a neighbor in distress) or malevolence (e.g., the obtaining of ransom or tribute payments).[3] Noncentric transfers can also arise for reasons that are less tied to individual motivation than to particular aspects of the social structure, e.g., the type of transaction explored in Chapter 4 on distribution among the Eskimo.

The institutional mechanisms underlying transfer transactions are extremely varied. In some societies transfers are distributed in a highly ritualized fashion (e.g., in the ceremonials of the Navajo Indians of Arizona or the ritualized theft that was practiced in the Fiji Islands of the Pacific Ocean), while in other societies the transfers are made in highly informal ways (e.g., casual gifts by the Wolof of Sene-Gambia to lower caste individuals) or, indeed, in ways such that the transfer element is entirely hidden (e.g., among the Eskimo of Sugluk). Transfers are often easily granted between kin; in addition, a variety of fictitious kin arrangements exist to facilitate such transfers between individuals who, by some formal rules of the society, are not kin (e.g., the *compadre* ('godparent') arrangement found in Mexico and Central America; the cohusband arrangement found among Eskimo men who have at one time exchanged sexual privileges to their respective wives; the perceived kinship between two !Kung Bushmen of Botswana who have relatives with the same name; the claimed kinship of two Iroquois Indians of New York State who have the same clan emblem; and so forth).

Transfers can be classified as progressive or regressive, depending on whether the distribution of goods (or labor hours) is more or less equal after the transfer is made. Transfers that do not systematically affect the distribution of goods (or labor hours) in either direction can be classified as neutral. Transfers can also be classified as narrow or wide, depending on the size of the set of individuals to whom the transfers are made. For instance, among the Sirionó Indians of Bolivia, most men only make transfers to their mothers-in-law and to no one else, while among the Omaha Indians of Nebraska, the distribution of transfers may embrace many people.

Certain problems of classifying transactions as transfers or exchanges arise. As noted in Chapter 7, some transactions have both reciprocal exchange and transfer aspects. For instance, the sharing of meat among hunters in a hunting party implies reciprocity between men of equal hunting ability and a noncen-

[3]Although my delineation of positive and negative noncentric transfers appears at first glance quite similar to Marshall Sahlins' concepts of "generalized reciprocity" and "negative reciprocity," my concepts are somewhat broader and depend neither upon kin distance between participants in the transactions nor upon their motives (which Sahlins did not emphasize but which others have). Sahlins' analysis is contained in "On the Sociology of Primitive Exchange," Chap. V of his *Stone Age Economics* (1972).

tric transfer between men of unequal hunting ability. The holding of a potlatch by the Indians of the Canadian west coast also has both elements since in one act the host tries to pay back certain social debts and, in addition, outdo his previous creditors in generosity.

The problems of classification are compounded by certain problems of detection. Isolation of transfer or grant elements in modern economies in which most transactions are carried out using the media of money is an extremely difficult task.[4] Isolating these flows in nonmonetary economies is even more difficult since often we have no single simple common denominator of value to determine if the transaction is balanced except, perhaps, labor hours of production. Furthermore, there are certain ambiguities in what we mean by "balance," and certain ostensibly balanced transactions may indeed contain strong elements of imbalance that are overlooked if we do not have detailed information about the transaction.[5]

These problems of detection force us to focus our attention only on gross imbalances, as measured by some type of labor values or, when they exist, market prices. This means, in turn, that we classify as exchange certain types of noncentric transfers in which the element of imbalance is only slight.

Additional problems arise in distinguishing between centric and noncentric transfers. How shall we classify, for example, the large feast given by a rich person to many of his neighbors in order to try to improve his social standing or the ceremonial that a particular individual finances but to which he invites his friends who may never reciprocate? These transfers (for their exchange rates may be extremely uncertain) involve many individuals and have a distinct focal point; on the other hand, the group may not embrace the community as a whole (even though the act is designated to achieve some community goal), and, at different times, other individuals may give similar feasts or ceremonials. I have classified such cases of "floating centricity" as noncentric since the key relationship seems to be between pairs of individuals, rather than an individual and the community as a whole (in a static sense or when the entire community is viewed as a whole).

I exclude from the analysis in this chapter two types of transactions that are, or could be, classified as noncentric transfers. The first type of transaction occurs in the slavery relationship, a phenomenon explored in detail in the last chapter. The second type of transaction excluded from this chapter occurs when land is rented or interest is charged. Although I define these as market transactions in Chapter 5 because the underlying forces are quite similar in

---

[4]Some of the methodological issues and empirical problems of analysis are discussed in: Kenneth E. Boulding, Martin Pfaff, and Anita Pfaff, eds., *Transfers in an Urbanized Economy* (1973); or Kenneth E. Boulding and Martin Pfaff, eds., *Redistribution to the Rich and the Poor* (1972).

[5]For instance, there is considerable dispute as to whether international trade represents exchange or transfer, and such issues have been recently reraised in a forceful but highly dubious study by Arghiri Emmanuel, *Unequal Exchange: A Study of the Imperialism of Trade*, trans. Brian Pearce (1972) [originally published 1969].

kind to those of other types of market transactions, it can be claimed that these are really transfers since the balancing elements are social invisibles (i.e., permission to use a particular piece of land or a bribe to obtain a desired object from its owner now rather than having to save up and obtain it later). Be that as it may, such transactions are not analyzed below.

Specific Types of Noncentric Transfers

NONCENTRIC TRANSFERS OF GOODS

Before examining noncentric transfers in primitive and peasant societies, it is well to consider for a moment such transactions in a more familiar context where we have certain monetary estimates. (Although the items to be discussed are not included in the calculation of national income [NI], a comparison of the noncentric transfers with this aggregate is illuminating.) In the United States in 1970 intrafamily transfers accounted for roughly $313 billion (39.1% of the NI), interfamily transfers accounted for roughly $8.4 billion (1.0% of the NI), private philanthropy amounted to roughly $11.1 billion (1.4% of the NI), and business transfers were roughly $3.6 billion (0.4% of the NI).[6] In 1965 negative noncentric transfers in the form of various kinds of theft and direct illegal costs against human and physical capital amounted to roughly $6.6 billion (1.1% of the NI); in addition, certain other types of negative transfers accounted for roughly 1% of the NI.[7] (To place such data in perspective, in 1970 centric transfers in the form of government grants of money to individuals amounted to roughly $75.1 billion or 9.4% of the NI; and such centric transfers in the form of all governmental expenditures amounted to almost four times as much.[8]) Thus, in the U.S. market economy, which has allegedly outgrown "primitive" distributional modes, noncentric transfers play an important economic role and add up to an amount corresponding roughly to 44% of the national income. (It must be added, however, that the bulk of these transfers are accounted for inside the unit of observation, viz., the family.)

[6]These estimates are derived from survey data by Nancy A. Baerwaldt and James N. Morgan, "Trends in Inter-Family Transfers," in *Survey of Consumers, 1971–72: Contribution to Behavioral Economics*, (1973), ed. Lewis Mandell et al., p. 221. Their definition of transfers is much broader than mine, but the data are very suggestive. A somewhat higher estimate of private philanthropy plus business and foundation grants is made by Martin Pfaff and Anita B. Pfaff, "The Grants Economy as Regulator of the Exchange Economy," in *The Economics of Federal Subsidy Programs* (1972), Joint Economic Committee, Congress of the United States, especially pp. 147–149.

[7]These data come from The President's Commission on Law Enforcement and Administration of Justice, *The Challenge of Crime in a Free Society* (1967), p. 33. My own estimates of the cost of crime are somewhat lower and are contained in the U.S. Department of Health, Education, and Welfare, The Panel on Social Indicators, *Materials for a Preliminary Draft of the Social Report* (April 1968).

[8]These data come from the U.S. Council of Economic Advisors, *Economic Report of the President 1975* (1975), pp. 328–330. For the total figure I have netted out intragovernmental transfers but have included all other types of governmental expenditures.

Turning to primitive and peasant societies, most discussions of noncentric transfers of goods have focused on transactions to obtain some type of social invisible such as prestige or respect; such transfers include the giving of gifts (especially in the form of feasts) and theft. The bravura of the first type of transfer is captured well in the language of the Omaha Indians of the American Great Plains whose word for "charity" is also the same as "to be brave"; the implication (at least to us if not to the Omaha) is that the generous man does not fear poverty. The bravura of the second type of transfer is illustrated well in the same society in the prestige given to warriors who successfully steal horses from other tribes. Because prestige is so intimately associated with many types of transfers, we meet a dazzling array of specific types of noncentric transfer transactions.

Rather than review all of the various specific types of noncentric transfers, it seems more reasonable to survey the general field by examining particular groups of transfers. The most useful classification scheme for such purposes focuses attention on the progressivity or regressivity of the transfer, for this permits considerable insight into the impact of such transfers on the functioning of the economy.

The most obvious types of progressive transfers are, of course, the giving of alms to the poor, the helping out of distressed neighbors with food gifts, or the ritual grants of gifts to members of inferior castes.[9] In Fiji the practice of *kere-kere* (where a good is begged with the ostensible promise of a return good of equal value, which is never made) is a variant of begging which, in practice, usually has an obvious progressive impact. As noted earlier, the sharing of game among members of a hunting party, even if the hunting is carried out individually, also has a clearly progressive impact. Another extremely common type of progressive transfer is the holding of feasts, ceremonials, or potlatches in order to obtain some social invisible such as prestige. In this case the richer are giving the poorer a share of their material goods and are thus evening up the distribution of goods in the society. Cattle stealing by nomadic herding societies (a practice which is, in a sense, the opposite of a potlatch; the one is a prestigeful takeaway, the other a prestigeful giveaway) most often seems to occur when groups who have less than the minimum critical level for a self-sustaining herd steal from groups who have such an excess of herds that they are unable properly to guard them.[10] A more subtle progressivity occurs in the Trobriand Islands off the east coast of New Guinea where it was the practice of each man to deliver a large part of the yams he grew to his wife's brothers and, in turn, to receive yams from his sisters' husbands. This is progressive in the sense that a man who grew few yams in a particular year because of some

---

[9]All specific ethnographic examples that are not footnoted come from societies in the sample, whose references are given in Appendix E.

[10]This is discussed by Louise E. Sweet, "Camel Pastoralism in North Arabia and the Minimal Camping Unit," in *Man, Culture, and Animals* (1965), eds. Anthony Leeds and Andrew P. Vayda, pp. 129–153; and by Paul W. Collins, "Functional Analysis in the Symposium 'Man. Culture, and Animals'," in the same volume, pp. 271–283.

misfortune would receive more yams than he gave away, other things being equal.

Certain types of transfers must be classified as neutral in impact since they do not systematically affect the distribution of goods in the society either toward or away from greater equality. Gambling transactions are one example: Here one person (the loser) gives another person (the winner) some goods or money with no counterflow. If the transaction is honest, there is no greater probability of the richer or the poorer person winning. In primitive and peasant societies certain feasts that families hold for special and somewhat random occasions such as marriages or births have also a neutral effect, at least insofar as no relationship exists between wealth or income and the frequency with which the particular event serving as the excuse for the feast occurs. In modern societies several examples of such neutral transfers can also be found. For instance, in the controversial example cited in Chapter 2 of American high school boys paying for all of the cost of their dates with high school girls, we can say that the transfer is neutral as long as both are from the same socioeconomic stratum. (If the boy dates a girl of a lower socioeconomic stratum, then the transfer would be progressive.) Blood donations in the United Kingdom have a neutral effect insofar as the socioeconomic class of the givers is roughly the same as the socioeconomic class of the recipients.[11]

Although examples of regressive centric transfers are common, I have found relatively few instances of regressive noncentric transfers, especially in the sample societies. One well-known regressive noncentric transfer occurs in the redistributive transfers between castes in Indian villages where people of each occupation share in the production of other occupations and the final distribution of income is, in many cases, more unequal than what would have occurred in an alternative system.[12] Another example of regressive noncentric transfer is the seizing of war booty by a strong and rich group from a weak and poor group. A variant of this was the horse stealing by American Indian tribes of the Great Plains that was done to achieve honor and was often carried out by the strong at the expense of the weak. (This judgment about regressivity refers to the institution as a whole; particular instances of such horse stealing could well have redistributed wealth progressively.) The holding of ceremonials for sick people by their families (who presumably have less than normal income because the sick person can not work) is another example. Such cases can

[11]Most blood is pooled and then redistributed, so I am speaking of the net flows of blood between social classes. Such matters are discussed by Richard M. Titmuss, The Gift Relationship: From Human Blood to Social Policy (1971).

[12]A brief and interesting analysis of this system is presented by Walter C. Neale, "Reciprocity and Redistribution in the Indian Village," in Trade and Market in the Early Empire (1957), ed. Karl Polanyi, Conard M. Arensberg, and Harry W. Pearson, pp. 218–239. It should be emphasized that judgments about progressivity or regressivity of such distributional systems are not based on whether everyone is guaranteed enough to eat but rather on a comparison of what would have happened to the distribution of income if producers could keep what they produced and exchange them with others without following caste rules. Obviously, such a Gedankenexperiment raises some difficult methodological problems unless one uses some criterion of price ratios such as relative labor hours embodied in each product.

occur in a direct fashion (e.g., among the Navajo of Arizona) or also indirectly; for example, the Toba of northern Argentina have the practice of sick people paying curers extremely high food fees, but these fees, in turn, are redistributed by the curer to the entire society. A final type of regressive transfer occurs within households or lineages where the leader redistributes goods to his own advantage. (Such a transaction has centric elements, however.)

Noncentric transfers can be structured so that both regressive and progressive elements are present in a series of consecutive acts concerning the same objects. For instance, in eleventh-century Europe a great deal of plundering by various knights and other men of war seems to have occurred; insofar as this represented a plundering of the weak and the poor (rather than the strong and the rich, who could hire people to defend them), the transfer was regressive. However, the proceeds of such plunder were used not only to support a free-spending life-style but also to give alms to the poor and generous gifts to friends and retainers, transfers which had progressive elements.[13]

Excluding plundering and intracaste transactions, the most common examples of noncentric transfers in precapitalist societies appear progressive; the least common appear regressive. Noncentric transfers act in exactly the opposite manner as centric transfers, which, as I discuss in the next chapter, appear mostly regressive. Further evidence on this overall judgment about progressivity of noncentric transfers of goods can be gained from an examination of the type of goods that are transferred in such transactions. In most cases the transfers consist of food; and although one might predict this from the fact that food products are the most important production goods in primitive and peasant economies, there is more to it than this. There also seems to be a greater probability that nonfood items will be involved in regressive than in progressive noncentric transfers. Unfortunately, I did not collect my statistics on noncentric transfers in a manner to offer convincing empirical demonstration of these generalizations, but the nexus between food transfers and progressive transfers is extremely suggestive.

NONCENTRIC TRANSFERS OF LABOR

Once we remove from discussion of noncentric transfers of labor all of the various types of slave and serf relationships, we find that the remaining types of noncentric transfers of labor are relatively unimportant. Three types of such transfers embrace almost all cases.

As I discuss in Chapter 2, certain noncentric labor transfers take place in herding societies when the owners of a small and large flock temporarily combine their flocks and share the shepherding duties on a fifty–fifty basis. In this case the owner of the small flock gives more labor hours of service to the owner of the large flock than the reverse, and the transaction is definitely regressive.

[13]An informative discussion of this way of life can be found in Georges Duby, *The Early Growth of the European Economy: Warriors and Peasants from the Seventh to the Twelfth Century* (1974) [originally published 1973].

Another type of such a labor transfer occurs in societies that have a custom of holding informal work parties and that do not keep close accounts on who holds the "party" and who does the work. Depending on the circumstances in which such "parties" are given (e.g., if sick and poor people or if rich people hold them in order to obtain extra workhands), the transaction can be either progressive, neutral, or regressive.

A third type occurs when property rights are split in such a manner that the "owner" of a piece of land has absolute control over the land and its produce except that as a condition of such ownership he must pay labor dues to someone else (who usually has considerable political power in the area or who controls a vital input to the land). Such a transaction raises all sorts of classification problems, for it could be considered as a rent (and hence a market exchange), or it could be considered as a centric transfer of labor. Fortunately for our analysis, such a transfer is quite rare; among the societies in our sample it occurs to the greatest extent among the Amhara of Ethiopia.[14]

It is noteworthy that all of these various noncentric transfers of labor appear relatively rare, at least among the nonherding sample societies. As I later show, in only 10 societies out of the 60 does such a distributional mode appear important (and three of these number among the nine herding societies). Furthermore, in the nonherding cases it is almost impossible to generalize about the overall progressive or regressive impact of such transfers since they appear in such varied forms and since we have so little data to make such judgments.

THEORIES OF NONCENTRIC TRANSFERS

Specific Determinants

NONCENTRIC TRANSFERS OF GOODS

In the last two chapters I have discussed various evolutionary theories of distribution. In almost all of these theories the first stage was supposed to be characterized by noncentric transfers or, as it was usually called, "gift giving."

---

[14]In Europe in the eleventh and twelfth centuries, a somewhat similar situation arose in which there were three different kinds of seigneurial lords: There was domestic lordship, which consisted of ownership of slaves or serf; landlordship, which consisted of the ownership of land and the collection of rents; and "banal" lordship (seigneurie banale), which permitted the requisitions of anything that could be taken or, in the words of Georges Duby, a "kind of legitimized and organized pillage, tempered only by the resistance of village communities." Although the three types of lordship often overlapped, they were legally quite distinct. The domestic lordship was clearly based on a noncentric labor transfer; the landlordship was clearly based on a market exchange; but the basis of the "banal" lordship is difficult to classify. Insofar as it represented some type of political overlordship, the extraction of such provisions from the population must be considered as a type of regressive centric transfer; insofar as it represented simple pillage, it must be classified as a type of regressive noncentric transfer. (The three types of lordship are discussed by Duby, European Economy, especially pp. 174–177, in considerable detail.) The Amhara case is also difficult to classify since it lies close to the dividing line between centric and noncentric transfers. I classified it as a case of a noncentric transfer, but this judgment is open to legitimate criticism.

This conventional wisdom has, however, been challenged by others such as Thurnwald, who declared rashly that no such transfers appear at these low levels of development.[15] The empirical evidence presented in the next section shows that the conventional wisdom is correct and that Thurnwald is wrong.

If we turn from the empirical facts to the theoretical analysis of the conditions underlying such transfers, problems arise. Most of these developmental theories rest either on *obiter dicta* or on inductive evidence which is given no rigorous theoretical justification. If we read this dreary literature in a generous fashion, however, we can discern the outlines of two different types of theoretical arguments to explain the facts at hand that such transfers are more likely to be found in societies at the bottom end of the development scale.

One type of argument is based on the notion that extremely primitive societies act as single families and that, "as everybody knows," considerable transfers take place among family members. Both parts of this argument deserve inspection.

The conjecture that extremely primitive societies act as single families can be questioned on several counts. Some primitive societies break up into small hunting and gathering groups for considerable parts of the year, and it is quite unclear why, when they come together, they should suddenly act as one large sharing family. Furthermore, some well-known examples can be cited where interfamilial transfers are negligible. For instance, among the societies in my sample, the Sirionó engage in very few noncentric transfer transactions and, indeed, find it hard even to participate in reciprocal exchange for fear that such exchange will turn into a transfer to their disadvantage.[16] It might be added that Sirionó families of four may gorge themselves on an entire 60-pound peccary at one sitting or eat their food at odd hours of the night rather than share it with others. Anecdotes and fragmentary evidence of the type presented in this paragraph do not, of course, constitute a convincing argument, for they may represent merely extreme cases in the spectrum of primitive societies.

The conjecture that individual families engage in considerable noncentric transfers among themselves also raises questions. Although the previously cited data for the United States suggests that such intrafamilial transfers are considerable, counterexamples can also be given. For instance, an extreme case occurs among the Ik of West Africa in which parents did not find it necessary to give much food to their children over the age of 4 or so and made their children forage food for themselves.[17] Among the Kapauku of New Guinea intrafamily economic relationships are apparently quite commercialized.[18] Sirionó men

---

[15]Richard Thurnwald, *Economics in Primitive Communities* (1932), p. 136, declares that highly primitive peoples have no "feeling" for presents (transfers) and this phenomenon appears only at later stages of development.

[16]Sirionó men participate in only two major types of transfer: If several men form a hunting party, they sometimes share their game; and they also give meat to their mothers-in-law. The episodes described in the text are reported by Allen R. Holmberg, *Nomads of the Long Bow: The Sirionó of Eastern Bolivia* (1969) [originally published 1950].

[17]The Ik are discussed by Colin M. Turnbull, *The Mountain People* (1972).

[18]See Leopold J. Pospisil, *Kapauku Papuan Economy* (1963).

are also reported to hide game they have killed from their wives so that they may eat it exclusively by themselves. Again, we may say that these societies represent extreme cases of minimal intrafamily transfers. Although such evidence suggests we should exercise caution in accepting propositions about the importance of noncentric transfers in highly primitive societies, the conventional wisdom still seems intuitively a more reasonable approach than the reverse, although we can not be satisfied with it without examining the cross-cultural evidence in a systematic fashion.

A second type of argument for the presence of noncentric transfers of goods in extremely primitive societies is based on the considerations regarding uncertainty of food supply that I raised in Chapter 7. In hunting and fishing societies the daily catch varies sufficiently from family to family that various types of sharing arrangements are beneficial to all even though the flows do not necessarily even out, so that families with good hunters or fishers are, in the long run, transferring part of their catch to families with poor hunters or fishers. This argument suggests that it is not the low level of economic development per se that brings about noncentric transfers but the fact that hunting societies generally have a relatively low level of economic development. According to this argument, we would not expect to find such noncentric transfers among societies that rely primarily on gathered food and that have equally low levels of economic development.

Other than these types of arguments I have been unable to locate any theoretical discussions of noncentric transfers in either the anthropology or economics literature that would permit derivation of testable propositions about the determinants of this type of distributional transaction. Nevertheless, a number of testable propositions can be generated by considering some quite simple economic factors.

The principal mode of food production may affect the presence or absence of noncentric transfers of goods in ways other than introducing daily uncertainties of food supplies. In particular, herding might have several different kinds of influences. First, an important part of animal husbandry is maintaining one's herd above the critical minimum point at which the average rate of increase in herd size is above the food requirements of the herding family. If the herd size of a potential transfer giving family is close to this critical point, transfers may not be given because such a drain on resources may take the family below this critical point and set off a cumulative process resulting in the eventual disappearance of the herd. Second, in herding, particularly of a nomadic variety, there are constant daily risks of loss of a sizable part of one's herd through disease, theft, stampede, climatic events, or accidents, so that this problem of maintaining a critical minimum limit looms large even to those herding families who are well above the limit. Finally, if the herd size is extremely far beyond this critical minimum limit, the herds may be too large for the owning family properly to shepherd. In this case requests for a transfer by the herding family may result in a counterrequest for shepherding help, so that a wage relationship is created in the place of a transfer arrangement. From such considerations we would expect to find the absence of noncentric transfers of goods in herding societies, particularly nomadic herding societies that rely almost exclusively on their herds for their food supply.[19] Another aspect of herding could influence noncentric transfers in exactly the opposite manner. E. E. Evans-Pritchard has argued, "The fact that cattle can be confiscated easily while crops can't gives pastoral people a bias for arts of war, rather than peace . . ."[20] Indeed, of the three societies in my sample for which the evidence suggests that raids on other groups or societies play an important role in the domestic economy, two are nomadic camel-herding societies (the Rwala and the Tuareg). From this consideration we would expect herding societies to engage in more negative noncentric transfers than other societies. In the regressions presented below, I show that the consideration about the minimum critical limit seems far more important and that, as predicted, nomadic herding is negatively related to the presence of noncentric transfers of goods.

Another possible determinant of noncentric transfers is the size of the unit of observation (as defined in Chapter 2). As previously noted, intrafamily grants are extremely important, but these are not included in the coding of noncentric transfer payments. However, if the size of the production and consumption units is very small, the unit does not have the risk-pooling or sharing benefits of an extended family and, therefore, may be in much greater need of occasional interfamily transfers from other members of the society. From such considerations, two propositions can be generated. First, we would expect to find the existence of interfamily transfers inversely related to the size of the unit of observation. Second, we would expect to find the presence of such noncentric transfers positively related to the important presence of strong lineages where kin bonds are stronger between members of different units of observation. In the regression analysis presented in the next section I find positive evidence for the first proposition but not for the second.

Noncentric transfers of goods might also be causally connected to certain value configurations. A tolerance for nonreciprocity might be correlated to, or might underlie, nonsymmetrical economic relations between individuals lead-

---

[19]An implicit assumption in this argument is that such a critical minimum level of capital plays a more important social role in herding societies than in societies with other kinds of subsistence economies. I believe this assumption is correct. In hunting or gathering economies the minimum required capital stock is very small and can be easily made. The same is true for fishing societies where fishing is carried out on shore; for those which rely extensively on boats, the situation is quite different, but I do not have any such societies in my sample. Agricultural societies require certain minimum levels of seed inventories, but the structure of risks is quite different than in herding societies. In agriculture there are risks of loss of capital, but such risks arise primarily in bad harvest years and, in addition, usually happen to everyone in the society; if an individual farmer has had bad luck in a year in which no general harvest failure occurred, others are not risking falling below the critical minimum level by helping him out. In nomadic herding societies risks of substantial loss of capital stock occur daily; in addition, the risks of one person are not tied so closely to the risks of others as in agriculture. Therefore, if an individual herder has had bad luck while others have not, the others may still have good reason to fear falling below the critical minimum level at a later date.

[20]E. E. Evans-Pritchard, The Nuer (1950), p. 50.

ing to noncentric transfers. The selection of a proxy variable to reflect such an "atmospheric" causal factor is difficult, and in the initial exploration of this hypothesis I chose three such proxies: the presence of polygyny, the presence of noncentric transfers of labor, and whether or not the total amount of work carried out by women and men was greatly different. The first two variables were unpromising in the preliminary regression runs and were dropped. The relative work variable turned out to be correlated with the presence of noncentric transfers of goods and is shown in some of the regressions below.

Several hypotheses about the determinants of noncentric transfers have a certain theoretical appeal but turned out not to provide much explanatory power when the regressions were calculated. For instance, it can be argued that noncentric transfers of goods might be quite related to a high degree of socioeconomic inequality. Various theorists of the grants economy have emphasized that transfers are more likely to appear under certain critical circumstances, of which an important condition occurs when one group of the society suffers a relative decline of income below an acceptable norm to the society.[21] If we have great socioeconomic inequality in a primitive society in which the average income is none too high, then the poorer groups may on occasion hover on the brink of starvation unless aided. Although such aid may come from political leaders or the church (and thus be a centric transfer), a functionalist might argue that such conditions would induce noncentric transfers as well. A variable denoting the relative degree of socioeconomic inequality was entered into the regression equations; to my great disappointment, it had to be dropped later because it did not appear statistically significant.

Another hypothesis with great theoretical appeal, which later had to be abandoned, focuses on the presence of a great deal of ritualized activity on a subcommunal level which can be linked to noncentric transfers. For instance, among the Navajo Indians of Arizona and New Mexico it has been reported that adult men spend one-fourth to one-third of their productive time in various types of ceremonies and that women spend from one-fifth to one-sixth of their time in similar activities.[22] Since such ceremonial activity often involves transfers, a correlation might be found between such ritual activities and the presence of noncentric transfers. In trying to investigate this link empirically, difficulties arose, and I was never able to find the expected correlation.

Several other hypotheses of lesser theoretical interest were also tested and dropped because of negative results. We have left, therefore, hypotheses linking the presence of noncentric transfers of goods to the level of economic development, to various types of principal modes for obtaining food, to the size of the unit of observation, and to the presence of a value configuration in the society indicating a tolerance for nonreciprocities.

---

[21]This type of argument is presented at length by Robert Solo, "Approaches toward a Theory of the Grants Economy," mimeographed paper, Michigan State University, East Lansing, Michigan (n.d.).

[22]Clyde Kluckhohn and Dorothea Leighton, *The Navajo*, rev. ed. (1962), pp. 225–228.

THE DETERMINANTS OF GAMBLING

Gambling represents a transfer that has been analyzed in a number of different social science literatures. Therefore, we have a range of hypotheses on which to draw in order to explain the presence of gambling in the societies of the sample.

The economic theory of the utility of gambling is quite well developed,[23] and from the Friedman–Savage approach we can derive several important determinants. According to this approach, in certain situations the marginal utility of wealth increases (rather than showing diminishing marginal utility as the classic economists believed). For instance, in societies which have great differences in income and wealth, gambling offers a rapid avenue of social mobility for the winners, so that after a certain point the utility of wealth in such societies should begin to rise rapidly when such wealth permits a qualitatively different life style. Assuming that mobility is normally difficult and that the society does not have many other easy mobility channels, we predict that there would be a positive correlation between economic inequality and the presence of gambling.

The Friedman–Savage approach also leads to an interesting hypothesis at the lower end of the wealth scale. For those societies that are close or that feel themselves close to the biological subsistence level, the disutility of gambling should be very great since a gambling loss may mean starvation. Therefore, we should not expect to find gambling in these societies, either. However, the measurement of this "close to subsistence" limit raises some difficult problems. As I have pointed out in Chapter 2, considerable evidence exists that highly primitive hunting and gathering societies or agricultural societies employing highly primitive slash-and-burn farming techniques are not close to this subsistence point. Although it is difficult to specify which societies are actually close to subsistence, we can designate more easily societies that feel themselves close to this limit. As I have already argued, in herding societies maintenance of a minimum size herd is crucial, and there are daily risks of losing one's entire flock; such circumstances would certainly lead one to suspect that such a society would not gamble. In addition, societies living in very "hard" environments (e.g., arctic, subarctic, or desert) would also feel this great uncertainty and not gamble. Therefore, from simple economic considerations we predict that the presence of gambling should be directly correlated with social and economic inequality and inversely related to location in a hard environment or reliance on nomadic herding for subsistence production; these predictors all prove quite successful in the empirical analysis below.

[23]Two classic essays on this subject are: Harry Markowitz, "The Utility of Wealth," *Journal of Political Economy* LX (April 1952): 151–158; and Milton Friedman and L. J. Savage, "The Utility Analysis of Choice Involving Risk," *Journal of Political Economy* LVI (August 1948): 279–304. The very close relationships between the analysis below and this economic literature are discussed in my article "The Friedman–Savage Utility Function in Cross-Cultural Perspective," *Journal of Political Economy* LXXXIV (August 1976): 821–834.

In the anthropology literature we can find several different approaches toward the determinants of gambling. There is one wide-ranging correlational study that shows that gambling is found in conjunction with a wide number of other societal traits.[24] A number of studies link different child-raising and psychological variables to gambling[25]; unfortunately, the levels of causation that are explored in these studies are sufficiently different from those in this analysis that I could find no easy way of incorporating these findings into my regression calculations. Finally, gambling is discussed in passing by a great many ethnologists, and from such studies we can find a variety of hypotheses. For instance, some authors have implied that gambling is related to the level of economic development: the higher the developmental level, the greater the individualism and the greater the breakdown of "strict tribal morality," two factors that might contribute to violations of ethical or religious injunctions against gambling. In addition, economic development is related to the domestic use of money for commercial purposes, and such money serves as an ideal medium for gambling. We can not only test this relationship between economic development and the presence of gambling but also particular aspects of this argument. More specifically, we can test whether gambling is related to individualism by looking at such proxies for individualism as nuclear (rather than extended) families and the absence of important lineage structures. We can also test whether the presence of money influences or facilitates the presence of gambling. Of all these hypotheses, only the linkage between money and gambling receives confirmation in the empirical analysis that follows.

Robert Lowie has raised a diffusion argument regarding gambling, suggesting that this phenomenon is particularly important in North American tribes.[26] A geographical variable was added to the regressions, and Lowie's conjecture receives impressive support.

Several less successful hypotheses were also tested. One common proposition is that gambling arises from the cultural degeneracy which allegedly occurs upon extensive contact with the West. For instance, gambling is currently practiced among the Truk Islanders of the Pacific and the Callinago Indians of the Caribbean, although apparently it was not an aboriginal activity. Testing this hypothesis is difficult with my data since I tried to select societies for the

[24]John M. Roberts and Brian Sutton-Smith, "Cross-Cultural Correlates of Games of Chance," *Behavior Science Notes* I, 3(1966): 131–144. Another, less ambitious cross-cultural study is by John M. Roberts, Malcolm J. Arth, and Robert R. Bush, "Games in Culture," *American Anthropologist* LXI (August 1959): 597–605.

[25]These are summarized by Roberts and Sutton-Smith, "Games of Chance."

[26]Robert H. Lowie, *An Introduction to Cultural Anthropology* (1934), p. 169 declared, "No civilized nation has more inveterate gamblers than the American Indians." Lowie did not, unfortunately, specify the nature of the diffusion process, nor did he speculate whether this was a trait brought with the original groups that crossed the Bering Straits. A more detailed study of the type of diffusion process involved is contained in my article, "The Diffusion Probability Method: A More General and Simpler Solution to Galton's Problem," *American Ethnologist* 3(November 1976): 731–749.

sample that had not yet experienced such degeneracy; and the statistical results (using a contact with the West variable) did not appear promising.

Another unsuccessful hypothesis extends an intrasocietal argument to an intersocietal level: In some societies most members are "risk lovers" and therefore practice gambling in order to fulfill this personal and cultural need. Manifestations of risk loving are reliance on modes of subsistence in which the daily variation in supply is high (e.g., hunting and fishing) or in which the environment is "hard." Thus, the risk-loving hypothesis predicts that gambling will be positively correlated with the hardness of the environment, while the economic considerations discussed previously predict exactly the opposite relation. It turns out that the risk-loving hypothesis provides a very poor predictor of the presence of gambling.

NONCENTRIC TRANSFERS OF LABOR EXCLUDING SLAVERY

The anthropological literature on the determinants of noncentric transfers excluding slavery appears silent. The subject is seldom discussed, and as far as I have been able to determine, no one has tried to investigate either theoretically or empirically the determinants of this phenomenon. The major reasons for this lacuna are probably that it is very difficult to conjure up useful hypotheses about the matter and that noncentric labor transfers excluding slavery are *not* an important mode of distribution in most societies.

One possible determinant is the relative level of economic development. We would expect to find more examples of this type of transfer in societies with low levels of economic development for the same two reasons as those offered as explanations for the inverse relationship between the level of economic development and noncentric transfers of goods. This hypothesis was not provided support in the regression experiments.

Other factors influencing the presence or absence of this type of distributional mode might arise from relationships of substitution or complementarity. For instance, we might expect to find such transfers only in societies without slavery since the presence of slavery would permit any necessary tasks to be performed in an alternative manner. We might also expect to find a complementary relationship with noncentric transfers of goods since the latter would provide the proper "atmosphere" for the former. Neither of these propositions was convincingly validated in the empirical analysis, although the evidence suggests that the first hypothesis be further explored.

Finally, the primary mode of food production might influence the presence of such noncentric transfers of labor. For instance, the possibility of combining herds and sharing herding duties gives rise to a particular type of labor transfer that I have previously discussed. This hypothesis also did not prove successful.

In short, my attempts to isolate the determinants of noncentric transfers of labor met defeat. Isolation of the determinants of this type of distribution awaits solution by others.

Some Impact Propositions about Noncentric Transfers: A Digression

Marcel Mauss's analysis of reciprocal exchange emphasized the stabilizing aspects of this mode of distribution. Although the absence of reciprocity does not necessarily imply an unstable situation, some anthropologists seem to believe that noncentric transfers are destabilizing and that such transfers reflect the strains of society and the elements which augur societal change. Aside from the logical problem involved, I believe that this view is quite false for several reasons. First, I have offered evidence above that most transfers in primitive and peasant economies are food and act in a progressive manner, so that certain strains arising from the presence of inequality and the possibilities of starvation may be dampened. Second, the analysis of Eskimo exchange in Chapter 4 shows that considerable noncentric transfers can occur in a society well known for its unchanging mode of life and absence of open social strife.

I feel on theoretical grounds that any attempt to link the presence of noncentric transfers and social stability is doomed to failure. However, if these neo-Maussian views are correct, then we should expect some kind of correlation between the relative importance of noncentric transfers and various measures of social strife or instability. I examined the relationship between the presence of various types of noncentric transfers and indicators of internal and external fighting but found no significant correlations either positively or negatively. I did not have other proxies for strife or instability; but if I did, I doubt whether they would have shown a correlation, either.

Another kind of impact proposition relates the presence of particular social institutions to the presence or absence of noncentric transfers. Let us briefly consider societies where individuals practice (or where some members believe other individuals practice) witchcraft against the food supplies of other societal members by hexing cattle or crops, bringing about bad hunting luck, and so forth. It does not seem likely that gambling would take place, for if any loser harbored ill feelings against the winner, he would destroy the latter's livelihood and this would be a sufficient threat to discourage gambling activities. It turned out that indeed a correlation does exist between the presence of "economic witchcraft"[27] and the absence of gambling. However, from such considerations one would also conjecture that the presence of "economic witchcraft" would be positively correlated with the presence of noncentric transfers of goods since if a potential transfer giver turned down a request, he also might fear loss of his livelihood—an interesting type of extortion. Unfortunately, I could find no cross-cultural evidence of this relationship at all.

---

[27]In coding the presence of witchcraft, I excluded witchcraft directed solely against the person to be harmed and only coded witchcraft as occurring if it was directed against (or believed to be directed against) a person's crops, herd, or hunting, fishing, or gathering luck.

We might also expect to find different kinds of social institutions and beliefs in societies featuring progressive and regressive noncentric transfers. The latter might feature greater individualism, greater mutual distrust, and fewer group activities than the former. Unfortunately, I did not collect the proper data to explore systematically such conjectures.

EMPIRICAL TESTS OF IMPORTANT HYPOTHESES

Coding Problems

I believe that the ethnographic materials of the various societies contain a systematic bias toward understanding the noncentric transfers. Part of this is due to the great emphasis in the theoretical literature of anthropology on the importance of reciprocal and market exchange and the relative neglect of transfers, so that field-workers are conditioned to look for certain types of distributional mode and not for others. And part of this is due to the under-standable necessity of ethnographers to focus their attention on particular as-pects of the society, so that transfers occurring in the neglected areas are simply not reported. Regarding gambling, underreporting of its importance or, indeed, overlooking its presence may occur because in many societies such an activity runs against the moral rules and must be carried out in secrecy.

In addition to these problems arising from inadequacies in ethnographic materials, a number of problems of classification, some of which were pre-viously discussed, raise additional difficulties. In particular, game sharing among members of a hunting party is classified as a noncentric transfer of goods (as well as reciprocal exchange) but not as a noncentric transfer of labor, which introduces an artifact in my statistics that must be watched. I also classified potlatches as both a noncentric transfer of goods and a reciprocal exchange. Rent and interest payments were excluded from the codings of the noncentric transfers of goods; and slavery and serfdom were excluded from the codings of the noncentric transfers of labor. Certain problems also arose in distinguishing between centric and noncentric transfers, which I examined in the preceding discussion.

As in the case of the analysis of other modes of distribution, I have used a 5% cutoff limit in my coding. That is, noncentric transfers of goods were coded as present only if they accounted for 5% or more of the total goods produced in the society; similarly, noncentric transfers of labor were coded as present only if they accounted for 5% or more of the total labor services outside the home. And in this regard considerable difficulties arose. In the first step of the estima-tions I tried to determine the type and frequency of every different kind of noncentric transfer transaction in the economy. In the second step I tried to determine the relative amounts of goods involved and whether the 5% limit was reached. In many cases, unfortunately, this estimation could only be made very impressionistically.

A particular problem arose in my coding of the relative importance of gambling. In most cases it was impossible to make any type of very exact quantitative determination of this matter since most observers devoted few efforts toward an estimation of resources transferred in this activity. Therefore, I used a three-group classification scheme: no gambling reported; gambling reported but either relatively "unimportant" or importance unascertainable; and gambling reported and apparently an important activity with "appreciable" resources transferred in this manner.

As far as I have been able to determine, no other codings of noncentric transfers have been made except for slavery and for gambling. For gambling my codings were very similar to the codings of George Peter Murdock and his associates for the presence of games of change.[28] For other types of noncentric transfers of goods and labor I had no comparison. I do not believe that adequate alternative estimates can be made from the Human Relations Area files, and an independent coder preparing an alternative evaluation would have to read the same sources as I did, an expensive task for which sufficient research funds were not available. Thus, the accuracy of my codings of both noncentric transfers of goods and of labor must remain uncertain.

Given the uncertainties in coding these noncentric transfer variables (in comparison with the greater certainties in codings of market or reciprocal exchange), it seems likely that the coefficients of determination in the regression analysis should be lower. This pessimistic prediction turned out to be true except for the regression experiments dealing with the determinants of gambling.

Cross-Section Tests

NONCENTRIC TRANSFERS OF GOODS

Noncentric transfers of goods amounting to 5% or more of all produced goods occurred in somewhat more than half of the sample societies. The regression experiments to uncover the determinants were quite straightforward, and the results that appeared most interesting are presented in Table 9.1.

As predicted, noncentric transfers of goods are significantly more important in the societies at the lower end of the economic development scale than in

[28]The codings on "games of chance" come from the Ethnographic Atlas, 1972 computer card version, obtained from the Ethnographic Atlas project of the Department of Anthropology, University of Pittsburgh. Of the 43 societies for which codings could be compared, we agreed on the presence of absence of gambling in 37 (86%). There was no systematic bias shown in the error pattern of the six societies where our codings differed. It must be also noted that although "games of chance" include more activities than gambling, it should be obvious that among adults the former usually implies the latter.

TABLE 9.1

Determinants of Noncentric Transfers of Goods[a]

1. $NCTG = 1.3323 - .0137*ED - .3537\ NH - .2580\ UO$	$R^2 = .3128; n =$
$\qquad\qquad\quad (.0032)\qquad (.1839)\qquad (.1555)$	$PCP = 75.00\%$
2. $NCTG = 1.1943 - .0127*ED - .3448\ NH - .2685\ UO + .2218\ GIW$	$R^2 = .3619; n =$
$\qquad\qquad\quad (.0031)\qquad (.1788)\qquad (.1078)\qquad (.1078)$	$PCP = 76.67\%$

Key:

NCTG	= Noncentric transfer of goods accounting for 5% or more of the produced goods in the society (yes; 0 = no) [mean = .5833].
ED	= Rank order of the level of economic development (1 = lowest; 60 = highest) [mean = 30.50
NH	= If more than half of the society's food supply comes from animal husbandry and if the societ nomadic or seminomadic (1 = yes; 0 = no) [mean = .1000].
UO	= Unit of observation (defined in Chapter 2) (0 = nuclear or stem family; 1 = extended family) [m = 1.1500].
GIW	= Great inequality of total work between husbands and wives (1 = yes; 0 = no) [mean = .533:
R^2	= Coefficient of determination.
n	= Size of sample.
PCP	= Percentage of correct predictions.
( )	= Standard error.
*	= t statistic for calculated regression coefficient is over the acceptable limit (2.25) defined in Chapte

[a] The data used in these regressions come from Appendix A, Series 6, 10, 21, 22 and 54. Logit regressions presented in Appendix B.1.

those at the upper end. It is noteworthy that the hunting-fishing variable did not prove to be a significant explanatory variable, which means that appearance of noncentric transfers in these societies at low levels of economic development is not due to the special risk factor discussed above but rather to the stronger sense of community that has been argued for these societies.

The negative relationship between nomadic herding societies and the presence of noncentric transfers follows the proposition that I previously discussed; the calculated regression coefficients are, however, slightly below statistical significance at the acceptable limit. It is noteworthy that this negative relationship is less strong if we substitute a variable representing all herding societies for the variable representing nomadic herding societies. This appears reasonable since in nonnomadic herding societies diversification of food production is possible and the critical minimum herd size no longer plays such a crucial role.

The unit of observation is also, as predicted, negatively related to the presence of noncentric transfers of goods. The calculated regression coefficient also falls short of statistical significance but is included because coding difficulties may have partially obscured the relationship and because I feel the theoretical evidence for such a relationship is strong. Other variables relating to this phenomenon were investigated and later dropped because they were not as promising.

One "atmosphere" variable also seems to act perhaps as a significant explanatory variable, namely, the occurrence of great inequalities of total work between spouses (which is a proxy for a societal tolerance for nonreciprocities). Its calculated coefficient falls a shade short of statistical significance. Other "atmosphere" variables proved unrelated to noncentric transfers and were dropped from the final calculations.

Examination of the regression residuals revealed little of interest; the prediction errors occur for a very heterogeneous group of societies.

I also conducted a series of other regression experiments to isolate additional factors influencing noncentric transfers of goods. In one set of regressions I recoded the presence of noncentric transfers to be equal to 2 if the set of people among whom such transfers are made were large; equal to 1 if the set of people among whom such transfers are made were small; and equal to 0 if such transfers amounted to less than 5% of the total goods produced. In another set of regressions I recoded the transfer variable to reflect whether the transfers were progressive, neutral, or regressive. None of these experiments yielded much additional information.

GAMBLING

The final calculations of the regression experiments to isolate the determinants of gambling, a component of noncentric transfers of goods, are presented in Table 9.2. The results of this proved most gratifying, for a very high percentage of the variance of the gambling variable is explained. Although certain

BLE 9.2

terminants for Gambling[a]

$$PG = -.2811 + 1.3302*LNA + .4151*DCM + .2372*SI - .4299*NH \qquad R^2 = .6757*$$
$$ (.1514) \qquad (.1256) \qquad (.0746) \qquad (.1961) \qquad n = 60; PCP = 90.00\%$$

:

= Presence of gambling (0 = not present; 1 = present but unimportant or present and importance unascertainable; 2 = present and an important distributive mode) [mean = .6500].

A = Location in North America (excluding Central America and the Caribbean Islands) (0 = no; 1 = yes) [mean = .1833].

M = Presence of a domestic commercial money (0 = no; 1 = yes) [mean = .4667].

= Presence of socioeconomic inequality (a scale, 1 = little or no socioeconomic inequality; 5 = a considerable amount of socioeconomic inequality) [mean = 2.2617].

= If more than half of the society's food supply comes from animal husbandry and if the society is nomadic or seminomadic (1 = yes; 0 = no) [mean = .1000].

= Coefficient of determination.

= Percentage of correct predictions (simple prediction of presence of gambling).

= Size of sample.

= Size of sample.

= t statistic for calculated regression coefficient is over the acceptable limit (2.25) defined in Chapter 1.
The data used in this regression come from Appendix A, Series 1, 6, 37, 56, and 66. Logit regressions are not calculated because the dependent variable has three values.

problems arise in determining statistical significance,[29] the importance of the predicted causal variables seems quite clear.

The location variable explains a considerable portion of the variance alone (45%). If this variable is removed from the regression, the other variables act roughly in the same manner as reported in the table.[30] As noted in the preceding theoretical discussion, this appears to be one of the few variables investigated in this study where diffusion appears to play an important causal role.

The presence of gambling is also positively related to the use of a domestic commercial money. This money variable is also a better predictor of gambling than a simple economic development variable. Since the use of money is related to the level of economic development (as I show in Chapter 5), this suggests that economic development and the availability of a convenient medium for gambling are mutually reinforcing as determinants of gambling.

As predicted, gambling is positively related to the degree of social inequality. As I also argued in the preceding discussion, the absence of gambling appears related to whether or not the society can be characterized as a nomadic, herding economy. The Friedman-Savage approach toward gambling appears to receive in these empirical results an impressive confirmation.

It is worthwhile to note briefly the hypotheses about the determinants of gambling that received no support in the empirical analysis. First, there is no indication that gambling is positively related to the "risk preference" of the society, as manifested by whether it relies on hunting or fishing as its main subsistence mode. The cultural degeneracy hypothesis also does not prove successful, although this may be the result of my conscious choice in selecting societies for the sample to exclude whenever possible societies with extensive contact with the West. Finally, the presence of gambling does not seem associated with any social or family structural variables other than those previously mentioned. Some of the relationships predicted by other hypotheses discussed previously can be found, albeit the explanatory power is considerably less than the above combination of variables.[31] The combination of causal variables also proved to have good predictive powers when other researchers modified the sample and used different regression techniques. That is to say, my results are very robust.

The percentage of correct predictions is very high. A study of the errors of prediction gives us no useful clues about other causal factors that may have been omitted.

---

[29]The problem arises because of the loss of degrees of freedom caused by the influence of diffusion among the 11 societies in North America. It is noteworthy that the independent variables in the regression still show statistical significance when the location variable is removed. I do not feel, however, that this loss in degrees of freedom affects the interpretation in the text to any significant extent.

[30]Such results are reported in my article, "The Diffusion Possibility Method."

[31]These matters are discussed in detail in my article, "The Friedman–Savage Utility Function."

NONCENTRIC TRANSFERS OF LABOR EXCLUDING SLAVERY

Noncentric transfers of labor that account for 5% or more turn out to be difficult to explain on an empirical as well as a theoretical basis. A number of regressions were calculated and seldom were R^2s larger than .12 obtained. One conclusion of interest stands out: In none of the 10 cases with such a mode of distribution was there slavery; however, the absence of slavery only explained 8.6% of the variance of the variable representing these labor transfers. Such transfers also seemed to take place more often than by chance in herding societies and in societies at the lower end of the development scale. Because of my decision to code game sharing among hunters as a noncentric transfer of goods and *not* labor, the labor transfer variable was inversely related to the hunting-fishing variable.

Since the explanatory power of these and other variables that I investigated to isolate the determinants of noncentric transfers of labor is so low, I do not feel that anything important would be gained by presenting the different regression results.

In short, although quite useful regression results can be obtained in the analysis of the most important type of noncentric transfer of labor, namely, slavery, the other types of such transfers appear too infrequently and constitute too heterogeneous a phenomenon to permit success in the empirical investigation of determinants.

DEVELOPMENTAL RELATIONSHIPS OF DIFFERENT KINDS OF
NONCENTRIC TRANSFERS

The analysis in previous chapters of the emergence or disappearance of the different modes of distribution yielded useful insights, and it is worthwhile to continue such an analysis in this chapter as well. Two techniques can be employed: Technique A (the *ceteris paribus* method), in which we take the average values of all the independent variables in the regression formulae except the level of economic development and determine at which developmental levels the particular mode of distribution can be predicted; and Technique B (the *mutatis mutandis* method), in which we merely examine the relative frequency of the distributional modes at different levels of development. I present relevant data in Table 9.3.

For the noncentric transfers of goods the data show quite clearly that this distributional mode appears most frequently in the societies with lower levels of development. The level of economic development, above which the chance of correctly predicting the presence of noncentric transfers of goods is less than fifty–fifty, is roughly the same rank at which the predicted reciprocal exchange of goods also "disappears" (Table 7.3) and, in addition, roughly the level at which the market exchange of goods appears (Table 5.6). However, one particular type of noncentric transfer of goods, namely, gambling, has quite a

TABLE 9.3

Levels of Economic Development and the Appearance of Different Types of Noncentric Transfers[a]

Type of noncentric transfer	Formula numbers	Technique A: Holding other causal factors constant — Level of economic development (rank) where predicted noncentric transfers disappear	Technique B: Number of societies in different developmental groups			
			The 15 societies at the lowest level	The 15 societies at the second lowest level	The 15 societies at the second highest level	The 15 societies at the highest level
All goods	B9-1-1	37	13	10	9	3
All goods	B9-1-2	38	13	10	9	3
Gambling	9-2-1	—	4	6	7	12
All labor excluding slavery	none	—	2 (8)	6 (8)	2 (2)	0 (0)
Slavery A	none	—	0	5	10	7
Slaver C	none	—	0	3	3	3
All labor including Slavery A	none	—	2 (8)	11 (11)	12 (12)	7 (7)
All labor including Slavery C	none	—	2 (8)	9 (10)	5 (5)	3 (3)

[a]The formula numbers refer to the number of the table (the first two numbers) and the equation number (the last number); the B refers to the logit regressions presented in Appendix B.1. The data in parentheses include game sharing among hunting parties as a noncentric labor transfer (although it was not treated this way in the regression analysis). The definition for noncentric transfers of goods includes the 5% cutoff limit of importance; the definition of gambling does not include this limitation and merely indicates the presence of any kind of gambling. (The gambling variable has a value either of 1 or 2.) Slavery A and C are defined in Chapter 8. The data come from Appendix A, Series 50, 52, 54, 55 and 56.

different pattern, with the relative frequency rising at higher levels of economic development.

The data for the noncentric transfers of labor present a more difficult pattern to analyze. If we look simply at such labor transfers (excluding slavery), their frequency appears greatest in the middle levels of economic development. If we include as a labor transfer the sharing of game on hunting expeditions (in the regression analysis this is not included as a noncentric labor transfer; the redefined labor transfers are presented in parentheses in the table), then all we can say is that clustering appears most marked at the lower end of the development scale. If slavery, which appears most frequently in the middle levels of development, is included in the definition of labor transfers, then the pattern appears even more mixed.

Time-Series Tests

To determine whether the cross-section evidence can be used to generalize about events occurring over time, we can employ the statistical tests described in Chapter 3 and used in the investigation of other modes of distribution. The relevant data are presented in Table 9.4.

For noncentric transfers of goods the data reveal no geographical clustering of societies where this mode of distribution can be found, no clustering of societies where such transfers are predicted, and no diffusion. Geographical clustering of societies without this mode of distribution appears (comparing the data in columns M and L), but when the test of the pattern of prediction errors is made (comparing columns Q and R), such "negative diffusion" does not seem significant.

For gambling, as already noted, a pattern of diffusion is demonstrated by a marked clustering of the trait among the primitive societies in North America. However, once a dummy variable indicating location of the society in North America is introduced into the regression, it appears that the cross-section results can be used for time-series generalizations. That is, the clustering pattern suggesting diffusion does not appear.[32] What all of this adds up to is simple: Although gambling appears to be due to a diffusion phenomenon in North America, the other determinants which were isolated played a causal role in the appearance of gambling in particular societies over time.

It must be added that because I tried to select the societies at a time before Western influence obtained, the diffusion of gambling through contact with the West is not detected. For several societies in the sample direct evidence of such diffusion is available.

---

[32]A glance at the data in columns Q and R suggests a "negative diffusion." Since there is no clustering of societies that do not have gambling (columns M and L) nor a clustering of societies in which one would predict the absence of gambling (columns Z and Y), this is undoubtedly a statistical artifact that should be ignored. "Negative diffusion" also makes very little theoretical sense in this context.

TABLE 9.4

Average Distances between Groups of Pairs of Societies for Making Diffusion Tests[a]

Type of noncentric transfer	Formula number	Average distances, standard deviations, and sizes of sample[b]											
		Total	Between societies with and without designated noncentric transfer			Between societies with and without predicted designated noncentric transfer			Between societies with and without designated noncentric transfer after taking causal variables into account			
			K	L	M	X	Y	Z	P	P'	Q	R
All goods	B9-1-1	5519 [1964] (1326)	5578 [1998] (465)	5561 [1911] (651)	5260 [2030] (210)	5538 [2012] (496)	5921 [1614] (640)	4117 [2252] (190)	5852 [1674] (150)	3667 [2165] (15)	5553 [1899] (175)	6110 [1355] (42)
All goods	B9-1-2	5519 [1964] (1326)	5578 [1998] (465)	5561 [1911] (651)	5260 [2030] (210)	5569 [2019] (528)	5680 [1790] (627)	4780 [2221] (171)	5777 [1682] (130)	3880 [2300] (10)	5609 [1936] (182)	4940 [2231] (35)
Gambling	9-2-1	5519 [1964] (1326)	5383 [2084] (300)	5577 [1897] (675)	5526 [1979] (351)	5076 [2199] (300)	5708 [1810] (675)	5536 [1976] (351)	6092 [1390] (66)	6600 [0] (3)	4795 [2161] (66)	6111 [1383] (9)

Key:

Group K: All pairs of societies that have the designated type of noncentric transfer.

Group L: All pairs of societies, one of which has and one of which does not have the designated type of transfer.

Group M: All pairs of societies that do not have the designated type of noncentric transfer.

Group X: All pairs of societies that the explanatory variables lead us to predict the presence of the designated type of noncentric transfer.

Group Y: All pairs of societies, of which we predict to have and the other of which we predict not to have the designated type of noncentric transfer.

Group Z: All pairs of societies that the explanatory variables lead us to predict the absence of the designated type of noncentric transfer.

Group P: All pairs of societies, one of which is predicted to have the other of which is predicted not to have the designated type of noncentric transfer, but both of which actually have the designated noncentric transfer.

Group P′: All pairs of societies, both of which are predicted not to have the designated type of noncentric transfer, but both of which actually have the designated type of noncentric transfer.

Group Q: All pairs of societies, both of which are predicted to have the designated type of noncentric transfer, but one prediction is incorrect.

Group R: All pairs of societies, one of which is predicted to have and the other of which is predicted not to have the designated type of noncentric transfer, and both predictions are incorrect.

[a]Since the gambling variable has three values, and the statistical technique employed requires a dichotomous variable, gambling must be redefined. I have done this by considering merely the presence or absence of gambling (i.e., lumping together the presence of a small amount of gambling with the presence of a great deal of gambling). If the redefinition were made according to the presence or absence of a great deal of gambling, problems arise in interpretation because of the small number of cases that one finds in certain cells of the above table. The data come from Tables 9.1 and 9.2.

[b]The standard deviation is enclosed in brackets and the size of sample in parentheses.

Since the results of the regression experiments with noncentric transfers of labor excluding slavery and serfdom were so disappointing, this analysis of diffusion could not be attempted. However, it should be added that since such transfers occurred in so few societies and since these societies are in such different parts of the world, the probability of diffusion is nil.

SUMMARY AND CONCLUSIONS

Because anthropologists and economists have been dazzled by the appearance of various forms of exchange—either reciprocal or market exchange—the presence of noncentric transfers of goods has received relatively little analytic attention. And because slavery and serfdom are such striking phenomena, other noncentric transfers of labor have also been analytically slighted. In this chapter I have tried to begin to redress the balance.

Noncentric transfers of goods can be found in a variety of forms. It is important to note, however, that most types are either progressive or neutral and, furthermore, that most transfers consist of food gifts. Thus, in most cases such transfers seem to serve a role of modifying the existing distribution of consumption toward greater equality.

Both theoretical and empirical evidence are advanced to show that noncentric transfers of goods appear more frequently in societies at the lower end of the development scale. Because of the great importance of a minimum critical level of herd size and the great risks associated with nomadic herding, noncentric transfers of goods are found with less frequency in such societies (other things being equal) than in societies with other modes of production. In addition, in societies with small units of observation (production and consumption units) noncentric transfers of goods appear with greater frequency than in societies with large units of observation, in part because the latter permit much greater pooling of food, so that less need for interfamily transfers obtains. Finally, the presence of noncentric transfers of goods appears positively related to an "atmosphere" variable, namely, the presence of great inequality of total work of spouses. This variable seems to reflect a low societal value placed on balance in distributional transactions.

Gambling is a species of noncentric transfer and has some different and some similar determinants of the genus. The theoretical analysis, based primarily on the Friedman–Savage approach toward gambling, suggests that gambling should be directly related to social inequality and inversely related to nomadic herding. Furthermore, the presence of gambling should also be related to the presence of money since the latter facilitates the former. The empirical analysis confirms these hypotheses. Diffusion also seems to play a role in the presence of gambling, at least among the societies of North America and also perhaps among the societies that have had extensive contact with the West.

Noncentric transfers of labor excluding slavery and serfdom also appear in a variety of forms. However, their frequency of occurrence to any important degree is small. Unfortunately, I have not been successful in unearthing either on a theoretical or empirical level any important determinants of this mode of distribution. The only important generalization that can be made is that such transfers only appear in societies that do not have slavery or serfdom.

Much exploration of noncentric transfers of both goods and labor remains to be carried out. Nevertheless, I hope that I have been able to sketch the boundaries of this territory and to provide survey lines so that more detailed mapping can be carried out by others.

10

THE DETERMINANTS OF CENTRIC TRANSFERS

Lo que no lleva Cristo, lleva el fisco.
SPANISH PROVERB[1]

To tax and to please, no more than to love and to be wise, is not given to men.

BURKE[2]

Of the four major modes of distribution only centric transfers of goods and labor remain to be surveyed. Many types of such transfers of goods are quite familiar through our own experience: the exaction of taxes by the government, the provision of public services by the same institution, or the collection of tithes by a church. And many have also firsthand knowledge of transfers of labor that occur in corvée work, military drafts, and other types of governmental mobilizations of labor. However, additional types of centric transfers that I will discuss have received relatively little attention. Moreover, anthropologists and other social scientists have devoted relatively little time to exploring on a theoretical level the determinants of such transfers in primitive and peasant societies.

The investigation of centric transfers parallels the approach used in previous chapters. I start with a discussion of the definition of centric transfers and a survey of the major forms of this mode of distribution. I then explore a series of hypotheses on a theoretical and empirical level, showing that the centric transfers of both goods and labor are positively related to the level of economic development and that the latter transfers also seem inversely related to the size of the unit of observation. Some attention is also paid to the degree to which

---

Design from a Blackfoot parfleche; northern plains of the U.S.A.
[1]'That which the church does not take, the tax collector does.'
[2]"On American Taxation," speech delivered in 1774, *Burke's Writings and Speeches,* Vol. II, *The World's Classics,* LXXXI (London: Oxford University Press, 1930), p. 142.

such a mode of distribution occurs because goods can not be easily transferred by means of exchange; positive evidence is provided for an implication of this hypothesis for centric transfers of labor.

A SURVEY OF CENTRIC TRANSFERS

General Considerations of Definition

I have defined transfer as a distributional transaction in which the goods and services flowing from one person or group to another are not "balanced" by a counterflow of equal value. This imbalance can arise either because no counterflow occurs at all, because the counterflow is very uncertain, or because the value of the counterflow has only a very inexact relation to the value of the goods or services received.

The distinguishing feature of centric transfers is their community-wide focal point. Such a focal point can be either political, religious, or social leaders of the community or institutions that are headed by these leaders. The existence of such leaders or institutions does not automatically imply that centric transfers take place, but their appearance should sensitize us to a strong probability of finding such transfers.

The flow of goods or services to or from the focal point can be strictly one-way. This occurs when the flow is only from the populace to the leader (e.g., when the political leader levies taxes to finance his own consumption expenditures) or only from the leader to the populace (e.g., when a hunting society headman, who is often the most skilled hunter, gives away much of the game he has caught to less fortunate tribesmen and never receives any material return). The flow of goods or services can also be two-way, the transfer element entering because the amount that a person receives is only infrequently of the same value as that which he gave. This occurs whenever the political or religious leaders receiving goods redistribute them somewhat randomly or when the political leaders mobilize goods and services for some community activity (e.g., construction of irrigation ditches) that benefit various individuals in different degrees than their contribution. This concept of centric transfers is much broader than Karl Polanyi's concept of redistribution or Neil Smelser's concept of mobilization, neither of which include strictly one-way flows but focus on two-way flows with a transfer element.[3]

---

[3]Redistribution as a particular type of distributional mode is discussed in various essays by Polanyi in *Primitive, Archaic and Modern Economies: Essays of Karl Polanyi* (1968), ed. George Dalton, of which the essay "The Economy as Instituted Process" (pp. 139–175) is particularly important. Smelser's discussion of redistribution and his own concept of mobilization is discussed in his essay "A Comparative View of Exchange Systems," *Economic Development and Cultural Change* VII (October 1957): 173–182.

It should be noted that centric transfers can occur not only within particular societies but also between societies. One-way flows include the tribute levied by one society on another that is channeled through the political authorities, the occasional political gifts given by one nation to another, or the raids for booty that are led by the political leaders of one society on another (if the raids are the action of one or several families on a similar group in the other society, then the transfer is noncentric). Two-way flows would include certain types of cooperative efforts between societies that redistribute resources, for example, the aid-giving efforts of the United Nations that are financed by the various member governments.

A number of problems arise in trying to classify transactions. One difficulty occurs in determination of "balance" or "imbalance" of the transactions. In many kinds of primitive political exchanges the supplicant presents a gift to the political leader at the beginning of the transaction and receives a gift from the political leader at the end. If the gifts are of considerably different value, and if this difference in value is, in some sense, accounted for by a favor given by the political leader or a pledge of fealty by the supplicant, then the transaction is a centric transfer since we do not include social invisibles in the definition of balance.[4] The transfer is centric because the political leader presumably has the same type of relationship with a great many other people in the community as well.

Other problems arise concerning the centricity of the transfer, for centricity or noncentricity are only the end points of a continuum, and it is difficult to know exactly where the boundaries of classification into two groups should be drawn. Different kinds of problems of classification arise concerning centric transfers with political, religious, and social contents.

In the political realm classification of transactions of local political leaders raises problems. In one sense such transactions might be centric since they may embrace the entire local community; in another sense such transactions might be noncentric if they concern transactions of only a small part of the community and focus on one person of relatively little political consequence. These and other difficult cases of classification (e.g., in a feudal situation where several different lords operate within the same community) were fortunately very rare.

Problems in determining centricity also arise with regard to religious centric transfers. If the transfer is to a local church or cult that embraces the entire community or is part of a much broader religious movement (e.g., local repre-

---

[4]An attempt to capture these nonmaterial flows in a theoretical manner to balance them against the material flows is made by R. L. Curry, Jr., and L. L. Wade, *A Theory of Political Exchange: Economic Reasoning in Political Analysis* (1968). Although such exchange approaches provide an interesting interpretative framework, they do not—as far as I can determine—permit us to derive any kind of interesting and testable propositions. They also mask the important element of coercion that governments exercise on their citizens.

sentatives of the Islamic faith), the transfers are treated as centric even though the movement is not centralized or formally institutionalized in some type of administrative hierarchy. Transfers to or from one of several neighborhood cults are treated as noncentric. More difficult cases of transfers of local cults that embrace most of the local community and that are unattached to any wider movement are fortunately rare in the sample.

Centric and noncentric transfers with a social dimension also raise problems. As I note in the previous chapter, particular types of ceremonials that are individually sponsored and financed and that do not embrace most of the community are classified as noncentric; if they do embrace most of the community, they are centric. However, in many cases of such "floating centricity," it is quite unclear if the events are community-wide or not, for example, pot-latches and other prestige feasts; but in the few important cases of doubt that arose in the investigation, I arbitrarily classified such transfers as noncentric.

Centric transfers can be classified as progressive, neutral, or regressive, depending on whether the distribution of income or consumption is more equal, the same, or less equal after the transfer takes place. Although this classification is quite simple for the case of noncentric transfers, a certain ambiguity arises for centric transfers since the handling of the income of the distributor in any kind of redistribution process raises conceptual difficulties. Clearly, a redistribution in which goods are extracted from the rich by the political leader and given to the poor is a progressive transfer. But what if, in this act, the political leader retains 50% of the collected goods for his own purpose? In this case the poor in the society might become richer; the rich in general might become poorer; but the political leader in particular becomes still richer. Another example is the alms giving by the medieval European church that aided the poor and enriched most parts of the church except for a few odd mendicant orders that took the vow of poverty seriously. With different parts of the income distribution changing, different measures of inequality might give quite different answers about whether inequality in general was increasing or decreasing. I have classified such transactions as regressive. Fortunately for our purposes, such subtle problems did not often arise in my sample.

Another problem arises in the classification of transfers of labor as progressive or regressive. In this case I define these concepts in terms of the amount of transferred labor that people do in comparison to a "standard work year." Thus, a corvée requirement that the poor must work 10 days each year for the king while the rich must work only 5 days is regressive according to this definition. (If progressivity were defined according to the ratio of corvée work to the amount of other work performed, such a corvée might be progressive if the rich did almost no work other than the corvée. Other definitions of progressivity, e.g., comparing work done to total income, are also possible.)

Determination of the progressivity or regressivity of corvée work when the people doing the work benefit from it (e.g., working on maintaining irrigation systems or roads) is more difficult. If the rich irrigate more land for the same amount of corvée work, or if the rich use the corvée built roads for carrying goods more than the poor (who are more self-sufficient), then judgment is easy. More difficult cases arise when the corvée is regressive, but the benefits are progressive, and we must decide which effect outweighs the other; again, fortunately, in the sample of societies used in this study few such cases are very important.

It should be emphasized that regressivity of centric transfers does not necessarily imply coercion or lack of legitimacy. If the citizenry feels that the benefits they obtain from a government that is characterized by a regressive fiscal system are worthwhile (i.e., if the disadvantages of regressivity are more than outweighed by the benefits of the social invisibles that are given to the people by the government), then the system could be marked by acceptance by all parties, a situation occurring often in modern industrial societies with regressive tax and governmental expenditure patterns.

As in the case of noncentric transfers, centric transfers can be also classified according to the set of people that are included. A transaction between a small group of citizens and the king would be classified as narrow; a transaction between all the citizens and the king (e.g., a head tax) would be classified as wide; and cases falling in between would raise their usual classification problems.

Types of Centric Transfers

CENTRIC TRANSFERS OF GOODS

The two most ubiquitous centric transfers are, of course, associated with political and religious institutions. Taxes and tithes have hoary origins, and they arouse strong feelings, as suggested by the Spanish proverb heading this chapter.

Although it is often asserted in the popular press that taxes are a universal phenomenon, I later show that this is not true. In more serious discussions it is sometimes claimed that taxes appear in all societies with a state, but this raises problems of tautology because the existence of a state is often defined in terms of the collection of taxes. In any case taxes are found in a large number of societies and appear in a dazzling variety of forms that many scholars have commented on.[5] Some borderline cases raise problems of classification. For instance, I include as a type of tax the unusual "tax rent" mentioned in Chapter 5: This is the payment of farmers to political leaders for permission to use the land, a type of fee that may occur in addition to a payment to the landlord that more resembles what we call a rent. (The tax rent is found, for instance, among the Ganda of Uganda and the Fiji Islands of the Pacific Ocean.)

[5]See, for instance, Wilhelm Gerloff, "Die oeffentliche Finanzwirtschaft der Naturvolker," in his *Die oeffentliche Finanzwirtschaft* (1948), pp. 42–58.

Transfers from political authorities to the population that are not financed by some type of taxes are usually found in societies with quite low levels of economic development. Such cases occur particularly in hunting societies where the headman is often the best hunter, who secures and maintains his political position by means of giving some of his food to less fortunate hunters. In agricultural societies the aid given by the village "big man" in Melanesia is another example.[6] Other transfers from the political authorities to the population are financed by certain types of taxes or fees and include various types of support given by political authorities to their retainers, their visitors, or to the poor. In modern times such transfers include the free public education, the free hospitalization, and other such services that progressive governments supply their citizens and that, for any specific individual or family, are not linked with the taxes paid. In many countries there is a strong centric transfer element in the social insurance payments made to the aged, in that the poorer population groups receive on the average more than they paid in, while the reverse occurs with the richer population groups.

It is noteworthy that almost all of the tax systems of the societies in the sample are regressive or, occasionally, neutral in their incidence. Even if we look at modern economies, this is also true. For instance, in the United States, according to one of the most exhaustive studies of the matter: "Regardless of the incidence assumptions, the tax system is virtually proportional for the vast majority of families."[7] And in the Soviet Union it is believed that the tax system is mildly regressive.[8]

On the other hand, there seems to be a greater probability that transfers from the government to the people may be progressive. This is particularly true of aid to the poor and other social transfers found in most societies. This also occurs in special kinds of governmental aid to help those in distress from economic catastrophes (such as in herding societies where taxes in cattle are levied by the political authorities to replenish the herds of those whose herds have, for one reason or another, been decimated). In modern economies the progressivity of government expenditures seems even more certain since in most nations the largest share of these expenditures in peacetime are various types of social expenditures.[9] Of course, certain types of governmental transfers are not pro-

---

[6]A quantitative analysis of the former case is presented by Jules Henry, "The Economics of Pilagá Food Distribution," *American Anthropologist* LIII (1951): 187–219. The Pilagá are very closely related to the Toba of Argentina, who are included in my sample. A quantitative analysis of the latter case is presented by Marshall Sahlins, "The Domestic Mode of Production: Intensification of Production," in his *Stone Age Economics* (1972), pp. 101–148.

[7]Joseph A. Pechman and Benjamin A. Okner, *Who Bears the Tax Burden* (1974), p. 64.

[8]According to Franklyn Holzman, *Soviet Taxation: The Fiscal and Monetary Problems of a Planned Economy* (1955), Chap. XI, the Soviet tax system in the interwar period was quite regressive (because of the importance of the bread tax) but, after World War II and the decline in importance of this tax, became only mildly regressive.

[9]Data on these matters are presented by Frederic L. Pryor, *Public Expenditures in Communist and Capitalist Nations* (1968), Chap. VII, especially Table 7.2. Many of these expenditures are for services rather than goods or money and should be classified as centric transfers of labor.

gressive, for example, the grants given by political leaders to their favorites or the restricting of the benefits of certain types of government subsidies or grants to the rich such as subsidies to operas or polo clubs. (Theoretically, of course, operas and polo clubs are open to all; in practice, most of those attending operas or participating in polo clubs belong to the upper income groups.)

If we look at the entire fiscal system and consider not only the taxes and the governmental grants to the population but also the tax resources financing the personal needs of the political leaders, then a clear picture emerges: In almost all primitive and peasant economies where such transfers amount to 5% or more of total produced goods, the fiscal systems are either neutral or regressive. Or, to put the matter in a different way, in most primitive and peasant societies except those at the very lowest levels of economic development, the fiscal system usually results in a more unequal distribution of income than if it had not been imposed. A well-known example is that of the Incas, who had a highly intricate social welfare system that aided the destitute; this was financed by the poor themselves, who also supported a political and religious establishment of considerable size living in the sumptuous splendor reported by the marveling Spanish Conquistadores. Only in modern industrial states has the overall impact of the entire fiscal system (taxes and expenditures) sometimes been progressive, a situation occurring, for instance, probably in both the United States and the Soviet Union.[10]

The extraction of tribute from a conquered society that, as I noted above, is a centric transfer is also often regressive. This is because the conquered society (which is usually weaker and poorer) is forced to pay the conquering society (which is usually stronger and richer). Some counterexamples such as the sack of Rome by poor nomadic societies should also be noted.

Various reasons can be offered as to why most primitive and peasant societies have regressive fiscal systems. Some of these are narrowly economic or technical, for example, regressive taxes such as head taxes are easiest to collect; some are quite broad and deal with the nature of class or stratum domination. It would take us too far afield to explore these matters, and this must be left to other commentators.

Religious institutions and leaders also act as focal points for a large number of different types of centric transfers. Full-time religious specialists occur even in societies with very low levels of economic development; and at higher levels of development, societies can develop extremely large priestly establishments that are supported in opulence by levies from the population. Among the primitive Warao, a gathering society of the Orinoco Delta in Venezuela, an elaborate temple cult requires an impressive portion of the society's resources for support (allegedly this is a survival of a practice when the society was at a

---

[10]A breakdown of income class beneficiaries of United States governmental expenditures is found in W. Irwin Gillèspie, "Effect of Public Expenditures on the Distribution of Income," in *Essays in Fiscal Federalism* (1965), ed. Richard A. Musgrave, pp. 122–187. A qualitative study of these matters for the Soviet Union is made by Holzman, *Soviet Taxation*, Chap. XI.

much higher stage of development and part of the Meso-American temple cult system).[11] Among the Khalka Mongols of Mongolia the lamas and other religious figures in the monasteries may have amounted to almost 10% of the adult population, and they were, in large part, supported by various types of religious exactions.[12] It could be argued that these religious figures are selling a service—propitiation of the gods, warding off witchcraft, and so forth—and that such transactions should be classified as a market transaction. However, such priestly services fall more under my definition of "social invisibles," so that it is more fruitful, I believe, to classify them as centric transfers instead. Furthermore, the element of coercion that is present regarding these transactions in many societies also points toward such an approach. It is worth emphasizing that such religious extractions occurred in many societies in the sample: However, in only a few did they alone amount to 5% or more of total goods produced in the society.

Other types of centric transfers of goods occur when the focal points are social institutions, especially in situations in which such institutions play an important role in determining the rank or prestige of the individual in the entire society. For instance, in many villages in Mexico and Central America, the richest men finance (or vie to finance) community-wide ceremonials which, although such expenses may reduce or eliminate their fortunes, give them much prestige.[13] Such a transfer is, of course, progressive. A regressive transfer of a similar type occurs among the Omaha of Nebraska in the United States, where social prestige is determined in considerable part by membership in secret societies, and to obtain this membership, a series of expensive gifts to the officers of the societies is required.[14] (Since these societies have a community-wide focus, the transaction has a centric focus. For social groups without such importance, such transactions would be classified as noncentric.)

In looking over the societies where the sum total of centric transfers of goods amounts to 5% or more of the total goods produced in the society, it appears that in most cases the effect of the centric transfer is regressive; and the centric transfers in remaining cases are usually neutral. Such a result stands in strong contrast to the noncentric transfer of goods where the net effect in most cases is either progressive or neutral. The differences between these two types of transfers on the distribution of income tells us something interesting about the natures of these transfers and their underlying determinants.

---

[11]The temple cult and this controversial interpretation is argued by Johannes Wilbert, "The Fishermen: The Warao of the Orinoco Delta," in his *Survivors of Eldorado* (1972), pp. 65–115.

[12]Gerold M. Friters, *Outer Mongolia and Its International Position* (1949) p. 39, states that at the end of the nineteenth century, 25% of the population were lamas and church serfs. I. Maiskii, *Sovremennaia Mongoliia* (1921), p. 27, argues that only one-third of the lamas lived in monasteries. I am additionally assuming that one-half of the lamas and church serfs were actually lamas and 50% of the population were adults.

[13]This phenomenon is analyzed quantitatively by Frank Cancian, *Economics and Prestige in a Maya Community: The Religious Cargo System in Zinacantan* (1965).

[14]See especially Reo E. Fortune, *Omaha Secret Societies* (1932).

CENTRIC TRANSFERS OF LABOR

The most frequently found centric transfer of labor is the mobilization of labor by the government for some public purpose. This usually takes the form of some type of regular corvée work for the purpose of road construction or other public works. In some societies such as the Inca, such centric transfers took the form of a labor tax that was paid by people working particular fields whose produce belonged to the government. In other societies such as the Sinhala of ancient Ceylon this took the form of a labor service for building and repair of the irrigation works by all those using irrigated land and thus was a type of labor tax rent to the political authorities.[15]

Mobilization of men for the purposes of warfare, either for defensive or offensive wars, might also be considered a centric transfer of labor. Since warfare in primitive and peasant societies often has a certain element of sport or entertainment, and since quite a direct linkage between a person's participation and his benefits often exists (e.g., the collection of booty in the case of an offensive war; the defense of one's homestead in a defensive war), I have chosen to exclude such mobilization in my definition of centric transfers except in those societies having a standing army.

Discussion in the literature on centric transfers of goods and labor is often based on the implicit assumption that for any government, these two methods of public finance are substitutes for each other, and that a government usually selects one or the other method. Although I did not collect evidence on these matters in a manner sufficient to isolate all of the important variables in this problem, this assumption seems incorrect, for the two types of transfers often appear together. That is, some societies have both corvées and taxes; and the choice of whether a particular task is financed by taxes and carried out by contractors or state agents or whether it is carried out by means of some labor mobilization depends on administrative convenience and such factors as the extent of the money economy, the portability of what is produced, and the direct interests that the local population has in seeing that some type of public task is properly carried out.

Although centric transfers of labor have received extensive comments by historians, such transactions (especially when the focal point is a political institution) have been greatly neglected by anthropologists. For instance, in the ethnographic literature dealing with the Island of Truk (in the East Caroline Islands in the Pacific Ocean), we learn that following foreign occupation around the turn of the century, the population began to work 1 day a week for the purpose of carrying out various types of public works such as maintaining paths.[16] If, as the literature implies, this was not the case before, then an enormous change was introduced in this society that had implications not only for the daily lives of the population but the whole nature of political authority

[15]Edmund Leach, "Hydraulic Society in Ceylon," *Past and Present* XV (April 1959): 2–27.
[16]Thomas Gladwin and Seymour B. Sarason, *Truk: Man in Paradise* (1953), p. 138.

and economic processes. As far as I have been able to find out, no anthropologist has closely analyzed this societal change, even though the ethnographic research on this society is quite considerable and numerous articles have been written on less important but more spectacular facets of Truk life such as certain bizarre sexual practices.

Centric transfers of labor can also have a religious or social focal point. For instance, in certain societies such as the Inca tithes in the form of labor dues on church fields were collected. Another type of centric labor transfer occurs when ceremonials for the benefit of the entire community are put on by "private" individuals at considerable expense of time and goods. An example of this occurs with the Yaqui Indians: in a particular Arizona village an ethnographer estimated that men spent roughly 18% of their time preparing or participating in such ceremonials and this village did not number among the Yaqui villages with the richest ceremonial life.[17] In most of the other societies in my sample participation in community-wide ceremonials was not counted as a centric transfer of labor since either most of the labor is accounted for by specialists who are compensated or else because preparation is minimal and participants engage in such activities at little expense for their own private purposes and enjoyment.

Considerable problems arose in determining whether certain centric transfers of labor are progressive or regressive primarily because the ethnographers have not reported the data necessary for making such judgments. Nevertheless, it appeared to me that many of the political centric transfers of labor are regressive and in this way parallel the centric transfer of goods; but the data are not sufficient to permit a very comfortable judgment.

THEORIES OF CENTRIC TRANSFERS

Before turning to the various propositions about the determinants of centric transfers or the impact of centric transfers on the rest of the economy, one proposition about the relative importance of such transfers deserves brief mention.

Karl Polanyi, in discussing one particular type of centric transfer (redistribution) has asserted that this mode of distribution has predominance over other modes at particular stages of development: "Redistribution [is] the ruling method [of distribution] in tribal and archaic society beside which exchange plays only a minor part."[18] In a later essay he maintains that redistribution is the most important mode of distribution only in archaic societies,[19] by which he

---

[17]Edmund Spicer, *Pascua: A Yaqui Village in Arizona* (1940), p. 50.

[18]Karl Polanyi, "The Economy as Instituted Process," in *Primitive, Archaic, and Modern Societies*, ed. Dalton, p. 156.

[19]Ibid., p. 156: "Tribal societies practice reciprocity and redistribution, while archaic societies are predominantly redistributive, though to some extent they may allow room for exchange."

means a "sociological phase intervening between the 'primitive' and the 'modern',"[20] which some of his followers have said is characterized by several levels of government. The strong version of these ideas is that in societies with several layers of government, the volume of goods or services transferred through this mode of distribution is greater than through other modes. However, one of Polanyi's followers has suggested to me a weaker version of these ideas, namely, that the volume of transactions between the village and higher levels of government is carried out primarily through centric transfer but that within the village other modes of distribution prevail. A conclusive test of these conjectures requires data that I did not collect; however, a partial test performed in the empirical section of this chapter suggests that the strong version of Polanyi's ideas is incorrect.

Determinants of Centric Transfers of Goods

A large number of social scientists, both economists and anthropologists, have argued a positive relationship between the level of economic development and the relative importance of centric transfers. In the economics literature, this is part of the general analysis of Wagner's Law, which was propounded by Adolf Wagner in the latter part of the nineteenth century and which states (in a vague manner) that the share of public expenditures (and taxes) in the national income rises with increasing levels of per capita national income.[21] In the anthropology literature such an argument is usually part of some stage theory of development or a theory tying governmental expenditures to the rise of the state.[22]

The mechanisms underlying this alleged link between centric transfers of goods and the level of economic development are often not very clearly specified, but several different (and partially conflicting) arguments can be unearthed. One common argument is economic: At higher levels of economic development, a greater "economic surplus" can be extracted, and this, in turn, somehow encourages political leaders to attempt to do so. However, the level of economic development and average productivity (the latter allegedly determines the "economic surplus") are not necessarily directly related in primitive and peasant societies, as I argued in Chapter 2. This type of argument thus leaves a great deal to be desired.

Another argument linking economic development and centric transfers of goods rests on the reasonable assumption that a centralization of political

---

[20]Karl Polanyi and Abraham Rotstein, *Dahomey and the Slave Trade: An Analysis of an Archaic Economy* (1966), p. xxv.

[21]The best survey of Wagner's ideas is by Herbert Timm, "Das Gesetz der wachsenden Staatsausgaben," *Finanzarchiv*, N.F., Band 21, (September 1961): 201–247. Extensive discussions of evidence on Wagner's law is contained in Pryor, *Public Expenditures*, or Richard A. Musgrave, *Fiscal Systems* (1969).

[22]See, for instance, the citation of Karl Polanyi in footnote 19.

power accompanies economic development (in terms of societal complexity, the manner in which I have defined it). This centralization permits those holding the political power to extract resources from the powerless that, in turn, are used in part to further strengthen the power and economic position of the leaders. Such an argument implies, among other things, that centric transfers are primarily regressive,[23] a feature that I find generally to hold in primitive societies at higher levels of development. Such an approach has much to recommend it, especially over other approaches based on assumptions about the progressivity of such taxes.

A still different type of relationship between the level of economic development and centric transfers has recently been argued by anthropologists of an evolutionist bent such as Marshall Sahlins and Morton Fried.[24, 25] They maintain that centric transfers occur in most societies but that their nature changes with the level of development. In most primitive societies at very low levels of development headmen gain power by generosity; therefore, such transfers are progressive. In much more highly developed societies political leaders maintain power through accumulation and conspicuous display, and the centric transfers are regressive. When does this changeover occur? Although neither scholar is completely clear about this point, Sahlins has a telling note of a Tongan chief who is philosophizing about money:

> Certainly money is much handier and more convenient, but then, as it will not spoil by being kept, people will store it up, instead of sharing it out, as a chief ought to do, and thus become selfish; whereas if provisions were the principal property of man, and it ought to be, as being the most useful and the most necessary, he could not store it up, for it would spoil, and so he would be obliged either to exchange it away for something else useful, or share it out to his neighbors, and inferior chiefs and dependents, for nothing.[26]

This suggests that the presence of a domestic money should be a critical explanatory variable, an hypothesis that, unfortunately, my data does not support. As I argued in previous chapters, primitives are not necessarily better anthropological theorizers than Westerners.

We can quite easily test whether or not centric transfers of goods are related to the level of economic development, but the problem of progressivity or regressivity raises a peculiar issue about the nature of these tests. As in the case of the other modes of distribution, I use a 5% cutoff limit for coding the presence of centric transfers. In the very primitive societies where the headman

---

[23]Considerations of this type seem to underlie many of the arguments of Friedrich Engels, *The Origins of the Family, Private Property, and the State* (1972) [originally published 1884], Chap. IX.

[24]Marshall D. Sahlins, "Political Power and the Economy in Primitive Society," in *Essays in the Science of Culture in Honor of Leslie A. White* (1960), eds. Gertrude E. Dole and Robert L. Carneiro, pp. 390–416; and Morton H. Fried, *The Evolution of Political Society: An Essay in Political Anthropology* (1967). A variant of this argument is presented by Elman Service, *Origins of the State and Civilization: The Process of Cultural Evolution* (1975).

[25]This approach, which I find quite convincing, is different from that of earlier evolutionists such as Herbert Spencer (*The Principles of Sociology*, Vol. II, Chap. IV [1882]) who argue that the institution of taxes arose from subjects making voluntary contribution to their political leaders.

[26]Sahlins, "Political Power," p. 407.

distributes much of his food to his followers, such transfers seldom amount to 5% or more of the total produced goods; therefore, they are not coded. By and large the centric transfers become large enough to be recorded only after they become neutral or regressive. On an impressionistic basis I feel that Sahlins and Fried are probably correct; however, my data show that most coded centric transfers occur in more developed economies and, furthermore, that such transfers are regressive.

Turning to other considerations, we have a wide variety of propositions on which to draw. Some of these propositions are drawn from the considerations that I have raised in the analysis of other modes of distribution; some of the propositions come from the public expenditures literature; and some are taken from the seemingly endless literature dealing with the origins of the state.[27] I discuss only those that I felt were sufficiently plausible to test empirically. None turned out to be successful.

One set of theories concerns the relationship between the principal mode of production and the presence of centric transfers of goods. It is sometimes argued that agricultural or herding societies "require" more centric transfers than other societies, but calculated regression coefficients of variables representing these factors were very small and statistically insignificant. A more interesting proposition is drawn from the work of Karl Wittfogel, that economies relying upon irrigated agriculture require a stronger government and higher taxes (in both money, goods, and labor) properly to function.[28] This proposition was also tested and rejected, and closer investigation of the reasons for this failure revealed a set of circumstances that Wittfogel did not consider. In many parts of the world irrigation is carried out without central direction by each person's simply guiding water from rivers or wells into fields. It is only a particular type of intricate irrigation system that requires central direction, and even specification of this type raises many difficulties.[29] A final type of related argument focuses less on the mode of production than on the environment of production, namely, that in societies facing great climatic risks (e.g., arctic, subarctic, or desert), centric transfers are more needed and therefore likely to be found. None of these interesting propositions linking mode or environment of production and centric transfers of goods is validated by the evidence.

Another set of theories link different kinds of domestic conditions of the society to centric transfers. For instance, it can be argued with persuasiveness that centric transfers are more likely to be found in societies where the production and consumption units are small (e.g., nuclear families) rather than large;

[27]Much of the literature is summarized in a useful manner by Georges Balandier, *Political Anthropology*, trans. A. M. Sheridan Smith (1970), pp. 151–157 [originally published 1967]. Service, *Origins of the State*, also has some interesting interpretive comments.
[28]Karl A. Wittfogel, *Oriental Despotism: A Comparative Study of Total Power* (1957).
[29]Interesting case studies of possible nonoriental irrigation societies are presented by Leach, "Hydraulic Society in Ceylon," and Richard B. Woodbury, "A Reappraisal of Hohokam Irrigation," *American Anthropologist* LXIII, 3(1961): 550–560.

in the latter case the extended family can provide various types of welfare and defense services for itself which a smaller family can not. (This argument parallels the argument in the previous chapter linking noncentric transfers to small units of observation.) Another argument can be derived from Robert Carneiro's theory of the factors encouraging the rise of the state, namely, that the political control necessary for large-scale centric transfers can be found only in societies with circumscribed or scarce agricultural land.[30] We can test for this in a crude manner by testing the relationship between various measures of density and the presence of centric transfers. A much different type of linkage between domestic conditions and centric transfers rests on considerations of such transfers as a substitute for other modes of distribution. More specifically, we might expect to find centric transfers when exchange relationships are weak (e.g., among the Inca) or when noncentric transfers are not found. The regression analysis did not verify any of these conjectures linking domestic conditions and centric transfers.

A large set of propositions can be derived from the standard literature on the origins of the state, but before discussing these, several difficulties must be mentioned. Most origin-of-the-state theories rest either on considerations of internal social stratification or else the exigencies of external warfare; in both cases, problems in separating cause and effect arise. Did the state originate because of internal stratification, or did the development of the state cause such stratification? Did the exigencies of defense give rise to the state, or did the state give rise to a great deal of warfare? We might find strong correlations between stratification and/or warfare variables and centric transfers, yet the results might be impossible to interpret because of this problem. A second problem is much simpler: Although most centric transfers do indeed have a political focus, not all do; furthermore, the political centric transfers of which I speak do not necessarily rest on the exercise of coercion, which seems a central feature in many of these state origin theories. Therefore, propositions resting on such political considerations might not be relevant for certain important centric transfers.

The stratification argument comes in several variants. One variant focuses on the strong empirical relationship that is found between social stratification (focusing on problems of status levels and/or rank) and centralization of political power; since these social phenomena feed on each other, there is no need to disentangle cause and effect relationships. Considerable discussion about these matters has rested on comparative evidence from various Polynesian societies.[31] In my sample a significant relationship exists between social stratification and the presence of centric transfers, but because of the difficulties in

[30]Robert L. Carneiro, "A Theory of the Origin of the State," *Science* CLXIX (August 21, 1970): 733–738.
[31]Marshall D. Sahlins, *Social Stratification in Polynesia* (1958); and Irving Goldman, "Status Rivalry and Cultural Evolution in Polynesia," in *Comparative Political Systems: Studies in the Politics of Preindustrial Societies* (1967), ed. Ronald Cohen and John Middleton, pp. 375–395.

separating cause and effect, such a variable had to be dropped from the regression analysis. Another variant focuses on the correlation of the presence of castes and the existence of the state. Considerable critical evidence against this proposition can be found in the anthropology literature[32]; several caste variables were tested and were found unpromising.

The external exigencies argument also comes in several variants. Warfare as a prime mover of the origin of the state has been argued by a great number of scholars. This kind of argument, however, does not imply that centric transfers are associated with warfare, particularly because I have excluded most kinds of military activity from my definition. At an early stage of the empirical analysis I included variables representing the degree of external warfare and also variables representing certain social structural features that might be correlated with warfare.[33] Neither of these variables played a very important role in the regressions, and I later dropped both because of the difficulties in separating cause and effect of warfare and centric transfers of goods. Another variant of the external exigencies argument is that the state originated in order to facilitate and channel foreign trade[34]; my sample revealed no positive evidence of any link between the presence of significant amounts of foreign trade and of centric transfers.

The determinants underlying centric transfers with a religious or social focus are very difficult to specify. Many experiments were carried out to examine in an inductive fashion the determinants of this subset of centric transfers, and the results were quite disappointing. The level of economic development and the absence of market or reciprocal exchanges of goods to any important degree were found to be positively related, and the important presence of extensive lineages was found to be negatively related to such transfers. Nevertheless, the explanatory power of these variables is small, and for centric transfers as a whole they did not (except for the level of development) appear to play a significant explanatory role. As I show later, the lack of any special theory of the determinants of such religious or social centric transfers leads to an obvious error in prediction. Fortunately for our analytic purposes, this subset of transfers is not very important in most of the societies of the sample, so that we do not lose too much by failing to take the determinants of such transfers adequately

[32]At the turn of the century a number of scholars such as Franz Oppenheimer proposed conquest and caste theories of the origins of the state. These are examined critically by William Christie MacLeod, *The Origin of the State* (1924) and his *The Origin and History of Politics* (1931); and Robert H. Lowie, *The Origin of the State* (1927), especially Chap. II.

[33]Marshall D. Sahlins, "The Segmentary Lineage: An Organization of Predatory Expansion," in *Comparative Political Systems*, ed. Cohen and Middleton, pp. 89–121, argues that a particular social structural form encourages warfare. Although I was unable successfully to code this feature, I did introduce into the regression analysis certain proxy variables (e.g., a dummy variable indicating patrilineal, patrilocal societies) in order to capture a part of this phenomenon; but, as noted in the text, no significant correlations could be found.

[34]Marc J. Swartz, Victor W. Turner, and Arthur Tudon, "Introduction" in their edited volume *Political Anthropology* (1966), p. 30; or Jack Goody, *Technology, Tradition and the State in Africa* (1971), p. 18.

into account and by focusing our attention primarily on the political centric transfers.

Determinants of Centric Transfers of Labor

We would expect to find a greater frequency of centric transfers of labor in societies at more advanced levels of economic development for the same reasons that we expect to find a positive correlation between the centric transfers of goods and economic development. Indeed, this conjecture is validated in the empirical analysis that follows.

The complementary role of taxes in labor and taxes in goods also suggests several propositions. Surely centric transfers of labor would be more likely to occur in societies where the central political authorities find it administratively difficult to levy taxes in money or goods. One such situation would occur when markets and reciprocal exchange relationships are highly underdeveloped for the specified level of economic development, so that political authorities would have difficulties in obtaining the goods they wanted if they levied taxes in kind. Therefore, we would expect to find centric transfers of labor where goods distributed through market or reciprocal exchanges account for less than 5% of the total goods produced. Although the central premise of this argument—the complementary nature of the two types of centric transfers—raises some problems, this proposition turns out to be validated by the empirical analysis that follows. Another less extreme situation when taxes in labor might be levied is when the society does not possess a domestic, commercial money; however, no significant relationship between centric transfers of labor and the absence of a domestic, commercial money could be found.

The notion that centric transfers of goods and of labor, at least those with a political focus, are complements (and the correlation between these two modes of distribution) suggests that the various determinants of the origin of the state that have been discussed might also serve as determinants for the centric transfers of labor. Again, however, we run into the problems of separating cause and effect, and we can not, for this reason, include variables representing social inequality and also the frequency of external warfare even though the former is correlated with centric transfers of labor.

We might also expect centric transfers of labor to be related to the size of the unit of observation for the same reasons as those discussed concerning the centric transfers of goods. That is, centric transfers of labor would be more frequent in societies where the consumption and production units are nuclear families, than in societies where such units are extended families and large groups of people can be privately mobilized for particular purposes. This conjecture receives support in the regression analysis.

The determinants of centric transfers of labor with a religious or social focus are difficult to specify, as also is the case of centric transfers of goods with the same focus. However, such transfers of labor appear quite unimportant in practically every society in the sample, and nothing is lost by omitting any kind of special determinants for such transfers in the empirical analysis.

Impact Theories: A Digression

The difficulties that I have noted in separating causes and effects of the origin of the state and the close relationship between centric transfers and the centralization of political power also prevents us from specifying very many unique impact propositions. That is, because a variable such as social inequality is both a cause and an effect of the centralization of political power and the levying of centric transfers, we can not offer the correlation between these variables as a unique impact proposition.

This difficulty also arises in considering the relationship between various social structural variables and centric transfers. Some empirical evidence exists of a correlation between centric transfers and the breakdown of strong lineages and of postmarital residential rules. But it is impossible to say whether the rise of political centralization was brought about by such social structural changes, or whether the political centralization caused such changes.

Turning to different types of impact theories, it can be argued that centric transfers are functional (or dysfunctional) and should therefore be related to measures of internal stability. I found no relationship, either positive or negative, between centric transfers of goods or labor and my measure of internal fighting.

I have been unable to derive or find in the literature any other interesting impact theories about centric transfers that can be empirically tested. A great deal of future research on these transfers would, I believe, be quite profitable.

EMPIRICAL TESTS OF IMPORTANT HYPOTHESES

Coding Problems

As in the case of other modes of distribution, I counted centric transfers as occurring in a society only if, for goods, the aggregate of such transfers amounted to 5% or more of the total goods produced in the society; and, for labor, if the aggregate of such transfers amounted to 5% or more of the total labor services outside the home.

Considerable difficulties were encountered in making such determinations. In making my estimates, I tried to take into account all of the centric transfers in the society that I could find and then to make some quantitative assessment of the relative importance of each in terms of goods or labor. The greatest difficulties arose in gauging the relative importance of the goods and the labor time expended in ceremonials and deciding whether the labor time should be included as a labor service. As noted, I often did not include this labor expended as a service because of the strong recreational or nonutilitarian elements in the ceremonials.

All factors considered, my codings for the presence of centric transfers of goods and labor contain many uncertainties. Since others have not, to my knowledge, attempted such codings, and since I did not have the research funds to pay an independent coder to make such evaluations, I have no outside check on the accuracy of my results. As in the case of noncentric transfers, we should expect relatively low coefficients of determination in the regression analysis because of these data uncertainties.

Cross-Section Tests

Karl Polanyi's conjecture about the predominant importance of centric transfers as a mode of distribution can not be directly tested, for I have coded not the total quantitative importance of each mode of distribution but only whether their importance equals or exceeds the 5% limit. Therefore, the only test I could perform is whether a larger number of societies have this distributional mode than other modes.

If we take the entire sample of 60 societies, then it appears that Polanyi's conjecture is open to doubt, for centric transfers of either goods or labor appear in fewer societies than total market exchange, total reciprocity, or total noncentric transfers (including slavery).[35] The same results are also obtained for centric transfers of labor if only the 15 or 30 societies with the highest levels of economic development are examined. If we examine the same subsamples for centric transfers of goods, then we find that more societies have a total market exchange of goods than such centric transfers but that such centric transfers appear in more societies than the remaining two modes of distribution.

CENTRIC TRANSFERS OF GOODS

In the previous discussion on the determinants of centric transfers of goods, we have a rich harvest of propositions; the resulting seeds prove, however, quite unfertile. The most successful regression result is presented in Table 10.1.

As predicted, the level of economic development is positively related to the centric transfers of goods. None of the large number of other hypothesized variables turned out, in conjunction with the development variable, to provide a statistically significant degree of explanation of these transfers. Although the results of these many experiments with other hypotheses proved disappointing, at least the development hypothesis does work. The relatively low (but statistically significant) coefficient of determination can, in part, be traced to the uncertainties of the data. (The logic of this argument is discussed in Chapter 1 in conjunction with Table 1.4.)

---

[35]The data come from the Appendixes, Series 26, 32, 44, 46, 50, 54, 55, 57, and 58. A more complete analysis of relative frequencies of different modes of distribution is found in the discussion concerning Table 11.1.

TABLE 10.1

Determinants of Centric Transfers of Goods[a]

1. $CTG = .0262 + .0139*ED$	$R^2 = .2340$
$\qquad(.0033)$	$n = 60;\ PCP = 71.67\%$

Key:
CTG = Centric transfer of goods equal to 5% or more of total produced goods (1 = yes; 0 = no) [mean = .4500].
ED = Level of economic development (1 = lowest level; 60 = highest level) [mean = 30.5].
R^2 = Coefficient of determination.
n = Size of sample.
PCP = Percentage of correct predictions.
( ) = Standard error.
* = t statistic for calculated regression coefficient is over the acceptance limit (2.25) defined in Chapter 1.
[a]The data come from Appendix A, Series 22 and 57. A logit regression is presented in Appendix B.1.

In interpreting these regression results, the problem of tautology arises. That is, if the measure of the level of economic development is defined in major part by state or governmental activity, and if the presence of centric transfers with a political focus are a precondition of such political activity, then my results represent a definition rather than a causal relationship. It is quite true that my measure of development, namely, the degree of societal complexity, contains a number of variables related to political activity; but these directly constitute only a small part of the overall index. Furthermore, I do not believe that the other components of the index are really very dependent on such political activity; however, it must be added that I make this judgment on theoretical grounds rather than on the basis of an empirical investigation aimed at exploring the political and other variables in the index. Therefore, although my variables for centric transfers of goods and for the level of economic development are not as "cleanly" independent of each other as desirable, I believe their independence is sufficient for the regression results to represent the causal relation I have proposed. The same arguments used here also apply to the centric transfers of labor.

The two most important components of centric transfers of goods are transfers with political and religious foci. In some preliminary experiments using data merely indicating the presence of these transfers (without considering whether or not they amount to 5% or more of total produced goods), I found, for instance, that the level of economic development accounted for roughly one-third of the variance of political transfers but only one-tenth of the variance of the religious transfers.[36] Inclusion of additional variables indicated in the

---

[36]The apparently different determinants of political and religious centric transfers contrast strongly with the results of Chapter 7, where I show that nonceremonial and ceremonial reciprocal exchanges have the same determinants.

earlier discussion raised somewhat the coefficients of determination, and such results suggested that a number of the previously discussed propositions would be validated. When I turned to the actual examination of centric transfers of goods, taking into account the 5% limit, the results were, as already noted, quite disappointing.

In examining the regression residuals to determine where the largest prediction errors occur, it is quite clear that many of the societies in which we predict the absence of centric transfers of goods and actually find its presence are those where such transfers have strong social or religious facets rather than political. As noted previously, we have no adequate theories to deal with this type of transfer.

It is worth mentioning that somewhat higher coefficients of determination can be obtained if social inequality is used as an explanatory variable and if other variables such as density are included in the regression. As I have noted, however, problems in separating cause and effect prevent us from using such variables in our analysis.

CENTRIC TRANSFERS OF LABOR

The theoretical analysis of this distributional mode proved somewhat more fruitful than for the centric transfers of goods.

The most important component of centric transfers of labor is the corvée work mobilized by political leaders. In some preliminary experiments using data merely indicating the presence of such work (without considering whether or not such work amounts to 5% or more of services outside the home), I found that the level of economic development accounted for roughly 45% of the total variance of this variable. The degree of explanatory power for centric transfers of labor as a whole is unfortunately considerably less. Relevant data are presented in Table 10.2.

As predicted, centric transfers of labor are positively associated with the level of economic development. Furthermore, as argued previously, such transfers appear inversely related to the size of the unit of observation; that is, these transfers seem more likely to be found in societies composed of nuclear families than of extended families. (However, some problems of interpretation arose because of the peculiar behavior of this variable in the logit regression calculations.) Finally, as I have suggested previously, centric transfers of labor seem to occur more frequently in societies that do not have important market or reciprocal exchanges of goods, for the absence of such exchange impedes the collection of taxes in kind and encourages the collection of taxes in labor services. Because of questions about the basic premises underlying this argument, the regression results are presented with and without it.

The low coefficients of determination, as in the case of the centric transfers of goods, can in part be traced to the uncertainties in the coding of the centric transfer variable. It is noteworthy, however, that the calculated regression coefficients are statistically significant at the .05 level. And, in the light of the theoretical discussion, the results make sense.

TABLE 10.2

Determinants of Centric Transfers of Labor[a]

1. $CTL = .1468 + .0086*ED - .2254\ UO$	$R^2 = .2029$
$\quad\quad\quad\quad (.0025)\quad\quad (.1191)$	$n\ = 60;\ PCP = 85.00\%$
2. $CTL = .1451 + .0086*ED - .2457\ UO + .3921*MREG$	$R^2 = .2775$
$\quad\quad\quad\quad (.0024)\quad\quad (.1147)\quad\quad\quad (.1631)$	$n\ = 60;\ PCP = 88.33\%$

Key:

CTL	= Centric transfers of labor equal to 5% or more of total produced goods (1 = yes; 0 = no) [mean = .1500].
ED	= Level of economic development (1 = lowest level; 60 = highest level) [mean = 30.50].
UO	= Unit of observation[b] (1 = nuclear or small extended families; 2 = extended families) [mean = 1.1500].
MREG	= Market exchange or reciprocal exchange of goods equal to 5% or more of all produced goods (0 = yes; 1 = no) [mean = .06667].
R^2	= Coefficient of determination.
n	= Size of sample.
PCP	= Percentage of correct predictions.
( )	= Standard error.
*	= t statistic for calculated regression coefficient is over the acceptable limit (2.25).[c]

[a]The data come from Appendix A, Series 21, 22, 49, and 58. Logit regressions are presented in Appendix B.1. The particular algorithm used to calculate these regressions does not, however, appear to lead to convergent results for the calculated coefficient of the UO variable for either regression. For the ordinary least squares regressions, as I discuss further in the text, no positive cases of the dependent variable are predicted.

[b]Defined in Chapter 2.

[c]Defined in Chapter 1.

Examination of the regression residuals reveals little of interest other than a statistical problem discussed later that makes it impossible to carry out the analysis of the prediction errors for the time-series tests.

DEVELOPMENTAL RELATIONSHIPS OF CENTRIC TRANSFERS

Additional insight can be gained by examining briefly the levels of economic development at which the two types of centric transfers appear. As noted in previous chapters, this issue can be investigated by holding all factors constant other than the transfer under investigation and the level of economic development (the *ceteris paribus* method or "Technique A") or by looking at the relative frequencies of occurrence (the *mutatis mutandis* method or "Technique B"). Relevant data are presented in Table 10.3.

The relationship between the presence of centric transfers of goods and the level of economic development when all other causal factors are held constant is shown in the first column of results. We have more than a fifty–fifty chance of correctly predicting the presence of such centric transfers at roughly the middle level of economic development, in which internal goods markets and credit markets also emerge and in which reciprocal exchange of goods and noncen-

TABLE 10.3

Levels of Economic Development of Emergence of Centric Transfers[a]

Type of centric transfer	Technique A: Holding other causal factors constant		Technique B: Relative frequency in different developmental groups			
	Formula numbers	Level of economic development (rank) where predicted centric transfer appears	The 15 societies at the lowest level	The 15 societies at the second lowest level	The 15 societies at the second highest level	The 15 societies at the highest level
All goods	B10-1-1	35	3	4	10	10
All labor	10-2-1	72	0	1	3	5
All labor	10-2-2	72	0	1	3	5

[a]These data come from Appendix A, Series 22, 57, and 58; and Tables 10.1 and 10.2.

tric transfers disappear.[37] The data on relative frequency also reveal the same picture.

The relationship between centric transfers of labor and the level of economic development can also be clearly seen in the table. The level of development at which, other things being equal, we have more than a fifty–fifty chance of correctly predicting the presence of such transfers is somewhat above the level of development represented by any society in the sample. The relative frequency data suggest the same conclusion. In short, the centric transfers of labor appear to emerge at a much higher level of development than the centric transfers of goods, which suggests that the complementarity between these types of transfers is certainly not complete.

Time-Series Tests

To evaluate the extent to which we can generalize from the cross-section results to events occurring over time, we must once again take recourse to the methods developed in earlier chapters to explore these matters. Relevant data are presented in Table 10.4.

For all centric transfers of goods, a slight clustering of societies that have this mode of distribution occurs. However, no statistically significant difference exists in the average distance between societies with this mode of distribution and pairs of societies of which only one has such transfers. The clustering of societies where such transfers are predicted is startling, but this arises from the occurrence, already noted in previous chapters, that societies with roughly similar levels of economic development appear to cluster. In carrying out the most sensitive tests for diffusion, we note that no clustering of societies occurs that would suggest a usual type of diffusion (comparing the data in columns P and R). However, there does appear to be a unique type of diffusion between societies, neither of which is expected to have the predicted type of centric transfer (comparing the data in columns P' and R). The mechanism underlying such strange results is difficult to imagine, for such transfers seem very unlikely to diffuse. These results should not simply be written off as a statistical artifact, for they may have arisen because we were unable to predict correctly the appearance of centric transfers of goods in situations where such transfers have a strongly religious or social aspect. If the true determinants underlying this phenomenon of religious or social centric transfers occurred in societies that are somewhat clustered, then such circumstances would bring about the results shown in the table.

For centric transfers of labor, two statistical problems arise in this calculation to determine the presence of slow diffusion. First, a number of societies with such transfers are eliminated from the calculation in Table 10.4 because they are not coded for the second half of the nineteenth century; this means that the

---

[37]These data come from Tables 6.6, 7.4, and 8.3.

TABLE 10.4

Average Distances between Groups of Pairs of Societies for Making Diffusion Tests[a]

Type of centric transfer	Formula number	Total	Between societies with and without designated centric transfer			Between societies with and without predicted designated centric transfer			Between societies with and without designated centric transfer after taking causal variables into account			
			K	L	M	X	Y	Z	P	P'	Q	R
All centric transfers of goods	B10-1-1	5519 [1964] (1326)	5224 [2095] (253)	5554 [1951] (667)	5647 [1881] (406)	3996 [2263] (210)	5983 [1556] (651)	5558 [1987] (465)	6356 [960] (126)	5364 [2174] (36)	4137 [2312] (98)	6084 [1497] (63)
All centric transfers of labor (excluding slavery)	10-2-1	5519 [1964] (1326)	4880 [2629] (10)	5234 [2086] (235)	5587 [1922] (1081)	The predicted number of societies with centric transfers, after removal of societies falling outside the specified time period, are too few for meaningful results.						

Average distances, standard deviations, and sizes of samples[b]

All centric transfers of labor (excluding slavery)	10-2-2	5519 [1964] (1326)	4880 [2629] (10)	5234 [2086] (235)	5587 [1922] (1081)	The predicted number of societies with centric transfers, after removal of societies falling outside the specified time period, are too few for meaningful results.

Key:

Group K: All pairs of societies that have the designated type of centric transfer.

Group L: All pairs of societies, one of which has and the other of which does not hae the designated type of centric transfer.

Group M: All pairs of societies that do not have the designated type of centric transfer.

Group X: All pairs of societies that the explanatory variables lead us to predict the presence of the designated type of centric transfer.

Group Y: All pairs of societies, one of which we predict to have and the other of which we predict not to have the designated type of centric transfer.

Group Z: All pairs of societies that the explanatory variables lead us to predict the absence of the designated type of centric transfer.

Group P: All pairs of societies, one of which is predicted to have and the other of which is predicted not to have the designated type of centric transfer, but both of which actually have the designated centric transfer.

Group P : All pairs of societies, both of which are predicted not to have the designated type of centric transfer, but both of which actually have the designated type of centric transfer.

Group Q: All pairs of societies, both of which are predicted to have the designated type of centric transfer, but one prediction is incorrect.

Group R: All pairs of societies, one of which is predicted to have and the other of which is predicted not to have the designated type of centric transfer, and both predictions are incorrect.

[a]The "B" in front of the formula number indicates the logit regression presented in Appendix B.1. For centric transfers of labor, however, the ordinary least squares regressions presented in Table 10.2 have to be used because of convergence problems with the logit regressions.
[b]The standard deviation is enclosed in brackets and the size of sample in parentheses.

number of societies in the calculation having such centric transfers of labor is five (only 10 pairs of distances can be considered), which is too small a sample from which to draw conclusions. Second, because the average level of economic development at which such transfers are predicted to appear is quite high, only a few societies are predicted to have such transfers, and most of these are limited when the sample is reduced to include only societies within a specified time period.

I must conclude, therefore, that the technique does not permit evaluating the influence of slow diffusion on centric transfers of labor, given the data of the sample. Given the nature of these transfers, however, it does not seem likely that such diffusion played a very important role in their presence in various societies.

SUMMARY AND CONCLUSIONS

Centric transfers of goods or labor are transfer transactions with various types of focal points in the society; however, for the societies in the sample centric transfers with a political focus seem the most important. Because of this tie with the political sphere, the centric transfers can act as both cause and effect of the development of the polity; therefore, special analytic problems arise.

A survey of the various forms of centric transfers reveals that in the more developed primitive societies they usually act in a regressive fashion, in marked contrast to the noncentric transfers discussed in the previous chapter. The most frequent cases of progressive centric transfers occur in the least developed societies where the headman of the community is the best food provider. As I have noted, the regressivity of the transfers does not necessarily imply that coercion was used or that political authorities in these primitive and peasant societies are necessarily repressive in any obvious sense.

The primary determinant of centric transfers of goods is, as far as I have been able to determine, the level of economic development. The linkage between high levels of development and the presence of such transfers raises some analytic problems. Some have argued that this is due to the greater "surplus" that can be extracted from the economy, a justification that is open to doubt. Others have argued that a centralization of political power accompanies the measure of economic development and that centric transfers are linked to this political centralization, a justification with greater intuitive appeal. I also presented a large number of hypotheses linking centric transfers of goods to other variables; unfortunately, none of these proved very successful explanations of the presence or absence of such transfers. Of particular concern was the failure to be able to explain the presence of centric transfers, other than those with a political focus.

Centric transfers of labor, when measured in terms of labor amounting to 5% or more of total labor services outside the home, are a much rarer phenomenon. The major determinants of this mode of distribution are the level of economic development and the size of the units of observation in the society; the presence or absence of exchange modes of distribution of goods that facilitate the gathering of taxes also appear to play a causal role.

Centric transfers of goods and labor appear to some degree complementary to each other, at least in the sense that both are linked to a political focus in which the leaders are attempting to finance various types of projects in the most expeditious manner. In some cases this can be accomplished by labor services, in other cases by the paying of taxes in goods or money. That centric transfers of goods appear at lower levels of economic development than centric transfers of labor suggests that such complementarity has certain limits.

The statistical analysis of clustering of societies with centric transfers of the error patterns in the regressions suggests that the cross-section results for the centric transfers of goods can probably also be used to generalize about events occurring over time. Some uncertainties in this analysis did, however, arise. Unfortunately, the data do not permit such an analysis to be carried out for the centric transfers of labor.

Although much work remains to be carried out in the exploration of the determinants of centric transfers, some of the major boundary markers of the field should now be visible. Further research would probably require larger samples, so that more instances of centric transfers with a religious or social focal point (as well as any centric transfers of labor) can be included in the testing of hypotheses.

This analysis of centric transfers completes my survey of the four modes of distribution. I have explored a large number of forms of these various types of distribution; and I have proposed and tested a large number of hypotheses about the determinants of such transactions. The major questions posed in the first chapter have been, at least in part, answered. The hypothesis-testing approach using a sample of 60 primitive and peasant societies has permitted us to approach a number of important questions in the field of economic anthropology with considerably more rigor than usually found in the literature. It seems useful, however, to try to draw together some of the broader implications of this analysis and to attempt to gain a more integrated view of the whole. It is to these more comprehensive considerations that I now turn.

11

SOME BROADER CONSIDERATIONS

*Think you need all this might sum
Of things forever speaking,
That nothing of itself will come,
But we must still be seeking?*
WORDSWORTH[1]

The purpose of this chapter is to provide perspective to the previous analyses of the individual modes of distribution in primitive and peasant societies. To gain such an overview, several important types of analysis must be carried out.

The first task is to survey the relative frequencies of the various modes of distribution and to examine their major determinants together. This can be accomplished in short order with the aid of several summary tables.

The second task is to explore the configuration of these different exchange modes together in order to see how the individual parts can be fitted together into a comprehensible whole. I approach this problem by trying to define different types of primitive and peasant economic systems, using as the criteria of classification particular aspects of the system of distribution. I then try to demonstrate the usefulness of these new definitions of economic systems by showing how such a classification of economies can be used to help explain some noneconomic aspects of the sample societies that have not yet been explored in this book.

The third and final task is to examine briefly the implications of the analysis for the disciplines of anthropology, economic anthropology, and economics.

Design from an Aleut basket; Aleutian Islands, Alaska.
[1]William Wordsworth, "Expostulations and Reply" (poem, 1798).

A REVIEW OF THE MODES OF DISTRIBUTION

Relative Frequencies

As noted in Chapter 1, the sample of 60 primitive and peasant societies used in this study is roughly evenly distributed among the world's cultural areas, a choice made to minimize the influence of cultural diffusion. I also tried to code the societies for a period preceding important Western influence, so as to capture the modes of distribution in a relatively pristine state.

If we are cautious, we can gain some idea about the differential importance of the various modes of distribution by examining their frequency of occurrence in the sample societies. Such data are presented in Table 11.1 not only for the sample as a whole (the column on the far left) but also for groups of societies at different developmental levels.

Among the modes of distribution of goods in the 60 societies of the sample, market exchange appears to be the most frequent, and centric transfer seems the least frequent. Among the modes of distribution of labor, reciprocal exchange is the most frequent, and centric transfer is the least frequent. In general, the average society in the sample is characterized by more different modes of distributing goods than labor.

To a certain extent, the greater frequency of the market exchange of goods can be attributed to contact with the West. This occurs because the sample could not be as "aboriginal" as I wanted and because market exchange appears to be the only mode of distribution strongly influenced by such Western contact. In Chapter 5, some attempt is made to isolate those societies where such Western trade was important; taking these crude calculations into account, we must modify the conclusions of the last paragraph to read that either the market exchange of goods or the noncentric transfers of goods are the most frequent mode of distributing goods.

The results of this brief examination of relative frequencies of different modes of distribution appear to run counter to the vague conjectures by various anthropologists who have claimed particular modes (e.g., reciprocal exchange of goods or centric transfers of goods) to be the most "important." In their defense, it must be added that such data on relative frequency of distributional modes tells us nothing about the relative volume of goods or labor distributed in such transactions. If propositions about the relative importance of particular modes of distribution are to be made more rigorous, explicit mention must be made whether "importance" is defined in terms of frequency of appearance of the mode among societies or in terms of the volume of transactions within societies.

Determinants

The empirical analyses in each chapter of the determinants of the various modes of distribution have unearthed a variety of causal factors. Perspective

TABLE 11.1

Relative Frequency of Modes of Distribution at Different Levels of Economic Development[a]

	Relative frequency in the different development groups				
Type of mode distribution	The 15 societies at the lowest level	The 15 societies at the second lowest level	The 15 societies at the second highest level	The 15 societies at the highest level	Total number of societies with distributional mode
Goods					
Market exchange of goods	7	12	10	14	43
Reciprocal exchange of goods	13	8	8	3	32
Noncentric transfers of goods	13	10	9	3	35
Centric transfers of goods	3	4	10	10	27
Labor					
Market exchange of labor	2	7	7	14	30
Reciprocal exchange of labor	10	11	11	9	41
Noncentric transfers of labor					
Slavery C (narrow slavery)	0	3	3	3	9
Slavery A (maximum slavery)	0	5	10	7	22
Other transfers excluding slavery	2	6	2	0	10
Centric transfers of labor	0	1	3	5	9
Other Types of Distribution					
Presence of interest	2	6.5	10	9.5	28

[a]These data are drawn from Tables 5.1, 7.3, 9.3, and 10.3. For all types of distribution except interest and Slavery A, the 5% limit discussed in the text is used as the cutoff line for determining the presence of the particular mode of distribution. For the presence of interest in societies for which I could not make a determination, I assign a value of one-half.

can be gained by reviewing briefly some problems of interpreting the regression equations and then by examining all of the various determinants together in order to see how they are related.

SOME PROBLEMS OF INTERPRETING THE EMPIRICAL RESULTS

Since various parts of society reciprocally influence each other, cutting into the causal nexus to isolate the determinants of particular economic institutions raises some problems, for which several solutions are available. One method is to take explicit account of such reciprocal influences by setting up and calculating simultaneous equations systems. Given the uncertainties in the data and the present state of knowledge (or, more exactly, ignorance) about the determinants of various modes of distribution, such an exercise seemed quite premature. Another method is to focus on those causal relationships in which the direction of causation is primarily in one direction. This method is used in the previous chapters. On certain occasions, however, problems arise (particularly in the analysis of centric transfers) that receive appropriate comments. Nevertheless, the general problem still remains: The more reciprocal the causal relationships, the less adequate is my choice of statistical methods of analysis. Such reciprocal causation means also that the regressions presented in the previous chapters must be interpreted as demonstrating correlation and not causation.

A second problem lies in my choice of independent variables. This study contains a bias toward the choice of explanatory variables that can be quantified in a manner such that cross-cultural comparisons can be made. This means that more subtle causal connections might have been overlooked. Furthermore, I have primarily focused attention on causal variables with relevance to a large number of societies, which means that special causal variables of importance in one or two societies were not included. Finally, I have exercised some choice in the hypotheses that are tested (omitting, for instance, a number of psychological propositions linking such matters as toilet training or breast-feeding practices to the presence or absence of particular modes of distribution),[2] which means that certain other causal connections may not have properly been brought into the analysis.

A third problem lies in the use of the particular statistical methods employed. Generally, I have used a linear multiple regression form, which means that

---

[2]Several remarks concerning psychological variables must be made. I did code a number of variables reflecting alleged forces of psychological causation and dutifully tested a number of hypotheses linking child-rearing practices (e.g., breast-feeding) and the presence of certain modes of distribution. The number of such psychological variables I tried to code was somewhat larger than the number I ended up with because certain variables (e.g., reflecting toilet-training practices) could not be coded for a sufficient number of societies to warrant inclusion in the statistical tests. The correlations between these variables and the various distributional variables were so low that I soon gave up trying to give them serious consideration.

nonlinear relations are not properly taken into account.[3] As I noted in Chapter 1, certain problems also arise because dummy variables rather than continuous variables are used in the analysis.

Certain broader methodological difficulties and issues, especially regarding eclecticism, economic determinism, and "substantivism" versus "formalism," can also be raised. These dreary problems are discussed and put to rest in Appendix B.6.

I do not believe that these methodological problems are sufficiently serious to force us to abandon attempts to explore the determinants of the various modes of distribution using the relatively simple analytic methods I have employed. Rather, these problems indicate (as I have continually emphasized) that the regression results must be interpreted as indicating a probability warranting further study rather than as presenting a definite proof.

THE RESULTS OF THE REGRESSION ANALYSES

In Table 11.2 I present a summary of the different regression formulae that are discussed in the previous chapters. Since the economic development variable seems to play an important role in modes of distribution, I also include a summary of the levels of development at which there is more than a fifty–fifty chance of predicting the appearance of that mode from the regression equation, holding all other causal factors constant at their average levels. (That is, these are the results of the *ceteris paribus* analysis of the appearance or disappearance of these distributional modes; data for a *mutatis mutandis* analysis of the same phenomenon are presented in the previous table and yield the same results.) Several important conclusions can be drawn from the information presented in this table.

First, a preponderance of the determinants can be classified as "economic." Such determinants include not only the level of economic development and particular primary modes of food production (herding, hunting, fishing, farming) but also such variables as the capital intensiveness of production. Of course, we can also find some "social" determinants (the presence of lineages and the significant occurrence of polygyny), one "political" determinant (concentration of political power), and several "mixed" variables (population, size of unit of observation, and relative degree of work by spouses). Similar conclusions about the relative importance of economic, social, and political variables can also be drawn from the regressions reported in the various chapters and not included in Table 11.2. Given the efforts described in previous chapters to test in the regression analysis a wide variety of "social" and "political" hypotheses, these results are disappointing.

---

[3]In certain cases where I suspected nonlinearities, however, some tests were made. It must also be repeated, as I discussed in Chapter 1, that the use of the development ranks in the regression means that I am linearizing a nonlinear scale and this shortcut also introduces sources of error in the regression.

TABLE 11.2

A Survey of Determinants of Modes of Distribution[a]

Type of mode of distribution	Formula number	Determinants: Direct (+) and inverse (−) relationships	Level of economic development (highest = 60; lowest = 1) where mode appears (+) or disappears (−), other determinants held constant at mean value
Market exchange			
All goods	5-2-5	Economic development (+); contact with West (+); population (−); polygyny (−)	18 (+)
All labor	B5-3-5	Economic development (+); herding as most important food source (−)	32 (+)
Presence of interest	B5-4-2	Economic development (+); capital intensiveness of production (+)	34 (+)
Reciprocal exchange			
All goods	7-1-1	Economic development (−); hunting; fishing, farming as most important food source (+); unit of observation size (−)	33 (−)
All labor	B7-2-1	Economic development (−); important presence of socially defined lineage (+)	54 (−)

Noncentric transfers

All goods	B9-1-2	Economic development (–); nomadic herding as primary food source (–); unit of observation size (–); great inequality of work of spouses (+)	38 (–)
Labor			
Slavery C (agricultural societies only)	B8-2-1	Greater work by women (+); concentration of political power (+)	**
Slavery A	B8-3-1	Economic development (+/–); presence of polygyny (+)	**
All other labor	none	No determinants discovered	**
Centric transfers			
All goods	B10-1-1	Economic development (+)	35 (+)
All labor	10-2-2	Economic development (+); unit of observation size (–); presence of important market or reciprocal exchange of goods (+)	72 (+)

*a*The data are drawn from the specified tables as well as Tables 5.6, 7.3, 9.3, and 10.3. The B in front of the designated table indicates that the logit regressions presented in Appendix B.1 are used instead of the least squares regressions. For those cases where the dependent variable has more than two values or where the logit algorithm does not appear to converge, the least squares regression technique is used.

** = Calculation impossible to make or results not meaningful.

Second, the time-series tests carried out in each chapter suggest that in almost all cases, the findings do not appear to be influenced by slow cultural diffusion. Not all types of cultural diffusion could be tested for. Nevertheless, the choice of the sample and the distributional phenomena under examination suggest diffusion to be unlikely, and the statistical results obtained offer some confirming evidence to this a priori notion. What this means is quite important: The results derived from the cross-section tests can be used for generalizing about events over time.

Third, the levels of economic development at which certain modes of distribution can be predicted to appear or disappear reveal quite a distinct pattern using the *ceteris paribus* technique. Societies at very low levels of economic development seem to rely on the reciprocal exchange of goods and labor and the noncentric transfers of goods as their primary modes of distribution, while societies at higher levels of economic development seem to rely primarily on the market exchange of goods and labor and the centric transfers of goods and labor. In many cases the change in relative importance of the different modes of distribution occurs in the development ranks between 30 and 40. The market exchange of goods appears at a lower rank of development because of the role of foreign trade; if only domestic trade is considered, this mode appears at the thirty-seventh rank of economic development, other factors held constant. Of course, this general pattern linking modes of distribution with the relative levels of economic development admits of many exceptions because of the important role of causal factors other than the level of development. Nevertheless, the central relationship of these modes of development with the level of economic development permits an interesting type of classification of primitive and peasant economic systems that will be discussed.

CONCEPTS OF PRIMITIVE ECONOMIC SYSTEMS

The list of causal factors influencing the appearance or disappearance of particular modes of distribution is sufficiently diverse that an overview is hard to obtain. However, by using the information derived from this table and from the individual regression equations to classify primitive economic systems, we can not only see the patterns of distribution more clearly but also gain further insight into the operation of these societies.

Purposes of Systems Classification

Before embarking on such an exercise in classification, several warnings must be issued. Economies can, of course, be classified in an infinite number of ways, and it is a harmless pastime to devise such schemas. However, if anyone other than the author is to adopt such a classification system, a criterion for acceptance must be specified. Such a criterion is not, in any sense, the "truth" of the classification system, for this is meaningless. Rather, the criterion is usefulness, and this, in turn, requires a statement of purpose.

One common purpose of systems classification is simply to assist in the ordering of facts about the individual economies so that they can be more easily comprehended. A major problem arising with such classification schemas is their usefulness in ordering facts about different economies that lie outside the dimensions that were used in the classification. For instance, to what degree do socialist and capitalist nations (a classification of modern economic systems in terms of ownership of the means of production) have different relative shares of public consumption expenditures in their gross national products? (Answer: There is no essential difference.[4]) Another common purpose of systems classification is to be able to lump economies together that have certain common problems. Again, the systems classification usefulness depends on the degree to which comprehensibility of factual materials can be increased.[5]

Another less common purpose of systems classification is to facilitate the derivation of testable hypotheses. For instance, a group of psychological anthropologists have argued that certain primary modes of food production such as hunting and fishing (in contrast to herding and agriculture) functionally require certain psychological traits of the producers, so that in these societies child-training practices emphasize independence and achievement rather than obedience and nurturing qualities.[6] In this case hypotheses are tested after arranging societies according to primary mode of food production and obtaining certain data on child-raising practices.

My purpose in the exercise below is twofold: to define primitive and peasant societies so as to allow arrangement of descriptive materials and also to permit the deduction of interesting propositions enlarging our understanding of the operations of these societies.

Previous Classifications of Systems

Several major classification principles for defining economic systems can be distinguished in the literature. Each is briefly discussed.

A large group of anthropologists, economists, and historians have classified economic systems according to the level of economic development. In the nineteenth century, this was a procedure employed by the evolutionists,[7] who based their methods on several key assumptions;

---

[4]Frederic L. Pryor, *Public Expenditures in Communist and Capitalist Nations* (1968).

[5]Examples of this and the previously described descriptive uses of systems classifications can be found in Manning Nash, *Primitive and Peasant Economic Systems* (1966).

[6]Herbert Barry III, Irvin L. Child, and Margaret K. Bacon, "Relation of Child Training to Subsistence Economy," *American Anthropologist* LXI (February 1959): 51–63.

[7]A useful summary of some of the basic notions underlying this literature is by Gertrude E. Dole, "Foundations of Contemporary Evolutionism," in *Main Currents in Cultural Anthropology* (1973), ed. Raoul Naroll and Frada Naroll.

1. However they defined the level of economic development, these early evolutionists seemed to assume that this development variable is correlated with all other significant economic, social, social structural, and political variables. That is, they had a very strong notion of functional congruence that was unfortunately seldom argued in any rigorous fashion. This assumption of correlation has often been challenged, and it is a simple matter to show empirically that it is false.[8] The concept of economic system does not in actuality depend on any correlation with any variables except those that define the dimensions of classification; and the actual correlation with other significant variables is an open theoretical question.[9]

2. However they defined the level of economic development, these early evolutionists seemed to assume that in most cases the economic systems change in only one direction and according to one sequence.[10] The concept of economic system is not in actuality based on any assumption about invariant directions of change or invariant sequences; the degree to which invariance actually does appear is another open theoretical question.

Modern evolutionists often define economic system in terms of the level of economic development but handle other questions in a much different manner. That is, they may assume that economic development is the single most important causal variable, so that it is useful to define economic system in such terms, but they make no further assumptions about directions of change or all-embracing functional congruences between economic system and all other variables. This study provides some evidence of the usefulness of such a procedure by modern evolutionists; witness the strong correlations that many of the different modes of distribution have with the economic development variable. Noteworthy, however, is that the links between development and distributional modes were questions explored here on a theoretical and empirical basis rather than assumed.

Another large group of social scientists has classified primitive and peasant societies by the primary mode of production, for example, hunting, gathering, herding, fishing, or farming societies. Underlying this procedure is either a notion that production activities of the society are the most important causal factor underlying other social activities or else more complex notions about the causal importance of particular ecological variables that shape (either directly

[8]In my article, "Property Institutions and Economic Development: Some Empirical Tests," *Economic Development and Cultural Change* XX (April 1972): 406–437, I present evidence (footnote 20) of an attempt to correlate economic development with a large number of societal characteristics which are given in Robert B. Textor, *A Cross-Cultural Summary* (1967). Very few statistically significant correlations were found.

[9]Modern evolutionists such as Robert L. Carneiro ("The Four Faces of Evolution: Unilinear, Universal, Multilinear, and Differential," in *Handbook of Social and Cultural Anthropology* [1973], ed. John J. Honigmann, pp. 89–111) handle this problem in a much different manner than I, yet our conclusions are quite similar.

[10]In many cases the evolutionists dealt with change primarily at a much more general level than that of the economic system; nevertheless, I believe that my statement is a fair inference.

or indirectly) both production activities and other social activities resulting in a certain congruence between them. The present study also provides evidence on the usefulness of such a procedure since the inclusion of such production variables in some of the regressions adds a significant amount of explanatory power. Noteworthy is the fact that in many of the other regressions such variables were entered and dropped when they proved highly unsuccessful in explaining the presence of some type of distributional transaction.

A third group has combined the first two approaches, arguing that the level of economic development and the primary mode of production are highly correlated. In the twentieth century this approach seems to be followed particularly by orthodox Marxists too intellectually timid to stray from Engel's mechanistic unilineal schema.[11] I present evidence in Table 1.3 that such a correlation between the level of development and primary mode of food production does exist; however, the correlation is far from perfect and admits many important exceptions.

A final and much smaller group of anthropologists and economists have employed still different criteria for classifying primitive and peasant economies.[12] Such systems of classification, however, have not been widely discussed or adopted.

Economic Systems Defined by Criteria of Distribution

The data on distributional modes presented in the previous chapters can be used in a variety of ways for defining different types of economic systems. I present one such classification in detail below and discuss several others briefly.

THE CRITERION OF ORIENTATION OF DISTRIBUTION

If we glance at the societies in the sample arranged according to their relative levels of economic development and focus our attention on those particular distributional modes that I show to be related to the level of economic development, we find that only a few of the societies concur completely with the expected pattern. Most societies possess certain distributional modes that, according to predictions based solely on their level of economic development,

---

[11]A number of Western Marxist scholars have deviated considerably from the ideas and the rigid schema put forth by Friedrich Engels in his *The Origin of the Family, Private Property and the State* (1884). Many of the issues of the disputes among Marxist scholars are surveyed by Gianni Sofri, *Ueber asiatische Produktionsweise* (1972) [originally published 1969]; by Eric Hobsbawm in his Introduction to Karl Marx's *Pre-Capitalist Economic Formations*, trans. Jack Cohen (1964). Most readers find this book of Marx confusing, and Marx's notebooks offer little help on many of the controversial issues raised. The notebooks are reproduced by Lawrence Krader, Ed., *The Ethnological Notebooks of Karl Marx*, 2nd ed. (1974).

[12]E.g., Manning Nash, *Primitive and Peasant Economic Systems*; or Mary W. Helm, "The Purchase Society: Adaptation to Economic Frontiers," *Anthropological Quarterly* XLII (October 1969): 325–343.

they should not; or do not possess certain distributional modes that, according to our predictions, they should.[13]

By examining the error pattern of predictions concerning the various distributional modes, we can determine those economies that have particular orientations of distribution that can not be predicted by simple reference to the level of economic development. For simplicity I look at three "economically oriented" modes of distribution, namely, market exchange of goods, market exchange of labor, and the presence of an interest rate; three "socially oriented" modes of distribution, namely, reciprocal exchange of goods, reciprocal exchange of labor, and noncentric transfers of goods; and two "politically oriented" modes of distribution, namely, centric transfers of goods and centric transfers of labor. The error patterns among these three groups of modes of distribution permit us to isolate those economies that have more or less than the predicted number of economically, socially, and politically oriented modes of distribution; and from this grouping of errors, we can then label the different economic systems. (The exact method is described in detail in Appendix B.7.)

Such a way of classifying economic systems means that a particular economy may have several orientations (e.g., a negative "economic orientation" and a positive "social orientation") or no particular orientation (i.e., given its level of economic development, its modes of distribution fall roughly along the predicted pattern). Such an approach has the advantage of making operational some rather vague concepts that are sometimes encountered in the anthropology literature when one reads that Society X is "more political" or "less social" than Society Y.

What all this adds up to is quite simple. I have defined a "main line of economic development" as traditional evolutionists have done; and then I have defined economic systems in terms of deviations, either positive or negative, from this main line. Of the 60 societies in the sample, 34 have distinct distributional orientations; and of these 34, somewhat less than one-third have two or more distributional orientations. The remainder fit along the main line, that is, their distributional modes are by and large predictable by reference to the level of economic development alone.

Although the methods used in determining distributional orientation are crude, they eliminate at least one type of subjective element arising in classifying economies when one is influenced by the comparative judgments of the ethnographer whose criteria are often not clearly stated. The usefulness of such an approach can only be determined by seeing how the classification can be used in empirical research, a task that will be taken up in two paragraphs.

---

[13]The particular dividing lines on the economic development scale for predicting whether or not a society should have a certain distributional mode are determined from the various regression formulas in the previous chapters, in which all of the average values of the different explanatory variables except the level of economic development are placed in the derived formula so that the economic development dividing line can be determined. Such calculations are shown in Table 11.2.

OTHER DISTRIBUTIONAL CRITERIA

If we examine the number of modes of distribution that account for 5% or more of the distribution of produced goods (i.e., market exchange, reciprocal exchange, noncentric transfers, and centric transfers), we find that most societies have two or three of these modes. Similarly, if we examine the number of modes of distribution accounting for 5% or more of the distribution of labor outside the home (i.e., market exchange, reciprocal exchange, noncentric transfers, and centric transfers), we find that most societies have one or two of these modes. We can classify economies by the number of modes of distribution that they have, focusing particular attention on the societies that fall outside the above specified ranges. Experiments were conducted with such a classification, and although a number of interesting observations were made, I could demonstrate no very exciting propositions that employed this schema.[14]

We can also classify economies according to the degree to which they rely on exchange modes of distribution, rather than transfers. Although certain experiments along these lines were made, again I could generate and demonstrate no very interesting propositions that employed such a classification system.

Economic System as a Causal Variable

In the social science literature one finds a wide variety of hypotheses that can be used for examining the usefulness of my systems classification based on distributional orientation. In the paragraphs that follow, I very briefly discuss three such propositions, each one focusing on one of the three major types of systems that arise from the classification. A more detailed discussion of the hypothesis plus the statistical tests are presented in Appendix B.7.

The first proposition focuses on the notion that an "economically oriented" economic system appears to play a causal role in the manner in which children are raised. In a short book written quite late in his life, Sigmund Freud analyzed the relationship between "civilization" and child-rearing practices.[15] He argued that the "price" of higher levels of cultural development is much stricter

---

[14]I found it interesting that among those societies that had both a low number of modes of distribution of goods (i.e., 0 or 1) and a low number of modes of distribution of labor (0 or 1), all the societies are polygynous with large extended family structures and also have large units of observation (defined in Chapter 2); in addition, all have important unilineal descent groups with strict postmarital residence rules (i.e., postmarital residence is always either with the wife's family or always with the husband's family). All of the societies that had both a large number of modes of distribution of goods (i.e., four) and a large number of modes of distribution of labor (i.e., three or four) have monogamous families with small units of observation but with strong unilineal descent groups and strict postmarital residence rules. The other two extreme groups (high number of modes of distribution of goods; low number of modes of distribution of labor, and vice versa) are monogamous and for the most part have no strong unilineal kin groupings or strict postmarital residence rules.

[15]Sigmund Freud, *Civilization and Its Discontents* (1930), trans. Joan Riviere. This ranks among Freud's worst books, vying for this title with his other anthropological writings.

upbringing of children and much less permissive disciplinary practices. Although his discussion is quite murky, he seems to intertwine two causal variables underlying child-rearing practices: the general level of economic development and the degree to which the society places particular emphasis on economic motivations and activities. The causal connections are argued in terms of his theories about personality development, which have been strongly attacked and which would lead us too far astray to discuss. Nevertheless, we can easily test the hypothesized relationships statistically, and we find (much to my surprise) that the level of economic development and a variable designating whether the society has a positive "economic orientation" are both significantly and, as predicted, positively related to a variable designating degree of repressiveness in child rearing.

The second proposition focuses on the notion that a "socially oriented" economic system seems an important causal factor for quite different practices, namely, the deliberate killing of the old and the incurably sick in primitive and peasant societies. Many anthropologists have suggested that such practices occur primarily in those societies that are at the lowest levels of economic development. It can be further argued, following Durkheim's notions about "altruistic suicide,"[16] that senilicide requires not only a certain willingness on the part of the aged but also a strong social cohesiveness so that the society is not torn apart each time the act is carried out. The socially oriented economic systems variable would be a good proxy for such social cohesiveness. The statistical analysis shows indeed that the level of economic development and a variable designating whether the society has a positive "social orientation" are both significantly related to a variable designating the presence of senilicide and the killing of the incurably sick. The former variable has the expected inverse relationship; the latter variable has the expected positive relationship.

The third and final proposition focuses on the notion that a "politically oriented" economic system appears an important determinant of the degree of socioeconomic inequality. Such inequality, many have argued, is related to the level of economic development. But it also seems likely that strong political orientation permits a high degree of socioeconomic inequality to be maintained or even increased. The statistical analysis shows very clearly that the level of economic development and a variable designating whether the society has a positive "political orientation" are both significantly and positively related to a variable designating the degree of socioeconomic inequality.

The demonstration of these three hypotheses using my approach for defining economic systems is gratifying. However, I must add that for several other plausible hypotheses such systems variables did not prove very helpful. These varied results should not be cause for alarm, for a particular classification of primitive and peasant economic systems should not be expected to solve all problems in economics or anthropology but a specific subset.

---

[16]Emile Durkheim, *Suicide: A Study in Sociology* (1951) [originally published 1897].

IMPLICATIONS OF THE ANALYSIS

Anthropology

Before reviewing the possible contributions I have tried to make to anthropology, it is useful to specify what I have not tried to accomplish.

Throughout this study I focus on the similarities among primitive and peasant economies, not the differences. I do not try to explain entire societal configurations, rather the presence or absence of particular phenomena. I do not aim at complete explanations for any phenomenon but try to isolate several of the most important causal factors. In sum, I do not try to offer cross-cultural analysis as a substitute for intensive fieldwork of specific societies but as a complement to such work. The progress of anthropology depends on more knowledge both of particular societies and of general causal relationships. To this progress I hope to have made four contributions.

First, I have tried to show the usefulness of collecting new kinds of ethnographic data, particularly quantitative information about exchange and transfer transactions. Throughout this study I try to show how ethnographers and anthropologists have not paid sufficient attention to many different aspects of these exchange and transfer transactions that, in turn, are so critical in evaluating the distributional side of the economy.

Second, I hope to have increased the quantity and quality of the inventory of propositions that are used in anthropology. Throughout this study I have tried to frame and explore a variety of causal relationships in a manner that permits statistical testing. Although such a procedure leads, as I have noted, to a neglect of many subtleties, it has the advantage of weeding out many of the incorrect propositions that are found in the literature and suggesting a large number of new propositions for further examination.

Third, I hope to have added to the analytic toolbox of anthropology a number of statistical techniques. Some of these techniques are new, for example, my method of handling problems arising from diffusion. And some of these techniques are commonly used in other social science disciplines but are seldom employed in anthropology, for example, the multivariate regression analysis that is used to isolate the determinants of various modes of distribution. The advantage of such multivariate techniques, particularly in resolving disputes where each of the parties is claiming that one particular determinant is the sole causal force, should be readily apparent, especially in cases where both determinants are operating.

Finally, I hope to have provided a new perspective with which to analyze the economy of particular societies. By showing what kind of similarities exist among societies, I hope that the analysis of differences is sharpened. By providing comparisons from a worldwide sample of societies, I have tried to provide a useful benchmark for studying particular societies so that their uniqueness can be more systematically dissected and appreciated.

Economic Anthropology

Throughout this study I have avoided entering the dispute between the "formalists" and the "substantivists," which has taken up so many pages in the economic anthropology literature. Part of this is because I am dealing with a set of issues that have not been (or are only seldom) addressed by the participants in this debate. And part of this is because many of the questions discussed in this debate do not seem phrased in a manner to permit convincing answers to be given. I have tried to transcend this debate and take the contributions of both schools of thought into account.

I believe that the emphasis of the substantivists on the importance of non-market modes of distribution is extremely important. My classification of these transactions is, however, quite different. Moreover, I hope to have shown that a number of propositions offered by this school, especially its source of inspiration, Karl Polanyi, turn out to be false.

I believe that the emphasis of the formalists on model building and deductive analysis has been extremely useful and that many of their ideas about the linkages between economic phenomena are quite important in understanding distribution in primitive and peasant societies. However, I believe that they often have focused on uninteresting or untestable economic propositions and, moreover, that their analyses have often been too general to be of much use in analyzing particular economies or particular institutions.

I have, in addition, avoided entering other debates in the field of economic anthropology, for example, between the Marxists and non-Marxists, and to take advantage of the contributions of each side. Again, this avoidance can not be traced to any pacific tendencies on my part but rather to the realization that a good deal more can be accomplished by actually doing economic anthropology than by writing on the way it should be done. And in carrying out such work, I have had two aims.

First, I hope to have broadened the agenda of research in economic anthropology so that a wider range of phenomena will be investigated and so that the determinants and the impact of such phenomena will be approached with greater perspective and rigor.

Second, I hope to have shown how the analysis of the exchange of goods and the exchange of labor can be more closely linked. Too often empirical analyses of these two aspects of distribution are carried out separately, the former placed in the context of investigation of consumption activities, the latter placed in the context of investigation of production activities. Their juxtaposition and joint consideration provides many useful insights.

Economics

To economics I have tried to make several important contributions: First, I hope to have shown that the traditional ways in which the development of economic institutions and activities have been viewed is schematic and that both Marxists and non-Marxists have seriously neglected such matters.[17] With several major exceptions, most economists have paid relatively little systematic attention in recent years to the development of nonmarket modes of distribution and how such distributional modes influence the economy. They have also seriously underrated the importance of noneconomic forces in the development of economic institutions. I have tried to show how economists must draw from social, political, and social structural considerations if they are to understand more fully the origins of the economy.

Second, I have tried to show how institutions per se can be fruitfully analyzed. Most types of economic analyses deal with the behavior of different variables such as prices, quantities of goods or labor, gross national product, money supply, and so forth. But since these variables operate within an institutional matrix, it is often necessary to look at these institutions to gain fuller understanding of the variables. At the present time, however, we have few techniques to do this in a systematic manner, so that institutional analysis is a relatively ad hoc affair. The "new institutionalism" has, for the most part, focused on microeconomic problems and has left the macroanalysis of institutions to scholars of other disciplines. It should be clear, however, that if economics is to become a truly "social" science, and if we are to develop rigorous theories of political economy, then we must pay increasingly greater attention to the institutional dimensions of the economy.

Third, I hope to have provided an inventory of propositions from which specialists in economic history and economic development can draw. The economic historians are faced with recording and understanding the events of economically underdeveloped nonmarket economies, but as yet we have few tools and propositions in this area. The economic development specialists are faced with problems in understanding the operation of nonmarket economies in making policy proposals, and they face the same lack of tools and propositions as the economic historians.

FINAL REMARKS

Samuel Johnson spoke for us all when he explained to a friend:

> There are two things which I am confident I can do very well: One is an introduction to any literary work, stating what it is to contain, and how it should be executed in the most perfect manner; the other is a conclusion, shewing from various causes why the execution has not been equal to what the author promised to himself and to the publick.[18]

[17]The schematism treatment of these matters by non-Marxists and Marxists arises from different sources. Non-Marxist economists seldom pay much attention to primitive and peasant economic institutions, so in most cases the unsatisfactory treatment of such subjects is due to neglectful research. Marxist schematism can be traced to the patristic texts; Marx and Engels had at the time of their writing too small an empirical base at their disposal for adequate generalizations.

[18]Cited by James Boswell, *The Life of Samuel Johnson*, LL.D., Vol. I Aetat. 46 (1755).

I shall not burden the reader with excuses, with lamentations about the unavailability of reliable data, or with apologies. Rather, in this final statement I will summarize very briefly what has been done in the book and what should be done in the future.

The book begins with a simple definitional schema that distinguishes four distributional modes: market exchange, reciprocal exchange, noncentric transfers, and centric transfers. In the next part of the book, I deal with some of the most important methodological problems in trying to analyze such distributional modes. Such problems include difficulties arising in using cross-section evidence to generalize about events over time; calculating the degree of balance in transactions so that they may be classified as exchange or transfer; and dealing with problems of disequilibrium and the determination of economic value.

In the following part of the book, I explore and empirically test a variety of propositions about the determinants of the various modes of distribution. Some of these propositions are drawn from the literature; others are derived from simple deductive models; and still others are based on hunches that can hardly be dignified by the term "theory." I have offered no unified theory about the determinants of distribution in general but have presented a series of propositions about the various types of distribution that are related through a common framework of analysis. And in this final chapter I have shown one way in which the various modes of distribution can be studied together in order to provide insight into other aspects of the society.

A number of promising avenues for future research emerge from this study. Certainly much more research on the various types of transfers, both noncentric and centric, is required; market and reciprocal exchange have received disproportional attention from anthropologists and economists, and it is time to redress this balance. I believe that closer attention than I have paid to the type of environment and the type of subsistence production in explaining the presence or absence of particular modes of distribution would also be fruitful; the type of herding (different animals differ considerably in the type of herding work required) and the type of farming (not only farming techniques but also type of crops) seem to play a crucial role in distribution in some societies. Much more research is also needed on the impact of different types of distribution on the rest of the economy; although I have tried to discuss and test in a simple manner some such proposition, the field is wide open for some exciting research.[19] Finally, it should be apparent that much fruitful research could be conducted on the patterns of different distributional modes as a totality and the relationship of such patterns to other aspects of the society.

[19]One type of interesting research concerns the costs of various modes of distribution in terms of resources spent in distribution, the inefficiencies arising from various types of distributional disequilibria, and so forth. An example of such research for industrial economies can be found in my article, "Some Costs of Markets: An Empirical Investigation," *Quarterly Journal of Economics* XCI (February 1977): 81–102. This essay was originally written as a chapter of this book before I narrowed the focus almost exclusively to primitive and peasant economies.

In attempting to systematize the various propositions about the origins of the economy, I have been struck by how little is known and how little we shall ever know on certain topics. It has been often emphasized that truly primitive societies do not keep records and that archaeological evidence provides only a few clues about the economic institutions and distributional processes of the society. And many anthropologists have lamented the unfortunate fact that part of their field of inquiry is quickly evaporating, for few primitive economies remain in their pristine state, and peasant economies are, or are trying, to modernize quickly. It may be too late to find out all that we now want to know about these economies, but the comparative method that is employed in this book gives us many clues.

A comparative analysis can be carried out in a number of different ways; in this volume the reader has been marched through a particular type of analysis that I have found fruitful in the other two volumes of the comparative economics trilogy, of which this is the final book. If I have encouraged anyone to attempt such a comparative analysis for his own purposes, or if I have enraged anyone to a sufficient degree that he or she will try a different kind of comparative analysis to show how the method should be more properly used, then my most basic purpose has been served. For there are far too many scholars in both anthropology and economics who are engaged in methodological posturing about how comparative economic analysis should be carried out; and few—far too few—who are actually engaged in such vital scholarly work.

APPENDIX A

ETHNOGRAPHIC DATA USED IN THE CALCULATIONS

The major sources of information on which the codings below were based are listed in Appendix E. Documentation of each of the roughly 4500 bits of information listed below proved too extensive to be included.

For each of the 75 series the variable is briefly designated, a general evaluation of the accuracy of the entire coding is presented, notes on the coding method are supplied if clarification is necessary, and the different code values are discussed. For the accuracy evaluation (designated as "grade") three letters are used: A = I am quite confident of the accuracy of most of the codings for the particular variable; B = I am mildly confident of the accuracy of the codings; C = I have some misgivings about the codings but believe that the accuracy is sufficient for the purposes for which the data are employed. Pluses and minuses modify these designations. These general evaluations are, of course, subjective and are presented in the hope that my own state of mind about the different variables may be of use to the reader.

The variables are numbered sequentially and the individual codes are presented in Table A.1, which follows the discussion. All of the codings were made by the author; comparable codings of some of these variables are discussed in the text. For the individual codings some accuracy ratings are also made: An "A" placed on the right of the code in the table indicates some misgivings about the specific coding; a "B" indicates considerable misgivings; and a "9" in the place of a code indicates that I did not have sufficient information even to hazard a guess.

1. Geographical location of society. [Grade = A+]. 1 = Sub-Sahara Africa; 2 = Circum-Mediterranean area (all Europe, the Middle East, and the northern part of Africa); 3 = Central and East Asia (excluding the Middle East but including the Asiatic part of the Soviet Union); 4 = Insular Pacific or Oceania; 5 = North America (excluding Central America and the Caribbean Islands); 6 = South and Central America (including the Caribbean Islands).

2. Hardness of environment. [Grade = B+]. Hard environment reflects arctic, semiarctic, or desert environments. 1 = hard environment; 0 = not hard environment (all other societies).

3. Contact with the West in the years up to the pinpointed year for which the coding was made. [Grade = C+]. This variable is intended to reflect the amount of Western influence; unfortunately, it could only be rather subjectively coded. 1 = considerable contact of a general nature; or heavy missionary work; or many visits by traders, colonists, tourists, or government officials; 0 = no contact, or occasional contact, light missionary work, or few visits by Westerners.

4. Major mode of subsistence production. [Grade = A−]. For each society an estimate was made of the percentage importance of different food sources; importance was measured in terms of calories (if available) or food weight (if data on calories not available). The code represents the most important food source. 1 = agriculture (if agricultural products amount to more than 50% of all foods); 2 = incipient agriculture (if agriculture is the most important food source, but amounts to 50% or less of all foods); 3 = animal husbandry (including dairy products); 4 = fishing (both river and ocean fishing but excluding hunting of large aquatic mammals or collecting clams and mussels on the shore); 5 = hunting (including large aquatic mammals); 6 = gathering (including clams and mussels on the seashore); 7 = hunting and gathering of equal importance.

5. Animal husbandry contributes at least 10% of all food. [Grade = B+]. The codes based on the data underlying variable 4. 1 = yes; 0 = no.

6. Nomadic herding. [Grade = A−]. Two criterial are employed: First, a determination was made whether animal husbandry contributes the most important source of food (Variable 4); second, whether the society is fully or seminomadic. (See Variable 16.) 1 = the society can be characterized as nomadic herding according to the two criteria specified above; 0 = the society can not be characterized as nomadic herding since one or both of the criteria specified above are not met.

7. Hunting and/or fishing account for 50% or more of food supply. [Grade = A−]. The coding is based on the data underlying Variable 4. 1 = yes; 0 = no.

8. Percentage of food produced by women. [Grade = C]. For each type of food a rough estimate was made of the percentage of work hours contributed by men and women in a typical monogamous family. These percentages were then weighted by the percentage importance of the different food sources (the data underlying Variable 4). Although the data are presented to three significant

digits, the accuracy of the estimates is much less. The relation of my results to those of others is discussed in the text.

9. Relative amounts of total work performed by spouses. [Grade = C]. Many difficulties arise in trying to distinguish "work" from "leisure" in primitive and peasant societies. If ethnographic reports suggest that in an average year there were great discrepancies in the amount of obvious leisure or obvious work (in which work is defined in terms of subsistence production or household tasks or other unpleasant but necessary economic tasks) of adult men and women, then coding was easy. Difficulties arose when work and leisure occurred simultaneously, and in such cases attention was focused on the predominant activity (e.g., if handicraft work is performed while people gather primarily for social purposes, then this is considered "leisure"). +1 = an average wife spends considerably more time in economic activities than an average husband; 0 = an average spouse spends roughly the same time in economic activities than a spouse of the opposite sex; −1 = an average husband spends considerably more time in economic activities than an average wife.

10. Great inequality of work performed by spouses. [Grade = C]. The same as Variable 9 but coding either a +1 or a −1 simply as 1. 1 = yes; 0 = no.

11. Population of the entire society. [Grade = B]. Certain difficulties arose in determining the exact limits of the society and two criteria were employed: (1) A society is a group of people with a highly similar culture and language; (2) a society is a group of several cultures under the political leadership of one person or group. I always selected that criteria which yielded the largest population. 1 = population under 10; 2 = 10 to 99; 3 = 100 to 999; 4 = 1000 to 9999; 5 = 10,000 to 99,999; 6 = 100,000 to 999,999; 7 = 1,000,000 to 9,999,999; 8 = 10,000,000 and over.

12. Population density. [Grade = B]. The population (Variable 11) divided by the area. 1 = less than 5 persons per square mile (fewer than 1.9 persons per 100 ha); 2 = 5 to 25 persons per square mile (2 to 9.8 persons per 100 ha); 3 = 25.1 to 100 persons per square mile (9.9 to 38.6 persons per 100 ha); 4 = over 100 persons per square mile (over 38.6 persons per 100 ha).

13. A land scarcity index derived from nonvalue indicators. [Grade = B−]. This variable is based on information on population density (Variable 12) and agricultural fallowing practices (Variable 15), and the calculation of the variable is discussed in detail in Appendix C.3. It runs in value from 0 through 6; an 8 indicates that the society is a nonagricultural society or else relies very little on agriculture as its source of food.

14. An "open resources" index. [Grade = B−]. This variable is based on information about land rentals (Variable 36) and an index of the availability of land. It is described in detail in Appendix C.4. It runs in value from 0 through 6; an 8 indicates that the society is a nonagricultural society or else relies very little on agriculture as its source of food.

15. Land fallowing period. [Grade = B−]. Certain coding problems arose when two different fallowing techniques were used; in this case an arithmetic

average was taken. Other problems arise when the fallowing technique varied according to the area, in which case a similar solution was used. 0 = no agriculture; 1 = free land fallow (land is essentially unlimited and people may not ever return to the same piece of land after it is farmed once or several times); 2 = full forest fallow (more than 20 years fallow period but a return to the same piece eventually); 3 = intermediate forest fallow (11–20 years fallow period); 4 = bush fallow period (5–10 years fallow period); 5 = short fallow period (1–4 years fallow period); 6 = annual cropping (no fallow period and one crop per land piece per year); 7 = multicrop agriculture (no fallow period and more than one crop per land piece per year).

16. Degree of nomadism (settlement pattern). [Grade = B]. 1 = fully fixed residences; 2 = semisedentary (a large part of the year is spent at a permanent settlement and where periodic trips for hunting, gathering, herding, or fishing purposes are made); 3 = seminomadic (where the society occupies temporary camps for much of the year or which rotates between two or more semipermanent settlements); 4 = fully nomadic.

17. Capital intensiveness of subsistence production. [Grade = B+]. 1 = all herding societies, all fishing societies that have extensive reliance on boat fishing, or all agricultural societies with at least two out of the following three characteristics; plow agriculture, irrigation, terracing of land; 0 = all hunting and gathering societies, fishing societies not relying extensively on boat fishing, or agricultural societies not meeting the characteristics specified earlier.

18. Production unit. [Grade = B+]. The concept of production unit is defined in Chapter 2. 1 = nuclear family (monogamous, polygynous, or polyandrous) or small extended family (e.g., stem family) or nuclear family plus additional people not closely related to the family; 2 = large extended family; 3 = several major production units; 4 = other (hunting groups, herding camp, etc.).

19. Consumption unit. [Grade = B−]. The concept of consumption unit is defined in Chapter 2. 1 = nuclear family (monogamous, polygynous, or polyandrous) or small extended family (e.g., stem family) or nuclear family plus additional people not closely related to family; 2 = large extended family; 3 = several major consumption units.

20. Relative size of production and consumption unit. [Grade = B]. 1 = same size; 2 = consumption unit larger than production unit; 3 = production unit larger than consumption unit; 4 = several consumption or production units.

21. Unit of observation. [Grade = B]. This concept is defined in Chapter 2. 1 = nuclear family (monogamous, polygynous, or polyandrous) or small extended family (e.g., stem family) or nuclear family plus additional people not closely related to family; 2 = large extended family.

22. Rank order of level of economic development. [Grade = B]. This concept is defined and discussed in Chapter 2 and is calculated in terms of societal

complexity. The rankings run from 1 (lowest level) to 60 (highest rank). Inclusion of decimal point indicates tie ranks.

23. Presence of domestic market exchange of food. [Grade = B+]. Any market exchange except of the most casual sort is included. 1 = yes; 0 = no.

24. Domestic trade accounts for 5% or more of total production of goods used in the society. [Grade = B]. As in the case of all of the evaluations about the relative importance of different modes of distribution, this represents a subjective judgment derived by taking into account the quantity of various goods produced and the relative amounts of each that are distributed. Since all judgments about the different modes of distribution were made at the same time, there should be some consistency between the ratings for a given society. 1 = domestic trade does account for 5% or more of total production of goods; 0 = domestic trade does not.

25. External trade accounts for 5% or more of total production of goods used in the society. [Grade = B]. See caveat for Variable 24. 1 = yes; 0 = no; 9 = do not know.

26. Total trade accounts for 5% or more of total production of goods used in the society. [Grade = B+]. See caveat for Variable 24. 1 = yes; 0 = no.

27. Presence of a marketplace. [Grade = B]. 0 = no formal marketplace; 1 = a domestic marketplace at least 1–3 days a week; 2 = use of an external permanent marketplace; 3 = domestic marketplace at least 4 days a week; 5 = other (e.g., participation in annual external trade fairs; use of impermanent external markets, etc.).

28. Skilled domestic wage worker or worker whose skills are purchased in a market transaction account for 5% or more of total labor outside the home. [Grade = B]. See caveat for Variable 24. Services are defined in Chapter 2. 1 = yes; 0 = no.

29. Unskilled domestic wage worker or worker whose services are purchased in a market transaction account for 5% or more of total labor outside the home. [Grade = B]. See caveat for Variable 24. Services are defined in Chapter 2. 1 = yes; 0 = no.

30. Skilled and unskilled domestic wage workers and workers whose services or skills are purchased in a domestic market transaction account for 5% or more of total labor outside the home. [Grade = B]. See caveat for Variable 24. Services are defined in Chapter 2. 1 = yes; 0 = no.

31. Skilled and unskilled wage workers and workers whose services or skills are purchased in an external market (i.e., outside the society) account for 5% or more of total labor outside the home. [Grade = B]. See caveat for Variable 24. Services are defined in Chapter 2. 1 = yes; 0 = no.

32. Skilled and unskilled wage workers and workers whose services or skills are purchased either domestically or externally (i.e., outside the society) account for 5% or more of total labor outside the home. [Grade = B]. See caveat for Variable 25. Services are defined in Chapter 2. 1 = yes; 0 = no.

33. Interest or an interest proxy levied on any type of domestic loan. [Grade = B−]. The key terms are defined in Chapter 5. 1 = yes; 0 = no.

34. Importance of sales of land. [Grade = B−]. 0 = land sales do not occur; 1 = land sales occur but do not seem important; 1X = possibly occur but are not important; 1Y = land sales occur and may possibly be important; 2 = land sales occur and are important; 3 = land buying and selling only with nonmembers of society.

35. Presence of pseudorents, gift rents, and tax rents. [Grade = B]. These terms are defined in Chapter 5. 0 = none present; 1 = pseudorent or gift rents present; 2 = tax rent present; 3 = both present or other (e.g., Wolof, tax rent present; uncertain if pseudorent present); 9 = do not know.

36. Presence of land rent. [Grade = B+]. 0 = no land rent present; 1 = land rent present but not important; 1Y = land rent present and possibly important; 2 = land rent present and accounts for 5% or more of agricultural production; 3 = other (Basseri obtain rents from nonsocietal members and these may possibly be important; the Tuareg obtain rents from nonsocietal members, and these amount to more than 5% of agricultural production).

37. Presence of an internal commercial money. [Grade = A−]. The key terms are defined in Chapter 6. 1 = yes; 0 = no.

38. Presence of an external commercial money. [Grade = A−]. The key terms are defined in Chapter 6. 1 = yes; 0 = no; 9 = do not know.

39. Presence of an internal noncommercial money, using the "criterion of two." [Grade = B]. The key terms are defined in Chapter 6. 1 = yes; 0 = no.

40. Presence of an internal noncommercial money, using the "criterion of three." [Grade = B]. The key terms are defined in Chapter 6. 1 = yes; 0 = no.

41. Presence of exchange spheres. [Grade = B−]. The key term is defined in Appendix B.3. 2 = exchange spheres present and relatively unambiguous; 1 = exchange spheres probably present, but ambiguous; 0 = exchange spheres not present.

42. Reciprocal exchange of food accounts for 5% or more of total production of goods used in the society. [Grade = B]. See caveat for Variable 24. Key terms are defined in Chapter 7. 1 = yes; 0 = no.

43. Reciprocal exchange of nonfood items accounts for 5% or more of the total production of goods used in the society. [Grade = C]. See caveat for Variable 24. Key terms are defined in Chapter 7. 1 = yes; 0 = no.

44. Reciprocal exchange of goods (both food and nonfood items) accounts for 5% or more of total production of goods used in the society. [Grade = B]. See caveat for Variable 24. Key terms are defined in Chapter 7. 1 = yes; 0 = no.

45. Highly ceremonial reciprocal exchange of goods (both food and nonfood items) accounts for 5% or more of the total production of goods used in the society. [Grade = B−]. See caveat for Variable 24. Key terms are defined in Chapter 7. 1 = yes; 0 = no.

46. Reciprocal exchange of labor accounts for 5% or more of total labor

outside the home. [Grade = C+]. See *caveat* for Variable 24. Key terms are defined in Chapter 7. 1 = yes; 0 = no.

47. Reciprocal exchange of labor accounts for 5% or more of total labor outside the home and is conducted in an important degree by simple labor exchange. [Grade = C+]. See *caveat* for Variable 24. Key terms are defined in Chapter 7. 1 = yes; 0 = no.

48. Reciprocal exchange of labor accounts for 5% or more of total labor outside the home and is conducted in an important degree by festive labor exchange. [Grade = C+]. See *caveat* for Variable 24. Key terms are defined in Chapter 7. 1 = yes; 0 = no.

49. Both market exchange of goods and also the reciprocal exchange of goods account for less than 5% of the total production of goods used in the society. [Grade = B]. The data come from Variables 26 and 44. 1 = yes; 0 = no.

50. Presence of Slavery A ("maximal slavery"). [Grade = A−]. The key term is defined in Chapter 8. 1 = yes; 0 = no.

51. Presence of Slavery B. [Grade = B]. The key term is defined in the glossary (Appendix D). 1 = yes; 0 = no.

52. Presence of Slavery C ("narrow or minimal slavery"). [Grade = B]. The key term is defined in Chapter 8. 1 = yes; 0 = no.

53. Presence of Slavery D. [Grade = B−]. The key term is defined in the glossary (Appendix D). 1 = yes; 0 = no.

54. Noncentric transfers of goods account for 5% or more of total production of goods used in the economy. [Grade = B−]. See *caveat* for Variable 24. Key terms are defined in Chapter 9. 1 = yes; 0 = no.

55. Noncentric transfers of labor (excluding slavery or serfdom) account for 5% or more of total labor outside of home. [Grade = C]. See *caveat* for Variable 24. Key terms are defined in Chapter 9. 1 = yes; 0 = no.

56. Presence of gambling. [Grade = B]. 2 = gambling reported and an "important" distributive mode; 1 = some gambling reported but not important or importance unascertainable; 0 = none reported.

57. Centric transfers of goods account for 5% or more of the total production of goods used in the society. [Grade = B]. See *caveat* for Variable 24. Key terms are defined in Chapter 10. 1 = yes; 0 = no.

58. Centric transfers of labor account for 5% or more of the total labor outside the home. [Grade = C+]. See *caveat* for Variable 24. Key terms are defined in Chapter 10. 1 = yes; 0 = no.

59. Economically oriented economic system. [Grade = B−]. This type of economic system is defined in Chapter 11, and the actual determination is discussed in Appendix B.7. 1 = yes; 0 = no.

60. Socially oriented economic system. [Grade = B−]. This type of economic system is defined in Chapter 11, and the actual determination is discussed in Appendix B.7. 1 = yes; 0 = no.

61. Politically oriented economic system. [Grade = B−]. This type of eco-

nomic system is defined in Chapter 11, and the actual determination is discussed in Appendix B.7. 1 = yes; 0 = no.

62. Economic systems with no economic, social, or political orientation only. [Grade = B−]. The data come from Variables 59, 60, and 61. 1 = yes; 0 = no.

63. Postmarital residence. [Grade = A−]. The definitions employed in the coding are the same as those employed by others with one major difference: if the married couple usually live very close to both kin groups, then it is coded as 0 even though the physical proximity may be a few yards closer to one kin group or the other. +1 = patrilocal or virilocal (residence with or near husband's kin); 0 = ambilocal, neolocal, or bilocal (residence with or near both kin, neither kin, or no societal rule) or else very close to both kin groups; −1 = matrilocal or uxorilocal (resident with or near wife's kin).

64. Important presence of extensive lineages in which lineages are defined in terms of corporate economic activities. [Grade = B]. The criterion of importance implies that the corporate economic activities play a significant role in the society; the criterion of extensiveness implies that such lineages have generational depth. The lineages include patrilineal, matrilineal, duolineal, and ambilineal groups. Other aspects of this variable are discussed in Chapter 6. 1 = yes; 0 = no.

65. Important presence of extensive lineages in which lineages are defined in terms of corporate social activities. [Grade = B]. The key terms are discussed in Chapter 6 and also in the description of Variable 64. 1 = yes; 0 = no.

66. Socioeconomic inequality. [Grade = B−]. Five-point scales of inequality among married men of income, consumption, property, carrying out of menial work, leisure, and the holding of specialized technological knowledge were set up and subjectively coded for each society. These five scales were then averaged to obtain an overall socioeconomic inequality variable. The scores run from 1 (greatest socioeconomic equality) to 5 (greatest socioeconomic inequality).

67. Political inequality. [Grade = B−]. A five-point scale was set up, and codings were subjectively made regarding the concentration of political power with reference to the relative importance of political leaders and the rest of society in making various important decisions concerning war making, dispute resolution, and so forth. The scores run from 1.0 (greatest political equality) to 5.0 (highest political inequality).

68. Family potestality. [Grade = C]. The difficulties in coding such a variable should be clear. 1 = husband plays predominant role in important family decision making; 0 = spouses play roughly equal roles in important family decision making. No cases of wives playing predominant roles in family decision making appeared in the sample.

69. Presence of polygyny. [Grade = A−]. 1 = more than occasional polygyny in the society; 0 = monogamy, polyandry, or only occasional polygyny in society.

70. Divorce rate. [Grade = C]. I tried to assess quantitatively the percentages of marriages ending in divorce, a process that often had to be based only on the anecdotes about divorce that the ethnographer reported. 1 = 30% or more of all marriages end in divorce; 0 = less than 30% of all marriages end in divorce; 9 = do not know.

71. Height of brideprice. [Grade = C+]. The calculation represents the ratio of the average net brideprice (i.e., brideprice minus groomprice) to the average income (production) or wealth. These terms are defined in detail in Appendix B.2. 3 = high net brideprice (i.e., a brideprice amounting to roughly 100% or more of the average labor income of a man; or a bride service amounting to a year or more; or a brideprice of assets amounting to more than 35% of the productive assets of an average established married man); 2 = medium net brideprice (more than a token brideprice but less than a high brideprice); 1 = token net brideprice (i.e., a few inexpensive gifts or a very small amount of money); 0 = no net brideprice.

72. Female dower. [Grade = C]. The key term is defined in Appendix B.2. 2 = high dower (not only personal and household property but considerable money, cattle, land, or other items used in production as well); 1 = medium dower (clothes and other personal property plus a considerable amount of household furnishing as well); 0 = low dower (either no dower or dower consisting only of the most ordinary personal items such as clothes).

73. Net brideprice minus female dower. [Grade = C−]. The amounts of the net brideprice and dower were taken from Variables 71 and 72. 3 = high net brideprice minus female dower (i.e., amounting to roughly 100% or more of the average labor income of a man; or to more than 35% of the productive assets of an average established married man; or to labor services or its equivalent in goods of over a year); 2 = medium net brideprice minus female dower (i.e., more than a token amount but less than a high amount); 1 = token net brideprice minus female dower (i.e., a few inexpensive goods or a very small amount of money); 0 = no net brideprice minus dower. The negative numbers designate the same values, except that the dower exceeds the brideprice (e.g., −1 = a token dower minus net brideprice).

74. Child-rearing practices. [Grade = C]. This variable was coded rather subjectively. 3 = nonpermissive child-rearing practices with some corporal punishment; 2 = nonpermissive child-rearing practices with no corporal punishment; 1 = permissive child-rearing practices with some corporal punishment; 0 = permissive child-rearing practices with no corporal punishment.

75. Practice of senilicide (killing of the elderly) and killing of the incurably sick occurs with sufficient frequency to be noted by ethnographers. [Grade = B−]. 1 = yes; 0 = no.

Ethnographic Data Used in the Calculations

#	Society	1	2	3	4	5	6	7	8	9	10	11	12	13	14	15	16	17	18
1.	Alor	4	0	0	1	0	0	0	76.0	1	1	5	3	3	1	5	1	0	1
2.	Amhara	2	0	0	1	1	0	0	23.5	0	0	7	3	4	5	4	1	1	1A
3.	Ao Naga	3	0	0	1	0	0	0	47.5	0	0	5	3	5	3	3B	1	1	1
4.	Aweikóma	6	0	0	5	0	0	1	28.8	−1	1	3	1	8	8	0	4	0	4
5.	Azande	1	0	0	1	0	0	0	61.8	1	1	7	3	4	0	4	1	0	1
6.	Aztec	5	0	0	1	0	0	0	26.8	0	0	7	4	6	6	6B	1	1	1
7.	Basseri	3	0	1	3	1	1	0	50.0	0	0	5	1	8	8	0	4	1	1
8.	Batak	4	0	0	1	1	0	0	60.2	1	1	6	3	3	3	5A	1	1	1
9.	Bhil	3	0	1	1	1	0	0	34.8	0	0	7	3	3	5	5B	1	0	1
10.	Bribri	6	0	0	1	0	0	0	45.5	0	0	3	1	0	0	5B	1	0	2
11.	Callinago	6	0	0	4	0	0	1	46.5	1	1	4	2A	8	8	1	1	0	1
12.	China	3	0	0	1	0	0	0	29.8	0	0	8	4	6	6	7	1	1	1
13.	Comanche	5	0	0	5	1	0	1	25.5	1	1	5	1	8	8	0	4	0	4
14.	Copper Eskimo	5	1	0	5	0	0	1	39.0	−1	1	3	1	8	8	0	3	0	1A
15.	Dogon	1	0	0	1	1	0	0	46.0	−1	1	6	4	6	2	6	1	1	1
16.	Fiji	4	0	0	1	0	0	0	36.5	0	0	6	2B	1	3	4B	1	0	1
17.	Fon	1	0	1	1	1	0	0	49.5	1	1	6	3	2	0	6B	1	0	3
18.	Ganda	1	0	0	1	1	0	0	72.5	1	1	7	4B	6	0	6A	1	0	1
19.	Gheg	2	0	0	1	1	0	0	55.5	1	1	6	3	3	2	5	1	1	2
20.	Havasupai	5	0	0	2	0	0	0	44.5	0	0	3	4	6	2	5A	2	0	1
21.	Inca	6	0	0	1	1	0	0	46.2	0	0	7	2	0	1	6	1	1	1B
22.	Iroquois	5	0	0	1	0	0	0	58.2	0	0	4	1	0	0	1	1	0	1
23.	Khalka Mongol	3	1	1	3	1	1	0	66.5	1B	1B	6	1	8	8	0	3	1	1
24.	Koryak	3	1	1	3	1	1	0	15.8	0B	0B	4	1	8	8	0	4	1	4
25.	!Kung Bushman	1	0	0	6	0	0	0	52.5	0	0	5	1	8	8	0	3	0	1A
26.	Kwakiutl	5	0	0	4	0	0	1	25.0	0	0	4	1	8	8	0	1	0	1
27.	Lapp	2	1	1	3	1	1	0	27.5	0	0	4	1	8	8	0	3	1	4
28.	Lepcha	3	0	0	1	1	0	0	46.8	1	1	5	3	4	0	4	1	0	1
29.	Manóbo	4	0	0	1	1	0	0	65.0	1	1	5	2B	3	0	1	2B	0	1
30.	Maori	4	0	0	2	0	0	0	34.0	0	0	6	1	0	0	4B	1	0	1A
31.	Mundurucú	6	0	1	2	0	0	0	37.7	1	1	4	1	0	0	1	1	0	3
32.	Murngin	4	0	0	6	0	0	0	63.8	0	0	4	1	8	8	0	4	0	3
33.	Naskapi	5	1	1	5	0	0	1	37.2	1	1	3	1	8	8	0	3	0	3
34.	Navajo	5	1	1	3	1	0	0	53.0	1	1	5	1	8	8	6	2	1	2A
35.	Nuer	1	0	0	3	1	0	0	32.8	1	1	6	1	8	8	6	2	1	1
36.	Nyakyusa	1	0	0	1	1	0	0	39.4	1	1	6	3	4	0	4	1	0	1
37.	Omaha	5	0	1	2	0	0	0	48.8	0	0	4	1	0	0	1	2	0	1
38.	Pomo	5	0	0	6	0	0	0	53.2	0B	0B	4	1	8	8	0	2	0	1
39.	Rif	2	0	1	1	1	0	0	19.5	0B	0B	7	4	6	6	6	1	1	1
40.	Rwala	2	1	1	3	1	1	0	19.5	1	1	5	1	8	8	0	4	1	1
41.	Semang	3	0	0	6	0	0	0	62.0	0	0	4	1	8	8	0	4	0	1
42.	Serbia	2	0	1	1	1	0	0	50.0	0	0	7	3	3	3	5	1	0	1A
43.	Shavante	6	0	0	6	0	0	0	60.0	1	1	4	1	8	8	2B	3	0	3
44.	Siane	4	0	0	1	1	0	0	62.0	1	1	5	3	6	0	3	1	0	3
45.	Sirionó	6	0	0	7	0	0	1	31.0	−1	1	4	1	8	8	1	4	0	1
46.	Suku	1	0	0	1	0	0	0	80.0	1	1	5	2	2	0	2	1	0	1
47.	Tanala	1	0	0	1	0	0	0	43.8	0	0	6	1A	0	0	4	1	0	2B
48.	Thonga	1	0	0	1	1	0	0	60.2	1	1	6	2	2	0	2	2	0	1B
49.	Tikopia	4	0	0	1	0	0	0	56.5	0	0	4	4	6	1	5	1	0	1
50.	Tiv	1	0	0	1	1	0	0	63.2	0	0	6	3	4	1.5	4B	1	0	2
51.	Toba	6	0	0	7	0	0	1	37.5	1	1	5	1	8	8	1	2	0	1
52.	Toda	3	0	0	3	1	0	0	10.0	−1	1	3	3	8	8	0	1	1	1
53.	Trobriand	4	0	0	1	0	0	0	48.0	0	0	4	4B	6	0	4	1	0	1
54.	Truk	4	0	0	1	0	0	0	27.0	0	0	5	4	6	2	5B	1	0	2A
55.	Tuareg	2	1	0	3	1	1	0	30.2	1B	1B	4	1	8	8	0	4	1	4
56.	Turkey	2	0	1	1	1	0	0	39.5	1	1	8	3	3	5	5	1	1	1
57.	Warao	6	0	0	6	0	0	0	46.0	1	1	5	1	8	8	0	2	0	2
58.	Wolof	2	0	1	1	1	0	0	37.5	1	1	6	3	3	0	5	1	0	1A
59.	Yahgan	6	1	0	6	0	0	0	65.0	1B	1B	4	1	8	8	0	4	0	1
60.	Yaqui	5	0	1	1	0	0	0	30.2	0B	0B	5	2	0	1	7	1	1	1

Continued

TABLE A.1 —*Continued*

	19	20	21	22	23	24	25	26	27	28	29	30	31	32	33	34	35	36	37	38
1.	1	1	1	38	1	0	1	1	2	0	0	0	0	0	1	0	0	0	0	0
2.	1A	1	1	58	1	1	0B	1	3	1	0B	1	0	1	1B	1X	2	2	1	9
3.	1	1	1	33	1	1A	0	1A	0	0	0	0	0	0	1	0B	0	1	1	1
4.	1A	3A	1	6	0	0	0	0	0	0	0	0	0	0	0	0	0	0	0	0
5.	1	1	1	41	0	0	0	0	4	0	0	0	0	0	9	0	0	0	0	0
6.	1	1	1	56	1	1	9	1	3	1	0	1	0	1	1A	1Y	0	2B	1	1
7.	1	1	1	25.5	0A	0	1	1	2	0	1	1	0	1	1	3	0	3	1	1
8.	1	1	1	34	1	1	0	1	1B	0	0	0	0	0	1	0	0	1	1	1B
9.	1	1	1	47	1B	1B	9	1	2	0B	0B	0B	0A	1A	1	2	0	2	1	1
10.	1B	3B	2A	24	0	0	1A	1A	0	0	0	0	0	0	0	0	0	0	1B	1
11.	1	1	1	27	0A	0	0	0B	0	0	0	0	0	0B	0B	0	0	0	0	0
12.	1	1	1	60	1	1	0	1	3	1	1	1	0	1	1	2	0	2	1	1
13.	1	3	1	16	0A	0	1A	1A	0	0	0	0	0	0A	0	0	0	0	1	0
14.	1A	1A	1	9	0A	1B	0	1	0	0	0	0	0	0	0	0	0	0	0	0
15.	1	1	1	48	1	1	0B	1	1	0	0	1A	0	1A	1	0	1	0	1	1B
16.	1	1	1	45	1A	0B	9	1B	0	0B	0	0B	0	0B	0B	0B	2	1	0	0
17.	2A	4	2	51	1	1	0B	1	3	1B	1B	1	0	1	1	0	0	0B	1	9
18.	1	1	1	49	1	1A	0	1A	1B	1B	0	1B	0	1B	0A	0	2	0	1	9
19.	2	1	2	50	1	1	0	1	3B	1B	1B	1	0	1	1B	1Y	0	0B	1	1
20.	1	1	1	14.0	0B	1B	1	1	0	0	0	0	0	0	0B	0B	0	0	0	0
21.	1B	1B	1A	52	1	0B	0	0B	1B	1B	1B	1B	0	1B	9	0	2	0	0	0
22.	3B	4	1A	28	0	0	1A	1A	0	0	0	0	0	0	0A	0	0	0	0	0
23.	1	1	1	39	1	1	1	1	3	1A	0	1	0	1	1	0	0	0	1	1
24.	1	3	1	12	0B	0	1A	1	4	0	1	1	0	1	0B	0	0	0	0B	1B
25.	1	1A	1	4.0	0	0	0	0	0	0	0	0	0	0	0	0	0	0	0	0
26.	1	1	1	29	1	0A	1	1	0	0	0	0A	0	0A	1	0	0	0	1	1
27.	1	3	1	20.5	0B	0	1	1	3	0	1	1	0	1	9	0	0	0	1B	1
28.	1	1	1	40	1	0	0	0A	0A	1B	0	1	0	1A	1A	1	0	0	0	0
29.	1	1	1	22	1	1B	1B	1	0B	0	0	0	0	0	1	0	0	0	0	1
30.	1A	1	1	42	0	0	0	0	0	1A	0	1A	0	1A	0	0	1	0	0	0
31.	3	4	1	11	0	0	1	1	3	0	0	0	0	0	0	0	0	0	0	0
32.	1	4	1	4.0	0	0	0	0	0	0	0	0	0	0	0	0	0	0	0	0
33.	3B	4	1	7	0	0	1	1	0	0	0	0	0	0	1A	0	0	0	0	1
34.	3B	4	2A	23	1A	0	1	1	0B	1	1B	1	0	1	0	0	0	0	0	1
35.	1	1	1	19	0	0	0	0	0	0	0	0	0	0	1	0	0	0	0	0
36.	1	1	1	31	0	0	0	0A	0	0	0	0A	0	0A	1	0	0	0	0	0
37.	1	1	1	17	0	0	1A	1A	0	0	0	0A	0	0A	1	0	0	0	0	1
38.	1	1	1	18	0A	1	1	1	0	1A	0	1A	0	1A	0	0	0	0	1	1
39.	1	1	1	55	1	1	9	1	1.5	1A	1A	1	0	1	0	2	0	2	1	1
40.	1	1	1	37	0A	0	1	1	0	1A	1	1	0	1	1	0	0	0	1	1
41.	1	1	1	2	0	0	0	0A	0	0	0	0	0	0A	0	0	0	0	0	0
42.	1A	1	1	57	1	1	0A	1	3	0B	0A	1A	0	1A	1	2	0	1Y	1	1
43.	1A	4	1	8	0	0	0	0	0	0	0	0	0	0	0	0	0	0	0	0
44.	3	4	1	10	0A	0	0	0	0	0	0	0	0	0	1B	0	0	0	1	0
45.	1	1	1	1	0	0	0	0	0	0	0	0	0	0	0	0	0	0	0	0
46.	3B	4	1A	44	1	1B	1B	1	1	0A	0	0A	0	0A	1	0	0	0	1	1
47.	2B	1A	2A	43	0A	0	0	0A	0	0A	0	0A	0	0A	1	2B	0	0	1	1
48.	2B	2B	2A	35	0	1B	0B	1A	0	0	0	0B	0	1B	0	0	2	0	0	0
49.	1	1	1	30	0B	0	0	0	0	1B	0	1	0	1	0	0	1	0	0	0
50.	3B	4	2A	46	1	1	0	1	1B	0	0	0	0	0	0	0	0	0	1	0B
51.	1	1	1	14.0	0	0	1	1	0	1B	0	1B	0	1B	0	0	0	0	0	0
52.	1	1	1	20.5	0	0	1	1	2	0	1	1	0	1	1	0	0	0	0	1
53.	1	1	1	25.5	1	1	1A	1	0	1	0	1	0	1	0B	1	0	0	0	0
54.	2A	1A	2	32	0B	0B	9	1	0	1	0	1	0	1	0	1	0	1	1B	1B
55.	1	3	1	36	0	0	1	1	2	1A	0	1A	0	1A	9	3	0	2	0B	1
56.	1	1	1	59	1	1	0	1	3	1	1B	1	0	1	1	1	0	2	1	1
57.	2	1	2	14.0	0	0	0	0A	0	0	0	0	0	0	0	0	0	0	0	0
58.	1A	1	1	53	1	0	1	1	0	1	1	1	0	1	0	0	3	0A	1	1
59.	1	1	1	4.0	0A	1	0B	1	0	0	0	0	0	0	0A	0	0	0	0	0
60.	1	1	1	54	1	1	1	1	3	1	0	1	1	1	0	0A	0	0	1	1

Continued

TABLE A.1 —*Continued*

	39	40	41	42	43	44	45	46	47	48	49	50	51	52	53	54	55	56	57
1.	1	1	2	1	1	1	1	1	1	1	0	1	0	0	0	0	0	1	0
2.	1	0	0	0	0	0	0	0	0	0	0	1	1	1	1	0	0	1	1
3.	1	0	0	0A	0B	0A	0A	1	1	1	0	1	1	0	1	0A	0	1	1
4.	0	0	0	1	0	1	0	1	1	1	0	0	0	0	0	1	0	0B	0
5.	1	1	0	0	0	0	0	0	0	0	1	1	1	1	1	1	0	0A	1
6.	0	0	0	0A	0	0A	0A	1B	1B	1B	0	1	1B	0B	0	0B	0	2	1
7.	1	1	0	0	0	0	0	1	0	1	0	0	0	0	0	0	1	0	0
8.	1	1	0	1B	1B	1	0	1	1	1	0	1	1A	1	1	1B	0	2	0
9.	1	1	0	1	0	1	1	1	1	1	0	0	0	0	0	0A	0	0	0A
10.	0	0	0	0	0	0	0	1A	1A	1A	0	0	0	0	0	0	0	0	0
11.	0	0	0	1B	0B	1	0A	0	0	0	0	1	1	1	1	1	0	0B	0
12.	1	1	0	0	0	0	0	1	1	0	0	0	0	0	0	0A	0	2	1
13.	1	1	0	1	1	1	0	1	1	1	0	1	0	0B	0	1	0	2	0
14.	0	0	0	1	1B	1	0	1	1	1	0	0	0	0	0	1	0	1	0
15.	1	1	0	0	1A	1A	1A	1	1	1	0	1	0	0B	0B	0	0	1	0
16.	1	1	0	1	1	1	1	1	1B	1B	0	0	0	0	0	1A	0B	0B	1
17.	1	1	0	0	0	0	0	1	1	1	0	1	1	1	1	1B	0	1B	1
18.	1	1	0	0	0	0	0	0	0	0	0	1	1	0	1	0	0	0B	1
19.	1	1	0	0	0	0	0	0	0	0	0	0	0	0	0	0	0	1	0
20.	1	0	0	0	0	0	0	0	0	0	0	0	0	0	0	1	0	2	0
21.	1	1	1	0B	0A	0A	0A	1A	1A	1A	1B	0B	0B	0B	0	0A	0	1	1
22.	1	1	0	1	0	1	1	1	1	1	0	0	0	0	0	1	0	2	0
23.	0	0	0	0	0	0	0A	1	1	0	0	0	0	0	0	0	0B	1	1
24.	1	1	0	1B	1	1	0	0A	0A	0A	0	0	0	0	0	0A	0	0B	0
25.	0	0	0	1	1	1	0	1	1	0	0	0	0	0	0	1	0	0B	0
26.	1	1	0	1	1	1	1	0A	0A	0A	0	1	1	0	0	1	0	2	1
27.	1	1	0	0	0	0	0	1	1	0	0	0	0	0	0	0	1	0B	0
28.	1	0	0	1	1	1	1	1	1	1	0	1	0	0	0	1	0	0	0A
29.	0B	0	0	1B	1B	1	0	1	1	1	0	1	1	1	1	0	0	0B	0
30.	1	1	1	1	1	1	1	1	1	1	0	1	1	0	1	0	0	0	1
31.	0	0	0	1	0B	1	0	1	1	1	0	0	0	0	0	1	1	0	0
32.	0	0	0	1	1	1	1	1	1	1	0	0	0	0	0	1	0	0B	0
33.	0	0	1	1	0	1	0	1	1	1	0	0	0	0	0	1	0	1B	0
34.	1	1	0	0A	0A	0B	0B	1	1	1	0	1	1	1	1	1	0	2	0
35.	1	1	0	0	0	0	0	1	1	1	1	0	0	0	0	1	1B	0	0
36.	1	1	0	1	0B	1	0	1	1	1	0	0	0	0	0	1A	1A	0	0
37.	1	0	0	1	1	1	1	1	1	1	0	0	0	0	0	1A	0	2	1
38.	1	1	1	0A	0A	0B	0B	0	0	0	0	0	0	0	0	1B	1B	2	0
39.	1	1	0	0	0	0	0	1	1	1	0	0	0	0	0	0	0	0	1
40.	1	1	0	0	0	0	0	1	0	1	0	1	1	0B	1	1	0	0B	1
41.	0	0	0	1	0	1	0	0	0	0	0	0	0	0	1	0	0	0	0
42.	1	1	0	1	0	1A	1A	1	1	1	0	0	0	0	0	0	0	1	1A
43.	0	0	0	1	0	1	0	1	0	1	0	0	0	0	0	1	0	0	0
44.	1	1	2	1	1	1	1	1	0	1	0	0	0	0	0	1	1	0	1B
45.	0	0	0	1	0	1	0	1	1	1	0	0	0	0	0	1	0	0	0
46.	1	1	0	0	0	0	0	0B	0B	0B	0	1	1	0	0	1	0	1	1
47.	1	1	0	1B	0	1B	0B	1B	1B	1B	0	1	1	0	1	0	0	1	0
48.	1	1	0	0	0	0	0	0A	0A	0A	0	0	0	0	0	0B	0	0B	1A
49.	1	0	2	1A	1B	1A	1A	1	1	1	0	0	0	0	0	0B	1	0	1
50.	0	0	2	0	0	0	0	0B	0B	0B	0	1	1	0	1	0	0	1	0
51.	0	0	0	1	0	1	0	0B	0B	0B	0	0	0	0	0	1	0	1	1
52.	1	1	0	0	0	0	0	0	0	0	0	0	0	0	0	1	0	0	0
53.	1	1	2	1	1	1	1	1	1	1	0	0	0	0	0	1	1	0B	1
54.	0	0	0	1	0B	1	0	1	0	1	0	0	0	0	0	1A	1	1	1
55.	1	1	0	0A	0	0A	0A	0	0	0	0	1	1	1B	1	1B	0	0	1
56.	1	1	0	0	0	0	0	0	0	0	0	0	0	0	0	1	0	1	1
57.	0	0	0	0	0	0	0	0	0	0	1	0	0	0	0	0	0	0	1
58.	1B	0	0	0	0	0	0	1	1B	1	0	1	1	1	1	1	0	1	1
59.	0	0	1	1	0B	1	0	1	1	1	0	0	0	0	0	1	0	0B	0
60.	0	0	0	0A	0	0A	0A	0A	0A	0A	0	0	0	0	0	1	0	1B	0

Continued

TABLE A.1 —_Continued_

	58	59	60	61	62	63	64	65	66	67	68	69	70	71	72	73	74	75
1.	0	0	0	−1	0	1	1	1	2.0	2	0	1	0	3	0	3	2	0
2.	1	0	0	1	0	1B	1	0	4.0	4	1	0	1	0	1	0	2	0
3.	0	0	0	1	0	1B	1	1	2.2	2	0	0	1	0	0	0	2B	0
4.	0	0	0	0	1	0	0	0	1.4	1	0	1	1	0	0	0	0	0
5.	1	−1	0	1	0	1	0	1	2.0	4	1	1	1	3B	0A	3B	0	0
6.	1	0	0	1	0	1	1	1	4.5	4	1	0	0	0	1	0	2	0
7.	0	1	−1	0	0	0	0	1	2.5	4	1	0	0	2	1A	2	0	0
8.	0A	0	0	0	1	1	1	1	3.2	3	1	0	0B	2	2	2	0	1
9.	0	0	0	−1	0	1	1	1	2.5	3	1	1	1	2A	1	2A	2	0
10.	0	0	−1	0	0	1	1	1	1.5	2	1	1	0	2B	0	2B	0	0
11.	0	0	0	0	1	−1	0	0	1.8	2	1	1	1B	1	0	1	0	1
12.	0	0	0	0	1	1	1	1	3.3	4	1	0	0	2	2	0	2	0
13.	0	0	0	0	1	0	0	0	2.3	2	1	1	0	2	0	2	0	0
14.	0	0	0	0	1	0	0	0	1.4	2	0	0	1	1	0	1	0	1
15.	0	0	0	−1	0	1	1	1	2.7	3	0A	1	1B	2	1	2	3	1
16.	1B	−1	1	1	0	−1	1	1	2.3	4	1	0	0B	1A	0	1A	0	1
17.	0A	0	0	0	1	1	1	1	4.8	5	1	1	0	2B	1A	2B	2	0
18.	1	0	0	1	0	0	1	1	3.3	4	1	1	1B	2	1	2	2A	0
19.	0	0	0	−1	0	1	1	1	2.0	3	1	1	9	2	0	2	2	0
20.	0	0	−1	0	0	0	0	0	1.3	2	1	0	0	2	0	2	0	0
21.	1	0	0	1	0	0	0	0	4.7	5	1	0	0	0	0	0	2	0
22.	0	0	0	0	1	−1	1	1	1.8	3	1	0	1	0	0	0	0A	0
23.	1A	0	0	1	0	1	0	1	3.3	4	1B	0	1	2A	2B	−2B	2	0
24.	0	1	−1	0	0	1	0	0	2.2	1	1	0	0	3	1	−2A	1	1
25.	0	0	0	0	1	0	0	0	1.2	2	0	0	0	0	0	0	0	0
26.	0	0	0	1	0	1	1	1	2.5	4	1	0	1B	2	2	−2	1	0
27.	0	0	−1	0	0	0	0	0	1.8	2	0	0	0	0	2	−2	0	0
28.	0	0	1	−1	0	1	1	1	2.3	3	1	1	0	2A	0	2A	2	0
29.	0	0	0	0	1	1	0	0	1.8	3	1	0	0	3	0	3	0	0
30.	0A	−1	0	0	0	1	0	1	3.2	3	0B	0	9	0A	0	0A	0	0
31.	0	0	0	0	1	−1	1	1	1.3	2	1	0	1	1	0	1	0	1
32.	0	0	0	0	1	1	1	1	1.2	2	1	1	0	1A	0	1A	0	0
33.	0	1	0	0	0	0	0	0	1.1	2.5	1	1	0B	3	0	3	0	1
34.	0	0	0	0	1	−1	1	1	2.0	2	1	1	1B	2B	0A	2B	0	1
35.	0	0	0	0	1	1	1	1	1.9	2	1	1	0B	3	0	3	0	0
36.	0	−1	0	0	0	0	0	1	2.4	3	1	1	1	3	0	3	2	0
37.	0	1	−1	1	0	0	1	1	2.3	3.5	1	0B	1	0A	0A	0A	2	0
38.	0	0	0	0	1	0	0	0	1.7	2	1	0	0	1A	0A	1A	2B	1
39.	0	0	0	0	1	1	1	1	2.5	3	1	0	9	3B	1A	2B	0	0
40.	0A	0	0	0	1	1	1	1	2.4	3	1	1	9	1A	1A	1A	2B	0
41.	0	0	0	0	1	1	0	0	1.2	1	0	0	1	2	0	2	0	0
42.	0	0	−1	0	1	1	1	1	2.8	3	1	0	0	1A	1A	1A	2	0
43.	0	0	0	0	1	−1	1	1	1.0	2	1	1	0	0	0	0	0	0
44.	0	0	0	1	0	1	1	1	1.5	2	1	0	0	2A	0A	2A	0	0
45.	0	0	0	0	1	0	0	0	1.3	1	1	1	0B	0	0	0	0	1
46.	0	0	0	0	1	1	1	1	2.0	3	1	1	1	2	1	2	2	0
47.	0	−1	0	−1	0	1	1	1	2.3	3	1	1	0	1	1	0	0	0
48.	0A	0	−1	0	0	1	1	1	2.4	3	1	1	1B	3	1	3	0	0
49.	0	0	0	1	0	0	1	1	2.5	4	0	1	0	0A	1	0A	0	0
50.	0	−1	0	−1	0	1	1	1	2.3	2	1	1	0B	0	0	0	0	0
51.	0	1	0	1	0	0	0	0	2.2	3	0	0	1	1	0	1	0	1
52.	0	1	−1	0	0	1	1	1	2.2	3	1	0	1	2	1	2	2	0
53.	1A	0	0	1	0	1	1	1	2.3	3	1	0	1A	2A	0	2A	0	0
54.	0	0	0	1	0	−1	1	1	2.0	3	1	0	9	0	0	0	2	0
55.	0A	0	0	0	1	0	1	1	3.0	3	1	0	1	2A	2	−2A	2	0
56.	0	0	0	0	1	1	0	1	2.8	4	1	0	0	3	2	0	0	0
57.	0	0	−1	1	0	−1	1	0	2.0	3	1	1	9	2B	0A	2B	0	0
58.	0A	0	0	0	1	1	1	1	2.5	4	1	1	1	3	1	3	2	0
59.	0	0	0	0	1	0	0	0	1.0	1	1	0	1B	2	0	2	3	0A
60.	1	0	0	−1	0	0	0	0	1.8	3	0	0	9	0	0	0	3B	0

APPENDIX B

RESEARCH NOTES

B.1 RESULTS OF THE LOGIT ANALYSIS

As discussed in Chapter 1, it is statistically incorrect to use a least squares technique for calculating regressions in situations where the dependent variable takes only two values. One method of circumventing these problems is the use of logit analysis, which involves a maximum likelihood approach and a transformation of the variables. The results, however, are considerably more difficult to interpret than least square results because the predicted dependent variable (henceforth labeled z) must be transformed in the following manner to derive a transformed predicted value (TPV) which can be compared to the actual value of the dependent variable: $TPV = 1/(1 + e^{-z})$, where $z = a + b_1X_1 + b_2X_2 \ldots$ (the regression calculated using the logit analysis).

One manner of interpreting the logit regressions is to compute TPV when the various X values are placed at their means, and then calculate the derivative of the expression when the various X values are changed. This gives misleading results, however, when an X variable take on only two values and when the mean of this variable is close to one of these values; therefore, a modified procedure is used.

In the data presented below, the number on the far left indicates the formula number of the ordinary least squares regression presented in the text that corresponds to the logit calculation; the definitions of the different variables are also presented in the text table containing the regression. TPV = transformed pre-

TABLE B.1

Results of the Logit Analysis

B5-2-1 $z_{IME} = -5.5648 + .087113\,ED - 1.9482\,PG + .067946\,WSP$ $n = 60$
         (1.6846)   (.024505)   (0.8066)   (.026920) $PCP = 75.00$

$TPVMEAN$	$= +.3215$
ΔTPV, ED from 30.5 to 31.5	$= +.0193$
ΔTPV, ED from 30.5 to 29.5	$= -.0187$
ΔTPV, PG from 0 to 1	$= -.3927$
ΔTPV, WSP from 44.703 to 45.703	$= +.0150$
ΔTPV, WSP from 44.703 to 43.703	$= -.0146$

B5-2-2 $z_{EME} = .24322 - .017415\,ED$ $n = 55$
         (.53572)   (.016242) $PCP = 45.45$

B5-2-3 $z_{EME} = 5.9278 + .057267\,ED + 2.8961\,CW - 1.7515\,PO$ $n = 55$
         (1.8884)   (.034619)   (0.9960)   (0.5268) $PCP = 80.00$

$TPVMEAN$	$= +.3937$
ΔTPV, ED from 29.0 to 30.0	$= +.0138$
ΔTPV, ED from 29.0 to 28.0	$= -.0136$
ΔTPV, CW from 0 to 1	$= +.6120$
ΔTPV, PO from 5.0 to 6.0	$= -.2924$
ΔTPV, PO from 5.0 to 4.0	$= +.3954$

B5-2-4 $z_{TME} = -.2651 + .04292\,ED$ $n = 60$
         (.5605)   (.01871) $PCP = 78.33$

B5-2-5[a] $z_{TME} = 3.4709 + .10881\,ED - .99151\,PO + 10.521\,CW - 2.0277\,PG$ $n = 60$
         (1.9243)   (.03707)   (.48484)   (37.441)   (0.8357) $PCP = 83.33$

$TPVMEAN$	$= +.9736$
ΔTPV, ED from 30.5 to 31.5	$= +.0027$
ΔTPV, ED from 30.5 to 29.5	$= -.0029$
ΔTPV, PO from 5.1167 to 6.1167	$= -.0416$
ΔTPV, PO from 5.1167 to 4.1167	$= +.0164$
ΔTPV, CW from 0 to 1	$= +.1645$
ΔTPV, PG from 0 to 1	$= -.0655$

B5-3-1 $z_{IMSL} = -3.1878 + .079111\,ED$ $n = 60$
         (0.8468)   (.021944) $PCP = 70.00$

$TPVMEAN$	$= +.3154$
ΔTPV, ED from 30.5 to 31.5	$= +.0173$
ΔTPV, ED from 30.5 to 29.5	$= -.0168$

B5-3-2[b] $z_{IMUL} = -2.7703 + .043586\,ED$ $n = 60$
         (0.8382)   (.020630) $PCP = 78.33$

$TPVMEAN$	$= +.1914$
ΔTPV, ED from 30.5 to 31.5	$= +.0068$
ΔTPV, ED from 30.5 to 29.5	$= -.0067$

B5-3-3 $z_{IMUL} = -6.1394 + .10397\,ED + 4.2908\,H$ $n = 60$
         (2.0086)   (.04073)   (1.3491) $PCP = 83.33$

$TPVMEAN$	$= +.0891$
ΔTPV, ED from 30.5 to 31.5	$= +.0088$
ΔTPV, ED from 30.5 to 29.5	$= -.0081$
ΔTPV, H from 0 to 1	$= +.7407$

Continue

35-3-4	$z_{IML} = -3.8139 + .097046\,ED + 3.6476\,H$	$n\ \ = 60$
	$\quad\quad\quad (1.0569)\ \ (.026273)\quad\quad (1.2334)$	$PCP = 80.00\%$

TPVMEAN	$= +.4239$
ΔTPV, *ED* from 30.5 to 31.5	$= +.0239$
ΔTPV, *ED* from 30.5 to 29.5	$= -.0235$
ΔTPV, *H* from 0 to 1	$= +.6437$

35-3-5	$z_{TML} = -3.7537 + .10282\,ED + 3.4677\,H$	$n\ \ = 60$
	$\quad\quad\quad (1.0360)\ \ (.02683)\quad\quad (1.2276)$	$PCP = 78.33\%$

TPVMEAN	$= +.4756$
ΔTPV, *ED* from 30.5 to 31.5	$= +.0257$
ΔTPV, *ED* from 30.5 to 29.5	$= -.0256$
ΔTPV, *H* from 0 to 1	$= +.5950$

35-4-1	$z_{PI} = -1.6760 + .050270\,ED$	$n\ \ = 56$
	$\quad\quad\quad (0.6239)\ \ (.017845)$	$PCP = 67.86\%$

35-4-2	$z_{PI} = -1.7921 + .040259\,ED + 1.4547\,CI$	$n\ \ = 56$
	$\quad\quad\quad (0.6609)\ \ (.019273)\quad\quad (0.6609)$	$PCP = 67.86\%$

TPVMEAN	$= +.4645$
ΔTPV, *ED* from 30.5 to 31.5	$= +.0100$
ΔTPV, *ED* from 30.5 to 29.5	$= -.0100$
ΔTPV, *CI* from 0 to 1	$= +.3469$

36-1-1	$z_{CIM} = -2.7740 + .08446\,ED$	$n\ \ = 60$
	$\quad\quad\quad (0.7667)\ \ (.02192)$	$PCP = 73.33\%$

TPVMEAN	$= +.4506$
ΔTPV, *ED* from 30.5 to 31.5	$= +.0210$
ΔTPV, *ED* from 30.5 to 29.5	$= -.0208$

36-1-2a	$z_{CXM} = -1.7705 + .05906\,ED$	$n\ \ = 57$
	$\quad\quad\quad (.06360)\ \ (.01919)$	$PCP = 66.67\%$

TPVMEAN	$= +.4905$
ΔTPV, *ED* from 29.33 to 30.33	$= +.0148$
ΔTPV, *ED* from 29.33 to 28.33	$= -.0147$

36-1-2b	$z_{CXM} = -2.5563 + .06620\,ED + 2.6359\,CW$	$n\ \ = 57$
	$\quad\quad\quad (0.8233)\ \ (.02340)\quad\quad (0.9198)$	$PCP = 70.18\%$

TPVMEAN	$= +.5198$
ΔTPV, *ED* from 29.33 to 30.33	$= +.0165$
ΔTPV, *ED* from 29.33 to 28.33	$= -.0165$
ΔTPV, *CW* from 0 to 1	$= +.5320$

36-1-3a	$z_{CM} = -1.4502 + .05848\,ED$	$n\ \ = 60$
	$\quad\quad\quad (0.5991)\ \ (.01847)$	$PCP = 63.33\%$

TPVMEAN	$= +.5826$
ΔTPV, *ED* from 30.5 to 31.5	$= +.0141$
ΔTPV, *ED* from 30.5 to 29.5	$= -.0142$

Continued

B6-1-3b $\quad z_{CM} = -1.9994 + .06178\,ED + 2.1947\,CW$ $\qquad\qquad\qquad\qquad n\quad = 60$
$\qquad\qquad\quad$ (0.7158)$\quad$(.02098)$\qquad$(0.8846) $\qquad\qquad\qquad\qquad PCP = 71.66\%$

$\qquad\qquad$ TPVMEAN $\qquad\qquad\qquad\qquad\qquad\qquad\qquad = +.6154$
$\qquad\qquad$ $\Delta TPV,\ ED$ from 30.5 to 31.5 $\qquad\qquad\qquad = +.0145$
$\qquad\qquad$ $\Delta TPV,\ ED$ from 30.5 to 29.5 $\qquad\qquad\qquad = -.0147$
$\qquad\qquad$ $\Delta TPV,\ CW$ from 0 to 1 $\qquad\qquad\qquad\quad = +.4176$

B6-1-4 $\qquad z_{NC2} = -1.1572 + .06766\,ED$ $\qquad\qquad\qquad\qquad\qquad\quad n\quad = 60$
$\qquad\qquad\quad$ (0.5974)$\quad$(.02076) $\qquad\qquad\qquad\qquad\qquad\quad PCP = 78.33\%$

$\qquad\qquad$ TPVMEAN $\qquad\qquad\qquad\qquad\qquad\qquad\qquad = +.7123$
$\qquad\qquad$ $\Delta TPV,\ ED$ from 30.5 to 31.5 $\qquad\qquad\qquad = +.0137$
$\qquad\qquad$ $\Delta TPV,\ ED$ from 30.5 to 29.5 $\qquad\qquad\qquad = -.0141$

B6-1-5 $\qquad z_{NC3} = -1.2312 + .04804\,ED$ $\qquad\qquad\qquad\qquad\qquad\quad n\quad = 60$
$\qquad\qquad\quad$ (0.5768)$\quad$(.01730) $\qquad\qquad\qquad\qquad\qquad\quad PCP = 65.00\%$

$\qquad\qquad$ TPVMEAN $\qquad\qquad\qquad\qquad\qquad\qquad\qquad = +.5583$
$\qquad\qquad$ $\Delta TPV,\ ED$ from 30.5 to 31.5 $\qquad\qquad\qquad = +.0118$
$\qquad\qquad$ $\Delta TPV,\ ED$ from 30.5 to 29.5 $\qquad\qquad\qquad = -.0119$

B6-1-6 $\qquad z_{IM2} = -3.2948 + .2301\,ED$ $\qquad\qquad\qquad\qquad\qquad\qquad n\quad = 60$
$\qquad\qquad\quad$ (1.1585)$\quad$(.0696) $\qquad\qquad\qquad\qquad\qquad\qquad PCP = 91.67\%$

$\qquad\qquad$ TPVMEAN $\qquad\qquad\qquad\qquad\qquad\qquad\qquad = +.9764$
$\qquad\qquad$ $\Delta TPV,\ ED$ from 30.5 to 31.5 $\qquad\qquad\qquad = +.0048$
$\qquad\qquad$ $\Delta TPV,\ ED$ from 30.5 to 29.5 $\qquad\qquad\qquad = -.0059$

B6-1-7 $\qquad z_{IM3} = -2.6561 + .1474\,ED$ $\qquad\qquad\qquad\qquad\qquad\qquad n\quad = 60$
$\qquad\qquad\quad$ (0.8638)$\quad$(.0388) $\qquad\qquad\qquad\qquad\qquad\qquad PCP = 86.67\%$

$\qquad\qquad$ TPVMEAN $\qquad\qquad\qquad\qquad\qquad\qquad\qquad = +.8630$
$\qquad\qquad$ $\Delta TPV,\ ED$ from 30.5 to 31.5 $\qquad\qquad\qquad = +.0165$
$\qquad\qquad$ $\Delta TPV,\ ED$ from 30.5 to 29.5 $\qquad\qquad\qquad = -.0184$

B6-1-8 $\qquad z_{TM2} = -2.8554 + .2334\,ED$ $\qquad\qquad\qquad\qquad\qquad\qquad n\quad = 60$
$\qquad\qquad\quad$ (1.1049)$\quad$(.0743) $\qquad\qquad\qquad\qquad\qquad\qquad PCP = 90.00\%$

$\qquad\qquad$ TPVMEAN $\qquad\qquad\qquad\qquad\qquad\qquad\qquad = +.9861$
$\qquad\qquad$ $\Delta TPV,\ ED$ from 30.5 to 31.5 $\qquad\qquad\qquad = +.0029$
$\qquad\qquad$ $\Delta TPV,\ ED$ from 30.5 to 29.5 $\qquad\qquad\qquad = -.0036$

B6-1-9 $\qquad z_{TM3} = -1.9145 + .1328\,ED$ $\qquad\qquad\qquad\qquad\qquad\qquad n\quad = 60$
$\qquad\qquad\quad$ (0.7674)$\quad$(.03715) $\qquad\qquad\qquad\qquad\qquad\qquad PCP = 90.00\%$

$\qquad\qquad$ TPVMEAN $\qquad\qquad\qquad\qquad\qquad\qquad\qquad = +.8944$
$\qquad\qquad$ $\Delta TPV,\ ED$ from 30.5 to 31.5 $\qquad\qquad\qquad = +.0119$
$\qquad\qquad$ $\Delta TPV,\ ED$ from 30.5 to 29.5 $\qquad\qquad\qquad = -.0132$

B7-1-1[c] $\quad z_{REAG} = 3.4115 - .1228\,ED + 11.774\,HF + 3.7996\,AG - 1.8018\,UO$ $\quad n\quad = 60$
$\qquad\qquad\quad$ (1.4560)$\quad$(.0359)$\quad$(5.329)$\quad$(1.3043)$\quad$(1.0287) $\qquad\quad PCP = 81.67\%$

$\qquad\qquad$ TPVMEAN $\qquad\qquad\qquad\qquad\qquad\qquad\qquad = +.8089$
$\qquad\qquad$ $\Delta TPV,\ ED$ from 30.5 to 31.5 $\qquad\qquad\qquad = -.0197$
$\qquad\qquad$ $\Delta TPV,\ ED$ from 30.5 to 29.5 $\qquad\qquad\qquad = +.0183$
$\qquad\qquad$ $\Delta TPV,\ HF$ from 0 to 1 $\qquad\qquad\qquad\qquad = +.5317$
$\qquad\qquad$ $\Delta TPV,\ AG$ from 0 to 1 $\qquad\qquad\qquad\qquad = +.6487$
$\qquad\qquad$ $\Delta TPV,\ UO$ from 1 to 2 $\qquad\qquad\qquad\qquad = -.3694$

Continue

B7-1-2[c]

$$z_{REF} = 1.4189 - .1229\,ED + 11.962\,HF + 3.4246\,AG$$
$$(0.7781)\ (.0351)\quad(5.320)\quad(1.2060)$$

$n = 60$
$PCP = 81.67\%$

TPVMEAN	= +.7892
ΔTPV, ED from 30.5 to 31.5	= −.0212
ΔTPV, ED from 30.5 to 29.5	= +.0197
ΔTPV, HF from 0 to 1	= +.5682
ΔTPV, AG from 0 to 1	= +.6122

B7-1-3[c]

$$z_{RENF} = 10.441 - .05664\,ED + 1.8539\,AG - 10.597\,UO$$
$$(5.337)\ (.02502)\quad(0.9006)\quad(5.336)$$

$n = 60$
$PCP = 73.33\%$

TPVMEAN	= +.0862
ΔTPV, ED from 30.5 to 31.5	= −.0044
ΔTPV, ED from 30.5 to 29.5	= +.0046
ΔTPV, AG from 0 to 1	= +.1352
ΔTPV, UO from 1 to 2	= −.3162

B7-1-4[d]

$$z_{CREG} = -.02195 - .04889\,ED + 10.823\,PLSC + 2.1138\,AG - 10.960\,UO$$
$$(62.600)\ (.02972)\quad(3.578)\quad(1.1024)\quad(5.137)$$

$n = 60$
$PCP = 80.00\%$

TPVMEAN	= +.00426
ΔTPV, ED from 30.5 to 31.5	= −.00020
ΔTPV, ED from 30.5 to 29.5	= +.00021
ΔTPV, PLSC from 0 to 1	= +.11651
ΔTPV, AG from 0 to 1	= +.00867
ΔTPV, UO from 1 to 2	= −.02168

B7-2-1

$$z_{REL} = .7402 - .03465\,ED + 1.7015\,PLSC$$
$$(.5978)\ (.02058)\quad(0.7568)$$

$n = 60$
$PCP = 70.00\%$

TPVMEAN	= +.6997
ΔTPV, ED from 30.5 to 31.5	= −.0073
ΔTPV, ED from 30.5 to 29.5	= +.0072
ΔTPV, PLSC from 0 to 1	= +.3783

B7-2-2

$$z_{FREL} = .5401 - .07751\,ED + 1.8169 + 2.0235\,AG$$
$$(.6170)\ (.02924)\quad(0.8198)\ (0.9344)$$

$n = 60$
$PCP = 71.67\%$

TPVMEAN	= +.6529
ΔTPV, ED from 30.5 to 31.5	= −.0178
ΔTPV, ED from 30.5 to 29.5	= +.0174
ΔTPV, PLSC from 0 to 1	= +.4177
ΔTPV, AG from 0 to 1	= +.4502

B8-1-1[e]

$$z_{SC} = -2.8297 + .03238\,ED$$
$$(0.9131)\ (.02258)$$

$n = 60$
$PCP = 85.00\%$

B8-1-2[e]

$$z_{SC} = -5.1866 + .2004\,ED - .002434\,ED^2$$
$$(2.4038)\ (.1404)\quad(.001925)$$

$n = 60$
$PCP = 85.00\%$

B8-1-3

$$z_{SA} = -2.2448 + .05225\,ED$$
$$(0.6940)\ (.01834)$$

$n = 60$
$PCP = 63.33\%$

B8-1-4

$$z_{SA} = -7.6411 + .4168\,ED - .005155\,ED^2$$
$$(2.6191)\ (.1481)\quad(.001941)$$

$n = 60$
$PCP = 73.33\%$

B8-2-1

$$z_{SCA} = -8.5998 + 2.6866\,RWS + 1.5667\,PC$$
$$(3.3020)\ (1.3277)\quad(0.7839)$$

$n = 36$
$PCP = 86.11\%$

TPVMEAN	= +.0710
ΔTPV, RWS from 0 to 1	= +.2567
ΔTPV, PC from 3.1806 to 4.1806	= +.1969
ΔTPV, PC from 3.1806 to 3.1806	= −.0553

Continued

B8-3-1	$z_{SARSC} = -8.8475 + .40630\,ED - .0049224\,ED^2 + 1.2569\,PG$		$n = 51$
	$\quad\quad\quad\;\;(3.5579)\;\;(.20186)\quad\;\;(.0026690)\quad\quad(0.8180)$		$PCP = 82.35\%$

$TPVMEAN$ $= +.3429$
$\Delta TPV,\ PG$ from 0 to 1 $= +.2833$
$\Delta TPV,\ ED$ from 29.1 to 30.1 $= +.0263$
$\Delta TPV,\ ED$ from 29.1 to 28.1 $= -.0275$

B9-1-1	$z_{NCTG} = 4.6422 - .07530\,ED - 1.8804\,NH - 1.4021\,UO$		$n = 60$
	$\quad\quad\quad\;\;(1.4208)\;\;(.02182)\quad\;\;(1.0232)\quad\quad(0.8675)$		$PCP = 73.33\%$

$TPVMEAN$ $= +.6330$
$\Delta TPV,\ ED$ from 30.5 to 31.5 $= -.0177$
$\Delta TPV,\ ED$ from 30.5 to 29.5 $= +.0173$
$\Delta TPV,\ NH$ from 0 to 1 $= -.4345$
$\Delta TPV,\ UO$ from 1 to 2 $= -.3270$

B9-1-2	$z_{NCTG} = 4.1778 - .07586\,ED - 1.8565\,NH - 1.5520\,UO + 1.3447\,GIW$		$n = 60$
	$\quad\quad\quad\;\;(1.4695)\;\;(.02328)\quad\;\;(0.9848)\quad\quad(0.9240)\quad\quad(0.6774)$		$PCP = 76.67\%$

$TPVMEAN$ $= +.6481$
$\Delta TPV,\ ED$ from 30.5 to 31.5 $= -.0175$
$\Delta TPV,\ ED$ from 30.5 to 29.5 $= +.0171$
$\Delta TPV,\ NH$ from 0 to 1 $= -.4319$
$\Delta TPV,\ UO$ from 1 to 2 $= -.3693$
$\Delta TPV,\ GIW$ from 0 to 1 $= +.3018$

B10-1-1	$z_{CTG} = -2.2922 + .06653\,ED$		$n = 60$
	$\quad\quad\quad\;\;(0.6920)\;\;(.01938)$		$PCP = 71.67\%$

$TPVMEAN$ $= +.4346$
$\Delta TPV,\ ED$ from 30.5 to 31.5 $= +.0164$
$\Delta TPV,\ ED$ from 30.5 to 29.5 $= -.0163$

B10-2-1[f]	$z_{CTL} = 5.1998 + .08305\,ED - 9.8381\,UO$		$n = 60$
	$\quad\quad\quad\;\;(5.1997)\;\;(.03082)\quad\;\;(5.1975)$		$PCP = 83.33\%$

$TPVMEAN$ $= +.02709$
$\Delta TPV,\ ED$ from 30.5 to 31.5 $= +.00228$
$\Delta TPV,\ ED$ from 30.5 to 29.5 $= -.00211$
$\Delta TPV,\ UO$ from 1 to 2 $= -.10858$

B10-2-2[f]	$z_{CTL} = 4.5942 + .08858\,ED - 9.7384\,UO + 2.7378\,MREG$		$n = 60$
	$\quad\quad\quad\;\;(5.2521)\;\;(.03372)\quad\;\;(52.491)\quad\quad(1.5606)$		$PCP = 85.00\%$

$TPVMEAN$ $= +.02365$
$\Delta TPV,\ ED$ from 30.5 to 31.5 $= +.00213$
$\Delta TPV,\ ED$ from 30.5 to 29.5 $= -.00196$
$\Delta TPV,\ UO$ from 1 to 2 $= -.09450$
$\Delta TPV,\ MREG$ from 0 to 1 $= +.21792$

---

[a] Results are for the tenth iteration. Examination of the twentieth iteration suggests that convergence is not achievable for the calculated coefficient of the CW variable.

[b] For no case was the presence of markets predicted.

[c] Results are for tenth itertion. Examination of twentieth iteration suggest that convergence is not achieveable for the calculated coefficient of the HF variable.

[d] Results are for tenth iteration. Examination of the twentieth iteration suggests that convergence is not achievable for the calculated coefficients of the $PLSC$ and UO variables.

[e] For all societies, the absence of slavery is predicted.

[f] Results are for tenth iteration. Examination of twentieth iteration suggests that convergence is not achievable for the calculated coefficient of the UO variable.

dicted value of the dependent variable; *TPVMEAN* = transformed predicted value of the dependent variable when the independent variables are placed at their means; *n* = number of cases in the sample; *PCP* = percentage of correct predictions.

The logit regressions were calculated using a computer program written by Dr. Charles Mansky, to whom I would like to express my gratitude. I received help at various phases of this work not only from Dr. Mansky, but also from Dr. Larry Mannheim, Dr. Barry Fishman, and Dr. E. M. Mullins, to whom I would also like to express my appreciation.

B.2   SUBJECTIVE AND OBJECTIVE PERCEPTIONS OF DISTRIBUTION: TWO STUDIES OF THE ECONOMICS OF MARRIAGE

> *Si vous vous mariez pour de l'argent, que deviennent nos sentiments d'honneur, notre noblesse?*
>
> BALZAC[1]

Introduction

The purpose of this appendix is to explore analytic difficulties arising when the perceptions of the participants in a set of distributional transactions (i.e., "subjective perceptions") differ from the perceptions of an outside observer studying the transactions in a comparative framework (i.e., "objective perceptions"). These problems are explored in two contexts of the economics of marriage. The first study concerns whether or not a brideprice and/or dower accompanies a marriage and, if so, how high is the amount. The empirical investigation is carried out using the worldwide sample of 60 primitive and peasant societies. The second study concerns the relative amounts of work that American husbands and wives contribute to their families. The empirical investigation is carried out using sample survey data of almost 500 families participating in a study of the uses of their time.

In both of these studies two problems receive particular attention. The first issue concerns the types of transactions involved and whether or not an exchange rate can be determined (so that we can know if the transactions are exchanges or transfers). For both of the empirical studies I employ regression techniques to show the existence of such exchange rates and to demonstrate the strong elements of exchange involved in the marriage relationship. The second issue concerns the interpretation of the statistical results, once exchange is shown to occur in a particular manner. The confrontation of the

---

[1]Honoré de Balzac, *Le Père Goriot* (Boston: D.C. Heath, 1907), pp. 121–122: 'If you marry for money, what becomes of our honorable, high-minded sentiments?'

exchange norms that I derive from the statistical analysis and the norms of those engaged in these exchange processes provides some important insights into causal elements underlying the transactions.

Some readers may feel squeamish about applying economic analysis to the marriage relationship because marriage is sufficiently "sacred" that it "transcends vulgar economics." They are advised to skip this appendix.

Brideprice and Dower

In many primitive or peasant societies marriage payments constitute the single largest economic transaction of a person's life. The subject holds considerable fascination to ethnographers, and a flood of studies on such payments can be found in the anthropology literature. Most of these studies are primarily descriptive, for determining exactly how the marriage payment system works often requires a detailed study of the entire social structure. In such studies theoretical analyses are generally limited to discussions about the relationship of such marriage payments to other important social institutions or arguments about how such payments stabilize or solidify either marital relationships or relationships between the kin groups of the respective spouses (arguments with sufficient implausibility on the surface that considerable effort must be made to demonstrate the point). Comparative studies have, for the most part, concerned themselves with conceptual analysis and descriptions of the variations in marriage payment systems that can be found in different societies.[2]

In the following discussion I begin by surveying some highlights of the discussion of marriage payments in the anthropology literature. Then, after defining some crucial terms, I propose and test a series of hypotheses about which societies have and do not have different types of marriage payments. Such an analysis leads to some very definite ideas about causal factors underlying such payments, which are then compared and contrasted with perceptions of causal elements by the participants in such transactions.

SOME HIGHLIGHTS OF PREVIOUS DISCUSSION

Brideprice versus Bridewealth. Underlying the seemingly trivial terminological debate as to whether payments made by the groom's family to the bride's family should be called "brideprice" or "bridewealth" are important disagreements among anthropologists about the relative importance of economic and social causal factors of such payments.

At first glance, the economic elements of marriage payments appear extremely important. In many societies marriage payments are fiercely bargained between the representatives of the families of the prospective bride and groom,

---

[2]Two of the most interesting recent entries into this crowded literature are: Jack Goody and S. J. Tambiah, *Bridewealth and Dowry,* Cambridge Papers in Social Anthropology 7 (1973); and Lucy Mair, "The Cost of Getting Married," Chap. IV in her book *Marriage* (1971), pp. 48–73.

and supply and demand elements are very apparent: Other things being equal, the more desirable the woman (in terms of beauty, temperament, family status, and so forth), the higher the brideprice; or other things being equal, the poorer the family of the groom, the lower the brideprice. In certain primitive or peasant societies, the brideprice fluctuates according to the ratio of marriageable men to marriageable women in the manner predicted using a simple supply and demand approach.[3] In some societies a rise in per capita income or per capita monetary assets has been accompanied by an inflation in brideprices[4]; and other cases are recorded where price ceilings imposed by colonial governments have led to a reduction in the supply of available brides and black-market marriages in which the groom's family pays illegally a price above the imposed limit.[5] In certain societies marriage rights are relatively transferable (i.e., the husband may transfer his wife to another man or back to the wife's original family) and receive a rebate on the brideprice he paid; in some societies a depreciation factor is subtracted from this rebate.[6] Among the Wanyaturu (Turu) of Tanzania where women do most of the agricultural work, the brideprice of wives (in terms of cattle) is equal to the relative marginal productivities of women and cattle in agriculture, a result which a market model of marriage would predict.[7] Indeed, in some societies the economic element of marriage payments is explicitly recognized; for example, among the Gusii of Kenya, the women say of themselves: "We are bought like cattle."[8] However, only a very small minority of anthropologists stress such economic elements of marriage payments, and they differ widely among themselves in theoretical perspectives.

Since a famous and fierce debate on the subject of brideprice in the pages of the journal *Man* between 1929 and 1932, the vast majority of anthropologists seem to believe that marriage payments have little to do with economics per se and must be viewed primarily as social transactions. According to Lucy Mair, "The term 'bride-price,' which was formerly used for the *quid pro quo,* has been rejected by many anthropologists because of its suggestion of a sale."[9] And according to A. R. Radcliffe-Brown, "The idea that an African buys a wife

---

[3]Mair, *Marriage,* discussed this phenomenon among the peasants of Cyprus.

[4]Such inflations are analyzed for a number of societies. Two recent studies are: Philip Mayer, *Two Studies in Applied Anthropology in Kenya,* Colonial Office, Colonial Study No. 3 (1951), Chap. II; and R. F. Salisbury, *From Stone to Steel: Economic Consequences of a Technological Change in New Guinea* (1962), pp. 180 ff. These, as well as most other studies, focus on long-run brideprice inflations. In some societies, such as the Wolof of Gambia (which is included in this study), the brideprice fluctuated according to the price of the main cash crop, peanuts.

[5]Mayer, *Anthropology in Kenya,* Chap. II.

[6]Robert F. Gray, "Sonjo Bride-Price and the Question of African 'Wife Purchase'," *American Anthropologist* LXII, 1(1960): 34–47; and Harold K. Schneider, *The Wahi Wanyaturu: Economics in an African Society* (1970).

[7]Benton F. Massell, "Econometric Variations on a Theme by Schneider," *Economic Development and Cultural Change* XII, 1(1963): 34–41.

[8]Mayer, *Anthropology in Kenya,* Chap. II.

[9]Lucy Mair, "African Marriage and Social Change," in *Survey of African Marriage and Family Life* (1953), ed. Arthur Phillips, p. 5, cited by Gray, "Sonjo Bride-Price."

in the way that an English farmer buys cattle is the result of ignorance, which may once have been excusable but is so no longer, or of blind prejudice, which is never excusable."[10] This group of anthropologists favors the use of the neutral term "bridewealth" and have raised two basic arguments to support their case about the social nature of the transaction.

First, many aspects of marriage payments do not, on the surface, appear similar to those of modern commercial transactions. A. R. Radcliffe-Brown informs us that most marriage payments create lasting obligations on the parties involved and, in contrast, "it is characteristic of a transaction of purchase and sale that once it has been completed it leaves behind no obligation on either the buyer or the seller."[11] If Radcliffe-Brown were trying to make a distinction between transactions with more diffuse and more specific obligation, this statement might be acceptable; taking the statement at face value, it is wrong. That is, if Radcliffe-Brown had spent more time shopping in modern industrial cities, he would have discovered a great many "commercial" transactions that violate his assertion, for example, products with explicit or implied warranties, goods or services delivered long after the sale (such as insurance or annuity payments), agreements on the part of the buyer to resell bought equipment only to the selling company, obligations on the part of consumer of certain services to cooperate with the purveyor, and so forth. In sum, in some societies marriage payments imply lifelong economic obligations between one group and another, but certain commercial transactions have the same characteristic. Another alleged difference between marriage payments and modern commercial transactions is that in many societies, the former is not bargained but is relatively fixed or determined by third parties. But administered prices or price fixing by governmental authorities are certainly aspects of certain modern commercial transactions. Still another supposed difference between marriage payments and commercial payments is that in the former transaction the good or service involved is difficult or impossible to transfer or resell. Leaving aside the large number of societies in which a man obtains a full or partial rebate on his brideprice when he divorces his wife (which may be considered as functionally equivalent to "reselling" a wife, albeit in a "social context" and often at a reduced price), such a marriage transaction bears many similarities to the purchase of an extremely illiquid asset.

Second, George Dalton and others have argued that a commercial transaction is one in which primary emphasis is placed on the amount of money involved and relatively little or no attention is paid to the religion, sex, status, lineage, or political affiliation of the buyer and seller.[12] But if a service is being

[10]A. R. Radcliffe-Brown, "Introduction," in *African Systems of Kinship and Marriage* (1950), ed. A. R. Radcliffe-Brown and Daryll Forde, p. 47.
[11]A. R. Radcliffe-Brown, ibid.
[12]George Dalton, "Bridewealth versus Brideprice," in his *Economic Anthropology and Development: Essays on Tribal and Peasant Economies* (1971), pp. 193–201.

purchased, such a bundle of attributes of the buyer and seller can play an extremely important role in the transaction, and modern demand theory can deal quite adequately with the determination of price of bundles of qualities, even when such qualities are embedded in a social matrix.[13] Although for some analytic purposes this difference may be important, for the type of question I am asking, the "social" attributes can be taken care of with an "economic" analysis. A variant of this argument is that marriage payments are not commercial transactions, which are organized through "markets" because they, like other noncommercial transactions, are organized in other ways, a distinction that defines the essential difference between prostitution (a commercial transaction) and marriage (a noncommercial transaction). But this argument is weak: The essential difference between prostitution and marriage, as many have pointed out, may not be the degree to which economic forces influence the transaction but the different bundle of rights and obligations which are exchanged; furthermore, economic factors can play important roles in any kind of exchange, even though the transaction does not take place on an impersonal level in a formal market.[14]

The brideprice versus bridewealth dispute is a sterile debate, for the basic questions are not stated in such a manner that the various issues can be resolved.[15] The most important issue is not whether marriage payments are "in essence" economic or social, but rather what insights can be gained using particular "economic" or "social" approaches. In the empirical analysis that follows, I use an "economic" approach to examine several particular issues, but this should not be interpreted to mean either that I deny the importance of social elements in marriage payments or that I think everything about marriage transactions can be explained using an economic approach. Before turning to my empirical analysis, several types of economic approaches toward the brideprice which have been used in cross-cultural comparisons deserve brief exploration.

[13]See especially Keven Lancaster, *Consumer Demand: A New Approach* (1971).

[14]Many aspects of the American "marriage market" have been captured in a highly sophisticated model by Gary Becker, "A Theory of Marriage: Part I," *Journal of Political Economy* LXXXI (July 1973): 813–846; and "Part II," *Journal of Political Economy* LXXXII (March 1974): S-11 to S-27. This model has the advantage of generating a series of propositions which can be subjected to empirical test in a straightforward fashion. One aspect of the model is explored in the section "The Exchange Rate between American Spouses" in this appendix.

Descriptions of the process by which males choose mates in various primitive and peasant societies recall to mind many aspects of our commercial economy. There is market research, advertising (where eligible men or women wear special clothing or have "coming out parties"), comparative shopping, bargaining, and so forth. If goods are misrepresented (e.g., if virginity is claimed where it is not found), they can be returned or substitutes procured. Other parallels can also be described.

[15]In recent years the debate between brideprice and bridewealth has been waged by Gray, "Sonjo Bride-Price"; Dalton, "Bridewealth versus Brideprice," and Philip Gulliver, "Bridewealth: The Economic versus the Noneconomic Interpretation," *American Anthropologist,* LXIII (October 1961), Part I, pp. 1098–1100. These contain references to previous salvos over these issues.

A Simple Correlation Approach.   A number of studies have been published which start with some proposition about what economic valuable is obtained in marriage which warrants payment to the family of the prospective bride, for example, payment by the groom's lineage for the right to claim the children of the marriage for their group, payment by the groom's family for obtaining an able-bodied worker, and so forth. Such propositions are then empirically demonstrated by finding a simple correlation between the specified factor and the presence of specified marriage payment. The correlation analysis can be carried out either by using formal correlation techniques or by more informal methods such as cross tabulations of cross-cultural data or compilation of supporting examples.

Several anthropologists have demonstrated the proposition that brideprice payments are related to postmarital residence of the newly married couple, that is, brideprice payments seem to occur in those societies in which the married couple lives with or near the family of the groom and that no brideprice payments occur when the couple lives with or near the family of the bride, when they alternate residence between the two families, when they establish a residence away from both families, or when no set rule obtains.[16] Others have argued that a correlation exists between presence of a brideprice and lineage structure, that is, that brideprice payments occur where the children of the marriage are affiliated with the family of the groom.[17] Another has demonstrated that a correlation seems to exist between the relative amount of work carried out by men and women in food-producing activities and brideprice payments which occur most often in those societies in which the women carry out a relatively high percentage of such work.[18] Still other propositions can also be found in the literature.[19]

We can criticize such studies in several different ways. First, it is quite unclear what is meant by the claim that the brideprice "represents" some particular social or economic variable and whether the brideprice "represents" the same basic phenomenon in every society, so that the theoretical structure of such arguments seems shaky. Second, most of the studies are based on reasoning, suggesting that the variable to be explained should be the *amount* of the brideprice rather than the presence of brideprice per se; yet the empirical work

[16]This relationship has been argued and documented by a number of anthropologists, including George Peter Murdock, *Social Structure* (1949), p. 20; and David F. Aberle, "Matrilineal Descent in Cross-Cultural Perspective," in *Matrilineal Kinship* (1961), ed. David M. Schneider and Kathleen Gough.

[17]This relationship has been argued by a number of anthropologists, most of whom seem to focus on Africa. These include: M. D. W. Jeffreys, "Lobolo is Child Price," *African Studies* X (December 1951): 145–184; and Max Gluckman, "Kinship and Marriage among the Lozi of Northern Rhodesia and the Zulu of Natal," in A. R. Radcliffe-Brown and Daryll Forde, *African Systems*, pp. 166–206.

[18]This proposition is argued using cross-cultural data from Murdock by Dwight B. Heath, "Sexual Division of Labor and Cross-Cultural Research," *Social Forces*, XXXVII, October 1958, pp. 77–79.

[19]A wide range of such propositions are surveyed by William J. Goode, *Social Systems and Family Patterns: A Propositional Inventory* (1971), pp. 388–390.

focuses primarily on the *presence* of the brideprice. Now it is quite possible that matrilocal societies or societies where men play the most important role in food production might have a brideprice, but it could be very small in comparison with the brideprice in a patrilocal society with important female roles in food production. In short, the empirical investigations are misspecified. Third, none of the studies I have seen has attempted to investigate whether the observed correlation between the presence of a brideprice and some other variable is due to multicollinearity (i.e., where several explanatory variables are correlated) or whether some other explanatory variable might be more highly correlated than the single variable under examination.

Multivariate Approaches. Even the most casual reader of ethnographic studies should realize that rights and obligations which are transferred at marriage vary widely in different societies. And this trivial insight suggests that in explaining a phenomenon such as brideprice, it is necessary to bring into the analysis a number of explanatory variables. Yet, my search of the anthropology literature has unearthed only three large-scale multivariate comparative studies of the brideprice, two focusing on herding societies in all of Africa and the third focusing on a large number of societies in the Congo-Gabon area of Africa.[20] In addition, several studies also take into account a number of variables but focus on only a handful of societies, so that no convincing statistical demonstrations can be offered.[21]

For my purposes the most interesting of these multivariate studies is by Harold Schneider, who examines the correlates of brideprice in 48 African herding societies. He shows that high brideprice is correlated with patrilocality, patrilineality, low divorce rate, and inheritance of wife by the groom's kin, while low brideprice is correlated with matrilocality, matrilineality, high divorce rate, and return of wife to her home in case of her husband's death. He argues that the rights a man obtains in a wife are reflected in the social structure and that these with the brideprice form a single, related complex whole. His empirical evidence and argumentation are fascinating, and one wonders to what degree we can generalize from his results (based on societies in which strong historical connections can be presumed) to all primitive societies.

AN EXCHANGE APPROACH TOWARD BRIDEPRICE AND DOWER

In the following analysis I hypothesize: (a) that both the brideprice and the dower are payments for particular types of rights; (b) that the relative impor-

---

[20]These studies are: Marion Pearsall, "Distributional Variations of Bride-Wealth in the East African Cattle Area," *Southwestern Journal of Anthropology* III (Spring 1947): 15–31; Harold K. Schneider, "A Model of African Indigenous Economy," *Comparative Studies in Society and History* VII (October 1964): 37–56; and Anita Jacobson, *Marriage and Money*, Studia Ethnographica Upsaliensia, XXVIII (1967).

[21]Such studies include those by Goody and Tambiah, *Bridewealth and Dowry*; and Edmund R. Leach "The Structural Implications of Matrilateral Cross-Cousin Marriage," *Journal of the Royal Anthropological Institute* LXXXI (1951): 24–53.

tance of these rights is roughly the same in all societies; (c) and that we can determine which type of rights are involved with the application of a simple supply and demand model. Such an analysis thus divorces consideration of the brideprice and dower from any consideration of value or cultural orientation of the society. The results of the empirical tests of such propositions suggest that considerable insight into the phenomena of brideprice and dower can be gained from such an economic approach but that room is still left for the introduction of social or other causal factors.

A Few Definitions.   Marriage payments include a number of different types of payments which are necessary to distinguish. A brideprice is the flow of assets from the groom and his family to the bride's *family*; a groomprice is the reverse flow. In this discussion below I speak only of net flows (i.e., brideprice minus groomprice), and in none of the 60 cases under examination is there a net groomprice. A special kind of brideprice is the brideservice, where the prospective groom works for the family of his bride, a phenomenon vividly described in the Bible story of Jacob's brideservice for Rachel. A groomservice is where the prospective wife works for the family of her prospective husband, a phenomenon that usually occurs only on a symbolic level for several days.

A dower is a payment from either of the families of the prospective bride or groom to either the bride or groom *personally* (and not to the family).[22] In most cases the male is dowered by his family, and the female is dowered by her family, but this is not always the case. In sixteenth-century England the bride not only received a dower from her own family but a "jointure" from her prospective spouse's family as well.[23] Among the societies in my sample, the new bride is dowered by the husband's family by the Ganda of Uganda by being given a complete household. Among the Turkish peasants or the Rif peasants of Morocco, this process occurs somewhat more indirectly as the bride's dower is financed by the brideprice. In some societies the husband is dowered by the bride's family, a phenomenon occurring among the Kwakiutl of Vancouver Island in Canada and also the Alor Islanders of Indonesia.[24] A dower is sometimes considered an anticipatory inheritance; it is noteworthy, however, that the presence or absence of female inheritance is not a good predictor of the presence or absence of a female dower, at least for the societies under examination. Finally, it must be noted that societies differ considerably on the degree to which the husband can control his wife's dower.

An endowment is a payment made between the prospective bride and groom. An example, for instance, is the "Morgengabe," which was given in

[22]I use the old-fashioned word "dower" instead of "dowry," so that the concept can be applied to men as well as women. My use of "dower" must not be confused with the legal definition of the term (which refers to the portion of a deceased husband's real property allowed by the law to his widow for her life).

[23]Mair, *Marriage,* Chap. IV.

[24]The examples drawn from the Ganda, Turks, Rif, Kwakiutl, and Alor Islanders, come from ethnographic materials of the sample of 60 societies, which are detailed in Appendix E.

various societies in northern Europe by the groom to his bride after their first night of marriage. These payments are usually quite small and are not considered at all in the analysis below.

Several features of these definitions deserve emphasis. First, a dower is not the opposite of a brideprice but rather a quite different kind of exchange.[25] Second, both brideprice and dower can include many different kinds of transfers. Third, in order to code these phenomena, we must define them to include only those transfers directly connected with the marriage ceremony. In many societies obligations of support are assumed upon marriage (e.g., among the Sirionó of Bolivia, the groom assumes the responsibility of giving his wife's mother a certain amount of meat for the rest of her life; and among the Trobriand Islanders, the bride receives annual payments of yams from her family for the rest of her life), but I have not included these as part of the brideprice or dower since they are not concerned with the marriage ceremony per se. On the other hand, I have included long-term obligations directly connected with the marriage ceremony (e.g., in cases where payment of the negotiated brideprice occurs over a period of years, an installment plan occurring in many societies where the brideprice is high).

Brideprice and Dower as Elements of Exchange. In discussion of marriage payments, anthropologists usually analyze separately brideprice and dower because the payments flow between different sets of people and for different societal purposes. An economist's first impulse would be to consider both types of payments together, for they arise from the same circumstances. In the theoretical discussion below I focus on the separate determinants of each; in the empirical analysis, I analyze them separately and then combined (i.e., brideprice net of dower).

The exchange approach toward the phenomenon of brideprice and dower focuses not only on the presence but also on the amounts of these payments. I have found it possible only to code the amount of these payments in rough categories (i.e., low, medium, and high), and so the discussion of determinants is also cast in this mold.

An economist's way of explaining variations in the brideprice or dower within a single society, or in a given society over time, or in different societies, is to examine the underlying supply and demand factors. If we follow such a procedure, then several quite different general factors come to mind that are related to such supply and demand considerations: the explicit rights obtained by marriage; the relative balance of work inputs that the husband and wife contribute to the marriage; the relative decision-making powers that they receive from the marriage; the conditions and circumstances of the setting of the brideprice and dowry; and certain general features of the economy constrain-

---

[25]The conceptualization follows the lines argued by Goody and Tambiah, *Bridewealth and Dowry*, in contrast to the conceptualization of Murdock, *Social Structure*, or the codings of the *Ethnographic Atlas*.

ing or preconditioning the exchange. For each of these general factors relating to supply and demand, we can specify several quite distinct hypotheses, the most important of which are outlined below.

Explicit rights obtained in marriage.   The brideprice or dower often varies in a quite striking manner within particular societies whenever the explicit rights obtained in marriage differ. For instance, among the Batak of Sumatra, a fully paid (and high) brideprice is associated with a patrilineal, patrilocal marriage; a low brideprice is associated with a patrilineal and matrilocal marriage. Among the Fon of Dahomey, there are over 10 different kinds of marriages, each associated with different rights and obligations of the spouses and also with different brideprices.[26] Of the many possible rights obtained in marriage, the following might be tied most directly with marriage payments.

Postmarital Residence. High brideprices seem likely to be associated with patrilocal (or virilocal) residence patterns of married couples. The brideprice would serve either as payment for the advantages the husband's family obtains from an additional worker or for their enjoyment of any wealth transfers from the wife's family to her; it might also be considered compensation for the psychic pain experienced by the wife's kin by her removal. This positive association is validated in the empirical analysis. Patrilocal marriages might also be associated with a higher dower since the wife would be removed from close access to her kin's possessions, but this hypothesis was not validated in the regression experiments.

Lineage of Children. If the children belong to the husband's lineage, it seems likely that the brideprice would be higher. This proposition has been argued by many[27] and for small samples has been shown to hold.[28] I defined lineage in three different ways to test this proposition, but in no case did the lineage variable act as a statistically significant explanatory variable of either the brideprice or the dower.

Importance of Exclusive Sexual Privileges. Since in many societies the brideprice of a nonvirgin female is lower than that of a virgin, it is possible that such a factor might operate cross-culturally as well. Two hypotheses can be derived: Societies in which a high value is placed on premarital virginity of women are more likely to have a high brideprice.[29] And societies in which

---

[26]These are analyzed by Laura Bohannan, "Dahomean Marriage: A Reevaluation," *Africa* XII, 4(1949): 273–287.

[27]E.g., Jeffreys, "Lobolo"; and Gluckman, "Kinship and Marriage." One disadvantage of using only a few cases for generalization is that it is difficult to distinguish between the impact of type of lineage structure and pattern of postmarital residence since there is a certain correspondence between these phenomena.

[28]E.g., Schneider, *Comparative Studies,* shows such a relationship for African herding societies.

[29]Two recent articles arguing such propositions are: Jane Schneider, "Of Vigilance and Virgins: Honor, Shame and Access to Resources in Mediterranean Societies," *Ethnology* X (January 1971): 1–25; and Kenneth W. Eckhardt, "Exchange Theory and Sexual Permissiveness," *Behavioral Science Notes* VI, 1(1971): 1–19. The latter study bears many similarities to this empirical analysis but includes fewer explanatory variables.

strong emphasis is placed on sexual privileges in the wife being exercised exclusively by the husband might also have higher brideprices. Neither of these hypotheses was validated in the empirical analysis for either the brideprice or dower.

Other Rights. A variety of other types of rights obtained in marriage which might influence the amount of the brideprice or dower can also be specified. It can be argued that the brideprice might be lower (and the dower higher) in societies where the husband's family can not prevent the husband's widow from remarrying outside of that family after his death; or that the brideprice might be higher (and the dower lower) in societies in which the wife participates extensively in the division of her parents' wealth after their death. Both of these propositions were tested and rejected. Other propositions come to mind which I would like to have tested but for which I could not obtain sufficient data, for example, Leach's hypothesis that in societies where women marry into a higher social class, there is a female dower but no brideprice; and in societies where women marry into a lower social class, there is a high brideprice and no female dower.[30] (The number of societies in the sample in which the social ranking of the bride and groom were generally different was too few to permit testing.) Finally, there are a series of hypotheses that I did not test because either proper data were not available or the propositions did not seem plausible, for example, the brideprice is higher in those societies in which the average marriage age of women is low and the man obtains more potential years of female fertility.

Relative balance of marital inputs and powers. Certain societies feature a female dower but no brideprice among the upper classes or castes, where wives do relatively little work; and a brideprice but no female dower among the lower classes or castes, where wives do a great deal of work.[31] Thus, the brideprice or dower seems to be related to economically valuable inputs which the respective spouses contribute to the marriage. Among the Naskapi and Montagnais of the Canadian Labrador peninsula (who are very similar since they have had the same language, oral traditions, customs, racial characteristics, and so forth), quite different marriage customs prevail. The Montagnais had a 1-year brideservice and, after the marriage, the husbands often physically mistreated their wives, while the Naskapi had no brideservice, and after the marriage the husbands did not mistreat their wives.[32] Thus, the brideprice in the

---

[30]E. R. Leach, "Aspects of Bridewealth and Marriage Stability among the Kachin and Lakhler," *Man* LVII (April 1957): 50–55.

[31]This is discussed by Goody and Tambiah, *Bridewealth and Dowry,* as well as by others.

[32]This information comes from: L. M. Turner, "Ethnology of the Ungava District, Hudson Bay Territory," in *11th Annual Report, 1889–90* (1894), Bureau of American Ethnology, especially pp. 271 ff. and 320 ff.; and Frank G. Speck, "Ethical Attitudes of the Labrador Indians," *American Anthropologist* XXXV (October 1933): 559–594. One difficulty with this example is that the two ethnographic reports refer to different periods of time and the differences may merely represent societal changes.

former society can be interpreted as a *quid pro quo* to the wife's family to mistreat physically the wives afterward. The following cross-cultural propositions can be generated:

Relative Amount of Leisure and Work of the Husband and Wife. From simple economic considerations it can be argued that a high brideprice (and a low dower) should occur in those societies in which the wives do considerably more work than their husbands. And certain positive empirical evidence for this proposition is available.[33] To test this proposition, I defined work in two different ways: percentage participation in those activities directly connected with the production or obtaining of food; and work hours in all economic activities. The latter formulation receives empirical support in the regression calculations.

Family Potestality. Generalizing from the Naskapi–Montagnais case, it can be argued that the brideprice might be higher (and the female dower lower) in societies where the husband makes most of the important family decisions without participation by or consultation with his wife. This hypothesis also receives some support in the empirical analysis.

Women's Social Status in Society. This variable has been invoked in the anthropology literature to explain both the presence of and the absence of a high brideprice (or a lower female dower). Some seem to suggest that if women have a low status in the society and are treated as chattels, the brideprice might be high since her family has no compunction about treating the marriage situation as an opportunity for economic gain. Others seem to suggest that if women have a high status in the society, the bridepride should be high since their husbands are obtaining a valuable asset. Some difficult problems are, of course, involved in coding such a variable; no matter how I coded it, such a variable did not prove to be an important explanatory variable for either the brideprice or dower.

Other Variables. Some have argued that the brideprice is lower (and the female dower higher) in societies in which marriages are based more on romantic love than on "practical" considerations.[34] (Presumably, romantic love implies a greater equality of decision-making power in the marriage.) I did not test this or similar propositions because of data scarcity and/or lack of plausibility.

Conditions and circumstances of the brideprice and dower. Various kinds of conditions and circumstances influencing the brideprice and dower can be specified. One condition of extreme importance is the presence of polygyny. Among the Kuba of Zaïre, for instance, a man who pays a high brideprice for any wife usually obtains other wives as well, and all wives have a relatively inferior status in his family, while a man who pays a low brideprice remains

[33]See especially Heath, "Sexual Division of Labor." This is also discussed in a more qualitative fashion by Ester Boserup, *Woman's Role in Economic Development* (1970), Chapter II.
[34]Such propositions are discussed by William J. Goode, *Social Systems*, pp. 388–390.

monogamous and treats his wife as an equal partner in the marriage.[35] The conditions and circumstances of the brideprice and dower that have the most promising cross-cultural significance are listed below:

Presence of Polygyny. Polygyny permits the accumulation of wives and opens up the marriage system to economic forces which are checked when monogamy prevails (and when wealthy men eliminate themselves from further bidding after they become married). If a large subset of men in the society is permitted to have many wives, this acts to increase the demand for women (that is, to shift the demand curve rightward); thus, presence of "more than occasional" polygyny should be associated with a high brideprice and a low female dower. The latter conjecture receives support in the regression analysis.

Other Factors. A plausible argument can be made that both a high frequency of divorce and/or nonreturn of the brideprice upon divorce might be associated with a low brideprice since these increase the risk element of a brideprice investment. Unfortunately, neither of these hypotheses was validated in the empirical analysis.[36] Other hypotheses, for example, the brideprice is lower in societies with cross-cousin (or parallel cousin) marriage preferences could not be tested for lack of a sufficient number of societies with such marital rules in our sample.

General economic influences on marriage transactions. In addition to these direct exchange considerations, we can also specify several general economic factors that plausibly might influence either the brideprice or the dower:

The Level of Economic Development. It can be argued that higher levels of economic development permit greater accumulations of wealth; therefore, the brideprice and dower might be higher. Furthermore, at higher levels of economic development more equipment is required to set up a household; therefore, the female dower might increase. There is some positive empirical evidence on these hypotheses as well.[37] The way in which I defined the amount of the brideprice (i.e., in terms of the ratio between the brideprice and the average annual income) did not permit the kind of testing that such an hypothesis requires. On the other hand, the hypothesis could be tested using the female dower as the variable to be explained because I defined quantity in a different way and found positive evidence for the hypothesis.

Type of Major Subsistence Activity. Of the various subsistence activities, herding provides the most dramatic instance of a critical minimum inventory. If a group relies on herding for its major source of food, and if the ratio of animals to people falls below a certain level, food requirements of the people will be

---

[35]This example comes from Jacobson, *Marriage and Money.*

[36]Some fascinating and promising considerations about the role of risk are also raised by Steven N. S. Cheung, "The Enforcement of Property Rights in Children, and the Marriage Contract," *Economic Journal* LXXXII (June 1972): 641–658. Unfortunately, cross-cultural evidence for testing many of the considerations he raises is not available.

[37]Such a proposition is empirically explored by L. T. Hobhouse, G. C. Wheeler, and M. Ginsberg, *The Material Culture and Social Institutions of the Simpler Peoples* (1930), pp. 155 ff.

greater than the reproductive capacity of the animals, and the group is headed for starvation.[38] We might suspect, therefore, that in herding societies a woman's family might be inclined to give her a high animal dower to help insure the survival of the newly married couple, and for certain societies supporting evidence is available. For instance, among the Koryak of the Kamchatka peninsula, both the Koryak relying primarily on herding (the Reindeer Koryak) and the Koryak relying mainly on fishing (the Maritime Koryak) have a long brideservice, but only the Reindeer Koryak have a high female dower as well.[39] Although a number of complicating factors enter the analysis,[40] I hypothesize that a high female dower is associated with herding societies, other things being equal; the empirical analysis provides support for this hypothesis.

Other Factors. I would like to have introduced data on the ratio of marriageable men to women (if this is high, I would suspect that the brideprice would be high; or the female dower low) and the differential life expectancy of men and women (the shorter men live vis-à-vis women, the lower the brideprice would be); unfortunately, comparable data for the sample societies could not be located.

STATISTICAL TESTS

Data Problems. In the course of an extensive cross-cultural study, Guy Swanson remarks that there were greater discrepancies between his different coders in evaluating the relative amount of marriage payments than for almost any of his other variables.[41] I found this difficult to understand until I tried my hand at coding marriage payments and ran into a number of serious problems.

First, in many societies it is difficult to determine all of the different kinds of exchanges which occur at the time of a marriage and to whom these exchanges are directed. Particular problems arise when extensive feasts are given or when many people participate in the exchanges.

[38]This kind of argument is made in a considerably more rigorous manner by Paul Collins, "Functional Analysis," in *Man, Culture, and Animals in Human Ecological Adjustment,* ed. A. P. Vayda and Anthony Leeds. Publication of the American Association for the Advancement of Science (1965), pp. 271–283.

[39]Waldemar Jochelson, *Material Culture and Social Organization of the Koryak,* Museum of Natural History, I, Part II (1908), pp. 740 ff.

[40]One complication is that such a situation might arise in certain very special agricultural situations. For instance, Theodore W. Schultz has pointed out to me that in southern Ghana, it takes several years for cocoa plants to grow before they bear fruit; therefore, the young married couple moving out to the frontier must be "staked" by their parents so that a minimum survival is insured. However, such a set of circumstances seems quite unusual.

Another complication in such an analysis is illustrated by considering the Banyankole of Uganda, a society featuring both herding and agricultural groups. The farming group features a relatively high brideprice, while the herding group has a lower brideprice but apparently no higher female dower. The lower brideprice of the herding group seems not only a substitute for a higher female dower but also a reflection of the fact that in this society women in horticulture do considerably more work than women in herding. This situation is discussed by Kalervo Oberg, "Kinship Organization of the Banyankole," *Africa* XI (April 1938): 129–159.

[41]Guy E. Swanson, *The Birth of the Gods: The Origins of Primitive Belief* (1960), Appendixes.

Second, in many cases it is difficult to reduce the various types of payments to a single dimension because the society may have no apparent standard of value and the exchanges may be of labor services, common articles, and "valuables." In such cases I tried to reduce everything to labor-day equivalents.

Third, in certain societies it was difficult to separate the exchanges and transfers occurring directly as a result of the marriage and certain kinds of exchanges and transfers occurring as part of the complex rights and obligation of the marriage partners toward the families of their spouse. Although it is theoretically more correct to include all of these obligations and rights for support as part of the brideprice and dower, this proved impossible to carry out in a meaningful manner; therefore, the definition of marriage payments had to be restricted.

Fourth, in some societies it was quite difficult to ascertain what were the "average" marriage payments since sometimes only selected examples of marriage payments were reported by the ethnographer. It was also difficult to determine the "average" annual income or capital stock of an established married male in order to determine the "average" relative importance of marriage payments in a person's life. And where several different forms of marriage existed in the society, I had to select which form (with its particular bundle of rights, obligations, brideprice, and dower) was used in the most marriages.

Fifth, although ethnographers have often paid considerable attention to the amount of the brideprice or dower, they have often neglected to specify how much the male brought into the marriage, either from his own savings or from gifts from various members of his family. I finally had to give up trying to obtain information on the male dower and to focus attention exclusively on the brideprice and female dower. In the regression analysis I include a variable representing the brideprice minus the female dower; I would have preferred on theoretical grounds to analyze a variable representing the net brideprice plus the male dower minus the female dower since this seems more truly a measure of the net marriage transactions.

Since I have defined brideprice and dower in a manner quite different from that found in other cross-cultural studies, no alternative codings are available with which to make comparison. Although it would have been desirable to have an outside observer code the data according to my definitions (a procedure followed in certain cases for some of the variables examined in succeeding chapters), my research budget could not be stretched to carry out such an exercise. Therefore, I must present my codings, made as conscientiously as I could, without adornment. Some notion of the range of variation of the brideprice and dower variables can be gained from Table B.2.

For coding the explanatory variables the usual kinds of problems arose. Since many of the variables could not be very exactly coded, I used dummy variables and focused only on gross differences. Some of the variables were coded by making qualitative judgments and must be considered as containing many uncertainties (e.g., my evaluation of family potestality). Some of the variables

TABLE B.2

Data on Brideprice and Female Dower by Major Regions[a]

	Number of societies in each category												
	Brideprice levels				Female dower levels			Brideprice net of female dower levels					
Region	0	1	2	3	0	1	2	−2	−1	0	1	2	3
North America	4	2	4	1	9	1	1	1	0	4	2	3	1
Central and South America (and Caribbean)	4	3	3	0	10	0	0	0	0	4	3	3	0
Sub-Sahara Africa	2	1	4	4	5	6	0	0	0	3	0	4	4
Circum-Mediterranean area	2	2	2	3	1	5	3	2	0	2	2	2	1
East Eurasia	1	0	7	1	3	4	2	2	0	2	0	5	0
Insular Pacific	3	2	3	2	7	2	1	0	0	3	2	3	2
Total	16	10	23	11	35	18	7	5	0	18	9	20	8

[a]The data come from Appendix A, Series 1, 71, 72, and 73.

Definitions of levels:

Brideprice

    0 = No net brideprice (i.e., brideprice minus groomprice equals zero).

    1 = Token net brideprice.

    2 = Medium net brideprice (more than a token, but less than a high brideprice).

    3 = High net brideprice (a brideprice amounting to roughly 100% or more of the average annual labor income of a man; or a brideservice amounting to 1 year or more; or a brideprice of assets amounting to more than 35% of the productive assets of an average established married man).

Female dower

    0 = Low dower (either no dower or dower consisting only of the most ordinary personal property such as clothes).

    1 = Medium dower (clothes and other personal property plus a considerable amount of household furnishing as well).

    2 = High dower (not only personal and household property but considerable money, cattle, land, or other items used in production as well).

Brideprice net of female dower (net brideprice minus female dower)

    0 = Zero brideprice net of female dower.

    1 or −1 = A token brideprice or groomprice net of female dower.

    2 or −2 = A medium brideprice or groomprice net of female dower (see definition of medium brideprice above).

    3 or −3 = A high brideprice or groomprice net of female dower (see definition of high brideprice above).

were coded by trying to make rough quantitative evaluations (e.g., frequency of polygyny or relative importance of herding) and are probably more accurate. For evaluating the relative "work" of the spouses, I tried to estimate the hours of each spouse spent in economic activities (including housework), but this involved many guesses since in many cases "work" (e.g., spinning or the making of agricultural implements) is combined with "pleasure" (e.g., carrying out such activities in a festive group) and I had to make a judgment about which was the primary activity. The uncertainties in the coding of the explanatory variables combined with the use of dummy variables act to lower the calculated coefficients of determination.

Empirical Results. In trying to test my general hypothesis about the exchange element in marriage payments, I was faced with a plethora of possible causal variables. A stepwise regression technique was employed to cull down a list of over 30 possible causal variables to a manageable size. For all of the variables to be explained, I could obtain coefficients of determination over .50 (i.e., I could explain over 50% of the variance of the dependent variable) by including a considerable number of explanatory variables, but I have tried to select a much smaller number of explanatory variables which seemed to explain the largest portion of the variance and whose calculated regression coefficients were over or close to the acceptance limit specified in Chapter 1. The final calculations are presented in Table B.3.

The most important conclusion to be drawn from the results in Table B.3 is that the exchange approach toward the brideprice and dower permit us to derive a number of explanatory variables which appear to play important causal roles. That is, in the worldwide sample of primitive and peasant societies the extent of the brideprice and dower appears to be considerably influenced by the presence of a small number of socioeconomic variables specified in the regression equations. The invariance of this causal connection, the correctness of the hypothesized signs of the calculated coefficients, and the relatively impressive coefficients of determination (the independent variables account for roughly two-fifths of the variance of the brideprice and the female dower, and roughly one-third of the brideprice minus dower variable) are all impressive. The lower coefficient of determination of the brideprice minus dower variable is probably due, as I have already argued, to the failure of this "net" variable to include the male dower as well. The variance of the dependent variable that I am unable to explain can be attributed to the influence of variables excluded from the regression (either because data were not available or because of inadvertence), errors in the calculation of the explanatory variables, misspecification of the statistical model (e.g., using dummy variables rather than continuous variables; or not taking interactions between two independent variables properly into account), and finally special factors operating within the specific societies. In short, the exchange approach toward the brideprice and dower, as I have employed it, explains part, but not all, of the differences in these phenomena among the societies in the sample.

The signs of the calculated regression coefficients are all in the hypothesized direction. Thus, the probability of a higher brideprice is increased if the society has patrilocal postmarital residence, if women work harder than men, and if men make most of the decisions in the household. The probability of a female

TABLE B.3

Regression Equations with Brideprice and Female Dower as the Explained Variables[a]

		n	R^2
BP = .5682 + .5807*PMR + .7224*RW + .5103 FP (.1543) (.1866) (.2944)		60	.4103
FD = −.1089 + .0211*ED + .7605*H − .2546 PG (.0041) (.1990) (.1419)		60	.4267
BMD = .4521 + .9068*PG + .5941*RW − .9123 H + .2613 PMR (.3265) (.2564) (.4381) (.2178)		60	.3087

Key:
BP = Brideprice (levels described in Table B.2) [mean = 1.4833].
FD = Female dower (levels described in Table B.2) [mean = .5333].
BMD = Brideprice minus female dower (levels described in Table B.2) [mean = 1.0500].
PMR = Postmarital residence [mean = .4167].
    +1 = Patrilocal or virilocal (residence with or near husband's kin).
     0 = Ambilocal, neolocal, or bilocal (residence with or near both kin, neither kin, or no societal rule).
    −1 = Matrilocal or uxorilocal (residence with or near wife's kin).
RW = Relative work of spouses [mean = .3667].
    +1 = Wife spends considerably more time in economic activities than husband.
     0 = Spouses spend roughly the same time in economic activities.
    −1 = Husband spends considerably more time in economic activities than wife.
FP = Family potestality [mean = .8000].
    +1 = Husband plays predominant role in important family decision making.
     0 = Husband and wife play roughly equal roles in important family decision making.
    −1 = Wife plays predominant role in important family decision making (no cases in sample).
ED = Relative level of economic development (lowest level of economic development = 1; highest level = 60) [mean = 30.50].
H   = Herding [mean = .1500].
    +1 = Societies in which products from herding (meat and dairy products) account for 50% or more of all food.
     0 = All other societies.
PG = Presence of polygyny [mean = .4500].
    +1 = More than occasional polygyny in society.
     0 = Monogamy, polyandry, or only occasional polygyny in society.
n_2 = Size of sample.
R^2 = Coefficient of determination.
( ) = Standard error.
*   = t statistic for calculated regression coefficient over the acceptable limit (2.25) defined in Chapter 1.
   [a]The data come from Appendix A, Series 4, 10, 22, 63, 68, 69, 71, 72, and 73.

dower is increased if the society has a higher level of economic development, is a herding society, and does not have polygyny. And the probability of a higher brideprice minus dower is increased with patrilocal postmarital residence, with women working harder than men, with primary reliance on nonherding products for food, and with frequent polygyny. It is interesting that the "economic" variables seem to play a much more important role in explaining the female dower than the brideprice or the brideprice minus dower.

The importance of several variables in explaining the presence of the brideprice or dower in the regression equations provides further evidence for the usefulness of the multivariate approach and the sterility of arguments directed toward proving that these phenomena are uniquely explainable by a single factor. The regression approach has the further advantage in that the numerical values of the calculated regression coefficients can be interpreted to indicate the relative importance of the variable under consideration. Such coefficients can also be interpreted as relative price weights (or exchange norms; or reciprocity norms) of the variable in question. For instance, a change from occasional to frequent polygyny accounts for a decrease on the average of .2546 in the level of the female dower. Insofar as my sample is a random sample of all the world's primitive societies, these price weights can be used in analyzing the brideprice and female dower in any primitive or peasant society in the world.

In the anthropology literature there is no suggestion that customs concerning the brideprice and dower are the result of diffusion. Nevertheless, I conducted statistical tests for diffusion and found that for that type of diffusion for which I could test, such a phenomenon could *not* be used to explain the variance of brideprice and/or dower between different societies.[42]

Why are my results different from those who have made previous calculations on these matters?[43] Several reasons may be adduced: First, they have defined their variables, especially brideprice, somewhat differently than I have. Second, I have included in my calculations not only most of the variables which they used but a wide range of additional variables as well, so that I had a much larger set of possible causal variables with which to experiment. Third, previous studies have, for the most part, been confined to a particular area where some of my explanatory variables show little variations from society to

---

[42] I used a modification of tests which are described in Chapter 3. Both the brideprice variable and the female dower variable showed a geographical clustering, the latter to an important extent. That is, the average distance between societies with the same rating of brideprice or of dower were smaller than for societies in which the ratings were different. However, once the causal variables shown in Table B.3 were taken into account and the pattern of errors was analyzed, no pattern of diffusion could be detected. Because I am not generalizing from these cross-section results to events over time and because no anthropologist has ever suggested that diffusion was an important factor underlying marriage payments, I am not presenting the data of this diffusion analysis so as to save space for more important matters.

[43] In this regard, the work by Schneider, *Comparative Studies,* is important to consider. Among other things, he found a relationship between brideprice (measured in absolute terms) and lineage system which I could not find, even though I defined my lineage variable in several different ways.

society and where additional causal factors which are important to that area alone may be operating.

One other feature of these results deserves brief comment. The relationships revealed in the regression formulas seem neither to reflect the imperatives of individual self-interest per se nor any sort of functional necessities of the society. That is, I doubt if any type of "functional" explanation (either of the type discussed by Malinowski, Radcliffe-Brown, or, for that matter, Parsons) which tries to interpret these results in terms of societal necessities will take us very far toward further understanding than the exchange approach I have presented. It must be added that my approach does not explain how such relationships came into existence, but rather shows the relative importance of the most important causal factors, taking precapitalist societies as a group.

The regression results from the cross-cultural study can also be used to clear up several small ethnographic mysteries appearing in the individual societies in the sample. Why do we find in China a situation where the brideprice and female dower are of roughly equal value in lower-class households but where there is often no brideprice but a high dower in upper-class households? As we see from the equations in Table B.3, brideprice and also brideprice minus female dower depend in part on the relative work of the spouses. In lower-class Chinese households at the time at which my data are drawn, the wife in the lower-class family did a great deal of work and was an important economic asset to her husband, while in upper-class families the wife did relatively little work and was an economic liability to her husband (even though she may have been a great social asset). Why do we find among the Ghegs of Albania a situation in which there was a considerable brideprice but relatively little female dower in the countryside and the reverse in the cities? Again, the argument about relative work of wives in the two situations can be invoked to explain the differences. A more complicated case occurs among the Serbs in neighboring Serbia. Why do we find in the middle part of the nineteenth century (when herding played a very important part in the economy) high brideprices and low female dowers, while in the twentieth century (when the relative importance of herding to agriculture had shifted considerably in favor of the latter), we find little or no brideprice and a considerable female dower? Certainly the herding element in the nineteenth century would suggest a female dower, but this may in part have been offset in importance by a much higher level of economic development in the twentieth century. I suspect, however, that the answer lies more in a change in relative work. Since herding was carried out on individual farms, women participated in the milking of cattle and other heavy chores; moreover, since many young couples lived in extended families with the husband's kin, the young wife's work was supervised by the older women. In the twentieth century, when agriculture became relatively more important, the men carried out most of the heavy chores such as plowing and the women did less of the direct food producing; moreover, the extended family was breaking up, and the young wife's work was not supervised as before. I also suspect that the breakup of the extended family (if it ever were very important) considerably raised in importance the problem of a newly married couple's obtaining a critical minimum level of assets with which to carry out herding or agriculture. Let me add that a considerable literature exists on the subject of the reasons why the Serbs changed from a brideprice system to a female dower system, and the controversy still rages. My speculations, based on the regression formulas of Table B.3, differ in detail but not in flavor from those of a number of specialists on Serbian ethnography.[44]

"SUBJECTIVE" AND "OBJECTIVE" PERCEPTIONS

Ethnographers have paid considerable attention to marriage payments and have recorded a wide variety of rationalizations supplied by informants as to why particular payments customs exist in different societies. For instance, a brideprice is supposed to represent a compensation for the mother's pain in bearing the child, the cost of bringing up the child (called "upfostering costs" in England), the loss of labor power in her natal family as a woman moves to the family of her husband, the price of assigning any children of the marriage to the husband's family, and so forth. These rationalizations are not consistent between societies; for example, while in many societies the prospective wife's father graciously accepts a brideprice, in some societies this is expressly forbidden because it is "wrong for a man to take pay for his own semen."[45] I developed a typology of such explanations and tried to code them for analytic purposes, but difficulties arose in coding because in many ethnographies it is unclear whether the "explanation" of the brideprice was that of the native informants or that of the ethnographer; experiments with such a variable finally had to be abandoned.

Whatever the native explanation for brideprice or dower payments, we can be sure that no native informant would agree with the explanation of these payments that is offered for the regression equations of Table B.3. What, then, is the epistemological status of my "explanation"?

It must be strongly emphasized that native explanations and the explanations of brideprice and dower derived from cross-cultural statistical analysis focus on two quite different realms of reality. The former explanations focus on a perceived reality and the attempts of the individuals in the society to understand and justify it; the latter explanation focuses on an underlying cross-cultural regularity or, more strongly, a social structural element that may or may not have been perceived until now. The native explanations of brideprice and

---

[44]Various ethnographers emphasize the role in the transition from herding to agriculture or the breakup of the zadruga as the important causal factors in the change in the system of marriage payments. Vera St. Erlich, *Family in Transition: A Study of 300 Yugoslav Villages* (1966), p. 255, also argues that the presence and the amount of the female dower is related to the relative extent of the female surplus. Although this population argument is invoked to explain differences among villages at one point in time, it might have importance explaining changes over time as well.

[45]L. O. Langners, "Marriage in Bena Bena," in *Pigs, Pearlshells and Women: Marriage in the New Guinea Highlands* (1969), ed. Robert M. Glasse and J. J. Meggitt, p. 38–55.

dower focus our attention on subjective elements in each culture; the cross-cultural explanations on the elements of each culture that appear the same to an outside observer. The two explanations are complementary rather than competitive.

If the formulas in Table B.3 give correct predictions about the relative amounts of brideprice and dower in a particular society, this should not obviate the collection of information about native explanations of these phenomena in that society. For exploring why natives understand the phenomenon as they do gives us some important clues about the cultural orientations of the society. For instance, justification of the brideprice in terms of compensation for the mother's pain at childbirth, instead of compensation for the loss of work power if the prospective wife moves to her husband's family, gives us some leads about attitudes toward sickness and pain and toward the value placed on women's work that might be interesting to follow up. Native complaints about the "fairness" of the brideprice give important clues about cultural change in the society. Although attitudes and practices are sometimes difficult to separate, the attitudes and explanations that are offered may indicate more about the informant and his cultural patterns than about the phenomenon under investigation.

If the formulas in Table B.3 give incorrect predictions about the brideprice and dower for any particular society, then we also have some important leads for research. The discrepancy between prediction and actuality may be due to the factors discussed above in the analysis of the portions of variance which are not explained by the regressions. But the discrepancy may also be due to the operation of several causal forces that are quite specific to that society. Collection of native explanations for the brideprice and dower might give us some clues in this matter as well.

In short, the formulas give us an ethnological standard of comparison. As a result, we can gain additional perspective about the ideological structures of the societies we are investigating.

The Exchange Rate between American Spouses[46]

In this section I focus on another problem in the economics of marriage which, on the surface, appears quite different. Nevertheless, the model of exchange used in the previous section can also be applied in a manner to yield not only information about the immediate problem but also new insights into the model itself. In addition, we run into new difficulties arising from differences in "objective" and "subjective" perceptions which lead me to discuss facets of the problem not yet considered.

In the discussion I analyze a particular kind of exchange occurring in white, urban American families concerning the allocation of time of the married

---

[46]Much of empirical work in this discussion was carried out by Mr. Gary Wolfram, to whom I would like to express my appreciation.

couple between work in the labor force (which yields monetary income), work in the household (which produces household services), and leisure, which is presumably a more pleasurable activity. I try to show that these kinds of decisions can be described as a type of trading arrangement between spouses and that such an approach allows us to gain considerable insight into the decision-making processes of families.

Most of the quantitative work in this discussion is carried out using survey data in which the respondents were asked to estimate the time they and their spouses spent in various activities. Using other data, I show that these "subjective" perceptions about work time differ in a quite systematic way from more "objective" measures of work time. Confrontation of several types of "subjective" perceptions about this type of work exchange with more "objective" perceptions illumine certain previously hidden facets of the analysis of exchange.

PROBLEMS OF FAMILY TIME ALLOCATION AND SOME HYPOTHESES

In 1965 the Michigan Survey Research Center interviewed a nationwide random sample of 2214 American families and asked a series of questions about how much time in a week the husbands and wives spent working outside the home for money, traveling to such work, and carrying out "household work." They also asked a variety of questions about how much time other people in their household worked, as well as a variety of personal questions about income, assets, and so forth. Then they converted such data to annual estimates. The answers they received reflected not only the respondents' own definition of work but also his or her perceptions about work time which might or might not reflect "reality." From this sample I selected a homogeneous subsample of white, urban, middle-aged couples and calculated the average amount of time they reported spent in various activities; the results are presented in Table B.4.

If we look at the total sample, it appears that men work about 123 hr more a year than women, a difference that is statistically significant at the .05 level. If we divide the sample into those families in which the wife has and does not have a job outside the home, we find that the wife works significantly more hours than the husband in the former sample and significantly fewer hours in the latter sample.[47] Similar results can be obtained for many other Western nations.[48] From the table we also see that men with wives working outside the home spend significantly longer time doing housework than men whose wives

---

[47]Several errors in misinterpretation must be avoided. First, work hours should not be interpreted to indicate actual work performed, and there is some evidence that some housewives stretch out housework so that it takes much longer than necessary. Second, I have excluded all families with more than a small amount of involuntary leisure, so these problems do not muddy the data. Third, volunteer work outside the home is not included as "work."

[48]Data on such matters for 12 Western nations are published in Alexander Szalai et al., *The Uses of Time* (1972).

TABLE B.4

Annual Hours of Reported Work of White, Urban, American Families[a]

	Total sample (438 households)		Households with wives in the labor force (185 households)		Households with wives in the lab force (253 households)	
	Average	Standard deviation	Average	Standard deviation	Average	Stand deviat
Wives						
Annual work hours outside home (including transportation)	575	868	1360	846	0	—
Annual hours in household work	2125	992	1632	763	2486	98
Annual total work hours	2700	940	2993	786	2486	98
Husbands						
Annual work hours outside home (including transportation)	2535	485	2474	468	2579	49
Annual hours in household work	288	343	369	378	228	30
Annual total work hours	2823	576	2843	580	2807	57

[a]The data were extracted from a computer tape of this survey which was obtained from the Survey Rese Center of the University of Michigan. The full results of this survey have been published in a number of pa and books of the S.R.C., of which the most accessible are: James N. Morgan, Ismail A. Sirageldin, and N. Baerwaldt, *Productive Americans,* Survey Research Center Monograph No. 43, Institute for Social Resea University of Michigan (1966); and Ismail Abdel-Hamid Sirageldin, *Non-Market Components of Nati Income,* Survey Research Center, Institute for Social Research, University of Michigan (1969).

The way in which I selected my sample from this larger sample is described in Appendix C.5.

do not have such work. We can analyze such time allocation data in several different ways.

Recently, some economists have tried to conceptualize the family as a maximizing decision-making unit similar to a firm. The husband and wife are considered to be consuming a vector of outputs (goods and services bought in the marketplace or produced at home) which is obtained either from work (in the marketplace or at home) or from outside income (from transfers or explicit property income or implicit property income such as housing services obtained from owner occupied homes). Decisions are made in order to maximize the utility of the family as a whole and a number of propositions can be derived.[49]

[49]This type of model has been extensively analyzed, and such propositions have been derived by: Gary S. Becker, "Theory of Marriage," Reuben Gronau, "An Economic Approach to Marriage: The Intra-family Allocation of Time," paper presented at the Second World Congress of the Econometric Society, Cambridge, England, 1970; and unpublished Ph.D. theses at the University of Chicago by H. Ofek and A. Liebowitz. In addition, there are a number of papers on the subject which circulated in the early 1970s and were written by Reuben Gronau, Ronald Silberman, and M. Grossman.

One objection that noneconomists have to this model is that it does not take in working for

For instance, other things being equal, the greater the ratio of hourly wages earned by the husband to such wages earned by the wife, the more time the husband will spend in the labor force and the less time he will work in the household, while the wife will work less in the labor force and more at home (so that each specializes more in those activities for which he or she has a comparative advantage). Another proposition suggests that the greater the property income, the less the wife will work in the labor force; or the greater the number of hours worked in the household by nonhousehold members (e.g., a maid), the more the wife will participate in the labor force. Using the survey data, we can test these propositions by calculating a multiple regression with annual hours in the work force by wives as the variable to be explained (which is equal to zero if the wife does not work for money outside the home) and with such explanatory variables as those indicated in the propositions previously discussed. I calculated a number of such regressions, and one of these with the best statistical fit is presented in Table B.5.

As the propositions discussed above suggest, work force participation by wives is inversely proportional to ratio of husbands' to wives' wages, inversely proportional to property income, inversely proportional to the number of their children, negatively influenced by the presence of children under six in the family, and inversely proportional to the annual hours of work in the household performed by others (which, of course, is really a response and not a cause of wives' labor force participation). The response of female labor force participation to housing status does not appear as predicted; apparently, home ownership induces more (not less) labor force participation by married women, so that the mortgage on the home (which is a useful form of property accumulation by the wife in case of divorce or the husband's death) will be paid off. Although much can be said about the sizes of the calculated response coefficients, these seem sufficiently "reasonable" that we can pass over them without further discussion. The family utility maximization model provides for a statistically significant explanation of the phenomenon of female labor force participation, although it can explain only about 13% of the variation of actual hours, which is not particularly impressive.

The exchange approach toward family time allocation is based on the notion that work is unpleasant (whether inside or outside the home) and that the amount of work carried out by one spouse depends on the amount of work carried out by the other spouse. More specifically, just as "goods" are traded, so are "bads," and exchange rates between such "bads" can be calculated in the same manner as for "goods." If we assume the society has certain norms about the ratios of exchange of different types of work performed by the indi-

---

"self-actualization," a motive allegedly prominent in the increase in female labor force participation in America in the late 1960s and early 1970s. The degree to which this motive played an important role (as opposed to women working to obtain the funds to pay the rising costs of giving their children a college education) is questionable. If this motive were important, then the regressions I run that are derived from the model should show a poor fit.

TABLE B.5

Explaining Wives' Annual Work Hours outside the Home Using a Family Utility Maximization Model and American Family Data[a]

Explained (dependent) variable = annual hours of work by wives outside home
Explanatory (independent) variables listed below

	Calculated regression coefficients
Constant	1415.3
Ratio of hourly wages of husband	−116.21*
to hourly wages of his wife	(41.60)
Property income	−.03191*
	(.01678)
Logarithm of (number of children +1)	−457.80*
	(71.14)
Presence of children under 6	−297.78*
(1 = yes; 0 = no)	(84.42)
Housing status (1 = own; 2 = rent)	−104.81
	(89.00)
Annual hours or work in household	.3335*
by nonhousehold members	(.0755)
R^2 (coefficient of determination)	.1340
Standard error of estimate	814.38
Number of households in sample	438

[a]See footnote [a] of Table B.4 for sources. The standard errors are placed in parentheses below the coefficients; the asterisks denote statistical significance at the .05 level. The husband's hourly wage is calculated by dividing total labor income by total hours worked plus transportation time; if the wife is in the labor force, a similar calculation is made for her. If a spouse is not in the labor force, then an estimated hourly wage is used, employing the calculations of Sirageldin, *Non-Market Components of National Income,* p. 31.

A large number of explanatory variables were originally included in the regressions but were later removed for lack of statistical significance. These included: education of spouse, socioeconomic class, age of family head, total family income, length of marriage, and so forth. The failure of these variables to yield significant results casts some doubt on the current theory about such matters.

vidual spouses, then determination of this norm will permit us to make predictions about individual family behavior, especially regarding the annual hours of work by wives in the labor force. It is not necessary for us to assume that an hour of the wife's time is equal to an hour of the husband's time (which, as I show below, is not really the case) or for us to assume that an hour of work in the labor force by either spouse is considered equivalent to an hour of work in the home by that spouse (which, as I show below, is also not the case). If, for instance, society values a male's work 20% more than a female's work, we may find that in one family the man works 5 hours a day while the woman works 6; while in another family the man works 10 hours a day and the woman, 12. In both cases the societal exchange norm is fulfilled, but in the latter case the couple works twice as long as in the former case. The factors determining the total time both family members work may be traced to the presence of children, the stage in the life cycle, personal predilections, and so forth, and the societal exchange norm enters only in determining the relative amount of work performed by each.

Given the societal exchange norms and information about the amount of time spent by the husband in work, in the marketplace, and at home and about the amount of time spent by the wife in housework, we can predict how many hours the wife spends working outside the home. This exchange model is a different kind of model than the family utility maximization model, for it permits prediction of female labor force participation because time allocation decisions are made as a "package"; while the family utility maximization model permits prediction of female labor force participation because of the presence of unidirectional causal factors (at least in the form in which I have stated the model). Although the mechanics of the two models are different, the predictive powers of the two models can be meaningfully compared. The two models are, in addition, complementary and can be combined, as I will show.

STATISTICAL TESTS

Assuming that the exchange approach is useful, the crucial problem is to determine exactly what the societal norms are. This problem becomes more complicated when we introduce one-way transfers of labor times (i.e., "grants") from one spouse to the other. Upon reflection, such a problem appears quite parallel to one arising in the study of foreign trade: Given data on quantity flows of goods between nations, how can we determine the prices of the traded goods, as well as the capital flows between nations? Since regression techniques can be used to solve the latter problem, we can adopt similar methods to solve our problem of analyzing the trading of work between spouses.

Let us start with a basic trade identity:

$$aL_w + bH_w = T + cL_h + dH_h$$

where L is work in the labor force (work measured in labor hours); H is household work (also measured in labor hours); the subscripts w and h indicate the wife and husband; T indicates the net unilateral transfers of labor hours; and a, b, c, and d, the various societal exchange norms. If my approach is valid, use of such a formula would tell us that if a wife increased her participation in the labor force by a certain amount, this would be accompanied by any of the following: a decrease in her work at home, an increase in her husband's work outside the home, an increase of her husband's work inside the home, or a weighted combination of these three responses. Although this seems obvious, I am also saying something more: that the amount of such responses is not random but rather is roughly the same for all families. If I can determine such response weights, then the notion of societal exchange norms between different kinds of work performed by the spouses is validated; if I can not determine in a statistically significant fashion such norms, then the approach must be abandoned.[50]

First, let us rearrange this basic trade identity in the following manner:

$$L_w = T' - b'H_w + c'L_h + d'H_h$$

where the primes indicate the original coefficients divided by the coefficient a, that is, we use as a *numéraire* the coefficient indicating the relative importance of work time of wives outside the home. In order to make the discussion more concrete, let us substitute some plausible numbers for some of the coefficients in the equation, for example,

$$L_w = 0 - .75H_w + 3.33\ L_h + 2.00\ H_h.$$

This formula says that if a wife works an additional hour in the labor force, either she cuts back 1.33 hours of housework (1.33 = 1/.75), or her husband increases his labor force participation by .3 hours (.3 = 1/3.33), or he increases his work at home by .5 hours (.5 = 1/2.00), or else some weighted combination of these three events occurs (e.g., the wife cuts back on her housework by .67 hours and the husband increases his work outside the home by .05 hours and his work at home by .17 hours). The formula also indicates that in the trading relationship between husband and wife, the man's time is considered more valuable than the woman's time and, furthermore, that work in the home by either sex is considered less valuable than work outside the home (in that more hours engaged in household activity than market activity are required to "compensate" the other spouse for additional work). Only a statistical analysis can tell us if these assertions are really true or whether we should investigate some other type of time allocation model, for example, that other things being equal, the amount of time the spouses spend doing housework is inversely related rather than directly related, as I have predicted, using an exchange model.

In using the sample survey data to calculate such coefficients, I am making a double argument: (a) Some societal norms exist which give the members of that society valuations for the time spent by the spouses in various types of work activities; (b) these norms are reflected in the activities of the individuals in the society and, more concretely, in the time allocation decisions that are made in each family. If I can actually calculate regression coefficients b', c', and d' (any or all three) that are significantly different from zero and which have signs in the proper direction, then my approach is validated, and we can use the results as indication of the societal norms. If I can not calculate such coefficients, then this means: (a) Either there are no such societal norms nor any such trading arrangement; (b) or else there are trading arrangements, but each family uses different norms, so that no statistically significant coefficients can be determined.

---

[50]One implication of this approach is that it is not sufficient to look at one kind of work performed by one spouse to make meaningful value judgments; rather, one must look at the length of time in various types of work performed by both spouses.

In the preceding numerical exposition, I assumed that $T = 0$. If a large T' is calculated, this means that a considerable portion of the work carried out by the spouses is not decided on in the manner I have discussed. It is possible to have a large T', as well as statistically significant exchange norms, and this means that several types of mechanisms are at work in determining the different amounts of work that spouses do, of which the specified exchange mechanism is only one.

Before carrying out such a calculation, several problems arise that deserve brief consideration. First, since I have not included in the calculation one major block of time (leisure, which includes sleeping and eating as well as other activities), we can calculate regressions from the survey results to try to obtain the desired coefficients without seriously worrying about biases in the results. Second, I have implicitly assumed that exchange between husbands and wives occurs with labor hours as a type of currency. If money earned is somehow considered an equivalent to labor hours, then the model must be reformulated. I calculated a number of regressions using such alternative formulations and including not only money but other variables, but none of them had as great predictive power as the model considered above. Third, the model may be misspecified because of the existence of exchange spheres, a phenomenon discussed in detail in Appendix B.3. Another series of statistical experiments was carried out to test for the presence of this phenomenon, but unimpressive results were obtained. With these problems out of the way, let us turn to the results of the regression experiment which are presented in Table B.6.

Several important conclusions can be drawn from these results:

TABLE B.6

Application of the Exchange Approach to the Determination of Wives' Annual Hours of Work outside the Home Using American Family Data[a]

Explained (dependent) variable = annual hours of work outside the home by wives
Explanatory (independent) variables listed below

	Calculated regression coefficients
Constant	1538.9
Annual hours of work in the household by wives	−.4124*
	(.0355)
Annual hours of work in the labor force by husbands	−.1014
	(.0726)
Annual hours of work in the household by husbands	.5877*
	(.1017)
R^2 (coefficient of determination)	.3041*
Standard error of estimate	727.48
Number of households in the sample	438

[a]Sources are given in footnote [a] of Table B.4. Again, standard errors are placed below the coefficients in parentheses and an asterisk designates statistical significance.

1. The explanatory power of the exchange approach, as measured by the coefficient of determination, is much higher than of the family utility maximization model.

2. The type of work and the sex of the spouse are both important factors in the exchange arrangement. If we combine total work hours (i.e., work in the labor force and in the household) of the wife and of the husband and regress one against the other, we get a very much lower coefficient of determination.

3. The amount of work that a wife does in the labor force is, as predicted, inversely proportional to the amount of work that she does at home and directly proportional to the amount of time that her husband works in the home. Contrary to our predictions, it is not a significant function of the amount of time that the husband spends in the labor force. The meanings of this apparently puzzling result, as well as the meaning of the numerical values of all of the coefficients, will be explored in detail.

4. Unilateral transfers of labor hours from the wife to the husband are also important. (If neither spouse does any work at home, and if the husband does not work in the labor force, the wife "gives" her husband roughly 1500 work hours in the labor force.) The exact meaning of this peculiar gift will also be explored.

5. The exchange approach receives sufficient verification (in the form of statistically significant exchange norms) for us to pursue this matter further.

Since the family utility maximization model and the exchange model operate on two different levels of causality, it is possible to combine them to obtain even greater explanatory power. The results of such an experiment are presented in Table B.7.

The explanatory power of the combined approach, as reflected by the coefficient of determination, is sufficiently higher than the separate approaches to show that both types of causal forces appear to be operating. The calculated coefficients of the variables representing different types of labor hours are not greatly different from those presented in Table B.6; the calculated coefficients of the variables originally used in the utility maximization model (Table B.5) are somewhat lower but still in the same general range. We can therefore conclude that using the two approaches together gives us additional information, and the discussion that follows on the meaning of the numerical values of the coefficients refers to the regression in Table B.7 rather than to the earlier tables.

Two results of the regression analysis immediately strike the eye: The first is the large unilateral transfer (reflected in the constant coefficient) which the wife gives the husband (if the husband does not work at all, it amounts to 1953.2 hours minus the impact of children, housing status, and so forth). The second is the lack of a significant relationship between the hours spent in the labor force by

TABLE B.7

Explaining Wives' Annual Hours of Work outside the Home by a Combined Family Utility Maximization and Exchange Model Using American Family Data[a]

Explained (dependent) variable = annual hours in work outside the home by wives
Explanatory (independent) variables listed below

	Calculated regression coefficients
Constant coefficient	1953.2
Annual hours of work in the household by wife	−.3589*
	(.0380)
Annual hours of work in the labor force by husband	−.1058
	(.0748)
Annual hours of work in the household by husband	.5656*
	(.1004)
Ratio of hourly wages of husband to hourly wages of his wife	−91.31*
	(36.93)
Property income	−.03045*
	(.01470)
Logarithm of (number of children +1)	−194.12*
	(68.48)
Presence of children under 6 (1 = yes; 0 = no)	−153.81*
	(75.49)
Housing status (1 = own; 2 = rent)	−101.52
	(78.39)
Annual hours of work by nonhousehold members	.2162*
	(.0677)
R^2 (coefficient of determination)	.3448*
Standard error of estimate	710.81
Number of households in the sample	438

[a] The sources and methods are described in footnotes [a] of Table B.4 and [a] of Table B.5. Parentheses and asterisks have the same meaning as in the previous table.

husbands and the dependent variable, the amount of time spent by wives in the labor force. (The calculated coefficient is not statistically significant and also has the wrong sign.) These two results are, I believe, related to each other.

Of the four different kinds of work considered in this study, the data underlying Tables B.4 and B.7 show that the amount of time the husband spends in the labor force has by far the smallest percentage variation from family to family. Indeed, roughly 68% (two standard deviations) of all men annually work a "standard work year" (which includes travel to work) of 2535 hours, plus or minus 19%. That is, a rough societal standard appears to exist for the amount of time men spend outside the home in the labor force. If this is true, then any marked deviation from such a norm may be considered only as a "temporary aberration" (e.g., sickness) which will soon be corrected and which should not significantly influence the normal exchange arrangement between wives and husbands regarding those types of work for which society's absolute standards are sufficiently weaker (as manifested by the much higher coefficients of variation) that exchange is permitted.

The "gift component" of the calculated exchange formula (the constant coefficient) thus becomes a partial or full offset for the "gift" of work time in the labor force which men are expected to carry out as a matter of course. Only in the rare case where the husband does not participate in the labor force or do housework does this constant coefficient represent a true unilateral transfer.

The exchange norms derived from the regression coefficients thus represent the time allocation regarding the distribution of a wife's work between the marketplace and the home and the amount of time men spend working at home. And they give us a familiar picture: When a wife works an additional amount of time in the labor force, either she cuts back on the time she spends working at home, or her husband increases his amount of this housework, or a weighted combination of these two events occurs. What is most important in this picture is that very definite exchange norms can be determined and that we can analyze these exchange norms by holding all factors constant except the two we are interested in.

Our enthusiasm in finding such exchange norms is somewhat tempered when we begin to examine the numerical value of the derived exchange norms, rather than merely looking at the signs of the calculated coefficients, for a controversial picture emerges. As we might expect, the time a wife spends working in the house is valued less than the amount of time a husband spends working in the house: Other things being equal, if a wife increases her household work by 1 hour, the husband increases his work by .63 hours (.63 = .3589/.5656). However, the wife's work outside the home seems to be valued more than the housework of either spouse: Other things being equal, if a wife increases her work outside the home by 1 hour, either she cuts back on her housework by 2.79 hours (2.79 = 1/.3589), or the husband increases his work at home by 1.77 hours (1.77 = 1/.5656), or there is some weighted combination of these responses (e.g., the wife cuts back on her housework by .60 hours, and the husband increases his housework by 1.39 hours). These results do not correspond to the intuitive picture that many of us have about American families, that is, that the wife's work outside the home would be valued less, not more, than housework by either spouse.[51]

We have now arrived at an uncomfortable situation: Husbands and wives tell the survey worker that they behave in a particular manner, and from such data we are able to derive a predicted exchange pattern in that the coefficients are statistically significant and have the right signs. Nevertheless, when we

---

[51]Some may object because the results are not consistent with the aggregative data presented in Table B.4. However, these aggregate data do not hold all causal factors constant in the manner of the regression analysis, so that comparisons can not easily be made. It is the greater valuation of a wife's work outside the home in comparison with the husband's begrudged household work which does not ring true.

examine the derived exchange norms, we arrive at conclusions which run contrary to some intuitive notions about the subject. That is, husbands and wives talk as if they trade "bads" with each other following societal exchange norms, yet the norms do not correspond with what many believe to be reality. One answer to the problem is simple: Our intuitive notions are incorrect, but this seems too simple. Another answer is that my statistical methods of analysis lie at the root of our difficulties, but I do not believe that the calculated coefficients contain sufficient bias to so skew the results. A more plausible explanation, I believe, is based on differences between what people say they do and what they actually do. We are brought again to the problem of differences in subjective and objective perceptions of exchange (in this case time usage), and we must examine several new facets of this problem.

"SUBJECTIVE" AND "OBJECTIVE" PERCEPTIONS

The data used in the above calculations were made from subjective estimates. That is, the respondents defined the terms they used and estimated the amount of time they and their spouses spent in various types of activities. The "work" designated by the respondents may not have been the "work" which they and their spouses actually traded, or the work which either they or their spouses carried out. How can we obtain data about the real work which spouses carried out?

One year later the Michigan Survey Research Center conducted a second nationwide study of time usage, this time asking each respondent to keep time diaries for a week. The various types of activities were broken down much more carefully, and the results have recently been published showing average minutes per week spent in some 90 different activities. If we assume a 50-week work year (omitting two vacation weeks), we can compare these "objective" time estimates to the previous "subjective" estimates; the results of such an exercise are presented in Table B.8. Some startling differences are revealed, and in order to trace the source of difficulties, the results of the "subjective" estimates by each type of respondent are also given.

The two samples have remarkably similar estimates of household work by women and work in the labor force of men; and they show remarkable differences in estimates of work in the labor force by women and household work by men. The samples are somewhat different, especially since the "subjective" sample covers a more homogeneous group of people. However, both samples include families of a considerable income range, and in both samples roughly 40% of the wives work for money outside the home. Two questions arise: How can we explain the differences in the "subjective" and "objective" perceptions of time? And how do such differences affect our regression results of Table B.7 and the way in which we interpret them?

The difference in time perceptions can, I believe, be understood if we take into account several rather trivial sociological observations about American

TABLE B.8

"Subjective" and "Objective" Perceptions of Work Time of Husbands and Wives in American Families[a]

	Sample size	% of wives in labor force	Work of wives: Annual hours			Work of husbands: Annual hours		
			In labor force	At home	Total	In labor force	At home	Tota
"Objective" sample	1243	39	774	2125	2900	2625	445	3070
"Subjective" sample	438	42	575	2125	2700	2535	288	2823
Ratio of objective to subjective	—	—	(74%)	(100%)	(93%)	(97%)	(65%)	(92%
Respondents in "subjective" sample[b]								
Husband only	62	42	716	2077	2793	2722	353	3075
Wife only	25	42	495	2195	2690	2425	220	2645
Husband and wife together	198	42	545	2068	2613	2499	279	2778
Husband plus another	20	42	529	2389	2918	2567	366	2933
Wife plus another	20	42	148	2322	2470	2857	149	3006
Husband and wife plus another	113	42	617	2188	2805	2459	291	2750

Definitions:
Hours in work force:
  "Subjective" sample: Hours "working outside" in either a "main job" or a "second job" plus time spe getting to work and home again.
  "Objective" sample: Hours spent outside the home on either main job or second job plus hours of pr fessional and other work brought home plus time spent in travel to workplace ar back (only "primary" work).
Hours in household work:
  "Subjective" sample: Regular housework (cleaning, meals, and so forth) and child care.
  "Objective" sample: Food preparation, meal cleanup, cleaning house, outdoor chores, clothes cleanir and ironing, marketing and shopping, gardening, home animal care, time spe obtaining repairs or administrative services, upkeep of clothes and sewing, baby ar child care, helping child with homework, home repairs, and other upkeep (on "primary" work).

[a]The "objective" estimates are drawn from Szalai *et al.,* pp. 640–647. The sample is more heterogeneou than the "subjective" estimates, but for the purposes I use the results, I do not believe this to be a seriou problem. The data for men represent a weighted average of employed married men with and without childre the data for women represent a weighted average of time spent by married women with and without outsid employment and with and without children. The weights used are the number of respondents in each categor so that the data presented in this table represent only time spent by married couples for the sample covering th entire United States and not Szalai's entire sample.

The "subjective" estimates are drawn from the source listed in footnote [a], Table B.4.

[b]Subsamples of families with and without wives in the labor force reweighted so that relative weights of th subsamples are the same as the sample as a whole.

society. First, housework has traditionally been considered primarily as "woman's work," while jobs outside the home (especially those with wide public visibility) have been considered "man's work." Second, in the decades preceding the carrying out of this survey work, an increasing percentage of married women were entering the labor force. Third, considerable emphasis was being placed by various groups and organizations to make housework more "respectable" for men (e.g., the "togetherness" slogans or, more radically, the first public stirring of various segments of the American feminist movement that argued for a more general reallocation of time among activities by husbands and wives).

On a psychological level the respondents to the "subjective" survey may have been embarrassed to admit (either to themselves or to the survey worker) that they were engaged in work that was still socially defined as more proper to a member of the opposite sex. On a sociological level, the direction of misperceptions is exactly what one would predict, taking into consideration cultural lags, that is, the movement away from old norms of time allocation. It is interesting that both men and women underestimated the time that "objectively" men spent on housework (albeit, female respondents underestimated this datum more) and that both men and women also underestimated the time that "objectively" women spent working outside the home. The confrontation of the "objective" and "subjective" data on these accounts give an interesting picture of the basic misperceptions; if the data from the "objective" sample could be broken down by age and education of the couple and compared with similarly classified data from the "subjective" sample, an even more fascinating picture could be obtained. A whole range of more subtle issues can also be explored with such data (e.g., changes in responses when both spouses are answering the questions), but I must reluctantly leave these to the reader.

Discovery of such differences in "objective" and "subjective" estimates of time usage suggests two interpretations of the regression results in Table B.7. According to a more timid interpretation, the results show that an exchange mechanism of time usage exists in the "symbolic economy" of the family; moreover, this symbolic economy is sufficiently similar for all of the families in the society that societal exchange norms can be derived. Or, in other words, American married couples tell us that they allocate their time in particular ways and that we can induce a societal norm. However, whether the couples perceive the mechanism of exchange in the manner I have argued or, indeed, whether they believe that they trade work times following societal norms at all is not clear since societal norms can operate through the structuring of expectations and values in a manner such that the exchange norm in its nakedness is neither observed nor suspected. A bolder interpretation of the differences in the "objective" and "subjective" estimates of time usage would include one additional idea. Since there is no reason to suspect that misperceptions of time usage would bias the statistical analysis in a manner to cause an exchange mechanism to be revealed where none existed in reality, the "subjective" results demonstrate the actual existence of an exchange mechanism, even though the derived exchange coefficients are distorted. That is, since we are dealing with three calculated coefficients, misperceptions in two out of the three time variables would bring about distorted coefficients for all of the time usage variables, while still revealing the existence of an exchange mechanism.

Although I hold the bolder interpretation, it contains an inference that some may not wish to make. The common conclusion of both is that the exchange mechanism that is found by looking at the regression coefficients in Table B.7 is still considered to exist; the interpretations differ concerning the level of reality at which inferences may be made.

Ideally, we should explore exchange norms between husbands and wives using the statistical methods described earlier with "objective" time budget data and also with different definitions of "work" (since the way in which I "objectively" define work may not correspond exactly with the definition of work that is used in the intrafamilial exchange process). Unfortunately, I could not obtain such data and, therefore, must leave this further empirical examination of exchange norms and subsequent comparisons with the "subjective" data to some future social scientist. Another type of interesting confrontation between "subjective" and "objective" perceptions would be between the exchange norms derived from the statistical analysis of "objective" data and the exchange norms which the respondents believe to be "fair." Even though exchange norms derived from "subjective" and "objective" time usage data may be similar sometime in the future (which, superficially, suggests an equilibrium), if these norms differ from those perceived to be "fair," then it seems likely either that the norms will converge or there will be considerable conflict between husbands and wives. Finally, it would be useful to broaden this analysis of intrafamily exchange so as to include "subjective" and "objective" perceptions of exchange of positive "goods" and also long-term exchanges. (E.g., the wife works to put her husband through graduate school in hopes he will do the same for her.)

Summary and Conclusions

RESULTS OF THE EXPLORATIONS OF THE ECONOMICS OF MARRIAGE

In the first part of this appendix I examine variations in brideprice and female dower in different societies and argue that there are certain economic and social factors entering the marriage transaction that allow us to predict the amount and direction of the brideprice and the amount of the dower. Using a simple supply and demand approach, I propose a considerable variety of causal variables that might operate cross-culturally and then conduct a regression analysis to test empirically their relative importance. It turns out that three or four variables are sufficient to explain from one-third to two-fifths of the variation in the brideprice or dower variable. More specifically, the amount of the brideprice is influenced by postmarital residence pattern, the relative amount of work carried out by the spouses, and family potestality. The amount of the female dower is dependent on the level of economic development of the society, the frequency of polygyny, and whether or not herding is the most important subsistence activity. Finally, the amount of the brideprice minus female dower is influenced by the relative work of the spouses, the frequency of polygyny, the importance of herding, and postmarital residence. All of these factors influenced the explained variables in the direction predicted from the economic considerations. The calculated regression coefficients represent exchange norms that underlie marital transactions in the various cultures of the sample. Deviations from these exchange norms represent types of reciprocal exchange not included in the regression calculation or particular transfer elements that can best be explored by examining the individual societies more closely.

In the second part of the appendix I argue that the relative amounts of time that husbands and wives spend in various unpleasant activities (considered here as different types of work) is determined by societal norms in a manner such that the process can be conceptualized as a type of exchange. With survey data from white, urban American families I show that the amount of time that American husbands and wives perceive they are spending in different work activities reveals the existence of the postulated exchange norms. However, the exchange norms derived from the perceptions data seem quite different from those actually existing in the society, and confrontation of "subjective" and "objective" data on time usage reveals some systematic differences. The exchange norms derived from the "subjective" perceptions reveal an exchange process operating in the perceived realm of reality, and as I further suggest, they may indeed reveal an exchange process occurring in "actual" reality since the misperceptions of time should not cause a false discovery of exchange but merely distorted exchange norms.

SOME BROADER IMPLICATIONS FOR THE ANALYSIS OF
DISTRIBUTION

Since a major purpose of these empirical investigations is to explore implications of the reciprocity model of exchange and to carry forward themes from the analysis of Eskimo exchange in Chapter 4, it is useful to review quite explicitly some of the theoretical and methodological implications of these studies.

In both this appendix and Chapter 4 I start with the assumption that an exchange model is applicable and with the aid of a regression analysis investigate whether the data support such an assumption. The problems investigated are quite different—an intracultural study of all types of exchange outside the family, an intracultural study of certain types of exchange within the family, and a cross-cultural study of one particular type of exchange. The analysis shows that in all three cases the exchange model helps us to explain a certain part of the phenomenon under investigation but that certain flows of goods or services represent transfers for which other explanations are needed. In the case of the investigation of the Eskimo economy, a number of social, economic, and political variables are used in a systematic fashion to explain deviations from balanced exchange accounts; in the study of brideprice and dower and of exchange between husbands and wives I could not attempt an exploration of these transfer elements in such a formal manner.

One of the difficulties in applying the exchange model is determining the exchange rates between various goods and services. In the case of Eskimo exchange this problem could be circumvented because exchange accounts for each particular item were roughly in the same degree of imbalance. In the case of brideprices and dower or intrafamilial exchange, the exchange norms had to be calculated by means of a regression analysis, a procedure that can be fruitfully applied in a wide number of other cases of exchange as well. The determination of exchange norms can be applied not only to "objective" data (i.e., data of flows of goods or services as observed by someone outside the exchange process) but also to "subjective" data (i.e., data on flows of goods or services observed by the participants), which are not necessarily in accord with "objective" reality.

In each of these three cases, wide discrepancies appear between "objective" and "subjective" exchange data. Aspects of such discrepancies have been discussed in the vast literature dealing with differences between "value" and "price" or with "false consciousness," "cognitive dissonance," "defense mechanisms," or "neurosis," but such analyses do not greatly aid us in understanding the problems raised in the empirical investigations. In all three cases, however, confrontation of the "objective" and "subjective" realities yields many additional insights. In the case of Eskimo exchange I argued that the perception of reciprocity (balanced exchange accounts) leads to nonreciprocal exchange since people are not unduly alarmed at imbalance "in the short run" and do not bother to keep close exchange accounts; while a perception of nonreciprocal exchange leads to quite balanced exchange since everyone is watching out to see that accounts are balanced. In the case of brideprice and dower I suggest that societal explanations of the reasons underlying such transactions tell us less about the transaction itself than about the cultural matrix in which the transaction takes place. And in the case of intrafamilial exchange I argue that false perceptions of the exchange relation give us important clues about changing norms and cultural lags.

Several types of general conclusions can be drawn from these studies: First, even though we are examining nonmonetary exchange transactions, we can use many of the analytic tools developed by economists. In many cases such tools will permit us actually to impute the exchange norms expressed in physical quantities or other *numéraires.*

Second, distributional transactions often contain elements both of exchange and transfer or reciprocity and nonreciprocity. By refusing to recognize the existence of such amalgams and by trying to characterize particular types of exchange as exclusively one type or another, we may be missing important elements in the reality of the transaction. It must also be noted that in many cases there are important practical reasons why only one element of the amalgam can be studied at a time, and in such cases the other element must either receive attention at a later point, or if this is impossible, consciousness of its existence must be held to act as a spiritual grain of salt to add to the conclusions of the element under examination.

Third, distributional transactions have both objective and subjective realities; furthermore, each of these realities may have several levels. For instance, in the analysis of marital exchange of time there is one subjective reality corresponding to perceptions about actual time usages, another level of reality corresponding to the perceived norm of exchange (even if it is not followed), and still another level corresponding to ethical beliefs about what is fair. In cross-cultural work the primary focus of investigation is on a certain kind of "objective" reality that results from the analysis of events using standardized concepts and empirical methods. Some cross-cultural studies could focus on certain "subjective" realities, for example, rationalizations of the brideprice, creation myths, or particular ethical views concerning senilicide, but such studies would require enormous effort.

Fourth, primary attention to "objective" reality may result in misperceptions or misinterpretations because particular phenomena are not studied in their entirety. For practical reasons stemming from limited research time and resources, I focus in the test primarily on "objective" reality, using analytic categories of my own devising (rather than "native" concepts) and analytic methods of a standardized variety. In certain cases I try, albeit in an informal fashion, to bring into the analysis certain important considerations of some "subjective" realities in order to avoid particular distortions in interpreting my data. Obviously, problems arising from only such a partial analysis of the reality of particular economic transactions can not be avoided. My primary justification for plunging ahead with the cross-cultural analysis is that the importance of systematically investigating this particular realm of reality considerably outweighs the importance of the distortions introduced by using such analytic methods and such data. It should be clear that the closer one focuses on a single society, the more necessary it becomes to confront my cross-cultural results with the realms of subjective reality existing in the society. As I stress throughout this book, the cross-cultural results are a complement to, and not a substitute for, detailed case studies.

B.3 A NOTE ON EXCHANGE SPHERES

> *Un titre de baron, de vicomte, cela s'achète;*
> *une croix, cela se donne . . . je ne vois que la*
> *condamnation à mort qui distingue un*
> *homme . . . c'est la seule chose qui ne*
> *s'achète pas.*
>
> STENDHAL[52]

Introduction

Exchange spheres lead to a particular type of patterning of exhange, so that some valuables can not be exchanged for others. In no society—at least, none with which I am familiar—are all valuables (goods, services, or various types of social or political invisibles) freely and easily convertible into all other valuables. On the contrary, in all societies exchange is patterned, and the most usual form is a certain compartmentalization of exchange transactions such that exchange of valuables in a given set for valuables in another set is either manifestly impossible, extremely difficult, illegal, or likely to result in a loss of prestige of at least one of the exchange partners if the transaction is discovered by others.

In modern industrial societies, for instance, one particular commodity (money) can be exchanged for many other valuables, but its use in exchange is not unlimited. Example 1: Money can not be used to obtain a high position in most church hierarchies since prohibitions against simony are nowadays strongly enforced. Example 2: Although money can be used to obtain sexual services, the seller usually suffers a loss of prestige if the transaction becomes widely known (there is an interesting asymmetry in the consequences of the transactors; in a political bribe this asymmetry is in many cases less noticeable). Example 3: A person can not buy a Ph.D. (real or honorary) because this would lead to a violation of academic ethics. However, in many cases the use of money in indirect ways can facilitate the obtaining of a high church position, a temporary sexual partner (or, for that matter, a wife), or an academic degree, but the conversion of money into these desired valuables is considerably more difficult than buying a car, purchasing some type of patent rights, or hiring a servant.

The ways in which exchange is patterned—especially the size and content of these different sets of valuables—differ greatly among societies. In certain societies the size of one of these sets of valuables may be very large in relation to the types of valuables in the society. In modern industrial societies, for instance, the size of the set which includes money is very large. In certain

[52]*Le rouge et le noir*, Book II, Chapter VIII: 'The title of baron, of viscount, can be bought. A cross? It can be had for the asking. . . . I see that only the death sentence confers distinction on a man . . . for it alone can not be purchased.'

primitive societies such as the Kapauku Papuans of West New Guinea, the relative size of the monetary sector apparently is in some ways even larger, for the Kapauku not only use money for the buying, renting, and leasing of goods, land, and labor, but they also use money to obtain wives, evoke expressions of grief, and even commission services within the household.[53] In contrast, however, in most primitive societies the relative size of the exchangeable values obtainable by money is very much smaller than in industrial societies.

In this appendix I focus primary attention on the exchange of common goods and services where goods and services in one set can not be directly or easily exchanged for goods and services in another set. The existence of such exchange spheres (defined more precisely in the following discussion) gives rise to some obvious kinds of economic disequilibria deserving brief attention. Certain obvious problems in the calculations of economic values also arise that deserve examination.

Since the anthropological literature contains considerable confusion about how exchange spheres can be most fruitfully defined and employed in analysis, my first task is to carry out a necessary but tedious terminological exploration in order to separate related concepts such as exchange circuits and exchange media. I also examine a series of different types of exchange spheres and their implications for the operation of the economy. The empirical task is to determine the relative frequency of the phenomenon of exchange spheres, an exercise designed to rebut some extreme claims about their universality in the exchange of goods in precapitalist economies. I also exchange several hypotheses concerning the determinants of exchange spheres.

Clarification of Terms

The key tool for clarifying the concepts used in this chapter is an exchange matrix, a listing of all goods and services in the society on both axes of the matrix and a determination (which, if positive, is signified by an "x" in the matrix) of whether one good or service is exchanged (either market or reciprocal exchange) for another.[54] Such a matrix can also be used to handle cases of transfers by employing the convention of placing an "o" in the northwest–southeast diagonal (which is shown in Figure B.3). Three extreme cases of exchange matrices are presented in Figure B.1.

In Situation 1 no goods or services are exchanged or transferred; the society is without any distribution of goods or services. In Situation 2 goods only of a

---

[53]Leopold J. Pospisil, *Kapauku Papuan Economy* (1963).

[54]The notion of an exchange matrix is implicit in many discussions in economic anthropology, although I have never seen such matrices employed explicitly for the purposes for which I am using them. It must be emphasized that in using them, I am abstracting away from all considerations which limit exchange between particular groups of individuals or families. These barriers can also be analyzed using exchange matrices by listing on the two axes each group and each good for each group, so that one can show if Good A is exchanged not just within Group 1 or Group 2, but also between Groups 1 and 2.

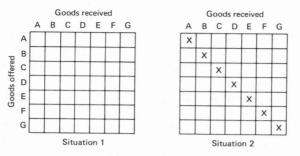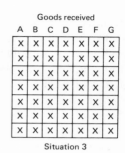

Figure B.1   Three extreme exchange matrices.

similar nature are exchanged, for example, food for food, bracelets for bracelets, and so forth. And in the third situation all goods are exchanged for all other goods. Situations that are more usual in moneyless primitive societies are shown in Figure B.2.

In Situation 4, Goods A, B, C, and D are not exchanged or transferred (they might be goods strictly produced in each household for its own use), while Goods E, F, and G are freely exchanged with each other. Some anthropologists have, by inference, suggested that this is an exchange sphere situation (two spheres: a traded and a nontraded set of goods). However, this does not seem a useful application of the concept since it does not distinguish economies from each other very well (almost all economies have a group of nontraded goods and services), and since it does not reveal the problem of trading across the boundary very clearly, that is, there may be no prohibitions against or loss of prestige occurring when A, B, C, or D are exchanged with E, F, or G, but such exchange may simply not occur because of lack of convenience (e.g., high transport costs) or because there is no specialization among households (if the good or service is simple to produce). In the discussion below, Situation 4 is not considered to represent an exchange sphere phenomenon. In Situation 5 not all goods are exchanged for all other goods, but with a particular good a person can carry out a series of exchanges to obtain any other good that he desires. In many cases such a situation arises when Goods A and B are very low in value

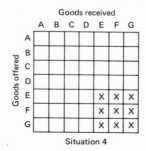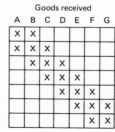

Figure B.2   "Normal" exchange matrices.

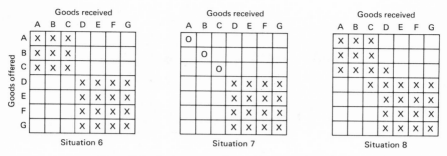

Figure B.3 Exchange matrices with true and overlapping exchange spheres.

(e.g., sweet potatoes and firewood), Goods C, D, and E are of medium value (e.g., spears, pigs, and mats), and Goods F and G are of high value (e.g., canoes and houses). Canoes are not exchanged directly for sweet potatoes because an inconveniently large pile of potatoes would be required to obtain the canoe— too many for the canoe owner to want for storage or for direct consumption.

EXCHANGE SPHERES

Exchange spheres occur when valuables belonging to one set can not be directly and easily exchanged for valuables belonging to another set without the breaking of some prohibition or without the loss of prestige on the part of at least one of the transactors if the exchange becomes widely known. In Situation 6 in Figure B.3 I have drawn a society with two spheres of exchange. The pattern shown in Situation 6 is a necessary but not sufficient condition for exchange spheres of this type, for the element of illegality or prestige loss in trading across the boundary must also be present. A different kind of exchange sphere phenomenon, shown in Situation 7, occurs when Goods A, B, and C (e.g., different types of goods) are distributed only in one-way transactions (i.e., they are transfers), while Goods D, E, F, and G (e.g., different types of handicrafts) are exchanged through market or reciprocal exchange for each other (and are never given in exchange for Goods A, B, or C).

Situation 8 is similar to Situation 6 except that there is a certain overlap, that is, two goods (C and D) can be exchanged for each other. This is not a "true" exchange sphere situation but could occur in cases in which the exchange spheres were disintegrating or the two "spheres" respectively contain very inexpensive and very expensive goods. Another case can occur when particular kinds of barter spheres exist but when one universal medium of exchange can be used to obtain any good or service.[55]

It is important to avoid confusing exchange spheres with several related phenomena, namely, exchange channels, exchange nexi, and dual valuational

[55]According to Pospisil, *Kapauku*, p. 341, the Kapauku economy has four different "spheres of barter" as well as a universal money which can be used to buy goods in each of these four sets of goods. Since exchange for money is much more important in this economy than barter exchange, these "spheres of barter" do not have a clearly ascertainable utility.

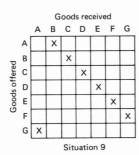 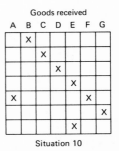

Figure B.4 Two examples of exchange circuits.

systems. Exchange channels occur when particular goods are exchanged within subsets of individuals in the society but not between individuals of different subsets.[56] Exchange nexi occur when different subsets of goods or services are distributed using different modes of distribution (defined in Chapter 2), but when some type of exchange also occurs between the goods of the different subsets.[57] (In the identification of exchange spheres, it is often difficult to decide whether an economy has exchange spheres or exchange nexi if the ethnographer has not fully described the exchange matrix; the concepts, however, are quite different.) Dual valuational systems are very rare and occur when the valuation of an exchange of two goods depends on the circumstances of exchange, for example, whether the exchange is part of "ordinary barter" or "ceremonial exchange" (so that if Person 1 gives A to Person 2 in the course of ordinary barter, and Person 2 gives B to Person 1 in the course of ceremonial exchange, both are in debt to each other in different circumstances and the two debts can not cancel each other out).[58] Exchange channels, exchange nexi, and dual valuational systems receive no further attention.

EXCHANGE CIRCUITS

Exchange spheres can feature either symmetric or asymmetric exchange. Symmetric exchange occurs if, when B can be obtained for A, A can also be

[56]Such a situation arises when different ethnic groups in a multiethnic society do not exchange particular goods and services (e.g., housing) with each other; or when sumptuary laws prevent the consumption or use of particular goods or services by a particular segment of the population.

[57]Such a case occurred among the Copper Eskimo where food was either given away or reciprocally exchanged for other food and where handicraft goods were exchanged through barter for other handicraft goods or for food. This is discussed by Diamond Jenness, *Report of the Canadian Arctic Expedition, 1913–18*, Vol. XII, *The Life of the Copper Eskimos* (1922).

[58]This type of phenomenon seems to have occurred among the Daly River tribes of Australia in which one valuational system was merely the acquiring of utilitarian goods for private purposes and the other valuational system rested on exchange to fulfill particular societal obligations; default in payment in the two types of transactions for the same goods with the same people could have considerably different societal consequences. This is described in more detail by R. F. Salisbury, *From Stone to Steel: Economic Consequences of a Technological Change in New Guinea* (1962), p. 201, who bases his information on some ethnographic reports of Stanner.

obtained for B. Asymmetric exchange occurs if, when B can be obtained for A, C but not A can be obtained for B. Asymmetric exchange implies a directionality of exchange, which is the distinguishing feature of exchange circuits. A simple and a complicated example of such exchange circuits are shown in Figure B.4.

In Situation 9 Good or Service A is given for B, B is given for C, and so forth, and finally G is exchanged for A. A well-known case occurs in the "circulating connubium" that is described in the standard anthropological analysis of preferential matrilateral cross-cousin marriage. A more complicated situation is shown in the next exchange matrix in which there are two circuits of exchange (Goods A, B, C, D, and E and Goods E, F, and G) with one overlapping good (E). Such a case was found to exist in the economy of the Mountain Fur of the Sudan Republic and gave rise to an interesting arbitrage situation.[59]

Although exchange circuits may exist within individual exchange spheres, the existence of the former are not a necessary or sufficient condition for the latter. Indeed, if the economy consists of one large exchange circuit (as shown in Situation 9), the society does not have exchange spheres.

EXCHANGE MEDIA

A brief exploration of the concept of "medium of exchange" is useful in illustrating certain aspects of exchange spheres which have not received proper attention. In addition, we establish some rigorous definitions that will be of great use in Chapter 6 which deals with the origins of money.

As used in this book, the concept of "medium of exchange" has three distinguishing characteristics. First, it is a "thing" which can be directly exchanged for a large number of other goods or services or valuables; second, it possesses this characteristic more than most other "things" (which means that in Situation 3, no medium of exchange exists); third, it serves this transfer function between other goods frequently. If a particular "thing" possesses the first two characteristics but not the third, it might be called a "medium of barter."[60] Certain implications of this concept can be seen from the exchange matrices in Figure B.5 and B.6.

---

[59]Frederik Barth, "Economic Spheres in Darfur," in *Themes in Economic Anthropology* (1967), ed. Raymond Firth, pp. 149–174. The circuits of goods and labor were: labor–millet–beer–labor (labor produced millet, from which beer was made, which was used as the main refreshment in the labor parties to plant more millet) and labor–tomatoes–cash–wives–labor (labor produces tomatoes, which were sold for cash to obtain goods and wives, which were used in turn to obtain labor to produce more tomatoes). Labor was the common element in both circuits. The arbitrage situation arose because cash did not enter the labor–millet–beer–labor circuit. Arab merchants bought millet from which beer was made to obtain labor to plant tomatoes for sale on the market, thus exchanging assets in the beer–labor circuit for cash. These were not exchange spheres since an overlapping service existed and because the boundary between the two circuits was not important, that is, arbitrage could be carried on without loss of prestige (except insofar as the cash obtained was not used to purchase more wives but was used to buy millet instead).

[60]The term "medium of barter" is borrowed from Paul Einzig, *Primitive Money*, 2nd ed. (1966), p. 319. Einzig's discussion of the concept is somewhat vague; I think, however, that my usage follows his.

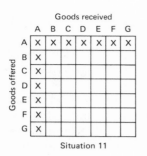
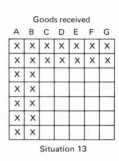

Situation 11   Situation 12   Situation 13

Figure B.5 Exchange media in simple situations.

In Situation 11 the first two criteria of a medium of exchange are clearly met, for Good A is the only good which can be exchanged for any other good; if it is used frequently for this purpose, which should not be difficult to determine, it is a medium of exchange. In Situation 12 the situation is more complicated: Clearly, Good A possesses the characteristic of exchangeability more than any other good; however, it may be much more difficult to determine the degree to which it serves a transfer function since considerable possibilities exist for direct exchange between goods. In Situation 13 two goods have general exchangeability and possess this characteristic more than other goods. If both are frequently used for this purpose, then we must conclude that the society has at least two media of exchange, a situation occurring in a number of societies in the sample.

In Situation 14 Goods A, B, and C are not exchanged at all, so that Good D serves as a medium of barter or exchange only for Goods D, E, F, and G. In other words, Good D is a limited purpose medium of exchange. Situations 15 and 16 illustrate different possible roles of media of exchange in economies that have exchange spheres. In Situation 15 each exchange sphere has its own medium of exchange or barter; A and D are limited purpose media of exchange or barter which serve their functions only within their own sphere. In Situation 16 the first sphere (Goods A, B, and C) has no medium of exchange or barter, so

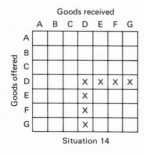
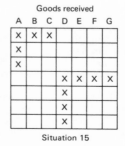
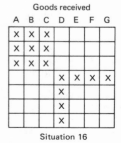

Situation 14   Situation 15   Situation 16

Figure B.6 Exchange media in complex situations.

that the economy as a whole has only one limited purpose medium of exchange or barter (Good D), which is used in only one of the spheres.

The existence of exchange spheres does not eliminate or enhance the role of media of exchange. However, exchange spheres do insure that any good serving as a medium of exchange has only a limited purpose, for otherwise no watertight exchange spheres would exist.

It should be apparent that there are often considerable difficulties in determining empirically whether a medium of exchange exists, not only because of the problems in determining the exchange matrix, but also in deciding the frequency with which the transfer function is carried out by the good under examination. This definition, however, has fewer subjective elements than others which have been proposed.[61]

Some Important Aspects of Exchange Spheres

Exchange spheres can occur in quite varied manifestations and can operate in the society in quite different ways. In the discussion of this section I outline some major types of exchange spheres and then point out some of the most important implications such an economic phenomenon might have on the society at large. In all of this discussion I use examples of exchange spheres that are drawn from the exchange of common goods since the empirical analysis in the following section is based on this narrow definition; thus, I omit consideration of exchange sphere in cases in which social, religious, or political valuables comprise the contents of the particular spheres.

DIFFERENT TYPES OF EXCHANGE SPHERES

Exchange Spheres Involving Similar or Different Types of Modes of Distribution.   In some primitive economies the same type of distribution modes are

---

[61]One additional difficulty arises when two types of "money" are used, one for large transactions, one for small change. The exchange matrix might show overlapping exchange spheres, with the "big bills" and "small change" being the overlapping elements. Although the two types of "money" are really one, more information than that contained in the exchange matrix is necessary to determine this unity.

An objection against the approach which I have followed in defining a medium of exchange is voiced by Jacques Melitz (*Primitive and Modern Money* [1974], pp. 75–79), who argues that because only certain groups in the society may use a medium of exchange, it is "dangerous" to reduce the percentage level for determining if a particular good serves the transfer function because many goods may be included as a medium of exchange which really are not. Melitz's own definition of a medium of exchange (which he equates with "money") is: "all goods that are held in significant measure in order to economize on transaction costs in the activity of trading a variety of other types of goods." It seems to me that such a psychological approach, while perhaps more in keeping with modern monetary conceptions, is considerably more difficult to apply to ethnographical situations than my definition, which only requires determination of the exchange matrix. Determination of motives even by the most skillful questioner is difficult, and problems are compounded by language barriers, suspicions of the natives against the anthropologist, and the inability of many people to verbalize their mental behavior. My approach, while less closely linked with modern monetary theory, seems more likely to yield useful information, an assertion which is put to test in Chapter 6.

found in all of the exchange spheres. For example, on the Western Polynesian island of Tikopia there were three spheres: the food–small objects (e.g., arm rings)–small services (e.g., loan of a canoe, unskilled labor) sphere; the bark cloth–sinnet cord–pandanus mats–timber–bows–coconut grating stool–specialist skills (e.g., canoe or house building) sphere; and the bonito hook–turmeric cylinder–canoe sphere.[62] Although these different spheres involved different ritual values, the primary mode of distribution in each was reciprocal exchange. It should be added that the labor value or scarcity value of the goods or services within each sphere was not the criterion for differentiation of these spheres since the time in making of small objects (first sphere) and bonito hooks (third sphere) was roughly the same.

In other societies the mode of distribution varies in the different spheres. For example, among the Siane of New Guinea there was a subsistence sphere (which included some but not all foods and all common agricultural equipment), a luxury sphere (which included particular types of consumer durables), and a prestige sphere (which included particular ritual goods, the most important of which were pigs).[63] Goods in the subsistence sphere were freely given (i.e., noncentric transfers) to fellow clansmen; luxury goods, on the other hand, were exchanged through barter (market exchange). And prestige goods were distributed in particular ceremonies (many of which were controlled by a few "big men" in each village) in a manner such that reciprocal exchange elements and centric redistributional elements entered into the exchange. In the exchange between various Melanesian societies, there were two spheres (or, perhaps, overlapping spheres)[64]: a subsistence sphere (food and handicraft items) that involved considerable market exchange and a valuable-goods sphere (the Kula ring) which was characterized by reciprocal exchange modes.

Exchange Spheres with and without Valuational Ranks. Ranking of exchange spheres can occur because the spheres are associated with different ritual elements (e.g., when there is a delineation between "sacred" and "pro-

---

[62]Raymond Firth, *Primitive Polynesian Economy* (1967), especially pp. 340–344.

[63]Salisbury, *From Stone to Steel.* Another society in which the mode of exchange was greatly different in the different spheres is described by Cora DuBois, "The Wealth Concept as an Integrative Factor in Tolowa-Tutuni Culture," in *Essays in Anthropology Presented to A. L. Kroeber* (1968), ed. Robert H. Lowie, pp. 49–67 [originally published 1936].

[64]Bronisław Malinowski, *Argonauts of the Western Pacific* (1961) [originally published 1922]. The overlapping element of the exchange spheres occurred on the Trobriand side in the domestic economy in which there was a certain exchange of food and labor for valuables. Between the Trobriand and other societies involved in the Kula exchange, true trade spheres seemed to exist. This is the only example of trade spheres in primitive international trade which I could find; many examples of such trade spheres can be noted in the international trade between modern societies in which there is governmental interference, for example, between the countries in Eastern Europe after the war certain nations (such as Poland) tried to achieve bilateral balancing of exports and imports with certain nations for individual goods or commodities (a ploy, in the Polish case, to increase Polish machine goods exports).

fane" spheres) or, more simply, because of differences in economic valuation (e.g., the goods in one sphere might involve more labor in production or be, in some manner, more scarce).

Unranked exchange spheres are sometimes found in societies in which few ritual elements are associated with any exchange. Both the Naskapi of Labrador and the Yahgan of Tierra del Fuego appear (although there is considerable uncertainty) to have had two exchange spheres[65]: a subsistence good sphere (primarily food) that was characterized by reciprocal exchange and one-way transfers and a handicraft goods sphere in which goods were bartered. In neither society does it appear that one of these spheres was, in any important sense, "higher." In the Polynesian Island of Tikopia items from the different exchange spheres were associated with different rituals; on the average, the items in the different spheres appeared to have different secular valuations; but the spheres, per se, do not appear to have been ranked.[66]

Ranked exchange spheres occurred among the Tiv of Nigeria where there was a subsistence sphere (foodstuffs, household utensils, some tools and raw materials), a prestige sphere (slaves, cattle, white cloth, metal rods, medicines, magic, ritual "offices," and so forth), and a "supreme sphere," which included only one item—marriage rights in women.[67] Goods in the subsistence spheres were bartered or given away without ceremony; exchange in the prestige sphere was usually accompanied by ceremony and apparently was carried out primarily by men; and exchange in the "supreme sphere" was carried out only reciprocally (i.e., woman exchange) and was considered the most important exchange of all. Both ritual and secular valuation entered into the ranking of these spheres. The previously cited example of the Siane of New Guinea is another case of ranked exchange spheres.

Exchange Spheres Involving Domestic and Imported Goods. Exchange spheres in a society can involve only those goods produced within the society, as many of the previous examples illustrate. The exchange spheres may delineate domestically produced and imported goods. The latter situation can arise because different modes of exchange are involved in obtaining such goods (a case which, to a certain extent, describes the Lele of Zaïre)[68] or

[65]Julius E. Lips, "Naskapi Law," *Transactions of the American Philosophical Society* XXXVII, Part 4 (December 1947): 329–492; Martin Gusinde, *Die Feuerland-Indianer,* Band II, *Die Yamana, Vom Leben and Denken der Wassernomaden* (1937).

[66]Firth, *Primitive Polynesian Economy.* This is a difficult case to decide since the ethnographer did not provide direct evidence on this matter.

[67]Paul Bohannan, "The Impact of Money on an African Subsistence Economy," in *Tribal and Peasant Economies: Readings in Economic Anthropology* (1967), ed. George Dalton, pp. 123–136.

[68]Mary Douglas, "Raffia Cloth Distribution in the Lele Economy," in *Tribal and Peasant Economies,* ed. Dalton, pp. 103–122. The domestic–foreign goods spheres were not completely separate since certain exchange transactions occurred between them. There seemed, however, to be a strong tendency to keep the transactions in the two sets of goods apart.

because the goods used in exporting and importing do not generally circulate (a situation which may have occurred in the Inca empire).[69]

Number and Content of Exchange Spheres.   Although I have focused primary attention on the various goods included in different exchange spheres, it should be added that labor services of different kinds might also be in different exchange spheres. In the Tikopian case just discussed, unskilled labor was in one sphere, whereas some types of skilled labor were in another sphere. In some societies the services of a wife can only be obtained by two families exchanging women, so we have an exchange sphere with only one type of object. As I noted at the beginning of this chapter, exchange spheres can exist to prevent direct exchange between particular economic, political, social, or religious valuables. The content of the exchange spheres is defined only by the total set of valuables that are exchanged (in the broad sense of this word) in a society. The sizes of the exchange spheres can vary from one valuable (e.g., women) to a set that embraces almost all of the valuables that are exchanged in the society.

In the statistical analysis presented later, I confine attention only to those exchange spheres that include common goods exchanged in the society. Restricting our focus in this manner, I have found no society in which the number of exchange spheres was any greater than three. In most cases only two spheres existed: A subsistence goods sphere (which might not include luxury or prestige foods and which might or might not include items other than food) and an "other goods" sphere (which might or might not include "prestige goods" and handicrafts).

SOME SOCIETAL IMPLICATIONS OF EXCHANGE SPHERES

The existence of exchange spheres implies that each society has multiple criteria for the determination of value and that great difficulties arise in easily converting values from one sphere to another. Such phenomena complicate economic analysis since certain analytic tools (e.g., those associated with general equilibrium analysis) may be inapplicable; however, many other analytic tools of economics can be usefully employed, an attempt which—aside from the fascinating analysis of R. F. Salisbury[70]—few anthropologists or economists

---

[69]John V. Murra, "Rite and Crop in the Inca State," in *Culture in History: Essays in Honor of Paul Radin* (1960), ed. Stanley Diamond, pp. 393–408; and John V. Murra, "Cloth and Its Function in the Inca State," *American Anthropologist* LXIV (August 1962): 710–728. The evidence on the Inca economy is very sketchy, but it appears two internal exchange spheres may have existed (basic subsistence goods such as potatoes; and higher status goods such as cloth and maize) and then a third sphere which embraced luxury goods produced domestically and also imported. Unfortunately, the evidence is not sufficiently clear for a clear statement about these spheres to be made; the first two spheres or else the last two spheres may have been combined.

[70]Salisbury, *From Stone to Steel*.

have attempted. Exchange spheres also have many implications in the social realm which deserve brief mention.

If a society has exchange spheres, the situation may arise where a person may be rich in goods and services in Sphere A but poor in goods and services in Sphere B and quite unable in the short run to bring about a more favorable balance for himself. Several important questions can be asked when examining such situations: To what degree is there a long-run correlation in the acquisition of goods and services in different spheres? How do situations of imbalance arise, that is, situations where a person is rich in the goods and services of one sphere and poor in those of another? What are the long-run mechanisms by which a person can achieve a more favorable balance of goods and services in the two spheres? Studies of such questions for primitive societies would have many parallels with the studies of industrial societies which focus on how economic wealth (or political power, religious sanctity, or wisdom) is converted into great "wealth" in political, social, religious, or educational realms.

Another important social implication of exchange spheres concerns their role in the distribution of privileges and social ranks, a question investigated by several anthropologists.[71] In some societies, especially in which exchange spheres are ranked, the exchange spheres may play a key role in the way in which social rank is achieved and maintained. That is, social rank may be obtained by judicious and imaginative exchange of goods and services of one particular exchange sphere. If the highest sphere contains only one or two objects which can be monopolized, this can have wide-ranging effects on the nature of political power (including the administration of justice and the waging of war) as well as on vital economic processes in other exchange spheres.[72]

Exchange spheres can also channel the impact of Western goods on a primitive economy in a manner resulting in quite different effects than if the economy had no exchange spheres at all. In certain cases the rigidness of the spheres was an important source of societal fragility, so that introduction of Western goods led to a breakdown of the spheres and a subsequent breakdown of important economic and social institutions, while in other cases, the Western goods could be incorporated into one of the existing exchange spheres (or made a separate exchange sphere), so that Western influences on the economy and society were blunted.[73]

Exchange spheres may also have few implications on the fabric of society, especially when the spheres are not ranked, and exchange of goods and ser-

---

[71]See especially Salisbury, ibid. and Douglas, "Raffia Cloth."

[72]An interesting analysis along these lines was carried out by Eva Krapf-Askari, "Women, Spears, and the Scarce Good; A Comparison of the Sociological Function of Warfare in Two Central African Societies," in *Zande Themes: Essays Presented to Sir Edward Evans-Pritchard* (1972), ed. André Singer and Brian V. Street, pp. 19–40.

[73]Examples of these two cases are, respectively, the Tiv (Bohannan, "Impact of Money") and the Siane (Salisbury, *From Stone to Steel*).

vices is not an important element in the society. It is difficult to generalize about the relative importance or unimportance of exchange spheres in the operation of primitive societies since we have only a few well-known case studies on which to base our opinion. Only a thoroughgoing comparative analysis of the operation of exchange spheres in a much larger number of societies than are contained in my sample can reveal the relative importance of the influence of this institution on the functioning of society, a task which must be left for others.

DETERMINANTS OF EXCHANGE SPHERES

At the present time there is no rigorous theory that will tell us very much about the occurrence, distribution, or form of exchange spheres in different societies; nor does such a theory appear on the horizon. To be sure, one can find assertions that exchange spheres, even in a limited sense concerning only the exchange of goods, are a very widespread phenomenon in precapitalist economies, but such statements are not argued and seem to represent inductions based on samples which are usually unspecified.[74]

Using a bit of imagination, one can extract several vague conjectures about the relationship between the relative level of economic development and the occurrence of exchange spheres. In discussions about primitive moneys some have argued that economic development is accompanied by the replacement of limited purpose moneys with a general purpose money. Such an argument suggests that perhaps exchange spheres should more likely be found in societies at lower levels of economic development. From other sources one can extract a contrary conjecture which is based on the notion that exchange spheres can serve as an important instrument in the central direction of production or in the rationing of consumption goods.[75] Since the desire (or necessity) for such control of production or consumption can occur at any level of development, we can infer that no relationship should exist between the level of economic development and the existence of exchange spheres. (Such an inference assumes, of course, that the existence of exchange spheres came about through conscious action toward some policy goal, an assumption which is quite questionable.)

In neither the economic nor the anthropology literature have I been able to find any other conjectures about the determinants of exchange spheres. Nor have I located any serious discussion about why the boundaries between sets of different goods and services defining what can and can not be directly ex-

[74]A number of anthropologists have stressed the widespread nature of exchange spheres within the realm of goods alone, for example, Richard Thurnwald, *Economics of Primitive Communities* (1932); or Fritz Steiner, "Notes on Comparative Economics," *British Journal of Sociology* V (June 1954): 118–129. More recently one finds such ideas in the writings of a number of anthropologists of the substantivist persuasion.

[75]This rationing aspect is particularly emphasized by Mary Douglas, "Primitive Rationing: A Study in Controlled Exchange," in *Themes in Economic Anthropology*, ed. Raymond Firth, pp. 119–148.

changed are drawn so differently in various societies that have exchange spheres. This is also one of the few phenomena discussed in this study for which I have been unable to generate any very convincing propositions on any important facet. For these reasons the empirical analysis must proceed quite inductively, in contrast to the approach in the text.

An Empirical Study of Exchange Spheres

DATA PROBLEMS

Determination of the existence of exchange spheres, particularly in ethnographies which do not focus on economic exchange, raises several difficulties that deserve brief discussion. Two types of errors may occur: failure to recognize exchange spheres when they actually exist and "recognition" of exchange spheres when they do not occur.

The first kind of error—failure to recognize exchange spheres—can arise in the original ethnographic work simply by oversight on the part of the ethnographer or because of his failure to follow lines of investigation to determine the existence of such a phenomenon. Since the concept of exchange spheres received general attention less than a half century ago, many of the earlier ethnographers may not have been looking for this phenomenon and, as a result, focused their research efforts on phenomena unrelated to exchange spheres. In spite of this, many of these ethnographers studied the general exchange problem in sufficient detail to leave important clues for us to determine the existence or nonexistence of exchange spheres. Unfortunately, the exchange situation in many societies was sufficiently complex that without tedious questioning and observing the general outlines of the trade matrix could not be determined. If the ethnographer did not follow such lines of investigation, we might conclude that exchange spheres did not occur in societies when they did.

The second kind of error—determining exchange spheres when they do not exist—arises primarily in the interpretation of published ethnographic materials. For instance, from an isolated statement in an ethnography that food is never traded, combined with another isolated statement that considerable trade of one handicraft for another occurs, we can conclude that exchange spheres featuring different modes of exchange exist. But if there is an unreported reciprocal exchange of food for handicraft, then we are dealing with exchange nexi, rather than exchange spheres, and have made a false inference. In reporting such interpretations, I have felt it necessary to include some measure of my certainty about the inference so as to alert the reader to errors of this type.

Is there any way to test the accuracy of my conclusions about the frequency of exchange spheres which I present below? If an error of identification arose because an ethnographer overlooked the phenomenon, the way to test the accuracy of my determinations is to consult as many different sources of information on the society as possible, a procedure which I tried to follow in making my original judgment. If error arose from false identification of exchange spheres, then replication tests can be performed. Such a test was performed and the results suggest that this type of error is probably not important.[76]

EMPIRICAL RESULTS

Since exchange spheres in a broad sense exist in all societies, I have used a very narrow definition of this phenomenon so that distinctions between societies could be made. More particularly, for the purpose of this empirical analysis I define exchange spheres as the existence of sets of common goods used often in exchange in which direct exchange of goods between the different sets is either impossible, extremely difficult, or likely to lead to a loss of prestige of one or both of the transactors if the exchange becomes widely known. This definition excludes exchange of services, goods for services, valuables whose ownership only seldom changes, or incorporeal valuables. Employing this narrow definition, only a small number of examples of exchange spheres could be found in the sample of 60 societies; these are listed, along with the degree of certainty of identification, in Table B.9.

In only 5 of the 60 societies can we identify exchange spheres in this narrow sense with any degree of certainty[77]; while in another 5 societies, exchange spheres may have been present, but we can not be very sure about the matter. Although, as I noted in Chapter 1, the sample is not sufficiently random to make any but the most gross generalizations about relative frequency of a particular phenomenon, I believe that the sample is sufficiently broad in a geographical sense for us to conclude that exchange spheres (using our narrow definition) are by no means a universal phenomenon in primitive economies and must be considered to occur only in a minority of such societies.

[76]A replicability experiment of the following nature was carried out. An independent coder (Carol Goldin, who performed not only this test but also the search for exchange spheres in societies outside the sample which is described in footnote 78) examined 14 societies in my sample which are also included in the Murdock–White SCC sample (George P. Murdock and Douglas R. White, "Standard Cross-Cultural Sample," *Ethnology* VIII (October 1969): 329–369) and for which there is a file on exchange in the Human Relations Area File. Using information from the latter source, the coder tried to determine the existence of exchange spheres (narrow definitions) in the subsample. The coder and I both recorded the same eleven societies having no exchange spheres; and the same two societies having exchange spheres. For the remaining case I recorded the existence of exchange spheres (but "quite uncertain"), and the coder recorded the society as having "no positive evidence of exchange spheres." Since I had considerably more ethnographic evidence on this society than the coder, this kind of difference in opinion is to be expected.

[77]For the Tiv, a special problem arises. Although the ethnographic evidence on this society is extremely rich, and since the phenomenon of exchange spheres was fully understood by the principal ethnographer (Paul Bohannan), I would ordinarily record this evidence as "very certain." A small cloud of doubt about this matter, however, has appeared in an article by A. J. H. Lathem, "Currency, Credit and Capitalism in the Cross River in the PreColonial Era," *Journal of African History* XII (1971): 599–605, who challenges Bohannan on the existence of exchange spheres. Lathem's evidence can also be challenged, and the issue is not completely resolved, although in my view Bohannan is most probably correct.

The relative infrequency of occurrence of exchange spheres in this narrow sense receives two additional types of confirmation. If we examine a subsample of societies from the Murdock–White SES sample, we find relatively few cases that we can positively identify as exchange spheres.[78] Moreover, outside the cases that I have discussed in this appendix, I could find few relatively well documented cases of exchange spheres.[79]

If we examine Table B.9 to derive generalizations about the forms of exchange spheres, we find few important patterns. In order to treat the uncertainties of the basic data with proper caution, I divide the societies in the table in two groups: Sample A comprises only those 5 societies in which exchange spheres can be identified with some certainty; Sample B comprises all 10 societies. With regard to whether the exchange spheres are ranked, we find that in Sample A, 4 out of the 5 have ranked spheres, but in Sample B this predominance is less striking as only 6 out of 9 have such rankings. (Ranking of spheres among the Pomo is unclear.) With regard to the presence of different exchange modes in the different spheres, we find that in Sample A this occurs in 2 of the 5 societies; and in Sample B, in 5 out of the 10 societies. Although the Trobriand Islands constituted the only case where the major focus of the exchange spheres was with exchange of goods with other societies, imported goods entered the exchange spheres of a number of the other societies.

The geographical spread of the exchange sphere phenomenon appears quite uneven. In the sample of 60 no cases of exchange spheres in its narrow meaning occur in Europe, Asia, or the Circum-Mediterranean area. Four out of 5 societies in Sample A and 5 out of 10 societies in Sample B are in the Oceania area. The remaining cases are scattered in North and South America and in Africa. None of the cases of exchange spheres in societies out of the sample

[78]Of a subsample of 70 societies in the Murdock–White sample ("Standard Sample") which are not included in my sample and for which information is contained in the Human Relations Area File, an outside coder was able to find only one society (New Ireland Islands in Oceania) which could be said with any certainty to have exchange spheres. For a number of societies the file materials were insufficient for a useful judgment to be made; and for several other societies exchange spheres possibly existed but the evidence was too skimpy to make a judgment with a reasonable degree of certainty.

[79]In addition to the cases discussed in this chapter, other instances are supplied by Elizabeth E. Hoyt, *Primitive Trade: Its Psychology and Economics* (1926), pp. 83–85; and Mary Douglas, "Primitive Rationing." Paul Bohannan and George Dalton, in their edited book *Markets in Africa* (1965), pp. 5–6, declare that (all?) small-scale societies without marketplaces as well as similar societies with peripheral markets have exchange spheres, but most of the examples they supply using a narrow definition are noted in my discussion. Nelson Graburn, "Traditional Economic Institutions and the Acculturation of Canadian Eskimos," in *Studies in Economic Anthropology* (1971), ed. George Dalton, pp. 107–122 suggests that exchange spheres exist in this society (which includes the Sugluk community discussed in Chapter 4) between "traditional goods" and "modern goods," although these spheres may overlap to some degree. Several anthropologists (notably Lorraine Baric, "Some Aspects of Credit, Saving and Investment in a 'Non-Monetary' Economy [Rossel Island]," in *Capital, Saving, and Credit in Peasant Societies* [1964], ed. Raymond Firth and B. S. Yamey, pp. 35–52; and George Dalton, "Primitive Money," in *Tribal and Peasant Economies,* ed. Dalton, pp. 254–284) have also argued that exchange spheres existed on Rossel Island in Oceania, although in a somewhat broader sense than I use the term in Table B.9.

TABLE B.9

Characterizations of Exchange Spheres in the Sample Societies[a]

Society	Certainty of identification	Characterization of spheres
Alor Island	Quite certain	Prestige goods and subsistence goods. Goods in both spheres traded but very much less frequently in the latter sphere. Prestige goods include (but not exclusively) imported commodities; also include some prestige foods
Inca	Quite uncertain	Basic subsistence goods (e.g., potatoes), prestige goods (e.g., cloth, maize), and luxury goods. Two of these spheres may have been combined. Goods in basic subsistence sphere traded to some extent domestically; luxury goods not traded domestically but used in foreign exchange and gift exchange
Maori	Quite uncertain	Subsistence goods (food and common articles) and prestige goods (ornaments, greenstone, heirlooms). Goods in both spheres used in reciprocal exchange and noncentric transfers. Greenstone exchanged for food, but only in foreign trade
Naskapi	Somewhat uncertain	Food and nonfood items. Nonranked spheres. Former goods distributed through reciprocal exchange and noncentric transfers; latter goods distributed in market exchange
Pomo	Quite uncertain	Food and nonfood items. Ranking unclear. Food supposedly not sold except in trade with other tribes, although some might have been sold domestically by specialists in certain food production
Siane	Very certain	Subsistence goods, luxury goods, ceremonial goods. Spheres ranked. Considerable noncentric transfers of subsistence goods; strong reciprocal exchange of luxury goods; reciprocal exchange and centric transfers of ceremonial goods
Tikopia	Very certain	Food and small items; bark cloth, ordinary sinnet, pandanus mats; and bonito hooks, canoe, turmeric cylinder spheres. Apparently spheres not ranked. Similar modes of exchange (reciprocity) in all three spheres
Tiv	Quite certain	Food and household goods, prestige goods (wives the "supreme" sphere). Ranked spheres. Market exchanges of goods in both spheres
Trobriand Island	Very certain	Food and handicrafts; valuables (armbands and necklaces). Spheres ranked. Food and handicrafts exchanged through a market; valuables, primarily through ceremonial reciprocity. Latter sphere important in foreign relations, although also a domestic reciprocal exchange of valuables

Continued

TABLE B.9—*Continued*

Society	Certainty of identification	Characterization of spheres
Yahgan	Quite uncertain	Food and nonfood. Spheres not ranked. More non-centric transfers of food than nonfood

[a]In addition, two societies (Mundurucú and Murngin) appear to have exchange nexi but possibly may have had exchange spheres. Unfortunately, the evidence is extremely thin, and no judgment can be made with confidence. Among the Dogon following the period for which my data apply, exchange spheres appear to have arisen: a "cowry sphere," which included only goods exchange among the Dogon, and a "franc sphere," which consisted only of foreign traded goods. These spheres may, however, have overlapped.

which I have been able to locate are in Europe, Asia, or the Circum-Mediterranean area, either. Whether the occurrence of the exchange sphere phenomenon only in Oceania, Africa, and the Americas arises from a biased sample, from diffusion of a cultural trait, or from the fact that ethnographic field workers in these areas were more sensitive to the existence of exchange spheres is quite unclear.

Is there any relation between the existence of exchange spheres in this narrow sense and the level of development of the economy or the type of major subsistence activity? These questions can be easily examined using the data presented in Table B.10.

TABLE B.10

Sample Societies with Exchange Spheres, Cross-Classified with Economic Variables[a]

	Groups of societies classified according to levels of economic development				Agricultural or incipient agricultural societies	Nonagricultural societies
	Lowest	Second lowest	Second highest	Highest		
Sample A: Societies with exchange spheres designated with relative certainty	1	2	1	1	5	0
Sample B: All societies with suspected exchange spheres	3	3	2	2	7	3
All societies in sample	15	15	15	15	36	24

[a]The rankings of societies according to the level of economic development and also according to the major subsistence activity are discussed in Chapter 2. Data are presented in Appendix A, Series 22.

Although the samples are too small for statistical tests to be performed with any assurance, several tentative conclusions can be drawn from these data. First, the existence of exchange spheres does not appear to be related to the level of economic development, for exchange spheres appear in roughly the same number of societies at every level of development. Thus, exchange spheres can not be linked to any particular stage of evolutionary progress, and if we look hard enough, we might find their existence in modern industrial societies. Indeed, in many nations in Eastern Europe in the 1950s and early 1960s, economic administrators instituted exchange spheres (e.g., between producer and consumer goods and between various categories of producer goods) in order to channel trade and control the pattern of production.[80] During World War II, most nations involved in the war instituted various consumption rationing devices which included the distribution of different types of nontransferable stamps or tokens with which only certain goods could be obtained.[81] Propositions linking exchange spheres to such purposes of control appear to have some validity.

Second, although the results from Sample A suggest that exchange spheres are found only in agricultural societies (or which can be rated as incipient agricultural), examples of nonagricultural societies with exchange spheres which can be identified with certainty can be cited (e.g., the Tolowa-Tututni of California). Furthermore, if we take all the sample societies in which exchange spheres are suspected, the representation of agricultural societies becomes less impressive.

I performed a number of other types of correlational tests and obtained similarly negative results. The presence of exchange spheres and the predominance of particular types of the different exchange modes was not correlated, for in Sample A each of these exchange modes was unimportant in at least one of the five societies. The presence of exchange spheres also appeared uncorrelated with various kinds of social variables, including the presence of particular types of lineage structure, marriage forms, or societal preferences for particular types of cousin marriages.

Exchange circuits seemed an even more rare phenomenon than exchange spheres; for among the 60 societies in the sample, I could find only one trivial example of such exchange circuits occurring. Among the Trobriand Islanders (and in the Kula exchange between the Trobriand Islanders and other societies)

[80]It might be argued that in East Europe exchange spheres did not exist because of the presence of a universal money. However, money alone could not be used to obtain certain producer goods, and although money or claims on bank accounts were transferred when ownership of producer goods was transferred, this was a passive reaction; indeed, such producer goods could be obtained without money if an order from the proper higher administrative organ were given.

[81]Again, money might accompany the buying of rationed goods, but since it was usually not a limiting factor in the transaction, it might be considered as a "passive" agent. Differences between active and passive money are discussed briefly in Chapter 6; and "passive money" is excluded from the definition of money used in this book.

necklaces were exchanged only for armbands (and never for other necklaces), and such armbands were exchanged only for the necklaces.

SOME IMPLICATIONS FOR THE ANALYSIS OF EXCHANGE
AND TRANSFER

Frequency of the Patterning of Exchange. In the sample of societies used in this book, exchange spheres within the circulation of goods appear in 8–17% of the cases. That is, although exchange spheres in a broad sense seem to occur in all societies, exchange spheres in a narrow sense appear to be somewhat more than an economic curiosum but considerably less than an economic universal. In any case this type of exchange sphere should not give rise to great alarm. Although more societies may have exchange spheres between particular sets of goods and sets of services, this should not greatly affect the analysis since I separate goods and services for analytic purposes, anyway. Exchange nexi and exchange circuits appear in the sample of 60 societies even less often than exchange spheres. And the patterning of exchange of goods by subsets of individuals (exchange channels) appears still rarer except in the trivial sense that handicraft workers may be the only people who trade in the goods which they make. Although the patterning of exchange can occasionally result in aberrant cases to the generalizations which I propose, the number of such cases should not be large enough to affect greatly the empirical generalizations drawn from all the societies in the sample.

Problems of Valuation. Since exchange and transfer are defined in terms of relative values of distributional flows, the presence of exchange spheres gives rise to an important problem, namely, that the society has no single indicator of relative value. That is, the exchange spheres imply the existence of several different sets of relative values, each relevant to just one sphere. Circumventing this problem is extremely simple. In examining whether a transaction is an exchange or a transfer, I only apply that standard of value which is relevant for the goods being distributed. The analysis that I apply does not rest on the existence of a single standard of value; I assume only that for a given transaction some standard of relative values exists in the society.

Economic Disequilibria. The existence of exchange spheres manifests an important economic disequilibria in the sense that arbitrage possibilities between the spheres may offer considerable economic rewards if successfully undertaken. However, the existence of such economic spheres also implies that there are certain social sanctions against achieving such "success," so that the possibilities of arbitrage may be utilized only by individuals who are not members of the society. However, none of the propositions argued in the succeeding chapters rests on any assumption about the existence or nonexistence of economic disequilibria, so the occurrence of such disequilibria should not affect the analysis in the slightest. As in the case of the existence of several standards of valuation, we can completely sidestep the problem.

Summary and Conclusions

With the aid of exchange matrices, relatively rigorous definitions of such phenomena as exchange spheres, exchange circuits, and exchange media can be made. In order to investigate empirically the occurrence of exchange spheres, it is necessary to narrow the definition of this concept to cover only commonly exchanged goods. Both empirical and methodological conclusions can be drawn from this survey.

The most important empirical result of the analysis is that exchange spheres in the narrow meaning of the concept occur in only a small percentage of the societies in the sample. Furthermore, there seemed to be no predominance of form of exchange sphere and no economic or social variable that could be correlated with the occurrence of such spheres. Exchange spheres are not correlated with the level of economic development, which excludes any type of evolutionary explanation of their existence. Such negative results in the correlation experiments means, among other things, that the search for other societies with exchange spheres can not be limited to societies with particular characteristics.

Although exchange spheres in this narrow sense seem to occur most often in societies in the Oceania area, followed by the Americas and Africa, the reasons underlying such a clustering pattern remain obscure, and it is unclear whether or not we can generalize from the sample to the whole universe of primitive economies. In those societies with exchange spheres this phenomenon can play a pivotal role in the society or can be quite peripheral in importance; as yet, we have no way of knowing in advance of empirical research on the society which will be the case.

The most important methodological conclusion is that the existence of various types of patterning of exchange should not greatly affect any empirical results obtained from the sample of 60 primitive and peasant societies. Furthermore, problems arising from multiple standards of valuation and from the economic disequilibria accompanying exchange spheres can be easily circumvented.

B.4   COLLECTION OF THE DATA ON ESKIMO DISTRIBUTION (FOR CHAPTER 4)

The discussion below focuses on the methods by which the data were gathered and the manner in which they were coded.

1. Designation of person, household, and family. Each individual Eskimo resident was assigned a number, and household designation followed a similar

procedure. Numbering was not complicated by deaths during the observation period. Problems arose because five households combined to form two larger ones. Households that merged late in the period of observation were still counted separately; the households that merged early in the observation were handled as a merged household for the entire period. Family membership was then assigned to nuclear family or less-than-nuclear family components within the households.

2. Designation of band. Sugluk was divided residentially, economically, and by origin into five subgroups, of which four were well defined and known by the name of the current leader, for example, Kaita-kut = the people, band of Kaitak. The ethnographer assigned individual and family membership in these bands through observation and considerable cross-checking of the few doubtful cases. Band membership may have varied before and after the period of field work because of economic and demographic conditions. The four well-defined bands were numbered one through four; all remaining individuals were lumped arbitrarily into a pseudoband that was numbered five.

3. Sex. Designation by sex provided no difficulties, as there were no berdaches (men who declare themselves women).

4. Age. Age in years was determined from year of birth until August 1959. The basis for age estimates was the extensive government and church records, but few Eskimos disagreed with these records. (As they got into their sixties, they sometimes claimed to be older.) The five age categories used in the text follow the categories of the Takamiut: (1) babies: *piarak, nutarak*; (2) boy children: *surusirk*; girl children: *niviaksiak*; (3) youth: *uvikak*; (4) male adults: *anguti*; female adults: *arngnak*; and (5) old men: *ituk*; old women: *ningiuk*.

5. Marital status. No one married or separated in Sugluk during the period of recording. We used categories significant to the Sallumiut: unmarried, betrothed (promised in marriage by parents), first marriage, widow/widower, and separated/divorced. There were none in the last category at the observation time.

6. Overall family status. We followed the judgments as expounded by the Sallumiut themselves in conversation and by other means. Such judgments were necessarily subjective; however, most of the Sallumiut seemed to make the same judgments about family status in spite of the obvious rivalries and the slightly differing criteria that various people might have employed. The basic criteria were how economically successful the family was, especially in hunting, and how well they obeyed the rules (of sharing, and of proper sexual and domestic behavior); historical and religious considerations also sometimes colored these judgments. A four-class set of categories was employed.

7. Individual prestige. Judgments about this dimension were made by criteria appropriate to the age and sex of the person under consideration and took into account the family status. This latter consideration was important because the son of the best hunter-leader would be expected to be of high prestige, but the son of a low-status family could successfully climb socially

through his prowess, and good works would be accorded an even higher prestige. A four-class set of categories was employed.

8. Position in the household/family. The following categories were used: head of household (a woman would be included if widowed), wife, first child of its sex (of all living children), other child of its sex, husband's relative of an older generation, husband's relative of the same generation, husband's younger-generation relative, wife's older-generation relative, wife's same-generation relative, wife's younger-generation relative, and unrelated boarder.

9. Adoption status. Adoption at birth was prearranged and was quite frequent in the Sallumiut area.

10. Legitimacy status. The Sallumiut placed significance on whether a child "had a father." The frequency of premarital births was increasing and was of some concern, although not grave enough that informants tried to hide the facts.

11. Total individual money income. This category represented the amount of the person's total monetary income for the first three quarters of 1959; to make such estimates, the ethnographer used the records of employment of the Canadian government, the Hudson's Bay Company, and the Christian mission, plus the records of the sale of all handicrafts, pelts, skins, clothing, and so on to these institutions and to all white residents, plus the records earned by some men from mining companies and the government outside the community. The calculation of money income does not include possible income from card play or sexual activities or from other inter-Eskimo transactions; however, these latter transactions were not important and were carried out mostly in non-monetary forms. A five-class set of categories was employed for the final ratings.

12. Total family money income. The individual money incomes of all family members were aggregated. A five-class set of categories was employed for the final ratings.

13. Individual hunting productivity. All men and women over 14 were asked how many of each significant species of animal, bird, and fish they had obtained from Christmas 1958 to September 1959. Although a few individuals were wary at first for fear that their answers might get back to local government officials, after reassurance by the ethnographer they soon became cooperative. They were helped both individually and collectively in estimating these data as accurately as possible. A five-class set of categories was employed for the final ratings.

14. Family hunting productivity. The individual hunting productivities of all family members were aggregated. A five-class set of categories was employed.

15. Individual total income. The individual money income and the individual hunting productivity were summed. The monetary value of the latter was estimated by using rough monetary equivalents of game animals and fish that prevailed in the village at that time. A five-class set of categories was employed.

16. Family total income. The individual total incomes for all family mem-

bers were aggregated. A five-class set of categories was employed for the final ratings.

17. Individual wealth. The bulk of the data was derived from a complete material culture survey of each household and of extradomestic possessions such as guns, sleds, boats, and shares in large boats. A five-class set of categories was employed for the final ratings.

18. Total family wealth. The individual wealth of all family members was aggregated. A five-class set of categories was employed for the final ratings.

19. Job status. This was a classification of the significantly different kinds of employment among the Sallumiut at the time of the survey. The following categories were used: individuals not working and not expected to work (such as small children); individuals on welfare (such as those who were sick or disabled) or on pensions (such as the aged, the blind, the widows); traditional hunter, trapper, or housewife ("average Eskimos" not employed but not disadvantaged thereby); those in low-status wage employment (manual laborers working at an hourly wage with low security as in unloading ships or in summer construction work); and those in high-status wage employment (usually employees with security, monthly pay, and sometimes with housing and rations provided such as the assistant manager at the store, the generator mechanic, government clerks, and the full-time school janitor).

20. Kin composition of household by types of family making up the domestic groups at that time. The categories included: less than nuclear family (e.g., one parent and children or a couple with no children); nuclear family; joint family (two or more coresident nuclear families related through siblingship, with perhaps one less-than-nuclear family); extended family (two or more nuclear families or part families, of which one is the parental family; nuclear family plus nonrelatives.

21. Type of house at the time of the middle of the survey. The categories included: single-walled duck tent; double-walled duck tent with moss insulation; patchwork house of scrap lumber, tarpaper, and other materials; well-made house, built with ample lumber and insulation; prefabricated house. A number of the latter were erected for the first time in Sugluk during the period of recording but were not occupied long enough to characterize any household. Since that time all Sallumiut have moved into government supplied prefab housing.

22. Size of house. This is an estimate of the actual volume of living space (excluding porches) taken from measurements of each household. It is a very good indicator of crowdedness, a significant factor in social life, as the regression analysis demonstrates. A five-class set of categories was employed for the final ratings.

23. Health status at time of survey. The following categories were employed: healthy; sick but continuing to perform some ordinary tasks; too sick to contribute economically to the family.

24. Able-bodiedness. The following categories were employed: able-

bodied; partially disabled but able to perform some ordinary tasks; totally disabled or blind.

25. Political status in the traditional system. The following categories were used: leader of a strong and well-defined band; leader of a weak band or a subband group; no political status. These statuses were self-evident to all within the community at that time.

26. Relation to political leader. The following categories were used: identity with leader; wife of leader; son or brother of leader; little direct blood or official relationship to leader.

27. Sugluk community political status. The following categories were used: past or present head of the elected community council; past or present membership on the community council; no past or present membership on the council. The council had only been in existence about 18 months, so that council membership records were readily available. Those elected as leaders tended to be those recognized as leaders in the "traditional" system.

28. Other political statuses. The following categories were used: head catechist, subcatechist, midwife, and no other political status.

29. Presence of head of household. The following categories were used: absent from the community for entire period of observation (e.g., in hospital, or engaged in wage labor elsewhere); absent part of the time (but more than for just a few days' hunting); present all the time except for a few days' hunting.

30. Presence of individual in community. The following categories were used: absent; partially absent except for a few days' hunting; present the whole time except for a few days' hunting.

B.5 ADDITIONAL NOTES ON ESKIMO DISTRIBUTION (FOR CHAPTER 4)[82]

The Pattern of Visiting

Both visiting and gift giving during visiting were highly patterned transactions. Perhaps the most important pattern was the greater frequency of interaction within bands than between members of different bands. Data to demonstrate this point are presented in Table B.11. If visiting or gift giving were random among people of the five bands, then intraband visiting and gift giving should constitute less than 20% of all such transactions. The data suggest, however, that such intraband transactions were roughly twice as high as predicted with such an assumption of randomness.

The visits were classified according to 35 different purposes so that some notion of motivations could be determined. If two purposes of a single visit were recorded, then each purpose was given a fractional weight. (A similar

---

[82]This appendix was jointly written with Nelson H. H. Graburn.

TABLE B.11

Intraband Visiting and Gift Giving as a Percentage of Total Visiting and Gift Giving among the Sallumiut Eskimo[a]

	Universe A[b]	Universe B[c]	Universe C[d]
Weighted visits	39%	38%	41%
Weighted gift giving	34%	36%	48%

[a]The weighting formulas used in the calculation of the overall visit and gift giving indices are described in Chapter 4. Visits or gifts of "Band 5" members with each other are considered extraband visits and gifts since this band is merely a residual category of individuals.

[b]All members of the society, excluding babies.

[c]Married youth, adults, and old people among each other.

[d]Children and unmarried youths among each other.

procedure was followed for gifts given by the hosts.) These data, aggregated into seven major categories, are presented in Table B.12.

Four features of the results deserve mention. First, the major purpose for transactions in all universes was "social." Second, those visits in which the visitor gave work services to the host were proportionately less, not more, rewarded with gifts. Third, those visits in which the purpose was courting or flirting were proportionately more rewarded with gifts, a not unexpected result. Finally, a considerable number of visits by children consisted of wandering in, obtaining something to eat, and quickly leaving.

We also computed relative frequency of participation in visiting and gift giving. Females generally did more visiting and participating in gift transactions than did males; and married people had the same pattern as unmarried people. Although children and unmarried youth did roughly the same amount of visiting as older members of the community, they did very much less gift giving. Much more could be said about such relative frequencies of participation in visiting and gift giving, but such results do not seem directly relevant to the major problem at hand, namely, the degree to which exchange accounts are balanced or unbalanced. Experiments to examine the impact of frequency of participation and the degree of imbalance in the exchange accounts did not reveal relationships which would affect our major conclusions; in the analysis in Chapter 4, therefore, we do not pursue these matters further.

Some Further Hypotheses

Many social scientists in the Maussian or neo-Marxian traditions appear to argue that important unbalanced distributional accounts are inherently destabilizing for any society. The evidence presented in Chapter 4 has considerable relevance for discussing this general proposition.

TABLE B.12

Purpose of Visits and Occasions at Which Gifts Were Given among the Sallumiut Eskimo[a]

	Percentage of total visits or gifts given					
	Universe A		Universe B		Universe C	
	Visits	Gifts	Visits	Gifts	Visits	Gifts
Quick in-and-out visits	2.8%	2.6%	0.9%	0.5%	1.7%	14.3%
"Social" (small talk, mutual recreation, listening to radio, visiting while doing own work, visiting other visitors)	82.8	86.3	82.0	87.1	93.7	83.9
Recruiting for work or obtaining work services	1.7	0.4	0.5	0.0	0.0	0.0
Helping out in household, performing work services	8.8	6.7	12.3	7.8	2.7	0.0
Business (borrowing or exchange something, other business)	1.4	0.3	1.7	0.1	0.4	0.0
Courting or flirting	1.6	3.3	2.6	4.5	0.0	0.0
Tagalong (coming along either with parents or friends)	0.8	0.4	0.0	0.0	1.5	1.8
Total	100.0	100.0	100.0	100.0	100.0	100.0

[a]For consistency with other tables we used weighted visiting and gift units as the basis of the calculations. Using unweighted units gives roughly the same picture but with a much higher percentage of quick visits and a correspondingly lower percentage of other types of visits. Universes A, B, and C are defined in Table B.6.

Until quite recently Eskimo society and social structure have demonstrated remarkable continuities in the several centuries since initial Western contact. Even though our numerical data and analyses have not been extended far back in the past, nor do they cover the duration since the period of intensive ethnographic work in the late 1950s, qualitative information about the society gathered in the course of carrying out the quantitative study permit several tentative generalizations. Although the Taqagmiut Eskimo, of which the Sugluk villagers are one group, are a classless society, family fortunes are identifiable over the generations. Reports from both native informants and from outside authorities[83] demonstrate that considerable continuity in the social placement and the political–economic prowess of genealogically connected persons (usually father to son) has been maintained for very long periods and that important

[83]E.g., F. F. Payne, "Eskimos of Hudson's Strait," *Proceedings of the Canadian Institute*, Series 3, Vol. VI (1888–1889), pp. 213–230.

instances of gross "account imbalances" have been reported for as many as nine decades before the period of our data collection. Although instability at one level (e.g., composition of particular villages) has long been a feature of Taqagmiut society,[84] the basic form of the society and the methods of distribution have remained the same during this long period with the same kinds of rules of behavior and the same economic activities esteemed and rewarded.[85] In this respect the important transfers among the Eskimo have not led to instabilities of basic Eskimo society.

On a less cosmic level of generalization Marshall Sahlins has argued a series of propositions about distribution which deserve brief notice. One hypothesis is that the level of transfers (which he designates as "generalized reciprocity") peaks on the occasion of a windfall such as an exceptionally successful hunt.[86] Our data contain a number of occasions labeled "feast," when a very successful hunter's family invited most of the rest of the community to eat and to take meat home. This situation is far different from the normal Eskimo hospitality which allows an uninvited guest to eat as he feels like it in the home of the host but not to take anything home.

Such a situation is complicated by another observation of Sahlins, namely, that typically people are stingy. Such a phenomenon was probably more prevalent in Sugluk than the ethnographer could observe. If a family, by caching its hunting or fishing products, did not announce its good fortune, then no feasting and inviting took place—and hence could not be recorded by the ethnographer. By taking such behavior into account, we might partially (but only partially) rescue the previously rejected hypothesis of Leach (and also of Sahlins) that an imbalance of tangibles may be balanced by a counterflow of intangibles such as prestige or social status.

We suggest that generosity might have been used in Sugluk in an attempt to *change* one's prestige or social status. The family caching its hunting kill was willing to forego a rise in prestige (and to risk a fall in prestige if their actions were found out) for the sake of later economic security. Certain groups might also have used generosity as a means of social climbing, so that instead of hiding their fortune, they were "putting it up front" and were especially generous with those with whom they wished to associate. Whether such a ploy was successful cannot be determined in an a priori manner; but it might explain in part why current prestige or family status was not related to the current balance of transactions. Our remarks should not be interpreted to mean that prestige or social status were solely functions of past generosity, for a number of other

[84]Nelson H. H. Graburn, "Eskimo Law in Light of Self and Group Interest," *Law and Society Review* IV (1969): 45–60.

[85]Nelson H. H. Graburn, *Eskimos Without Igloos: Social and Economic Development in Sugluk* (1960); and Graburn, "Traditional Economic Institutions and the Acculturation of the Canadian Eskimos," in *Studies in Economic Anthropology* (1971), ed. George Dalton, pp. 107–122.

[86]Marshall Sahlins, "On the Sociology of Primitive Exchange," in his *Stone Age Economics* (1972), pp. 185–277.

factors also determined how an individual was placed in these social categories. For instance, in our own society even the most generous unproductive cripple on welfare has relatively little prestige or social status.

Sahlins proposed a number of other propositions that, unfortunately, we cannot test with our data. For instance, he argued that marketable goods can never be subject to his propositions about reciprocity, for if internal leveling is carried out, then trade relations external to the household could not be sustained. He also argued that balanced reciprocity in isolation is not the prevalent form of exchange but is used particularly for formal friendship relations, affirmation of corporate alliances, peace making, and marital alliances. Although we have some doubt about the importance in overall distribution of some of these transactions, our Eskimo data do not lend themselves for testing these ideas. (The reciprocal nature of marital exchanges is tested with cross-cultural data in Appendix B.2.)

Further Analysis of the Distributional Data

In the following analysis we have aggregated all distributional transactions occurring between the natives of Sugluk who stand in different reciprocal kinship relations to each other and then have grouped the data according to kin distance. This is a different kind of analysis than that carried out in the test and represents an attempt to study more closely the impact of particular kinship relations on overall exchange. To simplify analysis, we examine data only for Universe A (all villagers except babies). Relevant data are presented in Table B.13.

For consanguineal near kin, the net exchange indices for both visits and gifts are highly positive in favor of the older of any dyadic set, especially when a generational difference obtained; this trend was the most marked between grandparents and grandchildren (none of the latter were, in fact, married) and is in accord with other results where we have shown that marital status is the significant factor and age a more spurious reflection of it. Within the same generation, older siblings tended to play host to the younger siblings and to a lesser degree, brothers and sisters; in the latter case the visiting index is one of near equality.

This section of the table reveals that affinal relationships obeyed an entirely different pattern. Contrary to expectations, the younger generation acted as hosts and gift givers, a reversal of the parent–child relationship. The son-in-law was insignificant as host, but perhaps the strong degree of interaction between parents-in-law and their daughters-in-law represented a concern for the welfare of their son's children on the part of the grandparents. The proximity of daughter-in-law households to their parents-in-law was much higher than of sons-in-law to theirs, for the Sallumiut are generally patrilocal. Affinals of the same generation, however, had relatively balanced net exchange indices, particularly for visits. They are also one of the few kinds of relationships that eliminate sex, age, and generational distinctions. Unfortunately, the net exchange indices of the relationship *aikulik* 'opposite-sexed sibling-in-law' are not calculable because the term is used reciprocally.

First-cousin relationships were relatively balanced, with a bias toward a negative gift index for the female cousin. Like the balanced *sakiak* 'sibling-in-law' group, this is also a set with no differences in age or generation. Unfortunately, the important *qatangutiksak* relationship 'first cousins of the same sex' is not taken into account for the same reasons as noted for *aikuluk* above. The pattern for second cousins of the same generation was entirely different from their relatively balanced first-cousin counterpart, the female being overwhelmingly the host for both visits and gift giving. Classificatory grandparents (siblings of one's "real" grandparents) followed the pattern of the lineal relationships by overwhelmingly hosting their classificatory grandchildren (grandchildren of one's siblings and cousins); contrastingly, the relationship between classificatory uncles and aunts (first cousins of one's parents) to classificatory nephews and nieces (children of one's first cousins) was very nearly balanced, overriding the expected generational/age bias.

More distinct affinal relationships repeat the pattern of the comparatively perverse close affinal relationships: The important person of the father's brother's wife was frequently hosted by her husband's brother's children, although gift exchange was fairly balanced. The more distant relationship between the spouses of older and younger orthosiblings was nearly balanced and did not follow the pattern of net exchange indices found between the older and younger sibling relationships on which it is based. Distant affinal relationships cannot be compared with closer affinal analogues, for Eskimos do not reckon second-order affinal relationships, as in American society.

In general, the net exchange indices are much more unbalanced than one would predict from the regression analysis in Table 4.1. For instance, we would predict that the brother:sister relationship might be 0.036 (visits) and .021 (gifts) since the only difference between the two is sex; but in actuality the signs are reversed, and the coefficients are much larger. If we measure "structure" by the deviation of the net exchange indices from zero (which would indicate balanced or randomness of relationship), then kinship relationships are the most highly structured exchange data that we have in the entire sample, much more than the analytic categories found to be most significant in the regression analyses in Table 4.1.

It might be argued that the data in Table B.13 prove Sahlins' kin-distance hypothesis. For instance, if we weight the absolute values of the net exchange indices in the table by the percentage of visits represented by such reciprocal kin pair transactions, then we derive the net exchange indices whose averages are shown in Table B.14.

As Sahlins predicted, the net exchange indices are much larger for near than for far kin, suggesting that reciprocity is more unbalanced for close

TABLE B.13

Average Net Exchange Indices for Selected Reciprocal Kin Pairs in Universe A[a]

Kin status and kin distance category		Net exchange indices		Percentage of transactions of total of kin distance			
Descriptive terms	Eskimo terms	Visits	Gifts	Visits	Gifts	Visits	Gifts
Near kin, not in the same household							
Older orthosibling: younger ortho-sibling	*angajuk:nukak*	−.402	− .531	3.31%	3.16%	11.16%	11.16%
Brother:sister	*anik:naiak*	−.210	− .586	0.73	1.07	2.44	3.77
Parent:child	*ataata/anaana:irnik/panik*	−.568	− .487	2.64	3.10	8.89	10.04
Grandparent:grandchild	*ataatacia/anaanacia:irngutak*	−.862	−1.000	1.43	0.57	4.82	2.03
Uncle/aunt:nephew/niece	*atkak/atsak/angak/ajak: qangiak/ujuruk/angak/nuak*	−.755	− .786	3.53	3.72	11.90	13.12
Parent-in-law:child-in-law	*sakik:ningauk/ukuak[b]*	+.152	+ .532	1.74	0.96	5.87	3.38
Man's wife's brother/ woman's husband's sister: man's sister's husband/ woman's brother's wife	*sakiak:ningauk/ukuak[b]*	+.043	+ .384	0.84	1.07	2.82	3.77
Subtotal				(14.22)	(13.65)	(47.90)	(48.18)
Far kin, not in same household							
Male first cousin:female first cousin	*anik:naiaksak*	−.055	+ .326	1.35	1.38	4.17	5.08
Male distant cousin:female distant cousin	*aniksak:naiaksak*	−.943	−1.000	1.39	0.68	4.30	2.51

Father's brother's brother's child	arngnaijuk:angutiakjuk/ paniakjuk	+.385	+.199	0.43	0.32	1.33	1.21
Spouse's older orthosibling's spouse:spouse's younger orthosibling's spouse	angajungruk:nukaungruk	+.022	−.163	0.34	0.70	1.04	2.59
Classificatory grandparent: classificatory grandchild	anaanacia/ataatacia:iirngutak	−.867	−.812	0.66	1.16	2.04	4.28
Classificatory uncle/aunt: classificatory nephew-niece	atkak/atsak/angak/ajak: qangiak/ujuruk/angak/nuak	−.201	−.008	3.41	2.20	10.56	8.10
Subtotal				(7.58)	(6.44)	(23.44)	(23.77)

[a]The table includes only reciprocal kin pairs in which the direction of exchange is indicated because the two people address each other by different terms. Thus, exchange between male first cousins is omitted because they used the same relationship term to each other.

The net exchange indices are presented in reference only to the first mentioned of the kin pairs; the net exchange indices of the second of the pair are, of course, the same as the first but with the sign reversed. (The index is negative if a person acts more as a host or gift giver and is positive if the person acts more as a visitor or gift receiver.)

For Universe A covered in the table, transactions are classified only according to the type of kinship relation between the visitor and the prime host or gift givers. It is vital to note that these accounts are calculated by aggregating the accounts of all people standing in the specified relation, a procedure different from that used in the tables in Chapter 4, in which the basis of our calculations is the net exchange index for each individual separately. The percentage of transactions is calculated by summing the visits (or gifts) received and given and taking this figure as a percentage of the total visits (or gifts) received and given.

Detailed discussion of the kinship terminology and relationships can be found in Nelson Graburn, *Taqagmiut Eskimo Kinship Terminology* (1964).

[b]We are able to distinguish between *ukuak* and *ninguak* as 'children-in-law' and as 'brothers- and sisters-in-law' because our kin categories were subdivided within the emic categories by such analytic devices as lineal versus collateral.

TABLE B.14

Average Net Exchange Indices of Reciprocal Kin Pair Transactions

	Visits	Gifts
Near kin	.505	.603
Far kin	.371	.352

kin. However, a closer inspection of Table B.13 suggests that such results occur because of particular aggregation biases and that the results of the weighted net exchange indices give spurious results. This may be seen by comparing near and far kin relationships that are actually comparable, point for point, with only kin distance different.

For instance, if we make a comparison of the net exchange indices between first-cousin relationship and second- and more distant cousin relationships, we see that the latter were very much more unbalanced. Similarly, although it appears that classificatory uncle/aunt:nephew/niece relationships were more balanced than their "real" counterparts, every single set *within* the former group is actually unbalanced: the aunts *ajak* (MoSi) and *atsak* (FaSi) repeat the expected intergenerational patterns, but these indices are counterbalanced by the behavior of the uncles *atkak* (FaBr) and *angak* (MoBr) who visit their male cousins' children to an unexpected degree. Perhaps, also, the average net exchange indices of near and far kin might be changed by the inclusion of data from the important *qatangutiksak* 'orthocousin' and *aikuluk* 'heterosibling-in-law' relationships but undoubtedly not enough to reverse the results of the weighted averages. Another factor was that within the aggregates there was more offsetting within the accounts of single individuals for near kin than for far kin. For instance, a man might have had a highly unbalanced account with his sister as well as with his older orthosibling, but these might cancel each other out. So his overall net exchange index among all near kin might be roughly 0.00, while such a balancing phenomenon was not so apparent among far kin.

B.6 SEVERAL METHODOLOGICAL CONSIDERATIONS (FOR CHAPTER 11)

The analytic methods used in this book have been, for the most part, drawn from the field of comparative economics. Although my results have a certain plausibility, several questions about the consequences of theoretical bias arise that deserve comment. To what degree are my results valid because of the eclectic hypothesis-testing approach? To what degree are my results acceptable because of a bias toward "economic determinism"? And to what degree are my results "tainted" because of "formalist" or "substantivist" tendencies?

The Question of Eclecticism

As noted in the first chapter, I have not started with an overarching theory about the dynamics of economic systems in general and of primitive economic systems in particular and then derived a series of hypotheses to test. Rather, I have searched the literatures of anthropology, economics, and history for hypotheses to test and, in addition, have derived a series of my own from quite simple considerations. This approach was adopted for several reasons.

First, no overarching theory has yet been proposed which permits the detailed derivation of a variety of hypotheses to explain the phenomena studied in this book. Nor, it should be added, does any such theory appear on the intellectual horizon. At the present time no person or group seems to know enough to be able to make a synthesis capable of coping with the vast variety of circumstances occurring in different primitive and peasant societies.

Second, the world may be sufficiently complicated that several quite disparate causal forces act separately to influence the presence or absence of some particular distributional phenomenon.

Third, the methods adopted in this book have led to the discovery of a number of causal forces that have previously received no attention, especially by those employing such overarching theoretical systems. Furthermore, the empirical studies of the sample of 60 primitive and peasant societies have shown that many hitherto accepted hypotheses derived from overarching theoretical schemas turn out to have very little or no explanatory power.

A basic methodological problem with the approach adopted in this book is that it is difficult to know whether as high a percentage of the phenomena under investigation is explained as possible. But such a methodological problem is common in all sciences and, indeed, separates science from ideology or religion, whose practitioners purport to explain everything.

The Question of Economic Determinism

Possible biases arising from economic determinism raise some more serious questions. Since this term has several meanings, it is necessary to disentangle the concept before an analysis of my alleged biases in this direction can be drawn.

To some scholars, economic determinism indicates that environmental and climatic conditions influencing production also shape or influence the variables under analytic examination such as the distributional variables I have been studying. (This argument comes in two versions: The first is that environment influences the activities of production, which, in turn, influence all other activities; the second is that the environment influences the activities of production as well as the other activities directly.) This type of determinism is also called "ecological" or "geographical" determinism and is so designated below. As I noted in Chapter 1, my use of such ecological variables did not prove very successful in any of the calculated regressions. Such negative results do not mean that the influence of such ecological variables is minor for particular subtypes of distributional transactions.

To others, economic determinism indicates that the level of economic development shapes or influences the presence of the variables under analytic investigation. In many of the equations for the determinants of the modes of distribution the level of economic development plays an important role; and in the exploration of child-rearing practices, senilicide, social–economic inequality, and female initiation ceremonies, the economic development variable also appears to be an important causal variable. It must be emphasized, however, that the development variable is usually only one of several variables acting as the determinants of a particular variable under examination.

To still others, economic determinism indicates that the economic system, however defined, plays the critical determinantal role in the presence or absence of the important variables under study. If the system is defined in terms of the level of economic development, this meaning of economic determinism is the same as the previous. But if the economic system is defined in terms of the principal mode of production or by some type of distributional criteria, then we have another distinct type of determinism. The role of the hunting–fishing variable as a determinant of noncentric transfers of goods or the role of the nomadic herding variable as a negative determinant of gambling are examples of such propositions using a production criterion for economic system. In the preceding pages I have presented several types of propositions using a distributional criterion of economic system.

To a final group of scholars, economic determinism indicates that a particular "economic" variable shapes or determines the presence of the important variable under examination. An example of such a proposition occurs in the analysis in Chapter 10 where the type of land tenure allegedly influences the existence of slavery.

Although this study has been strongly influenced by the mode of analysis employed by economists, and although this study contains scores of examples where "economic" (in one of the four senses outlined previously) is shown to be a determinant of the variable under examination, I would reject the charge that the results are strongly biased by an implicit assumption of economic determinism for several reasons:

First, in all cases I attempt to hypothesize and to test noneconomic determinants, and in many cases such noneconomic determinants appear to play important roles. Such noneconomic variables include various kinds of social structural, social, and political variables.

Second, I have not tried to argue that these noneconomic variables are caused by economic forces. Rather, I have focused on middle-level theories without attempting to reduce the determinants of all phenomena underlying the phenomena under investigation to a small set of economic variables. Indeed, I think that such a grand-system approach is not only premature but also, at the present time, unproductive.

Third, in the various regression equations I usually explain from 25–50% of the variance of the dependent variable (which indicates an R^2 of .25–.50 or a correlation coefficient of .50–.70). This means that from 50–75% of the variance is left unexplained. This, in turn, indicates that noneconomic variables that I did not explicitly consider can play a major causal role.

In short, starting from the analysis of Eskimo exchange in Chapter 4 where a variety of economic, social, and political variables are employed to explain the imbalances in the exchange accounts, I have tried to include for quantificative analysis all of the relevant causal variables, no matter how they are labeled.

As it turns out, economic variables do play a very important role as determinants for the phenomena under investigation. But this should not be surprising since most of these distributional phenomena are closely linked with the economic side of the sample societies. This does not mean that I am resuscitating the nineteenth-century version of the economic man, rather that I am exploring the role of economic forces within a social matrix. The relative importance of the economic and other forces has been in this study a matter for exploration, not of assumption. It must be added that this type of approach toward the relative importance of the different type of causal forces has been adopted by anthropologists and economists with theoretical orientations much different from mine.

The Question of "Formalism" and "Substantivism"

As noted in the text, I have drawn on the ideas of both contending schools of economic anthropologists; I do not consider myself an adherent of either school, however. Although the participants to the debate have apparently drawn a great deal of wisdom out of this interminable debate, I have not been so fortunate. Since I have been accused by adherents of both positions of being a follower of the opposing school, a few words of explanation are in order.

A major difference between the substantivists and me appears to be that I am trying to explain what is common to a diverse group of societies, while the substantivists are trying to explain their differences. This means that I am trying to frame propositions that can be demonstrated with statistical proof, while they are trying to interpret events or phenomena in a way that requires a much different method of proof. Furthermore, the substantivists and I differ strongly in our treatment of "invisibles." They wish to consider simultaneously material and invisible flows, while I try to examine the material flows first and then to turn to the flow of invisibles. This means that our definition of, and approach toward, "reciprocity" differs considerably. Finally, they seem to have a predisposition toward searching for balance in all relationships, while I do not. This means, for example, that in examining the slavery relationship, they might focus more attention on the food, room, and other services received by the slave in return for his work, while I focus more attention on the basic inequalities of the relationship. These differences between us are quite basic. However, the situations in this book where I have found myself in direct disagreement with the substantivists about some proposition have been relatively few because we usually focus on quite different questions. Only Karl Polanyi, from whom the substantivists have drawn their greatest inspiration, seems to have dealt with many of the problems discussed in this book, and this may be attributed to the fact that Polanyi was strongly influenced by the German historical school, which discussed many evolutionary problems.

A major difference between the formalists and me appears to be that they are wedded to a somewhat different brand of economics than I. It also appears, but I can not be sure, that they are less willing than I to attach causal significance to certain social and political mechanisms and more willing to focus on environmental factors as elements of causation. Since the formalists are less interested in issuing methodological *pronunciamentos* than the substantivists, their position must be inferred by reading between the lines of their anthropological writings, and I hope that I am being fair to them.

B.7. EXPERIMENTS WITH AN ECONOMIC SYSTEMS VARIABLE (FOR CHAPTER 11)

Defining Economic Systems Using Distributional Orientations as Criteria

The underlying rationale for defining economic systems in the terms discussed below is provided in Chapter 11. The paragraphs below describe how the actual calculations were made. The results of the calculations are presented in Appendix A, Series 59, 60, and 61.

For defining societies with a positive or negative economic orientation, I examine three distributional phenomena concerning market exchange that are positively related to the level of economic development: market exchange of goods accounting for 5% or more of the distribution of all produced goods; market exchange of labor accounting for 5% or more of the distribution of all labor outside the home; and the presence of an interest rate charged on loans. If a society deviates from the expected pattern (i.e., the prediction, given its level of economic development; see Table 11.2) in the same direction for two out of these three distributional modes, it is grouped among the societies with a positive or negative economic orientation. The societies with a positive economic orientation are on the lower end of the economic development scale and represent societies that have more types of market distribution than their level of economic development would indicate. The societies with a negative economic orientation are on the upper end of the economic development scale and represent societies that have fewer types of market distribution than their level of economic development would indicate.

For defining societies with a positive or negative social orientation I examine three distributional modes that are generally associated with "socialness" and that are negatively related to the level of economic development: reciprocal exchange of goods accounting for the distribution of 5% or more of total produced goods; reciprocal exchange of labor accounting for the distribution of 5% or more of labor services outside the home; and noncentric transfers of goods accounting for 5% or more of the distribution of total produced goods. If a society deviates from the expected pattern (i.e., the prediction, given its level of economic development; see Table 11.2) in the same direction for two out of these three distributional modes, it is grouped among the societies with a positive or negative social orientation. The societies with a positive social orientation are on the upper end of the economic development scale and represent societies that have more of these "social modes" of distribution than their level of economic development would indicate. The societies with a negative social orientation are on the lower end of the economic development scale and represent societies that have fewer "social modes" of distribution than their level of economic development would indicate.

For defining societies with a positive or negative political orientation, I examine two distributional modes tied up with political activity: centric transfers of goods accounting for the distribution of 5% or more of all produced goods; and centric transfers of labor accounting for the distribution of 5% or more of all labor outside the home. (For one society in the sample, namely, the Yaqui, the centric labor transfer variable was set equal to zero because such transfers were exclusively of a religious nature and unrelated to the political system, a situation that did not occur to such extremes in any of the other societies featuring centric labor transfers.) Both such centric transfer data are related with the level of economic development. If a society has either of such transfers when its level of economic development would lead to the opposite prediction (Table 11.2), it is classified among the societies with a positive political orientation; if a society does not have such transfers when its level of economic development would lead to the opposite prediction, it is classified among the societies with a negative political orientation. The societies with a positive political orientation generally appear at the lower end of the economic development scale and represent societies that have centric transfers of goods when, according to level of development, they should not. The societies with negative political orientation generally appear at the higher end of the economic development scale and represent societies with fewer centric transfers than they would be expected to have, given their level of economic development.

Economic System as a Causal Variable

DETERMINANTS OF PERMISSIVENESS IN CHILD-REARING PRACTICES

We can test in an illuminating manner several notions of Sigmund Freud about the relationship between "civilization" and repressive child-rearing

TABLE B.15

Determinants of Child-Rearing Practices[a]

$CRP = -.1399 + .0346*ED + .6888*EOS$	$R^2 = .3008$
$\qquad\qquad\quad$ (.0071) $\qquad$ (.2761)	$n = 60$

Key:

CRP = Child-rearing practices (0 = permissive child-rearing practices and no corporal punishment; 1 = permissive child-rearing practices but some corporal punishment; 2 = nonpermissive child-rearing practices but no corporal punishment; 3 = nonpermissive child-rearing practices and some corporal punishment) [mean = .9167].

ED = Rank on economic development scale (1 = lowest level; 60 = highest level) [mean = 30.50].

EOS = Economically oriented economic system (+1 = positive orientation; 0 = no orientation; −1 = negative orientation) [mean = 0].

R^2 = Coefficient of determination.

n = Size of sample.

( ) = Standard error.

* = t statistic for calculated regression coefficient is over the acceptable limit (2.25) defined in Chapter 1.

[a]The data come from Appendix A, Series 22, 59, and 74.

practices.[87] More specifically, in a short book written in 1930 that has received enormous criticism, Freud seems to argue that the "price" of higher levels of cultural and economic development is much stricter upbringing of children and much less permissive disciplinary practices. In his discussion Freud appears to intertwine two causal variables: the general level of economic development and the degree to which the society places emphasis on individualistic market activities.

Testing such notions raises two problems. The first is the problem of mechanism: Although the relationship Freud proposed may be correct, his explanation of the relationship may be quite incorrect. It would take us too far afield to explore these matters, and we must, for this argument, shunt such difficulties aside. The second is the determination of permissiveness of child-rearing practices. For each of the 60 sample societies I tried to determine whether or not the child-rearing practices were permissive, taking into account the ethnographic reports about the degree to which the children were allowed to behave as they pleased, the type and frequency of the disciplinary practices of parents, and so forth. These various considerations were combined into a single coding—either relatively permissive or relatively nonpermissive—in an impressionistic fashion. I also coded within each of the two categories whether

[87]Sigmund Freud, Civilization and Its Discontents (1930), trans. Joan Riviere.

or not corporal punishment was employed as a disciplinary technique for children, which results in a four-point scale of the dependent variable. This scale, admittedly, has strong subjective elements, but it captures in a crude manner the phenomenon under investigation.

For the explanatory variables I use the measure of economic development employed throughout this study plus the economically oriented economic systems variable. I also tested whether or not any of the other economic systems variables had any important influences on the results, but as expected, they did not. The results of the statistical analysis are presented in Table B.15.

The empirical implications of Freud's conjectures receive support from the regression results in Table B.15. Other independent variables that I introduced added little additional explanatory power. Such results encourage us to attempt a more precise coding of permissiveness of child-rearing practices (perhaps disaggregating so that such practices in different areas of activity can be separately examined) in order to explore Freud's notions with greater rigor. In short, although Freud's justifications of the relationship between the level of economic development, the type of economic system, and child-rearing practices can be strongly challenged, he seems to have isolated empirically two apparently important determinants of these practices that deserve more attention than they have previously received.

THE DETERMINANTS OF SENILICIDE

The deliberate killing of the old and incurably sick is a repellent topic that has received relatively little systematic attention.[88] Nevertheless, one can find a variety of hypotheses about the matter in the anthropology literature.

Among the most common conjectures about the determinants of senilicide is that such practices occur most often when the level of economic development is low, the environment is very severe, and the society is nomadic. The underlying arguments should be quite apparent. The first factor receives confirmation in the empirical analysis that follows; the latter two factors do not. The failure of the variable representing nomadism is particularly surprising to me.[89]

We might also hypothesize that this practice is related to the orientation of the economic system, and two hypotheses come to mind. The first is that such practices would occur in societies with positive economic orientation because such societies place relatively less stress on "human values." A second hypothesis is that such practices would occur in societies with a strong social orientation because such an act requires a certain willingness on the part of the

[88]A notable exception is Leo Simmons, *The Role of the Aged in Primitive Society* (1945). In the following discussion I draw especially on his hypotheses (especially those he discussed on pp. 228 and 240) but I do not use his coding definitions. There were too few overlapping societies in our samples to permit a meaningful comparison of our coding results.

[89]Many nomadic herding societies possess the means for transporting the aged and the incurably sick, so the "necessity-to-leave-behind" argument does not seem to apply. In addition, most nomadic herding societies also have low levels of economic development, a factor picked up by the development variable.

TABLE B.16

Determinants of Senilicide and the Killing of the Incurably Sick[a]

$PS = .4277 + .2932*SOS - .0062*ED + .2105\,EOS$	$R^2 = .1681$
$\quad\quad\quad\quad (.1272)\quad\quad (.0030)\quad\quad (.1259)$	$n\ \ = 60$

Key:
PS = Practice of senilicide and killing of incurably sick occurs with sufficient frequency to be noted by ethnographers (0 = no; 1 = yes) [mean = .2000].

SOS = Social-oriented economic system (+1 = positive orientation; 0 = no orientation; −1 = negative orientation) [mean = −.1333].

ED = Rank of economic development scale (1 = lowest level; 60 = highest level) [mean = 30.50].

EOS = Economically oriented economic scale (+1 = positive orientation; 0 = no orientation; −1 = negative orientation) [mean = 0.0000].

R^2 = Coefficient of determination.

n = Size of sample.

( ) = Standard error.

* = t statistic for calculated regression coefficient is over the acceptable limit (2.25) defined in Chapter 1.

[a]The data come from Appendix A, Series 22, 59, 60, and 75.

aged (i.e., the act bears a strong resemblance to Durkheim's "altruistic suicide")[90] and because a strong social cohesiveness is necessary so that the society is not torn apart each time the act is carried out. The results of the regression analysis are presented in Table B.16.

The empirical evidence from Table B.16 provides some confirmation to the hypothesis that senilicide practices occur in societies with socially oriented economic systems. Support is also given to the proposition that such practices occur primarily in societies at low levels of economic development. The economically oriented economic systems variable provides a certain additional explanatory power, but the standard error is too high in relation to the calculated coefficient for us to place much confidence in this relationship.

DETERMINANTS OF SOCIOECONOMIC INEQUALITY

As many have noted, socioeconomic inequality seems to rise as the level of economic development rises, and this relationship is borne out strongly by the data. In addition, socioeconomic inequality is probably also related to politically oriented economic systems for two reasons that I argue in Chapter 10. First, most centric transfers (which are the defining characteristic of politically oriented economic systems) are regressive and this increases the oriented economic systems) are regressive and this increases the socioeconomic inequality. Second, the resources obtained from such centric transfers permit

[90]Emile Durkheim, *Suicide* (1951), trans. John A. Spaulding and George Simpson [originally published 1897], especially Chaps. IV and V.

TABLE B.17

Determinants of Socioeconomic Inequality[a]

$SEI = 1.0612 + .0374*ED + .4386*POS$	$R^2 = .6469$
$(.0038)$ $(.1077)$	$n = 60$

Key:

SEI = Socioeconomic inequality scale (1 = least inequality; 5 = greatest inequality) [mean = 2.2617].

ED = Rank on economic development scale (1 = lowest level; 60 = highest level) [mean = 30.50].

POS = Politically oriented economic system (+1 = positive orientation; 0 = no orientation; −1 = negative orientation) [mean = .1333].

R^2 = Coefficient of determination.

n = Size of sample.

( ) = Standard error.

* = t statistic for calculated regression coefficient is over the acceptable limit (2.25) defined in Chapter 1.

[a]The data come from Appendix A, Series 22, 61, and 66.

the political leaders to increase their power and to widen the inequality. Therefore, we would expect that the social inequality variable would be related to the politically oriented economic systems variable both as cause and effect. The results of the empirical analysis are presented in Table B.17.

The coefficient of determination of the regression reported in Table B.17 is very high. Both hypothesized explanatory variables play their expected roles. Addition of other independent variables to the regression added little additional explanatory power.

Concluding Remarks

The short studies of the determinants of certain child-raising practices, the practice of senilicide, and socioeconomic inequality provide examples of the ways in which the economic system can serve as a causal variable. Other examples can also be provided. No tests for diffusion are carried out because in all three cases the nature of the phenomenon under investigation is such that diffusion is extremely unlikely.

APPENDIX C

STATISTICAL NOTES

C.1 THE RELATIONSHIP BETWEEN FREQUENCY OF DIVORCE AND THE RELATIVE EXTENT OF THE BRIDEPRICE (FOR CHAPTER 1)

As noted in the text, E. E. Evans-Pritchard once said: "It is therefore a common-sense inference that payment of brideprice has a stabilizing action on marriage."[1] If we interpret this statement as a cross-cultural generalization without modifiers and look at the 53 societies in my sample for which data for the relevant variables (as I understand them) are available, the truth of this seemingly obvious proposition seems quite doubtful. Such data are presented in Table C.1.

If we compare the data in the table with a distribution based on the assumption that divorce rates do not vary with the level of brideprice and calculate a chi-square statistic, we arrive at a chi-square of .6708, which suggests that there is not significant difference between the two distributions. Thus, Evans-Pritchard's proposition seems false. We can easily test a more sophisticated

[1]E. E. Evans-Pritchard, *Kinship and Marriage among the Nuer* (1951), p. 60. It must be noted that Evans-Pritchard seems to argue the reverse proposition several pages later in the same book. Regarding this proposition there was an acrimonious debate in the pages of *Man,* Vol. LIII (1953) Articles 75, 122, 123, and 279 and in Vol. LIV (1954) Articles 96, 97, and 153. The debate concerned what the proposition actually meant and, less interestingly, who said what about it.

TABLE C.1

The Relationship between Frequency of Divorce and the Relative Extent of the Brideprice[a]

	Number of societies	
	High divorce rate (30% or more of marriages end in divorce)	Low divorce rate (less than 30% of marriages end in divorce)
High brideprice (average brideprice amounts to more than 100% of the average annual labor income of a man)	4	6
Medium brideprice (average brideprice is less than "high" but more than a token)	12	9
Low brideprice (no brideprice or only token brideprice)	9	13

[a]The data come from Appendix A, Series 70 and 71. Problems arise concerning the cutoff line I make between "few" and "many" divorces as well as the fact that I define bridewealth in terms of a ratio of income rather than absolute terms (since the data can not be easily made comparable if an absolute measure of bridewealth is used). In addition to these conceptual problems there are coding problems. For a number of societies I found serious difficulties in deciding on which side of the cutoff line defining high and low divorce rates the societies fell. If the table is recalculated to include only those cases for which I am relatively sure that the data are accurate, the number of cases is reduced to 26 but roughly the same low chi-square statistic is obtained.

version of this proposition offered by Max Gluckman[2] and we obtain similar results.[3]

C.2 SAMPLE SIZES OF TABLES ON ESKIMO DISTRIBUTION (FOR CHAPTER 4)

TABLE C.2

Sample Sizes for Table 4.3

	Universe A		Universe B		Universe C	
	Visits	Gifts	Visits	Gifts	Visits	Gifts
$Q = -1.00$ to $-.40$	65	95	50	58	24	22
$Q = -.40$ to $+.40$	89	58	39	35	31	30
$Q = +.40$ to $+1.00$	28	29	23	19	12	15

[2]Max Gluckman, "Kinship and Marriage among the Lozi of Northern Rhodesia and the Zulu of Natal," in *African Systems of Kinship and Marriage* (1950), ed. A. R. Radcliffe-Brown and Daryll Forde, pp. 166–206. Gluckman tries to link lineage structure, bridewealth, and several other factors to relative divorce rates.

[3]I used regression techniques of the same nature as those presented in the following chapters; in none of my attempts did I obtain statistically significant coefficients of determination.

TABLE C.3

Sample Sizes for Table 4.4

	Universe A		Universe B		Universe C	
	Visits	Gifts	Visits	Gifts	Visits	Gifts
$KDI = -1.00$ to $-$ .40	51	70	34	36	24	21
$KDI = -$ .40 to $+$ .40	105	87	55	53	40	46
$KDI = +$ .40 to $+1.00$	26	25	23	23	*	*

*An asterisk indicates that too few transactions were recorded for meaningful comparison.

C.3 DETERMINATION OF THE OPEN RESOURCES INDEX (FOR CHAPTERS 5 AND 8)

The open resource index ranges from 0 to 6 and consists of two components: an index of the relative importance of rented land (which ranges from 0 to 4) and an index of the availability of agricultural land (which ranges from 0 to 2). The relative weights of these two components reflect my confidence in their coding.

In the rented land index two problems of coding arose. In some societies there is a gift rent, that is, a person can farm another person's land (often without permission) if a small gift is presented the owner at the end of the season to signify recognition of some type of claim on the land by the owner. In other societies there is a political rent, that is, a person can farm any piece of unused land in a given area if he agrees to pay a given amount to the political leader as a type of tax payment. I have excluded both of these types of rent and have only included more ordinary types of land rents (in commodities, money, or labor). If there is no land rent present in the society, the rating is 0; if the phenomenon of land rent is present, the rating is 2 points; if land rent is present and amounts to more than 5% of total agricultural production, the rating is 4.

The availability of land index was constructed in a more subjective manner. If the ethnographic materials suggested that a landless adult member of the society could obtain good farmland with relative ease (i.e., if he did not need to engage in very elaborate manipulations of his kin ties, or if land was bought and sold, the price was relatively low), the rating is 0; if a landless adult could obtain farmland of indifferent quality with relative ease, the rating is 1; if a landless adult could not obtain any land with relative ease, the rating is 2.

C.4 CALCULATION OF A LAND SCARCITY INDEX FROM NONVALUE INDICATORS (FOR CHAPTERS 5 AND 8)

As noted in the text, land scarcity depends not only on the density of population but also on the fallowing technique for farming the land. A society with 75

TABLE C.4

Calculation of Land Scarcity (Series 13) Using Nonvalue Indicators[a]

Land density (Series 12)	Fallow land system (Series 16)[b]						
	1	2	3	4	5	6	7
1 = Less than 5 persons per square mile							
(3.1 persons per km²)	0	0	0	0	0	0	0
2 = 5–25 persons per square mile							
(3.1–15.5 persons per km²)	3	2	2	1	1	0	0
3 = 26–100 persons per square mile							
(3.2–62.1 persons per km²)	6	6	6	4	3	2	1
4 = Over 100 persons per square mile							
(62.1 persons per km²)	6	6	6	6	6	6	6

[a]The series numbers refer to the data presented in Appendix A.
[b]For series 16 (fallow land and crop rotation variable):
  1 = Free land fallow (where land is essentially unlimited and people may not ever return to the same piece of land after it is farmed)
  2 = Full forest fallow (more than 20 years fallow period but a return to the same piece of land eventually)
  3 = Intermediate forest fallow (11–20 years fallow period)
  4 = Bush fallow period (5–10 years fallow period)
  5 = Short fallow period (1–4 years fallow period)
  6 = Annual cropping (no fallow period and one crop per land piece per year)
  7 = Multicrop agriculture (no fallow period and more than one crop per land piece per year)

people per square mile that uses a double cropping system of agriculture may have less land scarcity than a society with 25 people per square mile which uses a 20-year fallow system.

Unfortunately, I could find no objective evidence that would permit us to construct a land scarcity index from data on density and crop rotation schemes. Therefore, following intuitive notions I constructed the Table C.4 and assigned values from 0 through 6 to the various density–fallow system combinations.

C.5   ADJUSTMENT OF THE SAMPLE DATA FOR THE ANALYSIS OF MARITAL EXCHANGE (FOR APPENDIX B.2)

The data used to examine the exchange between American husbands and wives came from a computer tape purchased from the Survey Research Center (S.R.C.) of the University of Michigan. The S.R.C. obtained the data through nationwide personal interviews with a representative sample of 2214 families in January and February 1965. These data have been used and discussed in a number of S.R.C. publications, especially those of Morgan and Sirageldin.[4]

[4]James N. Morgan, Ismail Sirageldin, and Nancy Baerwaldt, *Productive Americans* (1966); and Ismail Sirageldin, *Non-Market Components of National Income* (1969).

I tried to select a homogeneous subsample from this larger sample, and therefore eliminated the following subgroups:

1. All farm families or families deriving income from the sale of agricultural products
2. All families headed by a nonwhite
3. All families that did not have both a husband and a wife
4. All families in which the respondent was not either the husband or the wife
5. All families with more than four adults in the household
6. All families in which a family member was disabled or one spouse could not work because of illness
7. All families in which the husband was under 30 or over 60 years old
8. All families in which one spouse was laid off or in which the two spouses had more than 100 hours of involuntary leisure in the year
9. All families with roomers, live-in servants, or other family units living in their home
10. All families in which either of the spouses earned less than $0.90 an hour in work outside the home
11. All families in which either of the spouses worked (either at home or outside the home or both) less than 500 hours or more than 5000 hours in the year
12. All families in which the interviewer was not able to obtain all of the data used in the regression experiments

In addition, I also removed several cases where I suspected that the original tape contained keypunching errors.

APPENDIX D

A GLOSSARY OF TECHNICAL TERMS

Terms defined and used only in one chapter are not listed below. The definitions of anthropological terms are mostly adapted from definitions given by Charles Winick, *Dictionary of Anthropology* (1970). All terms in italics are defined below.

Affine: A relation by marriage rather than by "blood."

Ambilocal: See *postmarital residence* rules.

Arbitrage: The purchase and sale of the same commodities or things in different markets for different prices for the sake of profit.

Balance: Used in this study in the sense of an equality of exchange values, where exchange values are defined in terms of the goods or services exchanged and from the point of view of the members of the society.

Bilateral descent: See *lineage*.

Bilocal: See *postmarital residence* rules.

Brideprice: Goods given by a groom and his family to the family of the bride in connection with the marriage. The services supplied by the groom or his family to the family of the bride are designated as the *brideservice*. The goods given by a bride and her family to the family of the groom are called the *groomprice*. These terms should not be confused with *dower*.

Brideservice: See *brideprice*.

Centric: Used in this study to characterize a pattern of distribution in which the goods or services move to or from a relatively permanent societal focal point such as a political or religious leader or a political or religious institution. The concept is discussed in greater detail in Chapters 9 and 10.

Chi-square: A statistical test devised by Karl Pearson for determining goodness of fit of a curve to a frequency distribution or, more generally, to determine the statistical significance of a relationship.

Coefficient of determination: A statistic used in *regression* analysis to designate the goodness of fit of a hypothesized curve to a set of points. It ranges from 0.0 to 1.0 and indicates the proportion of the variation of value of the set of points (more properly speaking, the variance) that is explained by the curve.

Consumption unit: A group of people who receive a set of goods and services and who, by means of some type of internal decision-making process, divide and consume them together. These are discussed in greater detail in Chapter 2. See also *production unit*.

Cross-section: A set of observations referring to different points in space. Usually, but not always, the observations are drawn at a single point in time; in this study this is not the case, and the data for the different societies refer to different years (specified in Appendix E). In anthropology such observations are sometimes called synchronic data.

Dependent variable: See *regression*.

Diffusion: A process by which a particular trait of one society is "borrowed" by another society; such "borrowing" can also be imposed by military conquest or can occur when one group splits off from another, yet continues to be characterized by the trait under examination.

Distribution: A process by which a particular good changes hands so that it is consumed by someone other than the producer or a particular service is "consumed" or enjoyed in an immediate sense by someone other than the person carrying out the service.

Dower: Goods given by the family of a bride to the bride or to the groom in connection with the marriage. The goods given by the family of the groom to the groom or to the bride are called an *endowment*. These terms are not to be confused with *brideprice* or *groomprice*.

Economic development: A term used in this study to designate the relative societal complexity. The concept is discussed in considerable detail in Chapter 2.

Economic system: A characterization of the economy according to some set of criteria. Several types of primitive and peasant economic systems are defined and analyzed in Chapter 11, including economically oriented, socially oriented, and politically oriented economic systems. See also Appendix B.7 for operational definitions.

Endowment: See *dower*.

Exchange: A *balanced* transaction of goods or services, that is, where goods or services of equal exchange value change hands. This concept is discussed in detail in Chapter 2.

Exchange matrix: A table showing the type of things (goods or services) that are exchanged for each other in the society. Such matrices receive considerable analysis in Appendix B.3 and are used to arrive at a definition of *medium of exchange*.

Exchange sphere: A set of goods which are exchanged among themselves but never with goods belonging to another set. These are discussed in Appendix B.3.

Exogamy: The practice of a person seeking a mate outside his "group" (which may be a clan, moiety, or community).

Floating centricity: A pattern of distribution in which goods or services move to or from a relatively impermanent societal focal point, for example, a person giving a one-time ceremonial in which a large number of people are invited. Transfers characterized by floating centricity are classified as noncentric transactions.

Futures market: A *market* in which claims on goods or services that will be actually exchanged at a future specified date are bought and sold.

Galton's problem: A problem arising in *cross-sectional* analysis in which the functional relationships under investigation may be masked or distorted because of the occurrence of *diffusion* at some past time. This problem and the manner in which it is circumvented is discussed in great detail in Chapter 3.

Groomprice: See *brideprice*.

Guttman scale: A technique devised by Louis Guttman for ranking whole units (e.g., societies, persons) composed of characteristics demonstrating a monotonic relationship with some scaling attribute (such as economic development for societies or intelligence for people).

Householding: A situation where the production unit produces only for itself and does not *exchange* or *transfer* goods and services. In short, a self-sufficient economy.

Independent variables: See *regression*.

Least squares: A technique used for calculating *regressions* where the regression line or plane is calculated in a manner to minimize the squared distances of differences between the predicted and actual observation points.

Lineage: A "consanguineal" kin group consisting of members with a common relation in the prevalent line of descent as the result of a specific group of genealogical ties. Such genealogical ties can be differently defined. A *patrilineal descent group* is one in which the transmission of name, property, or authority passes through males, for example, father to son. A *matrilineal descent group* is one in which such transmission passes through females, for example, mother to daughter. *Bilateral descent* refers to the transmission through both the female and the male in a manner that is either equal or does not emphasize either line (a situation existing in the

United States and Europe at the present time, except in peculiar cases such as royal families and aristocratic families). A lineage is defined as "important" if it has considerable generational depth. Important economically defined lineages occur when the corporate activity of the lineage concerns important economic matters; important socially defined lineages occur when the corporate activity of the lineage concerns important social matters. These terms are not mutually exclusive, and a lineage can be defined both as important economically and socially.

Logit analysis: A special type of *regression* calculations in a situation in which the *dependent variable* is either zero or one. In such a case a logistics curve is fitted to the points rather than a straight line. More explanation is given in Appendix B.1.

Market exchange: Exchange transactions where the economic forces of supply and demand are highly visible, in contrast to *reciprocal exchange* where they are not. The concept is discussed in detail in Chapter 5.

Matrilineal descent: See *lineage.*

Matrilocal residence: See *postmarital residence rules.*

Medium of exchange: A thing which an *exchange matrix* shows to be directly exchangeable for many other things, where it serves this function more than most other things and where it is often exchanged.

Mode of distribution: One of the four types of *distribution* that are defined in an exhaustive typology in Chapter 2. These modes include *market exchange, reciprocal exchange, noncentric transfers,* and *centric transfers.*

Money: Any standardized object serving in an active fashion as a *medium of exchange* for commercial purposes or as a medium of payment for domestic noncommercial purposes. This definition is discussed in detail in Chapter 6.

Multicollinearity: This occurs in the calculation of a *regression* equation when two or more of the *independent variables* are correlated with each other. It introduces bias into the calculation if a *least squares* method is employed.

Multiple Regression: See *regression.*

Multivariate analysis: A type of statistical analysis that takes into account simultaneously several explanatory variables. Using a *regression* analysis, this involves the calculation of a *multiple regression.*

Neolocal residence: See *postmarital residence rules.*

Noncentric transfer: A transfer which is not characterized by a *centric* pattern.

Orthosibling: A sibling of the same sex.

Orthocousins: Cousins of the same sex.

Patrilineal descent: See *lineage.*

Patrilocal residence: See *postmarital residence rules.*

Postmarital residence rules: In many societies there are generally accepted customs concerning where a man and woman shall live after they are married. *Patrilocal or virilocal* means that the couple lives in the home or the community of the husband's kin; *matrilocal or uxorilocal,* that the couple lives in the home or community of the wife's kin; *neolocal,* that the couple establishes a home away from both kin groups; *ambilocal,* the couple alternates residence between the kin groups; *bilocal,* that there is no set custom and the couple may live near either set of kin.

Production unit: A group of people who, by means of some type of decision-making process among themselves, are able to produce goods or services together in an organized fashion.

Regression: The calculation of the relationship between variables when the functional form is specified. A *simple linear regression* is the calculation of a relationship between two variables that are linked in a simple linear form ($Y = a + bX$), in which Y is the *dependent* or explained variable, X is the *independent* or explanatory variable, and a and b are the calculated *regression coefficients.* In the diagram the regression line was estimated by the method of *least squares.*

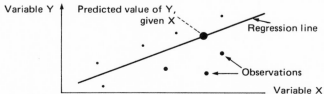

The regression *residual* is the difference between the observed value of *Y*, given any particular *X*, and the predicted value. A *multiple regression* is a regression with two or more independent (explanatory) variables. A *stepwise regression* technique is one in which the variables are entered into the multiple regression one at a time, with the variable chosen that results in the greatest increase in the *coefficient of determination*.

Reciprocal exchange: Exchange transactions characterized by weak or relatively hidden forces of supply and demand, in contrast to *market exchange*.

Service: Activities that are organized in a manner such that there is a close connection between a person carrying out the activity and his obtaining material means for satisfying his wants. This concept is discussed at greater length in Chapter 2.

Slavery: A type of dependent labor of a nonfamily member where one or more of the following three conditions is met: The superior has the right to kill the subordinate even when the latter has not committed a crime; the superior has the right to transfer the subordinate any time over his lifespan to another superior without the subordinate's permission; the superior has considerable more long-term legal rights than the subordinate not only with regard to participation in political decision making but also with regard to participation in other kinds of activities as well. *Slavery C* is a narrower definition that includes only those cases in which slaves constitute 5% or more of the labor force and have a markedly lower standard of living than their superior. *Slavery A* embraces all types of slavery specified in the definition (discussed at length in Chapter 8). *Slavery B* occurs when conditions for *Slavery A* are met and, further, such slaves constitute more than 5% of the labor force. *Slavery D* occurs when conditions for *Slavery C* are met or the conditions for *Slavery B* are met and, in addition, the children of slaves are considered to be slaves belonging to the master of their parents.

Standard deviation: A statistic designating the variation of a variable around the average. It is calculated by taking the square root of the mean variation of the various observations from the sample mean.

Standard error: In a *regression* analysis this is a statistic designating the variation in the calculated regression coefficient that would occur if different samples were drawn from the same universe. The smaller the standard error, the better the fit of the *regression* equation. Dividing the calculated *regression coefficient* by the *standard error* gives a *t statistic* which can be used in making *tests of statistical significance*.

Stepwise regression: See *regression*.

Test of statistical significance: A test to see whether or not the results obtained are random or not. In this study results were generally rejected unless there was *less* than 1 chance in 20 that the results could have come about as the outcome of random events.

t test: See *standard error*.

Transfer: A *distributional* transaction that is not *balanced*. The concept is discussed at length in Chapter 2. Transfers can be either *centric* or *noncentric*. A progressive transfer is one in which the transfer leads to a more equal distribution of consumption between rich and poor; a regressive transfer is the reverse.

Time-series: Data on a unit observed at different points in time, in contrast to a *cross-section*. In anthropology, sometimes called diachronic data.

Unit of observation: The unit for which the various types of distributional transactions vis-à-vis the outside world are examined and within which the transactions are neglected in this analysis. The *consumption* and *production* units play a major role in the selection of the unit. This concept is analyzed in detail in Chapter 2.

Uxorilocal residence: See *postmarital residence rules*.

Virilocal residence: See *postmarital residence rules*.

APPENDIX E

SOCIETIES IN THE SAMPLE AND PRINCIPAL ETHNOGRAPHIC SOURCES

Roughly 1200 sources were consulted, of which over 800 were used in coding the data. Although little use would be served in listing all of these sources, the most important sources for each society are listed below.

1. **Alor:** Atimelang Village, Alor Island, Lesser Sunda Islands, Indonesia; 1900 (before extensive contact with Chinese or Dutch).
    A. Cora Dubois. *The People of Alor: A Social Psychological Study of an East Indian Island.* Cambridge, Massachusetts: Harvard University Press, 1960 [originally published 1944].
    B. Cora DuBois, "How They Pay Debts in Alor." *Asia* XL (September 1940): 482–486.
    C. Cora DuBois, "Attitudes toward Food and Hunger in Alor." In *Language, Culture and Personality: Essays in Memory of Edward Sapir,* edited by Leslie Spier et al. Menasha, Wisconsin: Sapir Memorial Publication Fund, 1941.
    D. Personal communication from Cora DuBois.
2. **Amhara:** Gondar district, Ethiopia; 1900 (before extensive reforms and changes).
    A. Simon D. Messing, *The Highland-Plateau Amhara of Ethiopia.* Ph.D. dissertation, University of Pennsylvania, 1957 (also published by Human Relations Area File).
    B. Donald N. Levine, *Wax and Gold.* Chicago: University of Chicago Press, 1965.
    C. Allan Hoben, *Land Tenure among the Amhara of Ethiopia.* Chicago: University of Chicago Press, 1973.
    D. Personal communications from Allan Hoben, Donald N. Levine, and Simon Messing.
3 **Ao Naga:** Assam Valley, India; 1885 (shortly before British conquest).
    A. J. P. Mills, *The Ao Nagas.* London: Macmillan, 1926.
    B. William Carlson Smith, *The AoNaga Tribe of Assam: A Study in Ethnology and Sociology.* London: Macmillan, 1925.
    C. S. N. Mazumder, *Ao Nagas.* Calcutta: Majumder, ca. 1925.
4 **Aweikóma:** Dalbergia, Santa Catarina state, Brazil; 1913 (before "pacification").
    A. Jules Henry, *Jungle People: A Kaingáng Tribe of the Highlands of Brazil.* New York: Random House, 1964 [originally published 1941].

B. Dr. Bleyer, "Die wilden Waldindianer Santa Catharinas: Die Schokleng." *Zeitschrift fuer Ethnologie* XXXVI, 6(1904): 830–844.

C. José Maria de Paula, "Memoria sobre os Botocudos sob a inspeccao do Paraná e Santa Catharina, organisada pelo serviço de protecçao selvicolãs," *Annaes do XX Congresso Internacional de Americanistas,* Vol. I. Rio de Janiero: Imprensa Nacionale, 1924, pp. 117–139.

5. **Azande** (Zande, Niam-Niam): primarily in northeast Zaïre, but also in Sudan and the Central African Republic; 1905 (before European administration).

A. E. E. Evans-Pritchard, *The Azande: History and Political Institutions.* Oxford: Clarendon Press, 1971.

B. C. R. Lagae, *Les Azande ou Niam-Niam.* Brussels: Vromant and Co., 1926.

C. P. T. W. Baxter and Audrey Butt, *The Azande, and Related Peoples of the Anglo-Egyptian Sudan and Belgian Congo.* London: International African Institute, 1953.

D. P. M. Larkin, "Further Impressions of the Azande." *Sudan Notes and Records* XIII, 1(1930): 99–115.

E. Personal communications from Conrad Reining.

6. **Aztec** (Tenochca): Central Mexico; 1519 (shortly before arrival of Cortes).

A. Jacques Soustelle, *The Daily Life of the Aztecs on the Eve of the Spanish Conquest.* New York: Macmillan, 1962.

B. Alonso de Zorita, *Life and Labor in Ancient Mexico.* Translated by Benjamin Keen. New Brunswick, N.J.: Rutgers University Press, 1963.

C. Albert Idell, trans. and ed., *The Bernal Diaz Chronicles.* New York: Doubleday, 1957.

D. Arthur Monzon, *El Calpulli en la Organización Social de los Tenochca,* Universidad Nacional Autónoma de Mexico, Instituto de Historia; Publication, 1st Series, No. 14. Mexico City, 1949.

E. Friedrich Katz, *Die sozialoekonomischen Verhaeltnisse bei den Azteken im 15. und 16. Jahrhundert.* East Berlin: Verlag Die Wirtschaft, 1956.

7. **Basseri** (Khamseh): Fars, Iran; 1955 (shortly before Barth's fieldwork).

A. Fredrik Barth, *Nomads of South Persia: The Basseri Tribe of the Khamseh Confederacy.* New York: Humanities Press, 1961.

B. Fredrik Barth, "Nomadism in the Mountain and Plateau Areas of Southwest Asia." In *The Problems of the Arid Zone.* Paris: U.N.E.S.C.O., 1962, pp. 341–355.

C. Fredrik Barth, "Capital Investment and Social Structure of a Pastoral Nomad Group in South Persia," in *Capital, Saving and Credit in Peasant Societies,* edited by Raymond Firth and B. S. Yamey. London: Allen and Unwin, 1964, pp. 69–82.

D. Personal communication from Fredrik Barth.

8. **Batak** (Toba-Batak): Sumatra; 1880 (shortly before intensive missionary work).

A. Jacob Cornelis Vergouwen, *The Social Organization and Customary Law of the Toba-Batak of Northern Sumatra.* Koninklijk Instituut voor Taal-, Land-en Volkenkunde. Translation Series 7. Translated by J. Keuning. The Hague: Martinus Nijhoff, 1964 [originally published 1933].

B. Wilhelm Volz, "Die Battak-Laender in Zentral-Sumatra." *Zeitschrift der Gesellschaft fuer Erdkunde zu Berlin* LVIII, 10(1907): 662–693.

C. E. M. Leob, *Sumatra,* Wiener Beitrag zur Kulturgeschichte and Linguistik, III. Vienna: Institut fuer Voelkerkunde der Universitaet Wien, 1935.

D. Milan Stuchlik, "Batak Social and Political Organization, Part I." Annals of the Náprstek Museum, Prague, I, 1962, pp. 101–122. "Part II." Annals of the Náprstek Museum, Prague, II, 1963, pp. 69–139.

E. Alexander Bruch, *Der Batak, wie er leibt und lebt, von seiner Geburt an bis zu seinem Tode.* Rheinische Missionsschriften Nr. 193. Barmen: Verlag des Missionshauses, 1925.

9. **Bhil:** Area around Rajpipla, Gujurat, India; 1935 (shortly before the fieldwork of Koppers).

A. Wilhelm Koppers, *Die Bhil in Zentralindien,* Wiener Beitraege zur Kulturgeschichte und Linguistik, VII. Horn-Vienna: Verlag Berger, 1948.

B. T. B. Naik, *The Bhil, A Study.* Delhi: Bharatiya Adimjati Sevak Sangh, 1956.

C. Y. U. S. Nath, *Bhils of Ratanmal: An Analysis of the Social Structure of a Western Indian Community.* Baroda: Maharaja Sayajirao University, 1960.

D. P. Paul Konrad, "Zur Ethnographie der Bhil." *Anthropos* XXXIV, 1(1939): 23–117.

E. Personal communication from T. B. Naik.

10. **Bribri** (Talamanca): Costa Rica; 1866 (before strong Western influence).
    A. Doris Stone, "The Talamancan Tribes of Costa Rica." Papers of the Peabody Museum, XLIII, No. 2. Cambridge, Massachusetts: Peabody Museum, 1962.
    B. William Gabb, "On the Indian Tribes and Languages of Costa Rica." Proceedings of the American Philosophical Society, XIV, 1875, pp. 483–602.
    C. Personal communication from Doris Stone.
11. **Callinago** (Island Carib): Dominica, Lesser Antilles Islands; 1640 (at the time of early French visits).
    A. Raymond Breton and Armand de la Paix, An Account of the Island of Guadeloupe. HRAF translation from Joseph Rennard, ed., Les Caraïbes, La Guadeloupe, 1635–1656. Paris: Librairie Générale et Internationale, 1929, pp. 45–74.
    B. Jacques Bouton, Concerning the Savages called Caribs. HRAF translation from Bouton, Relation de l'establissement des François depuis l'an 1635 en l'isle de Martinique. Paris: S. Cramoisy, 1640.
    C. Douglas Taylor, "Kinship and Social Structure of the Island Carib." Southwestern Journal of Anthropology II, 2(1946): 180–212.
    D. Personal communication from Douglas Taylor.
12. **China** (Kwangtung province peasant): Nanching village, Kwangtung province, China; 1930 (before modern road put in).
    A. C. K. Yang, "A Chinese Village in Early Communist Transition." In his Chinese Communist Society: The Family and the Village, Cambridge, Massachusetts: MIT Press, 1965.
    B. Daniel Harrison Kulp, Country Life in South China: The Sociology of Familism, Vol. I, New York: Teachers College, Columbia University, 1925.
    C. Maurice Freedman, Chinese Lineage and Society, Fukien and Kwangtung. London School of Economics Monograph in Social Anthropology 33. London: Athlone Press, 1958.
    D. Personal communication from C. K. Yang.
13. **Comanche:** Texas, Oklahoma, U.S.A.; 1850 (before "pacification").
    A. Ernest Wallace and E. Adamson Hoebel, The Comanches: Lords of the South Plains. Norman: University of Oklahoma Press, 1952.
    B. E. Adamson Hoebel, The Political Organization and Law-Ways of the Comanche Indians. Memoirs of the American Anthropological Association, No. 54. 1940.
    C. Robert S. Neighbors, "The Na-ü-ni or Comanches of Texas." In Information Respecting the History, Conditions, and Prospects of the United States, Vol. II., edited by Henry E. Schoolcraft. Philadelphia: Lippincott, 1853, pp. 125–134.
    D. Personal communication from E. Adamson Hoebel and Ernest Wallace.
14. **Copper Eskimo:** Coronation Gulf, Northwest Territories, Canada; 1910 (before extensive Western contact).
    A. Diamond Jenness, Report of the Canadian Arctic Expedition, 1913–18, Vol. XII. The Life of the Copper Eskimos. Ottawa: F. A. Acland, 1922.
    B. Vilhjálmur Stefánsson, The Stefánsson–Anderson Arctic Expedition of the American Museum: Preliminary Ethnological Report. Papers of the American Museum of Natural History, Vol. XIV, Part 1. New York: 1914.
15. **Dogon** (Habe, Kado): Sanga region, Mali; 1900 (before extensive Western contact).
    A. Marti Palau, Les Dogon. Monographies ethnologiques africaines, Institut International African. Paris: Presses Universitaires de France, 1957.
    B. Denise Paulme, Organisation sociale des Dogon (Soudan Français). Paris: Domat-Montchrestien, 1940.
    C. Germaine Dieterlen, "Parenté et mariage chez les Dogon (Soudan Français)." Africa XXVI (April 1956): 107–149.
    D. Personal communication from Denise Paulme.
16. **Fiji:** Vanua Levu Island, Fiji; 1820 (before extensive Western contact).
    A. Basil Thomson, The Fijians: A Study of the Decay of Custom. London: Heinemann, 1908.
    B. Thomas Williams and James Calvert, Fiji and the Fijians, edited by George Stringer Rowe. New York: Appleton, 1860.
    C. Marshall D. Sahlins, Moala: Culture and Nature on a Fijian Island. Ann Arbor: University of Michigan Press, 1962.
    D. A. M. Hocart, Lau Islands, Fiji. Bernice P. Bishop Museum Bulletin 62. Honolulu, 1929.

E. Laura Thompson, *Southern Lau, Fiji: An Ethnography.* Bernice P. Bishop Museum Bulletin 162. Honolulu, 1940.

F. Buell Quain, *Fijian Village.* Chicago: University of Chicago Press, 1948.

17. Fon (Dahomey): Dahomey; 1860 (before the end of the slave trade and the beginning of extensive Western influence).

A. Melville J. Herskovits, *Dahomey: An Ancient West African Kingdom,* Vol. I. New York: J. J. Augusten, 1938.

B. A. Le Hérisse, *L'Ancien Royaume du Dahomey.* Paris: Emile Larose, 1911.

C. Richard F. Burton, *A Mission to Gelele, King of Dahome,* 2nd ed. Vol. I. London: Tinsley Brothers, 1864.

D. Karl Polanyi and Abraham Rotstein, *Dahomey and the Slave Trade.* Seattle: University of Washington Press, 1960.

E. J. A. Skertchly, *Dahomey as It Is.* London: Chapman and Hall, 1874.

18. Ganda (Baganda): Uganda; 1855 (before extensive Western contact).

A. John Roscoe, *The Baganda: An Account of their Native Customs and Beliefs.* 2nd ed. New York: Barnes and Noble, 1966 [first edition 1911].

B. John Roscoe, "Notes on the Manners and Customs of the Baganda." *Journal of the Anthropological Institute,* N.S. XXXI, 6(1901): 117–130.

C. John Roscoe, "Further Notes on the Manners and Customs of the Baganda." *Journal of the Anthropological Institute,* N.S., XXXII, 2(1902): 25–80.

D. Lucy P. Mair, *An African People in the Twentieth Century.* New York: Russell and Russell, 1965 [originally published 1934].

E. Lucy P. Mair, *Native Marriage in Baganda.* International Institute of African Languages and Culture, Memo XIX. London: Oxford University Press, 1940.

F. C. C. Wrigley, "The Changing Economic Structure of Baganda." In *The King's Men: Leadership and States in Baganda on the Eve of Independence,* edited by I. A. Fallers. London: Oxford University Press, 1964, pp. 16–63.

G. C. C. Wrigley, "Baganda: An Outline Economic History." *Economic History Review* X (August 1957): 69–81.

19. Gheg: Albania; 1912 (at year of independence from Turkey).

A. M. Edith Durham, *Some Tribal Origins, Laws and Customs of the Balkans.* London: Allen and Unwin, 1928.

B. Carleton S. Coon, *The Mountain of Giants: A Racial and Cultural Study of the North Albanian Ghegs.* Papers of the Peabody Museum, XXIII, No. 2. Cambridge, Massachusetts, 1950.

C. Margaret Hasluck, *The Unwritten Law in Albania,* Cambridge: University Press, 1954.

D. Margaret Hasluck, "Bride Price in Albania: A Homeric Parallel." *Man* XXXIII (December 1933): 191–195.

E. Personal communications from Hatip Jemali.

20. Havasupai: Arizona, U.S.A., 1890 (before extensive Western contact).

A. Leslie Spier, *Havasupai Ethnography.* Anthropological Papers of the American Museum of Natural History, Vol. XXIX, Part 3. New York, 1928.

B. Carma Lee Smithson, *The Havasupai Woman.* Anthropological Papers, Department of Anthropology, University of Utah, No. 38. Salt Lake City, 1959.

C. Elman Service, "Recent Observations on Havasupai Land Tenure." *Southwestern Journal of Anthropology* III (Winter 1947): 360–367.

D. John Eranklyn Martin, *Continuity and Change in Havasupai Social and Economic Organization.* Ph.D. dissertation, University of Chicago, 1966. Ann Arbor: University Microfilms, n.d.

E. Field notes, August 1973.

F. Personal communication from John Franklyn Martin.

21. Inca: Peru, Bolivia, Equador; 1532 (shortly before Spanish conquest).

A. John Howland Rowe, "Inca Culture at the Time of the Conquest." In *Handbook of South American Indians,* edited by Julian H. Steward, Vol. II, Smithsonian Institution, Bureau of American Ethnology, Bulletin 143. Washington, D.C.: G.P.O., 1944, pp. 183–300.

B. John Murra, *The Economic Organization of the Inca State.* Ph.D. Dissertation, University of Chicago, 1956. Ann Arbor: University Microfilms, n.d.

C. Sally Folk Moore, *Power and Property in Inca Peru.* New York: Columbia University Press, 1958.
D. Alain Gheerbrant, ed., *The Incas, the Royal Commentaries of the Incas, Garcilas de la Vega.* New York: Orion Press, 1961.
E. Louis Baudin, *Daily Life in Peru under the Last Incas.* Translated by W. Brandford. New York: Macmillan, 1962.

22. Iroquois: New York State, U.S.A.; 1700 (before intensive contact with the West).
   A. Lewis H. Morgan, *Houses and House-Life of the American Aborigines.* Department of the Interior, U.S. Geographical and Geological Service of the Rocky Mountain Region, Contributions to North American Ethnology, Vol. IV. Washington, D.C.: G.P.O., 1881.
   B. Lewis H. Morgan, *League of the Ho-de-no-sau-nee or Iroquois.* Vol. I. New York: Dodd, Mead and Co., 1904.
   C. Halliday Jackson, *Sketch of the Manners, Customs, Religion and Government of the Seneca Indian in 1800.* Philadelphia: Marcus Gould, 1830.
   D. Sara Henry Stites, *Economics of the Iroquois.* Ph.D. dissertation, Bryn Mawr, 1904. Lancaster, Pennsylvania: New Era Printing Co., 1905.

23. Khalkha Mongol: Mongolia; 1910 (before gaining independence).
   A. Herbert Harold Vreeland, *Mongol Community and Kinship Structure.* New Haven: HRAF, 1953.
   B. I. Maiskii, *Sovremennaia Mongoliia.* Irkutsk: Gosudarstvennoe Izdatel'stvo, Irkutskoe Otdelenie, 1921.
   C. Personal communication from Owen Lattimore.

24. Koryak (Reindeer Koryak) [Chavchuven]: Kamchatka peninsula and adjacent area, U.S.S.R.; 1901 (at time of fieldwork of Jochelson).
   A. Waldemar Jochelson, *Material Culture and Social Organization of the Koryak,* American Museum of Natural History, X, Part II. Leiden: Brill, 1908.
   B. V. V. Antropova, *Kul'tura i byt koryakov,* Leningrad: Izdatel'stvo Nauka, 1971.

25. !Kung Bushman: Southwest Africa, Botswana; 1950 (shortly before fieldwork of the Marshall family).
   A. Lorna Marshall, "The !Kung Bushmen of the Kalahari." In *Peoples of Africa,* edited by James L. Gibbs. New York: Holt, Rinehart and Winston, 1965, pp. 243–278.
   B. Richard B. Lee, *Subsistence Ecology of !Kung Bushmen.* Ph.D. dissertation, University of California, Berkeley, 1965.
   C. Lorna Marshall, "!Kung Bushman Bands." *Africa* XXX (October 1960): 325–354.
   D. Lorna Marshall, "Marriage among the !Kung Bushmen." *Africa* XXIX (October 1959): 335–365.

26. Kwakiutl (Southern Kwakiutl): Vancouver Island, British Columbia, Canada; 1860 (before extensive contact with the West).
   A. Homer G. Barnett, *The Nature and Function of the Potlatch.* Mimeographed. Eugene, Oregon: University of Oregon, Department of Anthropology, 1968 (originally 1938 as Ph.D. dissertation).
   B. Helen S. Codere, *Fighting with Property: A Study of Kwakiutl Potlatching and Warfare, 1792–1930.* American Ethnological Society Monograph 18. New York: J. J. Augustin, 1950.
   C. Philip Drucker and Robert Heizer, *To Make My Name Good: A Reexamination of the Southern Kwakiutl Potlatch.* Berkeley: University of California Press, 1967.
   D. Franz Boas, *The Social Organization and the Secret Societies of the Kwakiutl Indians.* Smithsonian Museum, U.S. National Museum, Report for 1895. Washington, D.C.: G.P.O., 1897.
   E. Franz Boas, *Ethnology of the Kwakiutl.* Smithsonian Institution, Bureau of American Ethnology, Annual Report, XXXV, 2 vol. Washington, D.C.: G.P.O., 1921.
   F. George M. Dawson, "Notes and Observations on the Kwakiool People of the Northern Part of Vancouver Island and Adjacent Coasts." *Proceedings and Transactions of the Royal Society of Canada,* V, Sec. 2, 1887. Ottawa, 1887, pp. 63–99.
   G. Philip Drucker, "Culture Element Distributions: XXVI, Northwest Coast." *Anthropological Records* IX, 3(1950): 157–294.
   H. Personal communications from Helen Codere and Ronald Rohner.

27. **Lapp** (Mountain Lapp): Käresuando Parish, Sweden; 1950 (shortly before fieldwork of Whitaker and Pehrson).
   A.   Ian Whitaker, *Social Relations in a Nomadic Lappish Community*. Samiske Samlinger Redaksjon Asbjørn Nesheim, Bind II. Oslo: Utgitt av Norsk Folkemuseum, 1955.
   B.   Robert N. Pehrson, *The Bilateral Network of Social Relations in Könkämä Lapp District*. Indiana University Research Center in Anthropology, Folklore, and Linguistics, Publication 3. Bloomington, Indiana, 1957.
   C.   Arne Furumark *et al.*, eds., *Lapponica: Essays Presented to Israel Ruong*. Studia Ethnographica Upsaliensia, Volume 28. Upsala, 1964.

28. **Lepcha (Rong):** Sikkim; 1870 (before extensive Western contacts).
   A.   Geoffrey Gorer, *Himalayan Village: An Account of the Lepchas of Sikkim*. London: Michael Joseph, 1938.
   B.   Amal Kumas Das and Swapan Kumar Banerjee, *The Lepchas of Darjeeling District*. Special Series 2, Bulletin of the Cultural Research Institute. Calcutta: Tribal Welfare Department, Government of West Bengal, 1962.
   C.   Halfdan Siiger, *The Lepchas: Culture and Religion of a Himilayan People*. National Museum of Denmark, Ethnographical Series XI, Part I. Copenhagen, 1967.
   D.   Personal communications from Geoffrey Gorer and Halfdan Siiger.

29. **Manóbo:** Agúsan Valley, East Mindanáo, Phillipines; 1905 (at time of fieldwork of Garvan).
   A.   John M. Garvan, *The Manobós of Mindanáo*. Memoir of the National Academy of Sciences, XXIII. Washington, D.C.: G.P.O., 1941.
   B.   Personal communications from James N. Anderson, Richard E. Elkins, and Stuart A. Schlegel.

30. **Maori:** North part of North Island; 1800 (before extensive white contact).
   A.   Te Rangi Hiroa (Peter Buck), *The Coming of the Maori*. Wellington: Whitcombe and Tombs, 1950.
   B.   Elsdon Best, *The Maori*. Vol. I. Memoirs of the Polynesian Society, V. Wellington: Tombs, 1924.
   C.   Raymond Firth, *Economics of the New Zealand Maori*. 2nd ed. Wellington: Owen, 1959 [originally published 1929].

31. **Mundurucú:** Cabruá Village, Pará, Brazil; 1952 (at time of fieldwork of Murphy).
   A.   Robert F. Murphy, *Headhunter's Heritage*. Berkeley: University of California Press, 1960.
   B.   Robert F. Murphy, "Matrilocality and Patrilineality in Mundurucú Society." *American Anthropologist* LVIII, 3(1956): 414–434.
   C.   A. M. Gonçalves Tocantins, "Estudos sobre a tribu 'Mundurucú'." *Revista trimensal do Instituto Historico Geografico e Ethnographico do Brasil* XL, 2(1877): 73–161.
   D.   C. F. P. Martius, *Beitraege zur Ethnologie Amerikas, zumal Brazilien*. Leipzig: Fleischer, 1867.
   E.   Personal communication from Robert F. Murphy.

32. **Murngin** (Wulamba): East Arnhem Land, Northern Territory, Australia; 1926 (at time of fieldwork of Warner).
   A.   W. Lloyd Warner, *A Black Civilization: A Social Study of an Australian Tribe*. New York: Harper and Brothers, 1937.
   B.   Donald F. Thomson, *Economic Structure and the Ceremonial Exchange Cycle in Arnhem Land*. Melbourne: Macmillan, 1949.

33. **Naskapi:** North Labrador peninsula, Canada; 1880 (shortly before fieldwork of Turner).
   A.   Frank G. Speck, *Naskapi: The Savage Hunters of the Labrador Peninsula*. Oklahoma: University of Oklahoma Press, 1935.
   B.   Frank G. Speck, "Ethical Attitudes of the Labrador Indians." *American Anthropologist* XXXV (October 1933): 559–594.
   C.   Frank G. Speck and Loren C. Eiseley, "Montagnais-Naskapi Bands and Family Hunting Districts of the Central and Southern Labrador Peninsula." *Proceedings of the American Philosophical Society* LXXXV (July 1942): 215–242.
   D.   Julius E. Lips, "Notes on the Montagnais-Naskapi Economy." *Ethnos* XII (January–June 1947): 1–78.
   E.   Eleanor Leacock, "The Montagnais 'Hunting Territory' and the Fur Trade." American Anthropological Association, Memoir No. 78, *American Anthropologist* LVI (October 1954) Part 2, pp. 1–59.

F.   Julius E. Lips, "Naskapi Law." *Transactions of the American Philosophical Society* XXXVII, Part 4 (December 1947): 329–492.

G.   L. M. Turner, "Ethnology of the Ungava District, Hudson Bay Territory." Smithsonian Institution, Bureau of American Ethnology, *11th Annual Report,* 1889–90. Washington, D.C.: G.P.O., 1894, pp. 167–389.

H.   Personal communication from Nelson Graburn.

34. Navajo: Arizona, New Mexico, U.S.A.; 1860 (before surrender to U.S. Army).

A.   Dane Coolidge and Mary Roberts Coolidge, *The Navajo Indians.* Boston and New York: Houghton Mifflin, 1930.

B.   Malcom Carr Collier, *Local Organization among the Navaho.* New Haven: HRAF, 1966 [originally published 1951].

C.   Clyde Kluckhohn and Dorothea Leighton, *The Navaho.* Rev. ed. Garden City: Doubleday, 1962.

D.   Gladys A. Reichard, *Social Life of the Navajo Indians; with Some Attention to Minor Ceremonies.* Columbia University Contributions to Anthropology 7. New York: Columbia University Press, 1928.

E.   Franciscan Fathers, *An Ethnologic Dictionary of the Navaho Language.* St. Michaels, Arizona, 1910.

F.   W. W. Hill, *The Agricultural and Hunting Methods of the Navaho Indians.* Yale University Publications in Anthropology, No. 18. New Haven: Yale University Press, 1938.

G.   James F. Downs, *The Navajo.* New York: Holt, Rinehart and Winston, 1972.

35. Nuer: A Āl̄i A-N̄il, Sudan; 1920 (before "pacification").

A.   Edward Evan Evans-Pritchard, *The Nuer: A Description of the Modes of Livelihood and Political Institutions of a Nilotic People.* Oxford: Clarendon Press, 1940.

B.   Edward Evan Evans-Pritchard, *Kinship and Marriage among the Nuer.* Oxford: Clarendon Press, 1951.

C.   P. P. Howell, *A Manual of Nuer Law.* International African Institute. London: Oxford University Press, 1954.

D.   Personal communication from P. P. Howell.

36. Nyakyusa (Banyakyusa, Wanyakyusa): Southern Highlands, Tanzania; 1890 (shortly before missionary arrival).

A.   Monica Wilson, *Good Company: A Study of Nyakyusa Age Villages,* International African Institute. London: Oxford University Press, 1951.

B.   Monica Wilson, *The Peoples of the Nyasa-Tanganyika Corridor.* University of Cape Town Communication, School of African Studies, N.S. 29, October 1958.

C.   Monica Wilson, "Nyakyusa Kinship." In *African Systems of Kinship and Marriage,* edited by A. R. Radcliffe-Brown and Daryll Forde. International African Institute. London: Oxford University Press, 1950, pp. 111–140.

D.   Philip Hugh Gulliver, *Land Tenure and Social Change among the Nyakyusa.* Kampala; East African Institute of Social Research, 1958.

E.   S. Charsley, *The Princes of Hyakyusa.* Makerere Institute of Social Research. Nairobi: East African Publishing House, 1969.

F.   Personal communication from Monica Wilson.

37. Omaha: Nebraska, U.S.A.; 1850 (before extensive Western contact).

A.   Alice C. Fletcher and Francis LaFlesche, "The Omaha Tribe." Smithsonian Institution, Bureau of American Ethnology, *27th Annual Report 1905–6.* Washington, D.C.: G.P.O., 1911, pp. 29–643.

B.   J. Owen Dorsey, "Omaha Sociology." Smithsonian Institution, Bureau of American Ethnology, *3d Annual Report 1881–2.* Washington, D.C.: G.P.O., 1884, pp. 205–370.

C.   Reo E. Fortune, *Omaha Secret Societies.* Columbia University Contributions in Anthropology, XIV. New York: Columbia University Press, 1932.

D.   Margaret Mead, *The Changing Culture of an Indian Tribe.* New York: Columbia University Press, 1932.

38. Pomo (Eastern Pomo): Clear Lake, California; 1847 (shortly before California gold rush).

A.   Edwin M. Loeb, "Pomo Folkways." *University of California Publications in American Archaeology and Ethnology* XIX, 2(1926): 149–405.

B.   Edward Winslow Gifford, "Clear Lake Pomo Society." *University of California Publications in American Archaeology and Ethnology* XVIII, 2(1926): 287–390.

   C.   Edward W. Gifford and Alfred L. Kroeber, "Culture Element Distributions, IC: Pomo."
        University of California Publications in American Archaeology and Ethnology XXXVII,
        4(1937): 117–254.
   D.   Alfred L. Kroeber, *Handbook of the Indians of California.* Smithsonian Institution, Bureau
        of American Ethnology, Bulletin 78. Washington, D.C.: G.P.O., 1925.
   E.   Personal communications from Robert Oswald, Burt W. Aginsky, Michael J. Lowy, and
        Robert Wharton.
39. Rif (Aith Waryaghar Rif): Morocco; 1920 (before major changes).
   A.   Carleton Stevens Coon, *Tribes of the Rif.* Harvard African Studies IX. Cambridge, Mas-
        sachusetts: Peabody Museum of American Archaeology and Ethnology, 1931.
   B.   David Montgomery Hart, "An Ethnographic Survey of the Riffian Tribe of Aith
        Waryaghar." *Tamuda* II, 1(1954): 55–86.
   C.   David M. Hart, "Clan, Lineage, Local Community and the Feud in a Riffian Tribe (Aith
        Waryaghar) Morocco." In *Peoples and Culture of the Middle East: An Anthropological
        Reader,* edited by Louise E. Sweet, Vol. II. Garden City, New York: Natural History Press,
        1970, pp. 3–76.
   D.   Paul S. Lunt, ed., *Morocco.* Subcontractor's Monograph, HRAF, No. 62, New Haven:
        HRAF, 1956.
   E.   Personal communication from David M. Hart.
40. Rwala (Rwala Bedouin): Syria, Jordan, North Arabia; 1905 (at beginning of fieldwork of
     Musil).
   A.   Alois Musil, *The Manners and Customs of the Rwala Bedouins.* American Geographical
        Society, Oriental Explorations and Studies No. 6. New York, 1928.
   B.   Louise E. Sweet, "Camel Pastorialism in North Arabia and the Minimal Camping Unit." In
        Environment and Cultural Behavior, edited by Andrew P. Vayda. Garden City, New York:
        Natural History Press, 1969, pp. 157–180.
   C.   Carl Raswan, *Im Land der schwarzen Zelte: Mein Leben unter den Beduinen.* Berlin:
        Ullstein, 1934.
41. Semang (Orang-Utan, Sakai): Northwest Malaysia; 1924 (at time of first fieldwork by
     Schebesta).
   A.   Paul Schebesta, *Die Negrito Asiens,* Vols. I and II. Studia Instituti Anthropos. Vienna-
        Moedling: St. Gabriel Verlag, 1954.
   B.   Paul Schebesta, *Among the Forest Dwarfs of Malaya.* Translated by Arthur Chambers.
        London: Hutchinson, n.d.
   C.   Ivor H. N. Evans, *The Negritos of Malaya.* Cambridge: University Press, 1937.
42. Serbia: Sumadija region, Serbia, Yugoslavia; 1910 (before Serbian–Turkish war and World
     War I).
   A.   Joel Martin Halpern, *Social and Cultural Change in a Serbian Village.* Ph.D. dissertation,
        Columbia University, 1956. New Haven: HRAF, 1956.
   B.   Eugene A. Hammel, *Alternative Social Structures and Ritual Relations in the Balkans.*
        Englewood Cliffs, New Jersey: Prentice Hall, 1968.
   C.   Jeremija M. Pavlović, *Folk Life and Customs in the Kragujevac Region of the Jesenica in
        Sumadija.* Srpski etnografski zbornik, No. 22, book 12, Srpska Kraljovska Akademija.
        Translated by HRAF. New Haven: HRAF, n.d. [originally published 1921].
   D.   Vera St. Erlich, *Family in Transition: A Study of 300 Yugoslav Villages.* Princeton, New
        Jersey: Princeton University Press, 1966.
   E.   Personal communication from Joel Halpern.
43. Shavante (Akwe-Shavante) (Chavante, Xavante): Central plateau, east Mato Grosso, Brazil;
     1950 (before extensive Western contact).
   A.   David Maybury-Lewis, *Akwe-Shavante Society.* Oxford: Clarendon Press, 1967.
   B.   Personal communication from David Maybury-Lewis.
44. Siane: Goroka subdistrict, Eastern Highlands, New Guinea; 1944 (before Western contact).
   A.   Richard F. Salisbury, *From Stone to Steel: Economic Consequences of a Technological
        Change in New Guinea.* London: Cambridge University Press, 1962.
   B.   Personal communication from Richard F. Salisbury.
45. Siriono: Eastern Bolivia; 1940 (at time of fieldwork by Holmberg).
   A.   Allen R. Holmberg, *Nomads of the Long Bow: The Siriono of Eastern Bolivia.* Garden City,
        New York: Natural History Press, 1969 [originally published 1950].

46. **Suku** (BaSuku, Pindi): Kwango district, Zaïre; 1915 (before extensive contact with missionaries or West).
   A.   Igor Kopytoff, "The Suku of Southwestern Congo." In *Peoples of Africa,* edited by James L. Gibbs. New York: Holt, Rinehart and Winston, 1965, pp. 441–477.
   B.   Igor Kopytoff, "Family and Lineage among the Suku of the Congo." In *The Family Estate in Africa,* edited by Robert F. Gray and P. H. Gulliver. London: Routledge and Kegan Paul, 1964, pp. 83–116.
   C.   Igor Kopytoff, "Labor Allocation among the Suku." Paper presented at the Conference on Competing Demands for the Time of Labor in Traditional African Society, October 1967.
   D.   F. Lamal, *Basuku et Bayaka des districts Kwango et Kwilu au Congo.* Musée royal de l'afrique centrale, Series In. 8, Sciences Humaines, No. 56. Turvuren, Belgium; 1965.
   E.   Personal communication from Igor Kopytoff.
47. **Tanala (Menabe Tanala):** Melagasy; 1890 (before extensive contact with the West).
   A.   Ralph Linton, *The Tanala: A Hill Tribe of Madagascar.* Field Museum of Natural History, Publication 317, Anthropological Series, Volume XXII. Chicago: Field Museum, 1933.
   B.   Ralph Linton, "The Tanala of Madagascar." In *The Individual and His Society,* edited by Abram Kardiner. New York: Columbia University Press, 1939, pp. 251–291.
   C.   Ralph Linton, *The Study of Man.* 2nd ed. New York: Appleton, Century, Crofts, 1936.
48. **Thonga** (BaThonga): Mozambique; 1870 (before beginning of fieldwork of Junod).
   A.   Henri A. Junod, *The Life of a South African Tribe.* 2nd ed. New Hyde Park, New York: University Books, 1962 [originally published 1912].
49. **Tikopia:** British Solomon Islands (Santa Cruz Islands); 1928 (at beginning of Firth's fieldwork).
   A.   Raymond Firth, *Primitive Polynesian Economy.* London: Routledge and Sons, 1939.
   B.   Raymond Firth, *We the Tikopia: A Sociological Study of Kinship in Primitive Polynesia.* Boston: Beacon Press, 1963 [originally published 1936].
   C.   Raymond Firth, *Social Change in Tikopia.* London: Allen and Unwin, 1959.
   D.   Personal communication from Raymond Firth.
50. **Tiv** (Munshi): Eastern central Nigeria; 1900 (before extensive Western contact).
   A.   Laura and Paul Bohannan, *The Tiv of Central Nigeria.* London: International African Institute, 1953.
   B.   Paul and Laura Bohannan, *Tiv Economy.* Evanston: Northwestern University Press, 1968.
   C.   Paul Bohannan, *Tiv Farm and Settlement.* London: H.M.S.O., 1957.
   D.   Paul Bohannan, "Some Principles of Exchange and Investment among the Tiv." *American Anthropologist* LVII (February 1955): 60–70.
   E.   Roy Clive Abraham, *The Tiv People.* Lagos: Government Printer, 1933.
   F.   Personal communication from Paul Bohannan.
51. **Toba (Eastern Toba or Toba-Pilagá)** (Pitilagá, Takshik, Komlik): Chaco and Formosa provinces, Argentina; 1860 (before lumber mills and military campaigns).
   A.   Rafael Karsten, *The Toba Indians of the Bolivian Gran Chaco.* Acta Academiae Aboensis, Humaniora IV:4. Abo:Abo Akademi, 1923.
   B.   A. Metraux, "Etudes d'Ethnographie Toba-Pilagá (Gran Chaco)." *Anthropos* XXXII, 1(1937): 171–194.
   C.   Jules Henry, "Some Cultural Determinants of Hostility in Pilagá Indian Children," *American Journal of Orthopsychiatry* X, 1(1940): 111–119.
   D.   Jules Henry, "The Economics of Pilagá Food Distribution." *American Anthropologist* LIII (April–June 1951): 187–219.
   E.   Elmer S. Miller, *Pentecostalism among the Argentine Toba.* Unpublished Ph.D. dissertation, University of Pittsburgh, 1967.
   F.   Personal communication from Elmer S. Miller.
52. **Toda:** Nilgrili Hills, Madras, India; 1901 (at time of Rivers' fieldwork).
   A.   W. H. R. Rivers, *The Todas.* London: Macmillan, 1906.
   B.   Murray B. Emeneau, "Toda Marriage Regulations and Taboos." *American Anthropologist* XLIX, 1(1937): 103–113.
   C.   Prince Peter of Greece and Denmark, "The Todas: Some Additions and Corrections to W. H. R. River's Book as Observed in the Field," *Man* LV (June 1955): 89–93.
   D.   Personal communications from Murray B. Emeneau and David G. Mandelbaum.
53. **Trobriand:** Kiriwina district, Boyowa Island, Trobriand Islands, Solomon Sea; 1914 (at time of Malinowski's fieldwork).

A. Bronisław Malinowski, *Coral Gardens and Their Magic,* Vol. I. New York: American Book Company, 1935.
B. Bronisław Malinowski, *Argonauts of the Western Pacific.* New York: Dutton, 1961.
C. J. P. Singh Uberoi, *The Politics of the Kula Ring.* Manchester: Manchester University Press, 1961.
D. H. A. Powell, "Genealogy, Residence and Kinship in Kiriwini." *Man* IV (1969): 177–202.
E. E. R. Leach, "Concerning Trobriand Clans and the Kinship Category *Tabu."* In *The Development Cycle in Domestic Groups,* edited by Jack Goody. Cambridge Papers in Social Anthropology No. 1. Cambridge: University Press, 1958.

54. Truk: Romónum Island, Truk Islands, East Caroline Islands group; 1895 (before extensive Western contact).
A. Ward H. Goodenough, *Property, Kin and Community on Truk.* Yale University Publications in Anthropology, N. 46. New Haven: Yale University Press, 1951.
B. Thomas Gladwin and Seymour B. Sarason, *Truk: Man in Paradise.* Viking Fund Publication No. 20. New York: Wenner-Gren Foundation, 1953.
C. Edward T. Hall and Karl J. Pelzer, *The Economy of the Truk Islands: An Anthropological and Economic Survey.* Honolulu: U.S. Commercial Company, 1946.
D. P. Laurentius Bollig, *Die Bewohner der Truk-Inseln: Religion, Leben und kurze Grammatik eines Mikronesiervolkes.* Internationale Sammlung ethnologischer Monographien. Muenster: Aschendorffsche Verlagsbuchhandlung, 1927.
E. Personal communication from Ward H. Goodenough.

55. Tuareg (Ahaggar Tuareg): Ahaggar area, Algeria; 1898 (prior to French military occupation of Sahara).
A. Henri Lhote, *Les Touaregs du Hoggar.* Paris: Payot, 1944.
B. Lloyd Cabot Briggs, *Tribes of the Sahara,* Cambridge, Massachusetts: Harvard University Press, 1960.
C. Johannes Nicolaisen, *Ecology and Culture of the Pastoral Tuareg with Particular Reference to the Tuareg of Ahaggar and Ayr.* Etnografisk Kaekke, IX. Copenhagen: National Museum of Copenhagen, 1963.
D. Personal communications from Lloyd Cabot Briggs and Johannes Nicolaisen.

56. Turkey (Turk): Sakaltutan and Elbasi villages, Central Anatolia; 1950 (at beginning of Stirling's fieldwork).
A. Paul Stirling, *Turkish Village.* London: Weidenfeld and Nicolson, 1965.
B. Joe E. Pierce, *Life in a Turkish Village.* New York: Holt, Rinehart and Winston, 1964.
C. Personal communication from Paul Stirling.

57. Warao (Warrau, Guaraunos): Orinoco delta, Venezuela: 1920 (before introduction of Western agricultural techniques).
A. Angel Turrado Moreno, *Ethnografia de los Indios Guaraunos.* Caracas; Lit. y. Tip. Vargas, 1945.
B. Maria Matilde Suarez, *Los Warao: indigenas del delta del Orinoco.* Departmente de Anthropologia, Instituto Venezolano de Investigaciones Cientificas. Caracas, 1958.
C. Johannes Wilbert, "Die soziale and politische Organisation der Warrau." *Koelner Zeitschrift fuer Soziologie and Sozialpsychologie* X (1958): 272–291.
D. Johannes Wilbert, "The Fishermen: The Warao of the Orinoco Delta." in his *Survivors of Eldorado.* New York: Praeger, 1972, pp. 65–115.
E. Heinz Dieter Heinen, *Adaptive Changes in a Tribal Economy: A Case Study Winikina Warao.* Ph.D. Dissertation, Department of Anthropology, University of California in Los Angeles, 1972. Ann Arbor: University Microfilms, n.d.
F. Personal communication from Johannes Wilbert.

58. Wolof (Ouolof): Senegal, Gambia; 1875 (before conquest by French).
A. David P. Gamble, *The Wolof of Senegambia, together with Notes on the Lebu and Serer.* Ethnographic Survey of Africa, Western Africa, Part IV. London: International African Institute, 1975.
B. David W. Ames, "The Use of a transitional Cloth Money among the Wolof." *American Anthropologist* LVII 5(1955): 1016–1024.
C. David W. Ames, "The Rural Wolof of Gambia." In *Markets in Africa,* edited by Paul Bohannan and George Dalton. Evanston, Ill. Northwestern U. Press, 1962, pp. 29–60.

D. David W. Ames, "Wolof Co-operative Work Groups." In *Continuity and Change in African Culture,* edited by William R. Bascom and Melville J. Herskovits. Chicago: University of Chicago Press, 1959, pp. 224–237.

E. Paul Pélissier, *Les paysans du Sénégal: Les civilisations agraires du Cayor à la Casamance.* Saint-Yrieix: Imprimerie Fabrègue, 1966.

F. Vincent Monteil, "The Wolof Kingdom of Kayor." In *West African Kingdoms in the 19th Century,* edited by C. Daryll Forde and P. M. Kaberry. International African Institute. London: Oxford University Press, 1967, pp. 260–281.

G. Personal communications from David W. Ames and David P. Gamble.

59. Yahgan (Yamana): Tierra del Fuego, Chile; 1850 (before missionaries).

A. Martin Gusinde, *Die Feuerland-Indianer.* Band II, *Die Yamana, Vom Leben und Denken der Wassernomaden.* Vienna-Moedling: Anthropos Verlag, 1937.

60. Yaqui: Sonora, Mexico and Arizona, U.S.A.; 1930.

A. Edward H. Spicer, *Potom: A Yaqui Village in Sonora.* Memoir of the American Anthropological Association No. 77, *American Anthropologist* LVI (August 1954) Part 2.

B. Edward H. Spicer, *Pascua: A Yaqui Village in Arizona.* Chicago: University of Chicago Press, 1940.

C. Ralph L. Beals, *The Contemporary Culture of the Cáhita Indians.* Smithsonian Institution, Bureau of American Ethnology, Bulletin 142. Washington, D.C.: G.P.O., 1945.

D. W. C. Holden et al., "Studies of the Yaqui Indians of Sonora, Mexico." *Texas Technological College Bulletin* XII, No. 1 (January 1936). Lubbock, 1936.

E. Personal communications from Edward H. Spicer, W. C. Holden, and Ralph L. Beals.

APPENDIX F

BIBLIOGRAPHY

PERIODICALS CITED IN TEXT AND APPENDICES

Acta Academiae Aboensis, Humanioia. Abo, Finland: irregular.
Africa. London: 4/year.
African Studies. Johannesburg, South Africa: 4/year.
American Anthropologist. Washington, D.C.: 4/year.
American Economic Review. Providence, Rhode Island: 5/year.
American Journal of Economics and Sociology. New York: 4/year.
American Journal of Orthopsychiatry. New York: 5/year.
American Journal of Sociology. Chicago, Illinois: 6/year.
American Sociological Review. Albany, New York: 4/year.
Anthropological Linguistics. Bloomington, Indiana: 9/year.
Anthropological Quarterly. Washington, D.C.: 4/year.
Anthropological Records. Berkeley, California: irregular.
Anthropos. Fribourg, Switzerland: 3/year.
Asia. New York, New York: 12/year.
Behavioral Science Notes. New Haven, Connecticut: 4/year.
Bijdragen tot de Taal- Land- en Volkenkunde. The Hague, Netherlands: 4/year.
British Journal of Sociology. London: 4/year.
Canadian Journal of Economics and Political Science. Toronto: 4/year.
Comparative Studies in Society and History. New York: 4/year.
Current Anthropology. Chicago, Illinois: 5/year.
Economic Development and Cultural Change. Chicago, Illinois: 4/year.
Economic History Review. Cambridge, England: 3/year.
Economic Inquiry. Long Beach, California: 4/year.
Ethnology. Pittsburgh, Pennsylvania: 4/year.
Ethnos. Lund, Sweden: 4/year.
Finanzarchiv. Tuebingen, Federal Republic of Germany: 3/year.
Journal of African History. Cambridge, England: 4/year.

Journal of Economic History. New York: 4/year.
Journal of Legal Education. Lexington, Kentucky: 4/year.
Journal of Personality and Social Psychology. Washington, D.C.: 4/year.
Journal of Political Economy. Chicago, Illinois: 6/year.
Journal of the Royal Anthropological Institute of Great Britain and Ireland. London: 2/year.
Koelner Zeitschrift fuer Soziologie und Sozialpsychologie. Cologne, Federal Republic of Germany: 4/year.
Law and Society Review. Buffalo, New York: 4/year.
Man. London: 4/year.
Oceanea. Sydney, Australia: 4/year.
Papers of the Peabody Museum. Cambridge, Massachusetts: irregular.
Past and Present. Oxford, England: 4/year.
Proceedings of the American Philosophical Society. Philadelphia, Pennsylvania: 6/year.
Proceedings of the Canadian Institute. Toronto: 1/year.
Quarterly Journal of Economics. Cambridge, Massachusetts: 4/year.
Revista trimensal de Instituto Historico Geografico e Ethnographica do Brasil. Rio de Janiero: 4/year.
Science. Washington, D.C.: 52/year.
Social Forces. Chapel Hill, North Carolina: 4/year.
Southwestern Journal of Anthropology. Albuquerque, New Mexico: 4/year.
Soviet Anthropology and Archeology. White Plains, New York: 4/year.
Sudan Notes and Records. Khartoum, Sudan: 1 or 2/year.
Tamuda. Tetuán, Morocco: 3/year.
Transactions of the American Philosophical Society. Philadelphia, Pennsylvania: irregular.
Transactions of the New York Academy of Sciences. New York: 8/year.
University of California Publications in American Archaelogy and Ethnology. Berkeley, California: irregular.
Zeitschrift der Gesellschaft fuer Erdkunde zu Berlin. Berlin: 12/year.
Zeitschraft fuer Ethnologie. Braunschweig, Federal Republic of Germany: 2/year.

A SELECTED BIBLIOGRAPHY OF CITED BOOKS

Only books cited in the text or the appendices excluding Appendix E are listed.

Adams, John W. 1973. *The Gitksan Potlatch: Population Flux, Resource Ownership and Reciprocity.* Toronto, Canada: Holt, Rinehart and Winston.
Antropova, V. V. 1971. *Kul'tura i byt koryakov.* Leningrad: Izdatel'stvo Nauka.
Balandier, Georges. 1967. *Political Anthropology.* Translated by A. M. Sheridan Smith. New York: Random House.
Banton, Michael, ed. 1965. *The Relevance of Models for Social Anthropology.* Association of Social Anthropologists, Monograph No. 1. London, England: Tavistock.
Barnett, Homer G. 1968. *The Nature and Function of the Potlatch.* Eugene, Oregon: Department of Anthropology.
Barth, Fredrik. 1966. *Models of Social Organization.* Occasional Paper No. 23, Royal Anthropological Institute of Great Britain and Ireland. London, England.
Becker, Howard. 1956. *Man in Reciprocity.* New York: Praeger.
Berger, Joseph; Zelditch, Morris; and Anderson, Bo, eds. 1972. *Sociological Theories in Progress,* Vol. II. Boston, Massachusetts: Houghton-Mifflin.
Blau, Peter M. 1964. *Exchange and Power in Social Life.* New York: Wiley.
Boehm-Bawerk, Eugen von. 1959. *Capital and Interest: A Positive Theory of Capital.* Translated by George D. Huncke. South Holland, Illinois: Libertarian Press.
Bohannan, Paul, and Dalton, George, eds. 1965. *Markets in Africa.* Garden City, N.Y.: Doubleday.
Boserup, Ester. 1965. *The Conditions of Agricultural Growth: The Economics of Agrarian Change Under Population Pressure.* Chicago, Illinois: Aldine.
————. 1970. *Woman's Role in Economic Development.* New York: St. Martin's Press.

Boulding, Kenneth E. 1973. *The Economy of Love and Fear: A Preface to the Grants Economy.* Belmont, California: Wadsworth.

Boulding, Kenneth E., and Pfaff, Martin, eds. 1972. *Redistribution to the Rich and the Poor.* Belmont, California: Wadsworth.

Boulding, Kenneth E.; Pfaff, Martin; and Pfaff, Anita, eds. 1973. *Transfers in an Urbanized Economy.* Belmont, California: Wadsworth.

Brown, Norman O. 1959. *Life Against Death: The Psychoanalytical Meaning of History.* Middletown, Connecticut: Wesleyan University Press.

Buecher, Karl. 1907. *Industrial Evolution.* Translated by S. Morley Wickett. New York: Holt.

Cancian, Frank. 1965. *Economics and Prestige in a Maya Community: The Religious Cargo System in Zinacantan.* Stanford, California: Stanford University Press.

Clifton, James A., ed. 1968. *Introduction to Cultural Anthropology.* New York: Houghton Mifflin.

Codere, Helen. 1950. *Fighting with Property: A Study of Kwakiutl Potlatching and Warfare, 1792–1930,* Monograph of the American Ethnological Society. New York: J. J. Augustin.

Cohen, Ronald, and Middleton, John, eds. 1967. *Comparative Political Systems: Studies in the Politics of Preindustrial Societies.* Garden City, New York: Natural History Press.

Cohen, Yehudi A., ed. 1961. *Social Structure and Personality.* New York: Holt, Rinehart and Winston.

Conrad, Alfred H., and Meyer, John R. 1964. *The Economics of Slavery.* Chicago, Ill.: Aldine.

Confino, Michael. 1969. *Systèmes agraires et progrès agricole: L'assolement triennal en Russie aux XVIIIe–XIXe siècles.* Paris: Mouton.

Curry, R. L., Jr., and Wade, L. 1968. *A Theory of Political Exchange: Economic Reasoning in Political Analysis.* Englewood Cliffs, New Jersey: Prentice-Hall.

Dalton, George. 1971. *Economic Anthropology and Development: Essays on Tribal and Peasant Economies.* New York: Basic Books.

————, ed. 1968. *Primitive, Archaic and Modern Economies: Essays of Karl Polanyi.* Garden City, New York: Anchor Books.

————, ed. 1971. *Studies in Economic Anthropology.* American Anthropological Association, Anthropological Studies, No. 7. Washington, D.C.

————, ed. 1967. *Tribal and Peasant Economies: Readings in Economic Anthropology.* Garden City, New York: The Natural History Press.

Davis, David Brion. 1966. *The Problem of Slavery in Western Culture.* Ithaca, New York: Cornell University Press.

Desmonde, William H. 1962. *Magic, Myth, and Money.* New York: Free Press of Glencoe.

Diakonoff, I. M., ed. 1969. *Ancient Mesopotamia: Socio-Economic History.* Moscow: Nauka Publishing House.

Diamond, Stanley, ed. 1960. *Culture in History: Essays in Honor of Paul Radin.* New York: Columbia University Press.

Dillon, Wilton S. 1968. *Gifts and Nations.* The Hague: Mouton.

Dole, Gertrude E., and Carneiro, Robert L., eds. 1960. *Essays in the Science of Culture in Honor of Leslie A. White.* New York: Crowell.

Duby, Georges. 1974. *The Early Growth of the European Economy: Warriors and Peasants from the Seventh to the Twelfth Century.* Translated by Howard B. Clarke. Ithaca, New York: Cornell University Press.

Durkheim, Emile. 1951. *Suicide.* Translated by John A. Spaulding and George Simpson. New York: Free Press.

Einzig, Paul. 1966. *Primitive Money: In its Ethnological, Historical and Economic Aspects.* 2nd ed. Oxford, England: Pergamon Press.

Ekeh, Peter. 1974. *Social Exchange Theories: The Two Traditions.* Cambridge, Massachusetts: Harvard University Press.

Emmanuel, Arghiri. 1972. *Unequal Exchange: A Study of the Imperialism of Trade.* Translated by Brian Pearce. New York: Monthly Review Press.

Engels, Friedrich. 1972. *The Origin of the Family, Private Property and the State.* New York: International Publishers.

Erasmus, Charles John. 1955. *Reciprocal Labor: A Study of its Occurrence and Disappearance Among Farming Peoples in Latin America.* Unpublished Ph.D. dissertation, University of California at Berkeley. Berkeley, California.

Evans-Pritchard, E. E. 1951. *Kinship and Marriage Among the Nuer*. Oxford, England: Clarendon Press.
———. 1950. *The Nuer*. Oxford, England: Clarendon Press.
Finley, Moses I. 1973. *The Ancient Economy*. Berkeley: University of California Press.
———, ed. 1960. *Slavery in Classical Antiquity*. Cambridge, England: Heffer and Sons.
Firth, Raymond. 1967. *Primitive Polynesian Economy*. London, England: Routledge and Kegal Paul.
———. 1959. *Social Change in Tikopia*. London, England: George Allen and Unwin.
———, ed. 1967. *Themes in Economic Anthropology*. Association of Social Anthropologists, Monograph 6. London, England: Tavistock.
Firth, Raymond, and Yamey, B. S., eds. 1964. *Capital, Saving and Credit in Peasant Society*. London, England: Allen and Unwin.
Fogel, Robert William, and Engerman, Stanley L. 1974. *Time on the Cross: The Economics of American Negro Slavery*. Boston, Massachusetts: Little, Brown.
Fortes, Mayer, and Evans-Pritchard, E. E., eds. 1940. *African Political Systems*. International African Institute. London, England: Oxford University Press.
Fortune, Reo E. 1932. *Omaha Secret Societies*. Columbia University Contributions in Anthropology, XIV. New York: Columbia University Press.
Freud, Sigmund. 1930. *Civilization and Its Discontents*. Translated by Joan Riviere. New York: Cape and Smith.
Fried, Morton H. 1967. *The Evolution of Political Society: An Essay in Political Anthropology*. New York: Random House.
Friters, Gerold M. 1949. *Outer Mongolia and Its International Position*. Baltimore, Md.: Johns Hopkins Press.
Genovese, Eugene D. 1965. *The Political Economy of Slavery in the Economy and Society of the Slave South*. New York: Pantheon.
Gergen, Kenneth J. 1969. *The Psychology of Behavior Exchange*. Reading, Massachusetts: Addison-Wesley.
Gerloff, Wilhelm. 1947. *Die Entstehung des Geldes und die Anfaenge des Geldwesens*. 3d ed. Frankfurter wissenschaftliche Beitraege, Kulturwissenschaftliche Reihe, Band 1. Frankfurt a.M.: Klostermann.
———. 1948. *Die oeffentliche Finanzwirtschaft*. Frankfurt a.M.: Klostermann.
Gladwin, Thomas, and Sarason, Seymour B. 1953. *Truk: Man in Paradise*. Viking Fund Publication No. 20. New York: Wenner-Gren Foundation.
Glasse, Robert M., and Meggitt, J. J., eds. 1969. *Pigs, Pearlshells and Women: Marriage in the New Guinea Highlands*. Englewood Cliffs, New Jersey: Prentice Hall.
Gol'tsberg, I. A., ed. 1972. *Agroklimaticheskii atlas mira*. Glavnaia gidrometerologicheskoi sluzbi. Moscow and Leningrad: Gidrometeorzdat.
Goode, William J. 1971. *Social System and Family Patterns: A Propositional Inventory*. Indianopolis, Indiana: Bobbs-Merrill.
Goodfellow, D. W. 1939. *Principles of Economic Sociology*. London, England: Routledge and Kegan Paul.
Goody, Jack. 1971. *Technology, Tradition and the State in Africa*. London, England: Oxford University Press.
Goody, Jack, and Tambiah, S. J. 1973. *Bridewealth and Dowry*. Cambridge Papers in Social Anthropology 7. Cambridge, England: University Press.
Graburn, Nelson H. H. 1969. *Eskimos Without Igloos: Social and Economic Development in Sugluk*. Boston, Massachusetts: Little, Brown.
———. 1964. *Taqagmiut Eskimo Kinship Terminology*. Northern Coordination and Research Center, Department of Northern Affairs and Natural Resources, N.C.R.-64-1. Ottawa, Canada.
Grierson, P. J. Hamilton 1903. *The Silent Trade*. Edinburgh, Scotland: W. Green and Sons.
Gross, Llewellyn, ed. 1959. *Symposium on Sociological Theory*. New York: Harper and Row.
Gusinde, Martin. 1937. *Die Feuerland-Indianer*. Band II. *Die Yamana, Vom Leben und Denken der Wassernomaden*. Vienna-Moedling: Anthropos Verlag.
Harris, Marvin. 1968. *The Rise of Anthropological Theory*. New York: Crowell.
Herskovits, Melville J. 1952. *Economic Anthropology: The Economic Life of Primitive Peoples*. New York: Norton.

Hobhouse, L. T.; Wheeler, G. C.; and Ginsberg, M. 1930. *The Material Culture and Social Institutions of the Simpler Peoples: An Essay in Correlation.* London: Chapman and Hall.

Holmberg, Alan R. 1969. *Nomads of the Long Bow: The Siriono of Eastern Bolivia.* Garden City, New York: Natural History Press.

Holzman, Franklyn. 1955. *Soviet Taxation: The Fiscal and Monetary Problems of a Planned Economy.* Cambridge, Massachusetts: Harvard University Press.

Homans, George Caspar. 1961. *Social Behavior: Its Elementary Forms.* New York: Harcourt, Brace.

Homer, Sidney. 1963. *A History of Interest Rates.* New Brunswick, New Jersey: Rutgers University Press.

Honigmann, John J., ed. 1973. *Handbook of Social and Cultural Anthropology.* Chicago, Illinois: Rank McNally.

Hoyt, Elizabeth Ellis. 1968. *Primitive Trade: Its Psychology and Economics.* New York: Augustus M. Kelley.

Hsu, Francis L. K., ed. 1972. *Psychological Anthropology.* 2nd ed. Cambridge, Massachusetts: Schenkman.

Hunt, George T. 1960. *The Wars of the Iroquois: A Study in Intertribal Trade Relations.* Madison, Wisconsin: University of Wisconsin Press.

Ilchman, Warren F., and Uphoff, Norman Thomas. 1969. *The Political Economy of Change.* Berkeley, California: University of California Press.

Jacobson, Anita. 1967. *Marriage and Money.* Studia Ethnographica Upsaliensia, XXVIII. Lund: Berlingska Boktrychkeriet.

Jenness, Diamond. 1922. *Report of the Canadian Arctic Expedition, 1913–18.* Vol. XII. *The Life of the Copper Eskimos.* Ottawa: F. A. Acland.

Jevons, W. Stanley. 1875. *Money and the Mechanism of Exchange.* New York: Appleton.

Jochelson, Waldemar. 1908. *Material Culture and Social Organization of the Koryak.* Museum of Natural History, I, Part II. Leiden: Brill.

Kluckhohn, Clyde, and Leighton, Dorothea. 1962. *The Navajo.* Rev. ed. Garden City, New York: Doubleday.

Kmenta, Jan. 1971. *Elements of Econometrics.* New York: Macmillan.

Knapp, G. F. 1924. *The State Theory of Money.* London: Macmillan.

Knies, Karl. 1885. *Das Geld.* 2nd ed. Vol. 1, *Geld und Kredit.* Berlin: Wiedmannsche Buchhandlung.

Krader, Lawrence, ed. 1974. *The Ethnological Notebooks of Karl Marx.* 2nd ed. Amsterdam: Van Gorcum Assen.

Lancaster, Keven. 1971. *Consumer Demand: A New Approach.* New York: Columbia University Press.

Laum, Bernhard. 1924. *Heiliges Geld: Eine historische Untersuchung ueber den sakralen Ursprung des Geldes.* Tuebingen: J. C. B. Mohr.

Leacock, Eleanor Burke, and Lurie, Nancy Oestreich, eds. 1971. *North American Indians in Historical Perspective.* New York: Random House.

LeClair, Edward E., Jr., and Schneider, Harold K., eds. 1968. *Economic Anthropology: Readings in Theory and Analysis.* New York: Holt, Rinehart and Winston.

Lee, Richard B., and DeVore, Irven, eds. 1968. *Man the Hunter.* Chicago, Illinois: Aldine.

Leeds, Anthony, and Vayda, Andrew P., eds. 1965. *Man, Culture, and Animals: The Role of Animal in Human Ecological Adjustment.* Publication No. 78, American Association for the Advancement of Science. Washington, D.C.

Lévi-Strauss, Claude. 1969. *The Elementary Structure of Kinship.* Rev. ed. Translated by J. H. Bell *et al.* Boston, Massachusetts: Beacon Press.

———. 1963. *Structural Anthropology.* Translated by C. Jacobson and B. G. Schoepf. New York: Basic Books.

Lindzey, Gardner, and Aronson, Elliot, eds. 1968. *The Handbook of Social Psychology,* Vol. II Reading, Massachusetts: Addison-Wesley.

Lowie, Robert H. 1934. *An Introduction to Cultural Anthropology.* New York: Farrar and Rinehart.

———. 1927. *The Origins of the State.* New York: Harcourt Brace.

———, ed. 1968. *Essays in Anthropology Presented to A. L. Kroeber.* Freeport, New York: Books for Libraries.

MacLeod, William Christie. 1931. *The Origin and History of Politics*. New York: Wiley.
―――. 1924. *The Origin of the State*. Philadelphia, Pennsylvania.
McKeon, Richard, ed. 1941. *The Basic Works of Aristotle*. New York: Random House.
Maine, Henry. 1861. *Ancient Law*. London: Oxford University Press.
Mair, Lucy. 1971. *Marriage*. London: Penguin.
Maiskii, L. 1921. *Sovremennaia Mongoliia*. Irkutsk: Gosudarstvennoe Izdatel'stvo.
Malinowski, Bronisław. 1961. *Argonauts of the Western Pacific*. New York: Dutton.
―――. 1926. *Crime and Custom in Savage Society*. London: Kegan Paul.
Mandell, Lewis, et al, eds. 1973. *Survey of Consumers, 1971–72: Contributions to Behavioral Economics*. Survey Research Center, Institute for Social Research, University of Michigan. Ann Arbor, Michigan.
Marshall, Alfred. 1948. *Principles of Economics*. 8th ed. London: Macmillan.
Marx, Karl. n.d. *Capital*, Vol. I. New York: Modern Library.
―――. n.d. *Grundrisse der Kritik der politischen Oekonomie*. Frankfurt a.M.: Europäische Verlagsanstalt.
―――. 1964. *Pre-Capitalist Economic Formations*, edited by Eric Hobsbawm and translated by Jack Cohen. New York: International Publishers.
Mauss, Marcel. 1967. *The Gift: Forms and Functions of Exchange in Archaic Societies*. Translated by Ian Cunnison. New York: Norton.
Mayer, Philip. 1951. *Two Studies in Applied Anthropology in Kenya*. Colonial Office, Colonial Research Study No. 3. London: H.M.S.O.
Mead, Margaret, ed. 1966. *Cooperation and Competition Among Primitive Peoples*. Boston, Massachusetts: Beacon Press.
Melitz, Jacques. 1974. *Primitive and Modern Money*. Reading, Massachusetts: Addison-Wesley.
Montet, Pierre. 1958. *Everyday Life in Egypt in the Days of Ramesses the Great*. Translated by A. R. Maxwell-Hyslop and Margaret S. Drower. London: Arnold.
Montias, John Michael. 1976. *The Structure of Economic Systems*. New Haven, Connecticut: Yale University Press.
Moore, Frank W. 1961. *Readings in Cross-Cultural Methodology*. New Haven, Connecticut: HRAF Press.
Morgan, James N.; Sirageldin, Ismail A.; and Baerwaldt, Nancy. 1969. *Productive Americans*. Survey Research Center, Institute for Social Research, University of Michigan. Ann Arbor, Michigan.
Murdock, George Peter. 1963. *Outline of World Cultures*. 3rd rev. ed. New Haven, Connecticut: HRAF Press.
―――. 1949. *Social Structure*. New York: Free Press.
Musgrave, Richard A. 1969. *Fiscal Systems*. New Haven, Connecticut: Yale University Press.
―――, ed. 1965. *Essays in Fiscal Federalism*. Washington, D.C.: The Brookings Institution.
Naroll, Raoul, and Cohen, Ronald, eds. 1973. *A Handbook of Method in Cultural Anthropology*. New York: Columbia University Press.
Naroll, Raoul, and Naroll, Frada, eds. 1973. *Main Currents in Cultural Anthropology*. New York: Appleton-Century-Crofts.
Nash, Manning. 1966. *Primitive and Peasant Economic Systems*. San Francisco, California: Chandler.
Nieboer, H. H. 1971. *Slavery as an Industrial System*. New York: Burt Franklin.
Parsons, Talcott, and Smelser, Neil J. 1956. *Economy and Society: A Study in the Integration of Economic and Social Theory*. Glencoe, Illinois: Free Press.
Pechman, Joseph A., and Okner, Benjamin A. 1974. *Who Bears the Tax Burden?* Washington, D.C.: The Brookings Institution.
Pfaff, Martin. *The Grants Economy*. n.d. Research Report, Computer Institute for Social Research, Michigan State University. East Lansing, Michigan. Mimeographed.
Phelps-Brown, E. H. 1962. *The Economics of Labor*. New Haven, Connecticut: Yale University Press.
Phillips, Arthur, ed. 1953. *Survey of African Marriage and Family Life*. London: Oxford University Press.
Polanyi, Karl. 1957. *The Great Transformation: The Political and Economic Origins of Our Times*. Boston, Massachusetts: Beacon Press.

Polanyi, Karl, and Rotstein, Abraham. 1966. *Dahomey and the Slave Trade: An Analysis of an Archaic Economy.* Monograph 42, American Ethnological Society. Seattle, Washington: University of Washington.

Polanyi, Karl; Arensberg, Conrad M.; and Pearson, Harry W., eds. 1957. *Trade and Market in the Early Empires: Economies in History and Theory.* New York: Free Press.

Pospisil, Leopold J. 1963. *Kapauku Papuan Economy,* Department of Anthropology, Yale University. New Haven, Connecticut.

Pryor, Frederic L. 1973. *Property and Industrial Organization in Communist and Capitalist Nations.* Bloomington, Indiana: Indiana University Press.

———. 1968. *Public Expenditures in Communist and Capitalist Nations.* Homewood, Illinois: Irwin.

Przeworski, Adam, and Teune, Henry. 1970. *The Logic of Comparative Social Inquiry.* New York: Wiley and Sons.

Quiggin, A. Hingston. 1956. *The Story of Money.* London: Methuen.

———. 1949. *A Survey of Primitive Money.* London: Methuen.

Radcliffe-Brown, A.R., and Forde, Daryll, eds. 1950. *African Systems of Kinship and Marriage.* London: Oxford University Press.

Rousseau, Jean-Jacques. 1955. *The Social Contract.* New York: Haefner.

Sahlins, Marshall. 1958. *Social Stratification in Polynesia.* The American Ethnological Society. Seattle, Washington: University of Washington Press.

———. 1972. *Stone Age Economics.* Chicago, Illinois: Aldine.

St. Erlich, Vera. 1966. *Family in Transition: A Study of 300 Yugoslav Villages.* Princeton, New Jersey: Princeton University Press.

Salisbury, R. F. 1962. *From Stone to Steel: Economic Consequences of a Technological Change in New Guinea.* London: Cambridge University Press.

Schaefer, James M., ed. 1974. *Studies in Cultural Diffusion: Galton's Problem.* New Haven, Connecticut: HRAF.

Schneider, David M., and Gough, Kathleen, eds. 1961. *Matrilineal Kinship.* Berkeley, California: University of California Press.

Schneider, Harold K. 1974. *Economic Man: The Anthropology of Economics.* New York: Free Press.

———. 1970. *The Wahi Wanyaturu: Economics in an African Society.* Chicago, Illinois: Aldine Atherton.

Schmidt, Max. 1926. *The Primitive Races of Mankind.* Translated by Alexander K. Dallas. London, England: Harrap.

Schumpeter, Joseph A. 1954. *History of Economic Analysis.* New York: Oxford University Press.

Schurtz, Heinrich. 1898. *Grundriss einer Entstehungsgeschichte des Geldes.* Weimar: Verlag Emil Felber, 1898.

Service, Elman R. 1975. *Origins of the State and Civilization: The Process of Cultural Evolution.* New York: Norton, 1975.

Shapiro, Harry L., ed. 1956. *Man, Culture, and Society.* New York: Oxford University Press.

Sills, David L., ed. 1968. *International Encyclopedia of the Social Sciences.* New York: Crowell, Collier and Macmillan.

Simmons, Leo. 1945. *The Role of the Aged in Primitive Society.* New Haven, Connecticut: Yale University Press.

Singer, Andre, and Street, Brian V., eds. 1972. *Zande Themes: Essays Presented to Sir Edward Evans-Pritchard.* Totowa, New Jersey: Rowman and Littlefield.

Sirageldin, Ismail Abdel-Hamed. 1969. *Non-Market Components of National Income.* Survey Research Center, Institute for Social Research, University of Michigan. Ann Arbor, Michigan.

Smelser, Neil J. Forthcoming. *Comparisons in the Social Sciences.*

Smith, Adam. 1961. *An Inquiry into the Nature and Causes of the Wealth of Nations.* London: Methuen.

Sofri, Gianni. 1972. *Ueber asiatische Productionsweise.* Frankfurt a.M.: Europäische Verlagsanstalt.

Speck, Frank G. 1919. *The Functions of Wampum Among the Eastern Algonkian: Memoirs of the American Anthropological Association,* VI. Lancaster, Pennsylvania.

Spencer, Herbert. 1882. *The Principles of Sociology,* Vol. II. London: Williams and Norgate.

Sorokin, Pitirim A. 1942. *Man and Society in Calamity*. New York: Dutton.

Spicer, Edmund. 1940. *Pascua: A Yaqui Village in Arizona*. Chicago, Illinois: University of Chicago Press.

Spooner, Brian, ed. 1972. *Population Growth: Anthropological Implications*. Cambridge, Massachusetts: MIT Press.

Sumner, William Graham, and Keller, Albert Galloway. 1927. *The Science of Society*, Vol. I. New Haven, Connecticut: Yale University Press.

Swanson, Guy W. 1960. *The Birth of the Gods: The Origins of Primitive Belief*. Ann Arbor, Michigan: University of Michigan Press.

Swartz, Marc J.; Turner, Victor W.; and Tuden, Arthur, eds. 1966. *Political Anthropology*. Chicago, Illinois: Aldine.

Szalai, Alexander *et al*. 1972. *The Uses of Time*. The Hague: Mouton.

Terray, Emmanuel. 1972. *Marxism and "Primitive" Societies*. Translated by Mary Klopper. New York: Monthly Review Press.

Textor, Robert B. 1967. *A Cross-Cultural Summary*. New Haven, Connecticut: HRAF Press.

Thibaut, John W., and Kelly, Harold H. 1959. *The Social Psychology of Groups*. New York: Wiley.

Thurnwald, Richard. 1932. *Economics in Primitive Communities*. London: Oxford University Press.

Titmuss, Richard M. 1971. *The Gift Relationship: From Human Blood to Social Policy*. New York: Random House.

Torgerson, Warren S. 1958. *Methods of Scaling*. New York: Wiley.

Triandis, H. *et al*. eds. Forthcoming. *Handbook of Cross-Cultural Psychology*.

Tullock, Gordon, ed. 1975. *Frontiers of Economics 1975*. Blacksburg, Virginia: University Publications.

Turnbull, Colin M. 1972. *The Mountain People*. New York: Simon and Schuster.

Tylor, Edward B. 1896. *Anthropology: An Introduction to the Study of Man and Civilization*. New York: D. Appleton.

Udy, Stanley H., Jr. 1959. *Organization of Work: A Comparative Analysis of Production Among Nonindustrial Peoples*. New Haven, Connecticut: HRAF Press.

U.S., Bureau of American Ethnology. 1894. *11th Annual Report, 1889–90*. Washington, D.C.: G.P.O.

U.S., Congress, Joint Economic Committee. 1972. *The Economics of Federal Subsidy Programs*. Washington, D.C.: G.P.O.

U.S., Council of Economic Advisors to the President. 1975. *Economic Report of the President, 1975*. Washington, D.C.: G.P.O.

U.S., Department of Health, Education, and Welfare, The Panel on Social Indicators. April 1968. *Materials for a Preliminary Draft of the Social Report*. Washington, D.C. Mimeographed.

U.S., President's Commission on Law Enforcement and Administration of Justice. 1967. *The Challenge of Crime in a Free Society*. Washington, D.C.: G.P.O.

Van der Pas, H. T. 1973. *Economic Anthropology 1940–1972: An Annotated Bibliography*. New York: Humanities Press.

Viljoen, Stephan. 1936. *The Economics of Primitive Peoples*. London: King and Sons.

Walter, Heinrich, and Lieth, Helmut. Various years. *Klimadiagramm Weltatlas*. Jena: VEB Fischer Verlag.

Weber, Max. 1961. *General Economic History*. New York: Collier Books.

Wilbert, Johannes. 1972. *Survivors of Eldorado*. New York: Praeger.

Wiles, P. J. D. 1968. *Communist International Economics*. Oxford: Basil Blackwell.

Winick, Charles. 1970. *Dictionary of Anthropology*. Totowa, New Jersey: Littlefield, Adams.

Winks, Robin, ed. 1972. *Slavery: A Comparative Perspective*. New York: New York University Press.

Wittfogel, Karl. 1957. *Oriental Despotism: A Comparative Study*. New Haven, Connecticut: Yale University Press.

Young, Michael W. 1971. *Fighting with Food*. Cambridge, England: University Press.

Zaremka, Paul, ed. 1974. *Frontiers in Econometrics*. New York: Academic Press.

INDEX

STUDIES IN SOCIAL DISCONTINUITY

Under the Consulting Editorship of:

CHARLES TILLY
University of Michigan

EDWARD SHORTER
University of Toronto

In preparation

Harry W. Pearson. The Livelihood of Man by Karl Polanyi

Richard Maxwell Brown and Don E. Fehrenbacher (Eds.). Tradition, Conflict, and Modernization: Perspectives on the American Revolution

Juan Guillermo Espinosa and Andrew S. Zimbalist. Economic Democracy: Workers' Participation in Chilean Industry, 1970-1973

Randolph Trumbach. The Rise of the Egalitarian Family: Aristocratic Kinship and Domestic Relations in Eighteenth-Century England

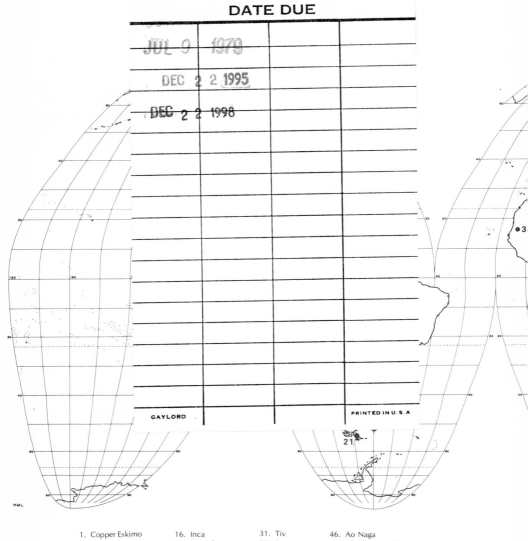

1. Copper Eskimo	16. Inca	31. Tiv	46. Ao Naga
2. Naskapi	17. Sirionó	32. Fon	47. Khalka Mongol
3. Kwakiutl	18. Shavante	33. Dogon	48. Koryak
4. Pomo	19. Toba	34. Wolof	49. South China
5. Havasupai	20. Aweikóma	35. Tuareg	50. Semang
6. Navajo	21. Yahgan	36. Rif	51. Batak
7. Comanche	22. Thonga	37. Gheg	52. Manóbo
8. Omaha	23. Tanala	38. Serb	53. Alor
9. Iroquois	24. !Kung	39. Lapp	54. Murngin
10. Yaqui	25. Nyakyusa	40. Turk	55. Maori
11. Aztec	26. Suku	41. Rwala	56. Siane
12. Bribri	27. Ganda	42. Basseri	57. Trobriand
13. Warao	28. Amhara	43. Bhil	58. Truk
14. Callinago	29. Nuer	44. Toda	59. Tikopia
15. Mundurucú	30. Azande	45. Lepcha	60. Fiji